# Green Management:
# A Reader

*Edited by*

Pierre McDonagh and Andrea Prothero

**The Dryden Press**

*Harcourt Brace & Company Limited*

London   Fort Worth   New York   Orlando
Philadelphia   San Diego   Toronto   Sydney   Tokyo

The Dryden Press
24/28 Oval Road,
London NW1 7DX

**A catalogue record for this book is available from the British Library**
ISBN 0-03-099040–8

Typeset by Mackreth Media Services, Hemel Hempstead
Printed in Great Britain at WBC Book Manufacturers, Bridgend, Mid Glamorgan

# Contents

# Introduction and Overview

*Pierre McDonagh and Andrea Prothero*

If we are to find the roots of the present ecological crisis, we must turn not to technics, demographics, growth, and a diseased affluence alone; we must turn to the underlying institutional, moral, and spiritual changes in human society that produced hierarchy and domination—not only in bourgeois, feudal and ancient society, nor in class societies generally, but at the very dawn of civilization. . . . Ecology . . . contains very radical philosophical and cultural implications (Bookchin, 1980).

There is no doubt that concern for the environment now plays a major role in our global society. Global environmental problems, such as ozone layer depletion and global warming, increased global concern for the state of the natural environment, environmental disasters and the like have all played their part in ensuring the state of the natural environment and our treatment of that environment have become a part of the rhetoric of everyday life. This is reflected in our consumption purchases, our political actions, our government's legislation and in the workplace. Thus when we discuss the *greening of management* we must remember that the development of ecological management theories and practices must be considered in conjunction with what is happening in the wider external environment. This is demonstrated by the introductory quotation by the social ecologist Bookchin.

We therefore attempt to provide a starting point for many and a focal point for others through the provision of a collection of readings on the greening of management from the contemporary management literature. We do this while also recognizing that in order to explore green management one must also be aware of wider ecological issues, and this again is reflected in this volume.

## GREEN—WHAT DOES IT MEAN?

There is confusion within the vast literature over the differing terms used when discussing the natural environment and green issues and this therefore has implications for what is meant by green management. Green transcends all aspects of our lives and is studied in various contexts in many disciplines. Figure 1 highlights some of the different meanings of 'green' for individuals in society and illustrates the variety of perceptions involved. For many people 'green' is a political viewpoint, while for others it is a particular lifestyle or a matter of having clean water or organic foods.

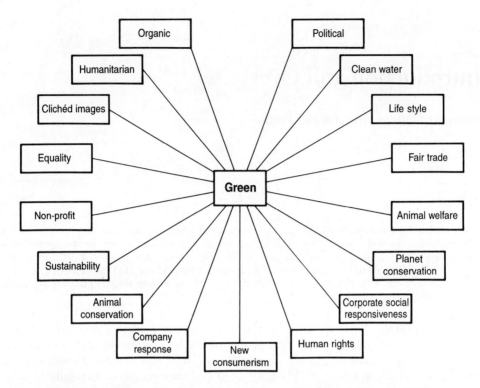

Figure 1. The Different Meanings of Green. (*Source:* adapted from McDonagh, 1994).

In contemporary society there is much preoccupation with the clichéd images used by companies when communicating about the environment and this is what some perceive 'green' to be about. Linked to this, as Figure 2 illustrates, is the fact that different issues are picked up and researched by different schools of academics and reported in their respective literature. In this respect, to assess a situation it is necessary to cover various sources in the literature.

Any study that considers environmental issues is a complex one, and attempting to define terms such as 'ecology' or 'environmentalism' in one or two sentences is not an easy task. As a number of authors have commented (Porritt and Winner, 1988; Bramwell, 1989; Eckersley, 1992), terms such as 'green', 'ecology', 'environmentalism' can be interpreted in various ways,

> Just as definitions of 'freedom', 'democracy', 'peace' and 'justice' vary according to the context in which they are used, so 'green' tends to mean very different things to different people. (Porritt and Winner, 1988).

Not only do we have various disciplines studying a variety of issues, within disciplines themselves there are sometimes differing schools of opinion. If, for example, we decided to explore the ecological philosophy literature, three main schools of thought would emerge. These are 'deep ecology' (see, for example, Naess, 1973; Norton, 1991), 'human ecology' (see the collection of works edited by Steiner

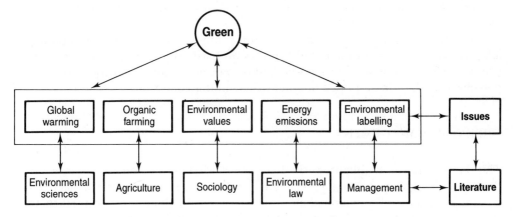

Figure 2. Green Issues and the Literature.

and Nauser, 1993) and 'social ecology' (see Bookchin, 1987). Linked to this, researchers have been known to use the same term as another author but applying a different meaning, or to use different terms that have the same meaning (Wall, 1994). It is therefore important to remember that, rather than trying simply to define the various terms, *one should aim towards understanding the different positions* associated with various green issues and try to understand why what means ecological to one individual could be referred to as environmentalism by another.[1] This is illustrated in the two quotations below:

> environmentalism, a reformist philosophy which maintains an essential distinction between the human species on the one hand and 'nature' on the other and a variety of more radical ideas which perceive humanity as inextricably linked with the rest of the biosphere (i.e. post environmentalism) (Young, 1990).

> Environmentalism does not bring into question the underlying notion of the present society that man must dominate nature; rather it seeks to facilitate that domination by developing techniques for diminishing the hazards caused by domination. The very notion of domination itself is not brought into question. . . . Ecology, I would claim, advances a broader conception of nature and humanity's relationship with the natural world. (Bookchin 1980).

Thus, one could argue that the ideology surrounding Young's post environmentalism could be similar to that which Bookchin associates with ecology. We believe that, rather than seeking a single universal definition of what we mean by green, we must aim towards *understanding* the issues across disciplines and be aware that different world views may exist within specific disciplines. Figure 2 illustrates that some people see issues in different ways and approach their research using differing terms; clearly one needs to be aware of these differences when examining green issues.

In our opinion we would like the term 'green' to have its *widest possible meaning*, where the greening of management, from both a process and a practical perspective, will be linked to the greening of society. It is our belief that the greening of management will ultimately depend on the greening of society and this is reflected in our choice of readings. Thus, the first two sections of this volume look at areas outside management readings.

When discussing the various readings in this volume we have used the terminology adopted by the writers in their work, and, as we have just noted, it is important for you, the reader, to note that what one author means by 'green' may be different in perception and/or focus to that of other writers in this collection.

## GREENING MANAGEMENT

This book aims to highlight work that details what is involved if organizations themselves are going to become green and introduce an environmental management system. A number of common themes have arisen and these are discussed in the readings in Parts III–V. Some of the main themes include the development of an environmental orientation and how both the strategies and structure of organizations (see also Stead and Stead, 1992; Shrivastava, 1994; Peattie, 1995) play a part in this process. The focus is thus not only on the development of an environmental management system via the introduction of environmental plans and policies but also on the role of top management and individual departments in contributing to this development. Thus, for example, the literature suggests environmental policies, like any others, will not be successful if they do not receive the support and commitment of top management (Burke and Hill, 1990; Shimel, 1991). Other factors for consideration include the communication of environmental policies, both internally and externally, and the status of the environmental policy for the company and its stakeholders. Linked to this one must also remember that, as well as considering practical developments, the whole 'soul' of the organization needs to be scrutinized (see Fineman, 1996) (Reading 10). It is important to stress that the authors are adopting a holistic approach to greening management and do not believe piecemeal responses by organizations will contribute to the greening of management as they see it, or indeed the greening of society. This idea of 'green' holism was best summarized by Wall (1994):

> Green philosophy . . . in its myriad forms always espouses holism, a method and outlook that examines the connections between things.

Throughout this volume we are attempting to draw the reader's attention to the connections between things, which here includes the connection between management and the wider external environment and also the connection within management of all the disciplines which affect organizations.

## STRUCTURE OF THE READER

In contemporary management literature, research in the *green area* has taken on a new perspective. Much has been published in recent years. The holistic and complex nature of *green itself* has meant, however, much of the work is outside the traditional management literature. This reader attempts to bring together a collection of readings from a wide selection of journals and books into one easily accessible volume. Since much of the literature published in recent years has been practitioner based, a number of these articles have been included alongside more theoretical works. Again, bringing the various perspectives together in one volume is of fundamental importance. It is hoped that this reader provides a collection of up to date theoretical, empirical and practical pieces that will enable the reader to identify the main issues of current importance as far as greening management is concerned, and thus examine how these relate to some of the more wider societal issues.

The reader can stand alone or be used alongside a number of existing textbooks, some of which have been referenced in the further information section at the end of the book. How much of the reader you will need to explore will ultimately depend on your reasons for studying the issues. Those only interested in green marketing, for example, may wish to lay their emphasis on Part V of the reader. It is ideal as an introduction to the issues for those who until now were unfamiliar with the arguments and, for whatever reason, want to inform themselves of key opinions. It is intended to be accessible and of use to students, academic researchers, managers, business people and the lay citizen.

The reader is divided into the following sections (Figure 3).

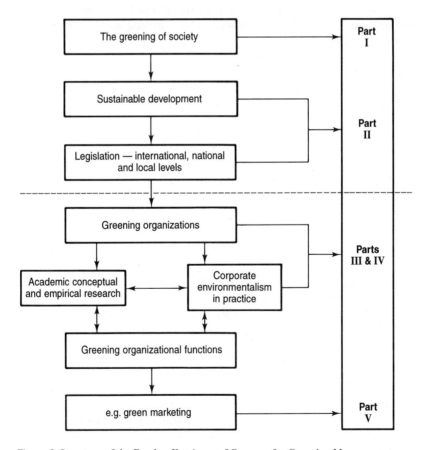

Figure 3. Structure of the Reader: Key Areas of Concern for Greening Management.

## Part I: General overview—the greening of society

This section provides a general overview of some of the main issues of importance with which people need to become acquainted if they wish to explore the concept of 'green management'. It provides a background to these issues from the point of view of society and also gives an account of some environmental trends in recent times. Whatever level of green you are examining, the authors recommend that the collection of readings in Part I should be consulted before moving on to some of the other issues discussed.

## Part II: Sustainable development—global, national and local issues

The readings in this part provide an account of recent environmental legislation at international, national and local levels. General environmental legislation and regulation is discussed as well as more specific legislation, such as the British Standard for environmental management systems BS 7750 which applies directly to business organizations. Some of the main issues surrounding the concept of sustainable development are also discussed throughout this section to help clarify this principle and also highlight the importance of applying sustainable development to society, the economy and politics.

## Part III: Greening organizations

This section has contributions that consider both theoretical and some of the more practical issues of importance involved specifically in the greening of organizations. Consideration is also paid to viewpoints from some of the professions—for example, accountancy and banking—that also impact upon the development of environmental management systems by organizations.

## Part IV: Corporate environmentalism in practice

This part provides examples of practical guidelines for companies to follow on their path towards implementing an environmental management system. Some empirical studies are also discussed, outlining some of the environmental strategies, pitfalls and benefits of 'going green' for particular companies and industries in recent years.

## Part V: Green marketing

Finally, the reader concludes by looking specifically at issues of importance raised in the marketing discipline, which has been implicated in generating many of the environmental problems in the first place. A general overview of what constitutes green marketing is detailed. This section also considers the role of the consumer in the greening process and explores the impact of green issues upon marketing communications, particularly advertising.

## NOTES

1. For further information in this area the reader can consult the following texts: Bookchin (1980), Porritt and Winner (1988), Bramwell (1989), Young (1990), Eckersley (1992).

## REFERENCES

Bookchin, M. (1980) *Towards an Ecological Society*, Black Rose Books, Montreal.
Bookchin, M. (1987) Social ecology versus deep ecology: a challenge for the ecology movement, *Green Perspectives*, Nos 4 and 5.
Bramwell, A. (1989) *Ecology in the 20th Century: A History*, Yale University Press, New Haven.
Burke, T and Hill, J. (1990) *Ethics, Environment and the Company*, The Institute of Business Ethics, London.
Eckersley, R. (1992) *Environmentalism and Political Theory: Toward an Ecocentric Approach*, UCL Press Ltd, London.
McDonagh, P. (1994) *Towards an understanding of what constitutes green advertising as a form of sustainable communication*, Cardiff Business School Working Paper in Marketing and Strategy.
Naess, A. (1973) The Deep Ecological Movement: Some Philosophical Aspects, *Philosophical Inquiry*, Vol. 8, 10-31.
Norton, B. G. (1991) *Toward Unity Among Environmentalists*, Oxford University Press, Oxford.
Peattie, K. (1995) *Environmental Marketing Management: Meeting the Green Challenge*, Pitman, London.
Porritt, J. and Winner, D. (1988) *The Coming of the Greens*, Fontana, London.
Shimel, P. (1991) Corporate environmental policy in practice, *Long Range Planning*, **24**(3), 10–17.
Shrivastava, P. (1994) Industrial and environmental crises: rethinking corporate social responsibility, *Journal of Socio-Economics*, **24**(1).
Stead, W. E. and Stead, J. G. (1992) *Management for A Small Planet: Strategic Decision Making and the Environment*, Sage, London.
Steiner, D. and Nauser, M. (eds) (1993) *Human Ecology: Fragments of Anti-fragmentary Views of the World*, Routledge, London.
Wall, D. (1994) *Green History: A Reader in Environmental Literature, Philosophy and Politics*, Routledge, London.
Young J. (1990) *Post Environmentalism*, Belhaven Press, London.

# Part I

General Overview—The Greening of Society

# CONTENTS

# Introduction to Part I

*Pierre McDonagh and Andrea Prothero*

Nature is man's *inorganic body*—nature that is, in so far as it is not itself the human body. Man *lives* on nature—means that nature is his *body*, with which he must remain in continuous interchange if he is not to die. That man's physical and spiritual life is linked to nature means simply that nature is linked to itself, for man is a part of nature (Marx, 1844).

One of the main issues in the recent green literature is the necessity of considering the holistic nature of the subject area. Thus, in this introduction any discourse of green management must be placed in the context of what is understood as the greening of society. This first collection of articles centres around providing you, the reader, with an overview of the environment in society. The main issue of importance for the first two sections is that, before delving into the literature for greening management, one must first be aware of the wider issues that will have an impact upon this process, as well as challenging our own contextualizations of what 'to manage' actually infers.

The first reading, by Macnaghten and Urry (1995), provides the central starting point to anyone examining environmental issues in any context (for example, management, social science, environmental science) for the first time. The central focus is on the problems that have been caused by society as a result of its historical separation of humans from nature, which, over time, has itself been constructed in many different ways. The authors emphasize that global environmental problems have arisen as a result of social patterns, which derive from the separation of humans and nature amidst a wider cultural process of *individualization* and *de-traditionalization*. Thus, before starting to examine green management we must first have an understanding of how society generally contributes to global environmental problems.

The authors highlight what Beck (1992) has coined a new dynamic of *subpoliticalization*, with the state confronted by an increasingly diverse and heterogeneous array of groups and minority *sociations*. They stress that many global environmental problems will only be solved by the creation of a new society (see also Dunlap, 1991; O'Connor, 1994) (Readings 4 and 5) which ultimately recognizes that nature and society are 'ineluctably intertwined.'

Shrivastava (1995) picks up on this theme in Reading 2 but examines these issues from a management perspective. As a result of living in the risk society the author argues for a fundamental shift in the way in which management is organized, namely a move away from an anthropocentric to an ecocentric world view (see also Kilbourne, 1995), (Reading 29). Table 1 in the article shows how ecocentric management may be gained by a move away from traditional management activities, which rely on anthropocentric values and are biased towards production, consumption and short term profit maximization.

This reading is a good starting point for those wishing to identify all areas affected by the deep greening of management. It must be remembered that the issues proposed in this, and many other readings in this volume, constitute substantial changes to the way in which academics consider the future of management theory and managers on a practical level consider their day to day activities. There are a number of serious issues that need to be considered, ranging from the view of the world we take as researchers, citizens or managers, to a practical consideration of, for example, the packaging materials used in producing items for consumption. This theme is also explored by Macnaghten and Urry (Reading 1), further by Shrivastava (Reading 9) and by Kilbourne (Reading 29).

Reading 3, by Caldwell (1991), considers the global nature of the environmental issue. Some good examples of global environmental issues are provided and the author explains very succinctly why environmentalism is a global issue. It shows that the environment is not purely a 1980s issue because there was widespread public concern in many countries during the 1960s and 1970s. The author's quote from *Life* magazine in January 1970 ('Ecology: a cause becomes a mass movement') should counter the cynics who say green is just a fad.

We believe this reading to be a good starting point for those wishing to gather background information on the environment. Areas covered include global environmentalism as a sequel to the globalization of international trade and commerce, the rapid speed of global environmental legislation and the links between environmentalism and other perceptions and values, such as freedom of speech and human rights.

Finally in this introductory section, Dunlap (1991) (Reading 4) explores the environmental movement (mainly from a US perspective) and examines public opinion towards various environmental issues over a 25 year period. Using Downs's 'issue-attention cycle' the author attempts to explain why the environment has remained an important issue and has not disappeared off society's agenda, as many people expected. Two issues of concern have been the perception of the seriousness of environmental problems and, linked to this, an increase in fear of the potential threat of environmental damage to human health (this can also be linked to the discussion centring on anthropocentrism and ecocentrism in Readings 2 and 29 by Shrivastava (1995) and Kilbourne (1995). While the environmental movement has been successful in creating awareness and 'converting the public to its cause', Dunlap argues it has been less successful in addressing the issues that initially cause these problems.

In concluding, Dunlap, as the first two readings in this introductory section also suggest, comments on the need to consider changes in society in order to address global environmental problems. This is a common theme throughout the reader and is the one major issue of importance, i.e. when we talk about greening management we must not fail to remember that this must be considered in conjunction with greening the economy, politics and society (see also O'Connor, Reading 5).

## REFERENCES

Beck, U. (1992) *Risk Society, Towards a New Modernity*, Sage, London.
Marx, K. (1844) *Economic and Philosophic Manuscripts*, Progress Publishers, Moscow (published 1977).

# 1

# Towards a Sociology of Nature

*Phil Macnaghten and John Urry*

This paper is concerned with the relationship between sociology and nature or the environment. We briefly summarise the various ways in which historically 'nature' has been conceptualised, including the connections between the 'natural' and the 'market'. We suggest that there are many 'natures' and then proceed to develop an agenda for a sociology of such natures. This comprises four elements: a sociology of environmental knowledges; social variation in the reading of natures; a sociology of the diverse forms of environmental damage; and a more general examination of environmentalism and society. We conclude with an examination of the relations between culture and nature suggesting that changes in this relationship now demonstrates what has always been the case, namely, that nature is elaborately entangled and fundamentally bound up with the social and the cultural. As the social and the cultural are both rapidly changing provides deciphering that relationship immensely fruitful but complex areas for future sociological work.

## SOCIOLOGY AND THE STUDY OF ENVIRONMENTAL CHANGE

In this paper[1] we want to examine a paradox, namely that sociology should be central to the examination of environmental change but that so far it has made only a rather modest contribution. It has not delivered what it could have delivered. Hence our argument is a rather tortuous one—we have to show that sociology's role should be central but with little empirical evidence to support this claim. Thus far sociology's contribution is not impressive, particularly as compared with some other social sciences, such as geography or planning—but its concerns are potentially central. To understand the under-representation of sociology in the understanding of environmental change we will first address the social and historical context in which sociology came to be situated, and then consider the ways in which this has contributed to how the 'social' has characteristically been addressed by those researching the nature of the environment and environmental change.

The discursive development of sociology was the product of a particular historical

Reprinted with permission from *Sociology*, Vol. 29, No. 2, 1995, pp. 203–220.
© 1995 British Sociological Association, Phil Macnaghten and John Urry.

moment, that of industrial capitalism in Western Europe and North America. Its key concept has been that of society. It tended to accept certain *a priori* assumptions about the consequent relationship between nature and society. Taking for granted the success of such modern societies in their spectacular overcoming of nature, sociology has concentrated and specialised on what it has been good at, namely describing and explaining the very character of modern societies. As such, sociology has generally accepted a presumed division of academic labour which partly stemmed from the Durkheimian desire to carve out a separate realm or sphere of the social which could be investigated and explained autonomously. In a way sociology employed the strategy of modelling itself on biology and arguing for a specific and autonomous realm of facts, in this case pertaining to the social or society. Such a realm presupposed its separation from, and antithesis to, nature.

Until very recently this academic division between a world of social facts and one of natural facts was largely uncontentious. *Inter alia* it was reflected in the conceptualisation of time, where it was presumed that the times of nature and of society are quite distinct (see Adam, 1990; Lash and Urry, 1994; Chap. 9). Moreover, this account made good sense as a strategy of professionalisation for sociology since it provided a clear and bounded sphere of investigation, a sphere parallel to but not challenging or confronting those physical sciences that unambiguously dealt with an apparently obvious nature.

Moreover, it is this model of sociology, and more generally of the social sciences, which is most visible in current investigations of so-called 'global environmental change'. Roughly speaking, the role of the social scientist is seen as that of addressing the social impacts and implications *of* environmental problems, which have been initially and accurately described by the natural scientist—a kind of 'Biology First' model (also see Grove-White and Szerszynski, 1992). This can clearly be identified in the major international research programmes on global environmental change.[2]

This suggests that the role hitherto of the social scientist in the analysis of global environmental change has been largely one of the social engineer, manipulating and 'fixing' society to aid in the implementation of a 'sustainable' society. As such, instrumentalist disciplines have been favoured, while there is little evidence of an emerging contribution from sociology to problems of global environmental change. We will now seek an explanation of why sociology has mostly failed to enter the environmental debate, even where there are now research programmes with a 'social science' focus. We will begin by returning to the complex relationship between the social and nature before suggesting some areas for sociological inquiry and engagement. It should be noted that this paper concentrates upon the society–nature relationship within the 'West' or the North Atlantic Rim societies and deals mainly with 'environmental' rather than 'biological' issues.

## NATURE—A HISTORICAL CONTEXT

In historical terms the juxtaposition of society and nature reached its fullest development in the nineteenth century in the 'West'. Nature was degraded into a realm of unfreedom and hostility that needed to be subdued and controlled.

Modernity involved the belief that human progress should be measured and evaluated in terms of the human domination of 'nature' rather than through any attempt to transform the relationship between humans and nature. This view presupposed the doctrine of *human exceptionalism*: that humans are fundamentally different from and superior to all other species; that people can determine their own destinies and learn whatever is necessary to achieve them; that the world is vast and presents unlimited opportunities; and that the history of human society is one of unending progress.

Williams, in an almost unique account of the cultural transformation of the language of nature, argues that our current understandings of nature derive from an immensely complicated array of ideas, linked to many of the key concepts of Western thought (1972, 1976). Perhaps one of the most significant historical transformations was the early usage of an array of *singular* natures which Williams identifies from the thirteenth century. For, once nature became separated from the wider multiplicity of things one can begin to propose social arrangements to be linked to a particular natural order. Williams proceeds to catalogue the forms of political relationships that have been subsequently justified through appeals to singular natures (such as property rights, parasitism, co-operation, aggression, democracy, slavery etc.) noting how many have been commonly achieved through a complex juxtaposition of personifications and metaphors. Thus, first as a goddess, then a divine mother, an absolute monarch, a minister, a constitutional lawyer, and finally a selective breeder, the appeal to a singular nature defined respectively the changing relationships (often bitterly contested) between a state of nature, a state of God, and humanity. However, two crucial transformations took place from the sixteenth and seventeenth centuries, both involving the separation and abstraction of a state of *nature*, from God and from *humanity*.

The first transformation involved the deadening of the state of nature: from a life giving force to dead matter, from spirit to machine. Through the new sciences of physics, astronomy, and mathematics, the study of nature became the study of how nature was *materially* constituted. Nature became a set of laws, cases and conventions, discoverable through the new rules of inquiry: forms of inquiry which could be carried out in their own terms without any recourse to a divine purpose or design.

The second transformation involved the construction of a state of nature thought of as prior to humanity, or at least prior to civilised society. Once nature became abstracted and, in effect, separated as a state prior to society, debate arose as to the essence of this state of nature as opposed to society. Two variants of this have been significant and these were grounded in a dispute over whether this 'pre-social state of nature' was the source of original sin or of original innocence. For example, while Hobbes described the pre-social state of nature as 'solitary, poor, nasty, brutish and short', Locke described this state as one of 'peace, goodwill, mutual assistance and co-operation'. As such Hobbes argued that the basis of a civilised society lay in overcoming 'natural disadvantages'; while for Locke the basis for a just society lay in organising society around 'natural laws'. These novel constructions of a separate nature had major consequences for the developing relationship between forms of social activity and a state of nature.

As described above, pre-modern cosmology involved the idea of an overarching order within which humanity, nature and God were bound together. Moral judgement was then largely understood in terms of whether human action conformed to this natural order. However, once nature became separated from humanity, it was possible to consider whether social activities did or did not fit into a pre-existing natural order. Williams argues:

> For, of course, to speak of man (*sic*) 'intervening' in natural processes is to suppose that he might find it possible not to do so, or to decide not to do so. Nature has to be thought of, that is to say, as separate from man, before any question of intervention or command, and the method or ethics of either, can arise (1972: 154).

These new abstracted natures not only legitimated theoretical inquiry: 'a separated mind looking at a separated matter', 'man looking at nature'; but also new applications. The separation of nature from society was a prerequisite for practices dependent on constituting nature instrumentally: as a set of passive *objects* to be used and worked on by people. The morality used to justify the enormous interference which occurred from the eighteenth century onwards arose from this construction of a separate nature, whose laws became the laws of physics. And since these were considered God's laws, physical interference came to represent the continuation of God's creation. Indeed, it led to systems of thought where it became considered fundamentally purposeful for people to interfere with passive matter for human use. And finally, it led to arguments proclaiming not only the 'naturalness' of interference, but to arguments where interference was considered so inevitable that any criticism of the argument became classified *itself* as interference.

It was around this time that another construction of nature arose. Just as 'improvers' were claiming the inevitability of their acts many people began to experience the environmental degradation and social exploitation deriving from this massive interference in 'nature'. Many of the side-effects of industrialism became criticised as inhumane, unjust, and 'unnatural'. However, while these negative effects were easy to acknowledge, developing a 'natural' alternative became more difficult. As the market became institutionalised in society, it was hard to criticise the very mechanism which was identified as the creator of wealth, prosperity, profits and liberal democracy. The market came to be understood as itself 'natural' and the laws of the market as analogous to the laws of the natural world, and therefore not to be interfered with or contested. Williams argues:

> The new natural economic laws, the natural liberty of the entrepreneur to go ahead without interference, had its own projection of the market as the natural (*sic*) regulator . . . a remnant . . . of the more abstract ideas of social harmony, within which self-interest and the common interest might ideally coincide (1972: 158).

This naturalising of the market strikingly showed how the restructuring of nature as 'natural science' was to cast its influence over humanity and the social world. All kinds of inquiry became subject to the same search for natural laws. The alternative conception of nature which emerged, out of Romanticism rather than Enlightenment, was more escapist than visionary. Instead of efforts to re-invoke a morality and ethics within nature by thinking through new ways to rework nature into the social, nature sustained 'her' separation by simply departing from the human sphere to the margins of modern society:

Nature in any other sense than that of the improvers indeed fled to the margins: to the remote, the inaccessible, the relatively barren areas. Nature was where industry was not, and then in that real but limited sense had very little to say about the operations on nature that were proceeding elsewhere (Williams, 1972: 159; this led to the notion in the USA of wilderness).

We have just referred to nature as female. This we now know has been a characteristic conception: that nature has often been constructed as 'female', as a Goddess or as a divine mother. It is further argued that the taming of nature through the industrial economy, reason and science has been viewed as involving its 'mastery' and that implicit in certain notions of nature have been male sexualised conceptions of its raping and pillaging. Some versions of eco-feminism presume that women are closer to nature than men. Many feminist utopias have been built around an all female society which is able to live at peace with itself and with the natural world (Merchant, 1980; Plumwood, 1993).

It should also be noted that the history of 'nature' further needs to account for how colonialism and racial oppression have been premised upon a separate nature which is there to be exploited by and for the West. This nature has been seen to consist both of separate 'virgin' territories, and of peoples more 'natural' as workers and as objects of the colonising tourist gaze (Shiva, 1988). Plumwood summarises:

> To be defined as 'nature' . . . is to be defined as passive, as non-agent and non-subject, as the 'environment' or invisible background conditions against which the 'foreground' achievements of reason or culture . . . take place. It is to be defined as . . . a resource empty of its own purposes or meanings, and hence available to be annexed for the purposes of those supposedly identified with reason or intellect (1993: 4).

Thus, there is no pure 'nature' as such, only natures. And such natures are historically, geographically and culturally constituted. Hence there are no natural limits as such, but each depends on particular historical and geographical determinations, as well as on the very processes by which 'nature' is culturally constructed and sustained, particularly by reference to the 'other'. Moreover, once it is acknowledged that ideas of nature both have been, and currently are, fundamentally intertwined with dominant ideas of society, we have then to address what ideas of society have been reproduced, legitimated, excluded, validated etc. through appeals to nature or the natural. And the project of determining what is a natural impact becomes as much a social and cultural project as it is 'purely' scientific.

## TOWARDS A CRITICAL SOCIOLOGY OF THE ENVIRONMENT

Current discourses of nature commonly appeal to variants of the nature/social distinctions as outlined above, and sociological research has only just begun to explore the ways in which current appeals can be linked both to a nature outside society (e.g. as in an appeal to a romantic, pre-human, original nature), and to the so-called 'naturalness' of current social arrangements (e.g. as in utilitarian appeals to the naturalness of pure market relations). While there exists a role for sociological research to explore further the social dimensions of current appeals to the natural, there are other contributions sociology can provide to current 'environmental' debates. These also arise from how the 'social' and the 'natural' are being reconstructed on contemporary societies. We will outline a tentative agenda for a critical, engaging, and reflexive sociology of the environment. This focuses on four interrelated areas: a sociology of environmental knowledges; reading 'natures' sociologically; a sociology of environmental 'damage'; and environmentalism and society.[3]

## A SOCIOLOGY OF ENVIRONMENTAL KNOWLEDGES

In many ways the current role ascribed for the social sciences pre-supposes a particularly 'modernist' account of nature. True, the world might be acknowledged as having finite limits and no longer identified as offering endless bounty, but research programmes still operate under a number of highly modernist assumptions concerning the physicality of the world, its accessibility through scientific and rationalistic inquiry, and the fundamental separation of people and human culture from the physical environment. One implication of this agenda lies in the assumption, currently largely shared in social scientific accounts of the environment, that nature should be viewed as primarily setting limits to what humans can achieve. The emphasis on absolute limits, typically defined by ecological science (see Newby, 1990), has passed from the agenda of a few visionaries in the 1960s into a commonly shared post-Rio agenda. Thus, in current programmes to promote sustainable development, the aim is primarily to identify ways to limit human activity so that economic and social development can proceed within the finite ecological capabilities of the planet, a description broadly shared across key inter-governmental documents such as the UNCED Brundtland Report *Our Common Future* (1987), and the European Communities *Fifth Action for the Environment and Sustainable Development* (1992).

Yet, in contrast to such an agenda, and not withstanding the reality of a certain physicality of the world, natures can be not only constraining but also enabling. There are many examples of the relatively beneficial ways in which 'nature' has enabled human activity of a non-environmentally destructive character to occur. For example, the current popular appeal to 'ecology' can be seen to reflect, not just a concern with the physical state of the environment, but also wider opportunities for developing a different basis to society. 'Nature' then should not be seen as something that has to be tamed or 'mastered' or something that is necessarily at odds with human endeavour. Indeed, to reify such an emphasis on limits, implemented with a series of 'don'ts', or 'do less', can promote the belief that environmental responsibility is something that is ultimately restrictive and disciplinary. Elsewhere we have examined the ways in which the emerging environmental policy agenda in the English countryside is associated with a paradoxical increase in the disciplinary *regulation* of visitors (see Macnaghten and Urry, 1993). Moreover, by defining limits in terms of physical quantities, the political focus lies in achieving commitments to limit economic behaviours, as opposed to the more fundamental questions concerning the very relationship between the natural and the social upon which current economic behaviour resides.

An area where this type of sociological research is beginning to contribute is in attempts to deconstruct the techniques and methodologies which currently 'fix' the environmental agenda. A current research programme at Lancaster is examining the sociology of the scientific knowledges informing global environmental change. Focusing on substantial environmental issues, including global warming, acid rain, habitat protection, and environmental risk perception, research has focused on the culturally contingent character of different forms of environmental knowledges. Early findings suggest that what counts as authoritative scientific knowledge is, to a considerable degree, a product of active processes of interaction and negotiation between scientists and policy makers. For example, models of global climate change, central to international policy responses to threats of global warming, implicitly correspond with questionable moral and epistemological commitments to modernist ideals of order, prediction, and standardised knowledges; where science and policy makers effectively mutually reconstruct political orders unreceptive to whether, for example, a unit of $CO_2$ refers to subsistence paddy fields or luxury air conditioning.

A related point lies in how a more critically informed sociology can challenge the technical and natural sciences more generally by demonstrating that science itself rests upon social assumptions which in the 'real world' mean that the predictions of the theory divided from the laboratory do not always work out in particular 'real world' circumstances. This point is also well shown by Wynne in the case of the effects of the fallout from Chernobyl on sheep farming in the English Lake District; he summarises as follows:

> Although the farmers accepted the need for restrictions, they could not accept the experts' apparent ignorance of their approach on the normally flexible and informal system of hill farm management. The experts assumed that scientific knowledge could be applied to hill farming without adjusting to local circumstances . . . Experts were ignorant of the realities of farming and neglected local knowledge (1991: 45).

By describing the social, human, and cultural contingencies of so-called objective science, sociology can contribute not only to better understandings of that agenda, but *also* to socially informed policies, more reflexive to the social assumptions upon which they rely.


## 'READING' NATURES SOCIOLOGICALLY


We can begin here by noting that sociology can help to illuminate the socially varied ways in which an environment can be evaluated. What is viewed and criticised as unnatural or environmentally damaging in one era or one society is not necessarily viewed as such in another. The 'reading' and production of nature is something that is learnt; and the learning process varies greatly between different societies, different periods and different social groups within a society.

Furthermore, sociology can contribute to the analysis of the social processes which have given rise to certain issues being taken to be 'environmental'. In contrast to a naïve realist perspective which assumes that environmental issues progressively come to light simply through the extension of scientific understandings, a sociologically informed inquiry looks to the cultural and political conditions out of which environmental issues emerge, and thereby to a more informed account of the social consequences.

The social and political threads to contemporary environmentalism are complex. They are tied to the emergence of other social movements (see Eyerman and Jamison, 1991; Melucci, 1989 for recent accounts), and to various other globalising processes. In this way, theorists have identified environmentalism as a new field of struggle against the 'self-defeating process of modernisation' (Eder, 1990), thereby tracing environmentalism to an emerging critique of a globally planned society, something initially reflected in the counter-culture of the 1960s. Grove-White (1991) argues that the very concepts that currently constitute the environmental agenda involved a process of active construction by environmental groups in the 1970s and 1980s, in response to concerns about the more general character of contemporary society. Using the particular examples of motorways, nuclear power, agriculture, and conservation, Grove-White argues that the particular forms of environmental protest were related as much to widespread public unease with a highly technocratic and unresponsive political culture, as with any specific evaluation of the health of the physical, non-human environment. Szerszynski notes two further processes had to develop here: first, that a range of empirical phenomena come to be regarded as environmental problems rather than as simply demonstrating environmental change. So motorways or nuclear power had to be viewed as novel and disruptive, not merely further changes which were in a sense 'naturally' part of the modern project (as much fossil fuel energy continued to be regarded. Szerszynski, 1993: 4). And second, there has to be gathering up of a whole series of issues so that they become viewed as part of an overarching environmental crisis, in which a striking array of different problems are regarded as part of *the* environment and subject to similar threats (also see Rubin, 1989).

It is also necessary to begin to analyse those more underlying social practices that have facilitated the social reading of the physical world as environmentally damaged. Urry (1992) argues that travel may in certain cases provide people with the cultural capital to compare and evaluate different environments and to develop that sense of what is environmentally degraded. He suggests that lack of travel in what was 'eastern Europe' partly explains the apparent blindness to the many kinds of environmental 'damage' that we now know were occurring throughout the region. Other social processes which may be contributing to an emerging environmental consciousness would include an emerging distrust of science, technology and the perceived significance of large transnational corporations in contemporary societies.

However, while environmentalism can be seen as mostly in contradiction with modernity, there are aspects of the latter which have facilitated a greater environmental sensibility, especially to the reading of nature as increasingly global. Thus, the emergence of global institutions such as the United Nations and the World Bank, the globalising of environmental groups such as the World Wildlife Fund, Greenpeace, and Friends of the Earth, and the emergence of global media conglomerates, have all helped to foster something of a new global identity in which environmental processes are increasingly identified as global and planetary. Of course, it is questionable whether these processes are really more global than many previous environmental crises which tended to be seen as local or national. The 'global' in global environmental change is partially a political and cultural construction (see Wynne, 1994).

We have thus taken for granted that strictly speaking there is no such thing as nature, only natures. In a recent study Szerszynski elaborates two key ways in which nature has been conceptualised in the recent period (1993; and see Dickens, 1992, for some mass observation data on how 'nature' is conceptualised). First, there is the notion of nature as 'threatened'. This sense can be seen in the panics over rare and endangered species especially those which are spectacular and aesthetically pleasing; in the perception of nature as a set of exhaustible resources which should be stewarded for future generations; in the sense of nature as a collection of rights-bearing subjects (Benton, 1993; Porritt, 1984); and in the notion of nature as a healthy and pure body under threat from pollution, a nature which according to Rachel Carson is fast becoming a 'sea of carcinogens' (1965; see Szerszynski, 1993; 19–20).

The second set of representations of nature construct it as a realm of purity and moral power. Here nature is characterised as an object of spectacle, beauty or the sublime; as a recreational space to be roamed across; as a state of presocial abundance and goodness as in the notion of natural healing; as representing a return from alienating modern society to an organic community; and as a holistic ecosystem which should be preserved in its diversity and interdependence, including of course the influential Gaia hypothesis (Lovelock, 1988).

These different constructions of nature have in part provided cultural resources *for* the development of the contemporary environmental movement, although we have also argued that they could only function in this way when the 'environment' as such had been discovered. Also it should be noted that many of these 'natures' were originally conceptualised in the context of the nation-state. Arguments for conservation, preservation, recreation and so on were couched in terms of national resources that could be planned and managed. Again contemporary environmentalism has had to 'invent' the entire globe or the one earth, which in its entirety is seen as under threat or alternatively through a oneness with nature is viewed as a moral source. A further research question is to identify in what ways it has been the modernist processes of globalisation which have laid the conditions for the emergence of this 'global' discourse around nature, or has this been much more the product of purely discursive shifts effected by movement intellectuals employing ideas and images, such as the blue earth, which are increasingly mobile in the current 'economy of signs' (see discussion in Szerszynski, 1993; chap. 1; Lash and Urry, 1994).

## SOCIOLOGY OF ENVIRONMENTAL 'DAMAGE'

A third way in which sociology can contribute to the understanding of environmental processes lies in research aimed at describing the social processes which currently produce what we recognise as environmental damage. Many of these social processes are currently theorised in sociology but rarely in terms of their environmental implications (such as consumerism, tourism, and globalisation). Almost all 'environmental' problems result from particular social patterns which are associated with the doctrine of human exceptionalism and the division between 'nature' and 'society'.

Consumerism is a particularly significant social pattern here. It is reasonably well-established now that there has been something of a shift in the structuring of contemporary societies such that parts of the pattern of mass production and mass consumption have been transformed. This is not to suggest that all economic activity was once 'Fordist'—much service industry was not—nor that there are not very significant elements of 'Fordist' production today. However, four shifts in the structural significance and nature of consumption are important: first, a huge increase in the range of goods and services which are currently available, as markets and tastes have been significantly internationalised; second, the increasing semiotization of products so that sign rather than use-value becomes the key element in consumption; third, the breaking down of some 'traditionalised' institutions and structures so that consumer tastes become more fluid and open; and fourth, the increasing importance of consumption patterns to the forming of identity and hence some shift from producer power to consumer power (see Lash and Urry, 1994, on much of this; see the sceptical comments in Warde, 1994).

Bauman's analysis is relevant here. He argues that:

> in present day society, consumer conduct (consumer freedom geared to the consumer market) moves steadily into the position of, simultaneously, the cognitive and moral focus of life, the integrative bond of the society . . . In other words, it moves into the self-same position which in the past—during the 'modern' phase of capitalist society—was occupied by work (1992: 49).

And as such the pleasure principle becomes dominant. Pleasure seeking is a duty since the consumption of goods and services becomes *the* structural basis of Western societies. Social integration thus takes place less through the principles of normalisation, confinement and disciplinary power, as described by Foucault or indeed by Bauman in the case of the holocaust (1989). Instead it takes place through the 'seduction' of the market-place, through the mix of feeling and emotions generated by seeing, holding, hearing, testing, smelling, and moving through the extraordinary array of goods and services, places and environments, that characterise contemporary consumerism organised around a particular 'culture of nature' (see Wilson, 1992). This contemporary consumerism for the affluent two-thirds in the major Western countries entails the rapid churning of demand for different products, services and places. Contemporary markets thrive on change, variety and diversity, on the undermining of tradition and uniformity, on products, services and places going out of fashion almost as quickly as they come into fashion. There is little doubt that these patterns of contemporary consumerism have disastrous consequences for the existing physical environment (not of course that that is 'natural'). This is reflected in holes in the ozone layer, global warming, acid rain, nuclear power accidents, and the destruction of many local environments.

Such Western consumerism in which nature seems turned into a mere artefact of consumer choice has been extensively critiqued by the environmental movement—

and this is in turn seen as part of the wider critique of modernity itself (see Strathern, 1992: 197 on how consumerism also leads to obtaining or purchasing new parts for the human body). But there is a further paradoxical point here. This is that the very development of consumerism has itself helped to generate the current critique of environmental degradation and the cultural focus upon nature. Environmentalism might be represented as presupposing a certain kind of consumerism. This is because one element of consumerism is a heightened reflexivity about the places and environments, the goods and services that are 'consumed', literally, through a social encounter, or through visual consumption (see Urry, 1992). As people reflect upon such consumption they develop not only a duty to consume but also certain rights, including the rights of the citizen as a consumer. Such rights include the belief that people are entitled to certain qualities of the environment, of air, water, sound and scenery and that these should extend into the future and to other populations. Contemporary Western societies have begun to shift the basis of citizenship from political rights to consumer rights and within the bundle of the latter, environmental rights, especially linked to conceptions of nature as spectacle and recreation, are increasingly significant. Some such rights also come to be seen as international since with mass tourism people in the West are increasingly consumers of environments *outside* their own national territory, and as such develop systematic expectations of such environments.

However, the processes of intensification involved in commodifying almost all aspects of social life has produced a corresponding intensification of non-market forms of behaviour and social relations. Building on different kinds of impulses (e.g. people trying to lead relatively altruistic, unselfish lives, operating in more relational, interdependent non-market behaviours), lies an emerging set of tensions between conflicting market and non-market rationalities. Indeed, in extreme forms, these critiques of consumer-oriented society have facilitated new forms of social organisation (in contrast to the consumer orientated groups as outlined above), whose social identity lies in explicit tension with consumer principles—a point which will be expanded in the following section on new social responses. These new social movements, often formed as a response to perceived threats of environmental abuse (e.g. such as 'Hunt Saboteurs', 'Animal Rights' groups, 'Earth First' actions, and other direct action groups), have effectively moved outside the legitimate sphere of state regulated, consumer-oriented action. Thus a future topic for research is what one might call 'environmental deviance'.

## ENVIRONMENTALISM AND SOCIETY

In this final section we will ask how sociology can contribute to understanding what role the environmental agenda is playing in the structural formation and cultural transformation of contemporary society.

One area, popular in current sociological theorising of the environment especially following the English translation of *The Risk Society* (Beck, 1992), lies in debates over the current state of post/late-modernity, and the cultural implications of new forms of reflexivity. Giddens, for example argues that in modernity reflexivity consists of social practices being constantly examined and reformed in the light of incoming information received about those very practices, thus altering their constitution. He says: 'only in the era of modernity is the revision of convention radicalized to apply (in principle) to all aspects of human life, including technological intervention into the material world' (1990: 38–39). This reflexivity leads the methods of Western science, the embodiment of modernity, to be constructed as no more legitimate an activity than many other social activities, each of which involves different forms of judgement. Science is not viewed as having a *necessarily* civilising, progressive and emancipatory role in revealing what nature is like. In many cases science and its associated technologies are seen as *the* problem and not the solution. This is especially the case where there are in effect massive and uncontrolled scientific experiments which treat the entire globe (or a fair part of it) as its laboratory (as with toxic waste, agro-chemicals, nuclear power and so on). In the risk society science is seen as producing most of the risks although these are largely invisible to our senses (Beck, 1992).

At the same time, science's loss of automatic social authority weakens the legitimacy even of the environmental (and medical) 'sciences'. The very identification of risk depends upon such science because of the 'disempowerment of the senses' that chemical and nuclear contamination produce (Beck, 1987: 156; Douglas and Wildavsky, 1982). This in turn causes problems for the green movement since such sciences have of necessity become central to many of the campaigns conducted by environmental NGOs, even though NGOs have hitherto tended to make tactical use of science in environmental campaigning (see Yearley, 1991; and Wynne and Meyer, 1993).

The above dynamics suggest opportunities for sociological inquiry into new forms of arrangement and structure arising from current social responses to environmentalism. One argument, in need of further elaboration, lies in interpreting the processes mentioned above as symptoms of a wider cultural process of individualisation and de-traditionalisation (see Beck, 1992; Beck, 1993; Giddens, 1990; Lash and Urry, 1994; Urry, 1993; Jacques, 1993). It is argued that such processes are leading to the emergence of less institutionalised forms of identity and social arrangement. Institutions, such as science, the church, the monarchy, the nuclear family, and formal structures of government are appearing to be de-legitimated (the emergence of the think tank DEMOS being one expression of this process), increasingly seen as part of the problem rather than the solution, leading to new, looser forms of social arrangement, including the development of new social movements or what we prefer to call 'new sociations' (see Urry, 1993). Indeed, the emergence of a new sphere of the political in the form of looser, non-party based and self-organising affiliations and associations, often in the form of self-help groups, community groups, and voluntary organisations, link to what Beck (1993) has described as a new dynamic of 'subpoliticalisation', whereby the state is confronted by an increasingly diverse and heterogeneous array of groups and minority sociations.

There are a number of characteristics of such sociations (Hetherington, 1993; Urry, 1993). First, they are not like those of traditional communities since they are joined out of choice and people are free to leave. Second, people remain members in part because of the emotional satisfaction that they derive from common goals or shared social experiences. And third, since membership is from choice many people tend to enter and leave such sociations with considerable rapidity. These characteristics effectively locate sociations as contemporary sites where people can experiment with new kinds of social identity. They may empower people, providing relatively safe places for identity-testing and the context for the learning of new skills. Research is required to explore the significance of this new style of social organisation; the extent of its political significance in contributing to a new realm of the political; and its implications for current research on environmentalism as a new social movement. The emergence of new sociations in the sphere of the environment suggests that particular forms of social identity are emerging which imply breaking down the relatively separate spheres of society and nature, and in forming a kind of reconstituted civil society (Jacques, 1993; and see Dickens, 1992; chap. 7 for some mass observation material on the processes of becoming 'green').

There are interesting connections between such new sociations and what we discussed earlier, namely, the perception of the environmental crisis as global. Evidence for the 'global' and holistic view of nature can be seen in the array of inter-governmental and governmental conventions, treaties, and documents arising from the current focus on sustainability—hence, the Brundtland Report talks of *Our Common Future*, partly because of the global character of certain of the threats posed to nature, beginning with the 'nuclear' threat.[4] This perception has been assisted by the development of global mass media which has generated an 'imagined community' of all societies inhabiting 'one earth' (hence Friends of *the* Earth). However, alongside an array of globalising processing lie a set of concerns with culturally situated local environments (such as the Common Ground approach to environmentalism). There are an extraordinary range of local concerns around which mobilisation can occur; examples in the north of England include efforts to conserve a slag heap in Lancashire, a campaign to prevent the painting of yellow lines on some of the roads in Buttermere, and intense opposition to the resiting of a burnt down market in Lancaster.

There are therefore multiple environmental identities, the local as well as the global; the rationalistic as well as the expressive; landscape-oriented as well as the use-oriented and so on (for much more detail, see Szerszynski, 1993). And further these multiple identities appear to be of increasing salience in post-modern societies. We need to develop a sociology which examines the apparently increasing significance of 'environmental identities' in contemporary societies, identities which often entail a complex intermingling of global and local concerns. Statistical evidence for the importance of environmental identities can be seen in the huge increases experienced across nearly all environmental organisations in the 1980s and 1990s.[5]

## CONCLUSION

We have thus set out some of the tasks of a sociological approach to the environment. It is a long and complex agenda which embraces questions of political economy, the state, gender, science, culture, deviance, new social movements, the 'other'—indeed all the issues currently under intense sociological interrogation. The environmental agenda provides opportunities for sociology to unravel the complex patterns emerging from current responses to 'nature', and to the adequacies or otherwise of official 'authoritative' accounts and policy agendas.

Reassessing the question of nature would also throw particular light on the topics of time and space which have so much entered the recent sociological agenda. Adam (1990) has very interestingly brought out how the conventional distinction drawn within sociology between natural time and social time cannot be sustained. It is commonplace of sociology that social time involves change, progress and decay, while natural phenomena are either timeless or can operate with a conception of reversible time. She argues that this distinction cannot now hold since much twentieth century science has shown that 'nature' is also characterised by notions of change and decay:

> Past, present, and future, historical time, the qualitative experience of time . . . all are established as integral time aspects of the subject matter of the natural sciences and clock time, the invariant measure, the closed circle, the perfect symmetry, and reversible time as our creations (1990: 150).

The social sciences have operated with an inappropriate conception of time in the natural sciences, an almost non-temporal time. The innovations of twentieth century science have rendered the distinction between natural and social time as invalid and lead us yet again to conclude that there is no simple and sustainable distinction between nature *and* society. They are ineluctably intertwined. There are therefore many different times (as indeed there are different spaces) and it is not possible to identify an unambiguous social time separate from natural time.

This relates to our more general project, to demonstrate the variety of 'natures'. Strathern (1992) points out a significant paradox about such contemporary developments. It is clear that empirically there is a greatly enhanced focus upon the importance of 'nature', upon valuing the 'natural', upon images of the 'natural' and upon 'nature conservation'. But Strathern notes that these emphases are fundamentally mediated by culture. In other words, culture has been necessary to rescue nature. Strathern argues that this produces: 'the conceptual collapse of the differences between nature and culture when Nature cannot survive without Cultural intervention' (1992: 174). And if so, is there any 'nature' left if it needs culture for its nurturance, so to speak? In the past the strength of nature lay in the way in which its cultural construction was in fact hidden from view (see Latour, 1993 for such an account). But in the contemporary world of reflexivity and ambivalence, this is no longer the case. A major task for the social sciences will be to decipher the social implications of what has always been the case, namely, a nature elaborately entangled and fundamentally bound up with the social.

However, it should also be noted that this nature is now less intertwined with individual national societies, with a national 'community of fate', and is much more interdependent with three other conceptions of the social: the global, including the informational and communicational structures; the local; and the complex diversities of identity and time (see Lash and Urry, 1994: chap. 11, for much more detail). The deciphering of these interconnections promises a rich and challenging research agenda which may even propel sociology out of the margins of the nature debate.

## NOTES

1. We would like to thank Bron Szerszynski, Robin Grove-White and an anonymous reviewer for helpful comments on earlier drafts.
2. This point was recently made by Newby (1993) in relation to the current structure of the Intergovernmental Panel on Climate Change (IPCC) and the Human Dimensions of Global Environmental Change Programme (HDP). Newby notes how both these programmes basically conceive of environmental change as a set of scientific problems requiring technological solutions. Similar features can be seen in UK government initiatives, including the UK Inter-Agency Committee on Global Environment Change, and the government-funded social science programme on Global Environment Change.
3. The last few years has seen a number of sociologists moving into modern environmental concerns. Two recent books which use social theory to elucidate the interrelationship between nature and society are Dickens' *Society and Nature* (1992) and Benton's *Natural Relations* (1993), both of which argue the value of ecological insights to more mainstream sociological questions of power, human rights, social justice and alienation.
4. Examples of key inter-governmental texts of sustainability which have helped to foster the idea of a 'global' nature are the *World Conservation Strategy* (WCS, 1980) and its successor *Caring for the Earth* (IUCN, 1991), the UNCED Bruntland Report *Our Common Future* (1987), the Rio-inspired UNCED *Agenda 21* (1992), and the European Communities *Fifth Action Programme for the Environment and Sustainable Development* (CEC, 1992).
5. Late 1993 membership of the more recognised environmental organisations indicate an increasing number with very large memberships. In the UK these include Greenpeace UK with 390,000 supporters, Friends of the Earth with 230,000 members, the National Trust with over 2,200,000 members, the RSPB with over 850,000 members, and the Royal Society for Nature Conservation with over 250,000 members.

## REFERENCES

Adam, B. (1990) *Time and Social Theory.* Cambridge: Polity.
Bauman, Z. (1989) *Modernity and the Holocaust.* Cambridge: Polity.
Bauman, Z. (1992) *Intimations of Postmodernity.* London: Routledge.
Beck, U. (1987) 'The Anthropological Shock: Chernobyl and the Contours of the Risk Society'. *Berkeley Journal of Sociology* **32**: 153–165.
Beck, U. (1992) *Risk Society: Towards a New Modernity* (M. Ritter, Trans.). London: Sage.
Beck, U. (1993) 'Individualisation and the Transformation of Politics'. Paper presented at the conference on De-Traditionalisation at Lancaster University, July 1993.
Benton, T. (1993) *Natural Relations.* London: Verso.
Carson, R. (1965) *Silent Spring.* Harmondsworth: Penguin.
Commission of the European Communities (CEC) (1992) *Fifth Environmental Action Programme for the Environment and Sustainable Development.* Brussels: CEC.
Dickens, P. (1992) *Society and Nature.* Hemel Hempstead: Harvester Wheatsheaf.
Douglas, M. and Wildavsky, A. (1982) *Risk and Culture: An Essay on the Selection of Technological and Environmental Dangers.* Berkeley: University of California Press.
Eder, K. (1990) 'Rise of Counter-Culture Movements Against Modernity: Nature as a New Field of Class Struggle'. *Theory, Culture and Society* **17**: 21–47.
Eyerman, R. and Jamison, A. (1991) *Social Movements: A Cognitive Approach.* Cambridge: Polity.
Giddens, A. (1990) *The Consequences of Modernity.* Cambridge: Polity.
Grove-White, R. (1991) 'The Emerging Shape of Environmental Conflict in the 1990s'. *Royal Society of Arts* **139**: 437–447.
Grove-White, R. and Szerszynski, B. (1992) 'Getting Behind Environmental Ethics'. *Environmental Ethics* **1**: 285–296.
Hetherington, K. (1993) *The Geography of the Other: Lifestyle, Performance and Identity.* PhD, Dept. of Sociology, Lancaster University.

International Union for Conservation of Nature (IUCN) (1991) *Caring for the Earth.* Gland, Switzerland: IUCN/UNEP/WWF.

Jacques, M. (1993) 'The End of Politics'. *Sunday Times: The Culture Supplement,* London, 18 July 1993.

Lash, S. and Urry, J. (1994) *Economies of Signs and Space.* London: Sage.

Latour, B. (1993) *We Have Never Been Modern.* (C. Porter, Trans). Hemel Hempstead: Harvester Wheatsheaf.

Lovelock, J. (1988) *The Ages of Gaia: A Biography of our Living Earth.* Oxford: Oxford University Press.

Macnaghten, P. M. and Urry, J. (1993) 'Constructing the Countryside and the Passive Body', in C. Brackenridge (ed.) *Body Matters: Leisure Images and Lifestyles.* Eastbourne: Leisure Studies Association.

Melucci, A. (1989) *Nomads of the Present: Social Movements and Individual Needs in Contemporary Society.* London: Radius.

Merchant, C. (1980) *The Death of Nature: Women, Ecology and the Scientific Revolution.* San Francisco: Harper and Row.

Newby, H. (1990) 'Ecology, Amenity and Society: Social Science and Environmental Change'. *Town Planning Review* **61**: 3–20.

Newby, H. (1993) *Global Environmental Change and the Social Sciences: Retrospect and Prospect.* (unpublished).

Plumwood, V. (1993) *Feminism and the Mastery of Nature.* London: Routledge.

Porritt, J. (1984) *Seeing Green: The Politics of Ecology Explained.* Oxford: Blackwell.

Rubin, C. (1989) 'Environmental Policy and Environmental Thought: Ruckelshaus and Commonor'. *Environmental Ethics* **11**: 27–51.

Shiva, V. (1988) *Staying Alive: Women, Ecology and Development.* London: Zed.

Strathern, M. (1992) *After Nature: English Kinship in the Late Twentieth Century.* Cambridge: Cambridge University Press.

Szerszynski, B. (1993) *Uncommon Ground: Moral Discourse, Foundationalism and the Environmental Movement.* PhD, Dept of Sociology, Lancaster University.

UNCED (1987) *Our Common Future.* UNCED, Switzerland: Conches.

UNCED (1992) *Agenda 21.* UNCED, Switzerland: Conches.

Urry, J. (1992) 'The Tourist Gaze and the "Environment"'. *Theory, Culture and Society* **9**: 1–22.

Urry, J. (1993) 'Social Identity, Leisure and the Countryside', in R. Grove-White, J. Darrall, P. M. Macnaghten, G. Clark and J. Urry (eds.) *Leisure Uses of the Countryside.* London: CPRE.

Warde, A. (1994) 'Consumers, Identity and Belonging; Reflections on some Theses of Zygmunt Bauman, in R. Keat, N. Whiteley and N. Abercrombie (eds.) *The Authority of the Consumer.* London: Routledge.

WCS (1980) *World Conservation Strategy.* Gland, Switzerland: IUCN/UNEP/WWF.

Williams, R. (1972) 'Ideas of Nature', in J. Renthall (ed.) *Ecology, the Shaping of Enquiry.* London: Longman.

Williams, R. (1976) *Keywords: A Vocabulary of Culture and Society.* London: Fontana.

Wilson, A. (1992) *The Culture of Nature: North American Landscape from Disney to the Exxon Valdez.* Cambridge, MA: Blackwell.

Wynne, B. (1991) 'After Chernobyl: Science Made too Simple'. *New Scientist* **1753**: 44–46.

Wynne, B. (1994) 'Scientific Knowledge and the Global Environment', in M. Redclift and E. Benton (eds.) *Social Theory and the Global Environment.* London: Routledge.

Wynne, B. and Meyer, S. (1993) 'How Science Fails the Environment'. *New Scientist* **1876**: 33–35.

Yearley, S. (1991) *The Green Case.* London: Harper Collins.

# 2

# Ecocentric Management for a Risk Society

*Paul Shrivastava*

A central feature of postindustrial modernization is the proliferation of technological and environmental risks and crises. These risks and crises emanate from corporate industrial activities. The traditional management paradigm is limited in several ways for responding to demands of the risk society and should be abandoned. I propose an alternative 'ecocentric' paradigm for management in the risk society context, which advocates an ecologically centered conception of interorganizational relations and internal management activities. Thus, organizations are viewed as situated within bioregionally sustainable *industrial ecosystems*, relating to each other through a logic of ecological interdependence. Within this context, *ecocentric management* seeks to minimize the environmental impact of organizational vision, inputs, throughputs, and outputs. Implications of this paradigm for management practice and research are examined.

## INTRODUCTION

The last quarter of this century has been a period of transition from an industrial to a postindustrial era. Previously, industrial societies were focused primarily on the creation of wealth through technological expansion and, secondarily, on distribution of the wealth (societal welfare). In contrast, postindustrial societies are centered on the *risks* that accompany the creation of and distribution of wealth. Consequently, the management paradigm that should be used for postindustrial societies is different from the management paradigm developed in the literature during the past three decades.

In this article, I examine the nature of postindustrial modernization. Important characteristics of postindustrial 'risk societies' and the worldwide proliferation of risks are described. Next, four key limitations of the traditional management paradigm are examined. Finally, I propose both an alternative ecocentric management paradigm and the implications it can have for organizational research and practice.

Reprinted with permission from *Academy of Management Review*, Vol. 20, No. 1, 1995, pp. 118–137
© 1995 Academy of Management

## BARE OUTLINES OF THE RISK SOCIETY

To set the stage for my argument, I must first distinguish between industrial and *postindustrial modernization.* Industrial modernization covered the period from the industrial revolution to the mid-20th century. This period of tremendous industrial progress was characterized by scientific and technological advancements in agriculture, medicine, communications, transportation, energy, chemicals, electronics, and other sectors. Such dazzling progress blinded people to the risks that were simultaneously imposed by industrialization.

Theories of industrial modernization proposed by Marx, Habermas, Parsons, and others share a utopian evolutionism. Proponents of these theories associate industrial modernization with steady progress, and they downplay discontinuities and crises, especially in the ecological arena. They use the concepts of development of means of production, communicative rationality, and structural differentiation and functional integration as the mechanisms behind the exceptional evolutionary economic and social transformation (Habermas, 1989; Parsons, 1982).

Postindustrial modernization represents the past 30 years in industrialized Western societies. Postindustrial societies are characterized by the following economic, social, and political attributes: (a) much of the economic production occurs in service and high-technology sectors; (b) there is increasing globalization of finance, production, labor, and product markets; (c) economic growth is confronted with ecological limits; and (d) there is a movement toward democratization of markets and politics (Bell, 1973; Giddens, 1990).

A number of social theorists have examined the transition that industrial societies make when they become postindustrial societies. These theories of reflexive modernity place *risk* at the center of the modernization process (Beck, 1992a; Douglas and Wildavsky, 1982; Giddens, 1990, 1991; Lash, 1992). These theories have viewed postindustrial modernization as processes of critically assessing and dealing with the risks created by industrialization, and their central concern has been with *technological and environmental risks.* The most compelling analysis in this genre is the work of Ulrich Beck (1992a,b), from which I draw generously in this section.

Risk is a complex concept that has been studied in numerous social science disciplines. Webster's *Ninth New Collegiate Dictionary* defines risk as 'exposure to possible loss, injury, or danger'. This basic idea of risk as possible loss has been interpreted differently in different disciplines. Psychologists define risk in terms of perceptions of people exposed to potential loss. They use psychometric measures of risk perceptions to measure risk (Slovic, 1987). Economists define risk as uncertainty about economic gains and losses. They use statistical probability models to measure this uncertainty. Financial analysts extend this economic concept of risk to include risks based on different sources of uncertainty (e.g. market risks, inflation risk, liquidity risk, credit risk, interest rate risk, currency risk, structural risk, reinvestment risk, and prepayment risk) (Bernstein, 1992). In risk management, authors use the probability of event times the impact of the event as a measure of risk (Kliendorfer and Kunreuther, 1987; Lave, 1987). Sociologists define risks as social processes and systems for dealing with hazards (Krimsky and Golding, 1992; Perrow, 1984; Short and Clarke, 1992).

Sociological definitions of risk best fit my needs for discussing the risks of postindustrial modernization. *Risk* is defined here as 'a systematic way of dealing with hazards and insecurities induced and introduced by modernization itself' (Beck, 1992a: 21). Modernization risks are produced concomitantly with the production of wealth. Modernization processes seek to fulfil human needs through the development of technological productivity and the creation of wealth. Exponential growth in productive forces unleashes hazards, potential threats, and risks. Thus, excessive production of hazards and ecologically unsustainable consumption of natural resources are the root sources of modern risks.

In the classical industrial society, the logic of wealth production dominated the logic of risk production; thus, risks were minor, and they could be treated as latent side effects or 'externalities' of production. In the postindustrial society, this relationship is reversed: the logic of risk production and distribution dominates processes of social change. Just as production and distribution of wealth (social welfare) were central organizing concepts in the classical industrial society, *risk* is the central organizing concept in the postindustrial society. Beck called postindustrial society, 'the risk society'—a society in which 'the productive forces have lost their innocence in the reflexivity of modernization processes' (Beck, 1992a: 12–13). Increasing production and accumulation of wealth also increases the potential for loss, in other words, risks.

Risks induce systematic and often irreversible harm in humans and the natural environment. They represent continued impoverishment of nature and often are invisible, at least when they begin, because knowledge about them is riddled with uncertainty.

Definitions of risk are based on causal interpretations; that is, risks exist only in terms of the *knowledge* about them. They can be changed, modified, magnified, channelled, and dramatized by knowledge. Risks are highly susceptible to social definition and social construction; consequently, perceptions of risk *are* reality for many practical purposes (Clarke, 1989).

In this perceptually and socially mediated relationship between risk and knowledge, science's monopoly on the rationality of risk decisions is broken. Multiple competing and conflicting 'scientific' claims about risk from different stakeholders are merged in the process of defining the causes and the effects of risk. Science does not provide unambiguous consensual answers to questions about risks. Scientific rationality is no longer an adequate arbiter of risk disputes. In resolving risk disputes, multiple (corporate vs. government vs. people's) scientific interpretations are moderated by their respective political interests.

Thus, knowledge of risks has great political significance. Knowledge or expertise is a source of political power. Risks politicize knowledge (scientific and otherwise) in unique ways; they cast doubts on scientific and social rationalities (Nelkin, 1979).

Risks are *ascribed* by epoch and civilization. A person is afflicted by risks by both being part of a civilization and by being aware of these risks. In this sense, risks have been part of every era; however, in earlier times the main sources of risks were acts of God or nature (earthquakes, plagues, pestilence, diseases, etc.). Blame for these risks lay outside of society. In contrast, modern risks are characterized by a *lack*: the impossibility of an *external* attribution of hazard. Instead, risks in modern times are acts of society or reflections of human actions and omissions. They depend on decisions—political, economic, social, and organizational ones. Risks are not caused by people's ignorance of solutions; they are caused by unintended and unforeseen effects of the solutions themselves. Thus, the source of danger is not ignorance but knowledge (scientific and technological) (Beck, 1992a).

Unlike the risks of earlier civilizations, modernization risks are rooted in ecologically destructive industrialization and are global, pervasive, long term, imperceptible, incalculable, and often unknown. Radioactivity and chemical contamination are exemplars of such risks. Risks emanating from the Chernobyl nuclear accident were geographically pervasive, temporally transgenerational, crossed national boundaries, and remain incalculable.

Ecological degradation contradicts the interests that advance industrialization, and it has differential impacts on people. Differential distribution of risks puts people in different *social risk positions*. Risks cross economic class, gender, ethnic, generational, and national boundaries. Risk positions exacerbate inequalities based on these variables, but wealth or power do not provide complete protection from modernization risks. These risks can have a boomerang effect on their producers; thus, producers are not immune to the risks they produce. Therefore, risks can transcend traditional boundaries of class, race, and nation (Clarke, 1989; Luhmann, 1990).

The logic of risk production, risk diffusion, and risk commercialization is only loosely coupled to the logic of capitalism or socialism (Communism), and it is *self-referential* (i.e., independent of the surrounding satisfaction of human needs). Modernization, in seeking economic growth, inadvertently but systematically unleashes risks and hazards. Once created, such risks can expand and evolve independently of economic gains.

**Risk proliferation.** Modernization risks have proliferated through population explosion, industrial pollution, environmental degradation, and the lack of institutional capacity for risk management. People in communities all over the world have been experiencing these risks in the form of visible negative influences on their quality of life.

The world population has doubled during the past 40 years; it is presently about 5.5 billion. It will double again during the next 40 years to approximately 11 billion. The tremendous ecological burden such a population explosion places on the earth's ecosystems is apparent from the depletion of natural resources (Ehrlich and Ehrlich, 1991). Widespread damage to world fishery (50% depletion during the last 50 years), wildlife, rain forests (42 000 square miles lost each year), soil degradation by industrial agriculture, and desertification (26 000 square miles lost each year) has now been documented (Brown *et al.*, 1990, 1991, 1992). To simply provide basic amenities to 11 billion people will require increasing world economic production by 5 to 30 times the current levels. At the most, probable rates of consumption growth, world reserves of oil, natural gas, coal, and all minerals will be depleted within the next century (Clark, 1989; Daly, 1977; McNeil, 1989; World Commission on Environment and Development, 1987).

Additionally, because of industrial pollution, risks to health and environment also have expanded, and urban air pollution, smog, global warming, ozone depletion, acid rain, toxic waste sites, nuclear hazards, obsolete weapons arsenals, industrial accidents, and hazardous products are manifestations of these risks. An idea of their scale may be gleaned from the data for one type of pollution—toxic wastes.

In the United States alone, there are over 30 000 documented uncontrolled toxic waste sites, and these are increasing at the rate of 2000 to 3000 per year. Of these sites, over 2500 are on the National Priority List because they represent active danger to human health. Estimates for cleaning up these sites range from $25 billion to $150 billion. Payment devoted for cleanup during the past 10 years has averaged approximately $0.5 billion per year. The net result of this incommensurate remedy is the cumulative increase of toxic wastes and risks each year (Carson, 1962; Commoner, 1990; Likens, 1987).

This pattern of *accumulating risks and inadequate remedies* is true for most of the other pollution problems I have listed. Such is the situation today in the United States, despite this country's immense financial and technological resources for cleanup, great public awareness of ecological problems, and stringent environmental regulations. The situation in the rest of the world is worse.

Environmental and technological risk have been created by institutions (corporations and government agencies) that also are in charge of controlling and managing these risks. This self-policing of risks is partly responsible for risk proliferation. Because of complexities and error proneness of technological systems, traditional risk managers' approaches have failed to prevent both accidents and the escalation of these risks (Perrow, 1984; Short and Clarke, 1992).

People who have been affected by 'technoenvironmental' risks are experiencing an increased dependency on obscure and inaccessible social institutions and actors. They have developed a sceptical attitude (private reflexivity) toward risk-related institutions, such as corporations and government regulatory agencies. Communities also progressively have taken risk decisions into their own hands. This action has been evidenced in the United States through the rise of the NIMBY (Not in My Back Yard) movement. NIMBY is a grass-roots resistance movement that opposes hazardous industrial and urban development projects within communities (Couch and Kroll-Smith, 1991; Douglas and Wildavsky, 1982; Goldstein and Shorr, 1991; Krimsky and Golding, 1992; Piller, 1991).

Public perceptions of technoenvironmental risks have been heightened by frequent high-profile industrial accidents. Chernobyl, the Exxon *Valdez*, and the incident in Bhopal have raised world consciousness about these techno-environmental risks. Heightened perceptions of risks have fostered political pressures for regulating environmental hazards. During the past two decades, increasing regulations worldwide have changed the competitive dynamics of many industries (Mitroff and Pauchant, 1990; Shrivastava, 1994; Smith, 1992).

This bare outline of the postindustrial risk society serves as the context for management problems of the coming century. Environmental degradation and risks, as central consequences of modernization, pose new challenges for corporate managers and public policy officials. Technological and environmental risks are the core management problems of the risk society.

In this context, it is not sufficient to manage corporations to optimize production variables, such as profits, productivity, jobs, and growth. Corporations must manage risk variables, such as product harm, pollution, waste, resources, technological hazards, and worker and public safety. This type of management does not mean simply an expansion of the management agenda to include new risks. It implies a fundamental reversal in the focus of managers' attention, that is, substituting the production orientation of existing paradigms with the risk orientation of a new paradigm proposed later in this paper.

The traditional management paradigm was developed for the industrial society; thus, it is inherently limited in many ways for meeting the challenges of the 'risk' society. I examine four key limitations of this traditional paradigm in the next section and then propose an ecocentric management paradigm compatible with needs of this risk society.

## LIMITATIONS OF THE TRADITIONAL MANAGEMENT PARADIGM

At the beginning, let me acknowledge that authors of the management literature do not agree on a single coherent management paradigm (Burrell and Morgan, 1978). There are many management theories and approaches that loosely fit into a dominant managerial worldview. In the traditional worldview, organizations have been described as economic and legal entities created by groups of people who have common or, at least, compatible goals. Organizational promoters invest their own and borrowed resources to accomplish their goals. Organizations are systems of production, serving the goals of stakeholders and operating in a dynamic economic, social, and political environment. Economic organizations or corporations have received much attention by researchers in organizational/management theory. Hence, this article also focuses on management in the context of modern corporations.

Within this general view of organizations, different management theorists have sought to optimize different types of productivity and returns from organizations. Organizational theorists examine the contingent match among organizational structure, size, environment, technology, resources, and decision processes (Aldrich, 1979; Hall and Quinn, 1983; Pfeffer, 1982; Scott, 1981). Strategic management theorists have sought to align organizational resources with environmental demands to achieve objectives and optimize returns to investors (Porter, 1980; Schendel and Hofer, 1979). In addition, organizational behavior and human resource management theorists have sought to optimize the use of organizational personnel (Miner, 1984).

Also, researchers of cultural theories of organization have examined organizational values, beliefs, assumptions, norms, and mores, seeking to understand these ideas as cultural entities (Frost, 1985; Deal and Kennedy, 1982). The corporate social responsibility (CSR) literature has examined the changing role of corporations in society, seeking to make corporations more responsive to societal needs (Freeman, 1984; Sethi and Steidlmeir, 1991; Wood, 1991).

All of these organizational theories (except for the CSR literature) do not address ecological issues seriously. CSR authors have periodically focused on ecological problems as a social issue of concern to management (Buchholz, Marcus and Post, 1992; Hoffman, Frederick and Petry, 1990; Post, 1991). However, ecology is not central even to the CSR literature. It is *one of many* social problems confronting corporations. Other problems include race and gender discrimination, business ethics and fraud, corporate philanthropy, minority concerns, community welfare, and stakeholder demands (Carroll, 1979; Preston, 1985).

Other theorists have argued for ethical and moral conduct of organizations (Etzioni, 1988; Goodpastor, 1989). Complex moral, social, and administrative motives are discernible in the creation and running of organizations. Not all organizations are driven by a single-minded objective to maximize profits; some, instead, pursue multiple objectives (March and Simon, 1958/1993).

Collectively, these organizational theories constitute a formidable body of literature. They cannot be described in the limited space of this article. Useful critical assessments have been conducted by other researchers (Alvesson, 1992; Burrell and Morgan, 1978; Fischer and Sirianni, 1993; Shrivastava, 1986; Whitley, 1984).

In this article, I simply want to identify four key assumptions (common to these organizational approaches) that act as limitations in dealing with the organizational challenges of a risk society: (a) a denatured view of organizational environment, (b) production/consumption bias, (c) financial risk bias, and (d) anthropocentrism. These assumptions are not equally and uniformly common to all theories in the traditional management paradigm. However, most traditional management theorists subscribe to some version of these assumptions.

**Denatured view of the environment.** In the traditional management paradigm a narrow concept of 'organizational environment' is used which emphasizes the economic, political, social and technological aspects of organizational environments. Economic aspects of environments, especially variables characterizing markets, industries, competitors, and regulations, receive primary emphasis. This approach virtually ignores the natural environment (Emery and Trist, 1965; Fahey and Narayanan, 1984).

Organizational environments are portrayed as abstract, disembodied, and ahistorical external influences on organizations. The environment has been described as a bundle of resources to be used by organizations. The emphasis is on understanding both how environments influence organizations and how organizations can procure, exploit, or compete for environmental resources. The reverse relationship—how organizations have an impact on their natural environment—has received little attention (Shrivastava, In press; Throop, Starik and Rands, 1993).

It is worth noting that, although management theorists have adopted a narrow view of environments, management practitioners have begun to incorporate a broader and more holistic view of the environment into their practices. The rise of environmentalism and environmental regulations have led corporations to acknowledge the physical environmental base of organizational activities.

To fully appreciate the ecological consequences of organizational activities, the relevant organizational environment must be viewed as an *economic biosphere*, which includes not only economic, social, technological, and political elements, but also biological, geological, and atmospheric ones. The environment of business consists of (a) the ecology of the planet earth; (b) the world economic, social, and political order; and (c) the immediate market, technological, and sociopolitical context of organizations (Davis, 1991; Smith, 1992; Stead and Stead, 1992).

**Production/consumption bias.** There are two linked assumptions of the traditional management paradigm that exacerbate environmental degradation. First is the assumption that business organizations are neutral, rational, technological 'systems of production' that serve the interests of many stakeholders. Business activities, education, and research are geared toward improving organizational *productivity and efficiency*, to benefit stakeholders. This focus on production ignores destructive aspects of organizations. Environmental destruction and harm caused by organizations, such as environmental pollution, toxic products and wastes, and technological and occupational hazards and risks, are ignored and treated as externalities.

Second is the assumption that unconstrained consumption is not a problem and should be promoted. Traditional management theorists accept the *consumerist* society ideal of Western industrialism. In the United States, over \$100 billion is spent each year in advertising aimed at increasing the consumption of goods. The basic logic of continually producing new products for limitless consumption has remained unquestioned by proponents of the traditional management paradigm (Commoner, 1990; Smith, 1992). These assumptions are now challenged by the mounting evidence of widespread environmental destruction and public health risks caused by organized industrial production and unsustainable consumption patterns.

**Financial risk bias.** Another limiting assumption of the traditional management paradigm involves the *concept of risk*. Financial risk dominates the idea of risk in business studies. Managers assume that the primary risks they face are related to financial and product markets. They assess and manage financial risks in relation to economic returns. They also manage product-market risks that involve uncertainty about product demand caused by changing economic conditions, consumer preferences, market demographics, competitive pressures, and regulatory changes.

They ignore the risks posed by technology, its location, its waste products, and its impact on the natural environment. This mindset ignores the numerous ecological, technological, and health risks emanating from industrial hazards that I described previously. Industrial hazards also impose risks due to the disruption of larger economic, social, political, and cultural systems.

This narrow-minded discussion of risks in organizations (i.e., how to face risks and how to manage them) (March and Shapira, 1989) predominates studies of organizations. Little attention has been paid to risks that have been imposed by organizations onto diverse stakeholders or the distribution of these risks among different sectors of society.

**Anthropocentrism.** Another fundamental limitation of the traditional paradigm is *anthropocentrism*, an ideology that asserts the separateness, uniqueness, primacy, and superiority of the *human* species. This concept legitimizes human welfare as the central purpose of societal institutions. Accordingly, nature is reviewed as an expendable resource for furthering the interests of humans. Humans, thus, have a right to exploit nature without any real concern for maintaining its integrity. Preservation of nature is meaningful only as a condition of human self-interest. Therefore, nature may be protected and conserved so that humans may use it to the 'max', both at the present time and in the future. According to anthropocentric assumptions, human beings have no moral obligation to minimize their impact of nature (Devall and Sessions, 1985; Nash, 1989).

Anthropocentrism is part of the traditional management paradigm at a very deep level. It is part of the basic assumptions borrowed from neo-classical economics, which is in itself anthropocentric. Thus, ideas such as 'property rights' over natural resources, 'free market' exchange with linked ecological externalities, 'economic rationality' in organizational decision making, denaturalized theories of the firm, and insatiable consumption needs of *homo economicus* are taken for granted in organizational studies (Daly and Cobb, 1989).

Under anthropocentric assumptions, organizational exploitation of natural resources is legitimate, even desirable. Concerns about natural resource extinction rarely surface as strategic organizational issues. When they do, they are prompted not by a preservationist sentiment, but rather by fears of price inflation and future shortages. This anthropocentric attitude has fostered the unchecked exploitation of resources by organizations (Pauchant and Fortier, 1990).

## SHIFTING PARADIGMS: ECOCENTRIC MANAGEMENT IN INDUSTRIAL ECOSYSTEMS

If organizations are to effectively address the ecological degradation inherent in risk societies, they must use a new management orientation. They need an orientation that focuses centrally on technological and environmental risks, that is, one that does not treat risks as externalities but treats them as the *core problems* of management.

Moving risk to center stage of organizational theory and practice can be accomplished in many ways. My approach here is to adopt the perspective of the stakeholder that bears the most risks from industrial activities: *Nature!* Why? Because nature is fundamental to all life, and certainly human welfare depends on it. Placing nature (and derivatively human health, not wealth) at the center of management/ organizational concerns is the hallmark of the alternative ecocentric management paradigm that I propose.

In this section I provide a preliminary description of the ecocentric management paradigm. My purpose is to help create a vision of ecologically sustainable organization-environment relations. This paradigm is simply a place for management researchers to start from, and consequently, it is tentative, provisional, and incomplete. In the next paragraphs I suggest two basic concepts—*industrial ecosystems* and *ecocentric management* that re-envision interorganizational relations and internal organizational elements. Industrial ecosystems provide a vision of organizational populations and interorganizational relations that are compatible with bioregional natural systems. Ecocentric management, in contrast, seeks ecologically sustainable organizational designs and practices.

## INDUSTRIAL ECOSYSTEMS

The ecocentric conception of organizational populations and interorganizational relations is based on both the ecological interdependence and ecological performance of organizational communities. Therefore, an industrial ecosystem concept parallels the natural ecosystem, which is a network of connected interdependent organisms and their environments that give and take resources from each other to survive. For example, in a marine ecosystem, big fish eat little fish; little fish eat insects; and insects eat weeds and plankton. Products of natural photosynthesis and waste of fishes and insects serve as nourishment of weeds, plankton, and fish habitats. This arrangement constitutes a self-sufficient, dynamically balanced ecosystem.

The industrial ecosystem seeks to emulate this idea of natural ecosystems. Conceptually, it consists of a network of organizations that jointly seek to minimize environmental degradation by using each other's waste and by-products and by sharing and minimizing the use of natural resources (Allenby, 1993; Ayres and Simonis, 1992).

Implicit in such an arrangement is the belief that it is possible to reduce the ecological impact of industrial activities and to use ecological resources more effectively through cooperative strategies. This cooperation can occur at several levels: (a) the simplest industrial ecosystem network could involve waste exchange among a few proximally located organizations and (b) more extensive industrial ecosystems could establish cooperative relations at the local, regional, and even national levels. Ideally, bioregionally bounded ecosystems are desirable because they make the most of natural bioregional capacities for resources, energy, markets, and waste sinks (Frosch and Gallapoulos, 1992; Tibbs, 1991).

A network of companies in Kalundborg, Denmark, exemplifies a simple industrial ecosystem. It consists of a power plant, an enzyme plant, a refinery, a chemical plant, a cement plant, a wallboard plant, and some farms. These plants use one another's wastes and by-products as raw materials. They coordinate their use of raw materials, energy, water, and their waste-management practices. Figure 1 shows the flow of resources among them.

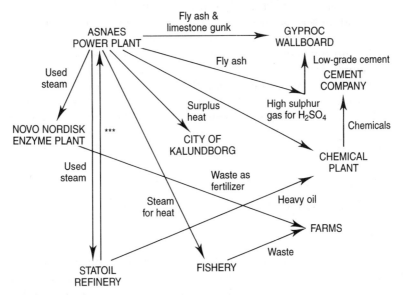

Figure 1. An Industrial Ecosystem.

The coal-fired Asnaes power plant sells its used steam to the Novo Nordisk enzyme plant and Statoil refinery, instead of condensing it and dumping it into the fjord. The power plant also sells its fly ash to a cement company and its surplus heat to the city for heating. Statoil, in turn, supplies Asnaes with treated waste water for cooling. It also sells the power plant desulphurized gas to burn, saving 30 000 tons of coal a year.

The power plant ships high-sulphur gas emissions to a sulphuric acid plant. Asnaes removes pollutants from its smokestacks and sells the limestone gunk to Gyproc, the wallboard plant. The wallboard plant also receives low-grade (below construction-grade specifications) cement from the cement plant, which cuts the import of mined gypsum. Asnaes warms a fishery that produces 200 tons of trout and turbot each year, and local farms use waste from the fishery and from Novo's enzyme plant as fertilizer.

The conservational impact of this industrial ecosystem on the natural environment is impressive. It saves water, which is pumped from Lake Tisso (seven miles away). The amount of waste sent to landfills is minimized. It reduces pollution that would otherwise be emitted into the atmosphere, and it conserves energy resources in the community. Thus, companies cooperate on ecological problems and are provided a forum for ongoing improvement of environmental performance. In addition, participating companies receive good publicity and enjoy a healthy image.

Viewing organizations as components of industrial ecosystems suggests fundamental changes in their operational scope, strategies, cost structures, location, and management practices. Creating organizations as parts of bioregionally desirable ecosystems requires very different criteria for new product development, venture financing, entrepreneurial forms, and infrastructural services.

Large-scale adoption of the industrial ecosystem model for restructuring interorganizational relations will require new economic and industrial regulations, new industrial infrastructure services, new roles for markets, and new markets for ecologically sound products. Many reasonable proposals for these larger societal changes at the regional, the national, and the international levels have been made in numerous studies. Due to space limitations and the organizational focus of this paper, I will not discuss these, but instead I refer the reader to the following authors: Allenby (1993), Costanza (1992), Daly and Cobb (1989), Naess (1987), and the World Commission on Environment and Development (1987).

## ECOCENTRIC MANAGEMENT

The second part of the ecocentric paradigm focuses on the management of organizational elements that have an impact on nature. The outcome would be to align organizations with their natural environments. This alignment involves a different view of organizational goals, values, products, and production systems as well as organization, environment, and business functions. Table 1 summarizes the key differences between traditional and ecocentric paradigms. The dichotomies and opposing ideal types represented by the two columns of Table 1 are an analytical artefact. In reality, the researcher is unlikely to find either paradigm in its 'pure' type.

Table 1. Traditional versus ecocentric management

| Traditional management | Ecocentric management |
|---|---|
| *Goals:* | |
| Economic growth & profits | Sustainability and quality of life |
| Shareholder wealth | Stakeholder welfare |
| *Values:* | |
| Anthropocentric | Biocentric or Ecocentric |
| Rationality and packaged knowledge | Intuition and understanding |
| Patriarchal values | Postpatriarchal feminist values |
| *Products:* | |
| Designed for function, style & price | Designed for the environment |
| Wasteful packaging | Environment friendly |
| *Production System:* | |
| Energy & resource intensive | Low energy & resource use |
| Technical efficiency | Environmental efficiency |
| *Organization:* | |
| Hierarchical structure | Nonhierarchical structure |
| Top-down decision making | Participative decision making |
| Centralized authority | Decentralized authority |
| High-income differentials | Low-income differentials |
| *Environment:* | |
| Domination over nature | Harmony with nature |
| Environment managed as a resource | Resources regarded as strictly finite |
| Pollution and waste are externalities | Pollution/waste elimination and management |
| *Business functions:* | |
| Marketing aims at increasing consumption | Marketing for consumer education |
| Finance aims at short-term profit maximization | Finance aims at long-term sustainable growth |
| Accounting focuses on conventional costs | Accounting focuses on environmental costs |
| Human resource management aims at increasing labor productivity | Human resource management aims to make work meaningful & the workplace safe/healthy |

The ecocentric paradigm aims at creating sustainable economic development and improving the quality of life worldwide for all organizational stakeholders. It is based on ecocentric and postpatriarchial values that seek freedom from domination of all types. These values reject human domination over nature. They appreciate the importance of intuition and understanding over scientific rationality.

The action consequences of ecocentric management proliferate all aspects of organizations—their mission, inputs, throughputs, and outputs. Ecocentric management seeks ecofriendly products through ecological designs, packaging, and material use. It encourages the use of low energy, smaller amounts of resources, and environmentally efficient and appropriate technologies of production.

Organizations in the ecocentric paradigm are appropriately scaled, provide meaningful work, have decentralized participative decision making, have low earning differentials among employees, and have nonhierarchical structures. They establish harmonious relationships between their natural and social environments. They seek to systematically renew natural resources and to minimize waste and pollution.

All business functions assume more ecologically centered roles. Marketing seeks to educate consumers about responsible consumption, instead of promoting unrestricted consumption. Finance aims for long-term sustainable growth, instead of short-term profits. Accounting seeks to incorporate social and environmental costs of production, instead of externalizing them. Management seeks to provide meaningful work and safe working conditions, instead of single-mindedly pursuing labor productivity.

The concept of total quality environmental management (TQEM) provides a framework for managing the environmental impacts. TQEM involves systematic greening of organizational missions, inputs, throughputs, and outputs (Council on Environmental Quality, 1993; Shrivastava and Hart, 1992).

**Mission.** Traditionally, corporate missions have had a national and financial orientation. They have aimed at satisfying the demands of a narrow set of stakeholders, primarily investors and customers and, secondarily, government and communities (David, 1989). Ecocentric management espouses corporate missions oriented toward long-term, global, and environmental issues. In addition to seeking financial gains, ecocentric companies actively seek harmony with the natural environment. Nature is a primary stakeholder, both in the regions where a company operates and globally. Ecocentric companies have their commitments to nature clearly articulated in mission statements (Campbell and Young, 1991).

Corporate missions and visions provide the 'glue' that holds together other elements of organizations. In fact, alignment of the organization's strategies, structure, systems, and processes is greatly facilitated by a widely shared vision. In ecocentric companies, such a mission and vision includes corporate commitment to

(1) Minimize the use of virgin materials and nonrenewable forms of energy.
(2) Eliminate emissions, effluents, and accidents.
(3) Minimize the life-cycle cost of products and services.

**Inputs.** Ecocentric managers reject uncontrolled organizational use of inputs in the form of natural resources and energy. They subscribe to the principle of *sustainable use* of natural resources. *Sustainable use* means pacing the exploitation of renewable resources in such a way that they can regenerate themselves through natural processes. It also involves minimizing the use of nonrenewable resources. The basis for this principle is recognition that the earth's resources are finite.

Ecocentric management seeks to *minimize the use of virgin materials and nonrenewable forms of energy*. This goal can be achieved by (a) reducing energy and material use through conservation measures, (b) making greater use of recycled or renewable materials and energy, or (c) offsetting consumption with replenishment.

The practical possibilities in resource and energy conservation are immense. Many companies are already developing innovative conservation programs. For example, the National Audubon Society's new headquarters building cut its use of energy by 40 percent through solar architectural design, use of energy-efficient lighting fixtures, and conservation-oriented maintenance and energy use programs. Herman Miller abandoned the use of virgin timber in their top lines of furniture, turning instead to wood grown on a sustained yield basis. The Body Shop is replenishing the fossil fuel-based energy it buys from utilities. It has established a wind energy plant in Scotland, which supplies energy back to the electric grid.

**Throughputs.** The throughput system or production process is often associated with environmental risks, occupational and public health risks, and inefficient use of material and human resources. Ecocentric management seeks to *eliminate emissions, effluents, workplace hazards, and risks of accident.* The production process aims at achieving a 'zero discharge' goal and a 'zero risk' goal. It focuses efforts toward the virtual elimination of waste. It espouses a preventative approach rather than a controlling approach after pollution and hazards are created.

The potential for ecocentric production systems is exemplified by Dow Chemical's new ethylene plant in Fort Saskatchewan, Canada. This facility was designed to minimize discharges of waste water. It will release only 10 gallons of waste water per minute, compared to 360 gallons per minute for a traditional plant. Corporations are realizing that throughput process improvements have a cost-saving effect and can even generate revenue. Evidence of these benefits is provided by 3M Company's Pollution Prevention Pays (3P) Program, Dow Chemical's Waste Reduction Always Pays (WRAP) Program, and Chevron's Save Money and Reduce Toxics (SMART) Program (Hunt and Auster, 1990; Kleiner, 1991).

3M saved nearly $500 million and prevented 500 000 tons of pollution between 1975 and 1989 through its 3P Program. This program has been based on pollution reduction at the source through product reformulation, process modification, equipment redesign, and recycling and reuse of materials. Each project undertaken by the 3P Program must meet four criteria: (a) eliminate or reduce pollution, (b) save energy or materials and resources, (c) demonstrate technological innovation, and (d) save money.

**Outputs.** Products and waste are the two primary outputs of organizations. Product choice and design have important implications for the natural environment. Products that lack durability or are difficult to repair place greater demand on the resource base of new materials and energy. Products that are difficult or expensive to reuse or recycle result in unnecessary costs for waste and disposal. Ecocentric management seeks to *minimize the life-cycle cost* of its products and services. Life-cycle costs attach a monetary figure to every impact of a product, that is, disposal costs, legal fees, liability for product harm, loss of environmental quality, and so on. Product-development decisions have been based not only on projected cash flow, but also on the projected future costs associated with each product design (Buzzelli, 1991).

Ecocentric managers view organizational waste both as an environmental problem and as a business opportunity. They seek to minimize and treat waste in a manner least harmful to the environment. Waste-management strategies include waste reduction, reuse, and recycling. The remaining waste is incinerated or placed in a landfill. The opportunities in waste management include both cost reduction and safe disposal of the enormous inventory of hazardous waste.

**Systems approach.** A systems approach to managing environmental impacts of organizational activities is central to ecocentric management. If managers consider jointly all of the aspects of the organizational system, this awareness helps to prevent the shifting of environmental harm from one subsystem to another. This approach can be facilitated by organizations' adopting life-cycle assessment methodology for minimizing the ecological impacts of products from 'cradle to grave'. Ultimately, the corporation should close the loop of output and input processes.

## CHALLENGES OF ECOCENTRIC MANAGEMENT

The ecocentric management paradigm has serious implications for management practice and theory. Corporate managers face many strategic and operational questions. For example, how should they redesign and navigate their business portfolios to meet ecological limitations and bottlenecks? What are the human resource needs of ecocentric organizations? How do ecological costs change the financial structure of investment projects and firm competitiveness? What are the market potentials for ecofriendly technologies and 'green markets?'

The ecocentric management paradigm also poses important challenges to the traditional management paradigm and theories. It calls for revising them significantly, that is, adopting a management theory that is not anthropocentric, a theory that acknowledges ecological risk and degradation as central variables in organizational analysis. This theory would not be biased toward ecologically unsustainable production and consumption. This theory would help researchers and practitioners alike to understand technological and environmental factors as key corporate risks.

Ecocentrism calls for questioning the very concept of organizations. If the organizational environment is viewed as an ecobiosphere, it forces those in the field of management to question the simplistic assumption that organizations are innocent *systems of production* that produce products desired by consumers. Accordingly, this theory suggests that organizations also must be seen as *systems of destruction* because they systematically destroy environmental value. This destruction cannot be dismissed as an 'externality' of production that the firm need not account for. It must be treated as a central and systematic feature of organized economic activity.

This view of firms suggests revising management's basic concepts of *organizational objectives and strategy.* Objectives of the firm that maximize (or satisfice) variables like profits, revenues, and productivity are incomplete and inadequate. Such objectives also must include minimizing the negative and destructive effects of organizational activities.

This new concept of strategy deals with the co-alignment of an organization with its environment. A firm's strategy cannot be limited to defining its domain of operation and scope at the corporate level and its competitive approaches at the business-unit level. This strategy must include some conception of the firm's relationship with the natural environment. It must address issues of impact of the firm's activities on the natural and social environments, and it must provide avenues for renewal of environmental resources that the organization uses.

Today, the challenge facing organizational researchers is momentous: for each management theory, proponents must reflexively identify implications of ecocentrism. Reconceptualizing fundamental concepts like *organizations, objectives,* and *strategies* forces researchers and practitioners to rethink much of what they know about organizations. Part of this rethinking involves making the functional areas of business (operations, accounting, marketing, finance, administration, and human resource management) more ecocentric. Fortunately, 'green marketing' and 'green accounting' have already been put to use in making progress toward ecocentrism in both theory development and practice (Gray, Bebbington and Walters, 1993). My hope is that in the coming years we (in management) will see the flowering of green organizational/management theories and practices.

## ACKNOWLEDGEMENTS

Many ideas and arguments in this article were stimulated by and discussed on the ONE-L network of the Organizations and the Natural Environment Interest Group of the Academy of Management. I would like to thank the ONE-L members for their contribution and support.

## REFERENCES

Aldrich, H. E. (1979) *Organizations and Environments*. Englewood Cliffs, NJ: Prentice Hall.
Allenby, B. R. (1993) *Industrial Ecology*. New York: Prentice Hall.
Alvesson, M. (1992) *Critical Organizational Theory*. Newbury, CA: Sage.
Ayres, R. U. and Simonis, U. (eds.) (1992) *Industrial Metabolism*. Tokyo: UN University Press.
Beck, U. (1992a) *Risk Society: Towards a New Modernity*. Newbury Park, CA: Sage.
Beck, U. (1992b) 'From industrial society to risk society'. *Theory, Culture and Society*, **9**(1): 97–123.
Bell, D. (1975) *The Coming of Post-industrial Society*. New York: Basic Books.
Bernstein, P. L. (1992) *Capital Ideas: The Improbable Origins of Modern Wall Street*. New York: Free Press.
Brown, L., Chandler, W. U., Flavin, C., Jacobson, J., Polock, C., Postel, D., Starke, L. and Wolf, E. C. (1991) *State of the World*. Washington, DC: Worldwatch Institute.
Buchholz, R., Marcus, A. and Post, J. *Managing Environmental Issues: A Case Book*. Englewood Cliffs, NJ: Prentice Hall.
Burrell, G. and Morgan, G. (1978) *Sociological Paradigms and Organizational Analysis*. London: Heinemann.
Buzzelli, D. (1991) 'Time to structure an environmental policy strategy'. *Journal of Business Strategy*, **12**(2): 17–20.
Campbell, A. and Young, S. (1991) 'Creating a sense of mission'. *Long Range Planning*, **24**: 10–20.
Carroll, A. B. (1979) 'A three-dimensional conceptual model of corporate social performance'. *Academy of Management Review* **4**: 497–505.
Carson, R. (1962) *Silent Spring*. Greenwich, CT: Fawcett.
Clark, M. (1989) *Ariadne's Thread*. New York: St. Martin's Press.
Clarke, L. (1989) *Acceptable Risk: Making Decisions in a Toxic Environment*. Berkeley: University of California Press.
Commoner, B. (1990) *Making Peace with the Planet*. New York: Pantheon Books.
Costanza, R. (1992) *Ecological Economics*. New York: Columbia University Press.
Couch, S. and Droll-Smith, S. (1991) *Communities at Risk*. New York: Peter Lang.
Council of Environmental Quality (1993) *Total Environmental Quality Management*. Washington, DC: Author.
Daly, H. E. (1977) *Steady State Economics*. San Francisco: Freeman.
Daly, H. and Cobb, J. (1989) *For the Common Good*. New York: Beacon Press.
David, F. (1989) 'How companies define their mission'. *Long Range Planning*, **22**: 15–24.
Davis, J. (1991) *Greening Business*. Oxford, England: Basil Blackwell.
Deal, T. E. and Kennedy, A. A. (1982) *Corporate Cultures*. Reading, MA: Addison Wesley.
Devall, B. and Sessions, G. (1985) *Deep Ecology: Living as if Nature Mattered*. Salt Lake City, UT: Peregrine Smith Books.
Douglas, M. and Wildovsky, A. (1982) *Risk and Culture*. Berkeley: University of California Press.
Ehrlich, P. and Ehlrich, A. (1991) *The Population Explosion*. New York: Touchstone.
Emery, F. E. and Trist, E. L. (1965) 'The causual texture of organizational environments'. *Human Relations*, **18**: 21–32.

Environmental Protection Agency (1990) *Environmental Investments: The Cost of a Clean Environment.* Washington, DC: US Government Printing Office.

Etzioni, A. (1988) *The Moral Dimension.* New York: Free Press.

Fahey, L. and Narayanan, V. K. (1984) *Environmental Analysis.* St. Paul, MN: West.

Fischer, F. and Sirianni, C. (1993) *Critical Perspectives on Bureaucracy.* (2nd rev ed.), Philadelphia: Temple University Press.

Freeman, R. E. (1984) *Strategic Management: A Stakeholder Approach.* Boston: Pitman.

Frosch, R. A. and Gallapoulos, N. E. (1992) Towards an industrial ecology. In A. D. Bradshaw (ed.), *The Treatment and Handling of Wastes.* London: Chapman Hall.

Frost, P., Moore, L. F., Louis, M. R., Lundberg, C. C. and Martin, J. (1985) *Organizational Culture.* Beverly Hills, CA: Sage.

Giddens, A. (1990) *The Consequence of Modernity.* Stanford, CA: Stanford University Press.

Giddens, A. (1991) *Modernity and Self Identity in the Late Modern Age.* Cambridge, England: Cambridge University Press.

Goldstein, R. L., Shorr, J. K. (1991) *Demanding Democracy After Three Mile Island.* Gainesville: University of Florida Press.

Goodpastor, K. (1989) *Business Ethics: The State of the Art.* New York: Oxford University Press.

Gray, R., with Beggington, J. and Walters, D. (1993) *Accounting for the Environment.* London: Chapman.

Habermas, J. (1989) *A Theory of Communicative Action.* Boston: Beacon Press.

Hall, R. H. and Quinn, R. E. (eds.) (1983) *Organization Theory and Public Policy.* Beverly Hills, CA: Sage.

Hannan, M. and Freeman, J. (1989) *Organizational Ecology.* Cambridge, MA: Harvard University Press.

Hoffman, W. M., Frederick, R. and Petry, E. S. (1990) *The Corporation, Ethics and the Environment.* New York: Quorum Books.

Hunt, C. and Auster, E. (1990) 'Proactive environmental management: Avoiding the toxic trap'. *Sloan Management Review,* **31**(2): 7–18.

Kleindorfer, P. and Kunreuther, H. (1987) *Insuring and Managing Hazardous Risks: From Seveso to Bhopal and Beyond.* New York: Springer-Verlag.

Kleiner, A. (1991) 'What does it mean to be green?' *Harvard Business Review,* **69**(4): 38–47.

Krimsky, S. and Golding, D. (1992) *Social Theories of Risk.* Westport, CT: Praeger.

Lash, S. (1993) 'Reflexive modernization: The aesthetic dimension'. *Theory, Culture and Society.* **10**(1): 1–23.

Lave, L. (ed.) (1987) *Risk Assessment and Management.* New York: Plenum Press.

Likens, G. (1987) 'Chemical wastes in our atmosphere—An ecological crisis'. *Industrial Crisis Quarterly,* **1**(4): 13–33.

Luhmann, N. (1990) 'Technology, environment, and social risk: A systems perspective'. *Industrial Crisis Quarterly,* **4**(3): 223–232.

March, J. G. and Shapira, Z. (1989) 'Managerial perspectives on risk and risk taking'. *Management Science,* **33**: 1404–1421.

March, J. G. and Simon, H. (1993) *Organizations.* New York: Wiley. (Original work published 1958).

McNeill, J. (1989) 'Strategies for sustainable economic development'. *Scientific American.* September: 155–165.

Miner, J. B. (1984) *Theories of Organizational Behavior.* New York: McGraw-Hill.

Mitnick, B. (1980) *The Political Economy of Regulation: Creating, Designing and Removing Regulations.* New York: Columbia University Press.

Mitroff, I. and Pauchant, T. (1990) *We Are So Big and Powerful Nothing Bad Can Happen to Us.* New York: Carol.

Naess, A. (1987) *Ecology, Community and Lifestyle: Ecosophy.* 1987. Cambridge, England: Cambridge University Press.

Nash, R. F. (1989) *The Rights of Nature.* Madison: University of Wisconsin Press.

Nelkin, D. (1979) *Controversy: Politics of Technical Decisions.* Newbury Park, CA: Sage.

Parsons, T. (1982) *On Institutions and Social Evolution.* Chicago: University of Chicago Press.

Pauchant, T. and Fortier, J. (1990) Anthropocentric ethics in organizations, strategic management, and the environment. In P. Shrivastava and R. Lamb (eds.), *Advances in Strategic Management*, Vol. 6: 99–114. Greenwich, CT: JAI Press.

Perrow, C. (1984) *Normal Accidents: Living with High-risk Technologies*. New York: Basic Books.

Pfeffer, J. (1982) *Organizations and Organization Theory*. Boston: Pitman.

Piller, C. (1991) *The Fail-safe Society: Community Defiance and the End of American Technological Optimism*. New York: Basic Books.

Porter, M. E. (1980) *Competitive Strategy*. New York: Free Press.

Post, J. E. (1991) 'Management as if the earth mattered'. *Business Horizons*, **34**(4): 32–38.

Preston, L. (ed.) (1985) *Research in Corporate Social Performance*. Greenwich, CT: JAI Press.

Scott, R. W. (1981) *Organizations: Rational, Natural and Open Systems*. Englewood Cliffs, NJ: Prentice Hall.

Schendel, D. and Hofer, C. W. (1979) *Strategic Management: A New View of Business Policy and Planning*. Boston: Little, Brown.

Sethi, S. P. and Steidelmeir, P. (1971) *Up Against the Corporate Wall*. Englewood Cliffs, NJ: Prentice Hall.

Short, J. F. and Clarke, L. (1992) *Organizations, Uncertainties, and Risk*. Boulder, CO: Westview.

Shrivastava, P. (1986) 'Is strategic management ideological?' *Journal of Management*, **12**(3): 79–92.

Shrivastava, P. (1994) *Greening Business: Towards Sustainable Corporations*. Cincinnati, OH: Thompson Executive Press.

Shrivastava, P. In press. 'Castrated environment: Greening organizational studies'. *Organization Studies*.

Shrivastava, P. and Hart, S. (1992) 'Greening organizations—2000'. *International Journal of Public Administration*, **17**(3–4): 607–635.

Siomkos, G. (1989) 'Managing product harm crises'. *Industrial Crisis Quarterly*, **3**(1): 41–60.

Slovic, P. (1987) 'Perception of risk'. *Science*, **236**(4799): 280–285.

Smith, D. (1992) *Business and the Environment*. London: Chapman.

Stead, W. and Stead, J. (1992) *Management for a Small Planet*. Newbury Park, CA: Sage.

Throop, G., Starik, M. and Rands, G. (1993) Sustainable strategy in a greening world. In P. Shrivastava, A. Huff and J. Dutton (eds.), *Integrating the Natural Environment into Strategic Management*, Vol. 9: 63–92. Greenwich, CT: JAI Press.

Tibbs, H. (1991) *Industrial Ecology: An Environmental Agenda for Industry*. Boston: Technology and Product Development Directorate, Arthur D. Little.

Tinker, A. (1989) *Paper Prophets: A Critique of the Social Role of Accounting*.

Whitley (1984) 'Management studies as a fragmented adhocracy'. *Journal of Management Studies*.

Williamson, O. E. (1985) *The Economic Institutions of Capitalism: Firms, Markets, and Relational Contracts*. New York: Free Press.

Wood, D. (1991) 'Corporate social performance revisited'. *Academy of Management Review*, **16**: 691–718.

World Commission on Environment and Development (1987) *Our Common Future*. New York: Oxford University Press.

# 3

# Globalizing Environmentalism: Threshold of a New Phase in International Relations

*Lynton K. Caldwell*

Sociologist Robert Nisbet conjectured that 'when the history of the twentieth century is finally written, the single most important social movement of the period will be judged to be environmentalism' (1982, p. 10). This assessment has been reinforced by subsequent events. Environmental concern has risen to the top of political agendas in the United States and many other countries, becoming a major consideration in international relations. A major force for the globalization of environmental politics in the United States has been the growing international concern of nongovernmental environmental organizations (NGOs). Almost all of the larger environmental NGOs now have significant international programs that attempt to influence public policies. Transnational collaboration between governments and NGOs on environmental issues has become a characteristic of contemporary politics in North America and Western Europe. Global issues such as climate change, ozone depletion, transboundary air and water pollution, endangered species, and uses of outer space will henceforth give an international dimension to national environmental policies.

## INTRODUCTION

As the twentieth century nears its close, environmental events have introduced new elements into the basic conditions under which nations relate to one another. 'The twentieth century may, indeed, come to be seen by future generations as the time in which the concept of sovereignty and the nation state reached its apogee and began to provide our human kind with diminishing returns' (Ramphal, 1987). Events have changed traditional relationships, and obligations declared through international law have gained relevance as national boundaries cease to be effective barriers against external environmental hazards. Discovery of the risks associated with global climate change and depletion of stratospheric ozone have added new dimensions to international environmental policy.

Reprinted with permission from *Society and Natural Resources*, Vol. 4, No. 3, pp. 259–272, Lynton K. Caldwell, Taylor & Francis, Inc., Washington. All rights reserved.
© 1991 Taylor & Francis

A series of catastrophic environmental events during the 1980s—Bhopal, Sandoz, Chernobyl, Exxon Valdez—captured public attention and pushed governments to assuage popular anxiety through reassuring rhetoric and intergovernmental declarations. Action, however, has been slower to materialize, in part because the institutional structures and managerial strategies available to implement international agreements have not been adequate to the needs. Worldwide communication made possible the rapid spread of information on all issues of universal concern, and threats to the human environment are prominent among them. The activities and goals of the U.S. environmental movement were interactive with similar efforts in other countries. U.S. environmentalism was essentially moving with a worldwide tide, but it was the nongovernmental sector that was leading rather than the government in Washington. The global concerns of U.S. citizens differed in no significant respect from those of environmentalists in Canada, Western Europe, and even in the Union of Soviet Socialist Republics (U.S.S.R), but the U.S. government tended toward indifference or resistance to international environmental protection efforts. Only at the end of the 1980s did a rhetorical concession to the importance of environmental protection achieve prominence.

## LEGITIMIZING GLOBAL ENVIRONMENTALISM: THE LEGACY OF STOCKHOLM

The term *environmentalism* predates its present popular usage. It has always implied a high, sometimes inordinate, level of concern for environmental influences and relationships. Ecologically informed environmentalism has been a factor in public affairs for hardly more than two decades, although it has deeper historical roots (McCormick, 1989; Petulla, 1980). Emerging as a popular movement in the United States during the 1960s, it gained political and international legitimacy at the 1972 United Nations Conference on the Human Environment in Stockholm. During the 1960s and 1970s, the United States was foremost among nations in environmental policy and law. After 1980, the Reagan administration reversed the environmental policies of the U.S. government and thereby diminished national credibility abroad (Caldwell, 1984).

The legacy of Stockholm was to lift a popular protest movement to an agenda item in international relations, hitherto largely confined to scientifically advanced industrial states. It stimulated a worldwide awareness of environmental concerns comparable with what Earth Day 1970 did in the United States. The 1972 United Nations Conference on the Human Environment gave political legitimacy to environmental issues in international affairs (Caldwell, 1991; McCormick, 1989). Although environmental factors previously had been present in international disputes (e.g., the Trail Smelter arbitration and the Corfu incident), the points in contest related more to economic damage and to safety in navigation than to environmental policy per se (Dinwoode, 1972; Livingston, 1968). In common law countries, notably in the United States, mere environmental degradation was rarely regarded as a contemporary cause in court. Unless monetary losses could be demonstrated, environmental effects were seldom regarded as legitimate claims for damages, particularly when large numbers of people were equally affected and class-action suits were not entertained. Moreover, environmental effects were often difficult to trace with certainty to demonstrably causal sources. For example, for many years the effects of photochemical smog were not regarded as cause for compensation because the specific harmful agent in the gaseous mixture could not be linked with positive assurance to a specific human complaint.

Four developments in the mid-twentieth century converged to change the status of the environment as an object of political action and legal prescription. Without this convergence over much of the world, the Stockholm Conference would not have occurred nor its aftermath have expressed a new dimension of international relationships. These convergent factors may be identified as (a) advances in environmental science, (b) proliferation of environment-altering technologies, (c) rise of public awareness of environmental deterioration, and (d) broadening concepts of law. These events occurred within roughly the same time period in all advanced industrialized countries. The environmental movement was inherently transnational.

**Advances in environmental science**

Although the attitude of many scientists toward early environmentalism may have been equivocal, the findings of science, notably after the International Geophysical Year (1957–1958) and the International Biological Programme (1963–1974), began to lay a factual foundation for science-based environmentalism. In 1969, while preparations for the Stockholm Conference were under way, the International Council of Scientific Unions (ICSU) established the Scientific Committee on Problems of the Environment (SCOPE). These efforts were complemented by many other multidisciplinary, multinational scientific investigations, some under ICSU sponsorship, some by specialized agencies in the United Nations (especially the World Meteorological Organization and the Educational, Scientific, and Cultural Organization), and some by nongovernmental organizations such as the International Union for Conservation of Nature and Natural Resources (IUCN) and the World Wildlife Fund (WWF).

These international collaborative efforts fed back into the agenda-setting mechanisms of national governments and intergovernmental organizations and, more important, into the perceptions of informed people and organizations at the national level. Moreover, research at the national level in atmospherics, soil science, oceanography, environmental toxicology, and especially ecology produced a rapidly expanding body of data on a wide range of environmental relationships and effects. Even in the medical profession, which for decades had tended to discount environmental influences, conferences were held to consider the 'rediscovery of the environment' (Rosen, 1964). Although these scientific developments occurred primarily in technologically advanced countries, scientists in the Third World emerged as focal points for the propagation of environmental awareness in their own countries. In 1971 at the 12th Pacific Science Conference meeting in Canberra, Australia, SCOPE convened a meeting of scientists from Third World countries to consider international environmental issues. Similar meetings were held in several parts of the world in anticipation of the Stockholm Conference.

## Proliferation of environment-altering technologies

In the United States, by the mid-1960s, the century-old love affair between modern society and technology had begun to cool. Rachel Carson's book *Silent Spring* (1962) became the most widely known of a number of books reporting the adverse effects of indiscriminate uses of technology. President Johnson spoke of 'the dark side to technology' and, in 1972, the U.S. Congress established the Office of Technology Assessment to test and forecast the effects of technological innovation on health, safety, and the environment. Broader in scope and inclusive of technological effects was the environmental impact statement requirement, Section 102 (2c) in the U.S. National Environmental Policy Act of 1969 (NEPA). In its 30 January 1970 issue *Life* magazine declared 'Ecology: A cause becomes a mass movement' (Caldwell, 1982).

The advent of nuclear energy was a factor, among many others, in globalizing environmental policy concerns. The environmental risks associated with peaceful uses of nuclear energy were recognized internationally as early as 1957 with establishment by treaty of the International Atomic Energy Agency. Popular apprehension over the effects of radioactive fallout from atmospheric testing of nuclear weapons led to the Partial Nuclear Test Ban Treaty of 1963. The race into space by the United States and the U.S.S.R. prompted the signing of the Treaty on Principles Governing the Activities of States in the Exploration and Use of Outer Space, Including the Moon and Other Celestial Bodies, on 27 January 1967 in London, Moscow, and Washington. Transboundary radioactive contamination from an accident in 1986 at the Chernobyl nuclear reactor in the Soviet Union led to the rapid consummation of two multinational treaties for prompt notification and emergency assistance in cases of nuclear accidents.

Thus, the globalizing of policy regarding atomic and space technology, beginning prior to the Stockholm Conference, has become an unequivocal fact in international relations. Environmental effects of technologies associated with industrial chemistry, extraction and transport of petroleum, biotechnology, and uses of the electromagnetic spectrum and of outer space had become objects of concern before Stockholm. Their global significance has been subsequently reinforced by continuing incidents and international political events, notably international conferences and declarations leading to multinational programs and treaties. The mere listing of environment-related political actions occurring between 1970 and 1990 could easily fill a small book (Caldwell, 1991). These were not inadvertent happenings; they were expressions of a popular movement that began in advanced industrial countries and spread around the globe with unforeseen speed.

## Rise of public awareness

International action to address environmental issues could not occur in the absence of national concern sufficient to place the issue on the agenda of international relations and negotiations. The practical expression of a globalized issue is its acceptance as an object of negotiation among national governments. No amount of popular concern over transboundary environmental problems—for example, over nuclear radiation, pollution of air, water, and outer space, export of hazardous materials, loss of the world's genetic heritage, or the spread of contagious disease— can lead to effective action without the involvement of government. However, governments (and private corporate organizations as well) seldom act in the absence of organized public demand. Uncoordinated individual discontent, however widespread, has little effect on politicians and bureaucrats. Governments did not concede the political legitimacy of environmental quality concerns until citizen organizations with political muscle and sophistication emerged during the 1960s and grew in numbers and strength during the 1970s and 1980s (Hays, 1987; McCormick, 1989). In the United States, environmentalism gained force through the new right of citizen review of environmental impact statements provided by the National Environmental Policy Act, facilitated by the willingness of the courts to hear class-action suits and by the rise of public interest law firms (Caldwell, 1982).

Public environmental awareness, moving to apprehension and leading to organized pressure on public officials, occurred in nearly every developed country during the 1960s and 1970s, especially in Western Europe and North America (Inglehart, 1990; Milbrath, 1984). During these decades, many volunteer, nongovernmental environmental organizations became international or established international networks. They were present in large numbers at the Stockholm Conference, and an NGO Environmental Forum was convened with the assistance of the Swedish government to provide an outlet for their complaints and agendas. This development helped conventionalize the involvement of environmental NGOs with official intergovernmental environmental policymaking. The relationship has continued and grown in association with the United Nations Environment Programme (UNEP), initiated in Stockholm (Caldwell, 1991; McCormick, 1989). The Environmental Liaison Centre at UNEP headquarters in Nairobi, Kenya, now interacts with more than 6000 environmental NGOs, representative of nearly every country on earth.

All of the foregoing developments have effected changes in both public opinion and national and international law. As previously noted, advances in science and technology have influenced environmentalism in varied ways and have extended the applicability of older statutes and conventions. For example, the technology of science has progressively led to refinements in chemical analysis. Pollutants (especially toxins) in air, water, and food can often be measured in parts per trillion, thus bringing into effect existing bans and restrictions regarding the presence of contaminants, in many cases contaminants whose presence had not previously been ascertainable. New laws and regulations have been adopted regarding the manufacture and distribution of new products. Concern for health has been a major impetus in environmentalism worldwide.[1]

## GLOBALIZING POPULAR CONCERN

During the years between 1965 and 1975 there was an upsurge of public awareness of the unity, finiteness, and interactivity of the planetary environment (Hays, 1987; Nicholson, 1970). The first landing on the moon on 20 July 1969 and pictures of the Earth from outer space brought to many people a realization that their environment had many of the characteristics of a closed system. 'Spaceship Earth' became a metaphor, and 'Only One Earth' was the motto of the 1972 United National Conference on the Human Environment. No specific action was indicated by this symbolism—the lives and prospects of people were not directly affected. However, by the mid-1980s, a series of highly publicized environmental disasters and revelation of environmental threats of global proportion brought home to people that nearly every environmental problem had personal and possibly international dimensions.

In recent years, several issues in particular have aroused concern that is leading to popular demand for both local and international action, including (a) transboundary transport of hazardous materials, chiefly wastes; (b) disintegration of the stratospheric ozone layer; and (c) global climate change, notably global warming. In each case, scientific findings, publicized in the news media, preceded public awareness and apprehension and eventually led to popular demands for governmental and international action. These were clearly not the types of issues that initiated U.S. environmentalism. Its first concerns were typically local or geographically restricted. In the United States, the legislative agenda during the 1960s and 1970s was characterized by measures to curb air and water pollution, to preserve wilderness areas and scenic rivers, and to protect specific endangered species.

Some commentators saw environmentalism as a largely American and transitory concern (Etzioni, 1970). However, during the decades since 1970, U.S. environmentalists have increasingly recognized the global dimensions of environmental problems and have identified their concerns with environmental movements around the world. Nearly every major U.S. environmental organization has an international component, and some (such as Friends of the Earth and the Sierra Club) have become international in membership. International organizations (e.g., Greenpeace) have become active in U.S. domestic environmental affairs, and growing numbers of U.S. citizens have joined it and other international coalitions (e.g., the Rainforest Action Network; McCormick, 1989). These developments reflect growing awareness that where formerly 'foreign and domestic policies could be shaped in isolation, now they must be merged' (Mathews, 1989).

U.S. NGO examples, initiatives by the IUCN World Conservation strategy, and national appeals by the WWF have stimulated the formation and growth of environmental NGOs in developing countries. Many U.S. NGOs, such as the Nature Conservancy, recognize the need for counterpart organizations in countries where they work. The gap between countries over environment or development priorities has narrowed as the concept of environmentally sustainable development has gained adherents.

Informed citizen groups, almost invariably ahead of the public policy makers, have already formed links with action groups in developing countries. Thus, when incidents and developments abroad are introduced into discussions of U.S. environmentalism, it is not a departure from the focus on the United States. It is recognition that U.S. environmentalists are influenced by and concerned with world trends because their roles cannot be fairly described by attention only to their domestic agendas. Previously noted events such as the escape of toxic gas at Bhopal, India (1984), the diffusion of radioactive material from an accident at an atomic nuclear reactor at Chernobyl, U.S.S.R. (1986), a massive chemical spill in the River

Rhine from the Sandoz chemical plant in Switzerland (1986), and the rupture of the oil tanker Exxon Valdez (1989) were covered at length and in detail in the U.S. environmental press.[2] Similar accidents in the United States have made it clear that the vulnerabilities are ultimately global, but these accidents are not as crucial for the global future as ozone depletion, global warming, and rainforest destruction.

### Transboundary transport of harmful materials

Expansion of world trade and transportation has carried with it an international flow of products, some of which have uncertain effects on health and environment. A phenomenal expansion of industrial chemistry, especially in relation to agriculture and medicine, has led to a large volume of regulatory protective legislation in the developed countries. In the United States, the Federal Environmental Pesticide Act of 1972 and the Toxic Substances Control Act of 1976 provided for government control over testing, manufacture, and use of chemicals believed to be dangerous. Similar measures have been enacted in other developed countries, but in the Third World protective legislation has as yet been minimal. In many of these countries, scientists and physicians have led efforts to restrict or at least identify hazardous materials imported from the industrialized world, and they have links with scientists and environmental organizations in the United States. Nevertheless, many less developed countries are threatened by dumping of hazardous wastes from industrialized countries and only recently have sought to reject this abuse. There is, moreover, the ethically dubious practice of exporting to less developed countries pesticides and pharmaceuticals banned in the countries of their origin (Caldwell, 1988).

The transboundary relationships needed to combat the spread of toxic chemicals have had a globalizing influence on the U.S. environmental movement. Faced with an intrusion of products whose safety has not been assessed and of substances banned for sale or use in their country of manufacture, Third World countries turned to the United States and the United Nations for relief. In many Third World countries, governments lacked the competence and sometimes the integrity to enforce national protective measures. Thus, on 17 December 1981 the General Assembly of the United Nations, by a vote of 146 to 1, adopted Resolution 37/137, Protection Against Products Harmful to Health and Environment. The United States cast the only negative vote, to the chagrin of U.S. environmentalists.

Earlier, in 1980, hearings on export of hazardous substances had been held in the U.S. House of Representatives. Environmental, health, and consumer organizations advocated control measures, and, shortly before leaving office, on 15 January 1981, President Carter signed Executive Order 12264, which would have placed restrictions on the export of hazardous substances by U.S. companies. Soon after taking office, President Reagan withdrew Carter's order, with the argument that control of imports in other countries was their business and that the United States should not impose its values and standards on them (Smith, 1982).

In Europe, circumstances were different. Hazardous materials moved both ways across national borders. Efforts by the Organization for Economic Cooperation and Development (OECD) to develop transboundary controls were opposed by the U.S.

(Reagan) delegate, reflecting the commercial interests of the U.S. chemical industry. Lobbying in Paris by the official U.S. representative against international protective measures was deplored by environmental groups in the United States and was resented by Europeans (Fouere, 1983).

Transhipments of solid and toxic wastes from industrial countries to poor countries of the Third World are often made without knowledge or consent of governments but increasingly are being monitored and exposed by environmental NGOs. For example, on 8 September 1987 the Greenpeace Toxics Campaign issued an International Action Alert protesting the shipment of toxic-laden incinerator ash from Philadelphia, Pennsylvania, to the remote province of Bocas del Oro in Panama. In Europe, attempts to dump hazardous wastes in Africa were frustrated by African governments that compelled the shipper to return the toxic wastes to their point of origin. In a similar vein, in 1987 a barge laden with 3168 tons of garbage from Long Island, New York, was forced to return to its home port after a 6,000-mile journey through the Caribbean in a vain effort to find a country that, for a price, would accept the noisome refuse (*Facts on File*, 1987).

Such events, and many more, led, after protracted negotiations, to the adoption on 22 March 1989 of the Convention on the Control of Transboundary Movements of Hazardous Wastes and Their Disposal by representatives of 35 nations and the Commission of the European Community. The United States, Great Britain, the Federal Republic of Germany, and the Soviet Union did not sign but indicated their intention to do so, contingent on further study of the terms of the agreement. The waste management issue illustrates the progression of what was at first (and still is) a local issue becoming a national and then an international and global issue. The neglected problem of waste and contamination is worldwide, expanding industrial society has been a major cause of the globalizing of environmentalism and the conversion to environmentalism of hitherto unaware or indifferent people and governments.

**Threats to stratospheric ozone**

The stratospheric ozone issue was influenced more by public confidence in scientific findings than by direct experience. The issue arose with relative suddenness with discovery in the 1970s of a thinning of the ozone layer in the stratosphere. The ozone layer shields the earth from excessive ultraviolet radiation from the sun. Discovery of a hole in the ozone layer, first detected by British scientists over Antarctica, was soon paralleled by evidence of thinning over northern latitudes. The effect of increased ultraviolet radiation on human health and the biosphere was scientifically predictable with a high level of probability and credibility. Estimates of effects on food supply and on diseases of the skin and eyes were sufficiently alarming that governments responded with unprecedented alacrity.

An international treaty to restrict the emission of ozone-thinning agents, notably chlorofluorocarbons (CFCs), was signed by representatives of 20 nations meeting in Vienna, Austria, on 22 March 1985. Negotiations on more rapid phaseout of CFCs continued, and on 16 September 1987, 28 nations agreed to the Montreal Protocol on Substances That Deplete the Ozone Layer. Although by early 1989, 36 nations had signed the Montreal Protocol, dissatisfaction with the agreed-on timetable for phaseouts led to international meetings in March 1989 in London, England, and in May in Helsinki, Finland. Eighty-one nations were represented at the Finland meeting, which, on 2 May 1989, issued the Helsinki Declaration on the Protection of the Ozone Layer, calling on all states to join the previous ozone agreements and to phase out all production and consumption of CFCs as soon as possible, but not later than the year 2000 (Whitney, 1989; *Facts on File*, 1989). The United States and the European Community countries had already legislated to end the use of CFCs. Thus, here was a highly visible and decisive example of the globalization of environmental policy in which U.S. environmentalists had taken an early lead. The concentration of the manufacture and release of CFCs in a few industrialized countries made this issue easier to negotiate in an international forum than the more widespread and less clearly established issue of global climate change.

## Global climate change

An issue of truly global proportions is the changing composition of the Earth's atmosphere, caused primarily by increasingly heavy emissions of carbon dioxide from the combustion of fossil fuels (oil, coal, and natural gas), methane (chiefly from agriculture), and CFCs. These emissions are residues of a rapidly populating and industrializing world. The effect of these so-called greenhouse gases in the atmosphere is to block the escape of infrared radiation (heat) from earth. If heat received from the sun is trapped on Earth, it will raise air temperatures and sea levels, melt the polar ice sheets, induce regional changes in rainfall, and vary the weather and the seasons. Increase in greenhouse gases in the atmosphere is exacerbated by massive burning of tropical rain forests for conversion to agriculture, with the consequential drop in emission of oxygen from a devegetated environment.

By the end of the 1980s, global warming and climate change had become the world's most publicized environmental issue. Here again, accumulating scientific evidence permeated the public consciousness and resulted in an unpredicted global political response. Scientists had been aware of the climate change issue for more than a decade before the issue 'exploded' in the legislative chambers of governments. Scientific studies published in the early 1970s identified the effects of human activities on the climate, and in February 1979 the World Climate Conference meeting in Geneva, sponsored by the World Meteorological Organization, adopted a program of international cooperative research to more precisely identify the elements of the problem. In 1978 the Climate Research Board of the U.S. National Research Council released a report, *International perspectives on the study of climate and society: Report of the International Workshop on Climate Issues.* Other studies and reports followed in the United States and other countries, and in 1981 the issue came to the fore in the U.S. Congress, setting off a series of committee hearings throughout the rest of the decade.[3] Here is a paradox that has yet to be fully explored. Although there is general agreement that local issues (e.g., toxic waste dumps or solid waste incinerators) are principal foci of U.S. environmentalism, the global climate change issue has probably received more high-level governmental attention than any other single environmental concern. It is too early to say, but the global climate change–ozone issue may prove to be the greatest single stimulus for the globalization of environmentalism.

## Other global issues and the U.S. response

Other issues now perceived to be of global significance have aroused concern and action among U.S. environmentalists. Among these are the destruction of tropical rain forests (diminishing the diversity of plant and animal species and the production of atmospheric oxygen), desertification over growing areas (notably in Africa), acid rain, and threat to survival of the world's wildlife (including marine life, especially whales and dolphins). U.S. NGOs have mounted campaigns against tuna fisheries and Japanese trawlers whose nets have caused the deaths of countless numbers of dolphins. Networking with environmental NGOs in other countries. Americans have kept pressure on the International Whaling Commission for phaseout of commercial whaling. They have forced a reluctant federal government to ban drilling for oil in sensitive coastal areas and have thus far successfully blocked efforts to weaken endangered species protective legislation.

U.S. environmental organizations have also been in the forefront of *debt-for-nature swaps* (Cody, 1988). One of them, Conservation International, privately purchased some of Bolivia's foreign debt in return for promises of environmental protection for endangered natural areas. U.S. NGOs were not alone in pressuring the U.S. Congress and the World Bank for changes in policy for development loans that encouraged environmental destruction. British groups were also active (Goldsmith, 1987). However, the ability of Americans to influence the World Bank's leading source of finance (the U.S. government) enabled them to play a leading role in reorienting the World Bank and its development bank partners.

Guided by economists with strong inclinations toward monetary strategies, the banks had encouraged Third World nations to grow crops for sale abroad and to exploit natural resources to pay for international loans. The loans were often put to use in development projects that proved to be environmentally unsustainable. Many less developed countries were burdened by heavy foreign debt, which they sought to pay off by further exploitation of their natural resources and agriculture. Third World countries today have widely adopted the sustainable development concept as advocated by the U.N. Commission on Environment and Development but have linked their cooperation on environmental protection to relief from international indebtedness (Cody, 1988; McCormick, 1989).

Although publicity, political pressure, and negotiations have been the principal strategies of NGOs, an ultimate goal of U.S. environmentalism has been to institutionalize its objectives in law. The growth of national environmental law in the United States. Canada, and Western Europe, and, in some respects, in Japan during the 1970s and 1980s has been phenomenal. In at least thirty-seven countries, statutory law has been to some extent reinforced by constitutional provisions.[4] International law has undergone a somewhat comparable expansion in the form of new conventions and other agreements and in the establishment of implementing agencies and programs that give international commitments greater force. Americans as private individuals and through the American Society for International Law and through World Peace Through Law have been leaders in the development of international law, including the U.N. Law of the Sea Treaty. They have often been more international in orientation than their governments, especially during the 1980s when official U.S. policy on environmental affairs was (with exception of the ozone issue) largely out-of-step with that of the rest of the world.

Realization of the Stockholm legacy occurred progressively but unevenly over an interval of 17 years. Nevertheless, by the July 1989 Paris summit meeting of the political heads of the seven major industrial democracies, the environment had become a top item on the world's political agenda. The threats of global climate change and of disintegration of the stratospheric ozone layer were the primary developments commanding attention at the highest international political levels. However, cumulative experience with international conferences, declarations, agreements, investigations, and cooperative programs since Stockholm made the Paris Communique of 7 July 1989 more of an overdue catch-up by chiefs of state than an excursion into the unknown (Markham, 1989). How high-level commitments were to be translated into action in the 1990s could not be foreseen, but global environmentalism was never more pervasive and Americans never more engaged in international environmental affairs.

Nevertheless, the commitment of the Bush presidency to the environment was ambiguous. Although candidate Bush made a major point of his environmental concern, the policies of President Bush often have seemed contradictory. The appointment of William Reilly as administrator of the Environmental Protection Agency was warmly applauded by environmental organizations. However, White House Chief of Staff Sununu, Office of Management and Budget Director Darman, and Interior Secretary Lujan are frequently described in the news media as unsympathetic to what they regard as excessive environmental concerns. Who speaks for the President? As of 1990 there was considerable doubt in the United States and abroad regarding the depth of the environmental commitment of George Bush, but even the sceptics consider him a great improvement over his predecessor.

## IMPLEMENTING GLOBAL ENVIRONMENTALISM: POLITICAL AND INSTITUTIONAL CHALLENGES

A phenomenon of the 1970s and 1980s, as previously noted, has been the burgeoning of nongovernmental organizations with international agendas (McCormick, 1989). There are many nongovernmental organizations around the world with many causes but it is unlikely that any exceed the environmental organizations in the United States in membership, in diversity, and in their commitment to international causes. NGOs from many nations have had an unofficial but organized presence at every United Nations environment-related conference since Stockholm, including those on population, food, science and technology for development, and new and renewable sources of energy. Links between these unofficial convenings and the actions of official national representatives may not be visible during these occasions. For some countries, notably the United States, there have been contradictions between positions taken by official delegations and the policies advocated by a majority of the NGOs present. This was frequently the situation during the Reagan years, and even some official representatives of the United States found themselves unable to support the President's positions.

On home fronts, environmental NGOs may press their governments for or against compliance with conference resolutions. Coalitions of NGOs have been formed to promote global environmental policies, and international nongovernmental conferences have been held in Europe and North America in which the agenda has been global (e.g., Giobescope in the United States, sponsored by the Global Tomorrow Coalition). In Europe, especially in countries with proportional representation in their elective legislatures, transnational voting for candidates to the Parliament of Europe facilitates transboundary collaboration among green parties and other environmentally concerned groups.

The principle of proportional representation, in effect in many European democracies, enables small parties to elect representatives to local and national legislative bodies. The result has been multi-party politics in which relatively minor parties may hold a balance of power when none of the major parties have sufficient votes to form a government. Green or ecological parties have emerged and have gained considerable influence over the traditional parties (Capra and Spretnak, 1986). The U.S. political system has been uncongenial to third- or fourth-party movements. U.S. environmentalists have fought or favored individual politicians on their environmental records, regardless of party affiliation. Should there be a break-up of the two-party system at some future time, environmentalism might become a more coherent force in U.S. politics.

Is global environmentalism a response to a climacteric in world affairs? If so, what might this signify for the future of U.S. politics? In human life, a *climacteric* is the point at which physical powers, having reached their climax, begin to decline. The human experience in populating the earth and in exploiting its resources may be analogous. During modern civilization's exuberant youth, roughly since 1492, it was possible for man to turn nature to his own purposes without regard to ecological or human consequences. Now, after half a millennium of unrestrained populating and developing the Earth, it seems that modern society has gone about as far as it can go with the policies and methods that it has heretofore used. The carrying capacity of the Earth in relation to humans may have been exceeded already (Catton, 1980). More care and caution will henceforth be required to sustain the human economy without progressive decline in the ability of the environment to maintain life on Earth.

Environmentalism in North America and throughout the industrially advanced world generally may be understood as a part of a more general shift in perceptions and values. During the last half of the twentieth century, parallel societal changes seem to have occurred spontaneously in North America, Western Europe, and other developed nations (Inglehart, 1990; Milbrath, 1984). Manners and morals, attitudes toward freedom of speech, dress, human rights, and lifestyles have followed similar courses, and growing concern for the environment has been a major dimension of the change. Globalizing of U.S. environmentalism is merely a particular case of the globalizing of environmentalism everywhere. It is a manifestation of a worldwide trend.

## Global environmentalism and sustainable development

In the course of history, global environmentalism is a sequel to the globalization of international trade and commerce, a process that began in the seventeenth century with British and Dutch enterprises in America, India, and the Far East. Colonialism was a globalizing process continued in our own time through reverse colonialism, wherein an overpopulated Third World overflows into the developed countries. To stem this flow, to improve the prospects for life in the Third World, and to save the biosphere, global environmentalism today has adopted the concept and goal of sustainable development (Redclift, 1987; Tolba, 1987). The report of the World Commission on Environment and Development (Bruntland Commission), entitled *Our Common Future* (1987), has become the closest approach to a scripture for global environmentalism. The report declares for sustainable development and undertakes to reconcile the environmental and developmental interests of developed and developing countries. The United States government (unlike those of many other countries) has chosen to ignore the report, which, however, is used widely in environment and development courses in U.S. colleges and universities.

It is anticipated that the Bruntland report will provide a conceptual basis for the projected United Nations Conference on Environment and Development to be held in 1992 in Brazil. By then the draft of an international convention on the atmosphere is expected to be ready for review. If by that time the Convention on the Law of the Sea has obtained the necessary ratification (for this, U.S. adherence is probably essential), human use of the two elements that encircle the globe will be brought under comprehensive international law. Dozens of treaties and other international agreements cover many of the uses of the land, its biota, and its inland waters. Global environmentalism will no longer be regarded as exceptional because, at least in context and awareness, all environmentalism must henceforth be global. Nor will it be possible for the government of the United States, as it did during most the 1980s, to remain aloof and often negative toward environmental issues that a large part of the world regards as requiring global cooperation.

## NOTES

1. It is paradoxical that a concept as broadly and diversely holistic as *environment* has come to be treated as an 'ism'—a sectoral or particularistic way of relating to practical affairs. Environmentalism is not a self-designating term used by the environmentally concerned. It has been applied often, with a pejorative undertone, among those interests in modern society in which more than a minimal concern for the environment is regarded as atavistic, impractical, utopian, and unprogressive. Thus, the broader ecological perspective is treated as if it were narrow, and a narrow economistic orientation, where dominant, tends to be regarded as practical and realistic.
2. For summary accounts of disasters receiving global news coverage, see *Keesing's Contemporary Archives: Record of World Events*: Seveso (June 1979: 29688; October 1983: 32475; March 1986: 34270), Bhopal (March 1985: 33467–33468), and Chernobyl (June 1986: 34460–34462). See *Facts on File* for Rhine River (7 November 1986: 845G1; 14 November 1986: 858E1; 31 December 1987: 89B2), and for Exxon Valdez (March 1989: 36541, 36606). See also *Challenges for International Environmental Law: Seveso, Bhopal, Chernobyl, the Rhine and Beyond*, edited by V. P. Nanda and B. Bailey (Washington DC: World Peace Through Law Center, 1987).

3. There is an extensive literature on the greenhouse effect and global climate change. See especially *The Potential Effects of Global Climate Change on the United States*, by the Environmental Protection Agency (October 1988), a draft report to Congress (Washington, DC: Author); the special issue of *Science* on 'Issues in atmospheric sciences' (10 February 1989); the special issue of *Scientific American* on 'Managing Planet Earth' (September 1989); and *Global Warming: Are We Entering the Greenhouse Century?* by S. H. Schneider (San Francisco: Sierra Club Books, 1989). For Congressional hearings and reports, see, for example, the following:

U.S. Congress, House of Representatives. *Carbon Dioxide and Climate: The Greenhouse Effect.* Hearing before the Subcommittee on Natural Resources. Agriculture and Environment and the Subcommittee on Investigations and Oversight of the Committee on Science and Technology, 97th Congress, 1st Session, 31 July 1981. Note testimony of Stephen Schneider. 'Carbon dioxide and climate: Research on potential environmental and societal impacts', pp. 39–59. Note also hearings before these Subcommittees, 98th Congress, 2nd Session, 28 February 1984.

U.S. Congress, Senate. *Global Warming.* Hearing before the Subcommittee on Environment and Public Works, 99th Congress, 1st Session, 10 December 1985.

U.S. Congress, Senate. *Ozone Depletion, The Greenhouse Effect and Climate Change.* Hearings before the Subcommittee on Environmental Pollution of the Committee on Environment and Public Works, 99th Congress, 2nd Session, 10–11 June 1986.

U.S. Congress, Senate. *Ozone Depletion, The Greenhouse Effect, and Climate Change.* Joint hearing before the Subcommittee on Environmental Protection and Hazardous Wastes and Toxic Substances of the Committee on Environment and Public Works, 10th Congress, 1st Session, 28 January 1987.

U.S. Congressional Research Service, Library of Congress. 1984. *Carbon Dioxide, the Greenhouse Effect, and Climate: A Primer.* Report, transmitted to the Committee on Science and Technology, U.S. House of Representatives, 98th Congress, 2nd Session, October 1984. Washington, DC: U.S. Government Printing Office.

See also *Society and Natural Resources*, Vol. 4, No. 4, a special issue entitled 'Global climate change: A social science perspective', ed. Martin F. Price, to be published in December 1991.

4. Information provided by the International Environmental Law Centre, Bonn, Germany. A slightly different list is provided by Edith Brown Weiss in *Fairness to Future Generations* (Dobbs Ferry, NY: Transnational, pp. 107–108). The total of combined lists is 45 countries in which some reference to the environment, natural or cultural, is made. In no more than a third of these, however, is the provision likely to have practical significance at present.

## REFERENCES

Caldwell, L. K. (1982) *Science and the National Environmental Policy Act: Redirecting Policy Through Procedural Reform.* University: University of Alabama Press.

Caldwell, L. K. (1984) 'The world environment: Reversing U.S. policy commitments'. In *Environmental Policy in the 1980s: Reagan's New Agenda.* ed. N. Vig and M. Kraft, pp. 319–338. Washington, DC: Congressional Quarterly Press.

Caldwell, L. K. (1988) 'International aspects of biotechnology: Guest editorial and review'. *MIRCEN Journal of Applied Molecular Biology and Biotechnology*, 4: 245–258.

Caldwell, L. K. (1990) *International Environmental Policy: Emergence and Dimensions*, 2nd ed. Durham, NC: Duke University Press.

Capra, F. and Spretnak, C. (1986) *Green Politics.* Sante Fe, NM: Bear and Company.

Carson, R. (1962) *Silent Spring.* Boston: Houghton Mifflin.

Catton, W. R. (1980) *Overshoot, the Ecological Basis for Revolutionary Change.* Urbana: University of Illinois Press.

Cody, B. (1988) *Debt-for-Nature Swaps in Developing Countries.* Washington, DC: Congressional Research Service.

Dinwoode, D. H. (1972) 'The politics of international pollution control: The Trail Smelter case', *International Journal*, **27**: 219–235.

Etzioni, A. (1970) 22 May. 'The wrong top priority', *Science*, **168**: 921 (editorial).

*Facts on File* (1987) 17 July, Vol. 47, p.518.

*Facts on File* (1989) 12 May, Vol. 49, pp.334–335.

Fouere, E. (1983) 'Clashing over the environment: U.S., Europe follow increasingly divergent paths. *Europe*, **237**: 12–15.

Goldsmith, E. (1987) Open letter to Mr. Conable, President of the World Bank. *The Ecologist*, **17**: 58–61.

Hays, S. P. (1987) *Beauty, Health and Permanence: Environmental Politics in the United States, 1955–1985*. Cambridge, MA: Cambridge University Press.

Inglehart, R. (1990) *Culture Shift in Advanced Industrial Society*. Princeton, NJ: Princeton University Press.

Livingston, D. (1968) 'Pollution control, an international perspective'. *Scientist and Citizens*, **10**: 173–182.

Markham, J. M. (1989) 12 April. 'Greening of European politicians spreads as peril to ecology grows'. *New York Times*, p.10.

Markham, J. M. (1989) 17 July. 'Paris group urges "decisive" action for environment'. *New York Times*, pp.1, 4–6.

Mathews, J. T. (1989) 11 June. 'Forging a policy to address global warming'. *New York Times*, p. 29.

McCormick, J. (1989) *Reclaiming Paradise: The Global Environmental Movement*. Bloomington, IN: Indiana University Press.

Milbraith, L. (1984) *Environmentalists: Vanguard for a new Society*. Albany: State of New York University Press.

Nicholson, E. M. (1970) *The Environmental Revolution*. New York: McGraw-Hill.

Nisbet, R. (1982) *Prejudices: A Philosophical Dictionary*. Cambridge, MA: Harvard University Press.

Petulla, J. M. (1980) *American Environmentalism: Values, Tactics, Priorities*. College Station: Texas A&M Press.

Ramphal, S. S. (1987) 'The environment and sustainable development'. *Journal of the Royal Society of Arts*, **135**: 879–909.

Redclift, M. (1987) *Sustainable Development: Exploring the Contradictions*. London: Methuen.

Rosen, G. (1964) 'Human health, community life, and the rediscovery of the environment'. *American Journal of Public Health and the Nation's Health*, **44** (Part 2): 1–6.

Smith, R. J. (1982) 'Hazardous products may be exported'. *Science*, **216**: 1301.

Tolba, M. K. (1987) *Sustainable Development: Constraints and Opportunities*. London: Butterworth.

U.S. National Research Council (1978) *International Perspectives on the Study of Climate and Society* (Report of the International Workshop on Climate Issues). Washington, DC: Author.

Whitney, C. R. (1989) 3 March. '12 European nations to ban chemicals that harm ozone' *New York Times*, pp.1, 4.

World Commission on Environment and Development (1987) *Our Common Future*. New York: Oxford University Press.

# 4

# Trends in Public Opinion Toward Environmental Issues 1965–1990

*Riley E. Dunlap*

A comprehensive review of available longitudinal data on public opinion toward environmental issues since 1965 suggests the following conclusions regarding trends in public concern over environmental quality: (a) Environmental concern developed dramatically in the late 1960s and reached a peak with the first Earth Day in 1970; (b) such concern declined considerably in the early 1970s and then more gradually over the rest of the decade, but remained substantial; (c) the 1980s saw a significant and steady increase in both public awareness of the seriousness of environmental problems and in support for environmental protection, with the result that by the twentieth anniversary of Earth Day in 1990, public concern for environmental quality reached unprecedented levels. This supportive public opinion provides a valuable resource for the environmental movement, and the future of the movement will depend heavily on the degree to which environmentalists can effectively mobilize this support.

## INTRODUCTION

About a quarter century ago, environmental quality began to emerge as a major social problem in our society. Issues such as wilderness protection and air pollution had previously received the attention of relatively small numbers of conservationists and public health officials, but in the mid 1960s a wide range of threats to environmental quality began to attract the attention of the media, policymakers, and the public. Due in large part to the efforts of a growing number of environmental activists, by 1970 the environment had become a major national concern, as reflected by the huge scale of Earth Day (22 April 1970) celebrations across the nation (see, e.g., Mitchell and Davies, 1978). Over the past two decades, environmentalism has evolved into a major sociopolitical force in our society, and one of the key reasons for this has been the widespread support that the environmental movement has received from the general public.

Reprinted with permission from *Society and Natural Resources*, Vol. 4, No. 3, pp. 285–314, Riley E. Dunlap, Taylor & Francis, Inc., Washington. All rights reserved. © 1991 Taylor & Francis

Social movements are spearheaded by activists and organizations, but their success or failure is often heavily influenced by the degree of support they receive from the broader public. Although contributions of money or time and political support (voting, petition signing, letter writing, etc.) are obviously crucial, the mere expression of support by the public in a scientific survey or an informal poll (as are often conducted by local newspapers and politicians) can also be a vital resource for a social movement. As Mitchell noted, 'Public support of environmental groups provides them with a key lobbying resource because it lends credibility to the claim that they represent the "public interest"' (1984, p. 52). Supportive public opinion thus not only lends legitimacy to a social movement but it provides a valuable resource in lobbying for new legislation or pressing for the effective implementation of existing legislation (Rosenbaum, 1991; Sabatier and Mazmanian, 1980). Some analysts even conceptualize the 'sympathetic public' as an outer layer of the environmental movement from which the core activists and organizations frequently can recruit members and solicit contributions and other resources (e.g., Morrison, 1986).

For such reasons the status of public opinion on environmental issues has received a great deal of attention over the past two decades. The degree to which the public supports efforts to protect environmental quality, and whether such support has increased or decreased, has been the subject of considerable debate over the years (see, e.g., Ladd, 1982). My goal here is to present a comprehensive overview of the evidence available on *trends* in public concern for environmental quality, beginning with the emergence of such concern in the mid 1960s and continuing through its evolution up to the twentieth anniversary of Earth Day in 1990.

The task is difficult because there are no data sets that have continuously monitored public opinion on environmental issues over this entire time period. However, by piecing together several sets of relevant longitudinal data—covering the late 1960s to 1970, the early 1970s, the mid to late 1970s, and the 1980s—I hope to provide an accurate portrayal of the broad contours of trends in public concern for environmental quality over the past quarter century. However, first I want to discuss a model of the evolution of public opinion toward social problems in general, and environmental problems in particular, in an effort to establish what was expected to happen to public support for environmental protection over this period.

## THE NATURAL DECLINE MODEL

As noted in the introduction to this volume, social scientists have discerned a pattern in which social problems are regularly discovered or 'created' by a group of activists who are successful in getting the larger society to accept their definition of various conditions as problematic and in need of amelioration. Such efforts are frequently transitory and seldom fully successful, however, and generally experience what can be termed a *natural decline*. One major reason seems to be the decline in public interest in and attention to the problem (Dunlap, 1989). Whether from basic boredom with the issue, from the fact that the media turn attention to newer issues, or from the sense that government is taking care of the problem and there is no longer any need to worry about it, the public is seen as inevitably losing interest in most social problems (e.g., Mauss, 1975; Sabatier and Mazmanian, 1980).

Given the thrust of social science thinking about the evolution of social problems and public concern with such problems, it is not surprising that a compatible model developed specifically for environmental problems by Anthony Downs—the *issue-attention cycle*—has been quite influential in analyses of public opinion on environmental issues. Writing a couple of years after the first Earth Day, Downs (1972) suggested that environmental problems would probably meet the fate experienced by most social problems: have a brief moment in the sun and then fade from public attention as newer problems take center stage on the national agenda.

Specifically, Downs (1972) suggested that, like most social problems, environmental problems would proceed through a five-stage cycle:

(1) the *pre-problem* stage in which the undesirable social conditions exist and may have aroused the interest of experts or interest groups but have not yet attracted much attention from the public;
(2) the *alarmed discovery and euphoric enthusiasm* stage in which one or more dramatic events or crises bring the problem to the public's attention and create enthusiastic support for solving it;
(3) a *realization of the cost of significant progress* stage in which public enthusiasm is dampened;
(4) a gradual *decline in the intense public interest* due to recognition of the costs of a solution, boredom with the issue, and decline in media attention to the problem; and finally
(5) the *post-problem* stage in which the issue is replaced at the center of public concern by new problems and moves into 'a twilight realm of lesser attention or spasmodic recurrences of interest' (Downs, 1972, p. 40), typically with little if any improvement in the original problematic conditions.[1]

Downs went on to suggest that in 1972 environmental quality was already about halfway through the issue-attention cycle.

Down's model, which is very much in line with social science models of the evolution of social problems, social movements, and public policy implementation, will be used as a benchmark in reviewing trends in public opinion toward environmental issues. Using it will enable me to determine the degree to which the environmental movement has managed to succeed in maintaining a high level of public attention to environmental problems and concern for environmental protection, thereby avoiding the natural decline in public support that is the fate of the typical, short-lived social-problem movement.

## TRENDS IN PUBLIC CONCERN FOR ENVIRONMENTAL QUALITY

### The early 1960s to 1970: emergence of widespread public concern

The fact that environmental issues were virtually ignored by public opinion pollsters in the early 1960s indicates the low level of societal attention to such issues at that time and suggests that environmental quality was still in Downs's (1972) pre-problem stage (of interest mainly to conservationists and air and water pollution officials). The situation rapidly changed in the latter half of the decade, however, because of several interrelated developments. First, conservation organizations such as the Sierra Club became more visible, both because they were appealing for widespread support in battles such as the fight to save the Grand Canyon and because they were broadening their focus beyond wilderness and scenic preservation to a wider range of environmental issues (Hays, 1987). Their activities coincided with a rapid increase in outdoor recreation, another factor contributing to the growth in membership of conservation organizations (McEvoy, 1972). At the same time, political leaders such as President Johnson and Senators Muskie and Jackson were pushing important environmental legislation through Congress, ranging from measures to improve air and water quality to protecting endangered species and culminating in the landmark National Environmental Policy Act (NEPA) of late 1969 (Hays, 1987). These trends and activities no doubt helped sensitize the mass media to environmental issues, and by the late 1960s environmental problems were receiving tremendous exposure in the media (Schoenfeld, Meier and Griffin, 1979). Finally, there was the enormous mobilization of citizen participation, facilitated by the widespread social activism of the 1960s, in celebration of the first Earth Day in the spring of 1970.

The effect of all of this on public opinion toward environmental issues is illustrated by several sets of trend data summarized in Table 1. The first set of data, from Gallup polls conducted in 1965 and 1970, show that the percentage of the public selecting 'reducing pollution of air and water' as a national problem that should receive the attention of government more than tripled (from 17% to 53%) during those 5 years. Almost as impressive an increase is documented in a series of Opinion Research Corporation surveys covering the same period, as the percentages viewing air and water pollution as 'very or somewhat serious' in their vicinity more than doubled, from 28% to 69% for air pollution and from 35% to 74% for water pollution. A bit less impressive was the increase in the percentage responding that there was 'a lot' or 'some' air pollution in their area, from 56% to 70%, in 1967 and 1970 Harris surveys, respectively.[2] The Harris surveys also asked respondents if they would be willing to pay $15 per year more in taxes for an air pollution control program, and over the 3 years those responding 'willing' rose from 44% to 54%, whereas those saying 'unwilling' dropped from 46% to 34%. The last set of Harris data covers only seven months, from August 1969 to March 1970, but reflects the impact of mobilization for Earth Day on public opinion: the percentage selecting 'pollution control' as one of the three or four government programs (from a list of ten) that they would 'least like to see cut' increased by nearly half, from 38% to 55%.

These trend data, especially those covering 1965 to 1970, indicate how dramatically public concern with environmental quality emerged during the last half of the 1960s. Especially notable is the fact that in the Gallup surveys the 17% selecting pollution reduction ranked it ninth overall among the ten problems in 1965, whereas the 53% selecting it in 1970 placed in second only to crime reduction. Such results led Erskine to conclude, 'A miracle of public opinion has been the unprecedented speed and urgency with which ecological issues have burst into American consciousness. Alarm about the environment sprang from nowhere to major proportions in a few short years' (1972, p. 120). The data also suggest that by 1970 environmental quality had definitely moved from the pre-problem stage to the alarmed discovery stage in Downs's

Table 1. Trends in public concern for environmental quality, mid 1960s to 1970

| National survey | Question | Percentage response by year (19–) | | | | | |
|---|---|---|---|---|---|---|---|
| | | 65 | 66 | 67 | 68 | 69 | 70 |
| (1) Gallup | 'Reducing pollution of air and water' selected as one of three national problems that should receive attention of government | 17 | — | — | — | — | 53 |
| (2) Opinion Research Corporation | Air/water pollution viewed as 'very or somewhat serious' in the area: | | | | | | |
| | (a) air pollution | 28 | 48 | 53 | 55 | — | 69 |
| | (b) water pollution | 35 | 49 | 52 | 58 | — | 74 |
| (3) Louis Harris | 'A lot' or 'some' air pollution thought to exist in the area | | | 56 | | | 70 |
| (4) Louis Harris | Willing to pay $15 a year more in taxes to finance air pollution control program | | | 44 | | | 54 |
| (5) Louis Harris | 'Pollution control' selected as government spending area 'least like to see cut' | | | | | 38 | 55 |

*Note.* For each survey, see the following reference for question wording and complete results: (1) Mitchell (1980, p. 404); (2) Erskine (1972, p. 121); (3) Erskine (1972, p. 123); (4) Erskine (1972, p. 132); (5) Erskine (1972, p. 129).

(1972) issue-attention cycle, the point at which the public clearly acknowledges the seriousness of a problem and enthusiastically supports efforts to solve it.

In the terminology of public opinion analysts (e.g., Pierce, Beatty and Hagner, 1982), environmental protection had become a consensual issue by 1970, as surveys found a majority of the public expressing pro-environment opinions and typically only a small minority expressing anti-environment opinions. The high and consensual level of concern for environmental quality at the beginning of what would become known as the 'environmental decade' was also reflected by cross-sectional data collected in 1969 to 1970 (Erskine, 1972). Yet, was environmental quality really that salient as an issue, one that was truly on the public's mind, even during this period of strong support for environmental protection? This is difficult to judge, but many public opinion analysts have argued that volunteered responses to most important problem (MIP) questions—that is, open-ended questions asking respondents what they see as the country's most important problem or problems— are the best way to measure the salience of an issue (e.g., Peters and Hogwood, 1985). MIP questions are stringent measures of salience, however, because responses are traditionally dominated by economic issues and foreign affairs/national security concerns (Smith, 1985).[3]

Unfortunately, MIP studies that report results for environmental problems are rare, and because the only two MIP trend studies that began in the 1960s extended past 1970, I have summarized them in Table 2 along with other longitudinal studies beginning in 1970. The sole trend study of the salience of environmental quality at the national level beginning in the 1960s was Hornback's (1974) analysis of MIP data collected in the Michigan National Election Surveys (NES), in which respondents were encouraged (through probes) to mention up to three problems facing the country. Hornback found that only 2% of the public volunteered any type of environmental problem in 1968, a surprisingly low figure in view of the data reported in Table 1 for other indicators of concern about environmental quality. In 1970 the figure was 17%, representing a dramatic increase but still only a small proportion of the public. The other MIP study from the 1960s was limited to the state of Wisconsin, in which Buttel (1975a, 1975b) found that the percentage of residents volunteering environmental problems as one of the two most important problems facing the state rose substantially, from 17% to 40% between 1968 and 1970. Although the degree of increase in Wisconsin was similar to that for the nation, the absolute levels of salience in Wisconsin were much higher in both years. Whether this reflects a higher than average level of environmental concern in Wisconsin or differences in study methodologies (or both) is impossible to determine.

Matters are not helped when the 1970 data from these two studies are compared with two other sets of MIP data beginning in 1970. First, Harris began reporting the results of an MIP question in late 1970. As shown in Table 2, fully 41% of a national sample volunteered some type of environmental problem as one of the 'two or three biggest problems' facing them in 1970—a figure comparable with the Wisconsin results. In contrast, three 1970 Gallup surveys included a question asking about the single 'most important problem' facing the country, and the percentages mentioning environmental problems ranged from only 2% to 10%. The Gallup results, taking into account that they asked for only one MIP, thus seem more in line with the results from the Michigan NES reported by Hornback.

Table 2. Longitudinal studies of public concern for environmental quality, late 1960s to mid 1970s

| Study | Question | Percentage response by year (19–) | | | | | | | | |
|---|---|---|---|---|---|---|---|---|---|---|
| | | 68 | 69 | 70 | 71 | 72 | 73 | 74 | 75 | 76 |
| **National survey** | | | | | | | | | | |
| (1) Michigan National Election survey | Pollution, ecology, etc., volunteered as one of the country's 'most important problems' | 2 | | 17 | — | 10 | | | | |
| (2) Louis Harris | Pollution, ecology, etc., volunteered as one of 'the two or three biggest problems facing people like yourself' | | | 41 | | 13 | 11 | 9 | 6 | |
| **State trend/panel studies** | | | | | | | | | | |
| (3) Wisconsin | Environmental problems volunteered as one of two most important facing the state | 17 | — | 40 | — | 15 | — | 10 | | |
| (4) Washington (panel) | Favour government spending 'more money' on: | | | | | | | | | |
| | (a) pollution control | | | 70 | — | — | — | 32 | | |
| | (b) protection of natural resources | | | 52 | — | — | — | 37 | | |
| (5) Washington (trend) | 'Reducing air and water pollution' selected one of two or three most serious problems in: | | | | | | | | | |
| | (a) state | | | 44 | — | — | — | — | — | 18 |
| | (b) respondents' community | | | 23 | — | — | — | — | — | 15 |

*Note.* For each survey, see the following reference for question wording, complete results, and response coding: (1) Hornback (1974, pp. 87, 233–234); (2) Mitchell and Davies (1978, Figure 2); (3) Buttel (1975a, pp. 83–85; 1975b, p. 58); (4) Dunlap and Dillman (1976, p. 383–384); (5) Dunlap and Van Liere (1977, p. 110).

The discrepant results obtained with MIP questions, especially those between the Michigan NES and Harris surveys in 1970, are difficult to reconcile. They do not seem attributable, for example, to differences in question wording. Despite the inconsistency in results, however, two conclusions can be drawn from the available MIP data. First, the salience of environmental problems increased substantially from 1968 to 1970. Second, even in 1970 only a minority (albeit a large one in some surveys) volunteered environmental problems when asked what they saw as the most important problems facing the country. The latter finding contrasts sharply with the results reported in Table 1 for other indicators of public concern for environmental quality and suggests that even around the time that our nation was celebrating the first Earth Day the salience of environmental problems did not match that of the traditionally dominant worries about war and the economy (Erskine, 1972; Hornback, 1974; Smith, 1985).

Overall, therefore, the available data indicate that public concern for environmental quality escalated rapidly in the 1960s and that by 1970 majorities of the public were expressing pro-environment opinions ranging from acknowledging the seriousness of pollution to supporting governmental efforts to protect and improve the environment. However, despite the relatively strong consensus in support of environmental protection, the state of the environment was viewed by only a minority of the public as one of the nation's most important problems. From a social movements perspective, it appears that a majority of the public had accepted environmentalists' definition of environmental quality as problematic and had become sympathetic to the goal of protecting the environment, but only a minority saw the environment as one of the nation's most important problems.

**The early 1970s**

As the high level of environmental activism stimulated by Earth Day inevitably began to decline, several commentators suggested that public support for environmental protection would likewise decline. The most influential was Downs (1972), who (as noted earlier) suggested that by 1972 environmental problems had already passed from the stage of alarmed discovery and enthusiastic support into one of sombre realization of the costs of environmental protection and improvement. The situation certainly seemed conducive for environmental quality to pass through the issue-attention cycle. At the beginning of the decade the government (both federal and state) passed a great deal of environmental legislation, set up highly visible environmental agencies (most notably the Environmental Protection Agency), and spent a good deal of money on behalf of environmental improvement and protection (Lester, 1989), thus giving the impression that government was taking care of environmental problems. In addition, media attention to environmental problems began to decline after 1970, and such problems were eclipsed when the energy crisis of 1973–1974 took over center stage on the public agenda (Schoenfeld et al., 1979). The setting seemed ripe for environmental problems to pass through the final stages of Downs's cycle and experience the natural decline posited by social scientists.

What, in fact, happened to public concern for environmental quality in the early

1970s? Sadly, data needed for providing a reasonably definitive answer to this question are not available. Not only did pollsters often stop asking the environmental questions they had used in the 1960s, but, surprisingly, they failed to start asking new questions in 1970 to provide a baseline for monitoring changes in environmental concern. The situation led Erskine (1972) to express consternation over public opinion pollsters' failure to collect good trend data on environmental issues, and forces one to rely on the very limited body of data shown in Table 2.

I have already referred to three of the data sets reported in Table 2, both of the national studies and the Wisconsin study. All three used MIP questions and all show a similar pattern: The salience of environmental problems declined substantially by 1972 from its peak in 1970, and even further by 1974–1975. The patterns in the Harris and Wisconsin data are especially similar, and indicate that the proportion of the public volunteering environmental problems as among the nation's or state's most serious problems declined from a large minority in 1970 to a small minority (10% or less) by mid-decade. A similar pattern was found in Gallup surveys using an MIP question asking for the *single* most important problem. As noted earlier, the percentage volunteering environmental problems reached a peak of 10% in 1970, and then fluctuated between 7% and 2% during 1971 and 1972 (Hornback, 1974). Unfortunately, in 1973 Gallup began asking respondents to name the *two* MIPs, making comparisons with prior years impossible. The environment continued to show up low on the Gallup MIP lists through 1973 but dropped off in 1974, when it was replaced by energy (Smith, 1985).[4]

Earlier I noted that public opinion analysts tend to regard responses to MIP questions as good indicators of the salience of an issue to the public. But it has been argued that responses to such questions are especially susceptible to media attention to particular problems (Funkhouser, 1973) and that—more broadly—salience as measured by MIP responses 'is transitory for all but the most momentous issues such as war or depression' (Mitchell, 1984, p. 55). Because media attention to environmental problems declined considerably in the early 1970s (Schoenfeld et al., 1979), perhaps these trends reflect little more than the public's susceptibility to the agenda-setting function of the mass media. The results also raise questions about the validity of MIP questions for measuring issue salience.[5] Some analysts of environmental concern have, in fact, argued that the obvious decline in the salience of environmental problems in the early 1970s was not matched by a decline in public commitment to environmental protection (Mitchell, 1984).

Remarkably, the only two sets of data available for testing this possibility are limited to the state of Washington. Fortunately, although the two studies used very different indicators of concern for environmental quality, they nonetheless produced similar results. In both cases a fairly sharp decline in environmental commitment was found by mid-decade, although not as great as the decline shown by the MIP indicators. The 1970–1974 panel study compared the priorities for spending government funds for 1600+ Washington residents over the 4 years and found significant declines in the percentage wanting more tax money spent on environmental protection. Those wanting more spending on pollution control declined from 70% to 32%, whereas those wanting more spent on protection of forests and other natural areas for public enjoyment declined from 52% to 37%. The 1970–1976 trend study compared different samples of 800+ residents in terms of their selection of reducing air and water pollution as one of the two or three most serious problems facing the state and their communities (out of a list of eleven potential problems). At the state level there was a large decline, from 44 to 18 in the percentage selecting 'reducing pollution' over the 6 years. The decline at the community level was smaller, from 23% to 15%, due in part to the fact that respondents were much less likely to see pollution as a community problem to begin with (Dunlap and Van Liere, 1977).

In short, the two Washington State studies found that public concern for environmental quality, measured both by spending priorities and by perceived seriousness of environmental problems, declined substantially between 1970 and mid-decade. Especially noteworthy is that in the 1970–1974 panel study, not only did the percentage wanting more spending on pollution control decline, but the percentage wanting less spending in this area increased as well (from 5% to 21%). Although great caution is called for in generalizing from a single state, the Washington results reveal a deterioration of the strong consensus on behalf of environmental protection that emerged with the first Earth Day in 1970.

To summarize, although the available evidence on trends in public concern for environmental quality in the early 1970s is sparse, it consistently indicates a significant decline in environmental awareness and concern among the public in the early 1970s. This seems to support Downs's (1972) contention that by 1972 environmental quality was about halfway through the issue-attention cycle, and his prediction that it would shortly move into the fourth stage (the decline of intense public interest) consequently seemed very plausible by mid-decade (see, e.g., Dunlap and Dillman, 1976).

## The mid to late 1970s

Although a few years late, by 1973 three items measuring public concern for environmental quality began to be used on a regular basis in national surveys, and more were added later in the decade. In reviewing the results obtained with these items (shown in Table 3), it must be kept in mind that by the time they were first used, public concern for the environment had already declined significantly from its peak in 1970.

In late 1973 (reflecting the emergence of the energy crisis), Roper began using a trade-off question in which respondents were asked if they were more on the side of producing adequate energy or more on the side of protecting the environment. For the sake of brevity I have reported only the percentages for these two positions, deleting the sizeable proportion of respondents who either volunteered 'neither' or 'no conflict' or indicated 'don't know'. In 1973 the two positions received equal levels of support (37% each), but after that the percentage siding with adequate energy began to exceed that siding with environmental protection (with the exception of 1976). By 1980 the gap had reached a modest 9% (45% vs. 36%), indicating that worries about energy supplies had clearly exceeded concern about environmental protection—but had not caused an erosion of support for environmental protection as was widely expected, for the latter held virtually constant from 1973 to 1980 (from 37% to 36%).

The second Roper question, asking respondents whether they think environmental protection laws and regulations have gone too far, or not far enough, or have struck about the right balance, shows a more substantial decline in public support for environmental protection. Table 3 shows the percentages indicating 'not far enough' or 'too far' (the percentages indicating 'struck about the right balance' or 'don't know' were deleted for brevity). In 1973 the percentage indicating that environmental protection efforts had not gone far enough sharply exceeded that indicating that such efforts had gone too far (34% vs. 13%). But the gap quickly began to close (with the exception of 1976) and reached a low point of only 5% in 1979 (29% vs. 24%).

The next item is from a question used by the National Opinion Research Center (NORC) in which respondents are given a long list of problems facing our nation and asked if they think we're spending 'too much money on it', 'too little money', or 'about the right amount' for each one. Surprisingly, as late as 1973 the percentage responding that 'too little' was being spent on improving and protecting the environment overwhelmed the percentage responding that 'too much' was being spent in this area; 61% versus 7% (the percentages indicating 'about right' and 'don't know' are not shown). In subsequent years there was a modest but fairly consistent decline in the percentage responding 'too little', and a small but relatively consistent increase in the percentage indicating 'too much'. The result is that the initial 54 percentage points difference between these two positions in 1973 declined to 33 percentage points by the end of the decade (National Opinion Research Center, 1989).

The fourth item, which Cambridge did not use until 1976, poses a broad trade-off between economic growth and environmental quality. It asks respondents whether we must sacrifice economic growth in order to preserve and protect the environment or sacrifice environmental quality for economic growth. In 1976 the public was almost twice as likely to prefer sacrificing economic growth for environmental quality as vice versa (38% vs. 21%). Although the percentage choosing to sacrifice economic growth held nearly constant over the next 3 years, the percentage indicating a willingness to sacrifice environmental quality steadily grew (with a consequent decline in the large proportion of volunteered 'don't knows,' which are not shown). The result is that by 1979 the pro-environmental position had only a 5 point margin over the pro-growth position (37% vs. 32%).

The final set of data in Table 3 covers only two points in time and is somewhat at odds with the other results in this table, and thus it should be viewed with caution. Nonetheless, the 1974 and 1980 Roper data on perceptions of the degree to which various environmental problems will probably be 'serious problems' in the future (25 to 50 years) reveal a remarkable degree of stability, with the percentages viewing air and water pollution as likely to be serious remaining identical (68% and 69%, respectively) and the percentages viewing water shortages as probable increasing slightly (from 53% to 57%) over the 6 years. The fact that majorities of the public saw pollution and water shortages as future problems suggests that although the saliency of environmental problems declined substantially and support for environmental protection declined modestly during the 1970s, the public apparently did not see environmental problems as disappearing.

The data covering the 1970s in Table 3 provide a generally consistent image of trends in environmental concern from the early part of the mid 1970s through the

Table 3. Trends in public concern for environmental quality, early 1970s to 1980

| National survey | Question | Percentage response by year (19–) | | | | | | | |
|---|---|---|---|---|---|---|---|---|---|
| | | 73 | 74 | 75 | 76 | 77 | 78 | 79 | 80 |
| (1) Roper[a] | More on the side of: | | | | | | | | |
| | (a) protecting the environment | 37 | 39 | 39 | 44 | 35 | — | 38 | 36 |
| | (b) having adequate energy | 37 | 41 | 40 | 33 | 43 | — | 43 | 45 |
| (2) Roper[b] | Environmental protection laws and regulations have gone: | | | | | | | | |
| | (a) not far enough | 34 | 25 | 31 | 32 | 27 | — | 29 | 33 |
| | (b) too far | 13 | 17 | 20 | 15 | 20 | — | 24 | 25 |
| (3) NORC[c] | U.S. spending on improving and protecting the environment: | | | | | | | | |
| | (a) too little | 61 | 59 | 53 | 55 | 48 | 52 | — | 48 |
| | (b) too much | 7 | 8 | 10 | 9 | 11 | 10 | — | 15 |
| (4) Cambridge[d] | Sacrifice environmental quality or sacrifice economic growth: | | | | | | | | |
| | (a) sacrifice economic growth | | | | 38 | 39 | 37 | 37 | |
| | (b) sacrifice environmental quality | | | | 21 | 26 | 23 | 32 | |
| (5) Roper[e] | Will be a 'serious problem' 25 to 50 years from now: | | | | | | | | |
| | (a) severe air pollution | | 68 | | | | | | 68 |
| | (b) severe water pollution | | 69 | | | | | | 69 |
| | (c) shortage of water supplies | | 53 | | | | | | 57 |

*Note.* NORC = National Opinion Research Center.

[a]Full question: 'There is continuing talk about an energy crisis and the idea that there won't be enough electricity and other forms of energy to meet consumer demand in the coming years. Some people say that the progress of this nation depends on an adequate supply of energy and we have to have it even though it means taking some risks with the environment. Others say the important thing is the environment, and that it is better to risk not having enough energy than to risk spoiling our environment. Are you more on the side of adequate energy or more on the side of protecting the environment?' Volunteered responses of 'neither', 'no conflict', or 'don't know' are not shown. Results are reported in Gillroy and Shapiro (1986, p. 275) and Dunlap (1987, p. 8).

[b]Full question: 'There are also different opinions about how far we've gone with environmental protection laws and regulations. At the present time, do you think environmental protection laws and regulations have gone too far, or not far enough, or have struck about the right balance?' Percentages responding 'struck about right balance' or volunteering 'don't know' are not shown. Results are reported in Gillroy and Shapiro (1986, p. 273) and Dunlap (1987, p. 9).

[c]Full question: 'We are faced with many problems in this country, none of which can be solved easily or inexpensively. I'm going to name some of these problems, and for each one I'd like you to tell me whether you think we're spending too much money on it, too little money, or about the right amount. First . . . Are we spending too much, too little, or about the right amount on . . . Improving and protecting the environment?' Percentages responding 'about right' or volunteering 'don't know' are not shown. Results are reported in National Opinion Research Center (1989, pp. 104, 108).

[d]Full question: 'Which of these two statements is closer to your opinion: We must be prepared to sacrifice environmental quality for economic growth. We must sacrifice economic growth in order to preserve and protect the environment.' Percentages volunteering 'don't know' are not shown. Results through 1986 are reported in Cambridge Reports, Inc. (1986, p. 9) and Dunlap (1987, p. 11).

[e]Full question: 'Here is a list of some different kinds of problems people might be facing 25 to 50 years from now. Would you please go down that list and for each one tell me whether you think it will be a serious problem your children or grandchildren will be facing 25 to 50 years from now?' Results are reported in Roper's *The Public Pulse*, (New York, NY), 'Research Supplement',June 1989, p. 1.

end of the decade: modest but continued decline in public support for environmental protection. These results, coupled with those reviewed in Tables 1 and 2, suggest the following evolution of public concern with environmental quality: concern grew rapidly in the late 1960s, reached a peak in 1970 after Earth Day, experienced a fairly sharp decline in the early part of the 1970s, and declined gradually throughout the rest of the decade.

The long-term trend I have just sketched is supported by one final piece of longitudinal data (covering too long a time span to be summarized in the prior tables). A 1980 survey for the Council on Environmental Quality (CEQ) repeated the question used by Gallup in 1965 and 1970 (listed in Table 1). Recall that respondents were given a list of ten national problems, including reducing pollution of air and water, and were asked to indicate which three they wanted to see government devote most of its attention to in the next year or two. As noted previously, reducing pollution was selected by only 17% in 1965, ranking it ninth out of the ten problems; in 1970 it was selected by 53%, hiking it to second. A decade later, in the 1980 CEQ survey, reducing pollution was chosen by 24%, ranking it sixth out of the same list of ten problems (Mitchell, 1980).[6]

In view of these data, should we conclude that at the end of the 'environmental decade', public concern for environmental quality had declined to the point that environmental issues had moved into the post-problem stage of the issue-attention cycle? This is not an easy question to answer, largely because Downs vaguely defines the final stage as when 'an issue that has been replaced at the center of public concern moves into a prolonged limbo—a twilight realm of lesser attention or spasmodic recurrences of interest' (1972, p. 40). It is clear that if one were to judge public concern by salience, as measured by MIP responses, then one should conclude that environmental quality had moved into the post-problem stage—indeed, it apparently did so as early as 1974 when it was supplanted by the energy crisis. However, the fact that the data in Table 3 indicate at least moderate levels of public concern with environmental quality throughout the decade, long after environment has disappeared from the list of the two or three most frequent responses to MIP questions, again suggests that salience may be a poor indicator of public concern for social problems.[7] Although it is the aspect of public opinion that best reflects the issue-attention cycle, salience may well be unduly influenced by mass media coverage, as argued by Funkhouser (1973).

Even if one ignores the salience dimension, it is difficult to determine if environmental concern had declined to the post-problem stage at the end of the decade.[8] First, note that Downs refers to this stage as a 'realm of lesser attention'; second, he later adds that 'problems that have gone through the cycle almost always receive a higher average level of attention, public effort, and general concern than those still in the pre-discovery stage' (1972, p. 41). The data reviewed thus far, indicating that environmental concern was lower at the end of the 1970s than at the beginning of the decade, but still higher than in the mid 1960s, would seem to indicate that environmental quality had at least settled into Downs's fourth stage, a period of less intense public interest, by the late 1970s (see, e.g., Anthony, 1982).

Regardless of what one concludes about the issue-attention cycle, it is apparent from Table 3 and from a large amount of cross-sectional data collected in the late 1970s (see Mitchell, 1980) that although public concern for environmental quality had become less consensual, it had by no means disappeared from the public agenda by the end of the 1970s. Although it is clear that the data can be interpreted differently, depending on whether one emphasizes the decline or the endurance of environmental concern throughout the decade, I would generally agree with Mitchell's assessment of the situation in 1980: 'Although the state of the environment is no longer viewed as a crisis issue, strong support for environmental protection continues . . . [F]ar from being a fad, the enthusiasm for environmental improvement which arose in the early 1970s has become a continuing concern' (1980, p. 423). Indeed, I think that public concern for environmental quality showed impressive staying power in the face of a continuing series of essentially competing concerns: the energy crisis of 1973–1974 and continuing concerns about energy supplies throughout the decade, a worsening economic situation, and a taxpayers' revolt begun by California's Proposition 13 in 1978 (Mitchell, 1984). In addition, the fact that the Carter administration was viewed as strongly committed to environmental protection may have contributed to public apathy about environmental problems.[9]

In sum, the environmental movement clearly seemed to have lost some of its broad-based public support throughout the 1970s. Yet, a full decade after the immensely successful Earth Day, and after a vast amount of government action on behalf of environmental quality, the movement had certainly not seen its concerns and goals fade totally from public attention. Public support may have waned, or experienced a natural decline, but it had definitely not disappeared.

## The 1980s and the rejuvenation of environmentalism

The public may have understandably assumed that government was taking care of environmental problems during the 1970s after watching so much governmental activity in the area, and this assumption was probably a contributing factor to the slow decline in public concern for environmental quality throughout the decade (Dunlap, 1989). However, the situation changed considerably when Ronald Reagan took office in 1980.

Environmentalists were wary of President Reagan because of his general emphasis on deregulation and his tendency to view environmental regulations in particular as hampering the economy (Holden, 1980). The Reagan administration quickly exceeded environmentalists' worst fears, deviating from a decade of generally bipartisan commitment to federal environmental protection. The Council on Environmental Quality was virtually dismantled, the budget of the Environmental Protection Agency (EPA) was severely cut, and the enforcement of environmental regulations was curtailed by administrative review, budgetary restrictions, and staff change. The last category received the most attention, with Anne Gorsuch at EPA and James Watt in the Department of Interior symbolizing the administration's commitment to changing the thrust of environmental policy (Hays, 1987; Portney, 1984; Vig and Kraft, 1984).

It is understandable that environmentalists were upset by the administration's policies and began to vigorously oppose and criticize them. Perhaps most notable was the issuance in 1982 of a well-publicized report, *Ronald Reagan and the American environment*, prepared by ten of the nation's largest environmental organizations and termed an indictment of the administration's environmental policies (Friends of the Earth, 1982). Opposition to these policies grew in Congress, where efforts were made to restore budget cuts and oversee effective enforcement of regulations. Most significant was the Congressional investigation of the EPA's handling of Superfund, which led to the registration of Gorsuch and several other EPA administrators. Congressional criticism, along with public pressure, also led to the resignation of James Watt, although an ethnic slur rather than the Department of Interior's policies was the precipitating event (see Rosenbaum, 1991).

In the face of mounting criticism, the administration defended its environmental initiatives in terms of its electoral mandate, arguing that Reagan's landslide victory was evidence of the voters' approval of his efforts to free the economy of the burden of governmental regulations (Mitchell, 1984). The President was a vigorous spokesman for deregulation and made the issue a test of his leadership capabilities. Because political leaders have long been recognized as potent forces in shaping public opinion (Pierce *et al.*, 1982), it might be expected that a popular president would have succeeded in convincing the U.S. public that environmental regulations had gone too far. Was President Reagan able to turn the tide against what his administration often termed *environmental extremism*?

The six sets of trend data on public support for environmental quality reported in Table 4 suggest that Reagan was not at all successful in lowering the public's commitment to environmental protection. Indeed, quite the contrary seems to have occurred. In each case there is a pattern of increasing commitment to environment protection during the Reagan administration, often followed by further increase during the first 2 years of the Bush administration.

The first four items are repeated from Table 3 because they all had been used during the last half of the 1970s. The first poses the trade-off between environmental protection and adequate energy; there was a 10% increase in those siding with the environment and a comparable decrease in those siding with energy from 1980 to 1982 (when Roper temporarily stopped using it). The 46% favoring environmental protection in 1982 was the highest figure recorded with this item, and the 11% margin it enjoyed over energy adequacy matches the previous high point of 1976. These results are especially impressive because a major theme of the Reagan administration was that environmental regulations had to be relaxed to allow for the increased energy production required for a strong economic recovery (Portney, 1984; Vig and Kraft, 1984). Roper began using the item again in 1989, by which time a majority chose environmental protection over energy adequacy, giving the former more than a two-to-one advantage (52% vs. 24%).

The second item, which asks respondents if they think environmental protection laws have gone too far or not far enough, provides an even more direct indicator of the public's evaluation of the Reagan administration's environmental policy agenda. The results indicate a growing rejection of the administration's position: after having reached a low point in 1979, the margin between those indicating not far enough and those indicating too far increased in Reagan's first year in office and in each subsequent year through 1983. In 1982 the 37% saying not far enough already exceeded the previous high of 34% from 1973, and the next year it jumped to 48%. Results from the end of the decade indicate that those wanting stronger rather than weaker environmental regulations outnumbered their counterparts five-to-one (54% vs. 11%)!

The next item, the NORC spending item, is also pertinent for judging the impact of Reagan's environmental policy because budget cuts for environmental protection agencies were a major aspect of that policy (Vig and Kraft, 1984). Although still fairly strong, support for increased spending on environmental protection had reached a low point in 1980, with 33% more people indicating 'too little' was being spent on the area than indicating 'too much' (48% vs. 15%). The gap between these two positions has begun to increase by 1982, and in 1984 it reached 51%, matching the 1974 level and approximating the previous high of 54% in 1973. The gap remained remarkably stable through 1986 and then increased steadily in each of the next 4 years to reach 67% in 1990—well in excess of the 1973 level.[10]

The fourth item, from Cambridge, forces respondents to choose between economic growth and environmental quality. Recall that in 1979, those preferring that economic growth be sacrificed for environmental quality held only a slim margin over those preferring the opposite (37% vs. 32%). At the outset of the Reagan administration the percentage preferring that economic growth be sacrificed rose to 41%, a new high, whereas the percentage opting to sacrifice environmental quality dropped to 26%, producing a margin that nearly equalled the 1976 level when the item was first used. Despite yearly fluctuations, the margin was the same in 1984 and then climbed to new peaks in 1986 (58% vs. 19%) and in 1990 (64% vs. 15%).

The *New York Times*/CBS News Poll began using the next item in September 1981, by which time the Reagan administration was under attack from environmentalists but before its environmental policies had gained the intense media attention of the EPA and Watt controversies. This item asks respondents to react to the extreme pro-environmental position that environmental improvements should be pursued regardless of cost. The public was almost evenly divided on the issue in 1981 (45% vs. 42%), but preference for the pro-environmental position over the rather mild anti-environmental position grew steadily throughout the Reagan years and then took a very large jump in 1989 to reach 56% (74% vs. 18%) and then held ground in 1990.

The final item in Table 4 was not used by Cambridge until March 1982. Like the second Roper item, it provides a good indicator of public reaction to the Reagan administration's overall environmental policy agenda, asking respondents if they think 'there is too much, too little, or about the right amount of government regulation and involvement in the area of environmental protection.' From the outset, the public clearly rejected the administration's contention that environmental regulations were excessive (by a margin of 35% to 11%), and this view has become more pronounced over time—peaking in 1986 (59% vs. 7%), dipping a bit the next 2 years, and then coming back strong in 1989 and 1990.

Taken together, the six sets of trend data in Table 4 provide a generally consistent view of recent trends in public support for environmental protection. After having declined moderately in the 1970s, public support for environmental protection began to rise shortly after Reagan took office and has continued to do so. This conclusion is bolstered by results obtained with several other items used at two time points only between 1980 and 1990 and reported elsewhere (Dunlap and Scarce, 1991). The trend data, along with a wide range of recent cross-sectional data, thus suggest that environmental protection has again become a consensual issue

Table 4. Trends in public concern for environmental quality, 1980 to 1990

| National survey | Question | Percentage response by year (19—) | | | | | | | | | | |
|---|---|---|---|---|---|---|---|---|---|---|---|---|
| | | 80 | 81 | 82 | 83 | 84 | 85 | 86 | 87 | 88 | 89 | 90 |
| (1) Roper[a] | More on the side of: | | | | | | | | | | | |
| | (a) protecting the environment | 36 | 40 | 46 | — | — | — | — | — | — | 57 | 52 |
| | (b) having adequate energy | 45 | 39 | 35 | — | — | — | — | — | — | 24 | 24 |
| (2) Roper[b] | Environmental protection laws and regulations have gone: | | | | | | | | | | | |
| | (a) not far enough | 33 | 31 | 37 | 48 | — | — | — | — | — | 55 | 54 |
| | (b) too far | 25 | 21 | 16 | 14 | — | — | — | — | — | 11 | 11 |
| (3) NORC[c] | U.S. spending on improving and protecting the environment: | | | | | | | | | | | |
| | (a) too little | 48 | — | 50 | 54 | 58 | 58 | 58 | 61 | 65 | 70 | 71 |
| | (b) too much | 15 | — | 12 | 8 | 7 | 8 | 6 | 6 | 5 | 4 | 4 |
| (4) Cambridge[d] | Sacrifice environmental quality or sacrifice economic growth: | | | | | | | | | | | |
| | (a) sacrifice economic growth | | 41 | 41 | 42 | 42 | 53 | 58 | 57 | 52 | 52 | 64 |
| | (b) sacrifice environmental quality | | 26 | 31 | 16 | 27 | 23 | 19 | 23 | 19 | 21 | 15 |
| (5) NYT/CBS[e] | Environmental improvements must be made regardless of cost: | | | | | | | | | | | |
| | (a) agree | | 45 | 52 | 58 | — | — | 66 | — | 65 | 74 | 74 |
| | (b) disagree | | 42 | 41 | 34 | — | — | 27 | — | 22 | 18 | 21 |
| (6) Cambridge[f] | Amount of environmental protection by government: | | | | | | | | | | | |
| | (a) too little | | | 35 | 44 | 56 | 54 | 59 | 49 | 53 | 58 | 62 |
| | (b) too much | | | 11 | 9 | 8 | 10 | 7 | 12 | 12 | 9 | 16 |

*Note.* NORC = National Opinion Research Center, NYT/CBS = *New York Times*/Columbia Broadcasting System.

[a] See footnote a of Table 3 for full question. Results for 1989 and 1990 were provided by the Roper Organization.

[b] See footnote b of Table 3 for full question. Results for 1989 and 1990 were provided by the Roper Organization

[c] See footnote c of Table 3 for full question.

[d] See footnote d of Table 3 for full question. Results through 1989 are reported in Cambridge Reports, Inc. (1989, p. 14). Results for 1990 were provided by Cambridge Reports/Research International.

[e] Full question: 'Do you agree or disagree with the following statement: Protecting the environment is so important that requirements and standards cannot be too high, and continuing environmental improvements must be made regardless of cost.' Percentages volunteering 'no opinion' are not shown. Results through 1989 are reported in *The Polling Report*, 24 April 1989, p. 3. Results for 1990 were provided by the *New York Times*.

[f] Full question: 'In general, do you think there is too much, too little, or about the right amount of government regulation and involvement in the area of environmental protection?' Percentages responding 'about the right amount' or volunteering 'don't know' are not shown. Results through 1989 are reported in Cambridge Reports, Inc. (1989, p. 16). Results for 1990 were provided by Cambridge Reports/Research International.

commanding support from an overwhelming majority of the public and eliciting opposition from only a very small minority. Perhaps most striking is a recent Harris survey that found an amazing 97% responding 'more' when asked. 'Do you think this country should be doing more or less than it does now to protect the environment and curb pollution?' (Harris, 1989, p. 3).

In staging this comeback, environmental issues have obviously halted their slide into the last stage of Downs's issue-attention cycle, the post-problem stage, and have reversed the natural decline that was the expected course for social problems. This is best illustrated by the only data I have located on environmental concern spanning the entire 1970–1990 period. In both years Gallup used the following item: 'As you may know, it will cost a considerable amount of money to control pollution. Would you be willing to pay the slightly higher prices for your goods and services business would have to charge to control pollution?' The proportion responding 'yes' increased from 63% to 79%, whereas that answering 'no' declined from 27% to 17%, over the two decades ('don't knows' dropped from 10% to 4%).[11] The results, along with other recent survey data (see Dunlap and Scarce, 1991), suggest that public concern with environmental problems is stronger now than it was in 1970.

What has accounted for this rejuvenation of environmental concern in our society? I have argued elsewhere (Dunlap, 1987, 1989) that much of the increased support for environmental protection in the 1980s probably stemmed from the public's apprehension that, unlike its predecessors, the Reagan administration could not be trusted to protect the environment (a perception that was obviously fueled by environmental organizations and the media, with the unwitting support of Watt, Gorsuch, and others). Indeed, large numbers of people became sufficiently concerned that they joined environmental organizations for the first time, producing sizable membership gains for many of the national organizations in the 1980s. This interpretation is strengthened by considerable evidence that the public was aware of the administration's poor environmental record and that, in general, the public believes that the government *should* assume responsibility for environmental protection (Dunlap, 1989).

What is notable about the growth of environmental concern in the 1980s, however, is that this concern did not decline after the Reagan administration's environmental scandals receded and that it has continued to climb since Reagan left office. Although President Bush has by no means proven himself to be a strong environmentalist, his efforts to portray himself as concerned about environmental quality have thus far shielded him from the intense criticism that environmentalists levelled at Reagan. This suggests that the other major factor stimulating rising public concern over environmental quality—increased awareness of the growing seriousness of ecological problems (Dunlap, 1989; Mitchell, 1984, 1990)—has probably become the critical force in driving public opinion.

## PUBLIC PERCEPTIONS OF ECOLOGICAL PROBLEMS IN THE 1980s

A combination of what might be called the institutionalized environmental movement (a collection of actors including government officials in environmental agencies; environmental scientists in government, academic, and other nonprofit research centers; and environmental organizations and activists; see Morrison, 1986), a sympathetic mass media, and ecological realities have combined to generate enormous societal attention to ecological problems in recent years. Scientists and government officials are constantly joining environmentalists in publicizing the latest aspects of ecological degradation, and their efforts have been validated by an endless array of newsworthy events (Bhopal, Chernobyl, frequent chemical spills, hazardous ocean beaches, oil spills, rainforest destruction, filled-up waste sites) that receive tremendous media attention. The success of these efforts in attracting public attention can be seen in newspapers, on TV news programs, and on the covers of our nation's most important news magazines (see, e.g., Mitchell, 1990). During 1988–1989 alone, *Newsweek* carried numerous cover stories on ecological problems, *U.S. News and World Report* had one on 'Planet Earth: How it works, how to fix it' (31 Oct. 1988), and *Time* captured the most attention by naming the 'Endangered Earth' as 'Planet of the Year' in lieu of its famous 'Man of the Year' for 1988 (2 January, 1989). Finally, there was the enormous amount of media coverage (radio and television as well as print) of the 22 April 1990 celebration of the twentieth Earth Day (Nixon, 1991).

**Increase in perceived seriousness of problems**

The impact of all of this on public awareness of what have become 'ecological' (rather than 'environmental') problems is aptly demonstrated by the range of trend data reported in Table 5. Unlike Table 4, in which the items focused on support for environmental protection, the items in Table 5 focus on perceptions of the seriousness of environmental problems. The results from these seven sets of trend data indicate a substantial rise in the public's perception of environmental problems as serious issues during the 1980s.

The first set of Roper data continues the results reported for 1974–1980 in Table 3 for three of the problems and shows sizeable increases in the percentages of the public viewing air and water pollution as likely to be 'serious problems' 25 to 50 years in the future (14% and 13%, respectively, from 1980 to 1988). There were also substantial increases of 9% for both water shortages and overpopulation (included by Roper since 1980). Most striking is the increase of 28% for the greenhouse effect that occurred between 1984 and 1988.

Whereas the items just discussed deal with future environmental problems, the first Cambridge item asks for respondents' perceptions of how 'overall quality of the environment around here' compared with that of 5 years ago. The results reflect a substantial increase in the percentage perceiving a worsening of their local environment from 1983 to 1989 (from 34% to 49%). Given the fact that surveys have consistently found the public more likely to see environmental problems as serious at the state or national levels than at the local level (e.g., Dunlap and Van Liere, 1977), it is striking that far more people see their local environment becoming worse than see it becoming better (in 1990, 31% indicated 'better', and the rest volunteered 'about the same' or 'don't know').

Table 5. Recent trends in the perceived seriousness of environmental problems

| National survey | Question | Percentage response by year (19–) | | | | | | | | | | |
|---|---|---|---|---|---|---|---|---|---|---|---|---|
| | | 80 | 81 | 82 | 83 | 84 | 85 | 86 | 87 | 88 | 89 | 90 |
| (1) Roper[a] | Will be a 'serious problem' 25 to 50 years from now: | | | | | | | | | | | |
| | (a) severe air pollution | 68 | | | | 70 | | | | 82 | | |
| | (b) severe water pollution | 69 | | | | 71 | | | | 82 | | |
| | (c) shortage of water supplies | 57 | | | | 53 | | | | 66 | | |
| | (d) the 'greenhouse effect' | — | | | | 37 | | | | 65 | | |
| | (e) overpopulation | 52 | | | | 56 | | | | 61 | | |
| (2) Cambridge[b] | 'Overall quality of the environment around here' worse than five years ago | | | | 34 | 33 | — | 32 | 32 | 46 | 49 | 55 |
| (3) Cambridge[c] | 'Most' or 'many' underground sources of water are contaminated with chemicals or other pollutants | | 28 | — | 29 | 37 | 40 | 39 | 50 | 54 | | |
| (4) Cambridge[d] | 'Quality and safety of your drinking water' is worse than five years ago | | | | | | 31 | 31 | 34 | 45 | 45 | 46 |
| (5) Cambridge[e] | Feel the 'greenhouse effect' is a 'very' or 'somewhat' serious problem | | | 43 | | — | — | 63 | — | 71 | 75 | 46 |

Percentage response by year (19–)

| National survey | Question | 80 | 81 | 82 | 83 | 84 | 85 | 86 | 87 | 88 | 89 | 90 |
|---|---|---|---|---|---|---|---|---|---|---|---|---|
| (6) Roper[f] | 'Environmental pollution' viewed as 'very serious' threat' to citizens | | | | | 44 | — | — | — | 62 | | |
| (7) Cambridge[g] | Environment volunteered as one of 'the two most important problems' facing the U.S. today | | | 2 | — | — | — | — | 5 | 8 | 16 | 21 |

[a] See footnote e of Table 3 for full question.

[b] Full question: 'Do you think the overall quality of the environment around here is very much better than it was five years ago, somewhat better than it was five years ago, slightly better than it was five years ago, slightly worse, somewhat worse, or very much worse than it was five years ago?' Results show three 'worse' categories combined. Results for 1983–1986 are reported in Cambridge Reports, Inc. (1986, p. 3). More recent results are reported in Cambridge Reports/Research International (1990, p. 4).

[c] Full question: 'There are a lot of sources of underground water in the United States. Some people say many of these sources are contaminated with chemicals and other pollutants. I'd like to know how you feel about this. Do you think most underground sources of water are contaminated, as many underground sources are contaminated as are uncontaminated, not very many are contaminated, or none are contaminated?' Results show 'most' and 'as many are as are not' combined. Results are reported in Americans for the Environment (1989, p. 5–25).

[d] Full question: 'Do you think the quality and safety of your drinking water is very much better than it was 5 years ago, somewhat better than it was 5 years ago, slightly better than it was 5 years ago, slightly worse, somewhat worse, or very much worse than it was 5 years ago?' Results are reported in Cambridge Reports/Research International (1990, p. 5).

[e] Full question: 'Actually, the greenhouse effect, which is a gradual warming of the Earth's atmosphere, is believed to be caused by carbon dioxide and other gases accumulating in the atmosphere and preventing heat from escaping into space. Some people have expressed concern that the greenhouse effect could lead to harmful changes in ocean levels and weather patterns. Just from this information, do you feel the greenhouse effect is a very serious problem, a somewhat serious problem, not too serious a problem, or not a serious problem at all?' Results are reported in Cambridge Reports, Inc. (Cambridge, MA), *Trends and Forecasts*, October 1989, p. 7.

[f] Full question: 'Here is a list of some different things people have said are threats to our society. For each one would you tell me whether you think it is a very serious threat these days to a citizen like yourself, a moderately serious threat, not much of a threat, or no threat at all? First, environmental pollution.' Results are reported in Roper's (New York, NY) *The Public Pulse*, Research Supplement, June 1989, p. 1.

[g] Full question: 'What do you think are the two most important problems facing the United States today?' Results show combined first- and second-choice responses. Results are reported in Cambridge Reports, Inc., *Trends and Forecasts*, June 1989, p. 5, and September 1989, p. 6, and Cambridge Reports/Research International (1990, p. 3).

In recent years, one of the most publicized ways in which local environmental quality deteriorates has been through contamination of water supplies, and the next two sets of Cambridge data reflect the importance of this problem to the public. First, between 1981 and 1988 the percentage indicating that they believe 'most [underground sources of water] are contaminated with chemicals or other pollutants' or 'as many are contaminated as are uncontaminated' nearly doubled, from 28% to 54%. Second, those indicating that the 'quality and safety' or their drinking water has worsened over the past 5 years increased by half, from 31% to 46%, in only 5 years.

Although fear of water contamination and toxic contamination in general have led to growing apprehension among the public about the quality of their local environment, the past few years have also seen an explosion of attention to large-scale environmental problems, ranging from regional problems such as acid rain to global problems such as ozone depletion and global warming. The fifth item taps the last issue, asking respondents about the degree to which they see the greenhouse effect as a problem, and it is clear that there has been a major increase in the proportion of the public viewing this phenomenon as problematic. By 1989, fully three-fourths of the public had come to see the greenhouse effect as at least somewhat serious.

Not only has there been a significant increase in the degree to which the public perceives environmental problems, ranging from local to global, as serious over the past several years, but there has been a concomitant rise in the perception of such problems as real threats to human well-being. This increase can be seen in the responses to the sixth item (although there are only two data points), in which by 1988 Roper found that 62% indicated that environmental pollution was a 'very serious threat . . . to a citizen like yourself' (up from 44% in 1984), a response that probably reflects the emergence of hazardous and toxic wastes as major pollutants in the 1980s. Although I am not aware of any comparable items being used in the 1970s, it is hard to imagine that such a large majority of the public would have seen environmental pollution as a 'very serious threat' to themselves in the 1970s.

Finally, mirroring the significant rise in the perceived seriousness of environmental problems that has occurred during the 1980s, such problems have begun to re-emerge as leading responses to MIP questions in the last half of the decade. The Cambridge MIP data reported in Table 5 show that in 1990, fully 21% volunteered some type of environmental problem as one of the two most important problems facing the United States today, ranking it fourth behind drugs at 39%, government spending at 26%, and other social problems at 22%. This is the highest percentage of respondents volunteering environmental problems since the April 1970 Harris survey reported in Table 2, and it exceeds the 13% reported by Harris for 1972. This strongly suggests that the environment has re-emerged as a salient issue (even judged by the extremely stringent criterion of showing up on volunteered MIP lists) to the public.[12]

## Increasing threat and declining quality

I argued above that there has been an increase in the degree to which environmental problems are perceived as real threats. Because I believe that this represents a major shift from the 1970s, and that it is a prime factor in the significant rise in public concern over environmental quality documented in Tables 4 and 5, I want to focus on the issue in more detail. In 1987 and again in 1989 Cambridge presented lists of environmental problems to samples of the public and asked them to rate the degree of threat posed by each problem—first to 'the overall quality of the environment' and then to 'personal health and safety'—on a scale of 1 to 7 (1 = no threat at all, 7 = a large threat). Table 6 shows the percentages of '6' and '7' responses (clearly indicating a high degree of perceived threat) for both environmental and personal threats over the 2 years. (The problems are ranked in the order of their rating as 'high personal threats' in 1989).

Several aspects of the results in Table 6 are worth mentioning. First, there was substantial increase (over 10%) in the perceived threat, both to the environment and personally, for nearly all of the problems over the 2-year period. Second, by 1989 majorities of the public (often around two-thirds) were rating most of the problems as large threats to the environment as well as to themselves. Third, there is considerable correspondence between the rating of problems as threats to environmental quality and as threats to personal health and safety, indicating that the two aspects of environmental problems increasingly go hand-in-hand. Finally, the overall ranking of the problems indicates that the threat posed by hazardous wastes, especially the possibility of water contamination, is the leading concern of the public. This finding is in agreement with other recent surveys in which the public is asked to rate the seriousness of a range of environmental problems (e.g., Hart/Teeter, 1990).

Reinforcing the increase in the perceived seriousness of environmental problems and the growing threat attributed to such problems is a sense that the overall quality of the environment is clearly deteriorating. Although I have come across no trend data besides the Cambridge item (which asks about changes in the local environment over the past 5 years) that bear directly on this issue, several recent surveys have found that a substantial segment of the public sees environmental quality as deteriorating. For example, a 1990 NBC/*Wall Street Journal* poll asked, 'Overall, do you think the environment in the United States has gotten better, worse, or stayed about the same over the last 20 years?' Although two-thirds felt it had gotten worse, only 16% felt it had gotten better, and 16% that it had stayed about the same (Hart/Teeter, 1990). In a similar vein, a recent Harris (1989) survey that asked, 'do you think that in 50 years' time the environment in the world as a whole will be much better, a little better, a little worse, or much worse than it is today?' found 81% responding 'worse' and only 18% indicating 'better'.

In short, despite considerable governmental and societal efforts at environmental protection over the past two decades, there is a widespread perception that the quality of the environment—from the local to the global level—is deteriorating. Furthermore, this deterioration is seen as posing a direct threat to the health and well-being of humans. I believe that this growing sense that environmental conditions are becoming truly threatening to our future provides a depth to environmental concern that was largely absent in 1970.

That environmental problems are seen increasingly as threatening, that they are threats to the public at large (rather than to only a segment of the population), and that their effects are ambiguous as well as ominous, are among the conditions that Downs (1972) recognized as possibly forestalling the disappearance of environmental

Table 6. Perceived environmental and personal threats from various problems, 1987 and 1989

| Problem | High environmental threat[a] | | | High personal threat[b] | | |
|---|---|---|---|---|---|---|
| | 1987 | 1989 | Change | 1987 | 1989 | Change |
| (1) Disposal of hazardous waste material | 65 | 71 | +6 | 62 | 69 | +7 |
| (2) Contamination of underground water supplies | 52 | 67 | +15 | 47 | 65 | +18 |
| (3) Air pollution (general) | 47 | 67 | +20 | — | — | — |
| (4) Pollution of our rivers, lakes and oceans | 54 | 67 | +13 | 46 | 60 | +14 |
| (5) Using additives and pesticides in our food supply | 49 | 55 | +6 | 49 | 60 | +11 |
| (6) Depletion of the ozone layer in the atmosphere | 42 | 61 | +19 | 39 | 58 | +19 |
| (7) Air pollution caused by business and industry | — | — | — | 37 | 58 | +19 |
| (8) Air pollution caused by cars and trucks | — | — | — | 32 | 52 | +20 |
| (9) The greenhouse effect | 26 | 52 | +26 | 20 | 48 | +28 |
| (10) Acid rain | 38 | 53 | +15 | 33 | 43 | +10 |

*Note.* Results are reported in Cambridge Reports, Inc. (Cambridge, MA), *Trends and Forecasts*, October 1989, pp. 4–6.
[a]Full question: 'Here is a card with a scale from "1" to "7", where "1" means "no threat at all" and "7" means "a large threat". Now I am going to read you a list of potential threats to the overall quality of the environment. Please use the card to tell me how much you think each problem threatens the overall quality of the environment. The more you think the problem threatens overall environmental quality, the higher the number you would give it.' The percentages reported are the combined "6" and "7" responses.
[b]Full question 'Now I am going to read you several potential problems facing our society. As I read each one, please use the same card to tell me how much you think each problem threatens your personal health and safety. The more you think a problem threatens your personal health and safety, the higher the number you would give it.' The percentages reported are the combined "6" and "7" responses.

issues from the public's attention. The data reviewed above indicate that Downs was wise to add such qualifications to the issue-attention cycle's applicability to environmental problems.

## SUMMARY AND IMPLICATIONS

The foregoing evidence on trends in public opinion toward environmental issues strongly indicates that the environmental movement has been extremely successful in attracting and maintaining—for two decades—the public's attention to and endorsement of its cause. We have already seen that large majorities of the public accept environmentalists' definition of ecological problems as serious (increasingly so) and express support for efforts to ameliorate the problematic conditions. In addition, when asked to do so, growing proportions of the public express positive views of the environmental movement and identify with it. Over the past two decades, a number of surveys have asked the public how they feel about the movement, and majorities have indicated that they are at least sympathetic toward it, whereas a significant minority (usually around 10%–15%) claim to be active in the movement (Dunlap, 1989; Mitchell, 1984).

Recent surveys confirm the public's positive image of environmentalism and suggest that after two decades the movement is drawing increasing support from the general population. For example, between 1987 and 1990 Cambridge found that the percentage responding that either they or someone in the household has 'donated to or been active in a group or organization working to protect the environment' had risen from 15% to 40% (Cambridge Reports/Research International, 1990). More impressively, 1989 and 1990 Gallup surveys found three-quarters (76% and 73%, respectively) of the public responding 'yes' when asked, 'Do you consider yourself an environmentalist?' (Gallup and Newport, 1990, p. 7). Thus, it is not surprising that a 1990 survey by Environment Opinion Study (1990) found two-thirds of the public agreeing that 'threats to the environment are as serious as the environmental groups say they are' and only one-quarter saying that 'environmental groups are exaggerating these threats in order to get the public to pay attention to them'. Finally, a 1989 *Business Week*/Harris poll (1989) gave respondents a list of six groups, and for each asked, 'Do you think they do more good than harm or more harm than good?' Seventy-five percent indicated that environmentalists did *more good than harm*, second only to their Chamber of Commerce (76%), and well ahead of the third-place consumer advocates. These results reflect an extraordinary level of public participation in, and identification with, the environmental movement and indicate the high degree of credibility and legitimacy that environmentalism has attained within our society.[13]

Of course, as noted in the introduction, the ultimate objective of environmentalists is not simply to convert the public to their cause but to improve the problematic conditions that gave rise to, and continue to drive, the movement. In this regard, the environmental movement has clearly met with considerably less success. This highlights the obvious fact that attaining and maintaining strong and widespread support[14] from the public—and thereby avoiding the fate of passing through Downs's

(1972) issue-attention cycle—is not a sufficient condition for a social movement to achieve its goals. Supportive public opinion clearly does not automatically translate into the basic social changes needed for solving major environmental problems.

Yet, public support for environmental protection is extremely high, even higher than two decades ago, and those intent on protecting environmental quality should recognize the tremendous resource that this support offers them. The public is concerned about environmental deterioration and wants to see something done about it. Although it is easy to question the depth of this concern by noting its relatively limited behavioral impact (Dunlap, 1987; Rosenbaum, 1991), perhaps what is needed is better leadership for harnessing public concern and translating it into effective action. Although great emphasis has recently been placed on the necessity of adopting more ecologically sound lifestyles, it is clear that many important changes must be made within political and economic institutions as well as in individual behavior. Thus, environmentalists should continually improve their strategies for channeling the vast reservoir of public support into the political arena (through election campaigns as well as in lobbying efforts) and into the private sector (through direct actions such as economic boycotts as well as through green consuming). Likewise, ecologically aware public officials should realize that they are in a unique position for providing leadership on environmental issues, and the polls suggest that it might be politically astute for them to take the lead in environmental protection. The future of our environment, as well as that of environmentalism, will be heavily influenced by the effectiveness of such leadership.

## ACKNOWLEDGEMENTS

Thanks are due to Angela Mertig and Rik Scarce for helpful comments on earlier drafts.

## NOTES

1. One can think of Downs's five stages as describing the public's role in the five stages of Mauss's 'natural history' model of social-problem movements.
2. Note that the Harris and National Opinion Research Center (NORC) questions focused on perceived levels of pollution in the respondents' vicinity, whereas the Gallup question focused on national priorities. It seems logical that the former would be related more closely to actual pollution levels than would the latter and, because there was very little change in actual pollution levels during this period, the increases found by Harris and NORC are impressive.
3. For a more detailed discussion of conceptual issues concerning public opinion, such as the distinction between salience and the intensity of opinion, see Dunlap (1989).
4. The percentages mentioning the energy shortage also exceeded those mentioning environmental problems in the Harris surveys beginning in 1974 (see Mitchell and Davies, 1978).
5. For a more detailed discussion of this issue, see Dunlap (1989, pp. 124–130).
6. The comparison between the 1970 Gallup poll and the Council on Environmental Quality survey probably exaggerates the degree of decline in environmental concern. First, the 1970 Gallup poll was conducted in late April, immediately after Earth Day. Second,

changing societal conditions no doubt influenced the public's selection of priorities from the list. For example, 'reducing unemployment' jumped from a tie for seventh to second (25% to 48%) from 1970 to 1980, reflecting the substantial deterioration of the economy over the decade. Third, the results in Table 3 (especially for the National Opinion Research Center spending item), as well as a large amount of cross-sectional data (see, e.g., Mitchell, 1980), indicate the existence of a substantial degree of environmental concern in 1980.

7. A review of the *Gallup Opinion Index* throughout the 1970s reveals that environmental problems reappeared on the 'most important problem' list only once after 1973, with 4% in May 1977.

8. For example, two analyses of the state of public concern with environmental quality through the 1970s came to differing conclusions in this regard, with Lake concluding that 'it has defied the issue-attention cycle' (1983, p. 232) and Anthony noting that despite its continued strength, 'there is also nothing . . . to suggest that Downs' analysis was basically wrong' (1982, p. 19).

9. A good indicator of the degree to which the Carter administration was viewed as pro-environmental is the fact that environmentalists were expressing concern because so many of their leaders were leaving movement organizations for positions within the administration (e.g., Baldwin, 1977).

10. This occurred despite a slight change in the item's wording, from 'improving and protecting the environment' to simply 'the environment', given to subsamples in the National Opinion Research Center surveys since 1984. Generally, the new wording resulted in a couple of percentage points fewer responding that 'too little' is being spent on the environment, but the differences in responses to the two versions are seldom significant. See Dunlap (1989) and Jones and Dunlap (1991) for data on the minimal response differences for the two versions.

11. Unpublished results were kindly made available by The Gallup Organization.

12. Results from recent Gallup polls show a lower percentage naming environment as a 'most important problem'—thus far peaking at 8% in April 1990 (see Gallup and Newport, 1990)—but this is with a question that asks for only a single MIP. A 1989 Media General/Associated Press poll that asked what respondents think will be the country's single MIP 10 years from 'now' found the environment mentioned by 12%, placing it second only to drugs with 17% (reported in *The Polling Report*, New York, NY, 4 December, 1989, p. 1).

13. For additional data on public involvement in and perceptions of the environmental movement, see Dunlap and Scarce (1991).

14. Support for environmental protection has always been widely dispersed among the major segments of society, and there has been minimal change in this regard over the past two decades (see Jones and Dunlap, 1991; Morrison and Dunlap, 1986).

## REFERENCES

Americans for the Environment (1989) *The Rising Tide: Public Opinion, Policy and Politics.* Washington, DC: Author.

Anthony, R. (1982, May) 'Polls, pollution, and politics: Trends in public opinion on the environment'. *Environment*, **24**: 14–20, 33–34.

Baldwin, D. (1977, June) 'Environmentalists open the revolving door'. *Environmental Action*, **9**: 13–25.

*Business Week*/Harris Poll (1989, 29 May) 'The public is willing to take business on'. *Business Week*, p. 29.

Buttel, F. H. (1975a) 'Class conflict, environmental conflict, and the environmental movement: the social bases of mass environmental beliefs, 1968–1974'. Unpublished Ph.D. dissertation. University of Wisconsin—Madison.

Buttel, F. H. (1975b) 'The environmental movement: Consensus, conflict and change'. *Journal of Environmental Education*, **7**: 53–63.

Cambridge Reports, Inc. (1986) 'Paying for environmental quality'. *Bulletin on Consumer Opinion*, No. 112. Cambridge, MA: Author.

Cambridge Reports, Inc. (1989) *The Rise of the Green Consumer*. Cambridge, MA: Author.

Cambridge Reports/Research International (1990) *The Green Revolution and the Changing American Consumer*. Cambridge, MA: Author

Downs, A. (1972) 'Up and down with ecology—the "issue-attention cycle".' *Public Interest*, No. 28, 38–50.

Dunlap, R. E. (1987, July/August) 'Polls, pollution and politics revisited: Public opinion on the environment in the Reagan era'. *Environment*, **29**: 6–11, 32–37.

Dunlap, R. E. (1989) 'Public opinion and environmental policy'. In *Environmental Politics and Policy*, ed. J. P. Lester, pp. 87–134. Durham, NC: Duke University Press.

Dunlap, R. E. and Dillman, D. A. (1976) 'Decline in public support for environmental protection: evidence from a 1970–1974 panel study'. *Rural Sociology*, **41**: 382–390.

Dunlap, R. E. and Scarce, R. (1991) 'The polls—a report: Environmental problems and protection'. *Public Opinion Quarterly*, **55**: In press.

Dunlap, R. E. and Van Liere, K. D. (1977) 'Further evidence of declining public concern with environmental problems: A research note'. *Western Sociological Review*, **8**: 108–112.

Environment Opinion Study, Inc. (1990) *A Survey of American Voters: Attitudes Toward the Environment*. Washington, DC: Author.

Erskine, H. (1972) 'The polls: Pollution and its costs'. *Public Opinion Quarterly*, **36**: 120–135.

Friends of the Earth (1982) *Ronald Reagan and the Environment*. San Francisco: Author.

Funkhouser, G. R. (1973) 'The issues of the sixties: An exploratory study in the dynamics of public opinion'. *Public Opinion Quarterly*, **33**: 62–75.

Gallup, G., Jr., and Newport, F. (1990, April) 'Americans strongly in tune with the purpose of Earth Day 1990'. *Gallup Poll Monthly*, No. 295: 5–14.

Gillroy, J. M. and Shapiro, R. Y. (1986) 'The polls: Environmental protection'. *Public Opinion Quarterly*, **50**: 270–279.

Harris, L. (1989, 14 May) 'Public worried about state of environment today and in future'. *The Harris Poll*, No. 21, 1–4.

Hart/Teeter (1990) NBC News/*Wall Street Journal*: National Survey No. 6. Washington, DC: Author.

Hays, S. P. (1987) *Beauty, Health and Permanence: Environmental Politics in the United States 1955–1985*. New York: Cambridge University Press.

Holden, C. (1980) 'The Reagan years: Environmentalists tremble'. *Science*, **210**: 988–991.

Hornback, K. E. (1974) 'Orbits of opinion: the role of age in the environmental movement's attentive public, 1968–1972'. Unpublished Ph.D. dissertation, Michigan State University.

Jones, R. E. and Dunlap, R. E. (1991, August) 'The social bases of environmental concern: Have they changed over time?' Revision of a paper presented at the 1989 meeting of the Rural Sociological Society, Seattle, WA.

Ladd, E. C. (1982, February/March) 'Clearing the air: Public opinion and public policy on the environment'. *Public Opinion*, **5**: 16–20.

Lake, L. M. (1983) 'The environmental mandate: Activists and the electorate'. *Political Science Quarterly*, **98**, 215–233.

Lester, J. P. (1989) 'Introduction'. In *Environmental Politics and Policy*, ed. J. P. Lester, pp. 1–9. Durham, NC: Duke University Press.

Mauss, A. L. (1975) *Social Problems as Social Movements*. Philadelphia: Lippincott.

McEvoy, J., III. (1972) 'The American concern with environment'. In *Social Behavior, Natural Resources and the Environment*, ed. W. R. Burch, Jr., N. H. Cheek, Jr., and L. Taylor, pp. 214–236. New York: Harper and Row.

Mitchell, R. C. (1980) 'Public opinion on environmental issues'. In *Environmental Quality: The Eleventh Annual Report of the Council on Environmental Quality*. Washington, DC: U.S. Government Printing Office.

Mitchell, R. C. (1984) 'Public opinion and environmental politics in the 1970s and 1980s'. In *Environmental Policy in the 1980s: Reagan's New Agenda*, ed. N. J. Vig and M. E. Kraft, pp. 51–74. Washington, DC: Congressional Quarterly Press.

Mitchell, R. C. (1990) 'Public opinion and the green lobby: Poised for the 1990s?' In *Environmental Policy in the 1990s: Toward a New Agenda*, ed. N. G. Vig and M. E. Kraft, pp. 81–99. Washington, DC: Congressional Quarterly Press.

Mitchell, R. C. and Davies, J. C., III. (1978) *The United States Environmental Movement and its Political Context: An Overview*. Discussion Paper D-32. Washington, DC: Resources for the Future, Inc.

Morrison, D. E. (1986) 'How and why environmental consciousness has trickled down'. In *Distributional Conflicts in Environmental-Resource Policy*, ed. A. Schnaiberg, N. Watts and K. Zimmerman, pp. 187–220. New York: St. Martin's Press.

Morrison, D. E. and Dunlap, R. E. (1986) 'Environmentalism and elitism: A conceptual and empirical analysis'. *Environmental Management*, **10**: 581–589.

National Opinion Research Center (1989) *General Social Surveys, 1972–1989: Cumulative Codebook*. Chicago: Author.

Nixon, W. (1991, January/February) '1990—The year of the environment'. *E: The Environmental Magazine*, **2**: 30–37.

Peters, B. G. and Hogwood, B. W. (1985) 'In search of the issue-attention cycle'. *Journal of Politics*, **47**: 238–253.

Pierce, J. C., Beatty, K. M. and Hagner, P. R. (1982) *The Dynamics of American Public Opinion*. Glenview, IL: Scott, Foresman.

Portney, P. R., ed. (1984) *Natural Resources and the Environment: The Reagan Approach*. Washington, DC: Urban Institute Press.

Rosenbaum, W. A. (1991) *Environmental Politics and Policy*, 2nd ed. Washington, DC: Congressional Quarterly Press.

Sabatier, P. and Mazmanian, D. (1980) 'The implementation of public policy: A framework of analysis'. *Policy Studies Journal*, **8**: 538–560.

Schoenfeld, A. C., Meier, R. F. and Griffin, R. J. (1979) 'Constructing a social problem: The press and the environment'. *Social Problems*, **27**: 38–61.

Smith, T. W. (1985) 'The polls: American's most important problems: Part I. National and international'. *Public Opinion Quarterly*, **49**: 264–274.

Vig, N. J. and Kraft, M. E., eds. (1984) *Environmental Policy in the 1980s: Reagan's New Agenda*. Washington, DC: Congressional Quarterly Press.

# Part II

Sustainable Development—Global, National and Local Issues

# CONTENTS

# Introduction to Part II

*Pierre McDonagh and Andrea Prothero*

> The environment problems that will be prominent in the 1990s are just the same as those at the beginning of the 1980s. Climate change, acid rain, tropical deforestation, toxic waste management, ozone depletion, the loss of species and all the rest will still be with us as we go into the next millenium and beyond. All that we have done in the last decade is to recognize that they require political solutions. But that is simply to arrive at the starting gate. We have yet to get going. (Tom Burke, quoted in Rose 1990).

The greening of management will also be affected by the development of green legislation and regulations. International meetings and the development of regulation on environmental issues is not a recent phenomenon. The first United Nations convention on the human environment took place in 1972 and in recent years the world leaders of most countries have been addressing global environmental problems. The attendance of 166 world leaders at the Rio earth summit proves, if nothing else, that concern for our natural environment is one of the major topics for discussion amongst all nations.

In recent years the development of legislation at international, national and local levels has been linked with the development of the term 'sustainable development'. The modern discourse on sustainable development was probably first popularized at the World Conservation Strategy Conference in 1980, at which the need to acknowledge the link between development and conservation was accepted. The term itself has also been criticized; again, as with the term 'green' generally, there has been considerable discussion as to what it actually means (Tolba, 1987; Pearce *et al.*, 1989). Pearce *et al.* (1989) claim this is probably because 'development' is a value term and therefore 'sustainable development' means different things to different people. The most widely published explanation of sustainable development was that made by the Brundtland Report (WCED, 1987), suggesting:

> sustainable development is development that meets the needs of the present without compromising the ability of future generations to meet their own needs . . . Living standards that go beyond the basic minimum are sustainable only if consumption standards everywhere have regard for long-term sustainability.

It is this main focus that thus becomes important when one considers the greening of politics, the economy and society.

The second collection of readings explore some of the issues surrounding the polysemy of sustainable development (bearing in mind sustainable development has differing meanings in the literature) and sustainable capitalism, while also focusing on global, national and local legislation/regulations, which have been developed partly as a result of the focus upon sustainable development as a concept for the future. Some of the legislation discussed pertains to society generally and the political actions of governments, some focuses upon legislation that relates specifically to the activities of business, for instance the British Standard on Environmental Management Systems, BS7750 in the UK and the EU eco-management and audit scheme.[1]

The issues of sustainable development and sustainable capitalism are addressed by O'Connor (1994) (Reading 5), who concedes that in order to solve the global ecological crisis one must consider the way in which the state in developed capitalist countries operates. Thus, it is again important to emphasize that exploring the issue from a business and/or consumer perspective is not enough. The author contends that the question 'Is sustainable capitalism possible?' is ultimately a political one, and before one begins to examine the activities of business, the wider issues for discussion are the make-up of the economy, polity and society. It is only after these issues have been addressed and considered can one move on to contemplate environmental management systems.

As the introduction to the reader highlights, the environmental issue is a holistic, complex one and the articles in parts I and II of the reader provide some discussions in this area, suggesting there are no transparent solutions. The remaining articles in part II focus on specific legislation and regulations that have developed in recent years.

McCormick (1995) (Reading 6) begins by suggesting the importance we should place on maintaining a balance between environmental management and economic development in order to change 'the nature of co-operation between governments, business, science and people.' He then focuses on key global environmental developments in recent years, namely *Our Common Future* and the Rio earth summit, before providing a discussion of possible reasons for being both optimistic and pessimistic about the future. Finally, the author shows, with special consideration of the case of lesser developed countries (LDCs), that one of the main problems as far as global environmental action is concerned is the gap that exists between the development of environmental policies and the implementation of such policies (this issue is one which is also raised in the discussions centred around greening organizations in Part III). The author stresses that discovering what needs to be done is relatively easy in comparison to then implementing such programmes (see also McCloskey and Smith, 1995) (Reading 11).

Hildebrand (1992) (Reading 7), taking an institutional framework, provides an excellent summary of the development of environmental policies of the European Union up to 1992.[2] It provides a first-class account of how environmental policies in the European Union have been established: this is vital to our understanding of more recent developments in this area within the EU. The article considers whether the EU has become an international regime and the impact of this upon any examination of environmental regulations and legislation within the Union. It explains how the development of environmental policies have gone from initial 'ad hoc' measures to a more recent 'negotiated order'. It considers the evolution of the policies and the key factors that have played a part in this development. The discussion is split into three periods:

(1) **Incidental measures**—1957 (Treaty of Rome) to 1972.
(2) **Responsive period**—1973 (first Community Action programme on the environment) to 1985.
(3) **Initiative phase**—beginning with the ratification of the Single European Act up to '1992' when the article was published.

What has happened within each period is discussed at length in association with consideration for the development of an international regime and the extent to which institutionalization has taken place within the three periods. The author concludes by reminding us that, although the EU can be commended for its environmental policies, a word of caution for everyone is that 'in many ways the task has only just begun'. This is a theme that can be applied throughout the reader and is an issue of importance not only for greening society but also for greening organizations, as the collection of readings in Parts III and IV clearly illustrate.

Reading 8 (Macnaghten *et al*, 1995) is a short extract from a report conducted for Lancashire County Council which helps clarify the historical position of research into sustainability indicators and community participation, drawing on the experience of the UK Local Government Management Board. To illustrate the challenge of the local Agenda 21 initiatives the authors highlight the need to seek out and build accurate and meaningful indicators to which members of the public will be more likely to respond. The authors clearly depict a three stage process for the task in hand.[3]

## NOTES

1. There are a number of other books and articles that could have been included in this section; however, space constraints prevented this and you may wish to consult the further information section at the end of the book.
2. Readers who wish to update their knowledge should also consult more recent publications.
3. This reading is a short extract from the full report (McNaghten *et al.*, 1995) and has been included to show how sustainable development issues are important at a local government level.

## REFERENCES

Macnaghten, P., Grove-White, R., Jacobs, M. and Wynne, B. (1995) *Public Perceptions and Sustainability in Lancashire: Indicators, Institutions, Participation*, Lancashire County Council, Lancashire.

Pearce, D. Markandya, A. and Barbier, E. B. (1989) *Blueprint for A Green Economy*, Earthscan Publications, London.

Rose, C. (1990) *The Dirty Man of Europe: The Great British Pollution Scandal*, Simon & Schuster, London.

Tolba, M. (1987) *Sustainable Development—Constraints and Opportunities,* Butterworth-Heinemann, London.
World Commission on Environment and Development (WCED) 1987, *Our Common Future,* WCED, Oxford.

# 5

# Is Sustainable Capitalism Possible?

*James O'Connor*

## INTRODUCTION

There are few expressions as ambiguous as 'sustainable capitalism' and such sister concepts as 'sustainable agriculture,' 'sustainable energy and resource use,' and 'sustainable development.' This ambiguity runs through all of the most important discourses on economy and the environment today—U.N. and government reports, scholarly research, popular journalism, and green political thinking. Precisely this obscurity leads so many people so much of the time to talk and write about 'sustainability': the word can be used to mean almost anything one wants it to mean, which is part of its appeal.

'Sustainable capitalism' has both a practical and a moral ring to it. Who in his or her right mind would be against 'sustainability?' The earliest meaning of *sustain* is 'support,' 'uphold the course of,' or 'keep into being.' What corporate chief, treasury minister, or international civil servant would not embrace this meaning as his or her own? Another meaning is 'to provide with food and drink, or the necessities of life.' What underpaid urban worker or landless peasant would not accept this meaning? Still another definition is 'to endure without giving way or yielding.' What small farmer or entrepreneur does not resist 'yielding' to the expansionary impulses of big capital and the state, and thereby take pride in 'enduring'? There is a struggle, worldwide, to determine how 'sustainable development' or 'sustainable capitalism' will be defined and used in the discourse on the wealth of nations. This means that 'sustainability,' in the first place, is an ideological and political, not an ecological and economic, question.

In the present account, the word *sustain* is taken to apply to all three of the above senses: to 'uphold the course' of capitalist accumulation globally: to 'provide the necessities of life' for peoples of the world; and to 'endure without yielding' by those whose ways of life are being subverted by the wage and commodity forms. The question of sustainable capitalism thus pertains in part to whether or not sustainability defined in all three ways can be achieved, and how it can be achieved.

There is a fourth meaning of *sustain*, namely, 'ecological sustainability,' even though there is little agreement among ecological scientists about the exact meaning of this expression. For example, 'biodiversity' or 'planetary health' are rarely problematized in terms of ecological science and the ideologies embedded in this science, nor is the expression 'ecological crisis,' which is widely used by popular writers without benefit of a clear definition. One definition of the latter might be 'a turning point during which it is decided whether a species, ecosystem, bioregion, or the planet as a whole lives or dies.' Yet 'ecological crisis' defined in this way has no status within ecological science (nor could it, given that ecology is an ambiguous combination of atomistic and holistic assumptions about the laws governing living nature). Population ecologists and conservation biologists normally correlate population changes of a particular species; changes in 'carrying capacity' defined narrowly in terms of the needs of that species; and some coefficient that measures the relationship between the species and the carrying capacity in question, on the one hand, and the rest of the ecosystem, which the species in question may depend on in indirect ways, on the other. All these terms have some explanatory power. But this multiplicity of determinants means that there is no obvious way to really know whether or not threats to an individual species are self-inflicted, so to speak, or arise because of changes in the ecosystem as a whole. If this is so, talk about the 'sustainability' of particular species may be less precise, and the concept of 'environment crisis' more problematic, than would superficially appear to be true.

These ambiguities become even more pronounced when ecologists or greens mix social and economic with biophysical dimensions, and discuss the 'sustainability' of whole ecosystems or bioregions. In California's Monterey Bay region, for example, excessive pumping has lowered the water table, causing salinization from sea water, threatening the viability of agriculture. Is this a 'crisis?' In economic terms, not if the region imports water; in fact, imported water might breathe new life into local agriculture, as well as housing, commercial and industrial development. 'Sustainable agriculture' means one thing if a strict bioregional perspective is adopted and something else if the perspective is widened to include other bioregions. In this particular case, it turns out that the debate over importing water has less to do with the 'sustainability' of local agricultural capital and water quality, and more with normative judgments pertaining to what kind of community and culture people in the region want to have (i.e., in Pajaro Valley, whether to keep its present Mexican cultural flavor or to open the area more to commuter populations from Silicon Valley on the other side of the coastal range).

Defining *sustain* in these four ways, the short answer to the question 'Is sustainable capitalism possible?' is 'No,' while the longer answer is 'Probably not.' Capitalism is self-destructing and in crisis; the world economy makes more people hungry, poor, and miserable every day; the masses of peasants and workers cannot be expected to endure the crisis indefinitely; and nature, however 'ecological sustainability' is defined, is under attack everywhere.

In this chapter I will review some important evidence bearing on the problem of 'sustainable capitalism,' highlighting along the way the very different concepts of 'sustainability' deployed by greens and corporations. A brief account of the conditions of economic sustainability (or of profitability and accumulation), narrowly defined, is offered. I will then discuss the 'internal' or 'first' contradiction of capitalism, and the crisis-ridden and crisis-dependent nature of capitalist accumulation, appending a short review of the gathering world crisis in the 1980s. The argument is made that the prospects of global economic management are as dim as those of global environmental regulation. Next, I discuss another seemingly intractable problem (a 'second' contradiction) facing capitalism today, namely, a 'cost-side' profit squeeze generated by the contradiction between capital and nature (and other conditions of production), together with the adverse economic effects on capital of environmental and other social movements. The ways in which capital is trying to confront these issues is discussed. I discount capital's capacity to successfully deal with both the first and the second contradiction, thanks to the nature of the liberal democratic state and of capital itself. I then underline the very uncertain political—hence economic and ecological—consequences of a general economic depression. Finally, following a short review of environmental conditions in the poor countries (the South), I draw some conclusions about the possibilities of radical environmental or 'red green' social and political movements. While the prospects for some kind of 'ecological socialism' are not bright (so the argument goes), those of a 'sustainable capitalism' are even more remote.

## ENVIRONMENTAL POLICY AND THE DISCOURSE ON SUSTAINABILITY

The evidence favors the judgment that capitalism is not ecologically sustainable, despite the recent flood of talk about 'green products,' 'green consumption,' 'selective forestry,' 'low-input agriculture,' and so on. In the 1992 U.S. presidential campaign not one of the three major candidates made the 'environment' an important issue. The Reagan and Bush governments compromised themselves on issues ranging from the use of federal grazing land to logging old-growth forests to fighting pollution (abandoning tried and true methods of pollution control for 'market solutions'). Increasingly, state and local governments neglect the environment in their competition to attract scarce capital. In federal law, the definition of 'wetlands' was narrowed, as was that of 'endangered species.' Occupational health and safety enforcement measures established over decades were undermined. National and state parks are now more commodified, as managers search for ways to meet expenses. Oppositional movements are fragmented. True, the Clinton administration is showing a 'green' color in reforming the use of public grazing lands; nuclear power is temporarily stalled; some capital goods industries such as paper and pulp have begun to install cleaner technology; and organic farming has benefited from a surge of consumer interest in pesticide-free products. But the majority of union leaders oppose or are indifferent to most demands made by environmentalists, and established environmental organizations (with two or three notable exceptions) are more willing to compromise their positions in the name of 'economic growth.'

In most countries green parties remain small or are accommodating their demands in national and local politics. In Europe, the environment is not a central concern of the bureaucrats who run the powerful European Commission, despite representation by greens in the European Parliament. International agreements on ozone layer depletion are weak and those on global warming are merely symbolic.

Agreements with respect to protecting the world's 'commons'—watersheds, forests, rivers, lakes, coastlines, oceans, and air quality—are more often than not honored in the breach. Whaling may be revived and fisherpeople everywhere clamor to empty the waters of their bounty. Oil as an instrument of economic wealth and national power is more important than ever before. Energy and mining companies (often the same) are poised to massively exploit more mineral resources everywhere from upstate Wisconsin to Siberia. In the South, many governments are eager to sell their natural birthrights to transnational corporations, often under the pressure of big external debts, in the name of 'development,' and the landless and land-poor masses of the world's countrysides and the urban poor are forced to deplete and exhaust resources and pollute water and air respectively, simply to survive. The environmental records of the East Asian 'tigers,' the Southeast Asian 'little tigers,' and Mexico, Brazil, and other Latin American growth centers are not encouraging.

One necessary step, practically speaking, toward ensuring a sustainable capitalism—defined in some sense of 'ecologically rational or sound'—would be national budgets that put high taxes on raw material inputs (e.g., coal, oil, nitrogen) and certain outputs (e.g., gasoline, chemical building blocks), meanwhile slapping value-added taxes on a wide range of environmentally unfriendly consumer products (cars, plastic products, throwaway cans)—complete with an enforceable 'green label' policy that would exempt genuinely green products, with 'green' defined strictly in terms of ecological impacts at every stage of the production, distribution, and consumption process. Other steps would include national expenditure policies that heavily subsidize solar energy and other benign alternative energy sources; technological research that leads to eliminating toxic chemicals and other substances at their source; innovations in mass transit; improvements in occupational health and safety conditions coupled with national, regional, and community enforcement procedures; and a redefinition and reorientation of scientific and technological priorities generally. In few political entities is this kind of green budget—with appropriate changes in methods of national income accounting—being developed, except on paper by a marginalized group of green economists and activists.

At the level of the discourse on 'sustainability,' the prospects for an ecologically sound capitalism, recognizable to greens, seem problematic at best. In fact, behind a seeming convergence of vocabulary is a disjuncture or gap between green and capitalist discourse, with both sides talking past each other. One problem is the discourse of much of the environmental movement, supported by companies that seek to green themselves, or at least present a green image to the public. This discourse seeks to find ways for corporations to reform their economic practices to make them consistent with the sustainability of biodiverse forests, water quality, wildlife preservation, atmospheric conditions, and so on. Focus is placed on production processes, technology, recycling and reuse, and energy efficiency, as well as broader questions pertaining to the structure of consumption, finance, marketing, and corporate organization, and also government policies. For example, the reform-minded World Resources Institute recently stated that sustainability presupposes an 'unprecedented transformation' of technology. For reformist greens, then, the question is how to remake capital in ways consistent with the sustainability of nature.

In the boardrooms of many corporations, however, the problem is discussed in different terms. At a superficial level, the issue is simply one of how to present a plausible green image to consumers and the public (e.g., the U.S. chemical industry planned to spend $10 million in 1992 to paint itself as environmentally reasonable and friendly).[1] It is also a question of how to introduce practices into production that save energy and raw materials. However, this has a largely economic motive. Far from being a problem for capital as a whole, energy and material efficiency in a period of slow growth (or a world recession that threatens profits) is economically desirable. To take one instance, as much as 75% of aluminum produced by U.S. companies today is made from recycled aluminum cans and other products. New wood industry practices that make posts and beams from trees too small to cut up for lumber, thereby utilizing what in the past would have been discarded as waste, is another example. Also, 'recycling' rhetoric and (selective) practices can be used to facilitate new waves of planned obsolescence under the banner of environmental friendliness, thus legitimating consumerism and maintaining profitability.[2]

But at a deeper level corporations construct the problem of the environment in a way that is the polar opposite of that in which greens typically think about reform—namely, the problem of how to remake nature in ways that are consistent with sustainable profitability and capital accumulation. 'Remaking nature' means more access to nature as 'tap' and 'sink,' which has political and ideological as well as economic and ecological dimensions, for example, the assault on the lives of indigenous peoples. Remaking nature also means reworking or reinventing nature (the political and ideological aspects of which are also important), for example, by means of 'even-age industrial plantations' of pine and fir in the U.S. Southeast and Northwest—a monoculture that has been called 'forestry's equivalent to the urban tower block'; genetic alteration of food to reduce crop losses and increase land yields; microorganisms used in the semiconductor industry to 'eat' toxic wastes; and genetically altered ragweed plants that clean soil contaminated by lead and other metals.[3] However, each innovation has its potential dangers: plantation forestry destroys biological diversity and genetic changes in food crops and the use of microorganisms to reduce costs contain unknown biological dangers. Here we enter a world in which capital does not merely appropriate nature, then turn it into commodities that function as elements of constant and variable capital (to use Marxist categories), but rather a world in which capital remakes nature and its products biologically and physically (and politically and ideologically) in its own image.[4] A precapitalist nature is transformed into a specifically capitalist nature. And just as the labor movement forced capital to move from a mode of absolute surplus value to one of relative surplus value production, for example, from lengthening work hours to reducing the costs of wages, so the green movement may be forcing capital to end its primitive exploitation of precapitalist nature by remaking nature in the image of capital—also to lower the costs of capital, especially the costs of reproducing labour power (or the cost of wages).

Seen this way, nature would become unrecognizable as such, or as most people experience it. It would be, rather, a physical nature treated as if it is governed by the law of value, the process of capitalist accumulation through economic crisis, like the production of pencils and fast foods. Discourse theory will then have as much to say about the problem of sustainability as do political economy and ecological science. The reason is that the capitalist project to remake nature—still in its infancy—is also a project to remake (pretendedly) science and technology in the image of capital.

What this image is or will be depends on complex issues of representation, images of nature, and problems of social solidarity, legitimation, and power within scientific and university communities.

## DEMAND CRISIS: EXPANSION AND CONSUMPTION

A systematic answer to the question 'Is an ecologically sustainable capitalism possible?' is 'Not unless and until capital changes its face in ways that would make it unrecognizable to bankers, money managers, venture capitalists, and CEOs, looking at themselves in the mirror today.' This assertion, widely rejected by national politicians and spokespeople for big business, requires for its justification a brief account of how capitalism works, why it works when it works, and why it does not work when it does not.

Until the rise of ecological economics—which, despite precursors dating back more than a century, is still at the fringes of the profession—economists discussed the sustainability of capitalism in purely economic terms, for example, money capital, investment and consumption, profits and wages, costs and prices. The physical or material world appeared in models of economic growth in just two guises: first, in the form of location and rent theory; second, in the concept of the 'accelerator', or the amount of physical product that new productive capacity can be expected to produce (e.g., at a given rate of utilization, so many machines are needed to produce so many refrigerators).

From an economic point of view, sustainable capitalism must of necessity be an expanding capitalism (and represented as such). A capitalist economy based on what Marx called 'simple reproduction' and what many greens call 'maintenance' is a flat impossibility—the (unpaid) maintenance work of domestic labour and (paid) work organized by the state excepted. There is little or no profit in maintenance; capitalistic sustainability depends on profits. A positive overall rate of profit means growth of total product ('gross domestic product,' as measured in capitalist national income accounts). Profit is the means of expansion, for example, of new investments and technologies. Profit also functions as an incentive to expand. Profit and growth are thus means and ends of one another, content and context, as it were, and the average money manager does not really see or care about the difference between them. While there are many variations of economic growth theory, all presuppose that capitalism cannot stand still, that the system must expand or contract, that, that it is both crisis-ridden and crisis-dependent, and, in the last analysis, that it must 'accumulate or die,' in Marx's words.[5]

In the simplest (and most simpleminded) model of capitalism, the rate of growth or rate of accumulation of capital depends on the rate of profit.[6] The higher the profit rate (everything else being the same), the more sustainable is capitalism. A negative profit rate spells economic trouble: at the least, a recession, at the most, a general crisis, deflation of capital values, and depression. According to this model, anything or anybody that interferes with profits, new investment, and expanding markets threatens the sustainability of the system, that is, an economic crisis with unknown and unknowable economic, social, and political consequences.

In traditional Marxist theory, capital is its own worst enemy. Capital threatens its own profitability because of what Marx called the 'contradiction between social production and private appropriation.' This means that the greater the degree of capital's political power over labor, the greater will be the degree of exploitation of labor (or the rate of surplus value), and the more potential profits will be produced. However, precisely for this reason, the greater will be the difficulty of realizing these potential profits in the market, or to sell goods at prices reflecting costs of production plus the average profit rate. Here we identify the contradiction between capital's political power and the ability of the capitalist economy to work smoothly (or, at the limit, to work at all). This 'first contradiction of capitalism' (or 'realization' or 'demand crisis') states that when individual capitals attempt to defend or restore profits by increasing labor productivity, speeding up work, cutting wages, and using other time-honored ways of getting more production from fewer workers, meanwhile paying them less, the unintended effect is to reduce the final demand for consumer commodities. Fewer workers, technicians, and others in the labor process produce more, who by definition are able to consume less, absent a deflation of prices. Thus, the greater the produced profits, or the exploitation of labor, the smaller the realized profits, or market demand—all other things being equal. Of course, other things are never equal: government budget deficits, mortgage and consumer credit, business borrowing, and an aggressive foreign trade policy, among other things, may buoy up demand to keep capital 'sustainable'.

Today, a sustainable economy presupposes a global political economic system able to identify and regulate this 'first' or 'internal' contradiction of capitalism. This means first and foremost the capacity for macroeconomic regulation on a global scale, or, at least, between the industrial powerhouses of the Group of Seven (G7), that is, an international Keynesianism of the type installed in the leading national economies from the 1950s through the late 1970s. Defined in this immediate and practical way, world capitalism may be much less sustainable than most economists think. First, the systems of national Keynesian regulation have weakened or self-destructed since the late 1970s. Second, the central role of the United States in the global economy until the post-cold war period—as a kind of world cash register—has ended. This means that, until the weak recovery from the recession of 1990–1991, the U.S. economy was driven by consumer and military spending and private and public borrowing. The present recovery, however, is the first since 1876 to be led by export spending, with investment spending a close second. All of Germany's recent recoveries have been export-led, and the German government has said that any recovery from its present economic doldrums will be export-driven. If and when Japan recovers from its present economic troubles, it will do so because exports will expand faster than domestic consumption, investment, and government spending. Finally, all of the so-called newly industrializing economies are export-driven. In a period in which a consumerist United States can no longer absorb the world's surplus commodities, global macroeconomic management of a Keynesian type will be needed to avoid a general deflation and depression.

In fact, there is a sort of global macromanagement composed of the finance ministers of G7, the International Monetary Fund, the Bank for International Settlements, the World Bank, and the General Agreement on Tariffs and Trade. This quasi-global capitalist state, however, is in the hands of big capital in general and finance capital in particular. Hence, with the exception of G7's attempts to lower interest rates and stimulate demand in countries with export surpluses (especially Japan), the global state follows an anti-Keynesian policy, one that forces individual capitals and whole countries to cut costs, increase efficiency, and lower government spending, respectively, without a second thought about the effects of this policy on capital overproduction on a global scale—of the type Marx identified long ago—not to speak of the dangers of bitter trade wars, creative forms of beggar-my-neighbor policies, growing social decay, political instability, and regional trading blocks. Put another way, there is no global parliament to pass minimum wage laws and protective legislation, no World Ministries of Labor or Social Welfare, no World Ministry of Environment, no legitimate power spreading Keynesian economic literacy on an international scale. Instead, in the United States, for example, ex-President Bush demanded that the United States become an 'export superpower' and President Clinton's economic advisers called for an 'increasingly aggressive' export policy.

The prospects of global regulation today, organized in a truly cooperative spirit, are as poor as those of national regulation during the crisis of the 1890s, namely, zero. In those days nationalist policies of dumping, monopoly, and colonialism helped to create two world wars of imperialist rivalry and the Great Depression. Superficially, there might be two mitigating factors today: one is that Europe is an economic entity; France, for example, wants to join, not fight, Germany, economically. The other is that capital is no longer national, but rather global in scope, hence theoretically more open to global regulation. But G7 has done a poor job of macroeconomic regulation to date, and global finance capital and the rentier class living off interest on the huge piles of debt accumulated in the 1970s and 1980s are powerful enough to prevent governments from reflating their economies.

## COST CRISIS: CONDITIONS OF PRODUCTION

Today, this kind of economic thinking, while still valid, is one-sided and limited (as, in fact, it always was). The reason is that it presupposes limitless supplies of what Marx called 'conditions of production.' This traditional model presupposes that capitalism can avoid potential bottlenecks on the 'supply side,' that growth is demand-constrained only. However, if the costs of labor, nature, infrastructure, and space increase significantly, capital faces a possible 'second contradiction,' an economic crisis striking from the cost side. Famous examples include the English 'cotton crisis' during the U.S. Civil War; wage advances in excess of productivity in the 1960s; and the 'oil shocks' of the 1970s. However, here we are concerned with phenomena that are much more structured or generic than these isolated examples by themselves would suggest.

Cost-side crises originate in two ways. The first is when individual capitals defend or restore profits by strategies that degrade or fail to maintain over time the material conditions of their own production, for example, by neglecting work conditions (hence raising the health bill), degrading soils (hence lowering the productivity of land), or turning their backs on decaying urban infrastructures (hence increasing congestion costs).

The second is when social movements demand that capital better provides for the maintenance and restoration for these conditions of life; when they demand better health care; protest the ruination of soils in the name of 'environmental protection'; and defend urban neighborhoods in ways that increase capital costs or reduce capital flexibility—to stay with the same three examples. Here we are talking about the potentially damaging economic effects to capitalist interests of labor movements, women's movements, environmental movements, and urban movements. This problem of 'extra costs'— and their threat to profitability—obsesses mainstream economists and capitalist ideologists; the leaders of labor and social movements are rarely willing to discuss it in public, however.

In the real world, both types of cost-side crises combine and intermingle in complex and contradictory ways that no one has ever systematically theorized. For example, from a quantitative standpoint, no one knows how much urban congestion costs are the result of capital's celebration of the automobile and its neglect of urban mass transport, and how much the effects of community struggles to keep freeways from scarring their neighborhoods.

We need a more refined theoretical approach to the problem of what Polanyi called 'land and labor.' Marx inadvertently supplied a start for such an approach with his concept of 'conditions of production.'[7] Conditions of production are things that are not produced as commodities in accordance with the laws of the market (law of value) but which are treated as if they are commodities; that is, they are 'fictitious commodities' with 'fictitious prices.' According to Marx, there are three conditions of production: first, human labor power, or what Marx called the 'personal conditions of production'; second, environment, or what Marx called 'natural or external conditions of production'; third, urban infrastructure (we can add 'space'), or what Marx called 'general, communal conditions of production.' The fictitious price of labor power is the wage rate, and that of environmental and urban infrastructure and space is rent. Given that wage and rent theory are not and cannot be based on costs of production, it is understandable that both bourgeois and Marxist economic accounts of wages and rents are the least developed and least satisfying topics in the entire economics literature.

Sustainable capitalism would require all three conditions of production to be available at the right time and the right place and in the right quantities and the right qualities, and at the right fictitious prices. As I noted, serious bottlenecks in the supply of labor power, natural resources, and urban infrastructure and space threaten the viability of individual capital units—and even of entire sectoral or national capitalist programs. If generalized, these bottlenecks would thus threaten the sustainability of capitalism by driving up costs and impairing the flexibility of capital. 'Limits to growth' thus do not appear, in the first instance, as absolute shortages of labor power, raw materials, clean water and air, urban space, and the like, but rather as high-cost labor power, resources, infrastructure, and space. This immanent threat to profitability leads the state and capital to attempt to rationalize labor markets, supplies, markets for fuel and raw materials, and urban and rural land-use patterns and land markets to reduce costs of production.[8]

Supply-side bottlenecks or shortfalls pose especially difficult problems for capitalist enterprises and policymakers when the economy is weak, or when it faces a demand-side crisis or fresh competition from other countries. Stagnant or falling profits force individual capitals to attempt to reduce the turnover time of capital, that is, to speed up production and reduce the time that it takes to sell their products. This obsession with making money faster and faster to compensate for low or falling profits runs up against, for example, union-organized labor markets, OPEC-influenced oil markets, and traditional agriculture's defense of 'inefficient' uses of the soil and water. On the one hand, money capital seeks more of itself faster and faster; on the other hand, what Polanyi called 'society' and what capital regards as out-of-date patterns of land and labor utilization, and land and labor markets, combined with the resistance to capitalist rationalization by labor and social movements, all constitute themselves as obstacles, or 'barriers to overcome.' At the very least, capital must deal with social indifference and inertia.

One of capital's solutions to this dilemma, at least in the short term, is as simple as it is economically self-destructive. Money capital abandons the 'general circuit of capital'—that is, the long and tedious process of leasing factory space, buying machinery and raw materials, renting land, finding the right kind of labor power, organizing and implementing production, and marketing commodities—and finds its way into speculative ventures of all kinds. Money capital, based on the expansion of credit, or money that cannot find outlets in real goods and services, jumps over society, so to speak, and seeks to expand the easy way—in the land, in stock and bond markets, and in other financial markets. Hence, the present economic anomaly: the value of claims on the surplus or profits grows at the same moment that the real value of fixed and circulating capital stagnates or declines. This tends to make a bad economic situation worse, for it causes growing indebtedness and the danger of a financial implosion. It also tends to worsen ecological and other conditions of production: as financial interests assume hegemony over productive interests, the environment tends to be neglected even more.

During earlier periods of capitalist development, and defined in functional terms, there was sufficient precapitalist labor power, untapped natural wealth, and space. This was true, in fact, and also in terms of the perceptions of early generations of bourgeoisies. The (fictitious) prices of labor power, natural resources, and space were thus held in check. Nor did environmental movements or urban movements raise political and social barriers to capital that capital itself (with the help of imperialism and state oppression) could not overcome. Over time, capital seeks to capitalize everything and everybody; that is, everything potentially enters into capitalist cost accounting. For millennia, human beings have been 'humanizing' nature or creating a 'second nature,' and this has often been destructive, for example, deforestation and drought–flood cycles under the Roman plantation system; the devastating ecological consequences of the Punic Wars; and soil depletion and water scarcity in Mayan civilization. But in capitalist social formations, this second nature is commodified and valorized at the same time as it is being degraded. From the point of view of those who want capitalism to be ecologically sustainable, this is when problems start to appear. Labor markets become tight, and the North has to rely on imported labour from the South—with all the attendant economic and social costs and problems. Examples include the economic cost of settling newcomers who use a different language and the social costs of a resurgence of racism. Raw materials and unpolluted commons become scarce, driving up what Marx called the 'costs of the elements of capital', for example, U.S. domestic oil and gas; trees and lumber; and supplies of clean water. And last but not least, urban infrastructure and space become scarce, creating rising congestion costs, higher ground rents, and greater pollution costs. Lost Angeles is a good example; Mexico City and Taipei are better ones.

Thus the capitalization of the conditions of production in general and the environment and nature in particular tend to raise the cost of capital and reduce its flexibility. As I have noted, there are two general reasons. First, a systemic reason, namely, that individual capitals have little or no incentive to use production conditions in sustainable ways, especially when faced with economic bad times of capital's own making. Second, precisely for this reason, labor, environmental, and other social movements challenge capital's control over labor power, the environment, and the urban (and, increasingly, the rural as well, especially in the South). Examples in the United States include regional Toxics Coalitions, occupational health and safety and right-to-know struggles, direct action to save wild rivers and original-growth forests, and antifreeway and antidevelopment movements.

In summary, these lines of thinking suggests that there are two, not just one, contradictions of capitalism, two, not just one, types of economic crisis, and two, not just one, types of crisis resolution. The 'second contradiction' of capitalism results in economic crisis that strikes not from the demand side but from the cost side. Since the 1960s many economists, leftist and right-wing alike, have defended the thesis that cost-side (as well as demand-side) crises characterize the late 20th century, for example, the cost-push crisis of profitability due to wage increases, struggles against productivity, welfare state expansion, high oil prices, overregulation of business, and so on.

Put simply, the second contradiction states that when individual capitals attempt to defend or restore profits by cutting or externalizing costs, the unintended effect is to reduce the 'productivity' of the conditions of production, and hence to raise average costs. Costs may increase for the individual capitals in question, other capitals, or capital as a whole. For example, the use of pesticides in agriculture at first lowers, then ultimately increases, costs as pests become more chemical resistant and also as the chemicals poison the soil. Permanent-yield monoforests in Sweden were expected to keep costs down, but it turned out that the loss of biodiversity over the years has reduced the productivity of forest ecosystems and the size of the trees. In the United States, nuclear power promised to reduce energy costs. But bad design, problems of finance, safety measures, and most of all popular opposition to nuclear power had the effect of increasing costs. As for the 'communal' conditions of production, new highways designed to lower the costs of transportation and the commute to work tend to raise costs when they attract more traffic and create more congestion. And in relation to 'personal' production conditions, it is clear that the U.S. education system, which is supposed to increase potential labor productivity, produces as much stupidity as learning, impairing labor discipline and productivity.

It is important to stress the idea that the conditions of production are not produced in accordance with laws of the market. Nor does the market generally regulate capital's access to these conditions when and if they are produced. There must be some agency, therefore, whose task it is either to produce the conditions of production or to regulate capital's access to them. In capitalist societies, this agency is the state. Every state activity, including every state agency and budgetary item, is concerned with providing capital with access to labor power, nature, or urban space and infrastructure. For example, in the United States, there are the labor and education bureaucracies; the Department of Agriculture; national and state park services; the U.S. Bureau of Land Management and the U.S. Bureau of Reclamation; and urban planning bodies and traffic authorities. Examples of specific functions related to the three conditions of production are, first, with respect to labour power, child labour laws and laws governing hours and conditions of work and work safety; second, in relation to environment, laws governing access to federal lands and regulating coastal development and pollution; third, with respect to urban infrastructure and space, zoning laws, traffic planning, and land-use regulation. There is hardly any state activity or budgetary item that does not concern itself in different ways with one or more conditions of production. This also includes monetary and military functions, which safeguard and facilitate 'legitimate' access by capitalist mining companies, banks, merchants, and other enterprises to needed resources and markets. Bush's war in the Persian Gulf is only the latest and most dramatic example of the role of the military in capitalist societies; the World Bank and the International Monetary Fund (at the supranational level) are the most obvious examples of monetary functions oriented to capitalist expansion.

## MANAGING COST CRISIS

What is the solution to these cost-side crises, from the standpoint of individual capitals and also from that of capital as a whole?

The worst case is when individual capitals, faced with both higher costs and lower demand, cut costs even more, thus intensifying both the first and second contradictions. But this result is not the only possibility. As I noted, in relation to the environment, there are many examples of individual capitals responding to green consumerism, such as the public demand to reduce waste and recycle by finding new uses for waste products; and also many examples of companies that upgrade their capital equipment when forced to reduce their pollutants and other companies that specialize in environmental cleanup.

The best solution for capital as a whole (though not for society nor even for 'nature'; this would presuppose a logic of reciprocation rather than the logic of capitalist exchange value) is to restructure the conditions of production in ways that increase their 'productivity'. Since the state either produces or regulates access to these conditions, restructuring processes are typically organized and/or regulated by the state, that is, politically. Examples include banning cars in urban downtowns to lower congestion and pollution costs; subsidizing integrated pest management in agriculture to lower food and raw materials costs; and shifting emphasis from curative to preventative health (e.g., the fight against AIDS in the United States) to lower health care costs. However, huge sums of monies would have to be expended—to attain a real solution—to restructure production conditions in ways that restored or increased their 'productivity' and thus lower the costs of capital. Long-term productivity would be enhanced, but at the expense of short-term profits. New industries would produce environmentally friendly products, urban transport, and education systems, which (like the examples cited above) effectively lower the costs of the elements of capital and of the consumption basket, as well as of ground rent; at the same time, the level of aggregate demand would be increased, attacking the first contradiction in potentially noninflationary ways. (By contrast, if new systems of forest management, pollution control spending, urban planning, and so on, have no effect on costs, the result is an increase in effective demand and inflation or a reduction in profits).

So much for the idea of sustaining capitalism; practice is another question. In liberal democratic states the normal political logic of pluralism and compromise prevents the development of overall environmental, urban, and social planning. The logic of the state administration or bureaucracy is undemocratic, hence insensitive to environmental and other issues raised from below. And the logic of self-expanding capital is antiecological, antiurban, and antisocial. All three logics combined are contradictory in terms of developing political solutions to the crisis of the conditions of production; hence chances of instituting a systematic 'capitalist solution' to the second contradiction are remote.

Put differently, there is no state agency or corporatist-type planning mechanism in any developed capitalist country that engages in overall ecological, urban, and social planning. The idea of an ecological capitalism, or a sustainable capitalism, has not even been coherently theorized, not to speak of becoming embodied in an institutional infrastructure. Where is the state that has a rational environmental plan? Intraurban and interurban planning? Health and education planning organically linked to environmental and urban planning? Nowhere. Instead, there are piecemeal approaches, fragments of regional planning at best, and irrational political spoils allotment systems at worst.

Every day, therefore, new headlines announce another health care crisis, another environmental crisis, and another urban crisis. In many regions the ultra-image we have is of an increasingly illiterate labor force, many of whom are homeless because of low wages and high rents, living in fear in a polluted city, immobilized by gridlock, and unable even to obtain clean water. This picture may not fit Rome or New York yet, but it comes close to describing Mexico City and New Delhi, which by any measure are parts of the capitalist world.

## ECOLOGICAL CONSEQUENCES OF A GENERAL ECONOMIC DEPRESSION

However sustainability is defined from an ecological standpoint, one thing seems fairly certain. If capitalism is not sustainable in terms of international macroeconomic regulation, there will be a global crisis, a general deflation of capital values, and a depression. In this event, no one knows or can know how individual capitals, governments, and international agencies will respond.

It may be that great economic pressures from the demand side (or the cost side or both at the same time) arising from capital overproduction (or underproduction or both) would force individual capitals to try to restore profits by externalizing more costs, that is, by shifting more cost to the environment, land, and communities, with states and international agencies looking on helplessly. In fact, there is plenty of evidence that the slow economic growth since the mid-1970s has resulted in such cost shifting, especially by transnational corporations. There is also evidence that in many cases this plan has backfired in the sense that cost shifting by one capital has increased costs for other capitals. Also, it can be shown that in many cases environmental struggles and environmental regulation have forced individual capitals to internalize costs that would otherwise fall on the environment. There is a kind of war going on between capital and the environmental movements, a war in which these movements might have the effect (intentional or not) of saving capital from itself in the long run by forcing it to deal with the negative short-term effects of cost shifting.

There is also the possibility, however slight, that a real economic depression might be the occasion for a general program of environmental restoration. In the United States in the 1930s the New Deal created the political conditions for two types of environmental changes. The first consisted of massive efforts to restore the degraded soils of the Great Plains and the ecologically damaged south and western rangelands. In this sense, the depression was an 'environmentally sound' event. The second type of environmental change consisted of even greater efforts to start up or to speed up giant infrastructure projects, such as huge dams, great bridges, and tunnels, which were indispensable for urbanization in the West and for post-World War II suburbanization everywhere in the country. Without these projects, consumerism and the culture of the automobile could not have flourished in the 1950s and 1960s. These projects in important ways helped to create the present structure of individualist consumption, which is ecologically unsound.

The next depression may make environmental conditions much worse, or it may be the occasion for vast changes in the structure of individual and social consumption, for example, green cities, integration between cities and surrounding agricultural lands, public transport that people look forward to using, and so on. Or both, to varying degrees, in different places. What will actually happen, of course, will be decided by the course of political struggle, institutional adaptation, and even types of technological innovation.

All of which is to say that environmental destruction, environmental and related social movements, government policies and budgets, policies of international bodies, and economic conditions are as interrelated as any complex ecosystem modeled by professional ecologists. Anyone trying to think about these interrelations will run up against the same epistemological and methodological problems that ecologists face when they try to model the fate of some particular species, that is, the problem of atomism and reductionism versus holism. Worse, while bald eagles and microorganisms do not organize themselves politically as social agents, people sometimes do. Hence a strict systems theory approach to the question of the ecological effects of a general depression is of questionable usefulness. In the last analysis, everything depends on the balance of political forces, and the visions of those who want to transform our relation with nature, hence our material relationships with one another—in short, with the political objectives of the environmental, labor, women's and other social movements, 'is sustainable capitalism possible?' is in the last, as well as in the first, instance, a political question.

## CONDITIONS IN THE SOUTH

The crisis of the conditions of production is especially severe in the South, which explains the appearance of the discourse on 'sustainable development' there, which has become an ideological and political battleground of growing importance. As I have noted, practically everyone uses the expression, with different intentions and meanings. Sustainability is defined by environmentalists and ecological economists to mean the use of only renewable resources and also low or nonaccumulating levels of pollution. The South may be, in fact, closer to 'sustainability' seen in this way than the North is, but the North has more capital and technological resources than the South as the means to attain sustainability. Capital, of course, uses the term to mean sustainable profits, which presuppose long-run planning of the exploitation and use of renewable and nonrenewable resources, and of the 'Global Commons'. Ecologists define sustainability in terms of the maintenance of natural systems, wetlands, wilderness protection, air quality, and so on. But these definitions may have little or nothing to do with sustaining profitability. In fact, there is generally an inverse relation between ecological sustainability and short-term profit. The 'sustainability' of rural and urban existence, the worlds of indigenous peoples, the conditions of life for women, and safe workplaces are also inversely correlated with the sustainability of profits—if the history of the long economic crisis of the late 20th century is any guide.

Independent of the question of the desirability of the South following the industrial consumerist path of the North is the possibility of it doing this. Industrial capitalism in India, Brazil, and Mexico (to take three examples) occurs at the expense of vast poverty and misery and also erosion of ecological stability, however this expression is defined. East Asia is doing well economically, and some Southeast Asian countries are doing even better (in terms of growth of gross domestic product), but these regions have yet to prove that they can be industrial powerhouses and also pay good wages and provide decent working conditions, progressive social policies, good conditions of urban life, and meaningful environmental protection. Most of the rest of the South (including the North's and East Asia's internal colonies) is an economic, social, and ecological disaster zone. There are many barriers to capitalist development in the South, for example weak markets, due to hugely unequal distribution of wealth and income; the absence of agrarian reform favoring small and middle farmers; and instabilities in the demand for, and supply of, raw materials. Also, there are problems relating to foreign debt and balance of payments crises, not to speak of maintaining ruling blocks of propertied interests and stable governments. These problems exist independently of the state of ecological conditions in particular and the conditions of production in general. Needless to say, this situation creates permanent social and political instability; new migration patterns to the North; more economic and ecological refugees; and so on—which, in turn, spell continued trouble in the North.

## POLITICAL POSSIBILITIES

The majority of the center–right and rightist governments that have been governing most of the world since the late 1970s and early 1980s are incapable of steering capitalist development in ways that improve the conditions of life, labor, the cities, or the environment. These governments are too intent on expanding the 'free market' and the international division of labor; deregulating and privatizing industry; forcing economic 'adjustments' on the South and 'shock therapy' on the old socialist countries—hence marginalizing up to half the population of some third world countries, and pretending that the 'market' and neoliberalism generally will solve the growing economic crisis. But things are likely to get much worse before they get better, especially in the South.

Meanwhile, there has been a growth of various green and 'red green' movements in different countries. Politically speaking, arguably the most developed is New Zealand's Alliance.[9] A few labor unions in some countries are addressing environmental issues more seriously. Conversely, environmental movements are addressing economic and social issues that 5 or 10 years ago they ignored or downplayed. In multiple forms, labor and feminist movements, urban movements, environmental movements, and movements of oppressed minorities have organized themselves around the general issues of the conditions of life. While the prospects for a sustainable capitalism are dim, there may be hope for some kind of ecological socialism—a society that pays close attention to ecology along with the needs of human beings in their daily life, as well as to feminist issues, antiracism, and issues of social justice and equality generally. Globally, it is around these issues that there is movement and organization, agitation and action, which can be explained in terms of the contradictions of capitalism and the nature of the capitalist state I discussed above.

Politically, this means that sooner or later labour, feminist, urban, environmental, and other social movements need to combine into a single powerful, democratic force—one that is both politically viable and also capable of radically reforming the economy, polity, and society.[10] Individually, social movements are relatively powerless in the face of the totalizing force of global capital. This suggests the need for three general and related strategies.

The first is the self-conscious development of a common or public sphere, a political space, a kind of dual power, in which minority, labor, women, urban, and environmental organizations can work economically and politically. Here there could be developed not the temporary tactical alliances among movements and movement leaders that we have today, but strategic alliances, including electoral alliances. A strong civil society, defining itself in terms of its 'commons,' its solidarity, and its struggles with capital and the state, as well as of its democratic impulses and forms of organization within alliances and coalitions of movement organizations—and within each organization itself—is the first prerequisite of sustainable society and nature. The second is the self-conscious development of economic and ecological alternatives within this public sphere or 'new commons'—alternatives such as green cities, pollution-free production, biologically diversified forms of silviculture and agriculture, and so on, the technical aspects of which are increasingly well known today. The third is to organize struggles to democratize the workplace and the state administration so that substantive contents of an ecological, progressive type can be put into the shell of liberal democracy. This presupposes that the movements not only use political means to economic, social, and ecological goals, but also agree on political goals themselves, especially the democratization of some national and international state apparatuses, and the elimination of others.

These ideas may seem to be as unrealistic as that of an ecological capitalism. Perhaps this is the case. But we need to remember that while the existing structures of capital and the state do not seem to be capable of anything more than occasional reforms, social movements worldwide grow every day—hence it is possible that at some point there will be a general social and political crisis, as the demands of these movements clash with existing profit-oriented economic and political structures. If this point is reached, all kinds of 'social morbid forms' will appear. Some will say that this is precisely what is happening today—that the social and political fabrics are unravelling, and that the resurgence of racism, nativism, discrimination against foreign workers, male and antienvironmental backlash, and other reactionary trends and tendencies are becoming increasingly great dangers. Others link the revival of right-wing populism and reaction to rightward shifts in the political and economic mainstream. There are other analyses of the current world political situation— including the line that the globe is witnessing a rebellion of the well-to-do against the demands of the poor, the welfare state, redistributive economic policies, and the like—a war of the rich against the poor. Or all of the above may be true. Whatever the case(s), from the standpoints of progressives, red or left greens, and feminists, the last thing in the world we need is factionalism, sectarianism, 'correct lineism'— instead, we need to scrutinize critically all time-worn political formulae and develop an ecumenical spirit, and to celebrate our commonalities or 'new commons' as well as our differences.

## NOTES

1. *New York Times*, August 12, 1992.
2. See, for example, Simon Fairlie, 'Long distance, short life: why big business favours recycling', *Ecologist*, **22**(6), November–December 1992, pp. 276–283.
3. On forestry, see Edward Goldsmith *et al.*, *The Imperialist Planet* (Cambridge, MA: MIT Press, 1991), p. 94. Most timber in the United States is produced on industrial plantations. Examples of genetic modifications now abound, and there exist modified strains of almost all staples either in laboratory or in commercial use—corn, rice, soybeans, and many other foods, including a potato that kills one of its own pests, the Colorado potato beetle, by emitting a protein fatal to the insect. Wheat has been experimentally genetically altered by the University of Florida and Monsanto Co. to increase yields. They introduced a foreign gene into wheat that produces an enzyme that makes many herbicides harmless to the wheat. Of course, the gene introduced into the wheat is a trade secret (*New York Times*, May 28, 1992).
4. No more is it only a question of capital appropriating what is already found in nature, then breaking it down and recombining its elements into a commodity, but rather of creating something that did not exist before. There is no hard line between the two; nevertheless, there is a qualitative difference once you compare the extremes.
5. All growth theories presuppose certain relationships between the 'real' and money economies, physical production and incomes, and increases in investment and consumption goods, on the one hand, and profits and wages, on the other hand. Before the development of ecological economics, the question 'What exactly is growing?' was relatively neglected. Today, more economists are willing to admit that growth not only includes some vector of outputs (commodities, services, increments of durable stocks of goods), but also outputs of 'wastes' and increments of stocks of durable wastes. This complicates an already complex and arbitrary system of income accounting.
   In classical terms, disproportionalities between the investment/consumption good and

profit/wages ratios can cause economic trouble ('disproportionality crises'). The main type of crisis inherent in capitalism, however, is a 'realization crisis.' Marxists regard capitalism as 'crisis-ridden.' But the system is also 'crisis-dependent' in the sense that economic crises force cost cutting, 'restructuring,' layoffs, and other changes that make the system more 'efficient,' that is, more profitable. Marx wrote that 'capital accumulates through crisis,' meaning that crises are occasions for the liquidation of some capitals, and also the appearance of new capitals and reorganization of old capitals, not to speak of the diffusion of new and more 'efficient' technology throughout the system, such as computerization (see below).

6. 'Most simpleminded' in part because while there is a general tendency for the rate of profit in different industries to become roughly comparable (via movement of capital away from low-profit and toward high-profit sectors), profit rates vary widely from industry to industry, even from capital unit to capital unit. There are many reasons for this, among which (and arguably the most important) is that big capitals not only appropriate larger profits defined in absolute or total terms than small capitals, but also the former 'earn' a higher profit rate than the latter. The reason is that small capitals typically cannot compete with big capitals, while big capitals can compete with small capitals (as well as with each other).

7. 'Inadvertently' because Marx used the concept of 'conditions of production' in different and inconsistent ways: he never dreamed that the concept would or could be used in the way that I will use it in this chapter; and no one could have used the concept in this way until the appearance of Karl Polanyi's *The Great Transformation* (New York: Farrar and Rinehart, 1944). The 'land and labor' theme has, of course, been taken up in other ways by critical writers concerned with peasant subsistence, indigenous or 'First Peoples,' and the nexus of women, capital, and the environment—for example, Claudia von Werlhof, 'On the concept of nature and society in capitalism', in Maria Mies, ed., *Women: The Last Colony* (London: Zed Books, 1988), pp. 92–112.

8. This rationalization also includes reprivatization defined as a shift from paid labor to unpaid labor in the home and community, or the revival of self-help ideologies that throw more of the burden of reproducing labor power and environmental and urban conditions of life onto noncapitalized domains. What Martin O'Connor calls 'autonomous subsistence'—the somewhat autonomous (but simultaneously exploited) domains of household, peasant, and communal life and (re)production activities—furnishes a necessary undergirding of capitalist accumulation, and this assumes particular importance during crisis periods—on the one hand, providing degrees of freedom in capital's restructuring process, and, on the other hand, providing a subsistence possibility for people jettisoned through redundancies or social welfare cutbacks from the 'formal' economy. Exploration of this issue raises the larger subject of how to theorize this articulation between capitalist and subsistence domains—whether and how, for instance, unpaid domestic labor constitutes the exploitation of women by men, functions as a subsidy to capital, and so on—questions that have been much debated by feminists, Marxists, Marxist feminists, and ecofeminists since the 1970s.

9. See Wayne Hope and Joce Jesson, 'Contesting new terrain: red green politics in New Zealand', *CNS*, 4(2), no. 14, June 1993, pp. 1–17. The strongly developed and high-profile green political movement in (former West) Germany has had only limited success in building alliances with the labor left; see John Ely 'Red green ecological reconstruction in Germany: a project on hold', *CNS*, 2(3), no. 8, October 1991, pp. 111–126.

10. No one knows or can know when a 'single, powerful democratic force' will develop, or even if it will develop at all. Very difficult questions must be answered, practically and theoretically—for example, whether the very concept of such a 'force' is fatally grounded in the modernist–humanist tradition of Western political philosophy, a 'liberal' tradition that has been less than truly tolerant of 'difference', yet for all that remains firmly grounded in affirming individual rights vis-à-vis the state. Some believe, in Martin O'Connor's words (pers. comm.), that it is important 'at this moment in time, that is, the late 20th century, to explore what it means to have a coexistence of many, somewhat discordant voices, having in common their repudiation of capital's domination, yet ill-

reconciled in many other ways. This is an aspect of realism, of things being "likely to get worse before they get better".' The question being raised here is partly one of what constitutes a 'unified' force, and partly one of whether and in what sense, if desirable, it is felt to be attainable. On the one hand, even if one affirms the possibility of concordant voices, there may not be time to work through all of the tensions and to fully and mutually hear the plurality of voices, different grounds of knowledge, and so on, existing between and within social movements as they stand today. On the other hand, the need for unity against capital and for a nonexploitative, socially just, ecological society may be too great, given the configurations of political forces today, to delay efforts at development of a unified political strategy capable of confronting global capital and the developing global quasi-state (of International Monetary Fund, World Bank, and so on).

## ACKNOWLEDGEMENTS

Martin O'Connor's editorial help is warmly appreciated. This chapter is a much revised version of 'Is Sustainable Capitalism Possible?', which appeared in Patricia Allen, ed., *Food for the Future: Conditions and Contradictions of Sustainability* (New York: John Wiley and Sons, 1983), pp. 125–137, and a lecture, 'Discourse on Sustainability', given at the School for Environmental Studies, York University, Ontario, Canada, March 1993.

# 6

# Rio and Beyond

*J. McCormick*

The debate over achieving a balance between environmental management and economic development continued to build during the 1980s, and it became increasingly obvious that much more thought needed to be given to the means of achieving such a balance. Rich and poor nations continued to have very different perceptions about the relative place of the environment on the policy agenda, and about the relative priorities of short-term growth and long-term planning. The tension between the two sides of the debate dated back to the very beginnings of the environmental movement, and had grown steadily through the decades since. Stockholm had focused an unprecedented level of attention on the environment/development issue, but problems continued to grow, and it became increasingly obvious that there was much more that needed to be done.

## BRUNDTLAND PAVES THE WAY

In September 1983, 34 years after UNSCCUR and 11 years after Stockholm, the UN General Assembly passed a resolution calling for the creation of a new independent commission charged with addressing the question of the relationship between environment and development, and with listing 'innovative, concrete and realistic' proposals to deal with the question. The World Commission on Environment and Development held its first meeting in Geneva in October 1984, chaired by Gro Harlem Brundtland, the former prime minister of Norway. The Commission had 23 members—12 from LDCs, seven from Western MDCs (among them Maurice Strong), and four from the communist bloc.

An unprecedented growth in pressures on the global environment had made grave predictions about the future commonplace, the Commission noted; a more prosperous, just and secure future demanded policies aimed at sustaining the ecological basis of development, and at changing the nature of cooperation between governments, business, science and people. Avoiding a reiteration of problems and

Reprinted by permission of John Wiley & Sons Ltd. McCormick, J., *The Global Environmental Movement*, 2nd edn, pp. 251–264.

trends, the Commission selected eight key issues (including energy, industry, food security, human settlements, and international economic relations) and examined them from the perspective of the year 2000. Between March 1985 and February 1987, it sponsored more than 75 studies and reports, and held meetings or public hearings in ten countries, garnering the views of an impressive selection of individuals and organisations. In 1987, the report of the Commission was published as *Our Common Future*.[1]

The report concluded that environment and development were inextricable, and that policy responses were handicapped by the fact that existing institutions tended to be independent, fragmented, too narrowly focused, and too concerned with addressing effects rather than causes, and so tended to address issues such as acid pollution as discrete policy problems. The goals of these agencies were too often focused on increasing investment, employment, food, energy, and other economic and social goods rather than on sustaining the environmental resource capital on which these goals depended.[2] National frontiers had become so porous that the distinctions between local, national and international issues had become blurred; domestic policies increasingly had effects well beyond national frontiers (e.g., acid pollution again). Greater international cooperation was needed, but international agencies—notably the UN system—were under siege at the time they were most needed.

Furthermore, the Commission concluded, environmental policy was too often accorded a secondary status; environmental agencies often learned of new initiatives in economic, trade or energy policy (with possible consequences for resources) long after the effective decisions had been taken. It was time that 'the ecological dimensions of policy [were] considered at the same time as the economic, trade, energy, agricultural, industrial, and other dimensions—on the same agendas and in the same national and international institutions'.[3] The commission had several specific recommendations:

— national environmental protection agencies needed urgent strengthening, particularly in LDCs;
— UNEP's work needed to be reinforced and extended (notably through increased funding);
— monitoring and assessment needed better focus and coordination;
— policy-makers needed to work more closely with NGOs and industry;
— law and international conventions needed strengthening and better implementation;
— the UN should work towards a universal declaration and later a convention on environmental protection and sustainable development.

In the Brundtland Commission's critique of conventional environmental management and in its global view, Redclift sees the most radical departure yet from previous approaches to sustainable development. Yet, even before the final publication of the report, he felt it unlikely that MDCs or LDCs would act on the measures recommended by Brundtland; they could not do so 'without involving themselves in very radical structural reform, not only of methodologies for costing forest losses or soil erosion, but of the international economic system itself'.[4]

Whether this process of reform had begun, or whether it could make headway against conventional political and economic attitudes to natural resources, struck at the very heart of the goals and philosophies of the environmental movement.

## THE RIO SUMMIT

The findings of the Brundtland Commission added to those of the World Conservation Strategy and UNEP's own conclusions to increase the pressure for a new summit to follow up on Stockholm. The special session of the UNEP Governing Council held in 1982 to review progress in the decade since Stockholm had concluded that much more long-term planning was needed. The Brundtland Commission had argued the need to understand the links between environment and development, and argued that environmental protection should not be seen as an obstacle to growth so much as an integral and supportive element in that growth. It recommended that an international conference be convened to review progress and decide on future action.

In December 1989, the UN General Assembly passed a resolution agreeing to call the conference, which Brazil subsequently offered to host. The decision to hold it in an LDC obviously had enormous political significance and symbolism. The United Nations Conference on Environment and Development (UNCED) drew representatives from 178 countries to Rio de Janeiro during two weeks in June 1992, becoming the largest international conference ever held. It was criticised and even dismissed by many environmentalists as an exercise in public relations by national governments and international agencies, and once the media hype had died down, it was obvious that there was once again going to be a gap between word and deed. Nevertheless, Rio added further substance to the debate over global environmental issues.

Sustainable development was always going to be the major theme of UNCED, but events in the late 1980s made sure that other, more specific, problems also went to the top of the conference agenda. Notable among these were the growing concerns about global warming and threats to the ozone layer, and continuing concerns about species extinction and threats to biodiversity. Preparatory meetings for UNCED were held in Nairobi (August 1990), Geneva (March 1991) and New York (March 1992), during which a draft agenda was produced, the active participation of NGOs at Rio agreed, and much of the text of the Rio Declaration and Agenda 21 agreed.[5]

Governments were invited to draw up and submit national reports on their policies and their hopes for UNCED. Although many failed to meet the deadline, almost every state in the world had prepared a report by the end of 1992. Several conferences were also held involving UN agencies, national governments and NGOs to discuss sustainable development issues, many of which produced conclusions that fed into UNCED.

The outcomes of Rio can be summarised in five key agreements.

(1) The *Framework Convention on Climate Change*. Although this was a legally binding convention, it was focused less around specific action than around providing an

international framework and a set of principles that would guide future action. Negotiations on the convention began in early 1991 under the direct auspices of the UN General Assembly, and the convention was signed at Rio by 153 states and the European Union.

One of the key problems underlying the debate about global warming was the lack of scientific consensus on the existence (let alone the causes) of the problem. The major significance of the Rio convention was that it established the principle that climate change was a serious problem that needed 'precautionary measures' that could not await the resolution of questions about scientific certainty. It also emphasised the role of MDCs in the production of greenhouse gases. MDCs agreed to take steps to cut greenhouse gas emissions to 1990 levels by the year 2000, and agreed to meet regularly and to submit reports on their plans and policies.

Discussions were driven in part by concerns among some LDCs that the greenhouse debate was a conspiracy by MDCs to retard their development, so agreement was reached that MDCs should take the lead on action, and compensate LDCs for any additional costs they incurred. This would be done through the Global Environmental Facility, a body to be run on an interim basis by UNEP, UNDP and the World Bank. (In essence, the LDCs said they would do nothing unless MDCs paid).

The wording of the convention was so ambiguous that it was open once again to widely differing interpretation, and no hard commitments were made. Signatories, for example, agreed to take action subject to the measures being 'cost effective', and the convention emphasised the need for continued research, and re-evaluation of action in the light of new findings. The best that can be said about the convention was that it reflected growing political concern for the issue of global warming, and brought the economic and political conflicts over the issue into the open. It forced governments to at least discuss the issue, but did nothing to ensure that anything would actually be done.

(2) The *Convention on Biological Diversity*. Negotiated under the auspices of UNEP, this convention was aimed at preserving global biological diversity through the protection of species and ecosystems. Since most of the threats were being experienced in LDCs, and most biotechnology was based in MDCs, discussions were again based around attempts to reach a compromise between the needs of the two sides.

The convention was widely criticised as representing the absolute minimum that governments could get away with, and for including far too many of the opt-out phrases reminiscent of so many international agreements. Much like the climate change convention, the best that can be said is that the biological diversity convention was a step in the right direction. It was signed at Rio by 155 states and the European Union. The United States refused to sign, President Bush arguing that it posed a threat to the US biotechnology industry and to American jobs.

(3) *Agenda 21*. This was an action plan for sustainable development, integrating the goals of environmental protection and economic development, and based on local community and free market principles. Agenda 21 ensured that the concept of sustainable development became a permanent principle of the UN. The Rio conference secretariat estimated that about $125 billion per year would be needed to implement Agenda 21, a sum that was so unlikely to be forthcoming that the huge

gap between words and deeds was emphasised once again. A recommendation was made for the creation of a UN Commission on Sustainable Development to oversee the implementation of Agenda 21. The Commission was established in late 1992, and consists of ministerial representatives from 53 states who met in plenary session once a year for two to three weeks to review progress and set annual goals. It is due to complete a five-year review in 1997 in time for a special session of the UN.

(4) The *Rio Declaration on Environment and Development*. This consisted of 27 principles guiding action on environment and development, and building on the Stockholm Declaration of 1972. The preparatory debates over the declaration saw LDCs emphasising development and global equity, while MDCs emphasised environmental concerns.[6] Among the more contentious of the principles was the third, which affirmed the 'right to development', a clause intended to assure LDCs that their basic development plans would not be slowed or compromised. The United States issued a disclaimer, rejecting such a right on the grounds that it might be used to override other rights (such as civil rights).

(5) The *Forest Principles*. These were all that remained from controversial attempts to draw up a global forest convention in 1990–91. They emphasise the sovereign right of individual states to exploit forest resources, but within general principles of forest protection and management.

Rio perplexed many inside and outside the environmental movement. It drew unparalleled levels of public attention to the problems of the environment, and represented another major step along the road to a workable resolution of the tensions between environmental management and economic development. It also drew lines in the sand regarding the basic principles on which governments would approach environmental management. It brought national governments yet closer together in agreeing the underlying goals of their environmental policies. At the same time, though, it suffered most of the weaknesses common to all big international gatherings—and since Rio was that much bigger, involved so many states, and had such a complex and all-encompassing brief, those weaknesses were magnified. Its major weakness lay in the extent to which its outcomes were diluted by the need to reach consensus among the dozens of participating states. Given the size of its task, though, it is difficult to see how it could have produced anything more than diluted compromise statements. Despite the criticisms it attracted from many environmentalists, it stood as a clear benchmark of just how far the environmental debate had come in 20 years.

## INTO THE 21ST CENTURY

'The report of my death', once observed a robust Mark Twain, 'was an exaggeration.' He might have been speaking for the environmental movement. With a persistent and misguided regularity, environmentalism has been declared dead, dying or defunct since almost before it was born. As early as 1954, Grant McConnell lamented that the United States would never again see the like of the Progressive Conservation movement.[7] In 1972, Anthony Downs warned that most social issues eventually enter a stage of prolonged limbo (although he conceded that environmental issues might retain their interest longer).[8] In 1975, James Bowman perceived a gradual decline of intense interest in the environment.[9] In 1980, Francis Sandbach, quoting opinion polls and diminishing newspaper inches, saw no reason to disagree with Bowman.[10]

Against this background, the views of Clay Schoenfeld were in a notable minority. Far from being a passing fad, he argued in 1972, the environmental movement (in the United States at least) seemed destined to be a permanent fixture,[11] for several reasons. First, environmental degradation was a high-visibility problem that millions could see, smell, taste and hear. Second, environmentalism was not a wholly new movement; it had a long-established and solid infrastructure from which to operate and expand. Third, the diversity inherent in the movement boded well for its survival. Fourth, affluence gave more people the opportunity to make hard choices. Finally, the movement had a good deal of internal integrity in that it was part of a coherent, fundamental shift in values.

Certainly there were opinion polls in the 1970s that seemed to indicate declining support for the environmental movement. There have been as many since that indicate exactly the opposite.[12] They are all missing the point. The robustness and significance of a social movement cannot always be measured in opinion polls, because too many look at the environmental movement from a perspective limited in historical, geographical and ideological terms.

For those Europeans or Americans who lived through the emotional heyday of mass environmentalism in the 1960s and 1970s, the relative sobriety of the late 1970s and 1980s—distracted as they were by economic recessions, energy crises, and returning affluence and ideological conservatism—must have seemed anticlimactic. The environmentalism of the streets declined, it is true; but the broader movement did not. Rather, it was transformed. During the 1960s, it was fixed in the arena of mass protest and citizen action; by the 1980s, it had scaled (and in some places breached) the citadel of public policy. During the 1960s, activists demanded changes in policy-making, planning goals, and economic and social values; by the late 1970s, their demands were slowly being met.

Qualitatively, the actions of governments and the efficacy of law often have left much to be desired, but there is no denying the advent of the environment as a public policy issue. In manifestos, platforms and campaign speeches, energy and the environment regularly take their place alongside statements on economic and foreign policy, welfare, education, crime, health, agriculture and other more 'traditional' policy areas. By the late 1980s, it was regularly argued that the greens were on the wane because their environmental policies were being adopted by the older, larger parties. This is a debatable contention in itself, but it clearly showed that the environment was becoming increasingly non-partisan.

As the 21st century approaches, and as the nature of the environment continues to broaden and change, it is difficult to know whether to be optimistic or pessimistic about the future. In the credit column, there has been a notable change of attitude.

- At the most fundamental level, the lifestyle of the Western middle classes is changing, and green consumerism is on the rise: people are driving more fuel-efficient cars, recycling, conserving energy at home, reducing the size of their families, and supporting environmental groups and their aims. Environmental awareness is taken increasingly for granted.

- There are more examples of corporate responsibility, notably through the growing use of environmental impact assessments. The record is still far from perfect, and the roots of such change may not always be as honourable as they appear (social responsibility does not yet always exceed the profit motive), but the trend is hopeful.
- Citizen and grassroots movements in MDCs and LDCs alike are building impressive records of achievement. In Britain, the National Trust alone has ensured the protection in perpetuity of thousands of acres of countryside. In Kenya, the Green Belt Movement has helped turn tree-planting into a national crusade. In Mexico, Malaysia and India, citizen's movements play a growing role in planning decisions. In the United States, environmental groups have proved effective lobbyists, and have repeatedly made the environment an issue in national, state and local politics. Bill Clinton and Al Gore responded by making the environment a key element of their 1992 election campaign, but disappointed the environmental lobby by doing little to tighten environmental regulation in the first two years of their administration.
- Although still far from perfect, the number of national government agencies and institutions dealing with the environment has grown, their work supported by a growing body of local, national and international law. Environmental policy-making—while still bound too often by the confines of ideology and incomplete data—is improving. Green parties have had mixed fortunes, but older established parties have given more thought to the environment as a policy area.

    The environment has traditionally fallen more easily into the constituency of moderate/liberal political ideology, but 1988 saw signs of a new interest among anti-regulation conservatives. During the 1988 US Presidential campaign, for example, George Bush made it clear that he was not going to rely on free market mechanisms to resolve environmental problems, unlike his predecessor Ronald Reagan.

    Even more surprisingly, Margaret Thatcher—after years of ardent opposition to government regulations (especially on environmental questions) and growing pressure from environmentalists and members of her own party—apparently underwent an abrupt conversion to environmentalism. In October 1988, she suddenly declared that protecting the balance of nature was one of 'the great challenges' of the late 20th century, and called for emergency action to safeguard the ozone layer, curb acid pollution, and avoid global climatic warming. The announcement took many environmentalists by surprise; it seemed to some that the Conservatives were launching an attempt to claim the environment as the natural preserve of the Right.

- The data are still far from complete, but much more is known about the state of the environment and about the kind of protection it needs. Environmental research is more coordinated and effective; IBP, MAB, Earthwatch and GEMS have brought a better understanding of the interconnectedness of cause and effect in environmental problems. The new data have revealed more clearly the geographical scope of environmental problems.
- Whether green parties continue to exist in their present form, or wither away as their policies are adopted by the older parties, the advent of green politics has

already shaken our assumptions about the old left/right axis in politics. Many greens argue that an entirely new political philosophy is needed to respond adequately to the needs of environmentalism, and that conservatism, liberalism and socialism in all their existing hues are too 'unecological'. Jonathan Porritt argues that green politics 'challenges the integrity of [existing] ideologies, questions the philosophy that underlies them, and fundamentally disputes today's accepted notions of rationality'.[13]

- Environmentalism has moved beyond the despair of the prophets of doom and has entered a more mature and measured phase in which the accumulated knowledge of the past two centuries, and particularly of the past two decades, is increasingly being put to effective use. Planners in MDCs and LDCs have begun to agree in seeing many environmental problems as being as much global as local concerns. The nature and scope of the work of international agencies is evidence in itself of a broader and more rational view of environmental issues and problems.

Yet despite such progress, there are problems on the debit side of the balance sheet which cannot be ignored. Although there is more certainty about the threats to the environment, there is perhaps less certainty about the prospects for addressing those threats.

- Despite the creation of new environmental agencies and the passage of new legislation in MDCs, the political will to implement the spirit—let alone the letter—of environmental protection, has been patchy. The ratio of words to action is weighted too heavily towards the former, and while public understanding of environmental imperatives was increased since Stockholm, and new institutions have evolved, many of the social, economic and technological causes of environmental problems have continued unchecked.[14]
- The break-up of the Soviet Union began to reveal the extent of environmental devastation in much of Eastern Europe and the former USSR, a problem long suspected by Western environmentalists. The extent to which the upheavals of the post-Soviet transition will interfere with attempts to address environmental problems in Eastern Europe and the former Soviet republics remains to be seen.
- The litany of problems afflicting LDCs meanwhile grows with worrying persistence. Incidents such as Bhopal and Ixhuatepec not only cast a shadow over planning and development priorities, but—as most of their victims were shanty-dwellers— also underline the dire social and economic problems of LDC cities, where economic inequality is creating a growing underclass, and where population growth frequently outpaces the provision of housing, clean water and sanitation.

  The rapid and dramatic growth of countries such as Brazil, Argentina, China, Malaysia and Thailand will bring new wealth to poorer states, and underpin political stability, but it also raises the prospect of the same kind of severe environmental problems as Western Europe and the United States saw during the early phase of their industrialisation.

  Sub-Saharan Africa gives the greatest cause for concern. Spiralling population growth, widespread soil erosion, falling food production, political instability, bureaucratic incompetence, and economic corruption and mismanagement have all too often combined to produce a sub-continent in crisis. If current trends continue, the region is promised continuing human and environmental catastrophe.

- Overarching almost everything has been the emergence first of problems affecting many different parts of the planet (acid pollution, toxic wastes, nuclear contamination, deforestation, and the killing of wildlife), and then of problems affecting the planet as a whole. Agreement on dealing with the threats to the ozone layer was reached remarkably quickly; more serious now, though, is the greenhouse effect. With the increased use of coal, oil and natural gas, the concentration of carbon dioxide ($CO_2$) in the earth's atmosphere has risen steadily since the industrial revolution. Acting like a greenhouse, this $CO_2$ has been trapping solar radiation in the earth's atmosphere.

Warnings of a global warming were made as early as 1970. Then, they sounded very much like science fiction, with seemingly fantastic suggestions that a warmer climate would lead to changes in crop production patterns, the melting of the polar ice caps, and a rise in global sea levels, inundating many coastal areas. By the late 1980s, those warnings had begun to seem much more real as records for extreme weather began to be broken over much of the northern hemisphere. Whether this really was part of the greenhouse effect, or simply the latest cyclical extreme in continental weather patterns, it provided many with a taste of the possible consequences of global warming. But the level of doubt was enough to give governments the excuse they needed to limit their responses.

In 1982, UNEP published *The World Environment 1972–1982* as an audit of 'the first ten years in which mankind [had] consciously and co-operatively attempted the rational management' of the earth. In his foreword, UNEP Executive Director Mostafa Tolba noted that 'preventive rather than curative actions have been gaining momentum and wide acceptance' and that the importance of international cooperation had been brought into focus. But, he warned, 'ten years after Stockholm it is clear that we still have a very imperfect knowledge of the state of the major components of our environment and of the interacting mechanisms', and he emphasised the need for long-term planning: 'the problems which overwhelm us today are precisely those which, through a similar [lack of foresight], we failed to solve decades ago'.[15]

UNEP repeated the exercise in 1992 with *The World Environment 1972–1992*. Tolba noted the paradox between growing public concern and media interest in the environment, and a faltering political response. There had been isolated achievements, he noted, but progress had slowed, and the gap between commitment and action persisted.[16]

At the global level, finding out and understanding what is needed in the management of resources is much easier than actually implementing multi-national management programmes. Science provides an understanding of the mechanics of environmental problems, but the causes and solutions are ultimately a question of human behaviour. In the final analysis, the environment is a political issue. Whether or not solutions are effectively applied will continue to depend upon politics and policy, upon the attitudes of leaders, parties, industry and the public, and upon a complex cross-referencing and cooperative system involving international agencies, national environmental agencies, NGOs, and a series of often non-binding international conventions and agreements.

Whatever the short-term prognosis, however, the longer-term changes in attitude have been heartening for the environmental movement. Bowman sees environmentalism as the last stage in a process that has taken humans 'from fearing, to understanding, to using, to abusing, and now, to worrying about the physical and biological world' around them.[17] There has been a marked trend away from the notion of environment as divorced from humanity and towards a new focus on the human costs of environmental deterioration and mismanagement. It is no longer simply a question of what we are doing to the environment, but of what the despoliation of the environment is doing to us. Environmentalists argue that we can no longer take the environment for granted. It is already too late to save many species and habitats, and more will undoubtedly suffer through ill-advised development. Pollution has been curbed or reduced in some parts of the world, but it is worsening in others. Forests and fertile land are being lost in some parts, and restored in others. Sooner or later, a workable balance must be achieved. However long this takes, the rise of the global environmental movement has made sure that the relationship between humans and their environment will never be quite the same again.

## REFERENCES

1. World Commission on Environment and Development, *Our Common Future* (Oxford: Oxford University Press, 1987).
2. *ibid.*, 310–312.
3. WCED, reference 1, 313.
4. Redclift, Michael, *Sustainable Development: Exploring the Contradictions* (London: Methuen, 1987), 14.
5. For details on the preparations for UNCED, see Chapter 2 of Grubb, Michael, Matthias Koch, Koy Thomson, Abby Munson and Francis Sullivan, *The Earth Summit Agreements: A Guide and Assessment* (London: Earthscan Publications, 1993).
6. Thompson, Koy, 'The Rio Declaration on Environment and Development' in Grubb *et al.*, *ibid.*, 86.
7. McConnell, Grant 'The conservation movement—past and present', *Western Political Quarterly*, **7**(3), September 1954, 463–478.
8. Downs, Anthony, 'Up and down with ecology—the "issue-attention" cycle', *The Public Interest*, **28**, Summer 1972, 38–50.
9. Bowman, James, S. 'The ecology movement: a viewpoint', *International Journal of Environmental Studies*, **8**(2), 1975, 91–97.
10. Sandbach, Francis. *Environment, Ideology and Policy* (Oxford: Basil Blackwell, 1980), 1–10. See also Dunlap, Riley E and Kent D Van Liere, 'Further evidence of declining public concern with environmental problems: a research note', *Western Sociological Review*, **8**: 1977, 108–112; Honnold, J. and L. D. Nelson, 'Age and environmental concern: some specification of effects', Paper presented at annual meeting of the American Sociological Association, Toronto, 1981.
11. Schoenfeld, Clay, 'Environmentalism: fad or fixture', *American Forests*, **78**(3): March 1972, 17–19.
12. See, for example, Milbrath, Lester W. *Environmentalists: Vanguard for a New Society* (Albany, New York: State University of New York Press, 1984); Council on Environmental Quality, *Environmental Quality 1980* (Washington, DC: US Government Printing Office, 1980), 401–423.
13. Holdgate, Martin, Mohammed Kassas and Gilbert White, *The World Environment 1972–1982* (Dublin: Tycooly Publishing, 1982), 629.

14.  Eckholm, Erik, *Down to Earth* (New York: W. W. Norton and Co., 1982), 199.
15.  Holdgate *et al.*, reference 13, xvi.
16.  Tolba, Mostafa, Osama El-Kholy, E. El-Hinnawi, Martin Holdgate, D. F. McMichael and R. E. Munn (eds), *The World Environment 1972–1992: Two Decades of Challenge* (London: Chapman and Hall, 1992).
17.  Bowman, reference 9.

# 7

# The European Community's Environmental Policy, 1957 to '1992': From Incidental Measures to an International Regime?

*Philipp M. Hildebrand*

This contribution describes and analyses the evolution of the European Community's environmental policy. The chosen time frame covers the period from January 1958, when the Treaty of Rome came into effect, to '1992', the target-date for the completion of the Single European Act (SEA) which entered into force on 1 July 1987.[1] The Treaty of Maastricht and its environmental consequences will be considered briefly in a final section. In light of the difficulty of a reliable interpretation so shortly after the treaty's signature and the fact that it is unlikely to go into effect before the middle of 1993, the reviewed legislative acts are drawn from the pre-Maastricht period.

It is often stated that, prior to 1973, there was no EC environmental policy. In principle this assessment is correct. Nevertheless, a number of pieces of environmental legislation had been adopted during that period. For that reason and in order to present an historically and analytically complete picture, the entire period will be assessed here.

At the outset it is necessary to ask two questions. First, how did the EC environmental policy evolve? Secondly, what were the determining factors of this evolution? At a time when the EC's environmental policies are increasingly being followed by the public, private corporations as well as various interest groups (Sands, 1990: 2), it is important to gain a thorough understanding of the historic evolution of European[2] environmental policies as a whole. The introduction of the Single European Act has brought about significant changes. Yet, relatively little has been written on the subject and, although '1992' has become every European's catchword, few seem to be aware of the potential environmental consequences of these recent developments.

Before laying out the structure of this study, it is necessary to discuss briefly the legal instruments that the relevant Community institutions are equipped with, in 'order to carry out their task'.[3] They are applicable to all issue-areas within the

Reprinted with permission from *Environmental Politics*, Vol. 1, No. 4, pp. 15–44. Published by Frank Cass & Company, Ilford, Essex, England. Copyright © 1992 Frank Cass & Co. Ltd.

competence of the European Community and have not been changed by the amendments introduced by the Single European Act or the Maastricht Treaty creating the European Union. Article 189 of the EEC Treaty sets out five different types of legal instruments. The first paragraph states: 'In order to carry out their task the Council and the Commission shall, in accordance with the provisions of this Treaty, make regulations, issue directives, take decisions, make recommendations or deliver opinions.' The last two have no binding force and should therefore not 'properly be regarded as legislative instruments' (Haigh, 1990: 2).

A regulation has general application and is 'binding in its entirety and directly applicable in all Member States' (Article 189/2). It has generally been used for rather precise purposes such as financial matters or the daily management of the Common Agricultural Policy (CAP). Only rarely has it been used for environmental matters (Haigh, 1990: 2).

A directive is 'binding, as to the result to be achieved', while it leaves it to the national authorities as to the 'choice of form and method' (Article 189/3). According to Nigel Haigh, 'it is therefore the most appropriate instrument for more general purposes particularly where some flexibility is required to accommodate existing national procedures and, for this reason, is the instrument most commonly used for environmental matters' (Haigh, 1990: 2)[4].

Finally, a decision is 'binding in its entirety upon those to whom it is addressed' (Article 189/4). With respect to environmental protection, decisions have been used in connection with international conventions and with certain procedural matters.

For analytical purposes I have divided the period to be covered here into three different phases. The first one begins with the entry into force of the Treaty of Rome and the establishment of the European Economic Community in 1957 and ends in 1972 with the Stockholm Conference on the Human Environment. With the approval of the first Community Action Programme on the Environment by the Council of Ministers in November 1973, the second phase begins which, according to this chronology, lasts until the adoption of the Single European Act in Luxembourg in December 1985. On 17 and 28 February the SEA was signed in Luxembourg and The Hague and, after ratification by the twelve national parliaments (and referenda in Denmark and Ireland), it came into force on 1 July 1987. The ratification of the SEA represents the onset of the third phase, in the midst of which the European Community's environmental policy is presently unfolding.[5]

I have attempted to describe and label each of the three phases in a distinct manner. According to this typology, the first one, from 1956 to 1972 is best understood as a time of pragmatic measures as opposed to proper policy. The overriding objective of the European Community during that time was to harmonise laws in order to abolish trade impediments between the member states. The pieces of environmental legislation that were adopted throughout those years were, as one observer has described them, 'incidental' to the overriding economic objectives (McGrory, 1990: 304).

After 1972 one begins to witness the emergence of an EC environmental policy. Specific actions and measures were initiated in a response to a number of circumstances and events. First, mounting public protest against environmental destruction exerted a considerable degree of pressure upon elected government officials. This pressure, in turn, seems to have had a positive effect on the dynamics and innovation of official EC policy. Secondly, during the 1970s and the early 1980s the world was witness to a number of environmental disasters which provided a dramatic backdrop to the emerging environmental sensitivity. Last but by no means least, member states became concerned about uncoordinated local environmental protection measures causing intra-community trade distortions.

With the third phase, which essentially coincides with the SEA, EC environmental policy becomes more substantive. The Title VII amendment to the original Treaty of Rome introduced important new ideas and methods of environmental policy. Within this context, it is important to keep a proper perspective and avoid a sense of 'euphoria'. The new provisions of the Single European Act are, although potentially far-reaching, rather abstract. Dirk Vandermeersch (1987: 407) describes them as giving a 'constitutional' base to the Community's environmental policy, and as defining its objectives. Nigel Haigh and David Baldock (1989: 20) take this line of thought one step further arguing that, depending on how one views the relevant articles of Title VII, they may 'do no more than legitimise what was happening anyway'. Yet, at the end, their final judgement is a positive one. They conclude that the new provisions contain interesting elements and result in subtle consequences. Ernst von Weizsäcker (1989: 49) arrives at a similar, though slightly more optimistic, conclusion. According to him, it will be up to us Europeans to convert the formal provisions into legal and economic reality.

This brings me to the concept of an international regime, to which I referred in the title of this contribution. Throughout the past decade, a significant amount of international relations and political science literature has been concerned with the concept of international regimes. As a result, a whole range of different definitions and approaches has emerged. Arguably, the most promising path is the one that perceives an international regime as a form of international institution or 'persistent and connected set of rules (formal and informal) that prescribe behavioural roles, constrain activity, and shape expectations' (Keohane, 1989: 3). Within this tradition, Robert Keohane defines international regimes as institutions with explicit rules, agreed upon by governments, that pertain to particular sets of issues in international relations'. Similarly, Oran Young (1992: 165) defines international regimes as 'institutional arrangements that deal with specific issue-areas'.

Another recent and related definition stems from Otto Keck (1991: 637) who views an international regime as an institutional arrangement for the collective management of problematic interdependencies of action, meaning problems that simultaneously touch upon the interests of several states and that cannot, or only inadequately, be resolved by individual states without resorting to coordination or co-operation with other states.[6] Applying this kind of concept of an international regime to the ECs environmental policy allows us to embark upon a dynamic analysis. Regimes do not just come into existence; they develop over time. The same applies to the EC's environmental policy. This development takes place via a process of increasing institutionalisation, which is the gradual recognition of participants that their behaviour reflects, to a considerable extent, the established rules, norms and conventions and that its meaning is interpreted in light of this recognition (Keohane, 1989: 1).

Throughout the following discussion of the evolution of the environmental policy of the European Community I shall pause at the end of each of the three phases mentioned above in order to assess to what extent this process of institutionalisation can be said to have taken place. In the conclusion I shall briefly address the question of the benefits of using a regime or institutional framework in an analysis of the European Community's environmental policy.

## 1957–1972: 'INCIDENTAL' MEASURES

When the Treaty of Rome, establishing the European Economic Communities (EEC), was signed on 25 March 1957, it did not include any explicit reference to the idea of environmental policy or environmental protection. The primary aim of the six founding Member States was to establish a 'common market' in which goods, people, services and capital could move without obstacles (Article 3). There are two articles in the original treaty that can be regarded as a direct indicator that, as Rolf Wägenbaur (1990: 16) has pointed out, 'the ambitions of the founding fathers went far beyond' the objective of the common market. First, Article 2 of the Treaty of Rome calls for the promotion throughout the Community of 'a harmonious development of economic activities, a continuous and balanced expansion, an increase in stability, an accelerated raising of the standard of living and closer relations between the states belonging to it'. The Community institutions tend to interpret this mandate to include not only an improved standard of living but also an improved quality of life (Rehbinder and Steward, 1985: 21). Although this interpretation, which suggests that environmental protection might be among the Community's objectives, it not uncontroversial, the general view of the literature seems to be that it is 'reasonable to interpret the Preamble and Article 2 of the EEC Treaty as including economic concepts of environmental pollution, such as those of external cost and of the environment as a common good' (Rehbinder and Steward, 1985: 21).

Secondly, Article 36 refers, at least implicitly, to the protection of the environment. It states that it is justifiable to restrict imports, exports or goods in transit on grounds of 'public morality, public policy or public security; the protection of health and life of humans, animals or plants; the protection of national treasures possessing artistic, historic or archaeological value'. In both cases, therefore, there exists a certain obligation to safeguard the environment. However, given the very general phrasing of Article 2 and the negative provision of Article 36, allowing for trade restrictions for reasons of public health and the protection of humans, animals and plants only as a derogation from the supreme principle of freedom of exchange, it is obvious that it was the 'common market' and the four 'freedoms' that constituted the core of the treaty's objectives (Wägenbaur, 1990: 16). Within this context it is worth noting that the European Court of Justice made an attempt to define the substance of the common market, stating that it involves 'the elimination of all obstacles to intra-Community trade in order to merge the national markets into a single market bringing about conditions as close as possible to those of a genuine internal market'.[7] Again, there is some room to perceive environmental protection as being related to the objective of such a common market but only insofar as it touches upon intra-Community trade obstacles, particularly non-tariff barriers.

During those early years, EC environmental legislation was therefore subject to a twofold restriction. First, there were no explicit, formal legal provisions to support any Community-wide action and, secondly, whatever action could be taken under the available general provisions had to be directly related to the objective of economic and community harmonisation (McGrory, 1990: 304). This meant that the pace of environmental protection was essentially set by strongly environmentally-oriented member states as opposed to anyone on the Community level.

As a result of the uncertainty about the jurisdictional basis for Community environmental protection measures, the Community institutions have, at least until the Single European Act, based their environmental policy primarily on Article 100 and, to a lesser extent, on Article 235 of the Treaty of Rome. Article 100 authorises the Council, provided it acts unanimously, to 'issue directives for the approximation of such provisions laid down by law, regulation or administrative action in Member States as directly affect the establishment for functioning of the common market'. Article 235 is also based on unanimous decision. It accords the Council the authority to take 'appropriate measures' to 'attain, in the course of the operation of the common market, one of the objectives of the Community' where the 'Treaty has not provided the necessary powers' to do so. Obviously the 'justification for using these two articles as the foundation of a common environmental policy depends ultimately on basic Community goals' (Rehbinder and Steward, 1985: 20). According to Article 3 of the EEC Treaty, 'approximation of the laws of the member states' is to 'promote the proper functioning of the Common Market and the Community's objectives set out in Article 2' (Rehbinder and Steward, 1985: 20). As a result, the use of Article 100 and Article 235 was essentially dependent on a generous reading of Article 2.[8] To sum up, while politically it was possible to use Article 100 and Article 235 for environmental objectives, these provisions were, as Rehbinder has pointed out, originally 'designed to give Community institutions powers to ensure the establishment and functioning of the Common Market as an economic institution and were not aimed at environmental protection as such' (Rehbinder and Steward, 1985: 16).

Despite the absence of a coherent framework, the Council passed several concrete pieces of environmental legislation prior to the First Action Programme on the Environment. Between 1964 and 1975 a number of initiatives were adopted under Articles 30, 92, 93 and 95 of the EC Treaty to prevent excessive subsidisation of the regeneration or incineration of used oil (Rehbinder and Steward, 1985: 16). In 1967 a directive was used for the first time to deal with environmental matters, establishing a uniform system of classification, labelling and packaging of dangerous substances.[9] The jurisdictional basis for Directive 67/548 was Article 100 of the Treaty of Rome. In March 1969 this directive was modified, again on the basis of Article 100.[10] In 1970, Directives 70/157, regulating permissible sound level and exhaust systems of motor vehicles, and 70/220, limiting vehicle emissions, were again passed with reference to Article 100 of the EEC Treaty, while Regulation 729/70 with respect to countryside protection in agriculturally less favoured areas was based on Articles 43 and 209. In 1971, the only 'environmental' directive that was passed extended the deadline for the implementation of the 1967 directive on dangerous substances. In the last year of the first phase, the Council passed three directives that can be considered to have an environmental impact, two of which were related to agricultural issues and therefore took their jurisdictional basis from Articles 42 and 43 of the EEC Treaty. Directive 72/306, regulating vehicle emissions caused by diesel engines, once again referred to Article 100.

While environmental measures were not altogether absent during the first fifteen years of the European Community's history, they cannot be regarded as adding up to any sort of proper and coherent policy. Only nine directives and one regulation were adopted during that time and, on the whole, these measures were incidental to the overriding economic objective (McGrory, 1990: 304). This is reaffirmed by the fact that all 'environmental' directives, with the exception of the ones pertaining to agriculture, were adopted on the basis of Article 100 and thus perceived as approximation measures with respect to the 'establishment or functioning of the common market'.

During this first phase, it is inappropriate to speak of an institutionalisation process in terms of environmental protection. A limited number of pieces of legislation were passed but these were not based on an established set of rules pertaining to the protection of the environment. In fact, the issue-area of the environment did not yet exist *per se*. It was therefore impossible for the participants to perceive their behaviour as a reflection of a set of rules within this issue area.

## 1972–86: THE 'RESPONSIVE' PERIOD

The Paris Summit Conference on 19 and 20 October 1972 marks the onset of the second phase in the evolution of Community environmental policy. In Versailles, the heads of state or government of the six founding member states and of the new members (United Kingdom, Denmark and Ireland) called upon the institutions of the Community to provide them with a blueprint for an official EC environmental policy by 31 July 1973. Accordingly, the Commission forwarded a 'Programme of environmental action of the European Communities' to the Council on 17 April 1973. Pursuant to this Commission initiative, the First Community Action Programme on the Environment was formally approved by the Council and the representatives of the member states on 22 November 1973.[11] The programme must be regarded as a landmark in the evolution of Community environmental efforts. It marked the beginning of an actual policy in that it set the objectives, stated the principles, selected the priorities and described the measures to be taken in different sectors of the environment for the next two years. As Eckhard Rehbinder (Rehbinder and Steward, 1985: 17–18) states, it 'opened up a field for Community action not originally provided for in the treaties' and, according to the Commission, 'added a new dimension to the construction of Europe'.[12]

The objective of Community environmental policy, as expressed in the First Action Programme, was 'to improve the setting and quality of life, and the surroundings and living conditions of the Community population'.[13] In order to achieve this objective, the Council adopted 11 principles, determining the main features of the policy. Three of these principles deserve particular mention here. First, the emphasis was laid on preventive action. Secondly, it was asserted that 'the expense of preventing and eliminating pollution should, in principle be borne by the polluter'.[14] Finally, the programme stipulated that 'for each different type of pollution, it is necessary to establish the level of action' befitting the type of pollution and the geographical zone to be protected.[15] With respect to the Commission this meant that it had the authority to act 'whenever lack of action would thwart the efforts of more localised authorities and whenever real effectiveness is attainable by action at Community level'.[16] Overall, the First Action Programme called for measured in three different categories: the reduction of pollution and nuisances as such; the improvement of the environment and the setting of life as well as the joint action in international organisations dealing with the environment. The second category of measures essentially fell under common policies, such as the common agricultural policies (CAP), social policy, regional policy, and the information programme.[17]

The first Action Programme was followed in 1976 by a second, more encompassing programme covering the period from 1977 to 1981. It was approved by the Council on 9 December 1976 and formally adopted on 17 May 1977.[18] With the transition from the first to the Second Action Programme coincided the publication of the first report by the Commission on the state of the environment in the Community, as provided for in the 1973 programme, reviewing all the environmental measures taken up to the end of 1976.[19] The aim of the Second Action Programme was to continue and expand the actions taken within the framework of the previous one. Special emphasis was laid on reinforcing the preventive nature of Community policy. Furthermore, the programme paid special attention to the non-damaging use and rational management of space, the environment and natural resources. With respect to the actual reduction of pollution, the programme accorded special priority to measures against water pollution. Prior to the adoption of the third environmental programme in 1983, the second programme was extended by one and a half years. Due to the problems of institutional transition caused by the accession of Greece and the upgrading of the Environment and Consumer Protection Service to a Directorate-General for Environment, Consumer Protection and Nuclear Safety, the extra time was needed to make the necessary adjustments (Rehbinder and Steward, 1985: 18).

The continuity of Community environmental policy was assured on 7 February 1983 when the Council adopted a resolution on a Third Community Action Programme covering the years 1982 to 1986.[20] While the third programme certainly remained within the general framework of the policy as outlined in the previous two, it introduced a number of new elements. Most importantly, it stated that, while originally 'the central concern was that, as a result of very divergent national policies, disparities would arise capable of affecting the proper functioning of the common market',[21] the common environmental policy is now motivated equally by the observation that the resources of the environment are the basis of—but also constitute the limit to—further economic and social development and the improvement of living conditions. It therefore advocated 'the implementation of an overall strategy which would permit the incorporation of environmental considerations in certain other Community policies such as those for agriculture, energy, industry and transport.[22] According to the resolution, the EC environmental policy could, in fact, no longer be dissociated from measures designed to achieve the fundamental objectives of the Community.

This acceptance of environmental policy as a component of the Community's economic objectives was fundamental in that it was the first attempt to do away with the clear subordination of environmental concerns vis-à-vis the overriding economic goal of the common market. Admittedly, the wording of the resolution was carefully chosen. Yet, with the Third Action Programme, environmental policy had clearly gained in terms of its political status. Besides the integration of an environmental dimension into other policies, the programme again reinforced the preventive character of Community policy, specifically referring to the environmental impact assessment procedure. It also established a list of actual priorities, ranging from atmosphere pollution (Directive 89/779/EEC), fresh-water and marine pollution (Directive 76/464/EEC: Directive 78/176/EEC), dangerous chemical substances (Directive 79/831/EEC; Directive 67/548/EEC), waste management (Directive 78/319/EEC) to the protection of sensitive areas within the Community and the co-operation with developing countries on environmental matters. Finally, the programme also included a commitment by the Commission to use certain considerations as a basis for drawing up their proposals such as, for instance, the obligation to evaluate, as much as possible, the costs and benefits of the action envisaged.[23]

Not surprisingly, these novelties resulted in a significant increase in terms of environmental legislation. Between February 1983 and the adoption of the SEA in December 1985, over 40 directives, eight decisions and ten regulations that all had at least some regard to the environment were adopted by the Council.

1986 was the designated final year of the Third Action Programme. The negotiations about a follow-up fourth programme were well under way by 1985, at which time it had become clear that the EEC Treaty would be supplemented by the SEA by way of which a separate chapter on the environment would be introduced in the Treaty. Although the Fourth Action Programme was not formally adopted until October 1987,[24] a new phase in the evolution of Community environmental policy was about to begin by the end of 1985, the legal basis of which would be provided by the Single European Act.

The preceding paragraphs have outlined how the Community's environmental policy evolved quite significantly during the second phase; both in terms of the underlying political attitude towards environmental protection as well as the actual number of adopted pieces of legislation. It must be remembered, however, that the actual legal basis for the policy remained relatively weak. In other words, even by the mid-1980s the Community lacked the formal competences to deal with many environmental problems. Two writers have evoked the image of a 'grey zone' of Community competences in this respect (Teitgen and Mégret, 1981: 69). Rehbinder and Steward (1985: 19) have gone even further by stating that the 'Community's expansion into this policy area is a considerable extension of Community law and policy at the expense of member states without any express authorisation'. To put it differently, until the SEA, the evolution of Community environmental policy took place in the absence of an evolution of its formal legal basis. Articles 2, 36, 100 and 235 of the Treaty of Rome were discussed within the context of the first phase. Of these, Article 100 and Article 235 continued to serve as the principal legal instruments to forward EC environmental policy. There are other specific provisions in the Treaty of Rome which can be regarded as a source of Community competence with respect to environmental policy. Article 43(2) has been used in connection with the common agricultural policy while Article 75(1)(c) and Article 84(2) had some relevance to the common transport policy. Their relevance, however, is marginal, since their scope is too limited to have any significant impact on the general evolution of Community environmental policy.

All said, the second epoch of the EC environmental policy portrays a peculiar image. On the one hand, the jurisdictional basis, being limited from the outset, did not evolve until the adoption of the SEA. On the other hand, the development towards a common environmental policy framework was, though arguably far from satisfactory, remarkable. Within the context of this dichotomy, I shall, in the following paragraphs, make an attempt to shed some light upon the driving forces behind Community environmental policy during these years.

With the unequivocal establishment of economic growth as the goal for post-war Europe, there was simply no room for environmental concerns at the time of the foundation of the European Economic Communities. This situation was accentuated by the fact that, at the time, the majority of the public and certainly most politicians probably did not perceive the need for particular efforts in the domain of the environment. The general degree of environmental degradation had not yet reached today's dimensions and even where that was not necessarily true, relatively little reliable scientific information was available. Within this context, it is interesting to note that even progressive politicians such as, for example, Lester Pearson had little doubt as to the political supremacy of economic growth.[25]

By the early 1970s, this premise was no longer uncontested. In many parts of the developed world, environmental concerns started to surface on political agendas. In the United States, the Environmental Protection Agency was founded in 1970, accompanied by the Clean Air Act and the subsequent Clean Water Act of 1972. American public opinion was mobilised through organisations such as Friends of the Earth and the Conservation Foundation which later merged with the WWF USA. During the late 1960s Europe witnessed the emergence to prominence of environmentalists such as Bernhard Grzimek in Germany and Jacques Cousteau in France. They made effective use of the mass media to sensitise the public to their causes. Greenpeace International also started to make an important impact with its much publicised and often spectacular missions on behalf of the environment. In the Federal Republic, Willy Brandt put environmental protection on his 1969 election platform. As Chancellor, he then set a precedent by granting environmental protection a high political priority. In fact, in October 1971, his government launched an official environmental programme (Hartkopf and Bohme, 1983: 84–118; Bechmann, 1984: 55–65; Müller, 1986: 51–96). At least formally, France went even further, becoming the first European country to establish its own environmental ministry. Finally, in the summer of 1972, the United Nations convened the Stockholm Conference on the Human Environment with the extensive acid rain damage to a large number of Swedish lakes as a dramatic backdrop. Under the leadership of Maurice Strong the conference succeeded, despite diplomatic isolation of the West, in establishing a United Nations Environmental Programme (UNEP).

Within the context of this newly emerging international sensitivity towards environmental protection, France seized the opportunity of her EC presidency to bring about the decision to establish the first Environmental Action Programme on the Environment at the 1972 Paris Summit in Versailles. Juliet Lodge has pointed out that the Member States' interest in an EC environmental policy was spurred not so much by upsurge of post-industrial values and the Nine's[26] endeavours to create a 'Human Union' or to give the EC a 'human face' as by the realisation that widely differing national rules on industrial pollution could distort competition: 'dirty states' could profit economically by being slack (Lodge, 1989: 320).

It is clearly in light of the fear of trade distortions that the Federal Republic of Germany and the Netherlands were among the strongest supporters of a concerted Community environmental policy. Their actual and foreseen national environmental standards were relatively strict, causing some concern about the resulting economic burdens. The German and Dutch industrial lobbies therefore argued for equal economic cost of environmental protection throughout the EC via the adoption of their standards on a Community-wide basis.

To sum up, the impetus for the First Action Programme was essentially threefold. First and, as we have seen, most importantly, there prevailed an increasing concern among the Member States about the relationship of environmental protection and trade distortions. Secondly, governments felt the need to initiate a coherent response to the increasing political pressure from environmentalists both on the national as well as on the international level. Finally, considering the inherently transnational characteristics of much of Europe's pollution, it was recognised that, in order to be effective, concerted supranational efforts were needed which could be based on the existing political structures of the European Community (McCarthy, 1989: 3).

In the years following the 1972 'turning point', there is another factor that affected the further course of Community environmental policy. Environmental disasters demonstrated the urgent need for further strengthening of the existing principles of environmental protection. Flixborough in 1974 and Seveso in 1976 were perhaps the most dramatic representations of the 'daily environmental abuse by petro-chemical and other industries, urban programmes and "high-tech" agricultural methods' that grew exponentially during the 1970s and 1980s (Lodge, 1989: 319). The oil shocks of the 1970s resulted in a temporary deceleration of environmental policy.[27] At the latest by the late 1970s, however, environmental protection had once again become an important item on Europe's political agenda. Several European countries experienced fierce debates about the expansion of civil nuclear capacities and by 1982, with the disclosure of the widespread forest destruction in Germany, environmental policy had become a matter of first priority, a status that even surpassed the one it enjoyed in the early 1970s (Weizsäcker, 1989: 27).[28]

Not surprisingly, the 1983 Stuttgart European Council reacted to these developments. Reviewing the state of Community environmental policy, it concluded that there is an 'urgent need to speed up and reinforce action', drawing special attention to the destruction of the forests (Johnson and Corcelle, 1989: 3). With the 1985 Brussels session of the European Council, the status of environmental protection policy was once again upgraded in so far as it was now perceived as a fundamental part of economic, industrial, agricultural and social policies within the Community (Johnson and Corcelle, 1989: 3). What this meant is that, by the mid-1980s, the view had emerged that environmental protection was an 'economic and not simply a moral imperative' (Lodge, 1989: 321). This final step in the evolution of Community policy during the second phase must be understood as a result of the increasing realisation of the link between economic growth stimulated by further integration and the resulting costs in terms of adverse environmental encumbrances (Haigh and Baldock, 1989: 45). The ensuing integrated approach towards environmental protection leads directly to the last of the three phases that were outlined at the outset.

The second phase of Community environmental policy can be summarised as an active one that undoubtedly furthered environmental protection in the European Community. At the same time, however, it was characterised by a considerable degree of uncertainty. It lacked the truly integrated approach based on a sound legal basis that emerged in the third phase with the Fourth Action Programme and the SEA. The policy until 1985 was a 'responsive' one in that it evolved according to the momentary economic, political and social circumstances. Its initial and probably most important impetus was, as described above, the general concern of environmental protection as a potential cause for trade distortions. Public pressure and the direct effects of environmental accidents later accelerated the process. Finally, there was the realisation that economic progress and the protection of the environment are so closely interlinked that one cannot be considered without the other. The nature of the policy evolved at each stage depending on the given set of circumstances. Generally speaking, the circumstances as they presented themselves during the second phase favoured a progressive evolution of the policy although, in the case of the 1973 oil shock, they temporarily worked in the opposite direction.

This type of policy had certain advantages. As a whole it remained flexible, not having to rely on rigid principles that quickly become outdated. In other words, it was possible to readjust quickly the policy to a newly arisen situation or set of circumstances. The disadvantage rested in the fact that under these conditions, environmental protection would always be relegated to a subordinate position in relation to Community economic aims. Whether this disadvantage has successfully been eliminated without undermining some of the positive aspects of the second phase will be discussed in the following section. Before that, however, I shall briefly review the most important pieces of legislation of the second phase. Given the significant number of environmental directives, regulations and decisions between the First Action Programme and the Single European Act, it would, of course, exceed the limits of this study to review them all. I have therefore chosen a small representative selection.

Ernst von Weizsäcker (1989: 42) had identified just over 20 directives as being the most important pieces of Community environmental legislation between 1973 and 1985. For the sake of simplicity I shall base my review on this selection.[29] The relevant directives can conveniently be grouped together in six different categories according to the environmental problem they are addressing:

(1) Water
(2) Air
(3) Noise
(4) Waste
(5) Emissions
(6) Lead in petrol.

In addition there are a number of other directives that do not readily fit into any of these categories: the 'Seveso' directive, a directive on chemicals, one on birds and their habitat and one on sewage sludge. Weizsäcker's selection of directives is useful in that it more or less represents the full spectrum of EC environmental activities.

In the fight against water pollution, there are four directives, all of which are based both on Article 100 and Article 235 of the EEC Treaty. Directives 74/440 and 80/778 are concerned with drinking water while directive 76/160 regulates bathing water.[30] Directive 76/464 deals with dangerous substances in water.[31] The air quality efforts are represented by three directives: 80/779 on smoke and sulphur dioxide, 82/884 on lead and 85/203 on nitrogen dioxide.[32] Again the legal basis for all three directives rests in Article 100 and Article 235 of the Treaty of Rome. The same applies to the three directives on waste: 75/442 outlines a general waste framework while 78/319 and 84/631 deal with toxic waste and transfrontier shipment of waste respectively.[33] In terms of emission standards, Directive 83/351 on vehicle emission only refers to Article 100, whereas Directive 84/360 on emission from industrial plants is again based on Article 100 and Article 235.[34] The two directives on the approximation of laws of Member States concerning lead content in petrol (85/210 and 78/611) are solely based on Article 100 of the Treaty of Rome.[35] The same is true of Directive 79/831, amending for the sixth time directive 67/548 on the approximation of the laws, regulations and administrative provisions relating to the classification, packaging and labelling of dangerous substances, as well as Directive 79/117 on use restrictions and labelling of pesticides.[36]

Directive 79/409 on birds and their habitat, on the other hand is exclusively based on Article 235. This is, of course, to be expected, since animal protection has hardly any direct effect on the 'establishment or functioning of the common market' as expressed in Article 100 of the Treaty of Rome.[37] Finally, there are two more directives that need to be mentioned here, both of which were adopted under Articles 100 and 235. Directive 82/501 on the major accident hazards of certain industrial activities was a Community response to the dioxine disaster in Seveso, and Directive 85/337 on the assessment of the effects of certain public and private projects on the environment set out an important new priority of Community environmental policy.[38]

This selective review of EC environmental 'legislation' between 1973 and 1985 reemphasizes a point made earlier. Although the Community institutions were engaged in a considerable amount of environmental activity, the available legal foundations remained limited. There was no explicit jurisdictional mandate for the protection of the environment; the Community therefore proceeded with its environmental efforts on the basis of what Ernst Weizsäcker has called a 'Kunstgriff', or knack, using Articles 100 and 235 of the original EEC Treaty. This is, of course, the most fundamental difference with respect to the final phase of Community environmental policy as it has been unfolding since the adoption of the SEA.

During this second phase, the institutionalisation process mentioned at the outset is becoming discernible. Member states begin to understand that certain collective actions are necessary in order to address a more or less specific set of problems in the newly defined issue-area of the environment. As I have pointed out, however, the environment does not stand on its own feet yet. It is still at least partly subordinated to the paramount objective of economic growth. Furthermore, although explicit rules exist in form of the various directives passed, their ability to prescribe behavioural roles, constrain activity and shape expectations is limited because of the absence of an unambiguous legal foundation. Despite an ongoing gradual process of institutionalisation, no proper EC environmental regime can therefore be in place. Though explicit and agreed upon by the member states' governments, the rules in fact remain weak and exert little independent compliance pull.

## 1985–'92': THE 'INITIATIVE' PHASE

An analysis of EC environmental policy after 1985 is rendered more complicated by the fact that, although there exists an element of continuity, it would be too simplistic to regard it as a mere continuation of previous policy developments. In terms of its general approach, the Fourth Action Programme is certainly related to the previous one, despite the fact that it was differently structured and that it initiated a number of new policy directions such as environmental educational efforts and a focus on gene-technology. It essentially completed and formalised the notions of earlier Community policy. In fact, EC policy, as laid down in the programme, is virtually all-encompassing. It demands integration of social, industrial, agricultural and economic policies, an objective that, as mentioned earlier, began to emerge with the Third Action Programme in 1983. Besides this factor of continuity, however, post-1985 EC environmental policy is shaped by a second strand of influence which manifests itself in the SEA amendment to the Treaty of Rome. Interestingly enough, the forces behind the emergence of the SEA have little to do with the environment. As Rolf Wägenbaur (1990: 17) has stated, the impetus stemming from the original EEC Treaty gradually weakened in the 1980s and 'it was felt that a new initiative was necessary. The so-called Single European Act came to the rescue'. The initiative was also related to the enlargement of the Community from the original six Member States to the present 12 (UK, Ireland, Denmark: 1973; Greece: 1981; Spain and Portugal: 1986). In light of the extended membership, the original treaty was clearly in need of revision. There were intensive discussions as to what sort of reform the treaty should undergo: a social charter, an environmental chapter, research and development programmes, a regional policy, the strengthening of the European Parliament, majority voting in the Council: all these issues were brought onto the agenda. The most important outcome of these negotiations, however, was the decision to go ahead with the completion of the internal market.

The commitment to achieve this goal within a specific time limit was laid down in Article 8a of the Treaty. This states that the Community 'shall adopt measures with the aim of progressively establishing the internal market over a period expiring on 31 December 1992'. The internal market is defined as 'an area without internal frontiers in which the free movement of goods, persons, services and capital is ensured'. In Lord Cockfield's White Paper, the Commission presented a plan as to what it perceived to be the specific measures that needed to be adopted in order to complete the internal market (*COM 85/310*).[39] This relatively sudden acceleration in the process of European integration put an end to perceptions of 'eurosclerosis' and caused great optimism as to the economic effects of the Single European Market.[40] The Cecchini Report on 'the economics of 1992' estimated that the internal market would result in an economic gain of 4.5–7 per cent of the Community's GNP. Such an increase in economic activities would affect the state of the environment. In the absence of any changes in policies or technologies, the environment could clearly be expected to deteriorate. It is within this context that, in 1989, a Commission Task Force published a report on 'The Environment and the Internal Market' in which it stated that the creation of a single market, as well as the need to decouple economic growth from environmental degradation requires a fundamental review of existing environmental policy at EC level and in the Member States' (Wägenbaur, 1990: 18). By including Title VII on 'Environment' in the new EEC Treaty, the authors of the SEA provided the formal legal foundation on the basis of which such a fundamental review could take place.

Figure 1 shows the two strands that define the post-1985 EC environmental policy. As mentioned earlier, it is the formal legal foundation as expressed in the SEA that distinguishes Community policy after 1985 from the earlier one. The chart indicates that the dynamics of the first and second phase are still operating (b). However, it is strand (a) that is the primary determinant of the third phase of Community environmental policy.

Obviously, the distinction between the two strands is somewhat schematic and therefore not entirely correct. The connecting line between the two strands suggests that the SEA amendment is also a result of Community environmental policy as it had been developing since 1972, culminating in the Fourth Action Programme in 1987. Nigel Haigh and David Baldock (1989: 20) make this point, arguing that the lack of a clear legal base for the EC's environmental policy had been much criticised. Within this context they see the 'Environment' title as a 'response to this criticism'. Nevertheless, the distinction is analytically useful if one works with the hypothesis that the adoption of the SEA had a significant effect on the nature of EC environmental policy. The following pages attempt to shed some light upon the question of whether or not this hypothesis is valid.

The SEA affects Community environmental policy in three different ways: first, through the general institutional changes—majority voting and the co-operation procedure; secondly, through the objective of completing the internal market; and thirdly through the new legal provisions that actually define Community environmental policy (Haigh and Baldock, 1989: 12).

## INSTITUTIONAL CHANGES

The first of the two institutional changes instigated by the SEA is the 'co-operation procedure' with its second reading by Parliament as expressed in Article 149 of the

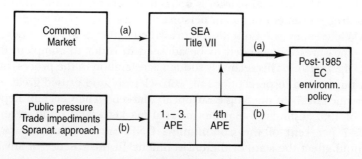

Figure 1.

EEC Treaty. In response to criticism of lack of openness of the EC legislation process and charges of a 'democratic deficit', the 'cooperation procedure is designed to allow the European Parliament to play an effective but qualified role in the legislative process' (Lodge, 1989: 69).[41] In terms of environmental protection, there is some significance to Article 149 in that it effectively allows public opinion, represented by the Parliament, to have more of an impact on the process of environmental policy formation. Considering that environmental consciousness has undoubtedly been heightened throughout the Community in the past few years, this source of public influence could prove to become quite relevant.[42]

The cooperation procedure is limited in that it only applies when a vote is taken in Council by qualified majority. Qualified majority voting, as laid down in Article 148 of the EEC Treaty, is not a new phenomenon; it was already contained in the original treaty. What is new, however, is that under Article 100A, it is now possible to use it for environmental purposes (Haigh and Baldock, 1989: 14). This stands in contrast to Article 100 and Article 235 on which most pre-1985 pieces of environmental legislation were based, as well as to the new Article 130s which I will discuss below. In all three cases, unanimity is a requirement for any action. As Nigel Haigh and David Baldock (1989: 15) point out, one of the problems with majority voting in the context of the environment is the uncertainty that prevails about how 'a choice is made for environmental measures between Article 130s (unanimity) and Article 100a (majority voting)'. Although Article 100a is, in principal, reserved for traded products, it is difficult to categorise all cases along these lines. Not surprisingly, the Commission and the Council do not see eye to eye on this question. The Commission's view is that Article 100a is the proper legal base whenever the specified conditions are fulfilled. According to this view, Article 130s 'only comes into consideration when the conditions of Article 100a are not fulfilled or when, for instance, the impact of the product on competition is very small as compared with the impact on the environment as such' (Wägenbaur, 1990: 21).

The European Court of Justice had been expected for some time to clarify the legal confusion arising out of the tension between these two articles. With the June 1991 ruling in the titanium dioxide[43] case 300/89, it has finally done so. The Court clearly gives preference to Article 100a, thus supporting majority voting. This could well set the path for future EC environmental legislation. In anticipation of the actual effect of the Court's position, Nigel Haigh's conclusion can be accepted that, while majority voting may not have revolutionized environmental policy, it has made it more difficult for one or two countries to block certain proposals as Denmark had to experience when it failed to prevent the adoption of Directive 88/76 on emission from large cars (Haigh and Baldock, 1989: 15).

## Completion of the 'internal market'

In order to achieve the objective of completing the internal market by 31 December 1992 (Article 8a), the SEA has introduced Articles 100a and 100b concerning the harmonisation of national laws, including environmental laws. Article 100a(3) states that the Commission essentially takes as a base a 'high level of protection' in its harmonisation efforts. Article 100a(4) allows member states to apply more stringent national environmental standards provided they are 'not a means of arbitrary discrimination or a disguised restriction on trade between member states'. There is also a safeguard clause (Article 100a(5)) that allows member states to opt out of harmonisation efforts in appropriate cases as provided for in Article 36. Article 100b requires the Community to draw up an inventory of national measures 'which fall under 100a and which have not been harmonized pursuant to that Article'. By majority voting, the Council then is to decide which of these can 'be recognised as being equivalent'. All others presumably have to be harmonised at that point (Haigh and Baldock, 1989: 18). These harmonisation measures designed to complete the internal market have an impact on environmental policy to the extent that most environmental protection standards that affect the functioning of the internal market will be set at EC level. Whether or not the EC will seek to harmonise standards for emission (to air or water) or for environmental procedures (e.g. safety requirements at factories, disposal standards at vast sites), which 'have the potential to affect the "functioning of the common market" (Article 100) or the "establishment of the internal market" (Article 8a) remained uncertain' (Haigh and Baldock, 1989: 19).

## Environmental title

The SEA has inserted Title VII entitled 'Environment' in part III of the EEC Treaty which is concerned with the 'policies' of the European Community. This is worth noting since it suggests that with the SEA it is no longer just de facto but de jure correct to speak of an environmental policy. The relevant treaty provisions are numbered 130r to 130s. Article 130r specifies the objectives of Community environmental policy and lays down the principles and guidelines that such a policy must follow. It also deals with member state versus Community competences in terms of environmental protection and finally calls for co-operation with third countries and international organisation in matters involving the environment. Article 130s, as discussed earlier, stipulates the legislative process for the formulation of environmental laws and Article 130t allows states to introduce more stringent protective measures as long as they are compatible with the rest of the treaty.

There are a number of ways in which these new provisions have affected Community environmental policy. First, title VII has given symbolic importance to environmental protection policy, reinforced by the preamble to the SEA in which the Community commits itself to 'promote democracy on the basis of the fundamental rights recognised in the constitutions and laws of the Member States'. As Haigh and Baldock (1989: 21) have pointed out, 'more than a third of the member states have accorded constitutional status to the protection of the environment or recognise environmental rights'. Secondly, the Community environmental policy objectives outlined in Article 130r(1) are sufficiently broad—to preserve, protect and improve the quality of the environment; to contribute towards protecting human health; to ensure a prudent and rational utilisation of national resources—to bring almost any environmental issue within the competence of Community legislation. Thirdly, Article 130r(2) gives legal force to the principle which, as discussed earlier, gradually evolved in the 'Action Programmes on the Environment': principle of prevention, rectification at source and polluter pays. In addition, Article 130r(2) formalises the new principle that environmental 'protection requirements shall be a component of the Community's other policies'. Fourthly, Article 130r(3) states four basic factors that the Community needs to consider in its policy adoption: (a) available scientific data, (b) environmental coordination in the various regions of the Community, (c) the potential benefits and cost of action or lack of action and (d) the economic and social development of the Community as a whole and the balanced development of its region. Fifthly, Article 130r(4) lays down the principle of subsidiarity which determines whether appropriate action is to be taken at the Community or at the member states level. The article states: 'The Community shall take action relating to the environment to the extent to which the objectives referred to in paragraph I can be attained better at Community level than at the level of the individual Member States', thus expressly reserving residual jurisdiction to the Member States (Vandermeersch, 1987: 422).

Before addressing the question of whether or not these effects are negative or positive in terms of actual environmental protection, I shall, once again, turn to a brief review of environmental legislative measures of the third phase. As was the case for the second phase, this review is highly selective. I have, however, tried to make the selection as representative as possible of the totality of measures adopted. The survey begins with the entry into force of the SEA on 1 July 1987 and ends in August 1990.

Of the nine directives and two regulations that I have selected to review, there is not a single one that is based on Article 100 and/or Article 235. Regulation 3143/87, amending Regulation 3626/82 on the implementation in the Community of the convention on international trade in endangered species of wild fauna and flora, and Directive 88/302, amending for the ninth time Directive 67/548 relating to the classification, packaging and labelling of dangerous substances, make no reference to any specific legal foundations at all. They simply have 'regard to the Treaty of the EEC'.[44] There are four directives and one regulation that take Article 130s as their legal basis: Directive 87/416 amending Directive 85/210 on approximation of the laws of the member states concerning lead content of petrol;[45] Directive 88/347, an amendment of Directive 86/280 on DDT, carbon tetrachloride and pentachlorophenol;[46] Regulation 3322/88 on certain chlorofluorocarbons and halons which deplete the ozone layer;[47] Directive 90/219 on the contained use of genetically modified micro-organisms[48] and Directive 90/415 on dangerous substances in water.[49] The remaining four directives—88/76 and 88/77, both on emissions from vehicles; 88/436, amending an earlier directive on vehicle emission (70/220); and 90/220 on the deliberate release into the environment of genetically modified organisms[50]—were adopted on the basis of Article 100a of the EEC Treaty which, of course, implies that they were essentially harmonisation measures agreed on by qualified majority voting and subject to the co-operation procedure.

This limited survey reveals a number of interesting points. First, it is clear that the legal basis used during the first and second phase—mainly Article 100 and Article 235—have been replaced by the new provisions provided by the SEA amendments to the Treaty of Rome. Secondly, it reaffirms the fact that, prior to the titanium dioxide case, there reigned uncertainty about which article—100a or 130s—was to serve as the legal foundation for a given piece of environmental legislation. The range of problems that qualify as having an effect on the 'establishment of the internal market' does not seem to have been rigorously established. Finally, the evidence from our review indicates that Article 100a, implying majority voting and the co-operation procedure, was not used as frequently as one might have expected. Thus, at least until late 1991, much of the Community's environmental policy continued to be contingent on a unanimous decision by the Council.

Whilst it is difficult to assess unfolding events, there are, however, a number of observations about European Community environmental policy since the Single European Act that can already be made. For this purpose it is useful to recall that I set out to examine the hypothesis that the SEA is likely to result in a dramatic change of EC environmental policy. There are a number of indications that would validate such a hypothesis. Community environmental policy has undoubtedly gained momentum since the SEA. Title VII of the EEC Treaty has important symbolic consequences. The protection of the environment is now formally of equal or even superior status to all other Community objectives. The possibility of majority voting provides a framework for adopting a much greater amount of environmental legislation. The principle of subsidiarity, as expressed in Article 130r(4), may well have significant psychological effects on member states. Using the example of the United Kingdom, Nigel Haigh and David Baldock (1989: 24) have demonstrated how, in terms of the environment, Europe, including its sub-national units, is likely to increasingly perceive itself as a whole, thus moving ever closer to the 'union among the peoples of Europe' called for in the preamble to the Treaty of Rome. From such a point of view, the SEA has indeed had dramatic effects; not only in terms of a much broader and more effective environmental policy but also in terms of accelerating the process of integration among the European people in general.

As so often in international politics, there is, however, a perspective that points in the opposite direction. It is conceivable that the new provisions on majority voting could have negative effects in that they allow some member states to overrule others which will then, in the absence of an effective European enforcement agent, be tempted to simply ignore their implementation obligations. Anxiety has also been expressed with respect to the subsidiarity principle, arguing that, from a Community perspective, it is clearly a step backwards (Vandermeersch, 1987: 422). While, prior to the SEA, 'the issue was whether or not the EC had competence to act or not, now measures can be challenged in terms of whether or not the EC or the member states could better deal with the issue' (Lodge, 1989: 323). In that sense, the SEA has widened the possibilities for challenging EC environmental action which could result in an overall weakened and less effective Community environmental policy.

These examples should suffice to demonstrate that there is indeed significant potential in the Community environmental policy as laid down in the SEA amendments to the EEC Treaty. At the same time, many of the provisions are abstract and leave much room for manoeuvring the thrust of the policy in either direction. Much will therefore depend on the political interpretation of the policy and the nature of future amendments to its jurisdictional basis.

## MAASTRICHT AND BEYOND

The signing of the Maastricht treaty represents the first step towards such an amendment. It introduced important institutional and jurisdictional changes to the foundation of the European Community's environmental policy. The traditional economic growth ethos of the community has been 'greened' considerably. According to the preamble, the European Community is now determined 'to promote economic and social progress for their peoples within the context of the accomplishment of the internal market and of reinforced cohesion and environmental protection'. Title I, Article B sets the objective 'to promote economic and social progress which is balanced and sustainable'. Article 2 of the Treaty of Rome has been amended. It no longer simply refers to a 'continuous and balanced expansion', but 'a harmonious and balanced development of economic activities, sustainable and non-inflationary growth respecting the environment'. Finally, article 3(k) stipulates that the activities of the Community shall include 'a policy in the sphere of the environment'. With Maastricht, the environment has therefore 'acquired full status as a policy falling within the Union's priority objectives'.[51]

Specifically, the environment is covered by title XVI of the new treaty, articles 130r to 130t. Again, the reference is to 'Community policy on the environment' as opposed to 'action by the Community relating to the environment' under the previous article 130R. The concept of making environmental consideration a part of the other community considerations has been strengthened by the obligation to integrate environmental policy requirements into other Community policies as opposed to merely making them components.

More importantly, qualified majority voting has been introduced for most matters of environmental policy. The exceptions are provisions that are primarily of a fiscal nature, policies with limited transnational effects such as town and county planning, some aspects of water pollution control as well as measures that affect a Member State's choice between different energy sources and the general structure of its energy supply. With that, another step has been taken to reduce the prevailing uncertainty under the SEA amendments to the Treaty of Rome between unanimity and qualified majority voting as the proper procedure for environmental legislation.

The Maastricht treaty also increased the European Parliament's say over environmental standards. In addition to the cooperation procedure, introduced by the Single European Act, it contains the new 'co-decision procedure' under Article 189b.[52] The new procedure for the adoption of an act is characterised by a Conciliation Committee which can be convened at two different stages as well as the possibility for a total of three different readings by the Council and the Parliament.

It will be some time before a reliable judgement on the new environmental provisions can be made. On the one hand, there are indications that the EC's environmental regime has been strengthened by the new treaty. Environmental policy has gained in prestige with respect to the other, particularly economic, objectives of the Community. The new voting rules and the additional power of the European Parliament have increased the policy's political potential. Indeed, one observer judges that 'the notions of sovereignty in the area of environmental policy have become increasingly irrelevant' (Wilkinson, 1991). On the other hand, the possibility of overruling recalcitrant states could once again amplify the already existing implementation problems. Also, the new procedures are so complicated that the objective of increasing legislative transparency has slipped away further than ever. Beyond that, the wording concerning the exceptions to the qualified majority voting procedure is 'sufficiently vague to allow many exceptions and endless wrangles' (Wolf, 1991).

Rather than trying to give a positive or negative verdict on the new provisions, it is perhaps more important and more relevant to emphasise once again the dynamic characteristics of the European Community's environmental policy. The Maastricht treaty has not created an unambiguously powerful Europe-wide environmental regime. Neither has it made a radical departure from the environmental objectives as set out in the SEA amendments. It has, however, moved the policy yet another step on the road towards an institutional framework which will, sooner or later, have to be taken seriously by the Member States. Clearly this road is covered with obstacles, one of which could soon prove to be the ratification processes in some of the Member States. Nevertheless, it is bound to evolve further. The Fifth Action Programme was presented by Commissioner Carlo Ripa di Meana in March 1992. There are now well over 100 new environmental proposals in the policy pipeline, covering a wide range of issues. This will entail significant costs to the business communities of the member states. At the same time, there are new opportunities opening up as a result of the new policy thrusts. There will be community funding to support companies investing in new environmental standards, not to speak of the investment opportunities in environmental protection industries. It is also important to keep in mind that the treaty itself states 1996 as the date for a new intergovernmental conference. This will almost certainly set off another reform round in the European Community. By then, the discussions will need to take into account the membership of Austria, Sweden and possibly other EFTA states. All these factors will influence the further development of the EC's environmental policy. Therefore, while it might be too early to predict the exact course the policy will take, it appears safe to conclude that it will play an increasingly important role in the future development of Europe.

But is it possible to argue that the institutionalisation process as described at the start of this study has progressed to the point where it is useful to describe the present state of the European Community's environmental policy in terms of an international regime? Let us once again look at Robert Keohane's definition of an international institution as 'persistent and connected sets of rules (formal and informal) that prescribe behavioural roles, constrain activity, and shape expectations'. The rules are clearly established. There is a large and growing body of legislation in the various areas of European environmental protection. This legislation is based on a relatively unambiguous jurisdictional basis. Formally, there is no doubt that it prescribes behavioural roles, constrains activities and shapes expectations. In fact, its tendency to shape expectations has even reached beyond the present Community member states. The central and eastern European countries which are aspiring to an eventual accession to the European Community are already involved in adjusting or, in some cases, establishing their domestic environmental legislative bodies in such a way as to make sure that they will eventually be compatible with the expectations as expressed in the Community rules. Within this context the conclusion imposes itself that the institutionalization process of the European Community's environmental policy, notwithstanding the above-mentioned weaknesses, has progressed far enough to warrant the description of an international environmental regime.

# CONCLUSIONS

As mentioned above, the question imposes itself whether there is any added value in introducing the potentially ambiguous concept of an international regime in this attempt to describe the evolution of the European Community's environmental policy up to the most recent amendments. Critical voices might, after all, point out that all it does is to bring conceptual confusion to what amounts to a relatively simple task of description.

Such criticism is inappropriate for two reasons. The first one I have already discussed. An institutional framework is useful to assess the dynamic nature of the Community's environmental policy. Through the process of institutionalisation, the participants' behaviour gradually converges around the established rules. These rules, in turn, evolve as a reflection of the participants' experiences during the process of institutionalisation. In that sense, what has been labelled the tradition of neo-liberal institutionalism provides us with the conceptual tools to understand how a number of ad hoc environmental measures can, over time, evolve into an international regime or, what Oran Young calls a 'negotiated order' (Young, 1983: 99).

The second reason why regime or institutional approaches are useful is perhaps even more significant. To study and explain the formation and the maintenance of an international institutional arrangement is important. Many students of international relations have, in recent years, been preoccupied with this problem. It is now time, however, to move on to the next stage and assess the effectiveness of international regimes. Do regimes matter? This is a fundamental question. In the long term, the emphasis on international institutions can only be justified if it is possible to demonstrate that there is a link between 'institutional arrangements on the one hand and individual and collective behaviour on the other' (Young, 1992: 160).

Very little work has been done in this area. The ideas emerging out of the institutional literature are probably the most promising ones to follow up. As Oran Young has pointed out,

> we must look at the behaviour of states not only in responding to the dictates of international institutions on their own behalf but also in implementing the provisions of regimes in such a way as to ensure that those operating under their jurisdiction (for example, corporations, non-governmental organisations, and even individuals) comply with institutional requirements as well (Young, 1992: 161–162).

This brings the concept of compliance to the forefront of future international institutional studies. To determine when and to what extent international regimes matter, systematic studies need to be undertaken that take into account both domestic and international variables. The conclusion that the European Community's environmental policy has reached the state of an international regime is therefore no cause for complacency. In many ways the task has only just begun. We are, after all, not dealing with an obscure intellectual puzzle. The issue at hand is the increasing threat to our environment. It is in our immediate interest to start examining the effectiveness of the European Community's environmental regime as one of the available institutional arrangements to address this situation. The first set of conceptual guideposts has been provided by the advocates of international institutional approaches. It certainly seems worthwhile and, for the time being, promising to try to build on them.


## ACKNOWLEDGEMENTS

The author wishes to thank Andrew Hurrell, Andrew Walter, David Wartenweiler and David Judge for their helpful comments on earlier versions of this study.


## NOTES

1. The first time '1992' was officially mentioned was in the Commission president's statement to the European Parliament on 14 January 1985. Referring to the next European Council, he said: 'now that some Heads of State and Government have decided to set an example... it may not be over-optimistic to announce a decision to eliminate all frontiers within Europe by 1992 and to implement it' (Commission of the European Communities (1985b), 'The thrust of Commission Policy', Bulletin of the European Communities, Supplement 1/85, 14 and 15 January. The idea was formally approved by the Brussels European Council on 29–30 March 1985 and adopted in December 1985 in Luxembourg. See Lodge 1989: 9.
2. The terms 'European' and 'European Community' are used interchangeably throughout this article. When referring to other parts of Europe, the proper specification will be made, i.e. 'Eastern European', 'Southern Europe', and so on.
3. Article 189, Treaty Establishing the European Economic Community as Amended by Subsequent Treaties, Rome, 25 March, 1957; subsequently referred to as Treaty of Rome.
4. See also, House of Lord's Select Committee on the European Communities Transfrontier Shipment of Hazardous Wastes, 9th Report Session 1983–1984, HMSO.
5. It remains to be seen whether the changes incorporated in the Maastricht treaty, creating a European Union will, in itself, represent a new phase of Community environmental policy or follow in the footsteps of this third phase. I will briefly comment on this question in the final section on Maastricht.
6. Citation translated by author.
7. Gaston Schul Judgement of 1982, Case 15/18, 1982 ECR 1409, p. 1431.
8. For a thorough discussion of the legal details of Article 100 and Article 235 see Rehbinder and Steward (1985: 21–8).
9. Directive 67/548 EEC of 27 June 1967 on classification, packaging and labelling of dangerous substances, JO No. 196, 16.8.1967, p. 1 (French ed.).
10. Directive 69/81 EEC of 13 March 1969 modifying the directive of 16.8.1976 on classification, packaging and labelling of dangerous substances, JO No. L68, 19.3.1969, p. 1 (French ed.)
11. OJ No. C112, 20.12.1973, p. 3. See also Seventh General Report of the EC (Brussels, 1973), point 258; Bulletin of the EC, 11–1974, point 1203, pp. 11–12.
12. 7th Report EC, 1973, point 258, p. 235.
13. See OJ No. C112, 20.12.1973, p. 5.
14. 7th Report EC, 1973, point 262.
15. OJ No. C112, p. 7.
16. 7th Report EC, 1973, point 263.
17. *Ibid.*, point 264.
18. OJ No. C139, 13.6.1977; Bulletin EC 5–1977, point 2.1.40.
19. See, 'State of the Environment: First Report', 1977.

20. Action Programme of the European Communities on the Environment (1982 to 1986) in OJ No. C46, 17.2.1983, p. 1.
21. OJ No. C46, 17.2.1983, p. 3.
22. Seventeenth General Report on the Activities of the European Communities, 1983, point 372, p. 158.
23. See OJ No. C46, p. 2.
24. In December 1986, the Council adopted a resolution on the strengthening of Community action in favour of the environment in which it welcomed 'the submission by the Commission of detailed proposals for a Fourth Environmental Action Programme and considers that such a programme provides an opportunity to strengthen decisively Community action in this area, building on the achievements of the past, and to determine a coherent framework within which specific Community actions can be formulated, coordinated and implemented over the period of 1987–1992'. It also refers to the SEA which 'will constitute a new legal basis for the Community environmental policy'. OJ No. C3, 7.1.1987, p. 3.
25. See, Pearson Report, Bericht der Kommission für Internationale Entwicklung, Wien, München, Zürich, 1969, pp. 48–51.
26. By the time of the Paris Summit, the adherence to the Community of the United Kingdom, Ireland and Denmark was already decided. Weizsäcker argues that one of the objectives of the 1972 Action Programme was to get it through and then present it to the New Member States as a 'fait accompli'.
27. For a discussion of the German example, see Müller (1986: 97–102).
28. It is worth noting that 1982 was also the year when the Greens were first elected to the German 'Bundestag'.
29. The total number environmental legislative pieces for the entire second phase amounts to 120 directives, 27 decisions and 14 regulations.
30. Directive 75/440, OJ No. L194, p. 26; Directive 80/778, OJ No. L229, 30.08.1980, p. 11; Directive 76/160, OJ No. L31, 05.02.1976, p. 1.
31. Directive 76/464, OJ No. L129, 18.05.1976, p. 23.
32. Directive 80/779, OJ No. L229, 30.08.1980; Directive 82/884, OJ No. L378, 31.12.1982; Directive 85/203, OJ No. L87, 27.03.1985, p. 1.
33. Directive 75/442, OJ No. L194, 25.07.1975, p. 39; Directive 78/319, OJ No. L84, 31.03.1978, p. 43; Directive 84/631, OJ No. L326, 13.12.1984, p. 31.
34. Directive 83/351, OJ No. L197, 20.07.1983, p. 1; Directive 84/360, OJ No. L188, 16.07.1984, p. 20.
35. Directive 85/210, OJ No. L96, 03.04.1985, p. 25; Directive 78/611, OJ No. L197, 22.07.1978, p. 19.
36. Directive 79/831, OJ No. L259, 15.10.1979, p. 10; Directive 67/548, OJ No. L196, 16.08.1967; Directive 79/117, OJ No. L33, 08.02.1979, p. 36.
37. Directive 79/409, OJ No. L103, 25.04.1979, p. 1.
38. Directive 82/501, OJ No. L230, 05.08.1982, p. 1; Directive 85/337, OJ No. L175, 05.07.1985, p. 40.
39. Commission of the EC, Completing the Internal Market: White Paper from the Commission of the European Council (the Cockfield White Paper), Luxembourg, 1985.
40. Although the phrase 'Single European Market' has come into widespread use, it is not used in the SEA. It simply combines the SEA and the internal market, at the expense of conferring the original meaning of the word 'Single' in the SEA 'which was so called because it combined in a single legal instrument two texts that had different origins, one amending the Treaty of Rome (Title II) and one dealing with co-operation in the sphere of foreign policy'. See Haigh and Baldock (1989: 10).
41. For a detailed discussion of the 'cooperation procedure' see Lodge (1989: 68–79).
42. This is illustrated by the case of Directive 88/76 on Emissions from small cars. See Haigh and Baldock, 1989: 51–54.
43. Titanium dioxide is a white pigment, generally thought to be harmless. It is used in paints, plastic and other products in order to reduce reliance on toxic substances such as lead and zinc. The problem is that its manufacture results in the discharge of acid waste

contaminated by metals. EC legislation on titanium dioxide dates back as far as the early 1970s.

44. Regulation 3143/87 OJ No. L299, 22.10.1978, p. 33; Regulation 3626/82 OJ No. L384, 31.12.1982, p. 1; Directive 88/302 OJ No. L133, 30.05.1988, p. 1.
45. Directive 87/416 OJ No. L225, 13.08.1987, p. 33; Directive 85/210 OJ No. L96, 03.04.1985, p. 25.
46. Directive 88/347 OJ No. L158, 25.06.1988, p. 35; Directive 86/280 OJ No. L181, 04.07.1986, p. 16.
47. Regulation 3322/88 OJ No. L297, 31.10.1988, p. 1.
48. Directive 90/219 OJ No. L117, 08.05.1990, p. 1.
49. Directive 90/415 OJ No. L219, 14.08.1990, p. 49.
50. Directive 88/76; Directive 88/77; Directive 88/436; Directive 70/220; Directive 90/220.
51. Bulletin of the European Community, Supplement 1/92, p. 30.
52. On British insistence, the term of 'co-decision procedure' has been dropped from the treaty. Interestingly enough, this has not deterred Jacques Delors from using it. See Bulletin of the European Community, Supplement 1/92, p. 31.


## REFERENCES

Bechmann, Arnim (1984) *Leben wollen*, Köln.
Haigh, Nigel (1990) *EEC Environmental Policy and Britain*, 2nd revised edition, Essex: Longman.
Haigh, Nigel and David Baldock (1989) *Environmental Policy and 1992*, London: British Department of the Environment.
Hartkopf, Günther and Eberhard Bohme (1983) *Umweltpolitik, Band 1: Grundlagen, Analysen und Perspektiven*, Opladen.
Johnson, Stanley P. and Corcell, Guy (1989) *The Environmental Policy of the European Communities* (International Environmental Law and Policy Series), London: Graham & Trotman.
Keck, Otto (1991) 'Der neue Institutionalismus in der Theorie der Internationalen Politik', *Politische Vierteljahresschrift*, **32**, Jahrgang, Heft 4, pp. 635–653.
Keohane, R. O. (1989) *International Institutions and State Power: Essays in International Relations Theory*, Boulder, Co: Westview Press.
Lodge, J. (1989) 'Environment: towards a clean blue-green EC', In Juliet Lodge (ed.), *The European Community and the Challenge of the Future*, London: Pinter.
McCarthy, E. (1989) *The EC and the Environment*, European Dossier Service II.
McGrory, D. P. (1990) 'Air pollution legislation in the United States and the European Community', *European Law Review*, **15**(4), August.
Müller, E. (1986) *Innenwelt der Umweltpolitik*, Opladen.
Rehbinder, E. and Steward, R. (eds.) (1985) *Environmental Protection Policy, Volume 2, Integration Through Law: Europe and the American Federal Experience*, Firenze: European University Institute.
Sands, P. (1990) 'European Community Environmental Law: legislation, the ECJ and Common Interest Groups', *Modern Law Review*, **53**(5), September, 685.
Teitgen, P-H and Mégret, C. (1981) 'La fumée de la cigarette dans la "zone grise" des competences de la C.E.E.', *Revue Trimestrielle de Droit Européen*, 68.
Vandermeersch, D. (1987) 'The Single European Act and the Environmental Policy of the European Economic Community', *European Law Review*, **12**(6).
Wägenbaur, R. (1990) 'The single market programme and the protection of the environment', in *Environmental Protection and the Impact of European Community Law*', Papers from the Joint Conference with the Incorporated Law Society of Ireland, Dublin: Irish Centre for European Law.
Weizsäcker, E. U. von (1989) *Erdpolitik. Oekologische Realpolitik an der Schwelle zum Jahrhundert der Umwelt*, Darmstadt: Wissenschaftliche Buchgesellschaft.
Wilkinson, D. (1991) 'Eurovision conquest', *The Guardian*, 29 November.
Wolf, J. (1991) 'Environmentalists bemoan watered down and draft chapter', *The Guardian*, 7 December.

Young, O. R. (1983) 'Regime dynamics: the rise and fall of international regimes', in Krasner, Stephen (ed.) (1983), *International Regimes*, Ithaca, NY: Cornell University Press.
Young, O. R. (1992) 'The effectiveness of international institutions: hard cases and critical variables', in James N. Rosenau and Ernst-Otto Czempiel (eds.) (1992), *Governance Without Government: Order and Change in World Politics*, Cambridge: Cambridge University Press.

# 8

# Sustainability and Indicators

*Phil Macnaghten, Robin Grove-White, Michael Jacobs and Brian Wynne*

## 1. A SHORT HISTORY

Sustainability and sustainable development have emerged over the past decade as central concepts in the discourse of government organisations and other institutions concerned with the environment.[1] Following the 1987 Brundtland report (UNCED, 1987) (in which the term was first given political currency and credibility), the 1992 United Nations Conference in Rio de Janeiro on Environment and Development (at which the implications of the term were explored in detail and endorsed by national governments), and subsequent initiatives such as the international action plan, Agenda 21 (UNCED, 1992) (setting out a programme of sustainability), and the creation of the new United Nations body, the 'Commission for Sustainable Development' (through which its implementation is being monitored), sustainability has become a new common language framing the formal environmental agenda of the 1990s.

In a British context, the UK Government launched its national strategy document, 'Sustainable Development—the UK Strategy' (HMG, 1994), outlining its detailed response to the Rio initiatives, and launching three new initiatives designed to stimulate lifestyle change and create new levels of partnership between government and other environmental actors. These were: a new panel of environmental advisors to government; the 'UK Round Table on Sustainable Development'; and a new citizen's environment initiative, 'Going for Green'.

Even before the 1992 Rio Earth Summit, local government bodies across the globe had begun to take initiatives with respect to environment and development issues (e.g. such as the global cities initiatives). Thus, an important outcome of the Rio meeting was the idea of a Local Agenda 21, in which the principles and targets for local sustainability could be developed in a partnership between local authorities and local 'stakeholders'. In the UK at local government level, the Local Government Management Board (LGMB) has subsequently developed and submitted to national government its own 'Framework for Local Sustainability', and is currently undertaking a 'Sustainability Indicators Research Project' as part of a wider 'Local Agenda 21' initiative which aims to advance sustainability at a local level.

Reprinted with permission from Macnaghten, P., Grove-White, R., Jacobs, M. and Wynne, B., *Public Perceptions and Sustainability in Lancashire*, March 1995, pp. 7–11

Given that working definitions of sustainability have been broadly accepted by governments, NGOs and business (e.g. cast in terms of living within the finite limits of the planet, of meeting needs without compromising the ability of future generations to meet their needs, and of integrating environment and development), there is now a growing impetus towards developing tools and approaches which can translate the goals of sustainability into specific actions and assess whether real progress is in fact being made towards achieving them. Within this framework, the aspiration to develop indicators as tools of measurement is acquiring increasing prominence.

## 2.  SUSTAINABILITY INDICATORS

There is already a wide variety of local, national and international initiatives designed to devise and measure key factors relevant to sustainability. As outlined in a recent LGMB report (LGMB, 1994a) these include projects as diverse as an OECD set of Environmental Indicators: a UK Audit Commission set of indicators designed to enable local government to monitor its performance in service delivery; a DoE project designed to develop environmental capacity indicators for historic cities; and programmes of 'Eco-feedback' and 'Global Action Plan' designed for individuals to monitor their own consumption and lifestyles and to devise their own targets. In addition, the LGMB have noted a number of regular reports which provide data relevant to sustainability, including: the World Bank's annual 'Social Indicators of Development'; the UNEP Environmental Data Reports; the Worldwatch Institute's annual 'State of the World Reports'; and the World Resources Institute's 'Guide to the Global Environment'. At a country level, a number of specific projects on sustainability have also emerged including several 'Sustainable Communities' projects across Canada and the United States; a National Environment Policy Performance Indicator Project in the Netherlands; and a number of highly publicised local projects such as the Sustainable Indicators project in Seattle in the U.S.

Within the above framework, in 1993 the U.K. Local Government Management Board set up its 'Sustainability Indicators Research Project', designed to develop indicators for local government bodies to use in advancing towards local sustainability. To date, with the assistance of consultants (the United Nations Association, the New Economics Foundation, and Touche Ross), a framework for measuring sustainability has been developed, a scoping study completed, and 13 themes and a menu of 113 'draft' indicators produced (LGMB, 1994a). Phase 2, involving the 'road testing' of sustainability indicators by selected 'pilot' and 'shadow' local authorities with their local communities, has been completed and findings are shortly to be published.

A number of factors help explain the current popularity of such indicators and their different roles and functions. First, they are seen in a managerial context as tools for planning government and local government environmental initiatives. Coupled to 'State of the Environment' information, their role is seen as being to provide information for managers to assist in the setting of targets, the implementation of programmes, and the measurement of progress. By devising indicators linked to specific targets, managers can help operationalise the concept and thereby facilitate genuine action towards sustainability at a local level.

Secondly, indicators are envisaged as having a role in political objective-setting. By providing and publicising indicators of environmental quality, it is intended to move environmental questions to the foreground of public decisions. The very act of defining indicators for sustainability is a way of seeking to provide new political objectives, such as reduced energy use or increased recycling. Indeed, there is growing recognition that alternative forms of measurement are required to reflect cogently the sustainability concept, given the sheer inadequacy of existing commonly used indicators (most of which tend to be narrowly economic). And, given the power of current indicators (such as measurements of GNP) to set the boundaries of discussion of societal change in the media and public policy generally, many have commented on the potentially 'subversive' merits of well-designed sustainability indicators, which, if popular, will lead discussion (and hence policy) to areas more in line with a wider conception of economic and social progress.

Thirdly, as a counterweight to the managerialism which prompted the initial development of indicators, there has been a growing move towards developing programmes of sustainability indicators which promote public communication and participation. Indeed, this has become the principle aim of the LGMB 'Sustainability Indicators Project'.

## 3.   COMMUNITY PARTICIPATION AND SUSTAINABILITY

Moves towards sustainability will affect everybody, so public involvement is seen as vital. The concept of sustainability challenges the still dominant political and social assumption that indiscriminate economic growth can be reconciled with environmental protection, advocating, in contrast, patterns of development based on a new synthesis of social, economic and ecological dimensions. The discourse of sustainability emphasises the links between basic needs, long-term quality of life, and short-term economic considerations; and the need to ensure that human well-being is met only within the finite limits of the planet. Hence, programmes of action for sustainability increasingly involve measures for community participation and involvement, not least via the Local Agenda 21 process. Indeed, the role envisaged for the public in the emerging model of sustainability is crucial.

Since Rio there has been a growing official recognition that governments alone cannot solve what is seen as a looming global environmental crisis. One of the more striking achievements by NGOs at Rio was to ensure that a new language of 'empowerment', 'citizen participation', and 'multi-stakeholder partnership' became integrated into Agenda 21—the action plan for sustainable development adopted by world governments.

In line with local Agenda 21 initiatives, a variety of new 'partnerships' involving local environmental fora have begun to consolidate. The Lancashire Environment Forum illustrates these developments. The Forum is a partnership of 90 organisations who, under the aegis of Lancashire County Council (LCC), have collaborated since 1989 in the development of a 'Green Audit' of the county, and of a subsequent Lancashire Environmental Action Programme as elements in Lancashire's own contribution to local and global environmental improvement. Related local authority initiatives and partnerships are emerging increasingly around the country. Similarly, the DoE's 'Going for Green' campaign, designed to look at ways to increase people's awareness of the role they can play in making a reality of sustainable development, is being overseen by a committee involving business, the media, local authorities, environment groups, 'women's institutes' and the church. Likewise, the LGMB's 'Sustainability Indicators Project' reflects an understanding that widespread partnership and consensus between stakeholders is required to promote a sense of individual and community responsibility and to encourage action.

However, whilst there has been considerable talk of the need for community participation and involvement in wider processes of public decision making as an integral part of sustainability, to date there has been little evidence of such participation outside the impressive but still limited arena of academics, NGOs, government and business. Thus, while environmental fora have begun to be successful in reaching out to so-called 'stakeholder' groups (e.g. consortia of business interests, utilities, environment groups and to a lesser extent community groups), there have been few initiatives and little response from ordinary individuals (i.e. those who are not members of this limited set of groups). Against such a background, indicators are now being identified both as a mechanism to promote popular participation in sustainability initiatives, and as a way to provide a climate of public support for local and national government initiatives.

Through consideration of the above developments, it is possible to deduce some of the relationships that appear to be assumed, as articulated in the emerging literature and programmes of sustainability.[2] First, there is the assumption that sustainability implies moving from a current unsatisfactory state to a more satisfactory one. While there is little overall agreement about how to describe the current and proposed state vis à vis sustainability—alternative categorisations used to represent our current state include environmental, social and economic categories (perhaps the most familiar distinctions); economic development and environmental categories (favoured by the UK Government's 'Sustainable Development—the UK Strategy'); quality of life and carrying-capacity categories (favoured by the LGMB 'Sustainability Indicators Project'); or equity, quality of life, futurity and environment principles (favoured by the LGMB 'A Framework for Local Sustainability')—most frameworks tend to distinguish an environmental realm, a social (or quality realm of life), and an economic realm. Moreover, such frameworks tend to assume that current priorities aimed at promoting economic welfare can be at the expense of both the environment and of people's wider quality of life needs, and to imply that an 'ideal' state of sustainability is signalled when people's economic welfare and quality of life needs can be met in ways which respect local and global environmental limits.[3]

Secondly, there is the assumption that moves towards sustainability require action from government, NGOs, business, other stakeholders and the public. One key element to any programme of action is thus the identification and monitoring of indicators, which are envisaged as helping inform government and other stakeholders, including the public, of on-going progress towards sustainability. Through accurate and meaningful indicators, the argument runs, members of the public will be more likely to participate in government and business initiatives and to modify their own individual behaviours. Indicators are also pictured as having a more managerial function for government, to help plan and implement sustainability programmes and initiatives.

Most reports on the subject to date thus imply a three-stage process, in which:

(1) the present 'unsustainable' situation is defined (largely by 'experts', whether within government, NGOs, industry and/or academia);
(2) new mechanisms and relations are generated (including 'indicators'), to enable progress to be made towards improving matters; and
(3) through such mechanisms and relationships the desired state of 'sustainability' is approached.

These processes can be pictured schematically (Figure 1).

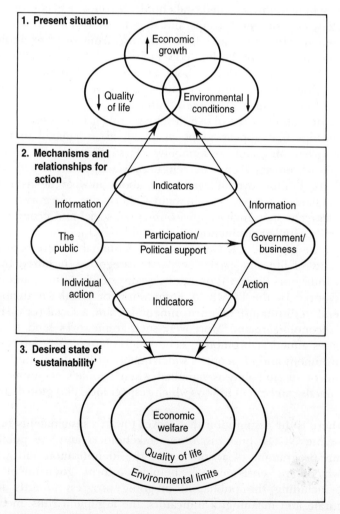

Figure 1. Model of Sustainability and the Rôle Envisaged for Indicators.

But is such a picture realistic? So far there has been little analysis of the key cultural and social assumptions on which it rests. In particular, despite the importance of the role envisaged for the public in this model, there has been little research into the question of whether or not the envisaged mechanisms and relationships for action (as in box 2 of Figure 1) will be likely to prove credible or effective with the public in practical terms.

Against this background, the present research study focuses on the question—How do ordinary people in Lancashire feel about 'sustainability' issues, and how will they be likely to respond to 'indicators' aimed at advancing sustainability?'

## NOTES

1. For the purpose of the report no distinction is made between the concept of sustainability and that of sustainable development.
2. In a UK context these relationships are most developed in the literature emerging from the Local Agenda 21 initiative. This includes the LGMB's 'A Framework for Local Sustainability' (LGMB, 1993); the LGMB's Sustainability Indicators Research Project's 'Report of Phase One' (LGMB, 1994a); and the LGMB's Local Agenda 21 Round Table Guidance Notes on 'Principles and Process' and 'Community Participation' (LGMB, 1994b, 1994c). However, the same relationships can also be partly or wholly recognised in national and international reports on sustainability including: the UN's 'Agenda 21 Programme for Action for Sustainable Development' (UNCED, 1992): the EC's Fifth Environmental Action Programme 'Towards Sustainability' (CEC, 1992); and the UK's 'Sustainable Development— The UK Strategy' (HMG, 1994).
3. While no distinction was applied between quality of life and economic welfare in the LGMB Sustainability Indicators Project, the above model can still be applied. In the development of indicators, the LGMB project divided the category of 'quality of life' into 9 themes (these were basic needs, health, access to information, education, freedom to participate in decision making, freedom from fear, access to services, income, work, leisure and aesthetics), and the category of the environment into three themes (these were resources, pollution and biodiversity).

## REFERENCES

CEC (1992) *Towards Sustainability: The Fifth Environmental Action Programme for the Environment.* CEC, Brussels.
HMG (1994) *Sustainable Development—The UK Strategy,* Cm 2426. HMSO, London.
Local Government Management Board (1993) *A Framework for Local Sustainability.* LGMB, Luton.
Local Government Management Board (1994a) *Sustainability Indicators Research Project: Report of Phase One.* LGMB, Luton.
Local Government Management Board (1994b) *Local Agenda 21 Roundtable Guidance Notes: 'Principles and Process'.* LGMB, Luton.
Local Government Management Board (1994c) *Local Agenda 21 Roundtable Guidance Notes: 'Community Participation'.* LGMB, Luton.
UNCED (1987) *Our Common Future.* Conches, Switzerland.
UNCED (1992) *Agenda 21.* Conches, Switzerland.

# Part III

## Greening Organizations

# CONTENTS

# Introduction to Part III

*Pierre McDonagh and Andrea Prothero*

The first issue of importance to note in the literature surrounding the greening of management is the lack of both conceptual and empirical research (see, for example, Gladwin, 1993; Simintiras *et al.*, Reading 24). It is hoped that in future years both of these problems in the green management arena will be addressed. In this volume we have taken the broadest meaning in attempting to explain what is meant by the greening of organizations. This suggests the whole organization must become green and this is illustrated in the selection of articles we have chosen.

Reading 9, the second article by Shrivastava (1994), is an excellent starting point for illustrating the importance of considering green management in a holistic manner, taking account of the broader natural environment. It shows that organization studies have neglected the area of green research and future organizational theories need to be more 'nature centred', where the natural environment plays a central role in our understanding of organization studies. The reading signifies the importance of seeing nature and humans as interdependent, i.e. one is 'not better' than the other. The article discusses the CASTRATED (Competition, Abstraction, Shallowness, Theoretical immaturity, Reductionism, Anthropocentrism, Time independent (ahistorical), Exploitable and Denaturalized) way in which previous green research has been conducted in this area and then moves on to consider new perspectives for greening in the future.

The author provides a good discussion of some of the key multiple discourses on environmental issues and the reading should be read in conjunction with Kilbourne (Reading 29). Shrivastava concludes by emphasizing the importance organizations must place on providing centrality to nature, therefore they need new ways of doing things. New management tools include environmental management programmes and elaborate ecological strategies, discussed in more detail in Readings 11–13.

Fineman (1996) (Reading 10) offers a useful insight into our understanding of the process of greening an organization as the author focuses on greening the manager. He suggests that within organizations a person's private moral position is distinct from and in conflict with the conventional morality of the corporation.

Fineman's work is based on a qualitative study of 37 top and middle managers in six major automotive manufacturers and is part of a wider project sponsored by the UK Economic and Social Research Council. The results of the research show that managers responsible for the environment vary in both seniority and background—

ranging from the health and safety executive to the company lawyer. The author concludes that the meaning of business must change, and if it fails to do so '*it is unlikely that managerial greening will progress beyond the formulaic.*' Thus, some of the practical issues discussed in the readings by Elkington with Burke and Barnard in Part IV will not be enough on their own to help green organizations. According to Fineman such practical issues must also be considered in conjunction with changing the 'soul' of the organization and this will only occur if both 'organizational thinking and practice' see a paradigm shift. This fundamental issue is a theme that is discussed at various points throughout this reader for both the greening of society and the greening of management. Ultimately one must remember piecemeal responses to one of the most important issues of the millennium, the destruction of our natural environment, will not help in slowing down this destruction.

Reading 11 by McCloskey and Smith (1995) considers the relationships between '*business activities and environmental quality in the light of post-industrial economic decline*'. The need to turn the environmental policies of companies (included in the mission statement and strategic plan) into activities that can be operationalized within the company is of vital importance. Thus the emphasis is very much on *implementing environmental strategies*. The article looks specifically at the strategy process areas of environmental analysis, resource analysis, strategy formulation and implementation, and how this process is affected by environmental issues. The authors suggest that what we need is a 'more open democratic approach to the strategic process'. This will require changes to the dominant way in which decisions are currently made within organizations. Again it is important to stress that some of the key themes as far as greening organizations are concerned, such as implementation, are issues of concern not only for business managers but also the government, the organization of the economy and society generally.

At this stage in the reader the articles begin to explore some of the practical issues involved for organizations who wish to implement environmental management systems in their company.

The next two readings (12 and 13), by Roberts (1995) and Ledgerwood *et al.* (1992), consider various methods and procedures that have been established to help organizations in developing environmental management systems. The first of these, by Roberts, explains in detail environmental impact assessments, environmental auditing and environmental information systems and provides background legislative information on these environmental procedures. Examples of the two environmental auditing schemes detailed are the UK's BS 7750 environmental management system and the EU's eco-management and audit scheme. Some of the criticisms associated with the various methods are also explored.

The author (Reading 12) emphasizes the importance of the adage *prevention being better than cure* and suggests the methods explained can provide valuable help for those organizations who wish to adopt an environmental management system within their company. He suggests the company will then be in a position which highlights environmental areas of concern before they become major problems. Organizations are not only enabled to develop environmental strategies but also to consider the implementation of such polices within the wider external environment.

The article by Ledgerwood *et al.* (Reading 13) further explores the environmental audit. A detailed summary and comparison of the EU eco-management and audit scheme and the British Standard for Environmental Management Systems BS 7750 is provided; comparison is also made between BS 7750 and the British Standard for quality systems BS 5750. The authors conclude by proposing their own framework for environmental auditing based on the two schemes and what they perceive as best practice in industry. The practicalities of carrying out such an audit are discussed and this section of the reading is an excellent starting point for those wishing to have an overview on what is actually involved in conducting an environmental audit.

The final three readings (14–16) in this section, by Gray (1992), Kopitsky and Betzenberger (1987) and Maltby (1995), show us that greening organizations applies across all organizational areas, using the examples of accountancy, banking and contaminated land, respectively. Thus the professions that have an impact on the business organization, such as banking and accountancy, also have a role to play as far as developing environmental management systems are concerned. The importance of suppliers, discussed in Part IV, further illustrates this.

Gray (1992) (Reading 14) focuses specifically on how the accounting function generally can take account of the natural environment. The reading provides an excellent account of how deep green thinking (see also Readings 1, 2, 9 and 29) can be applied to accountancy in a utopian vision of the future. Recognizing the difficulties in reality the author also provides a detailed account of how accounting principles may be altered in a non-green world to allow greater transparency of the issues involved. Gray suggests that the two channels of progression, namely 'the intellectual and the immediately practical', be addressed together in working towards a utopian vision for the future. Practical examples are provided and Table 3, for instance, provides examples of environmental accounting and information systems— for example, environmental and social reporting and environmental assessment accounting.

Kopitsky and Betzenberger (1987) (Reading 15), both senior bankers in American companies, debate whether banks should lend money to companies with environmental problems, an issue also raised in the discussion of contaminated land in Reading 16 by Maltby (1995). The argument is centred around lending to companies who generate hazardous waste. Kopitsky argues that banks should not make loans with environmental risks because of the reduced potential for any loan recovery in a situation of environmental risk. Betzenberger counters this argument, explaining why it is that banks must continue to lend despite environmental liabilities, and after detailing the A to Z of the loan application procedure suggests that an environmental risk category be included in the pricing procedure. Ultimately the aim as far as both authors are concerned is to protect the lenders: this debate is therefore typical of the anthropocentric nature of business discussed throughout the reader. Neither author, in weighing up the pros and cons for lending to companies with an environmental problem, goes into any detail about implications for the natural environment and how potential borrowers could try and reduce the so called 'environmental risk'. As this whole area of liability is one that is continuing to grow globally, it is hoped that future debates will not only consider the needs of the borrower and lender but also those of the natural environment.

Maltby (1995) (Reading 16) considers the subject of contaminated land in relation to corporate social reporting. Government regulations in the area of information disclosure are raised, with the author concluding that the government has interfered in the reporting of information by business. This interference has enabled business to provide information based on its own interests rather than those of society. This article thus shows very clearly that one must not only consider how business voluntarily responds to the environment but that the role of other stakeholders, such as the government, within society is vital. Thus, in order for society to become greener, governments must impose stricter rather than more lenient measures and businesses must abide by these regulations. This again takes us back to the issues of importance raised in Readings 1 and 2, and also discussed in Reading 29.

## REFERENCES

Gladwin, T. (1993) The meaning of greening: a plea for organizational theory, in Fischer, K. and Schot, J. (Eds) *Environmental Strategies for Industry*, Island Press, Washington DC.

# 9

# CASTRATED Environment: GREENING Organizational Studies

*Paul Shrivastava*

Over the past hundred years organizational activities have caused devastating damage to the natural environment. In response, environmentalism has emerged as an influential intellectual current, and as a worldwide mass movement. Despite these trends, Organizational Studies as a field has failed to engage seriously in environmental discourses.

Organizational theories cannot adequately address the environmental concerns because of their limited ideas of 'organizational environment'. This paper identifies and critiques these limitations. It proposes an alternative view of organizational environment as an economic biosphere. It examines the implications of this view for creating more nature-centred (green) organizational theories.

## INTRODUCTION

Organizations are a primary instrument by which humans impact their natural environment. Therefore, one would expect Organizational Studies (OS hereafter)[1] to be engaged in serious conversation with environmental discourses. Surprisingly, this conversation is virtually non-existent.

A primary reason for this non-conversation is that OS uses denatured, narrow and parochial concepts of 'organizational environment'. This term is an exclusionary signifier. It prevents and also devalues the incorporation of natural environment into organizational theorizing. Instead, it emphazises economic social, political and technological aspects of organizational environments.

At the present time, when environmental crises proliferates around the world, nature-centred organizational theories are particularly important. Examples of these crises include, depletion of stratospheric ozone, air pollution, acid rain, global warming, loss of biodiversity, extinction of non-renewable resources, toxic waste, major industrial accidents, transportation accidents, and other technological risks to the public.

Reprinted with permission from *Organization Studies*, Vol. 15, No. 5, 1994, pp. 705–726.

The purpose of this paper is to critique and theoretically reconceptualize 'organizational environment', in a way that gives centrality to the *natural* environment. Such reconceptualization could facilitate OS to appropriate environmental values and theoretical ideas. It could lead to the development of more nature-centred (green) organizational theories. It could also have the practical benefit of preventing ecological damage.

The first section of this paper argues the need for reconceptualizing organizational knowledge. The following section provides a critique of existing concepts of organizational environment, from an ecological perspective. The next section provides suggestions for greening OS by incorporating lessons from the many discourses on environmentalism. Part of the greening task involves accepting an alternative concept of organizational environment as economic-biosphere.

The paper is programmatic in scope. It seeks to open lines of conversation between OS and the various environmental discourses. It seeks to motivate organizational scholars to rethink organizational theories in the light of environmentalism. It urges redefinition of our most fundamental ideas of organizations, their objectives, strategies, technologies, structures and culture.

## THE NEED FOR RECONCEPTUALIZING ORGANIZATIONAL KNOWLEDGE

At this point in history, organizational research cannot pretend that the natural environment is peripheral to understanding organizations. Nor can OS ignore the affects of organizational decisions on nature. These destructive impacts are wide ranging and proliferating.

Organizations, particularly private corporations, may be viewed as systems of inputs, throughputs and outputs. Each of these organizational elements causes some environmental harm. Excessive wasteful use of inputs, such as energy and raw materials, is depleting them rapidly. At current rates of consumption, we have less than fifty years supply of oil, nickel and cobalt (Frosch and Gallopoulos, 1989). The use of fossil fuels for energy generation is also a major source of atmospheric pollution. It is responsible for acid rain and global warming (Likens, 1987).

Organizational throughput systems or production facilities impact nature through polluting emissions. Technological facilities have hazardous work conditions. Accidents at plants pose health risks to communities. Effluents from production plants pollute land and ground water. Production waste is a source of the toxic waste and landfill crisis facing many communities (Hoffman *et al.*, 1990; Pauchant and Fortier, 1990). Organizational outputs or products are another major source of environmental harm. Products such as Chloroflurocarbons (CFCs) released into the atmosphere rise to the stratosphere and destroy ozone. Disposable diapers and discarded product packaging contribute to the garbage crisis. Automobiles are a major source of urban air pollution and greenhouse-effect gases. Other products such as asbestos, tobacco and Dalkon Shield contraceptives have caused mass injuries to consumers (Throop, Starik and Rands, 1993; Shrivastava, 1990; Siomkos, 1989; Mitroff and Kilmann, 1984).

Modern organizational theory has barely addressed these important problems. In recent years a few organizational studies have begun to focus on these problems (Mitroff and Pauchant, 1990; Perrow, 1984; Roberts, 1989; Shrivastava, 1992a; Weick, 1988). More such studies are desirable to throw light on unexamined organizationally linked environmental problems.

However, giving more attention to environmental problems is not sufficient. Given the pervasive environmental impacts of all organizational elements, it is important for OS to reconceptualize organizational knowledge. It needs to rethink basic theoretical ideas in a way that allows discussion of the natural environment.

Only through a fundamental re-theorization of organizations will we be able to pay genuine attention to organization–nature relationships. We need new ways of theorizing 'the environment' to be able to re-theorize organizations. Instead of understanding 'the environment' from an organizational viewpoint, we need to understand 'the organization' from an environmental viewpoint.

The consequence of this reversal is not simply to make organizational environment a more inclusive signifier (including nature). This reversal changes the ontological status of organizations. It views organizations as part of a larger natural universe. The articulation of a complete ecological organizational theory is beyond the modest scope of this essay, which simply indicates some directions to take and initiates the greening of OS.

## FROM CASTRATED TO GREENING

My assumptions and values in this essay are different from traditional anthropocentric assumptions of OS. These should be stated at the outset. The most important assumption is that nature has a moral standing *in its own right*. It does not exist simply as a resource for humans, or for their welfare.

Another premise of this essay questions the taken-for-granted 'progress' of modern industrial development. Yes, industrialism has contributed significantly to human progress. However, it has also had many disastrous consequences. These include, environmental destruction, proliferation of technological risks, haphazard urbanization, underdevelopment of Third World countries, and the loss of cultural values (Berry, 1988; Carson, 1962; Devall and Sessions, 1985; Lovelock, 1988; Mckibben, 1989; O'Connor, 1987).

The essay also departs from the conventional format of theoretical writing in OS. Conventional theorizing involves the definition of concepts, constructs and variables. It involves identifying relationships between variables and statements of empirically testable hypotheses.

The purpose behind the present theorizing is to motivate organizational scholars to engage in a cross disciplinary conversation with environmentalism (Weick, 1989). Motivation implies memory. One must remember, before one can be motivated.

The paper adopts a stylistic strategy, therefore, that simplifies remembering. It develops the critique and re-orientation ideas using mnemonics. The use of mnemonics (or 'the arts of memory') as the analytical form for critique and theorizing has both symbolic and heuristic values (Fischer, 1986).

Symbolically, mnemonics help us to reclaim lost memory. In this instance, the memory of the ecological basis of organizational activities, and the memory of initial organizational concern for environmental conservation. Taylorism, the source of modern OS, was spurred, to some extent, by a drive for conserving natural resources. It sought conservation through a 'scientifically efficient' use of resources. It also calls attention to the short memory span of organizational theory. Its focus on current (past fifty years) organizational issues, ignores the long term (in geological time) organizational–environmental relationships.

Heuristically, this analytical approach emphasizes *not forgetting* ecological lessons in organizational theorizing. It urges us to permeate ecological concerns in all organizational ideas. Ecological lessons apply to the choice of products and strategies; to the design of structures and systems; to the hiring and training of employees; to the organizational missions and objectives; to energy use, waste management and production efficiency.

OS portrays organizational environments as disembodied external influences on the organization. It is one sidedly concerned about how the environment influences organizations. Its goal is to seek better ways of managing organizational resources under different environmental conditions.

The reverse relationship of how organizations impact their environments (particularly nature) has received very little attention (Shrivastava *et al.*, 1988). The next section examines these and other limitations of OS.

## CONCEPTS OF THE 'ENVIRONMENT' IN OS

In the early 1960s, several researchers argued that the *context* in which organizations operate, is an important determinant of their behaviour and performance. Since then, three streams of literature have addressed organizational environment as a theoretical construct. These include, Organization Theory, Strategic Management, and Corporate Social Responsibility perspectives.

I review these perspectives briefly to elicit their respective conception of organizational environment. This review has the limited objective of identifying what organizational environment means in each perspective. More comprehensive reviews of literature are available in Fahey and Narayanan (1984), Freeman (1984) and Starbuck (1976).

### The environment in organization theory

Organizational theorists originally examined organizational environments using the Systems Theory idea of 'open systems'. As complex open systems, organizations interact with many external forces. This theoretically includes natural forces. However, the influences most emphasized in the literature are economic and social. Managers have little or no control over these influences (Crozier and Thoenig, 1976).

There are two environments considered relevant to organizations—the task environment, and the general environment. The task environment influences narrowly defined tasks, such as purchasing, sales, and production. The general environment refers to the broad social and economic milieu of organizations. This environment consists of several component forces, possesses certain analytical dimensions, and is of several distinct types. *Components* of the general environment include economic, market, social, cultural, political and technological forces (Terreberry, 1968; Lawrence and Lorsch, 1967).

Emery and Trist (1965) used three *dimensions*—stability, concentration, and turbulence—to characterize environments. They posited the existence of four different *types* ('causal textures') of environments. These include placid randomized, placid clustered, disturbed reactive, and turbulent environments.

Several other analytical dimensions of the environment received frequent attention. Most important of these was environmental uncertainty. Uncertainty is a function of heterogeneity/homogeneity, stability/change, and interconnectedness/ isolation of environmental elements. Another important dimension is the degree of dependence of organizations on their environment. Dependence is a function of resource munificence, resource concentration, and level of coordination among environmental agents (Aldrich, 1979; Scott, 1981; Starbuck, 1976).

Some researchers argued that managerial perceptions of their environments were equally important. Managerial environmental perceptions vary because of personal experiences and knowledge. The perceived environment influenced managers' choices in decision-making situations (Duncan, 1972).

Weick (1979) suggested that managers enacted their organizational environments. Managers selectively perceived environmental influences based on their personal biases and cognitive limits. They selectively ordered and made sense of the plethora of their experiences and information received through limited cognitive maps. They collectively formed a consensus over what environmental influences were of consequence to the organization. Through group sense-making processes they enacted environmental constraints, opportunities and threats.

Organizational environment is also seen as a set of material, human, and information resources. Organizations depend on environmental resources for survival and prosperity. They are in continuous exchange relationships with their environments. Their success depends on skilfully managing these relationships, to exact resources and fulfil environmental demands (Aldrich, 1979; Pfeffer, 1982).

This resource-based view of organizational environments also underlies the organizational 'population ecology' perspective (Hannan and Freeman, 1989; Rosenzweig and Singh, 1991). This perspective borrows some basic ideas and methodological techniques from the discipline of Natural Ecology, but, ironically, it does not develop a nature-centred view of organizational environments. It brought sophisticated mathematical 'population ecology' models to OS, but did not reconceptualize organizational environments in the naturalist spirit of the parent discipline.

## The environment in strategic management

Most strategy analysts acknowledge that the environment is a multidimensional concept. It consists of economic, social, political, cultural and technological forces

(Fahey and Narayanan, 1984). However, the economic environment and industry/market environment is given the most importance.

Porter's (1980) concept of competitive market environment is the *de facto* reigning view of environment in the strategy field. Competition is a function of structural forces in an industry. These include, barriers to entry, rivalry among competitors, power of buyers and suppliers, threat of substitutes, and industry regulations. These forces determine the profitability and competitive structure of industries. By analyzing them, managers could identify opportunities and threats facing their firm.

There are several other multidimensional conceptions of the environment in the literature. Examples include mature product environments, declining industry environments, and high velocity environments (Eisenhardt, 1989; Hambrick, 1983; Harrigan, 1980). However, these concepts use only economic and market variables to characterize the environment. Often used variables include sales volatility, industry growth rate, product demand, industry concentration, and advertising expenditures.

Strategic Management researchers work within the neoclassical economic paradigm. Their primary concern is with firm competitiveness in free market economies. The natural environment has remained outside their domain of concerns. They regard environmental degradation as an externality of production, a subject for the field of public policy.

## The environment in the corporate social responsibility perspective

A more liberal conception of the firm's environment comes from researchers interested in corporate social responsibility. The idea of 'organizational stakeholders' provides one way of understanding environmental influences on the firm. Stakeholders are all those individuals, groups, and organizations that are influenced by, or who influence, the firm's performance. In this view, customers, suppliers, government agencies, bankers, owners, communities, the public, etc. are legitimate parts of the firm's environment. This view sees the public, and its interest in the natural environment, as legitimate forces in strategy making (Freeman, 1984).

Many researchers within this perspective explicitly acknowledge natural environment problems created by organizations. They see nature as a legitimate aspect of organizational environment. They acknowledge that corporations have significant environmental side effects. They seek to reform corporations and their production systems, products, and waste management processes. They advocate regulations and voluntary corporate actions to achieve corporate reformation (Bucholz, Post and Marcus, 1992; Hoffman *et al.*, 1990; Post, 1991; Smith, 1992).

However, this literature suffers from some important limitations. First, it is anthropocentric in that it treats natural environment as a social concern. It seeks to address nature related problems in terms of the welfare of consumers, producers, suppliers, and the public. Second, this type of acknowledgement of the natural environment as just one of many components of the firm's environment serves to marginalize its importance. It allows researchers and managers to treat the natural environment as a special topic or a 'social/public policy issue'. As a social issue it deserves consideration, but it is not central to organizational theorizing (Shrivastava, 1995).

## CASTRATED ORGANIZATIONAL ENVIRONMENT

These OS ideas of organizational environment are narrow, economistic, and anti-naturalistic. They preclude the discipline from addressing the central concerns of environmentalism that deal with degradation and extinction of natural resources.

The concepts and language of organizational environments are CASTRATED. Castrated literally means deprived of testes and ovaries, and signifies lack of vitality, potency, and effect.[2] It serves as a convenient mnemonic for critiquing these concepts. It represents the nine elements used to organize the critique. The letters stand for: Competition, Abstraction, Shallowness, Theoretical immaturity, Reification, Anthropocentrism, Time independent (ahistorical), Exploitable, and Denaturalized.

The mnemonic does not imply any particular order of importance of these elements. Nor are the elements mutually independent. There are some overlaps between elements and these overlaps reinforce some of the limitations.

### Competition

A fundamental assumption of the received views of organizational environment, is that it is a legitimate venue or turf for 'competition'. Competition has two dimensions. One involves competition for environmental resources. The second dimension also implies antagonistic exploitative relations between organization and their environments. Competition is regarded as an acceptable, legitimate, and perhaps the only way, of relating organizations to their environments.

These concepts de-emphasize the possibility that organizations and their environments may work in cooperative rather than in antagonistic competitive relations. They devalue the possibility that organizations can nurture environmental resources and be in trusteeship relations with them. They do not question the legitimacy of using the environment as the turf for competition. They do not explore the detrimental consequences of competitive relations on the environment, neither do they examine the environment's capacity to support competitive activities.

### Abstraction

These concepts regard the environment as an abstract social entity. It consists of abstract (and non-physical) economic, social, cultural, and technological components. Equally abstract ideas of 'uncertainty', 'stability', 'turbulence', 'domain consensus', etc. are used to characterize it. The environment is operationalized and measured by even more abstract market and accounting measures or contrived social and perceptual attitude scales.

Concrete substantive aspects of the environment are de-emphasized. Physical aspects of environments are barely even acknowledged. The natural environment, the *terra firma* of all organizational activities is largely ignored. There is little consideration of the relationship between firms activities and this physical/natural environment. The rare exceptions are discussions within the corporate social responsibility perspective.

## Shallowness

Received concepts of organizational environment are shallow. They are simply semantic definitions that distinguish the firm from its external milieu. They attempt to describe the fuzzy boundaries of organizations, in simplistic terms. They are thus descriptively inadequate. They do not provide deep definitions, nor do they examine its essence, its geo-spatial character, and its internal relations. They do not examine the relationship of the organizational environment with larger social and cultural issues.

## Theoretical immaturity

The concepts of organizational environment are theoretically immature. They do not go beyond mere empirical re-descriptions of immediate external influences on organizations. There is little analysis of the structural character of environmental influences, its historical origins, the interrelationships among structural and process elements, the complex dynamics of environmental changes, and relationships with larger social and historical processes.

Environmental analysis lacks anchors in broader social theories. There is little analysis of the impact of major social movements, radical social discontinuities, or social change patterns on organizations. With few exceptions, writing on environmentalism, consumerism, gender and race issues in organizations, are tenuously connected to social theories of these movements.

## Reductionism

Two reductionist tendencies are apparent in OS views of organizational environment. In principle, the concept includes *all* forces outside the firm that influences its actions and performance. However, in operationalizing it, researchers invariably reduce these forces to economic, social and technological forces that impact financial performance. They completely ignore natural influences such as physical space, location, and time, that influence all aspects of organizations.

Second, positivist tendencies in OS place heavy emphasis on measuring organizational environments objectively. Measurement is necessarily a reductionist activity. It increases precision, but reduces descriptive richness. Measurement techniques reduce the environment to its 'essential' dimensions. For example, studies try to capture the dynamic and complex changes in an industry deregulation, with the simplistic concept of 'environmental volatility'.

## Anthropocentrism

OS concepts of the environment presume that nature exists to fulfil *human and organizational* needs. Human needs unquestioningly receive priority over the natural environment. To the extent that firms attempt to fulfil human needs, they are considered to possess legitimate rights over natural resources. This generalization of human interests serves as a licence to harness and exploit nature.

Another aspect of anthropocentrism is that it fails to acknowledge any limits to the exploitation of nature. It legitimates exploitation to the point of extinction of natural resources. As a result, we have witnessed stupendous loss of natural species and biodiversity due to industrial activities. OS has not dealt with this loss in any serious way (Pauchant and Fortier, 1990).

## Time independent (ahistorical)

Organizational environment is regarded as a time independent, ahistorical idea. It is characterized by timeless dimensions, such as, uncertainty, heterogeneity and stability. These time neutral concepts obfuscate the historical roots and processes that shape organizational environments. Discussions of the environment sound as if they are equally valid at any period in time, and in any region of the world.

By neglecting the essentially historical roots of organizational environments, and critical historical relationships that shape them, OS neglects a fundamental explanatory idea. It also loses a way of understanding historically cumulative effects of organization–environment relationships. The one exception to this is the organizational Population Ecology approach. This approach examines organizational survival patterns *over time*. However, it does so by excluding nature from its idea of organizational environment.

## Exploitable

A fundamental assumption of these views is that the environment is a resource that may be exploited eternally for organizational benefit. Business organizations' sole objective is to exploit the environment to create economic value for its stockholders. No limits to this exploitation are ever acknowledged.

Environmental resources are scarce. This scarcity is exacerbated by organizations' competitive attempts to capture resources. Despite these limits, OS does not acknowledge any limits on exploitation of the environment. The ecological notion of 'carrying capacity' (capacity to sustain life and self-renew natural resources) of the environment receives little attention in the study of organizational environments. Even within the corporate social responsibility perspective there is little discussion about renewing natural resources and maintaining them at sustainable levels.

## Denaturalized

The literature portrays organizational environment as being entirely a product of human institutions and actions. It has no natural component. It is created by people, organizations, and social and political institutions. It includes pressures from scientific and technological changes, changing international relations, and changes in demographic and social relations.

This denaturalizing of organizational environments allows the field to view it solely as a social artifact. As an artifact it can be exploited, changed, used, and discarded. Nature remains at the margins of the definition of organizational environment. This exclusion prevents OS from seriously addressing environmentalists' concerns, which centre mostly on the status of nature and human–nature relations.

Working under the burden of these distorted assumptions, OS has failed to incorporate the environmentalist discourse in its own theoretical logics. To create a more nature-sensitive (if not nature-centred) OS, the values and goals of the field need to be reorientated and the concept of organizational environment reconceptualized.

## GREENING ORGANIZATIONAL STUDIES

To become responsive to environmental concerns, OS needs to be unshackled from its burdensome assumptions. It needs to incorporate lessons from the environmental discourses of the past century. It requires an alternative view of organizational environment that gives primacy to ecological/biological, ethical/moral, and social and political justice concerns. We begin this task by briefly reviewing environmental discourses.

## ENVIRONMENTAL DISCOURSES

The intellectual roots of modern environmentalism go back to the liberal impulse that spawned the American Revolution, the revolution vastly expanded the definition of liberty, freedom and democracy. It made possible and legitimate, the consideration of the rights of oppressed minorities and oppressed nature (Nash, 1989).

Reducing the oppression and degradation of nature was the focus of a diffused set of environmental theories and movements. Today there are many environmental discourses differentiated by their basic assumptions, and their cognitive and practical interests. For the limited purposes of introducing these discourses, they are simplified into four categories: Naturalism, Reform Environmentalism, Radical Environmentalism, Eco-Feminism. This is not to imply that all environmental discourses fit neatly into these categories. I simply want to acknowledge the existence of multiple discourses.

### Naturalism and ecology

Environmentally oriented writings of the great nineteenth-century writers, such as, Ralph Waldo Emerson, George Perkins Marsh, John Muir, and Henry David Thoreau, are the best examples of the naturalist stream of environmental thought. These humanist-naturalists attempted to expand the narrow anthropocentric conception of the human community to include the natural world. Their views of human community were holistic and organic, and included nature. Humans belonged to this larger community and related to it through complex interdependencies. Preserving nature was a means of preserving the human community.

Darwin (1859) scientifically codified this naturalist concern in his theories of evolution. By showing that man evolved from animals, he established the principle of continuity of life forms. He argued that species changed form over time. There was no basis for treating one (human) species as superior to others. He gave animal and plant species a new and heightened status. They played a role in the evolution of humans.

The scientific study of the natural environment took formal shape under the rubric of 'ecology'. This term, coined in 1866 by a German Darwinian, Ernst Haeckel, referred to the study of how organisms interacted with each other and to their total environment. It was the study of the whole system, the community, of living organisms. Ecology gave centrality to the ideas of holism and interdependence as defining features of nature, and of human relationship to nature.

Ecological understanding helped in a wide range of problems. These included the predator problem and policies for wildlife preservation (Worster, 1977); land use and management (Leopold, 1949); philosophical and theological inquiry (Whitehead, 1920); and ethics (Scwheitzer, 1923). Each application brought with it new ideas and insights into the planet's ecology. The first half of the twentieth century thus set the intellectual stage for reform environmentalism.

*Reform environmentalism*

With the advent of large-scale industrialization, the consequent environmental destruction became apparent. In response, a new mood—one that confronted industrialism—emerged within environmentalism. Rachel Carson's seminal study of environmental pollution caused by wide-spread use of pesticides and chemicals, *Silent Spring* appeared in 1962. It inspired far reaching reassessments and critique of industrialization and consequent environmental pollution. It prompted efforts to reform industrialization processes to minimize their environmentally destructive consequences.

The next two decades (1960s and 1970s) saw a burgeoning of the discourse on ways of improving the environmental performance of industries. Hundreds of universities developed courses on environmental problems and solutions. Governments around the world enacted thousands of new environmental regulations. The 1972 U.N. conference on the environment and human settlements led member countries to create environmental ministries. Research-and-policy-analysis centres mushroomed around the world to study environmental crises.

The underlying premise of reform environmentalism is still anthropocentric. It views the natural environment as a necessary, functional, and instrumental resource for the development of human communities. It is critical of wasteful industrial development that destroys the environment, thereby harming long-term human development.

Reform environmentalists also see the globally unsustainable use of natural resources. They acknowledge world hunger, exploding population, fossil-energy dependence, unmanageable urbanization, as major environmental problems. They urge conservation, moderation of consumption, and environmentally 'sustainable' economic development to ensure long-term viability of the planet earth (World Commission on Environment and Development, 1987).

*Radical environmentalism (deep ecology)*

Even as major environmental reforms were going into effect in the 1970s, a radical strain of environmentalism was gaining ground. Two factors, one theoretical and the other practical, fueled its growth. There was a strong theoretical critique and rejection of anthropocentrism. The environment could not be treated simply as a resource to be used for human welfare. The natural world was seen to have a moral standing in its own right, not simply as an accessory to human well-being (Ehrenfeld, 1978; Naess, 1987).

Deep-ecology theory redefined human–nature relationships through the idea of 'ecological egalitarianism'. This referred to the 'intrinsic' right to every form of life to function normally in the ecosystem; to blossom, live and flourish. It gave nature a status and rights similar to those that humans had arrogated to themselves. It made the protection and conservation of nature a part of our individual and collective moral responsibility (Devall and Sessions, 1985; Naess, 1987).

On the practical side, slowness of reforms fueled radical environmentalism. Environmental reforms failed to arrest rapid and progressive environmental destruction. In the 1980s, proliferating environmental crises heightened concern for the environment. Crises of ozone depletion, greenhouse effect, air pollution, acid rain, hazardous wastes, raised the public's environmental awareness. Episodic environmental disasters such as the Bhopal accident, the *Exxon Valdez* oil spill, and the Chernobyl nuclear-power-plant accident scared the public (Garelik, 1990; Gorbachev, 1990; Kirkpatrick, 1990). Activism spawned by deep ecology included 'bioregionalism', aggressive defense of the ecosystem, and the NIMBY (Not in My Back Yard) movement.


*Eco-Feminism*

Drawing on deep ecology, a distinctly feminist ecological position emerged under the rubric of Eco-Feminism. It uses the idea that women's attitudes toward, and relationship with, the natural environment are qualitatively different from men's.

Eco-Feminism sees many parallels between the oppression of women and the oppression of the natural world. The roots of this oppression lie in patriarchic thought, in which women receive the same abuse and ambivalence as nature. Men repudiate and dominate both, for their own benefit. They view nature and women as resources to be used. Both women and non-human life have subservient status (Merchant, 1980).

There is a connection and mutual reinforcement of exploitation and domination of nature and of women. Linking women with nature, allows urges for domination and control of nature, to expand and include domination and control of women. Women thus have a special stake in ending the domination of nature, because by doing so they would achieve a measure of emancipation (King, 1983).

Eco-feminists extend the basic right to live and flourish to the entire biosphere, not just to humans or to a select set of species. All species including humans are a part of a natural system, in dynamic symbiotic relationship with each other. They reject the 'man-in-environment' image. Instead, they favour the idea that organisms exist as elements in a network of intrinsic relations. Nature is not there for human consumption. Nature and humans do not have separate atomistic identities. They are one, in a holistic relationship.

In eco-feminism, preserving nature does not mean instrumental resource conservation and shallow anti-pollution environmentalism. It means preserving the integrity of the relationships that make up the natural world. It implies sustaining connections between elements of the biospherical community. It implies a contextual approach to caring for nature in our lives, wherever we are in the web of relationships. Nurturing relations with the environment is not an abstract moral value, but a part of the lived experience of women (Cheney, 1987).

From this perspective the protection of workers, the public and the natural environment, is not something to be done as an extra, in the tasks of organizing and producing. Instead, the organization of life and the creation of production systems must be geared to caring and nurturing the planet's ecology.

Several possibilities for the greening of OS and economic organizations emerge from these environmental discourses. They require correctly reassessing our responsibilities towards both human *and* natural environments. There are four possibilities for doing this. I depict them through the mnemonic GREENING discussed below.

## GR—good returns

Organizations pursue the goal of securing good returns. Reorientation of OS must begin by questioning what constitutes good returns. The definition of good returns is highly contested (Hall and Quinn, 1983). Historically, good returns were defined from the viewpoint of investors—as profits or economic wealth.

Environmentalism challenges the adequacy of such uni-dimensional measures of returns. It views returns in more holistic terms. Apparently organizations 'return' or produce more than just economic goods. They produce jobs, taxes, environmental pollution, technological risk, hazardous wastes, work places, power, and social milieus. They reproduce culture in their own image. Good returns cannot therefore be defined simply as economic returns. They must include socially, culturally and environmentally desirable outcomes (Daly and Cobb, 1989).

For organizational performance to be meaningful from the environmentalist perspective, it needs to be measured by criteria that at least include environmental performance. These include protection of human health and the natural environment, and the conservation of non-renewable natural resources. To do this OS needs an entirely new calculus that can merge traditional measures of economic performance with measures of environmental performance, without reducing one to the other.

## EE—economics to ethics

A second possibility for greening OS lies in shifting its focus from its current economic orientation to an ethical one. The legitimacy of economic goals of organizations, depends on their ability to respond to ethical demands of society.

Environmentalism suggests that successful business management cannot be measured in economic terms alone. Organizational goals and performance should be measured in community, ecological and ethical terms (Etzioni, 1988); in terms that involve responsible and responsive concern for social and political justice and for the natural environment (Rawls, 1971; World Commission on Environment and Development, 1987).

This ethical reorientation problematizes virtually everything that current organizational theory espouses. It calls into question the very reason for existence of business organizations. If the profit motive is not enough to justify their existence, then revered notions of efficiency, productivity, profitability, competitiveness, etc., become less meaningful.

An ethical base of organizational practice would include concerns and responsibilities of all stakeholders. Paying for environmental protection becomes a shared responsibility of stakeholders.

## NI—nature's independence

Environmental discourses forcefully argue that nature is independent and fundamental. Nature has a moral right to exist independently of the welfare or economic interest of humans. It does not exist for manipulation by humans for their own welfare. It is the fundamental base for all human and consequently organizational activities and is fundamental in the sense that it preceded and survived human agency.

This independence and fundamentalness imposes certain responsibilities on humans who seek to interact with nature. Our responsibilities toward the natural environment can be seriously addressed only if we acknowledge this. Denying it, is the arrogance of humanism and the social sciences (OS included) (Ehrenfeld, 1978; Naess, 1987).

Acknowledging nature's independence alters its status for OS. Nature cannot be viewed simply as a resource. It must be treated and respected as an independent force that casts many influences on organizations.

## NG—nature's goodness

Finally, OS must come to see the benefits of nature-centred theories. These benefits accrue from the inherent goodness and munificence of nature. Nature has historically provided and can continue to provide to humans a basis for reasonable, even bountiful living. Nature-linked pre-industrial societies were in more harmonious relationship with nature than modern industrial societies. Even today, 'nature's people' (indigenous people), wherever they exist around the world live with reverence for nature. They are more in touch with, and harvest the inherent goodness of, nature (Sale, 1992).

Modern industrialization severed the connection between the natural and social/economic worlds. It negated our experience of nature's goodness. It disrupted the generations-long equilibrium between human lifestyles and nature. It caused unequal and socially unjust development. As a result, 25 percent of the world population now enjoys unsustainably high levels of consumption, consuming 80 percent of world resources (and producing 80 percent of world pollution). Simultaneously, 75 percent of the world lives in hunger and extreme deprivation and these 3.5 billion people can industrialize only at the cost of catastrophic environmental damage.

Recognizing nature's goodness implies seeking alternatives to industrially based and environmentally destructive development. OS must expand its agenda to find environmentally sustainable economic-development strategies and lifestyles; lifestyles that allow people to reconnect their economic and social lives with their natural environment. Organization and economic theories must now find ways of reconnecting nature with organizational, economic and social life. They must create a more holistic understanding of economic and organizational development.

## THE ECO-BIOSPHERE: A NEW VIEW OF ORGANIZATIONAL ENVIRONMENTS

The greening of OS can be facilitated by redefining organizational environment as an ecologically grounded concept. As a starting point, I propose the eco-biosphere view of organizational environments. It provides the 'big picture' of the environment in which organizations operate.

Business organizations are economic institutions operating in a physical biological world. Therefore, their relevant environment is an *economic biosphere*. Organizational environments consist of (a) the ecology of the planet Earth, (b) the world economic, social and political order, and (c) the immediate economic, market, technological and socio-political context of organizations.

This eco-biosphere extends beyond the market economies that are the primary focus of much OS. It includes the natural economy of the ecosystem. Ecosystems maintain themselves in equilibrium by producing and consuming resources in natural production cycles. The ecobiosphere also includes the sustainence economy on which millions of people survive by directly taking resources (food, firewood, water, etc.) from nature (Shiva, 1991).

The earth's ecology is not simply an environment that sustains life, but an autonomously self-regulating system that carefully balances its component elements (Brown *et al.*, 1987; Myers, 1984). Some scientists have argued that the planet earth is a living organism (the Gaia hypothesis). It is a self-sustaining system, consisting of the atmosphere, the oceans, the climate and the earth's crust. It gradually created itself and continually modifies its surrounding and parts, to ensure its survival (Cohen and Swan, 1985; Lovelock, 1988). From this perspective, humans and other species are only parts of an indivisible whole.

The world economic, social and political order structures life within the natural environment. This order consists of many nation states with their unique economic, social, cultural and political histories, and mutual relationships. International treaties and laws govern economic relations between nation states and within regional clusters of nations. Despite the apparent separateness of nation states, their economies are linked and interdependent.

Within this world order operate organizations of various types, pursuing diverse objectives. They face specific economic, social, political, regulatory and technological circumstances which create opportunities and constraints for organizations.

Organizational environment is thus a system of tightly interconnected economies and ecologies. It cannot be separated without the loss of essential character and quality. The implication for OS is that it cannot operate under the neoclassical economic assumptions of the past. It must adapt itself to the emerging ecological economics (Costanza, 1992). It must rethink organizations through an eco-biosphere lens.

This way of conceptualizing organizational environments forces us to confront the environmental harm caused by organizational activities (such as technological risks, pollution and waste). Organizations can no longer be treated primarily as rational, neutral, technical *systems of production*, as is done in traditional OS. They must also be seen as *systems of destruction*. They systematically destroy environmental value. This destruction cannot be dismissed away as an 'externality' of production. Organizations must become accountable for these externalities, which are a central and systematic feature of organized economic activity.

This view of organizational environments suggests the need for a fundamental revision of OS concepts and theories. It offers the possibility of creating a more eco-centric OS and eco-centric management practice. Such theories and practices give centrality to nature. They seek to harmonize organization–nature relations. This requires revising our cherished notions of *organizational objectives and strategy*. Objectives of the firm that maximize (or satisfice) variables such as profits, revenues and productivity are incomplete and inadequate. Objectives must also include minimizing the negative and destructive effects of organizational activities.

The concept of strategy deals with the co-alignment of organization with its environment. A firm's strategies should not simply define its domain of operation and scope at the corporate level, and competitive approaches at the business-unit level. They must include some conception of the firm's relationship with the natural environment and an ecological strategy for the renewal of environmental resources and for managing environmental impacts.

The eco-biosphere view also has implications for organization–environment relationships. It emphasizes how embeddedness between organizational and environmental elements makes them mutually and reciprocally interdependent. Environmental analysis must therefore assess how organizational activities impact the environment (Pearce, Markandya and Barbier, 1989; Rees, 1989).

Organizations that view their environments in eco-biosphere terms would establish clear ecological missions, develop elaborate ecological strategies and have strong environmental management programmes. Organizational strategies, structures, systems and cultures would be designed to enhance environmental performance. Accounting systems would try to capture the unaccounted organizational and societal costs of environmental problems. Traditional accounting procedures systematically bias real costs and performance by ignoring environmental degradation.

Long-term organizational legitimacy depends on how organizations handle their ethical responsibilities toward the natural environment. Organizations can build legitimacy by addressing the environmental concerns of primary stakeholders such as customers, investors, suppliers, government, communities and the media.

Finally, moving toward eco-centric management requires changes in industrial policies and government regulations. The public-policy infra-structure within which businesses operate must create necessary inducements and fair competitive rules for protecting and enhancing the natural environment.

In this closing decade of the Twentieth Century, protection of the natural environment has become the primary concern of society. Many academic disciplines, societal institutions and social movements have given voice to this concern. OS has neglected to engage this environmental discourse seriously.

Considering the serious damage that organizational activities inflict on nature, we need to rectify this lacuna in OS. This paper takes a first step in this direction. It articulates a critique and proposes an alternative concept of organizational environment. It examines some implications for organizational theory of looking at the environment in these new ways. Fleshing out the implications further and developing ecocentric organizational theories and practices is the challenge facing OS researchers.

## ACKNOWLEDGEMENTS

I would like to thank Marta Cálas and Linda Smircich of University of Massachusetts and Denis Smith of Liverpool Business School for their insightful comments on earlier versions of this paper.

## NOTES

1. Organizational Studies is a broad and fragmented field. Delineating its boundaries is a difficult task. It includes the literature that deals with organizations from a number of disciplinary and interdisciplinary perspectives (Whitley, 1984). The core literature deals with behaviours in, and of, organizations. Organizational scholars usually operate out of an institutional base of management departments in business schools and public administration schools, and form sociology and psychology departments. It is the literature that gets published in journals such as *Administrative Science Quarterly, Academy of Management Review* and *Journal, Organization Studies, Journal of Management Studies,* etc. Other relevant literatures that contribute to organizational studies come from organizational sociology and psychology.
2. In choosing the mnemonic CASTRATED I was guided by the literal meaning of the term taken from *Webster's New Collegiate Dictionary,* 150th Anniversary Edition (G.C. Merriam Company, Springfield, MA, 1981):
   *Castrate:*
   derived from Latin *contratus,* or *contrare,* Greek *keazein* to split, akin to Sanskrit *sasati* he cuts to pieces, meaning 1. (a) to deprive of the testes: GELD, (b) to deprive of the ovaries: SPAY; 2. to deprive of vitality or effect: emasculate.
   Deprived of testes and ovaries signifies incapacity in *both* genders. I would like to avoid possible unintended Freudian interpretations where girls are seen as castrated boy, and hence mother nature as castrated father nature.

## REFERENCES

Aldrich, H. E. (1979) *Organizations and environments.* Englewood Cliffs, NJ: Prentice-Hall.
Berry, Thomas (1988) *The dream of the earth.* San Francisco: Sierra Club Books.

Brown, L., W. U. Chandler, C. Flavin, J. Jacobson, C. Polock, S. Postel, L. Starke, and E. C. Wolf (1987) *State of the world 1987.* Washington D.C.: Worldwatch Institute.

Bucholz, R., A. Marcus, and J Post (1992) *Managing environmental issues: a case book,* Englewood Cliffs, NJ: Prentice-Hall.

Burrell, G., and G. Morgan (1978) *Sociological paradigms and organizational analysis.* London: Heinemann.

Carson, R. (1962) *Silent Spring.* Greenwich, CT: Fawcett.

Cheney, Jim (1987) 'Eco-feminism and deep ecology'. *Enivironmental Ethics* (Summer): 115–145.

Cohen, M. J., and J. Swan, *editors* (1985) *Is the earth a living organism?* Proceedings of a conference by National Audobon Society Expedition Institute, Sharon, MA, August.

Commoner, B. (1990) *Making peace with the planet.* New York.

Costanza, R. (1992) *Ecological economics.* New York: Columbia University Press.

Crozier, M., and J. Thoenig (1976) 'The regulation of complex organized systems'. *Administrative Science Quarterly* **21:** 547–570.

Daly, H., and J. Cobb (1989) *For the common good.* New York: Beacon Press.

Darwin, C. (1859/1963) *On the origin of species.* New York: Heritage Press.

Devall, B., and G. Sessions (1985) *Deep ecology: living as if nature mattered.* Salt Lake City, UT: Peregrine Smith.

Duncan, R. B. (1972) 'Characteristics of organizational environments and perceived environmental uncertainty'. *Administrative Science Quarterly* **17:** 313–327.

Emery, F. E., and E. L. Trist (1965) 'The causal texture of organizational environments'. *Human Relations* **18:** 21–32.

Ehrenfeld, D. W. (1978) *The arrogance of humanism.* New York: Oxford University Press.

Eisenhardt, K. M. (1989) 'Making fast strategic decisions in high velocity environments'. *Academy of Management Journal* 32/3: 543–576.

Etzioni, A. (1988) *The moral dimension.* New York: The Free Press.

Fahey, L., and V. K. Narayanan (1984) *Environmental analysis.* St. Paul, MN: West Publishers.

Fischer, M. M. J. (1986) 'Ethnicity and the post modern arts of memory' in *Writing culture: the poetics and politics of ethnography.* J. Clifford and G. E. Marcus (eds.) Berkeley: University of California Press.

Freeman, R. E. (1984) *Strategic management: a stakeholder approach.* Boston: Pitman.

Frosch, R., and N. Gallopoulos (1989) *Scientific American* (September): 144–152.

Garelik, G. (1990) 'The Soviets clean up their act'. *Time,* January 29, pp. 64.

Gorbachev, M. (1990) 'Address to the global forum on environmental protection and development for survival'. Moscow, January 20.

Hall, R. H. and R. E. Quinn, *editors* (1983) *Organization theory and public policy.* Beverly Hills, CA: Sage.

Hambrick, D. C. (1983) 'An empirical typology of mature industrial product environments'. *Academy of Management Journal* **26:** 213–230.

Hannan, M., and J. Freeman (1989) *Organizational ecology.* Cambridge, M.A.: Harvard University Press.

Harrigan, K. R. (1980) *Strategies for declining industries.* Lexington, MA: Lexington Books.

Hoffman, W. M., R. Frederick, and E. S. Petry (1990) *The corporation, ethics, and the environment.* New York: Quorum.

King, Ynestra (1983) 'The ecology of feminism and the feminism of ecology'. *Harbinger: The Journal of Social Ecology* **1:** 16.

Kirkpatrick, David (1990) 'Environmentalism: the crusade'. *Fortune,* February 12, pp. 44–51.

Lawrence, P. R., and J. Lorsch (1967) *Organizations and environments.* Boston: Graduate School of Business, Harvard University.

Leopold, A. (1949) *A sand county almanac.* New York: Oxford University Press.

Likens, G. (1987) 'Chemical wastes in our atmosphere—An ecological crisis' *Industrial Crises Quarterly* 1/4: 13–33.

Lovelock, J. (1988) *The ages of Gaia: A biography of our living earth.* New York: Norton.

Marsh, G. P. (1965) *Man and nature: or, physical geography as modified by human action.* Cambridge MA: Harvard University Press.

Mckibben, R. (1989) *The end of nature*. New York: Random House.

Merchant, Carolyn (1980) *Death of nature: women, ecology and the scientific revolution*. New York: Harper and Row.

Mitroff, I. I., and R. H. Kilmann (1984) *Corporate tragedies*. New York: Praeger.

Mitroff, I., and T. Pauchant (1990) *We are so big and powerful nothing bad can happen to us*. New York: Carol Publishing.

Myers, N., *editor* (1984) *Gaia: an atlas of planet management*. New York: Anchor Press, Doubleday.

Muir, J. (1901) *Our national parks*. Boston: Houghton Mifflin.

Naess, A. (1987) *Ecology, community and lifestyle: Ecosophy T*. Cambridge: Cambridge University Press.

Nash, R. F. (1989) *The rights of nature*. Madison, WI: University of Wisconsin Press.

O'Connor J. (1987) *The meaning of crisis*. New York: Basil Blackwell.

Pauchant, T., and J. Fortier (1990) 'Anthropocentric ethics in organizations, strategic management, and the environment' in *Advances in strategic management*, Vol. 6. P. Shrivastava and R. Lamb (eds.). Greenwich, CT: JAI Press.

Pearce, D., A. Markandya, and E. Barbier (1989) *Blueprint for a Green Economy*. London: Earthscan Publication.

Perrow, C. (1984) *Normal accidents: living with high risk technologies*. New York: Basic Books.

Pfeffer, J. (1982) *Organizations and organizations theory*. Boston: Pitman.

Porter, M. E. (1980) *Competitive strategy*. New York: The Free Press.

Post, J. E. (1991) 'Management as if the earth mattered'. *Business Horizons* (July–Aug.) 32–38.

Rawls, J. (1971) *A theory of justice*. Cambridge, MA: Harvard University Press.

Rees, William E. (1989) 'The ecological meaning of environment–economy integration'. Unpublished paper, School of Community and Regional Planning, The University of British Columbia, Vancouver, B.C.

Roberts, K. H. (1989) 'New challenges to organizational research: High reliability organizations'. *Industrial Crisis Quarterly* **3/2:** 111–127.

Rozenzweig, R., and J. V. Singh (1991) 'Organizational environments and the multinational enterprise'. *Academy of Management Review* **16/2:** 340–361.

Sale, K. (1992) *The conquest of paradise*. New York.

Scott, R. W. (1981) *Organizations: rational, natural and open systems*. Englewood Cliffs, NJ: Prentice-Hall.

Scwheitzer, A. (1923) *Philosophy of civilization: civilization and ethics*. (Trans, John Naish). London: A & C Black.

Shiva, V. (1991) *Ecology and the politics of survival*. New Delhi: Sage.

Shrivasta, P. (1990) 'The ozone crisis: A multiple stakeholder solution'. *Business and Society Review* (October).

Shrivasta, P. (1992a) *Bhopal: anatomy of a crisis,* (revised ed.). London: Paul Chapman.

Shrivasta, P. (1995) 'Industrial/environmental crises and corporate social responsibility'. *Journal of Socio-Economics* **25/1:** forthcoming.

Shrivasta, P., I. I. Mitroff, D. Miller, and A. Miglani (1988) 'Understanding industrial crises'. *Journal of Management Studies* **25/4:** 285–304.

Smith, Denis (1992) *Business and the environment*. London: Paul Chapman.

Siomkos, G. (1989) 'Managing product harm crises'. *Industrial Crises Quarterly* **3/2:** 41–60.

Starbuck, W.H. (1976) 'Organizations and their environments' in *Handbook of industrial and organizational psychology*. M. D. Dunnette (ed.). 1069–1123. Chicago: Rand McNally.

Terreberry, S. (1968) 'The evolution of organizational environments'. *Administrative Science Quarterly* **12** (March): 590–613.

Thoreau, H. D. (1906) *The writings of Henry Thoreau*. (B. Torrey, Ed.) Boston: Farrar, Strauss, Giroux.

Throop, G. M. Starik, and G. Rands (1993) 'Strategic management in a greening world' in *Advances in Strategic Management*, Vol. 9. P. Shrivasta, A. Huff, and J. Dutton (eds.), 63–92. Greenwich, CT: JAI Press.

Weick, K. E. (1979) *The social psychology of organizing*. Reading, MA: Addison Wesley.

Weick, K. E. (1988) 'Enacted sense making in crisis environments'. *Journal of Management Studies* **25:** 305–317.

Weick, K. E. (1989) 'Theory construction as disciplined imagination'. *Academy of Management Review* **14/4**: 516–531.

Whitehead, A. N. (1920) *The concept of nature.* Ann Arbor, MI: University of Michigan Press.

Whitley, Richard (1984) 'Management studies as a fragmented adhocracy'. *Journal of Management Studies* **21**: 369–390.

World Commission on Environment and Development (1987) *Our common future.* New York: Oxford University Press.

Worster, D. (1977) *Nature's economy: the roots of ecology.* San Francisco: Sierra Club Books.

# 10

# Constructing the Green Manager

*Stephen Fineman*

This article applies a social constructionist approach to senior managers' 'green' selves and roles. In a qualitative, empirical, study of the UK automotive industry, the social/political contexts of managers' organizational lives are explored as they interact with, and define, the green corporate agenda. Ethical dimensions of environmentalism are stressed—particularly the distinctions and tensions between private moral positions, enacted morality, and the conventional morality as disseminated by the corporation. The study reveals the way different stakeholders are construed, and how 'green' territories are contested. The implications for organizational change and strategic formulation are discussed, especially the strengths and limitations of approaching corporate greening from enacted/normative moralities, or from a vision of a substantive transformation of values.

Since the 1970s there has been a surge in public concern about the responsibility and moral culpability of corporations for the environmental damage inflicted by their processes and products. Disasters, legislation, green education, green consumerism, environmental pressure groups and the media have kept 'business and the environment' alive as an issue. Although some of the most visible sources of industrial pollution have now faded, overall pollution from industrial enterprise continues to rise (Smith, 1993; Schot and Fischer, 1993). Of particular concern has been the greenhouse effect, depletion of stratospheric ozone, the exhaustion of fossil fuels, the effects of high uses of agro-chemicals, deforestation, and the extermination of plant and animal species.

The organizational sciences have been slow to address environmental worries. What Gladwin (1993, 39) terms 'a great paradox: the dearth of theory and empiricism in the face of one of the most important transformations of all time'. He, and others, seek a more systematic link to strategic analysis, organizational theory and change, morality and leadership (Mylonadis, 1993; Roberts, 1992; Beauchamp and Bowie, 1983; Pauchant and Fortier, 1990; Everett *et al.*, 1993). One key strand in this plea is a prescriptive one: that a substantial shift is required in the belief system and values of key organizational actors—away from the crisis prone and defensive

Reprinted with permission from *British Journal of Management*, 1996, in press towards one where 'ethical values and environmental sensibilities dominate' (Shrivastava, 1993, 30). Bolting on the 'false consciousness' of a 'green tinge' is regarded as inadequate (Smith, 1993, 9).

Surveys of UK executives and managers suggests that some things are indeed happening environmentally, but probably not because of their passion for protecting the planet. Large corporations have institutionalized and bureaucratized the environment. Typical symbols are public statements of environmental intent or mission and an official, or department to 'handle' environmental affairs (Burke and Hill, 1990; Touche Ross, 1990). Yet environmental work takes up a very small proportion of boardroom time, where compliance with legislative standards is of most concern (IOD, 1992; 1993). 'Deeper' structures devoted to 'total quality environmental management' are hard to find (Bennett *et al.*, 1993), and it is very rare to encounter companies raising environmental considerations at a product's inception (Schot and Fischer, 1993). Some firms will attempt to optimize production processes to reduce pollution, while others engage in greening in fragmented fashion, according to what they feel is affordable or looks right—such as energy saving, recycling or supplier auditing.

This mixed picture, from generally thin data, hints at how managers might be thinking. But we have yet to determine precisely how they construct 'the environment'. This paper attempts to do just this by taking a less-usual, social constructionist approach. It seeks to explicate the personal and social meanings of 'greening' as situated in managers' everyday working realities, illuminated by 'thicker', qualitative reports, grounded in managers' own experiences and observations (Geertz, 1983; Berger and Luckmann, 1966).

Can the moral imperative and ethical values underpinning the wider environmental debate be enacted by managers. The theme is explored through three related sub-questions:

1. *What are managers' private moral positions on the environment?* We are here concerned with an individual's 'internalized' views of right and wrong, reflecting parental, educational, community and religious influences. Some theorists (e.g. Kholberg, 1981; Snell, 1990) suggest that personal morality progresses from a fairly primitive self-interested notion of justice to a more collective, or 'relativistic' one. Fisher *et al.* (1987) hold that relativism includes a deep concern for social issues, and is a key to effective management in complex, 'post-bureaucratic' organizations.

2. *How do such beliefs transfer to managers' views about what is appropriate for their work roles, and how are they reconciled with the conventional morality of the corporation—its public statements of environmental intent?* Job roles contain their own 'oughts', contextualized in terms of meeting the local expectations of peers, supervisors and other staff. Conventional morality is reflected in high-profile corporate symbols of environmental intent—codes of ethical conduct and published mission statements.

3. *What emotions, rationalizations and political processes influence managers' enacted morality—what they do (or say they do) in terms of environmental protection?* Enacted morality refers to the moral tone and structure of manifest actions—which can be different from what people say they ought to do. It reflects the moral rules in use; a product of the social/political order of the moment and the situationally-specific needs and interests of the actors involved (Jackall, 1988). What is morally wrong at a level, is 'right' in action.

## DATA SOURCES AND METHOD

One industry is featured—UK-based automotive manufacture. The research forms part of a wider qualitative study of the author's on the 'greening of management'[1]. The present discussion is based on interviews with a cross-functional group of 37 top and middle managers in six major automotive-manufacturing companies. All companies are major international traders. Two have their corporate headquarters in the USA; the other in Scandinavia, Europe, UK and Japan.

The companies agreed to take part in the study in return for evaluative feedback from the researchers on their environmental performance. Interviewees include directors and other staff with special responsibility for the environment. The sample, therefore, comprises many of the main 'reality definers' on company environmental philosophy and practice. In semistructured interviews participants were asked about their company's past and present position on environmental issues, the structures and processes in place, their as-citizen feelings and beliefs, the realities of their role, the trade-offs and stakeholders, the external pressures and the interdepartmental politics. Information was also gleaned from observation—participant and non-participant—of company environmental meetings, from officials of the industry's trade association, from public relations documents and internal company papers.

## AUTOMOTIVE AND GREENING

The automotive industry is a particularly interesting case for greening. Arguably, its produce could be viewed as environmentally disastrous, whatever. Cars and trucks pollute, add considerable stress to land, plants, people and animals, and tend to saturate cities and villages. Its manufacturing processes involve the consumption and processing of a wide range of materials—steel, plastics, timber, chemicals, paints—and a huge use of energy. Its factories occupy vast tracts of town and city land, and, more recently, green-field sites.

Set against this, the sales and the ownership of vehicles have become one of the key indicators of individual and national prosperity. The industry feeds, and is fed by, a multitude of other industries; it creates employment and wealth. Cars have come to represent personal status and are prized as much for their image as for their apparent indispensability to personal mobility.

Within this split picture, the industry has been subjected to a range of pressures to respond to public environmental concerns. It has been targeted by green pressure groups and subjected to national and international legislation on environmental standards. It has also been confronted by various waves of green consumerism. In response most automotive companies (all in the present study) have published an expansive image of their green credentials. For example:

> We are the world's largest industrial corporation . . . a leader for the rest of the auto industry . . . dedicated to protecting human health, natural resources and the global environment.

Protecting the earth and its natural resources is indeed one of the most critical issues facing mankind. As a concerned corporate citizen and a manufacturer of automotive products that have environmental impacts, we are supportive of initiatives that have a positive effect on the environment.

Such rhetorical flourishes are a presentation of conventional corporate morality, and are a routine step towards company image transformation. However, they need to be understood in relation to actors' less-public beliefs.

### Greenness—out of, and within, role

Generally, respondents had a sober, relatively unimpassioned, view of their citizenship of an environmentally degrading world. They eschewed radicalism or active environmentalism outside of work. Not being 'lentils and sandals' types was a favoured, defensive, self-description. Concern for environmentalism in their private life ranged from the non-existent to mildly interested. Most managers would do a 'bit of recycling' at home, and were a touch apprehensive in the face of some of the 'trickier' environmental questions raised by their children. Few, however, felt that environmental care was something that (a) should be their personal mission (they were just 'a tiny cog in a huge wheel') or (b) should have some special meaning because of their position in the motor industry. As 'ordinary men' they acted in 'ordinary' self-interested ways:

I put petrol in the car, burn it and don't really think about it. I suppose it comes down to if you can't see it, it isn't there.

I could drive a smaller car. I know when I put my foot down I'm actually burning more fuel. So where's my personal conviction? I suppose it's a question of ease of availability.

I'm not a villainous polluter of the environment. I'm quite a tidy person. But I still prefer a car without a catalytic converter because of the better fuel economy.

Managers with a special responsibility for environmental affairs would, ironically, also step back from owning any special feelings for, or about, environmental damage. Indeed, some were decidedly uncomfortable with any implication that their work was, or should be, anything beyond a particular form of technical expertise:

I'm fairly pragmatic, not an idealist. I think there's a misconception that if you're an environmental manager then you are an idealist. To me it's simply a feature of good management.

The 'pragmatism' was often coupled with a rationalization, or cutting-down to size, of environmental fears: 'It's really not the mess that a lot of people would have us believe'; 'We're forecasting doom and gloom which is unnecessarily pessimistic'; 'It's an apocalyptic view of life that's never going to happen'. Such dissonance reduction (e.g. Festinger and Carlsmith, 1959) was supported by the managers' selective interpretation of technical arguments—to back up, or validate, their scepticism. One environmental director disclosed his reluctance to toe the corporate environmental line—underlined by tossing the interviewer a book which purported to show 'just how over-hyped the claims are'. He viewed himself as a source of reason and realism amidst the growing hysteria.

## Serving the great car economy

Some managers would concede that there was a problem 'out there' that they could not ignore. They would speak genuinely of their concern to avoid doing things that could cause harm to others. They wanted decent air to breath. A few had harsh words for the automobile: 'they've ruined town centres'; 'fouled the environment', 'clogged the countryside', 'killed more people than Genghis Khan'. But the dissonance was not irresolvable. Their rationalization proceeded as follows:

*Argument 1*  There is very little that we do that does not affect the environment. There must be a balance. So it is naive to blame the car.

*Argument 2*  There is always a price to pay for our civilisation, for our very basic needs for personal, private, transport. We all want to travel, and public transport simply is not enough.

*Argument 3*  Of course, public transport should be better, and we would support that. But that is for the government, not us.

*Argument 4*  Many people in the past have said the end of the world is nigh. There have been lots of false prophets.

*Argument 5*  But what is right? The environment or industry? If we went for a perfectly green world without industry and jobs, how is that progress. No. We must clean up our operations as quickly as possible, not get rid of the car.

In this manner managers would construct three key props to their beliefs to assuage any ethical anxieties and assist them to enact their corporate roles. The first was faith in the automobile—as absolutely essential to social and trading life as we know it. The car was regarded with some reverence, and often coupled with words such as 'value', 'respect', 'people's needs', 'worthwhile', 'essential convenience'. These were 'givens' which could not be compromised. The second was a vote of confidence in a competitive economic system in which automotive production plays a key part. Finally, a trust in the technical fix—to ameliorate or reduce 'necessary' environmental damage.

## Translating and shaping the environment

The construction of the environment soon became politicized and professionalized—notably in the partiality of its guardianship. It could rest with an engineer, a public relations executive, a commercial manager, a health and safety expert, a company lawyer, or an operations manager. Some would be top managers; others middle ranking. Their positioning amply symbolized the importance, or the ambiguity, of environmental affairs in the corporation. And their particular expertise suggested how the company preferred initially to interpret, or transform, the environment—into a PR issue, an engineering problem, a legal challenge, a marketing project, or an accounting activity. So one environmental director, also an engineer, spoke enthusiastically of their 'lean burn engines' as '*the* major way forward'. Another, an accountant by training, could not justify the payoff on any new investment on environmental issues. And a third, schooled in economics and law, asserted that 'the key task for us now is to ensure we comply with the legislation'.

There was some evidence that a strong environmental champion at the top of the organization could be heard, at least to junior management levels. The green message was normally orchestrated and amplified through company newsletters, internal television and publicized energy targets. But there was little evidence of a consistent internalization and passion for greening, along the lines of the corporate mission statement or the tenets of a 'strong' organizational culture. The one, pristine, Japanese company in the sample refused to accept that the environment was an issue per se—over and above normal quality control and engineering design. Most of the others were highly factionalized, with environmental interests fast dissipating after leaving their internal sponsors. They would get caught in the machinations of structural changes aimed at delayering and decentralizing; in the politics of recessionary survival; in the doubts and scepticism of managers tied tightly to specific production and cost targets; and in the promotion of particular functional interests.

Some of these processes were evident in the reports on, or direct observations of, managerial meetings devoted to environmental strategy and policy. Top policy meetings were described as 'really hard nosed'; 'quite pragmatic'; 'usually defensive', 'how to keep our nose clean':

> It's can we afford it? What will it give us in return? How long will we have to wait? Any competitive advantage? No fine moral sentiments in this! (Environmental Director)

While environmental directors varied in their professional expertise, they all expressed vulnerability in presence of their directorial colleagues. 'Selling' the environment internally, beyond legislative compliance, was regarded as a tough task, especially in a highly competitive market where customers were not calling for green products. Greenness was rarely afforded any intrinsic value, worthy of investment for its own sake. One company in the sample was an exception. It had a long history of social responsibility and its customers were described as 'buyers who wouldn't cut your throat for a pound'. Such attitudes reflected the Scandinavian roots of the company where pro environment values flourished, echoed by the company's shareholders. Yet, significantly, it was a glum, cautionary tale that was circulating. The company had recently failed spectacularly with a very expensive environmental state-of-the-art plant. The vehicles it produced were too expensive to sell competitively and the plant had to close.

Most directors could not assume acceptability for their environmental arguments, and they talked of the importance of 'correctly justifying' expenditure. 'It can't be presented as just rather a good thing to do. It's like this', commented one director:

People talk about all sorts of things as an expression of how green they feel, but that soon fades away. I managed to get my Board to accept that we needed to spend £1 million to go green in the factory, and that will meet the way public opinion is shifting over the next five years. But then up pops my Marketing colleague and says that he could spend that £1 million now on an advertising campaign which would actually sell another 20,000 cars and keep 500 employed for another month. Guess who won the day.

The social negotiation of the environment continued in middle-level environmental committees. Typically, these forums handled agendas ranging from the recylability of plastic cups from the company's coffee machines, to the details of energy conservation, environmental-award competitions, and environmental training and awareness. They were normally low key affairs, highly bureaucratized, with moderate to low commitment. Frequently, the drive and energy of the chairman was a crucial factor in maintaining the enthusiasm of colleagues who, while sympathetic to the agenda, rarely considered environmental issues as central to their work.

## External stakeholders

Some managers acted as environmentally-attuned gatekeepers, interacting directly with outside stakeholders—especially pollution inspectors, government environment officials and green pressure groups. Together, these could markedly influence what an organization did, or what new environmental company approach, or orthodoxy, emerged. The meaning of greening continued its mobile course.

Dealings with officials charged with enforcing pollution regulations were often likened to a game of poker. A company's ace card was its crucial role as a local employer—to be played against an inspector's 'unreasonable' (i.e. too expensive) demand for technical changes. The deal struck, and its cost to the company, depended very much on how well managers played their cards and 'read' the official's intent. While cost minimization was the overwhelming drive in these encounters, managers would also claim how misguided were many directives—such as consuming energy to eliminate one form of pollution, simply to create another.

Corporate power is also exercised with government civil servants and ministers to influence the shape of national and international environmental directives which could impinge on the company. Any legislative change could result in significant financial costs to the company, especially for research and engineering in product development. This was generally perceived as a commercial threat, to be minimized if possible—regardless of its environmental intent or public interest. 'Getting ahead of legislation' was a commonly stated aim to deflect criticism that the company was mainly reactive in its environmental stance. In practice proactivity was very carefully calculated and confined. Few managers were willing to speculate very much on the environment and, as the above discussion indicates, few would be permitted to do so. A senior engineer summed up his view:

I enjoy the technical challenges of improving the product and if that actually has the benefit that it makes it more environmentally friendly then that's a bonus. But I still think we're a long way from where the environmental issues are really driving the product development.

A final arena of concern is interfacing with environmental pressure groups. Although most managers wished to keep such groups at a distance, they had developed a grudging respect—borne of tussles which, whatever the official outcome, could inflict damage to the company' reputation. Public embarrassment was a potent emotion for organizational change, although this normally meant defensive strategies. Green claims were very carefully worded (e.g. 'recylable' does not mean it is actually recycled) or avoided, and 'fact sheets' were prepared to present the company view. Green groups were seen, generally, as becoming more sophisticated in their arguments and adroit in their techniques. A force to be reckoned with despite their 'misunderstandings' and 'emotionality'. This was patently clear to one middle manager who was urgently seeking ways to damage limitation after a Friends of the Earth named them 'sewer rat of the month'. Interestingly, and a somewhat wry comment on corporate morality, some managers were content to leave the custody of the organization's scruples in the hands of green pressure groups.

## DISCUSSION AND CONCLUSION

This brief, but variegated, sketch of corporate environmental life sheds some descriptive light on the questions raised at the beginning of this paper. The interpretative style of research is helpful in deepening our understanding of the less-obvious, and often multidimensional, processes that shape managerial reflection and action.

Thinking and feeling green is a fickle process in the automotive industry. It is clearly not related to strongly held private views on environmental care. The managers, as a group, seemed content to 'ride' the environment in their personal lives, both metaphorically and literally. If the automotive industry is typically (and indeed, the managers' responses were not dissimilar from those of other industries in the research programme), managers are not particularly good emissaries for the environment. They are less likely than their children to experience moral perturbation or outrage about environmental damage, and they are skilled at techno-rationalization—taking the emotional sting out of the environmental debate.

Prescriptive moral theory suggests organizational actors need to think that they are transgressing a universal moral imperative (e.g. 'it is quite wrong to create undue harm to the environment, regardless') if unqualified ethical behaviour is to follow (Brady, 1990; Oakley, 1993). In this respect, the managers in this study have some way to go. In terms of Kholberg's (1969) six stages of cognitive moral development, they rarely move beyond Stage 3 (living up to the expectations of key role-senders at work) or Stage 4 (being legally justified in their actions). The few who were mildly concerned about environmental degradation were unwilling to honour this at work, or to justify their work actions in terms of the environmental welfare of others (Stages 5 and 6). It would be surprising if a significant moral/value shift could be inculcated through exposure to corporate statements on environmental care, or from 'green' company training courses. At best, they might bring about first-order change (Levy and Merry, 1986)—adopting some of the vocabulary of environmentalism and minor adjustments to current procedures. Furthermore, as suggested earlier, moral conduct requires more than the application of certain ethical rules. It is 'felt'. The anxiety, guilt or shame that triggers feelings of responsibility for the broader effects of one's actions are learned in situations beyond those of just the organization (Soloman, 1991; Fineman, 1993).

If we take managers' *working* moralities as our starting point, we encounter a number of smaller environmental 'oughts'. Some are firmly located in organizational norms (e.g. 'we have faith in technology'; 'commercial survival comes first'; 'cars are crucial'), others are improvised when particular social encounters, or felt pressures, test the shape of green interest or commitment. Framing greening in this socially constructive manner connects well with the experiential and empirical realities of the actors in the study. It also supports a view that green organizational culture, like some other popularized brands of culture, will often run unevenly throughout an organization; more a series of swirls, or ebbs and flows, of mutual interest and direction (Aldrich, 1992; Martin and Siehl, 1983). Likewise, strategic choice to go green in order to maximize competitive advantage (a rational commercial approach) is rarely a dominant belief; it usually has to be haggled for by a 'committed', but ever vulnerable, champion. An agreements amongst top managers are not necessarily espoused by their subordinate staff. Perhaps the only green certainty is legislation— which ensures that environmental issues will exist somewhere on the corporate agenda. But for the corporate actor, legislation is fertile ground for the exercise of managerial talents for negotiation, game playing and persuasion. There is no straightforward relationship between 'out there' environmental legislation and 'in here' company reactions.

**Filling the moral vacuum?**

Our picture of the automotive industry leads to two rather different conclusions on greening. The first develops the thesis that working, or enacted moralities, essentially reflect what managers are and do, so any quest for green corporate change is best focused on these constructs. The second asserts that this is not good enough. As the environment 'belongs' to everyone, its damage is quintessentially a matter of broad-consensual moral concern and organizational actors are as culpable as anyone else. Environmental protection cannot be left to the vagaries of organizational political nuance. Here, the challenge for organizational theory is to find ways of bridging the enacted and absolute moral perspective (e.g. see Donaldson and Dunfee, 1994).

It is likely that environmental sensibilities can be fostered, or attuned, under the enacted morality perspective. Encounters with legislators and green pressure groups offer scope for wider, developmental, organizational learning beyond the defensive strategies typical of the sample in the present study. The organization's accounting system could begin to include environmental performance targets, against which individual managers could be judged (Owen, 1993; Gray *et al.*, 1993). Leaders of 'transformational' ilk could help promote the concrete, bottom-line, benefits of thinking and performing green, and green shareholders could be wooed. And there are examples of cultural engineering where 'passion' for a product, be it 'green', 'excellent', or 'quality' has been achieved to a degree (Kunda, 1992; Hochschild,

1983; Peters and Waterman, 1982). These processes are not without their pitfalls or ideological traps (Willmott, 1993). They offer promise of an organization that shifts some of its practices and espoused values towards environmentalism. Its soul, however, can remain relatively untouched; environmentalism comes and goes according to 'business priorities'.

Until there is a substantive change in the meaning of business, such that commercial and social value is inextricably tied to 'common-wealth' and 'non-anthropocentric' outcomes (Pauchant and Fortier, 1990), it is unlikely that managerial greening will progress beyond the formulaic. At present, the portentous sense of crisis generated by some readings of the planet's ecological state is not shared by managers; at least not to the extent to significantly challenge still-rewarding ways of doing business. The paradigm shift in organizational thinking and practice has yet to come (Khun, 1970). But this could change as new players arrive on the scene, and older ones gain strength—such as green pressure groups, national and international legislators, the media and a new generation of greener managers. This last group is particularly worthy of attention; they were noted for their challenging stance in the current study. They are, perhaps, the tip of an iceberg of new graduates and MBAs who have been a solid part of the social and educational environmentalism of the last two decades. They represent what Hannan and Freeman (1984, 1989) see as a shift in organizational ecology; inevitable organizational change through selection and replacement.

## NOTE

1. The study is financed by the UK Economic and Social Research Council.

## REFERENCES

Aldrich, H. E. (1992) Incommensurable paradigms? Vital signs from three perspectives. In M. Reed and M. Hughes, *Rethinking Organization*, London: Sage.
Beauchamp, T. L. and Bowie, N. E. (eds) (1983) *Ethical Theory and Business*. Englewood Cliffs, New Jersey: Prentice Hall.
Bennett, S. J., Freierman, R., and George, S. (1993). *Corporate Realities and Environmental Truths*. New York: Wiley.
Berger, P. B. and Luckmann, T. (1966) *The Social Construction of Reality*. New York: Doubleday.
Brady, F. N. (1990). *Ethical Managing*. New York: Macmillan.
Burke, T. and Hill, J. (1990) *Ethics, Environment and the Company*, London: Institute of Business Ethics.
Donaldson, T. and Dunfee, T. W. (1994) Towards a unified conception of business ethics: integrative social contracts theory. *The Academy of Management Review*, **19**: 2. 252–284.
Everett, M., Mack, J. E. and Oresick, R. (1993) 'Towards greening in the executive suite'. In K. Fischer and J. Schot, J (eds), *Environmental Strategies for Industry*, Washington, D.C.: Island Press.
Festinger, L. and Carlsmith, J. (1959) 'Cognitive consequences of forced compliance'. *Journal of Abnormal and Social Psychology*, **58**: 203–210.
Fineman, S. (ed) (1993) *Emotion in Organizations*. London: Sage.
Fisher, D., Merron, K. and Torbett, W. R. (1987) 'Human development and managerial effectiveness', *Group and Organization Studies*, **12**: 3, 257–273.

Geertz, C. (1983) *Local Knowledge*. New York: Basic Books.

Gladwin, T. (1993) 'The meaning of greening: A plea for organizational theory'. In K. Fischer and J. Schot, J (eds), *Environmental Strategies for Industry*, Washington, D.C.: Island Press.

Gray, R., Bebbington, J. and Walters, D. (1993) *Accounting for the Environment*. London: Chapman.

Hannan, M. T. and Freeman, J. (1984) 'Structural inertia and organizational change', *American Sociological Review*, **49:** 149–164.

Hannan, M. T. and Freeman, J. (1989) *Organizational Ecology*. Cambridge, Mass.: Harvard University Press.

Hochschild, A. (1983) *The Managed Heart*. Berkeley: University of California.

IOD (1992) and (1993) 'Members' Opinion Survey—Environment'. Institute of Directors, London.

IOD (1993) 'Members' Opinion Survey—Environment'. Institute of Directors, London.

Jackall, R. (1988) *Moral Mazes*. New York: Oxford University Press.

Kholberg, L. (1969) 'Stage and sequence: The cognitive development approach to socialization'. In D. A. Goslin (ed), *Handbook of Socialization Theory and Research*. Chicago: Rand McNally.

Kholberg, L. (1981) *Essays on Moral Development*. New York: Harper and Row.

Khun, T. (1970) *The Structure of Scientific Revolutions*. Chicago: Chicago University Press.

Kunda, G. (1992) *Engineering Culture: Control and Commitment in a High-tech Corporation*. Philadelphia: Temple University Press.

Levy, A. and Merry, U. (1986) *Organizational Transformation*. New York: Praeger.

Martin, J. and Siehl, C. (1983) 'Organizational culture and counterculture', *Organizational Dynamics*, **12:** 52–64.

Mylonadis, Y. (1993) 'Environmental concerns as a source of organizational learning'. Unpublished paper, The Wharton School of the University of Pennsylvania, August.

Oakley, J. (1993) *Morality and the Emotions*. London: Routledge.

Owen, D. (1993) The emerging green agenda: a role for accounting? In D. Smith (ed) *Business and the Environment*, London: Chapman.

Pauchant, T. C. and Fortier, I. (1990) 'Anthropocentric ethics in organizations. How different strategic management schools view the environment'. In W. M. Hoffman, R. Frederick and E. S. Petry (eds) (1990) *The Corporation, Ethics and the Environment*. New York: Forum.

Peters, T. J. and Waterman, R. H. (1982) *In Search of Excellence: Lessons from America's Best-Run Companies*. New York: Harper & Row, Publishers.

Roberts, P. (1992) 'Business and the environment: an initial review of the recent literature'. *Business Strategy and the Environment*, **1:** 2, 41–50.

Schot, J. and Fischer, K. (1993) 'Introduction: the greening of the industrial firm'. In K. Fischer and J. Schot, J. (eds), *Environmental Strategies for Industry*, Washington, D.C.: Island Press.

Shrivastava, P. (1993). 'The greening of business'. In D. Smith (ed) (1993) *Business and the Environment*. London: Paul Chapman Publishing.

Smith, D. (1993) *Business and the Environment*. London: Paul Chapman Publishing.

Snell, R. S. (1990) 'Managers' development of ethical awareness and personal morality', *Personnel Review*, **19:** 1.

Solomon, R. C. (1991) 'Business ethics, literacy, and the education of emotions'. In R. E. Freeman (ed), *Business Ethics: The State of the Art*. New York: Oxford University Press.

Touche Ross (1990) *Head in the Clouds or Head in the Sand? UK Managers' Attitudes to Environmental Issues*. London: Touche Ross.

Willmott, H (1993) 'Strength is ignorance; slavery is freedom: managing culture in modern organizations', *Journal of Management Studies*, **30:** 4, 515–552.

# 11

# Strategic Management and Business Policy-making: Bringing in Environmental Values

*Jo McCloskey and Denis Smith*

## INTRODUCTION

Accepted economic thinking in postwar industrial countries tended to promulgate ideologies which stated that the way forward for sustainable future development was through growth via increasing consumption of resources. Mass production resulted in what appeared to be limitless products and services, and industry developed a range of new technologies that enabled faster production and distribution of those products. The free enterprise system that prevailed in these economies ensured rapid economic growth and high productivity and encouraged mass consumption and freedom of choice by consumers. However, by the middle of the 1970s, changes in the physical environment were beginning to manifest themselves and this combined with the findings of research studies which revealed a correlation between environmental damage and industrial practices that had arisen from industrial activities. The publication of Rachael Carson's *Silent Spring* and the Club of Rome's work on the limits to economic growth combined with media coverage of environmental issues to heighten public awareness and concerns about the range and extent of environmental problems. These issues included the need stringently to treat water in order to make it safe for consumption, the extensive damage to landscape by intensive farming and forests, the risks from nuclear power production, the effects of pesticides and the eutrophication of lakes. By the early part of the 1990s, the extent of these issues had widened considerably to include global problems of environmental impact, such as the erosion of the ozone layer, acid precipitation, global warming and hazardous waste disposal. The biosphere, which had always been regarded as a free good that could be almost endlessly exploited, was under serious threat (McIntosh, 1991). Increased awareness of global environmental damage, combined with the downturn in productivity and consumption and mounting trade deficits, highlighted the need for societies to adjust their economic ideologies from those which had concentrated on short-termism to more sustainable strategies for development. This chapter seeks

Reprinted with permission from *Greening Environmental Policy*, Fischer, F. and Black, M. (eds), 1995. Paul Chapman Publishing, pp. 199–209 to explore the interface between business activities and environmental quality in the light of post-industrial economic decline.

## DEVELOPING ENVIRONMENTAL VALUES

The free enterprise system is characterized by the enormous amount of decisions which are reached independently by producers and consumers in order to promote a certain quality of life while preserving individual autonomy. However, rapid developments in information technology, consumer education and sophistication and numerous products and process scares have resulted in changes in individual purchasing behaviour. These changes, coupled with collective consumer pressure on producers, mean that it is no longer enough for manufacturers to supply products that simply fulfil narrowly based consumer requirements for product performance. Public groups are increasingly demanding environmentally friendly products that are produced by using materials and processes which do not threaten the environment or society. These social and political pressures are forcing manufacturers to consider the complete life-cycle of the product and this includes disposal and/or recycling of the product at the end of its useful life. This cradle-to-grave approach raises fundamental questions about the moral responsibilities of both producers and consumers alike and brings into sharp focus the global inequalities that exist between nation-states. Such a swing in consumer behaviour requires industry to redesign mass production, distribution and consumption mechanisms so that the lowest feasible level of resources can be used to provide society with optimal standards of living and commensurate quality of life. Such a shift to conservation requires that pollution be reduced through rigorous efforts to eliminate waste, inefficiency and mismanagement (Gunn, 1991).

While most organizations acknowledge that virtually all company operations today have some form of environmental implications, one of the major problems facing industry is the confusion as to what exactly constitutes 'environmentally friendly' initiatives or practices. Companies who proclaim to be environmentally aware and corporately responsible have formulated environmental policies into their mission statements and strategic plans. However, these initiatives rarely give specific practical guidance as to how and where environmental efforts should be applied within the range of activities undertaken by the organization (Hooper and Rocca, 1991). Without principles to guide such decisions, it is impossible to communicate how environmental affairs can fit into the broad strategies of the company. It is imperative that such principles should reflect the perspectives of operations, environmental affairs, legal, financial and other relevant functions and should be constructed to parallel critical decision-making processes and major activities.

## BUSINESS STRATEGY AND THE ENVIRONMENT

The strategic management process seeks to ensure that the organization achieves a fit with its environment and optimizes its resources to achieve competitive advantage. The means by which competitive advantage can be achieved are many and varied and there has been considerable debate within the literature concerning the role of technical expertise in achieving such an advantage. Indeed, a school of criticism has developed around the work of Mintzberg (1994) which is opposed to the rational planning school of thought. Critics of business planning, as epitomized by the rational planning school, have pointed to the difficulties faced by planners when attempting to plan beyond anything but the short term. In more recent years, some authors have suggested that the inherent chaos and uncertainty within the broad business environment necessitates that organizations revise their decision-making to incorporate such uncertainty and to recognize the limitations of technical expertise in the process (see, for example, Stacey, 1991).

In theory the incorporation of 'green' issues within discussions of strategic management should be relatively simple to accomplish. (In the context of our discussions, 'green issues' is used as a label in order to differentiate these problems from those more general issues which are grouped under the label of the 'business environment'. Although the term 'environment' is often used within the business literature, it is narrowly defined and often restricted to a discussion of environmentally based issues.) If the strategic management process is broken down into its constituent parts (Figure 1) then it is possible to identify a number of critical areas where attention could be focused across a range of 'green issues'. The strategic management process is essentially concerned with the interaction of business and its competitive environment. Consequently, the process should seek to help managers develop strategies that allow organizations to achieve a best 'fit' with the environment in which they operate. The use of the term 'environment', however, has usually been seen in terms of barriers to

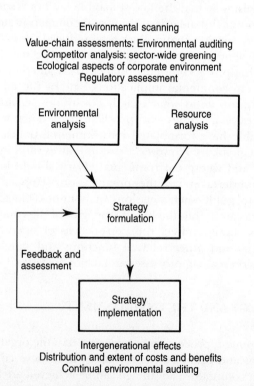

Figure 1. A Green Perspective on the Strategic Management Process. (*Source*: Smith 1992).

entry, the economic buying power of buyers and suppliers and the economic exploitation of the resource base in order to gain competitive advantage (Porter, 1985). There is now, however, a need to broaden this economic interpretation of the environment to encompass those factors in the micro and macroenvironment which present opportunities for, and/or threats to, environmentally benign business practices (see Shrivastava, 1993; Smith, 1992; 1993; McCloskey and Maddock, 1994). Some organizations, particularly those with a high environmental profile, have already incorporated both environmental audits and environmental impact assessments into their environmental and resource analysis procedure, and already apply an ecological perspective to their existing economic considerations. Those organizations that carry out both ecological and economic environmental scans and audits will benefit from improved statutory compliance, along with a more accurate identification and management of environmental risk. Such a process should also lead to enhanced environmental awareness and corporate responsibility throughout the organization (Smith, 1991). Ultimately, this will lead to better financial and insurance planning and will provide the organization with ever-increasing opportunities for gaining competitive advantage and increasing profits (North, 1992). Put simply, incorporating environmental (ecological) values into corporate decision-making will ultimately result in greater organizational sustainability.

## ENVIRONMENTAL VALUES AND THE STRATEGY PROCESS

The strategic management process places considerable weight on the values held by senior staff within the organization. Indeed, there are those who have suggested that, ultimately, 'Almost all questions of corporate strategy are questions of ethics... [and] ... the very best corporations can and should be managed in a way that is consistent with a strategy built on a foundation of ethics' (Freeman and Gilbert, 1988, pp. 7–8). If we accept this relationship between values and strategy, then it should be a relatively simply matter to incorporate more radical ecologically based values into the main strategy theories. However, the transformation of business strategy in this regard has proved to be problematic and business schools have shown some considerable reluctance to take such an ecologically and ethically based transformation on board (see Smith, Hart and McCloskey, 1994). Events such as Bhopal, Chernobyl, Love Canal and the pollution problems in the former communist-bloc countries will eventually force through change in organizations as social concerns transform political pressures into tighter regulatory frameworks. It is our contention here that organizations can gain a long-term competitive advantage by anticipating such changes and improving their environmental performance now before they are forced to make expensive changes by the governments.

Analysing the environment and measuring environmental impact therein is crucial to the implementation of any environmental strategy. However, the pollution process recognizes no political or economic boundaries and any systematic attempt at analyzing the global effects of specific businesses and industry sectors on the biosphere is at present virtually impossible. None the less, it is now widely recognized that business has a major role to play in providing the answers to many of our pollution problems through resource reduction and better managerial processes.

Within a resource analysis it is desirable to assess the effective utilization of resources and their subsequent influence on environmental impact. Porter's (1985) value chain provides a useful framework within which to consider such issues. The value chain attempts to profile those activities that will add value through its business strategy. The value chain includes both direct *value creating* activities—inbound logistics, operations, outbound logistics, marketing and services—as well as *support activities* such as procurement, technological development, human resource management and management systems. For example, an organization pursuing a low-cost strategy will attempt to focus its attention on operations and logistics and less on marketing and sales. In capital-intensive industries (which have been accused of being among the major polluters) such as the automobile, chemical, steel and heavy electrical industries, significant value is usually added in logistics and operations. These industries typically opt for global standardization as customized or country-specific products would be prohibitively costly. However, if the value-chain analysis was to be linked with the process of environmental auditing, it would be possible to highlight those aspects of the organization's activities which contribute significantly to its 'portfolio of degradation' and take necessary corrective action. Alternatively, more value could be added through the various marketing and services activities by formulating or marketing new environmentally benign products and processes, thereby creating opportunities to gain a competitive edge.

If we move away from viewing the environment as a common 'good' towards an ecologically driven model, then the value of the organization's products and services need to take into account the environmental impact associated with its production (Smith, 1992). If polluters were unable to see pollution as an externality on the production process but had to incorporate the costs of such pollution, then we would see a move towards waste minimization strategies being incorporated into the strategic decision-making process. The costs of pollution, if calculated to account for the spatial and temporal dynamics of that pollution process, would force many organizations to reassess their modes of production and sectoral activities. This would also provoke changes in consumer behaviour as the costs of greater pollution control would be passed on to the consumers who would revise their preferences accordingly.

Table 1 illustrates some of the elements that are likely to prove of importance in securing an ecologically based competitive advantage. The value chain can serve as a useful framework for assessing the impact that an organization and its activities have on environmental quality; and the potential for organizations to take a more fundamental approach to greening their activities is considerable, given the range of activities listed. After completing the processes of environmental and resource analysis, the strategy process moves into the formulation and implementation stages. Here it is possible to identify a number of important areas which have an impact on the greening process. These include the limits of technical expertise in decision-making; the process of short-termism; and the nature of competitor activity.

## The use of technical expertise

There is a large and varied literature that examines the process of human reasoning and the role of bias therein (Evans, 1989). A considerable element of research has

Table 1. Greening Porter's value chain

|  | Inbound logistics | Operations | Outbound logistics | Marketing and sales | Service |
|---|---|---|---|---|---|
| *Procurement* | Transportation impacts Storage modes | 'Green consumables' Clean technologies Recyclable packaging | Storage modes Transportation modes | Raw materials sourcing and supply | Receipt and environmental disposal of used product or product components |
| *Technology development* | Waste minimization through source reduction Alternative raw material sources | Clean technologies Pollution minimization and control | Finished product recyclability | Packaging minimization and disposal innovatory 'Green' products and products | Dissembly and reconstruction |
| *Human resource management* | Staff selection Supplier selection | Corporate culture training programmes Corporate environmental awareness | Subcontractual arrangements | Internal and external communications and community liason | Incentives Rewards for environmental ideas and practices |
| *Management systems* | Inventory reduction Recyclability | 'Just-in-time' processes | 'Cradle-to-grave' responsibility for products Recycling and recovery infrastructure | Green new-product development committees Research & development | Quality circles and environmental standards assurance |

sought to explore the role of technical expertise within decision-making and the often debilitating effects that technocracy can have with regard to environmental performance and, more specifically, technological risk (see, Collingridge and Reeve, 1986; Fischer, 1990; 1991; 1993; Smith, 1990; 1991; 1994).

Environmental affairs have long been a technical or scientific function performed by specialists, with little emphasis placed on developing a broad management perspective among environmental personnel. Such specialism allows a technocratic approach to environmentalism to prevail and this can create the illusion of infallibility of science and technology (see Collingridge and Reeve, 1986). These specialists, whether external or internal, are aware of, or may even be part of, the company culture. They are, or will be made aware, of the corporate image that the company wishes to portray to the outside world and the need to preserve the status quo. They are often under pressure, real or imagined, to produce reports that side-step the issue by referring to the historical record of the business practice (or process) without acknowledging an adequate enough time lag between the polluting activity and the pollution damage. For example, the causal relationship between asbestos pollution and lung cancer proved difficult to verify because of the latency period needed for cancer to develop, by which time blame can be levelled at other forms of exposure. Similar comments can be made over the relationship between smoking and lung cancer and with the disposal of hazardous chemical waste, which also display a longevity and toxicity that creates major intergenerational problems for those concerned with environmental policy. Alternatively, specialist reports can be couched in such scientific and technical language that it is difficult either to prove or disprove their findings, or to assess the thoroughness of the investigations. The high degree of uncertainty that accompanies new technologies and scientific developments, and the imbalance in the distribution of expertise, highlights the need for a more open, democratic approach to the strategic process (see Fischer, 1990). Participative management, involving a range of specialist personnel covering the whole spectrum of the organization's activities, could provide a foundation for reciprocal accountability and would produce a more egalitarian communication and control system than the current specialist, hierarchical management structures found in most organizations. Such a move, while essential to achieving sustainability, will require fundamental change in the dominant forms of decision-making used by industry and government alike (see Sheldon and Smith, 1992).

## THE PROCESS OF SHORT-TERMISM

As has already been mentioned, economic growth through mass production, distribution and consumption has been the tenet for sustainable development in free market economies since the 1940s. This philosophy rests on the growth of wealth and assets and is loosely measured in material living standards and gross national product (GNP). However, living standards are measured in material terms only and GNP simply records total output regardless of what resources have been used. The fast accumulation of wealth brought about by quick turnover led to increased capital expenditure on plant and machinery and investment in more efficient manufacturing and distribution processes. The upwards spiral of production, growth and profits justified the free market ideology until the 1980s when evidence of environmental degradation and decline in production and consumption became apparent. The focus on 'growth assets' has started to lose ground to a philosophy of 'productivity of assets'. Organizations have begun to operate strategies that maximize the value that their activities add to the economy and, while profit maximization will always be fundamental to any business organization, there is now another fundamental objective that must be addressed if businesses are to be sustainable in the longer term—that objective is the minimization of environmental mismanagement. Unfortunately, the environmental perspective has hitherto been pitted against, or imposed on, manufacturing initiatives by legislation and regulation rather than being integrated with a more proactive operations management. This conflict has developed from the erroneous belief that environmental activities rarely contribute to profit generation and can even hinder such efforts. However, the business community has now begun to realize that there is a need to improve their environmental performance if organizations are to remain competitive. This realization is due to the growing concerns currently being expressed by a variety of stakeholders, some of which can be listed as follows:

(1) Consumers are not only demanding environmentally friendly products but are now also starting to question the material and processes used in production.
(2) Forthcoming EC legislation could decree that banks and other lending institutions would be at least partially liable for environmental damage caused by companies with whom they do business. Future legislation could mean that banks who hold a mortgage over contaminated land may be sued for any resulting pollution damage associated with that investment.
(3) Environmental damage claims accounted for over 50 per cent of the £509 million losses reported by Lloyds of London in June 1991. Latest policies now include specific time limits and are much more specific as to the damage claims which will be covered. It is conceivable that insurance companies will not insure against environmental damage unless businesses adhere to strict environmental policies and processes (Greenpeace Business, 1991).

As major stakeholders become increasingly wary about investing in companies that are engaged in unsound environmental processes, more organizations are realizing that unless they comprehensively clean up their activities they will not be sustainable in the market-place.

**The nature of competitive activity**

The notion of competition remains one of the most fundamental and pervasive conditions of business practice. Business rivals capitalize on their strengths and efficiencies to gain competitive advantage and the ultimate objective is to force their rivals out of the market and thereby to achieve total dominance. The total cost of such competition must include loss of productivity and expenses incurred in bankruptcies and liquidation (Gunn, 1991). These costs have to be absorbed in the cost of operating the economy, which, in turn, lowers the standards of living and the quality of life—the foundation on which free enterprise is based! The purpose of competition should be to increase the chances of survival by achieving maximum productivity, while simultaneously conserving resources and minimizing waste and costs. Some companies (notably The Body Shop and Loblaws Industries) have shown that it is possible to achieve competitive advantage through conforming to high environmental standards, irrespective of the actions of their competitors.

As the criterion for success in organizations changes from 'growth of assets' to environmentally sound productive efficiency, competition will become a cost-effective form of rivalry whereby organizations compete against their own past performance. Self-competition will dominate and accentuate the use of cooperation, collaboration and teamwork to achieve optimal output using environmentally benign materials and processes.

## CONCLUSIONS

It is evident that consumers are becoming increasingly concerned about environmental issues and industry has begun to think more carefully about the effects their products and processes may have on the environment. Given the more stringent demands of key stakeholders such as banks, lending institutions, insurance companies and the media, organizations have realized that they must incorporate ecological issues into their business practices and processes if they are to survive in the market-place in anything other than the short term.

Managing environmental affairs is no longer an incidental or secondary function of company operations. Product design, manufacturing, transportation, customer use and the ultimate disposal of a product should not merely reflect environmental considerations but must be driven by them. While many models and techniques for greening business have been developed, one of the major difficulties remaining for organizations is that of implementing a green strategy and integrating environmental management systems and policies with the strategic management process. The main areas of controversy centre around the interaction of technical and scientific expertise, the continuing ethos of short-term profit rather than long-term sustainability and the nature of competition which currently favours 'survival of the fittest' rather than 'survival of the species'. In addition, the conflict of interest between the competitive and ecological environments on the one hand, and between societal concerns and political manoeuvring on the other, provide for a complex setting within which the strategic management process is framed.

Organizations must realize that to be effective they need to articulate practical principles to guide the organization's environmental efforts; integrate environmental affairs within the company operations; and develop environmental professionals to meet mounting environmental requirements (Hooper and Rocca, 1991). However, while a small number of industries lead the way in new technology, the majority of organizations are still trying to keep abreast of the ever-increasing developments in new technology. It is important that industry realizes the significance of the changes that are brought about by such developments and recognizes the need to communicate the implications for business and the impact on the environment clearly to the public, if conflict and controversy are to be avoided.

# REFERENCES

Chakravarthy, B. S. and Lorange, P. (1991) *Managing the Strategy Process.* Prentice-Hall, N.J.
Collingridge, D. and Reeve, C. (1986) *Science Speaks to Power.* Francis Pinter, London.
Evans, J. St B. (1989) *Bias in Human Reasoning: Causes and Consequences.* Lawrence Erlbaum Associates, Hove.
Fischer, F. (1990) *Technocracy and the Politics of Expertise.* Sage, Newbury Park, Calif.
Fischer, F. (1991) 'Risk assessment and environmental crisis: towards an integration of science and participation', *Industrial Crisis Quarterly*, Vol.5, no. 2, pp. 113–32.
Freeman, R. E. and Gilbert, D. R. (1988) *Corporate Strategy and the Search for Ethics*, Prentice-Hall, Englewood Cliffs, N.J.
Gunn, B. (1991) 'Competruism: strategic implications,' *Management Decisions*, Vol. 25, no. 5, pp. 16–27.
Hooper, T. L. and Rocca, B. T. (1991) 'Environmental affairs: now on the strategic agenda,' *Journal of Business Strategy*, May/June, pp. 26–30.
McCloskey, J. and Maddock, S. (1994) 'Environmental management: its role in corporate strategy,' *Management Decision*, Vol. 32, no. 1, pp. 27–32.
McIntosh, A. (1991) 'The impact of environmental issues on marketing and politics in the 1990s,' *Journal of the Market Research Society*, Vol. 33, no. 3, pp. 205–7.
Mintzberg, H. (1994) *The Rise and Fall of Strategic Planning.* Prentice-Hall, London.
North, K. (1992) *Environmental Business Management: An Introduction.* International Labour Office, Geneva.
Porter, M. (1985) *Competitive Advantage: Techniques for Analyzing Industries and Competitors.* Free Press, New York.
Sheldon, T. A. and Smith, D. (1992) 'Assessing the health effects of waste disposal sites: issues in risk analysis and some Bayesian conclusions,' in M. Clark, D. Smith and A. Blowers (eds) *Waste Location: Spatial Aspects of Waste Management, Hazards and Disposal.* Routledge, London.
Shrivasta, P. (1993) *Bhopal: Anatomy of a Crisis.* Paul Chapman Publishing, London.
Smith, D. (1990) 'Corporate power and the politics of uncertainty: risk management at the Canvey Island complex,' *Industrial Crisis Quarterly*, Vol. 4, no. 1, pp. 1–26.
Smith, D. (1991) 'The Kraken wakes—the political dynamics of the hazardous waste issue,' *Industrial Crisis Quarterly*, Vol. 5, no. 3, pp. 189–207.
Smith, D. (1992) 'Business strategy and the environment: what lies beyond the rhetoric of greening?' *Business Strategy and the Environment*, Vol. 1, no. 1, pp. 1–9.
Smith, D. (1993) 'The Frankenstein factor—corporate responsibility and the environment,' in D. Smith (ed.) *Business and the Environment: Implications of the New Environmentalism.* Paul Chapman Publishing, London.
Smith, D. (1994) *Bhopal as a Crisis of Ethics: Corporate Responsibility and Risk Management. Crisis Management Working Paper 3.* The Home Office Emergency Planning College/Liverpool Business School.
Smith, D., Hart, D. and McCloskey, J. (1994) 'Greening the business school: environmental eduction and the business curriculum,' *Management Learning*, Vol. 25. no. 3, pp. 485–98.
Stacey, R. (1991) *The Chaos Frontier: Creative Strategic Control for Business.* Butterworth-Heinemann, Oxford.

# 12

# Environmental Assessment, Auditing and Information Systems

*Peter Roberts*

Understanding the environmental impacts of business operations is an essential prerequisite for the development and introduction of a system of environmental management. It is impossible to manage environmental impacts in the absence of methods for measuring their severity, significance and locational characteristics. Measurement also implies that there will be a need to construct some form of database or information system; this information system can be used to provide the fundamental resource for the establishment of an environmental management system.

It is important at the outset to distinguish between environmental impact assessment (EIA), also known in the UK as environmental assessment (EA), and the variety of methods and procedures used to conduct initial environmental reviews, environmental surveys and environmental audits. Terminology presents a number of difficulties, because there is no single authoritive source or legal definition which encompasses all the terms. In this book the following definitions are used:

- *Environmental impact assessment (or environmental assessment)* is a procedure for predicting, analysing and evaluating the impacts of a proposed action on the environment and ensuring that information regarding these impacts is taken into account in decision-making.
- *Environmental auditing* is a process for checking, on a regular basis, the environmental performance of an existing organisation or activity.
- *Environmental review* is an initial or preliminary form of an environmental audit; it may provide the basis for the adoption of an environmental policy and the introduction of a full system of environmental auditing.

These definitions are also helpful in identifying the roles and purposes that are assigned to EIA and environmental auditing. Although the distinction may be blurred in certain forms of practice, in general the purposes of these methods are as follows:

Reprinted with permission from Roberts, P., *Environmentally Sustainable Business*, 1995
© 1995 Paul Chapman Publishing Ltd, London

- EIA is normally undertaken prior to making a decision. It is a preventative form of analysis; it offers an organisation the ability to review its proposals and to avoid taking an action that may have a negative impact upon the environment.
- Environmental auditing is normally undertaken by an organisation as part of its regular cycle of monitoring and evaluation; it is a systematic method for ensuring that information is collected in order to aid the process of management.

It is worth mentioning at this point that both methods are also related to the concept and procedure of life-cycle assessment. This method of assessment seeks to highlight particular activities during the environmental life of a product or project where specific environmental impacts may occur. These impacts can then be addressed and any problems can be rectified through the redesign of the product, process or project. For example, if an impact results from the use of a particular source of raw materials, then alternative sources may need to be identified or the process may have to be changed (Welford and Gouldson, 1993).

## COMMON FEATURES OF EIA AND ENVIRONMENTAL AUDITING

Both EIA and environmental auditing attempt to measure and evaluate a wide range of environmental impacts that are associated with an action or an activity. They use units of measurement that are appropriate to the action or activity which is the subject of analysis, although it may also be possible to assign monetary values. By using appropriate units of measurement (number of species, parts per million) these methods avoid the criticism frequently made in relation to cost-benefit analysis, that is, that it is impossible to assign a monetary value to many aspects of the environment. The measurement of actions and activities may, in some cases, also involve an assessment of the relative significance of certain aspects of the environment *vis-à-vis* the action or activity in question. Priorities may have to be set and assigned to the interactions that occur between the environment and the various elements or stages that are contained within an action or activity. The assignment of priorities will vary between actions or activities; for example, a proposal to construct a dam is likely to have a major impact upon the volume and flow of water in a river, and in an EIA a high degree of priority may be assigned to the possibility of a reduction in river flow and the implications for water supply. By way of comparison, an EIA of a proposed airport may place priority on the environmental consequences of the loss of good agricultural land and the generation of noise. In a similar manner, whilst an environmental audit of a transport business may place particular emphasis on energy use and the emission of exhaust gases, in an audit of a chemical company, even though road transport is used to move materials and products, it is likely that emphasis will be placed upon measuring process-related emissions rather than the emission of exhaust gases.

The commonality of approach, in terms of the use of appropriate units of measurement, that exists between EIA and environmental auditing can be extended to other characteristics of the methods. Other common features include the roles played by assessment and auditing within a hierarchy of decision-making, the need for adequate baseline information, the relationship of the methods to legal and other requirements, the importance of disclosure and communication, the wider application of such methods, and the importance of ensuring that any analysis takes into account the context within which an individual project or activity will take place.

Although many EIAs have been conducted in order to assess the likely environmental consequences of a particular project, EIA is equally valuable as a method for assessment of policies, programmes and plants (see Figure 1). It has also been suggested that EIA offers considerable potential for the analysis of individual subproject elements and of specific products, such as a motor vehicle. To ignore the role of EIA in the assessment or screening of policies, programmes and plans is to ignore the potential for reducing the need for, cost of, and time taken to conduct assessments. By assessing the environmental impact of a policy, programme or plan, undesirable options can be eliminated at an early stage in the development process, and before any such options emerge as proposals for specific projects. This concern with the strategic dimensions of EIA is of long standing (Lee and Wood, 1978; Roberts and Shaw, 1981), and it is currently reflected in calls for the introduction of strategic environmental assessment. The role, features and procedures of strategic environmental assessments are considered in the third section of this chapter.

Environmental auditing also has the potential to play a strategic role in the analysis and assessment of options. At the level of corporate strategy it is possible to filter out

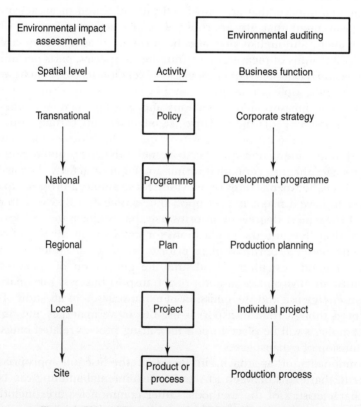

Figure 1. EIA and Environmental Auditing: A Total Approach.

policies which have undesirable environmental consequences, and at subsequent stages in the processes of business planning the application of environmental auditing can be effective in screening operational programmes and plans. As with EIA, the use of environmental auditing throughout a business is intended to ensure that an individual process or product is in accord with the requirements for environmentally sustainable business development.

Both methods necessitate the development of a baseline of information and understanding. In the case of EIA this is likely to involve the assembly of existing knowledge relevant to the spatial level at which the assessment is to be undertaken; for example, in order to make a policy decision as to the future forms of transport policy, it will be vital to gather information on the current split among the various modes of transport, forecasts of demand and other factors. An environmental audit will involve the gathering of information on subjects such as the sources of materials, the range of production processes and products used, and the generation of wastes. For both methods it is essential that this database is kept up to date. The information gathered as part of the process of preparing an EIA, or in conducting an audit at the lowest level in the hierarchy, should be fed into the database. Other relevant externally generated information will also need to be captured at regular intervals, including the implications of changes in legislation and environmental standards.

Current legislation and other regulatory standards provide a starting point for an EIA or environmental audit. Whilst an EIA is required for any major project proposed in the UK, or elsewhere in the European Union, the position is less clear with regard to environmental auditing. Nevertheless, it is important to be aware of the range of environmental standards that currently condition and constrain the activities of a company and to anticipate future limits and standards. In both EIA and environmental auditing, the emphasis is on anticipation and taking action to avoid problems that may emerge in the future.

For EIA and environmental auditing to give of their best, it is essential that the process of preparing the assessment or audit is an open one. Constructing a baseline of information will require extensive consultation, including efforts to seek the views of any individuals, organisations or groups who are likely to be affected by a proposed action. These views can provide a valuable source of information, and they allow for the generation of a feeling of involvement and participation. Ideally the results of an EIA or audit should be presented in non-technical language and should be widely disseminated. This will help to reassure those likely to be affected by the proposed action or activity that a full assessment or audit has been undertaken, and that any decision made is based upon a clear understanding of the impacts and consequences. In the case of environmental auditing, such an approach will also ensure compliance with the need for corporate disclosure and the requirements of a social responsibility audit (Clutterbuck, Dearlove and Snow, 1992).

EIA and environmental auditing can be applied to a wide range of activities. Both methods depend upon the gathering of information from a number of sources; they attempt to assess an actual or proposed action, and to evaluate the extent to which a particular option amongst a range of proposed actions can be seen to be to the mutual benefit of both the organisation and the environment. Early EIAs were mainly concerned with major infrastructure projects, such as dams, roads and airports, but the method is now used to assist in making decisions on a range of investments. Many decisions and functions within a company can benefit from the use of environmental auditing, including those related to product design, the configuration of the technology used in production processes, purchasing, marketing and human resource management. Both methods are vital elements in the construction of any form of strategic policy or corporate strategy.

Environmental auditing and EIA should be undertaken within an appropriate and relevant context. Whilst it may be convenient to assume that all projects or processes have the same impacts irrespective of their location in space, this assumption is both erroneous and dangerous. An individual plant or project is located in a local environment and each local environment displays distinctive and individual features. A local natural and built environment is unique, and it may be valued in different ways by various groups in a community, including residents, other business activities and local public policy organizations. Each of these groups may place a different interpretation or value on the component parts of the local environment, and these differences should be recognised and respected. It is also the case that the local environment will change over time, and this implies that an audit or an EIA should be anticipatory. For example, a factory may have been established in a remote location prior to the development of adjacent land for housing. In the past noise from production processes may not have generated a perceived environmental impact. However, following the development of housing, the current situation may be one in which residents complain about the noise which is generated. Any decision on changes to layout, the use of new production equipment and the siting of extensions should anticipate the future use of land adjacent to a factory. If necessary a safeguarding area of land may have to be purchased in order to comply with anticipated legal requirements and stated standards of corporate behaviour.

**Some common criticisms of the methods**

As well as sharing many common features, both EIA and environmental auditing have been the subject of a number of common criticisms. These criticisms relate to the precision of the methods, the feasibility or otherwise of allowing for participation, the absence of arrangements for the full disclosure of results, variations in the requirement to make use of EIA and auditing methods, and the extent to which the methods can inhibit good or rapid decision-making.

The degree of precision of an EIA, or an environmental audit, will depend upon the availability of baseline information, the resources available for the conduct of the audit or assessment, the amount of time available to conduct an analysis, and the degree of co-operation offered to the analysts by local and other actors who have a stake in the outcome. The need for a comprehensive and up-to-date baseline of information and understanding has already been discussed and, whilst it is recognised that adequate information is an essential prerequisite for a satisfactory outcome, the reality is often far removed from this ideal. In many areas, ecological and other surveys may be absent, incomplete or out of date. The absence of good information will inevitably affect the degree of precision that can be attained by an EIA or audit. This is not the fault of the method itself, although it does provide a powerful argument in favour of the development of procedures for assessment and auditing that are designed so as to minimise the need for the collection of data and which can produce reasonable results irrespective of the quality of the data available.

Whilst it is always possible to supplement an existing baseline of information by conducting direct surveys, the extent to which additional information can be collected will depend upon the resources available to the assessment team, in terms of both money and personnel. Other constraints include the amount of time allowed to prepare an EIA or audit, and the willingness of local and other actors to make available any specialist information and knowledge which they may possess.

The availability of financial, staff and other resources will also influence the precision and accuracy of an environmental assessment or audit. Given that many of the stages in any assessment or audit will involve the exercise of a high degree of professional judgement, the availability of trained and experienced staff is a crucial matter. Of equal importance is the provision of sufficient time to conduct a full and comprehensive EIA or audit. Co-operation from local and other actors who are likely to be affected by a proposed project or process may prove helpful in ensuring that sufficient information is obtained, and such co-operation may be essential in order to allow an audit or EIA to proceed with an analysis of the key issues, many of which are only likely to emerge through consultation and participation. Many environmental problems are virtually invisible or unseen, and participation by the workforce in an environmental audit, or by the local community in an EIA, is an important factor that may determine the successful application of either of the methods.

Lack of precision may result from all or any of the above causes. However, compared with many other business methods, both EIA and environmental auditing are relatively precise. As Muller and Koechlin (1992, p. 48) observe, 'the standards applied in environmental questions are stricter by far than in other management problems', and that if 'the same exactitude were to be demanded for, say, an investment decision, investment would virtually come to a standstill'.

The extent to which the participation and co-operation of a workforce or of a local community, can be secured will influence the accuracy and validity of an EIA or environmental audit. One criticism levelled at both EIA and environmental auditing is that they are procedures that allow for the assertion of the values held by the proposer of a project, or which can be dominated by the views of management. This need not be the case, and it is important to ensure that any assessment is carried out in a spirit of openness and full participation. Full disclosure of the method to be used, the criteria for assessment and the form and accessibility of the results can do much to guarantee the participation of all parties. In the USA this is provided for in terms of the public right-to-know principle (Cannon, 1992), but there is resistance to the adoption of this principle in certain other countries.

Considerable variations exist between countries with regard to the extent to which an EIA or an environmental audit is required. As will be discussed later in this chapter, EIA is now a legal requirement in the European Union if a major project is proposed. Determining the threshold above which a project is considered to be significant, and thereby requires an EIA to be produced, is a matter of debate. Environmental auditing is not a statutory requirement in the UK and most other countries but Norwegian company law now requires an environmental statement to be included within the annual report. In order to comply with the requirements of British Standard 7750 a company has to utilise a satisfactory form of audit.

The final criticism levelled at EIA and environmental auditing is that the use of such methods can hamper effective management and can delay vital decisions. This criticism has little validity, unless there is a need to achieve immediate cost savings. However, if a project or company is in such a difficult financial position that it can only be saved by pragmatism of this nature, then it is almost certain that the project or company should not continue in its present form.

## Intracompany and extracompany dimensions

Given the shared features of EIA and environmental auditing, and accepting that the methods share a number of weaknesses, it is important to consider the position of each of the methods in relation to the operation of business organisations. In analysing the relationship among a business, the environment and the other characteristics of an individual location, it is apparent that there is a need to consider both the way in which:

- this relationship is analysed and assessed within an organisation; this can be referred to as the intracompany dimension; and
- the relationship between a company and the wider environment can be assessed, this can be referred to as the extracompany dimension.

It is important to recognise the existence of both of these dimensions in analysing the relationship among business, environment and place, and to acknowledge that they reflect a range of broader social concerns. Both dimensions are vital because a business does not operate in isolation from other factors and actors in its immediate environment, nor can it hope to achieve the objectives of environmentally sustainable business development without taking action itself to improve the environment, and encouraging and supporting similar actions that are taken by other companies and organisations in a locality.

In contemplating the construction of premises, or the installation of new plant, it is both logical and cost-effective to use an EIA as a method for testing the sustainability of a project. In addition, it is sensible to prepare an EIA using a format that can provide a baseline for future environmental audits. Equally, an EIA can obtain much useful information from the results of successive rounds of environmental audits conducted at a similar plant located elsewhere.

This distinction between the intracompany and extracompany dimensions of environmental analysis and assessment is made in order to illustrate the importance to business of attempting to pay equal attention to both the internal and external characteristics of the environment. An example of the way in which the extracompany dimension can be assessed is provided by EIA, whilst the intracompany dimension can be analysed through the adoption of environmental auditing. As noted above, the former procedure is now a statutory requirement in the case of major projects, whilst the latter, in its broadest sense, is not.

# ENVIRONMENTAL IMPACT ASSESSMENT

On 27 June 1985 the Council of Environment Ministers of the European Communities adopted Directive 85/337/EEC on 'the assessment of the effects of certain public and private projects on the environment' (CEC, 1985). This directive, which is generally known as the European Environmental Assessment (EA) Directive, requires member states of the community to develop and implement procedures and methods for the comprehensive assessment of the environmental consequences of major projects. The directive, which was the outcome of over ten years of negotiation between the Commission of the European Communities and member states, came into force in July 1988 and is subject to detailed monitoring and review. In one sense, the directive can be viewed as an experiment in transnational environmental regulation, while in another sense it represents a logical extension to the long-standing programme for environmental protection and improvement, and the principle that prevention is better than cure.

## The origins of EIA

Whilst the directive was an important step forward in the development of a common European programme for environmental regulation, it was based upon over twenty years of experience of the application of EIA both in Europe and elsewhere. Much of the impetus for the adoption of a standard form of EIA within Europe came through a recognition of the benefits that were derived from the implementation of a nationwide approach to EIA in the USA. Following the enactment of the National Environmental Policy Act 1969 (United States Government, 1969), all federal agencies in the USA were required to prepare an Environmental Impact Statement in advance of all major projects. European experience, often built upon the foundations laid in the USA, is more varied. Some member states introduced detailed statutory systems of EIA at an early point in time; for example, the federal government of Germany has required that, since 1971, all measures undertaken by federal authorities should be subject to an examination for environmental compatibility, whilst other member states, including the UK, encouraged the preparation of EIAs outside the requirements of specific legislation (Roberts, Shaw and Adkins, 1980; Wathern, 1988).

This wide experience of the use of EIA, both generally and more specifically in the UK, has its roots in the 1960s. Early experience in North America demonstrated the benefits of undertaking the comprehensive environmental assessment of major civil engineering and other projects. In a number of cases these professional interests in capabilities of EIA were reflected in the growth of an increasingly powerful and vocal environment lobby. Similar lobbies emerged in many European countries, including the UK, during the late 1960s. The loose coalition of interests that comprised the environment lobby in the UK began in the late 1960s and early 1970s to analyse and contest proposals for the development of major projects. The earliest evidence of increasing concern was demonstrated, for example, in the opposition mounted to the proposed construction of a Third London Airport at Maplin, the mining of potash in the North York Moors, and the development of oil platform construction yards and servicing facilities in Scotland. Doubts also emerged regarding the competence and appropriateness of the traditional means of planning control to deal with these projects.

In Scotland, and to a lesser extent elsewhere in the UK, the experience of having to comply with the stricter national legislation encountered in the USA prompted many oil companies to submit EIA alongside any application for planning permission for the construction of oil-related facilities. Preparing an EIA had become second nature to such companies, and the practice of EIA was accepted as an integral part of the industry's standard approach to environmental issues. The result was the production of a series of informal EIAs, of many types and related to many different projects. In addition to these practical experiments in the use of EIA, the UK Department of the Environment commissioned a series of research investigations (Catlow and Thirwall, 1976; Clark *et al.*, 1976). These reports, together with the informal EIAs, set the standard for best practice and the debate which ensued. Despite the clear demonstration of the need for a formal system for assessing environmental impacts, which was presented by the aforementioned reports and the informal EIAs, it was not until 1985 that a statutory requirement for EIA (now renamed EA) was introduced. It is this statutory system, implemented in response to the European directive of 1985, that forms the basis for the operation of EA in the UK.

## The features of EIA

There are many different procedures and systems of EIA and they utilise a variety of techniques, criteria and methods of measurement. However, in general terms, most forms of EIA can be expected to conform to four basic principles:

(1) They identify the nature of the proposed and induced activities that are likely to be generated by an action including alternatives to the action and, if appropriate, alternative locations for an action.
(2) They identify the relevant elements of the environment that will be affected by an action.
(3) They evaluate the initial and subsequent impacts of an action, including alternatives and alternative locations.
(4) They are concerned with the management of the beneficial and adverse impacts likely to be generated.

In proposing the above principles, it is suggested that EIA provides not just a method of analysis but a comprehensive system for identifying, analysing, evaluating and managing the impacts of the introduction and operation of any action, be it a policy, a project or a process. The output from an EIA is a detailed assessment statement which provides an objective basis upon which a decision can be made. The purpose of an EIA is to help decision-makers to make better decisions; it does not, in itself, provide a decision.

It is also important to distinguish EIA from other forms of assessment, such as cost-benefit analysis. This can be achieved by examining the characteristics of EIA and setting them against those of other forms of testing, analysis or evaluation. Whilst many traditional forms of analysis and assessment are often specific to an individual process or project, and normally attempt to utilise measurement criteria that are individual in nature, such as monetary value, EIA measures all the major elements which are encapsulated within a proposed action and relates them to the overall operation environment. It is no longer realistic or possible to claim that individual actions that have an effect on a particular operational environment can be assessed solely by reference to the measurement of their inherent characteristics.

EIA attempts to examine and evaluate a project within the context provided by an existing (or future) operational environment. This implies that a hierarchy of actions exists, and that there are various levels of application of a specific action. In general terms this implies that a specific action, such as a motorway project, should be viewed as an individual element set within a nested set of actions, often occurring in a chronological sequence and generating impacts at different spatial levels. To paraphrase Lee and Wood (1978, p. 102) this offers the possibility of developing a 'tiered system of EIA' within which an 'action at one tier is inevitably conditioned by prior actions at higher tiers'. Such an approach suggests that EIA can be applied through a spatially nested hierarchy. The spatial sequence, or hierarchy, of policies, programmes, plans, projects and process has been demonstrated in Figure 1.

An approach such as that suggested in Figure 1 indicates the potential and the inherent strengths of EIA as a tool of analysis and assessment. It also indicates the possibility of developing a two-way interaction between the design and implementation of policy and the design and operation of an individual project or product. Thus, for example, national or international transport policy may contain an explicit consideration of the noise aspects of policy options, and this may be reflected in the specifications of noise limits which relate to a particular product.

A dynamic assessment system, which incorporates both positive and negative feedback links, provides a powerful tool that may be used both by the community and by those in business. It has the inherent advantage of providing explicit guidance for those who are responsible for the design, manufacture and evaluation of specific projects, and it also allows product assessment to coexist with the operational environment within which products are utilised.

By implication EIA is concerned with assessing the impacts of a specific proposed action upon the environment, and considering a range of alternative actions or products which could be adopted should the projected impact of such actions, or products, prove to be undesirable or unacceptable. It would, for example, be possible for an EIA to suggest that

(1)  a proposed action is acceptable at the site suggested;
(2)  a proposed action is not acceptable at the site suggested, but is acceptable at an alternative site;
(3)  the proposed action is unacceptable at any site; and
(4)  a modified action may be acceptable at the site suggested or at an alternative site.

The possible outcomes are not mutually exclusive, and there are potential trade-offs between the recommendations. In addition, it is important to recognise that the criteria and standards utilised in preparing an EIA will vary from one country to another, and even between areas within a single country (Murphy, 1981).

## The current system of environmental assessment in the UK

It is important to recognise that the broad description of EIA that has been provided above does not equate to a system of EA introduced in the UK in response to the EC directive. The more restricted system of EA now in use in the UK does not, for example, readily allow for the comparison of a series of alternative sites for an action or project, unless the proponent of the action has directly provided the possibility of such a consideration.

There were, and still are, many different views and opinions as to the merits of introducing a uniform statutory system for EA in the various member states. In order to minimise any delays in introducing a common European system for EIA, the European Community therefore opted in the directive to require that: 'Member States shall adopt all measures necessary to ensure that, before consent is given, projects likely to have significant effects upon the environment by virtue of their nature, size or location are made subject to an assessment with regard to their effects' (CEC, 1985, Article 2), and that: 'The environmental impact assessment may be integrated into the existing procedures for consent to projects in the Member States or, failing this, into other procedures to be established to comply with the aims of this Directive' (*ibid.*).

The directive recognised the diversity of legislation and procedures that exists within member states, whilst at the same time attempting to ensure that a common approach to EA was implemented. The success or failure of the directive and, by implication, the future development of EA within the member states of the European Union, depends on

(1)  the *quality* of EAs that are prepared;
(2)  the structure and *organisation* of the pre-existing procedures for decision-making and assessment; and
(3)  the *willingness* of member states to adjust and improve pre-existing procedures in order to allow for the specific consideration of the findings of EAs.

In practice, the UK decided to introduce a system for EA that operates in parallel with the normal planning requirements. The operational objective of the EA system is stated in the guide to EA published by the Department of the Environment in 1989:

> Properly carried out, EA will help all those involved in the planning process. From the developer's point of view the preparation of an environmental statement in parallel with project design provides a useful framework within which environmental considerations and design development can interact. Environmental analysis may indicate ways in which the project can be modified to anticipate possible adverse effects, for example, through the

identification of a better practicable environmental option, or by considering alternative processes. To the extent that this is done, the formal planning approval stages are likely to be smoother (Department of Environment, 1989, p.3).

This positive approach to the value of EA reflects the earlier findings of the House of Lords (1981) who observed that substantial benefits could be gained by developers who utilised EA as part of project design and development, for example, through the avoidance of costly modifications to plant once operational or by reducing delays in gaining approval for a project. British Gas, for example, claimed it had saved £30 million over a ten-year period, mainly because it had achieved quicker authorisation of projects.

The system introduced by the Department of the Environment conforms to the requirements of the EC directive. The directive and the UK regulations (Department of the Environment, 1988) classify projects into two major groups: Schedule 1 (or Annex I) projects for which an EA is required in every case, and Schedule 2 (or Annex II) projects for which an EA is required only if the particular project is likely to give rise to significant environmental effects. The activities classified under Schedule 1 are shown in Box 1.

---

**Box 1.** *Schedule 1 projects*

1. Crude-oil refineries and installations for the gasification and liquefaction of 500 tonnes or more of coal or bituminous shale per day.
2. Thermal power stations or other combustion installations with a heat output of 300 megawatts or more and nuclear power stations or other nuclear reactors.
3. Installations for the storage or final disposal of radioactive waste.
4. Major iron and steel works.
5. Installations for the extraction of asbestos or for the processing of asbestos or products containing asbestos.
6. Integrated chemical installations.
7. Construction of motorways, major roads, long-distance railways and airports.
8. Trading ports and inland waterways which permit the passage of vessels of over 1,350 tonnes.
9. Installation for the disposal of toxic and dangerous waste.

---

In the case of Schedule 2 projects an EA is required if the project is considered to be likely to give rise to significant environmental effects. The assessment of significance is a crucial matter and it is difficult to define precise screening criteria in order to determine if an EA is required. In general terms three criteria are used to determine significance:

(1) Is the project of more than local significance, principally in terms of its physical scale?
(2) Is the project located in a particularly sensitive location, such as a national park?

(3) Is the project likely to give rise to particularly complex or adverse effects, for example, will it discharge pollutants?

The projects specified in Schedule 2 (see Box 2) can be tested by reference to a number of quantified thresholds. For example, a sand and gravel working of more than 50 hectares may require an EA, as will a new manufacturing plant requiring a site in the range of 20–30 hectares or above. A particular problem in practice is how to judge the cumulative impact of a number of projects, each of which is just below the threshold size, that are located adjacent to one another.

---

**Box 2.** *Schedule 2 projects*

1. Major agricultural projects.
2. Extraction industry—peat, deep drilling, coal mining, petroleum, natural gas, ores, bituminous shale, open-cast mining, surface installations, coke ovens, cement works.
3. Energy industry—except those in Schedule 1.
4. Processing of metals—except those in Schedule 1.
5. Glass making.
6. Chemical industry—except those in Schedule 1.
7. Food industry.
8. Textile, leather, wood and paper industries.
9. Rubber industry.
10. Infrastructure projects—except those in Schedule 1.
11. Other major projects.
12. Modifications to Schedule 1 projects.
13. Developments within a description mentioned in Schedule 1, where they are for the development and testing of methods or products for no more than one year.

---

In the case of a project that is subject to EA the developers must collect and present certain information about the impact of the project in the form of an environmental statement (ES). The information to be provided in the ES includes a description of the project and the major effects upon the environment, including noise, vibration, emissions of pollutants and the production of residues. In addition, the developer is required to indicate the aspects of the environment that will be significantly affected by the project, including: the human population, fauna, flora, soil, water, the climate, the built environment, landscape and the inter-relationship among these factors. Further information is required on measures to prevent and reduce any adverse effects upon the environment. The developer is obliged to provide a non-technical summary of the above information. These conditions place a major responsibility upon the developer, especially in relation to the need to provide the information in a form which is easily understood by decision makers.

The procedure for preparing an EA is complex and has been outlined by Wood and Jones (1991, p. 2) as consisting of the following steps:

(i)    Determining the need for EA in a particular case.
(ii)   Determining the coverage of the EA.
(iii)  Preparing the ES.
(v)    Consultation and participation
(vi)   Synthesising the findings from consultation and reaching a decision.
(vii)  Monitoring the impacts of a project if it is implemented.

The major output of the process of EA is an ES. This is prepared by the developer and submitted to the competent authority (in the UK this is the local planning authority). Whilst the preparation of the ES is the responsibility of the developer, there are sound reasons why a developer (or a developer's agent) should consult with the local authority at the outset. As the Department of the Environment (1989) indicates, local authorities can offer advice and provide baseline information which may assist in the definition of the project or the choice of site, and this may help to minimise any delays caused by the EA process.

Key issues worthy of particular consideration in the preparation of an ES include

(1)  the determination of the scope of an assessment; formal guidance as to scope and content is available, but additional special or local factors also occur;
(2)  the consideration of the need to investigate alternative ways of proceeding with the project and alternative sites for the project;
(3)  the range of consultations (above and beyond the statutory consultations) which need to be undertaken; and
(4)  the range of techniques and methods to be employed in preparing the ES.

Given the additional time required to consider and determine an application for a project that requires the preparation of an EA, the period allowed to a UK local planning authority to determine an application is extended from the normal 8 weeks to 16 weeks. In practice this formal period of time may prove to be insufficient, especially if the local authority has not been involved at the outset in determining the specification for an EA.

## Preparing an environmental assessment

The procedure for preparing an environmental assessment (EA) was introduced above. However, this presented a simplified version of the methodology which inevitably requires further expansion. In particular, as already indicated, there are many methodologies and procedures available for use by an environmental assessor. Most methodologies make use of an impact matrix that seeks to relate the characteristics of an action or project to the relevant features of the local environment. A typical environmental impact matrix is illustrated in Figure 2.

As demonstrated in Figure 2, the impact matrix can be used to record either a beneficial or an adverse impact. In a simple recording matrix this may be indicated

Action resulting from the project

| | Dam construction | River control | Road building | Water emission | Atmospheric emission | Noise |
|---|---|---|---|---|---|---|
| Soils | | | | | | |
| Land form | | | | | | |
| Water quality | | | | | | |
| Air quality | | | | | | |
| Temperature | | | | | | |

Features of the environment

Figure 2. An Environmental Impact Assessment Matrix.

by a plus or a minus sign. It is also possible to record the severity of the impact; is the interaction between the project and the local environment likely to bring about serious and lasting change? As some features of a local environment are of greater significance and value than others, the importance of any interaction can also be noted. Overall, the benefit of using a matrix to record environmental impacts is that it allows for the pattern of interaction to be clearly demonstrated and readily appreciated, especially by a lay audience.

Preparing an environmental assessment is not, however, simply a matter of determining the incidence and importance of any inter-relationship that exist between the features of a local environment and the characteristics of a proposed project. There are a number of other important steps in the preparation of an EA; these are intended to ensure that the actual process of assessment complies with the requirements of the legislation, and to allow for the assessment to be focused on the most important impacts. The procedure commences with the determination of the need for an EA and is followed by the definition of the scope of the assessment, the specification of the characteristics of the project and the identification of the features of the local environment that require consideration. Other important features of the procedure include the need to make provision for public participation, the methods employed for the actual assessment of impacts, and the desirability of considering alternatives to a proposed project. The production of the final ES is followed by a process of decision-making which may approve the proposed projects, suggest modifications to the proposed projects, or reject it. This procedure is illustrated in Figure 3.

This outline of procedure describes the overall approach to the use of EIA and attempts to demonstrate, in a general manner, the various stages that are involved in constructing and applying EIA. The specific procedure for EA that is used in the UK is described in detail in the Department of the Environment's *Guide to the Procedures* (Department of the Environment, 1989). More detailed information on the methods

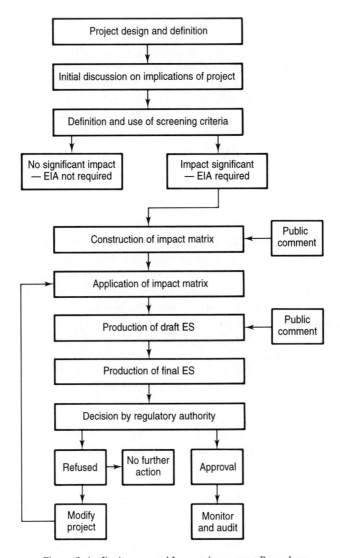

Figure 3. An Environmental Impact Assessment Procedure.

available for conducting an EIA is available from a number of specialist texts (for example, Wathern, 1988).

**EA in practice in the UK**

A major review of the operation of the EA system in the UK has been conducted by Manchester University on behalf of the Department of the Environment (Wood and Jones, 1991). This review examined all known environmental statements submitted between 15 July 1988 and the end of 1989. In addition, it surveyed 24 local authorities who had not received an ES, and it looked in more detail at a number of cases where an ES has been submitted.

The Manchester research team experienced some difficulty in identifying the precise number of statements which had been submitted. The Department of the Environment notifies the *Journal of Planning and Environment Law (JPEL)* on a regular basis of the number of ESs submitted. During the review period some 138 ESs were referred to *JPEL*; one was later excluded. The Manchester team also established the existence of 16 other ESs, bringing the total recorded to 153. Of these, 121 ESs were submitted to English authorities, 13 were submitted in Wales and 19 were in Scotland. Some 13 per cent of ESs were associated with Schedule 1 projects and 87 per cent with Schedule 2 projects.

In total, 107 ESs were submitted to district councils (70 per cent), some 39 (25 per cent) to county or regional authorities, 6 (4 per cent) to urban development corporations and 1 to a national park authority. Voluntary submission occurred in 89 per cent of cases. In 9 per cent of cases an ES was submitted in response to an opinion, and in 2 per cent of cases following a directive from the competent central government department. Some 36 per cent of developers were large companies, 54 per cent small companies and 10 per cent local authorities. In 73 per cent of cases consultants were employed to prepare the ES. Some 32 per cent of ESs were prepared for projects located in urban areas, and 25 per cent of projects were located in areas, such as national parks, that are subject to specific forms of environmental regulation and protection.

Of the cases which had been decided at the time of the publication of the Manchester report, permission had been granted in 22 cases (56 per cent) and refused in 17 cases (44 per cent).

In the case studies of authorities where an EA was conducted, the Manchester team reviewed the ESs. Of the 24 cases reviewed, 15 were considered to be unsatisfactory because they did not fulfil the requirements of the EA scheme and were not in broad compliance with the EC directive. In 10 of the 24 cases examined, the local authority took less than four months to reach a decision.

The implementation of the directive allows for an initial judgement to be made to the extent to which business has responded to the implications of the introduction of a stricter regime of project development and assessment. A number of concerns have emerged from the review undertaken by the Manchester researchers and from a broader experience by using EA. These include

- difficulties related to the precise definition of projects and their assignment to Schedules 1 or 2;
- issues related to the definition of what is considered to be a significant impact;
- a number of problems related to the specification of the items considered necessary for inclusion in an EA;
- issues related to the availability of sufficient information about a project and the characteristics of a local environment, and the availability of methods and techniques for environmental assessment;
- doubts regarding the degree of skill and experience of some developers, and their agents, in relation to their ability to conduct an EA;
- factors related to the extent and quality of public consultation and involvement;

● issues related to the means by which the results of an EA are presented, and the inadequacy of some of the non-technical summaries which have been prepared.

These and other issues form the basis from which EA itself can be assessed; such matters will figure prominently in the review of the 1985 European directive which will take place during 1994. Most observers of EA expect that the European Commission will press for EA to be extended to include a capacity for strategic environmental assessment (SEA).

## Strategic environmental assessment

Project or product-related EIA or EA is seen by some observers as only the tip of the iceberg of environmental assessment (Glasson, 1994). Although the application of EIA is a good example of the use of the precautionary principle, that prevention is better than cure, many problematical projects would not have been developed to the state at which they require an EIA if the policy, upon which they are based, had been assessed for its environmental impact at the outset. In addition, as well as the conventional coverage of EIA, a case has been made for the inclusion of socioeconomic impacts within EIA. These two additional dimensions, strategic assessment and the widening of the scope of EIA, are likely to figure as major issues in the future development of environmental assessment.

Strategic environmental assessment has been described by Therivel *et al.* (1992) as the application of EIA to policies, plans and programmes. These higher-level tiers of the policy process were illustrated in Figure 1 and the application of principles of EIA at these levels can be seen as the next step towards prevention rather than cure. There are two approaches to the development of a system of SEA: the refinement of project EIA and the trickling down of the objective of sustainability (*ibid.*). The former approach, whilst possessing the merit of extending the use of already known and familiar methods and procedures, suffers from a number of drawbacks. These include the inherently responsive nature of the project-based EIA—it reacts to proposals rather than initiating them—and this limits the extent to which project-based EIA can satisfy all the objectives of sustainability. Difficulties are also experienced in project EIA when it is faced with having to assess the cumulative impacts of more than one project. Problems also arise with the need to assess alternatives to a specified project. Equally, it is difficult for conventional EIA to consider measures for the mitigation of impacts; to deal with difficult projects rapidly or within a tight timescale; and to incorporate fully the requirement for public participation (*ibid.*). Whilst these weaknesses are not, in themselves, incapable of rectification through revisions to present methods and procedures, they could prove to inhibit the development and introduction of SEA.

A more satisfactory basis for the development and introduction of SEA is offered by using the generic principles of sustainability as a starting point. By using such an approach, which first defines the objectives for the achievement of sustainability, the principles of sustainability can be trickled down through policies, programmes and plans. A first step, at the level of the individual plan, towards the introduction of SEA has been taken in the revised guidance published by the Department of the Environment on the structure and content of development plans (Department of the Environment, 1992b). This guidance plans to take environmental considerations into account.

Over the next decade it is likely that, at both European level and in the UK, SEA will become an established feature of the policy landscape. As such, it will prove essential for the environmentally aware business to assess its policies for their environmental sustainability and to ensure that the principles of sustainability trickle down into all aspects of operational programming and business planning.

The translation of these objectives into reality is likely to involve a number of elements:

- A commitment to sustainability and its interpretation in relation to an individual activity.
- The definition of the parameters for the achievement of sustainability.
- The definition of the carrying capacity of an environment within which an activity occurs.
- The preparation of an SEA for all policies, programmes and plans that will have an effect on the environment.
- The assessment of individual projects (or products) within the constraints set by SEA.
- The introduction of monitoring and auditing to trace the consequences of a project (Therivel *et al.*, 1992).

The introduction of a requirement for regular monitoring and auditing provides a feedback loop that can be used to inform the future policy process. A knowledge of the impact of past actions can allow for the avoidance of future mistakes. The following section considers how a capacity for monitoring and auditing can be introduced into business procedures.

## ENVIRONMENTAL AUDITING

As was noted earlier in this chapter, environmental auditing can be viewed as the intracompany dimension of the linked processes of environmental assessment and auditing. It is chiefly concerned with the regular monitoring and evaluation of the environmental performance of a business.

Environmental auditing is now well established as good business practice. There are many approaches to auditing, but they share a common concern to ensure that a systematic, documented, periodic and objective evaluation is conducted of how well an organisation's systems are performing in relation to the environment when assessed against internal objectives and procedures, and the need to comply with statutory requirements. The point made earlier, that environmental auditing in its broadest sense is not a statutory requirement, needs to be qualified by reference to those aspects of a company's operations, for example, in relation to health and safety matters in the work environment, that are regulated through legislation.

## An approach to environmental auditing

It is interesting to note that many companies have sought a form of statutory validation for their audits, initially through extending the coverage of the British Standard on total quality management and more recently through meeting the requirements of the new BS 7750 for *Environmental Management Systems* (British Standard Institution, 1991).

The component parts of a typical environmental audit are as follows:

(1) Defining the objectives of the audit—what is required from the audit?
(2) Setting the scope and span of the audit—will it relate to the entire company, to a division or to an individual aspect of the company's operation?
(3) Defining the baseline—identify the major production activities carried out by a company (and possibly on behalf of it), the range of supporting activities, the key aspects of the legislation and the broader environmental context within which a company operates.
(4) Agreeing on the action to be taken following the completion of the audit—it is important to understand the implications of conducting an audit and to determine what limits, if any, will be placed on its implementation.
(5) Selecting the audit team—insiders and outsiders—ensuring that the team has knowledge of, or access to, all aspects of a company's activities and that the workforce knows the reason for conducting the audit.
(6) Gathering information and evidence in relation to prespecified requirements and the means of assessment—this will require substantial assistance from staff. This procedure will look at many aspects of the operation of a company including

- the overall environmental policy of a company;
- production issues—raw materials, sources of materials, production processes, products and packaging;
- staff awareness, training and recruitment;
- energy use;
- water use;
- waste disposal and recycling;
- discharges;
- the transport of goods and people;
- accident and emergency procedures; and
- the adequacy of management and technical control systems.

(7) Assessing the performance of all aspects of a company's operations in relation to the objectives of policy and specified targets.
(8) Evaluating the audit findings—this is likely to employ many different techniques and procedures, but a non-technical summary is essential.
(9) Reporting the findings—there is likely to be a need for interim reports (to individual units) for clarification and further work, and a final report; again a non-technical summary is essential.
(10) Developing an action plan—this might, for example, classify outputs and possible actions into:

- major changes required  at low cost, and
                          at high cost
- minor changes required at low cost, and
                          at high cost

At this stage it is important to re-examine company policy and to redefine the objectives and targets of policy. It is also important to look at the time spans required for successful implementation and the need to gain approval and help from regulatory agencies, other companies and advisers.

(11). Monitoring is vital; there is a clear need to follow up the action plan and to assess the changing operational features of a company, the industry generally and the scope of environmental regulation.

An outline procedure for conducting an audit is illustrated in Figure 4.

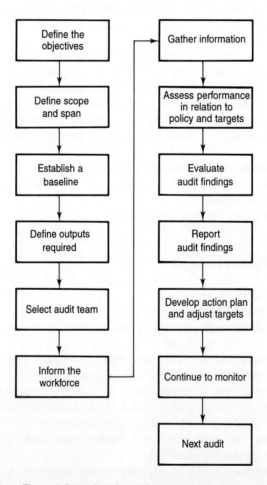

Figure 4. Procedure for an Environmental Audit.

## The role of environmental auditing

Environmental auditing is now well established, and many companies have undertaken an audit as part of their regular review of company strategy. Other organizations have widened the scope of a statutory COSHH (control of substances hazardous to health) audit to include environmental auditing, or have extended existing procedures that were initially designed to monitor and audit total quality management.

Although not a statutory requirement in itself, environmental auditing is now seen as playing an essential role in the sustainable management of a business. Governments, the International Chamber of Commerce, the CBI and other business organisations consider auditing to be a normal and highly desirable central aspect of corporate strategy. In his introduction to the CBI guidance on environmental auditing, Sir Brian Corby, the CBI President, noted that

> Companies must not wait for restrictive legislation to bring about change. Whilst many companies have a good record, there is a gap between what a business could do to reduce its impact on the environment and what it actually does, which could be closed with better information and instruction (CBI, 1990, p.3)

Environmental auditing is increasingly seen as an essential element in achieving total quality. Welford (1992a) has argued that the concept of total quality management implies the elimination of any negative impacts on the environment. He also suggests that the main elements of a system of environmental management and auditing are

- *team work*—the workforce needs to be involved in any system of auditing;
- *commitment*—a company-wide commitment is essential from the chief executive down;
- *communications*—essential in order to ensure that accurate information is available and that feedback flows throughout the company;
- *organisation*—clear channels of responsibility and reporting need to established;
- *control and monitoring*—the existence of a system can generate a false sense of security; checks and inspections are vital elements in ensuring compliance;
- *planning*—processes need to be well planned and implemented in order to monitor, record and adjust processes; and
- *inventory control system*—this is essential both in order to minimise costs and to ensure that materials and energy costs are reduced.

## Audits for specific purposes

In Chapter 5 one of the many forms of environmental audit was discussed: the initial environmental review. The review was presented as a one-off exercise, conducted in order to allow a company to establish a baseline from which an environmental policy may be established or elaborated. The full environmental audit, which has been illustrated above, can be viewed as a general-purpose approach to auditing that is applicable to most business situations.

However, many companies have also discovered that an audit is required for a particular purpose, or to assess a specific aspect of operation. Owen (1993) has illustrated the need for such audits by reference to the range of procedures used by British Petroleum. The different forms of audits used by BP include

- *compliance audits*—these are designed to allow a company to check its performance in relation both to statutory requirements, and to voluntary codes and internal standards;
- *site audits*—spot checks may be required at individual sites, including sites to be acquired;
- *activity audits*—in some cases it is important to examine activities that cross the boundaries between activities within a business;
- *corporate audits*—a full audit of an entire business sector;
- *associate audits*—examining the activities of companies associated with the business; and
- *issues audits*—these concentrate on specific issues or topics such as energy use or the consumption of scarce raw materials.

The use of specific forms of audit is growing rapidly. One of the clearest examples is found in relation to the acquisition of companies, or of sites and premises. Given the potentially expensive and time-consuming problems that are associated with having to clean up a business operation or site that fails to comply with statutory or other regulations, many companies now seek assurance through an environmental audit that the prospective new acquisition does not harbour unknown environmental problems.

Legal practices, consulting engineers and management specialists offer a range of auditing services that are designed to provide a client with the assurance that a potential acquisition is free of any major environmental problems. The services offered by such organisations range from searches and inspections of public registers in order to identify land which may be contaminated to a full assessment of the environmental implications of the activities of a company.

## Environmental auditing schemes

Two main schemes for environmental auditing have been introduced in recent years: the European Eco-Management and Audit Scheme and the British Standard 7750 on environmental management systems. Although the two schemes differ in terms of their details of approach, they are, in Welford's (1992b, p. 26) view, 'completely compatible and it is up to firms which scheme to choose although there is no reason why both cannot be simultaneously adhered to'.

The European Union scheme was introduced in the form of a council regulation on 29 June 1993. The scheme has the following objectives:

(1) The establishment and implementation of environmental policies, programmes and management systems by companies, in relation to their sites.

(2) The systematic, objective and periodic evaluation of the performance of such elements.
(3) The provision of information on environmental performance to the public.

Key elements in the scheme include the definition of an environmental policy, the setting of targets for achievement within a given time, the provision of plans and systems to achieve the targets, the auditing of progress made, the reporting of the results of an audit, and the setting of new targets for the next time period (*ibid.*). Within the cycle of auditing, illustrated in Figure 5, particular attention should be paid to the following environmental effects:

● Controlled and uncontrolled emissions to the atmosphere.
● Controlled and uncontrolled emissions to water or sewers.
● Solid and other wastes, particularly hazardous wastes.
● Contamination of land.
● Use of land, fuels and energy, and other natural resources.
● Discharge of thermal energy, noise, odour, dust, vibration and visual impact.
● Effects on specific parts of the environment and ecosystems.

The effect of a company's activity upon the environment can, in Tanega's (1994) view, be seen to imply that certain decisions should be taken in response to specific environmental issues:

● *Critical*—threatening loss of life, property, environmental catastrophe or the production of hazardous waste.
● *Major*—tending to make environmental objectives fail.
● *Minor*—falling short of an intended function but not necessarily causing a failure of an environmental objective.
● *Incidental*—having no unsatisfactory effect.

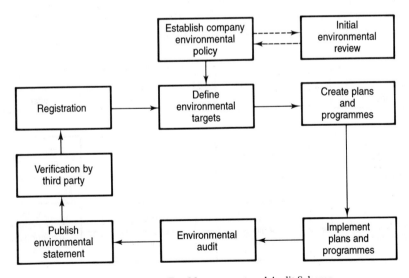

Figure 5. European Eco-Management and Audit Scheme.

An important element in the European scheme is the role played by an accredited environmental verifier. The role of the verifier is to confirm that all stages in the scheme have been complied with and that the information presented in the audit report is accurate. The verifier should be involved in all stages of the audit and can also be used as a source of additional information.

The Eco-Management and Audit Scheme is applicable to both public and private organisations. A guide to the scheme for local government has been prepared by CAG Consultants (1993). The local government scheme provides a useful context for the development of an approach to auditing at local level, and it can be used to guide local economic development procedures. As such, it is of relevance to small and medium enterprises who are members of a local environmental business club or forum.

British Standard 7750 was introduced in 1992 with the intention of enabling an organisation 'to establish procedures to set an environmental policy and objectives, achieve compliance with them, and demonstrate such compliance to others' (British Standards Institution, 1992, p. 3). The scheme shares many of the features and characteristics of the European scheme.

The British Standard requires the establishment of a baseline of company environmental policy through the preparation of an initial environmental review, the assessment and recording of the environmental effects of an organisation's activities and the regular audit of policy and operations. Auditing is at the heart of the environmental management system suggested by BS 7750 in order to 'assess the compliance of the system with the Standards' requirements' and to ensure that management activities and procedures 'meet those requirements' (Gilbert, 1993, p. 50). The British Standard system is illustrated in Figure 6.

## Environmental auditing in the future

As has already been discussed in Chapter 5, an environmental audit is a vital element in the development of a capability to assess the impact of a company's operations upon the environment. It is likely that commercial and legal pressures to adopt

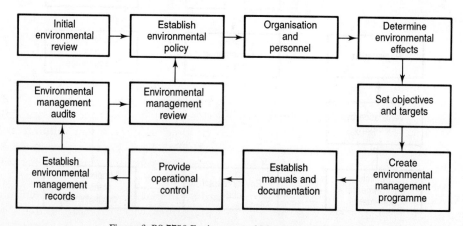

Figure 6. BS 7750 Environmental Management Scheme.

environmental auditing will become more intense and, as a consequence, companies will have to incorporate methods for the regular auditing of the environmental effects of their activities within their standard operational procedures. In some industries and sectors of the economy it is already clear that companies now regard environmental auditing as a normal and essential part of the portfolio of management methods. Gray, Bebbington and Walters (1993) stress two points with regard to the current and future use of environmental audits:

(1) It is essential to ensure that terminology is clear and that the objective of auditing is stated in an unambiguous manner.
(2) It is vital to treat environmental auditing as a serious matter; an audit by itself is little use, it needs to be matched by a commitment to action and a change in attitudes and behaviour.

An environmental audit provides a means of ensuring that future problems can be avoided. It is a proactive and powerful management tool, and it implies the need for an evolutionary approach to be adopted to the continuous raising of the environmental performance of a company. In the view of one observer, environmental audits, and the management systems of which they are an essential component, 'cannot be seen simply as a competitive edge, they will in time become a means of survival' (Welford, 1992b, p. 26).

## ENVIRONMENTAL INFORMATION SYSTEMS

In the introduction to this chapter it was noted that it is important to identify or establish sources of information and knowledge upon which systems and procedures for environmental assessment and auditing can be based. Whilst systems of assessment and auditing generate substantial quantities of information that can be used in subsequent exercises, the initial starting point in any system will be to assemble the necessary data. Having established a system it is equally important that the database is kept up to date.

A substantial part of the information required in order to conduct an environmental audit and assessment is likely to be available from the internal records of an organisation. However, it is likely that much of this information will be dispersed throughout the organisation and it is unlikely to be available in a readily usable form. In the case of the development of a specific project (or new plant) the parameters and characteristics of the project (or plant) will be known and this information can be used to develop a project (or plant) specification report. The information contained in such a report can be used to inform and calibrate the horizontal axis of an environmental impact assessment (as shown in Figure 2), or to specify the operational characteristics of a company, or part of a company, that will be the subject of an environmental audit.

An important task is to ensure that any information that is collected and held in a database is available in a form that is compatible with external sources of information. For example, specified international units of measurement should be adopted if possible and efforts should be made to convert historic data to current units of measurement.

In constructing an environmental information system, it is equally important to be aware of the availability of the major sources of information that are held by external organisations, such as government departments, local authorities, regulatory agencies, nature conservation bodies, local amenity groups, business organisations and research organisations including universities and commercial research bodies. An overview of the information that is available from such sources can be obtained from publications such as the Department of the Environment's *The UK Environment* (Department of the Environment, 1992a) and the *European Environmental Statistics Handbook* (Newman and Foster, 1993).

It has been noted that any information system should be organised in a manner that is compatible with similar systems that are used by other organisations. A basic element of organisation is the use of a spatial or geographic method of data referencing. A geographical information system (GIS) relates individual items of information to a specific set of spatial co-ordinates, allowing information to be mapped and manipulated in a way that allows for the environmental effects of an activity, or proposed activity, to be presented or simulated. Modern GIS methods allow data to be collected, analysed and compared over time and between places. Many GIS data and information systems are based upon the pooling of information that is held by various organisations present in a locality. This common user approach implies that individual organisations have to accept a degree of disclosure of information in exchange for access to other information that they may require. A pooling arrangement also implies the need to harmonise the methods used to collect data, the units of measurements utilised, and the formats employed for the recording of data.

The major elements of an environmental information system are illustrated in Figure 7. As can be seen from this figure, the major component parts of a system are

- information internal to an organisation;
- published external sources of information;
- unpublished external sources; and
- sources derived from legislation and regulation.

An organisation's individual information system may be linked to other systems or may be freestanding. A more comprehensive business environmental information system has been developed by the International Institute for Sustainable Development (1992).

## CONCLUSIONS

In this chapter attention has been focused on procedures and methods that allow for assessment and auditing of the environmental standards and performance of business and other organisations. Such procedures and methods provide an organisation with a capacity to understand the way in which it operates, the effects of

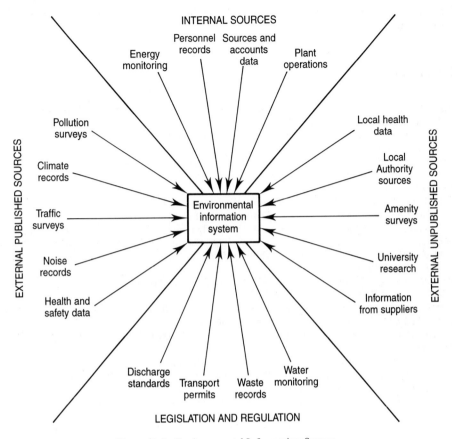

Figure 7. An Environmental Information System.

its operation upon the environment and the alternative ways in which it can respond to any undesirable consequences.

By adopting EIA or environmental auditing an organisation can better understand its ability to bring about change and it can develop a proactive capacity that will allow it to avoid any undesirable environmental effects in future. These methods and procedures have, until now, been mainly applied to specific projects, or to the operation of particular items of plant and equipment. However, it is likely that they will become commonplace in the future. Increasingly, companies and public bodies are applying the principles of environmental assessment and auditing to the development of their policies, programmes and plans. The adoption of strategic environmental assessment and auditing aims to avoid the emergence, in the future, of projects, products and processes that are environmentally unsustainable.

Prevention is better than cure. Organisations that wish to avoid costly and time-consuming errors of judgement, and the possible rejection of their proposals on environmental grounds, would be well advised to consider the adoption and integration of environmental assessment and auditing within their procedures for corporate strategy and operational management. An essential element in the adoption of such an approach is the establishment and maintenance of an environmental information system.

## REFERENCES

British Standards Institution (1991) *Specification for Environmental Management Systems*, British Standards Institution, Milton Keynes.
CAG Consultants (1993) *A Guide to the Eco-Management and Audit Scheme for UK Local Government*, HMSO, London.
Cannon, T. (1992) *Corporate Responsibility*, Pitman Publishing, London.
Catlow, J. and Thirwall, C. G. (1976) *Environmental Impact Assessment*, Department of the Environment, London.
Clark, B. D., Chapman, K., Bisset, R. and Wathern, P. (1976) *Assessment of Major Industrial Applications: A Manual*, Department of Environment, London.
Clutterbuck, D., Dearlove, D. and Snow, D. (1992) *Actions Speak Louder*, Kogan Page, London.
Commission of the European Communities (1985) Council directive of 27 June 1985 on the assessment of the effects of certain public and private projects on the environment, *Official Journal L175*, pp. 40–8.
Confederation of British Industry (1990) *Narrowing the Gap: Environmental Auditing*, Confederation of British Industry, London.
Department of Environment (1988) *Town and Country Planning (Assessment of Environmental Effects) Regulations*, Department of the Environment, London.
Department of the Environment (1989) *Environmental Assessment: A Guide to the Procedures*, HMSO, London.
Department of the Environment (1992a) *The UK Environment*, HMSO, London.
Department of the Environment (1992b) *Planning Policy Guidance Note 12: Development Plans and Regional Planning Guidance*, HMSO, London.
Gilbert, M. J. (1993) *Achieving Environmental Management Standards*, Pitman Publishing, London.
Glasson, J. (1994) EIA—only the tip of the iceberg? *Town and Country Planning*, Vol. 63, no. 2, pp. 42–5.
Gray, R., Bebbington, J. and Walters, D. (1993) *Accounting for the Environment*, Paul Chapman Publishing, London.
House of Lords Select Committee on the European Communities (1981) *Environmental Assessment of Projects*, HMSO, London.
International Institute for Sustainable Development (1992) *Business Strategy for Sustainable Development*, International Institute for Sustainable Development, Winnipeg, Manitoba.
Lee, N. and Wood, C. (1978) EIA—a European Perspective, *Built Environment*, Vol. 4, no. 2, pp. 101–10.
Muller, K. and Koechlin, D. (1992) Environmentally conscious management, in D. Koechlin and K. Muller (eds) *Green Business Opportunities*, Pitman Publishing, London.
Murphy, T. (1981) EIA and developing countries, *Planning Outlook*, Vol. 24, no. 3, pp. 109–12.
Newman, O. and Foster, A. (1993) *European Environmental Statistics Handbook*, Gale Research International Ltd, Andover.
Owen, D. (1993) The emerging green agenda: a role for accounting? In D. Smith (ed.) *Business and the Environment*, Paul Chapman Publishing, London.
Roberts, P. and Shaw, T. (1981) EIA: links to practice, in M. Breakell and J. Glasson (eds) *Environmental Impact Assessment*, Oxford Polytechnic, Oxford.
Roberts, P. W., Shaw, T. and Adkins, M. G. (1980) *Environmental Impact Assessment: A Practice Guide*, Department of Urban and Regional Planning, Lanchester Polytechnic, Coventry.
Tanega, J. (1994) *Eco-Management and Auditing: A Practical Guide to the EC Regulations*, IFS International, Kempston, Beds.
Therivel, R., Wilson, E., Thompson, S., Heaney, D. and Pritchard, D. (1992) *Strategic Environmental Assessment*, Earthscan, London.

United States Government (1969) *National Environmental Policy Act,* United States Government Printing Office, Washington, D.C.

Wathern, P. (ed.) (1988) *Environmental Impact Assessment: Theory and Practice,* Unwin Hyman, London.

Welford, R. (1992a) Linking quality and the environment: a strategy for the implementation of environmental management systems, *Business Strategy and the Environment,* Vol. 1, pt. 1, pp. 25–34.

Welford, R. (1992b) *A Guide to Environmental Auditing,* European Research Press, Bradford.

Welford, R. and Gouldson, A. (1993) *Environmental Management and Business Strategy,* Pitman Publishing, London.

Wood, C. and Jones, C. (1991) *Monitoring Environmental Assessment and Planning,* HMSO, London.

# 13

# A Model Protocol and International Standards for Environmental Audit

*G. Ledgerwood, E. Street and R. Therivel*

This chapter discusses the proposed EC Directive on Eco-Audit and the British Standard on Environmental Management Systems, both of which are likely to have a profound impact on environmental auditing in future years. It discusses links between them, and to other relevant legislation, including the UK Environmental Protection Act 1990 and BS 5750 on quality systems. It proposes an environmental auditing protocol with advisory comments. On the basis of this protocol, an environmental manager can devise, with adjustments for local circumstances, a procedure for carrying out an environmental audit in his or her own organisation.

## EC DRAFT ECO-AUDIT DIRECTIVE

The EC's 'Eco-Audit' Directive will make environmental auditing a voluntary but regulated activity throughout all Member States. It applies directly in all Member States; in other words, it does not require Member States to pass enabling legislation. The legislation features a voluntary system for the introduction of environmental auditing and is targeted primarily at manufacturing and processing industries.

Once a company decides voluntarily to seek registration for an eco-audit, it agrees to abide by the rules on a site-by-site basis. Participating companies must do the following.

(1) Undertake a comprehensive environmental review of their activities, impacts and regulations, which include the following topics:
— management;
— saving and choice of energy;
— raw materials;
— water;
— selection of production processes;

— planning;
— design;
— packaging and transportation of the product; and
— communications with the public.

(2) Prepare or refine a detailed environmental policy, programme and objectives. This includes:
— a company environmental policy, i.e. broad intentions of the company with respect to the environment;
— a company action plan;
— objectives and targets—objectives will usually be broad-brush (e.g. reduce $SO_2$ emissions), targets will be quantified and attached to a timescale (e.g. 10 per cent $SO_2$ reduction in two years); and
— an environmental programme or strategy to achieve this (e.g. install scrubbers).

(3) Put in place an environmental management system to deliver this package. The system organises people, documentation, equipment, systems, monitoring etc. to ensure that the strategy is carried out. It includes regular audits at sensible frequencies.

(4) Prepare a statement according to eco-audit rules, setting out objectives and background. This statement includes:
— a description of the company's activities, as relevant;
— an assessment of the relevant environmental issues, including factual data;
— a summary of quantitative data on the organisation's emissions, waste, raw materials, energy and water consumption during the period before the report;
— company policy, plans, targets for the site;
— an evaluation of environmental performance at the site; and
— an agreed deadline for the next statement.

(5) Get the statement verified, and submit it to the competent authority. This provides assurance to the public that statements are fair and gives credibility to the whole scheme. Verification entails confirmation that the factual part of the statement is true and fair, that results reported are correct and that no significant issues are omitted. It also entails confirmation that reports are based on adequate environmental audit procedures and that the necessary management system components exist. The verifier should not, however, repeat the audit process.

Registration is achieved once the audit statement is validated by an accredited verifier, and is received by the competent national registration body. The company is then registered and entitled to use the logo. The logo only refers to the site that the company has submitted for eco-audit. It does not refer to the company as a whole unless the company had submitted all its sites and holdings to the eco-audit process.

In order to remain registered, the company has to perform the audits as promised in the first statement and submit statements outlining the audit results. De-registration occurs if a registered organisation fails to provide a verified audit statement by the date previously agreed. There is no judgement by the competent body of the 'quality' of the company's environmental performance.

Figure 1 presents the main features of the EC's eco-audit scheme. The role of the external verifier and the need for standardised criteria, protocols and procedures are

| | |
|---|---|
| Objectives | — Systematic, objective and periodic review of environmental performance of certain industrial activity<br>— Provision of information to the public |
| Sectors to be covered in initial phase | — Mining, quarrying<br>— General manufacturing<br>— Production of electricity, gas, steam, hot water<br>— Solid or liquid waste recycling<br>— Waste treatment, destruction, disposal<br>— Other commercial activities could be included under a pilot scheme |
| Registration | Voluntary, based on individual sites |
| Validating authority | To be designated by Member States |
| Compliance | Once registered, companies would be obliged to comply with the eco-audit scheme in full; entitled to use a logo so testifying |
| Elements of eco-audit | — Planning<br>— Review of environmental programmes<br>— Assessment of organisation and equipment<br>— Identification of areas for improvement |
| Stages of eco-audit | — Internal<br>— Validation by independent expert; this stage would have specific detailed rules and protocols to be adhered to and harmonised across Member States |
| Areas of focus | — Energy management<br>— Waste reduction, recycling<br>— Raw materials and water savings<br>— Accident prevention |
| Publication | Company required to publish annual 'environmental statement' for submission to national authority and general public |

Figure 1. EC Draft Eco-Audit Directive: Principal Aspects.

key to the eco-audit regulation, to ensure that a level playing field exists across the Single Market. Owen and Mundy (1991) comment:

A wide range of factors will be considered, from the procurement of raw materials to the use of energy and the disposal of waste. In assessing the overall impact and the relationship that an industrial installation has on both man and the surrounding environment, the proposals represent a radical departure from the current forms of EC pollution control which are sector-specific and aimed only at particular pollutants. The frequency of the audits (probably annual) will mean that a company's compliance with the rules and regulations and its policy and management systems relating to areas such as pollution discharge, choice of raw materials, waste management and product planning will constantly be under review. Not only will they cover current environmental performance, but they should also stimulate improvements in a company's management.

European legislation on the environment has developed to such an extent that many of the data-gathering exercises of environmental audit already have to be undertaken to ensure compliance with other legislation such as the UK Environmental Protection Act 1990. Nevertheless, eco-audit takes the concept of environmental responsibility of firms a step further. It forces firms to review all their activities from resource use to disposal (from cradle to grave) in an environmentally sensitive manner.

## THE BRITISH STANDARD FOR ENVIRONMENTAL MANAGEMENT SYSTEMS

Organisations faced with the cost of implementing environmental programmes often seek to gain some benefit or advantage from implementation. One such benefit is certification of the successful implementation through a government agency such as the British Standard Institution (BSI). In 1992, the BSI adopted its own environmental management systems standard based on a talk by Michael Gilbert (1992). This standard may well form the basis for a similar standard by the International Standard Organisation (ISO), the global agency which has emerged in recent years. Therefore, it is useful to examine the BSI approach in detail, as this approach will no doubt serve as an important international prototype in coming years.

Broadly, the BSI uses performance standards in environmental audit which spell out expected outcomes for:

- each part of the auditing protocol;
- the final outcome of the protocol's operations; and
- the various forms and systems an organisation may use in achieving the required standard.

The British Standard is in three parts:

- Part 1 introduces the concept of the standard;
- Part 2 specifies the elements of the system; and
- Part 3 is a guide to the specification, designed to give more detailed information about the specification requirements.

The procedures of the British Standard entail the following steps.

- A *commitment* by the organisation to establish an environmental management system.
- An *initial review* and assessment of the organisation's environmental position concerning its environmental policy, adherence to environmental standard etc.
- Formulation of an environmental *policy* in the form of a corporate environmental programme. It is this environmental policy which will be the basis for a statement of *targets and objectives* toward which the environmental management system will strive.
- An *inventory of the organisation's activities,* and an *assessment of the activities' environmental impacts,* consistent with the stated policy.
- An *inventory of pertinent regulations and requirements* to ensure compliance.
- The development of an *environmental management plan* and of a supporting *manual* which details all relevant parts of the system.

- The application of the management plan in both the company's *operations* and *record-keeping*.
- A cycle of *audits* of the company's performance to test whether objectives and targets are being met.

*Part 1* of the standard focuses on 'concepts, elements and applications'. Covering matters similar to the EC's eco-audit provisions, the standard details, the costs, benefits, risks and rewards of establishing an environmental management system in a firm. Consistent with the view taken by many observers, the BSI standard emphasises that environmental management is integral to the organisation's management system. In particular, issues of health, safety and quality assurance are interlinked and implicit in environmental standards.

The standard's aims are summarised as follows:

> . . . to facilitate:
> (a) the achievement and demonstration of compliance with environmental regulations and with organisational policies which establish more stringent requirements;
> (b) effective use of personnel skills and other resources;
> (c) accreditation schemes for environmental management.

In adopting this standard, an organization will thus aim to accomplish two objectives:

(1) sustained achievement of environmental performance necessary to meet the requirements of its environmental policy, including compliance with regulatory requirements; and
(2) provision of confirmation to its own management that the intended environmental performance is being achieved and sustained efficiently.

Figures 2 and 3 show respectively the organisational model and the life-cycle model based upon the British Standard.

*Part 2* of the standard deals with specifications for the development, implementation and maintenance of an environmental management system. The key performance standard for Part 2 is as follows:

> The organisation's management shall define and document its environmental policy. The management shall ensure that this policy is understood, implemented and maintained at all levels in the organisation.

The need for in-company verification procedures is inherent to this. An important standard is that:

> . . . investigations of incidents and accidents, and of resulting corrective actions, shall be carried out by personnel independent of those having direct responsibility for the work being performed.

Provision for inventories, audits and reviews of all aspects of environmental systems are established. Procedures include standards for three different operating modes: normal operating procedures; abnormal operating procedures; and incidents, accidents and potential emergency situations.

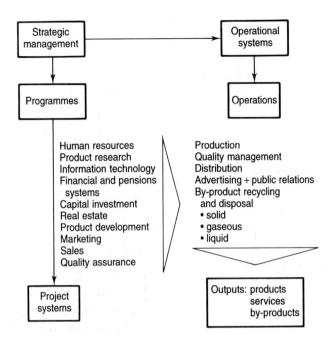

Figure 2. Organizational Model for Environmental Audit. (*Source*: IMRIC University of Greenwich Business School 1992).

The inventory of environmental systems must include compositions, quantities and paths of releases to air and water, and of wastes generated; consumption of materials, fuels and energy; and effects upon specific parts of the environment and ecosystem, including the workforce and workplace.

Internal environmental audits will focus on whether the operation of the environmental systems are bringing them into line with the organisation's adopted environmental plan. The audit will be conducted by following a protocol, which will involve the use of:

- questionnaires;
- checklists;
- interviews;
- measurements; and
- direct observations.

*Part 3* of the standard focuses on additional details of implementation and verification. It discusses different responsibilities of management, reporting systems, training and other details which need to be specified when applying for BSI certification.

In sum, the BSI standard allows an organisation to gain public recognition for the expensive and painstaking implementation of 'environmental management systems'. This recognition may be important both in assisting compliance, and in achieving maximum efficiency in insurance arrangement, and acquisition and disposal

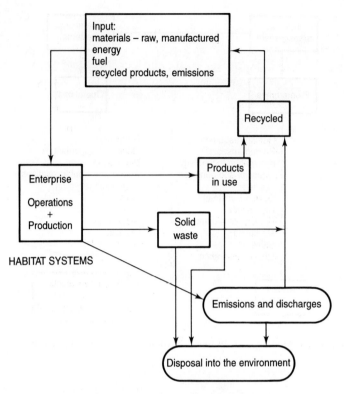

Figure 3. Life-Cycle Model for Environmental Audit. (*Source*: IMRIC University of Greenwich Business School 1992).

planning. Importantly, while the BSI standard requires many details of provisions, its specification allows for a wide array of different mechanisms in arriving at the required standard.

## LINKS BETWEEN BRITISH STANDARD 7750 FOR ENVIRONMENTAL MANAGEMENT SYSTEMS AND BRITISH STANDARD 5750 ON QUALITY SYSTEMS

The British Standard for Environmental Management Systems is closely linked to, and complements, BS 5750 on quality systems. BS 5750 was adopted in 1979, was updated and adopted as an International Standard (ISO 9000 series) in 1987, and has been adopted by the European Committee for Standardization as the EN 29000 series.

The major difference between the proposed Standard on Environmental Management Systems and the Quality System Standard is that currently the Quality System Standard addresses the organisation's outputs as products or services of the organisation, and tries to establish criteria for the management system of the organisation that will meet customer needs. The Standard on Environmental

Management Systems, on the other hand, focuses much more on the by-products or product or service delivery, with the customer being less easy to define, namely the general public.

The European Organisation for Testing and Certification would have to establish a common protocol for assessment and certification to fulfil the requirements of both standards. This would ensure that assessment and verification against proposed standards would be carried out in a common way. The regulation would cover a multitude of environmental issues that the environmental management system should be addressing. To meet these requirements an organisation would need to take a holistic view of its operations to focus on those areas that are most important in terms of environmental impacts.

To develop an environmental management system, the company would carry out assessments of all of its activities to decide which are the most important from an environmental point of view. Implicit in the proposed legislation is a cradle-to-grave approach to the environmental effects of companies' activities. Upstream the organisation would need to examine where raw materials and manufacture materials come from. Downstream, what happens after the product or services leaves the organisation in terms of its 'in use' effects and disposal would be the centre of analysis. The company would then come to a judgement about where to focus its environmental effects analysis, and its plans and programmes related to product lifecycle.

## LINKS BETWEEN EC DRAFT ECO-AUDIT DIRECTIVE AND BRITISH STANDARD FOR ENVIRONMENTAL MANAGEMENT SYSTEMS

It is intended that the proposed EC Eco-Audit Directive and the British Standard for Environmental Management Systems are co-ordinated activities which link to one another. This reciprocity ensures that the standard requirements are compatible with the legislative requirements of environmental audit regulations. The British Standards Institution is confident that this approach will enable UK industry to have at their disposal a national standard which sets the scene for the development of international standards.

There is a close similarity between the two. The EC Directive includes four key areas that are relevant to the proposed BSI standard.

(1) The requirement for participating organizations to establish an *internal evaluation of the environmental management system*, the output of the system being a defined and achieved level of environmental performance. An element of the system is the organisation's evaluation of the system's effectiveness by self-assessment or internal audit. Most organisations will integrate this into their existing management system as part of the way they run their business.

(2) The system will have a *common approach*. It will start with the *company's policy for performance* and, from that, policy objectives and targets for management and operations will be identified. This will be summarised into a plan. At the lowest level these are work instructions that are integrated into the way people actually

carry out their day-to-day job, be it on the production line or in services or management. Day-to-day operations are translated into control, testing, verification and measurements; all those things that are normally necessary to ensure that work instructions are being appropriately followed to meet requirements.

(3) On a regular basis *operations will be reviewed* to ensure that they are meeting objectives and targets. There will be a need to consider at the very senior level whether the policy that established the objectives and targets is appropriate. The company will draw on audit results at a high level to ensure that the policy and programmes are appropriate.

(4) The regulation will require the preparation of a *public statement*. Thus, the results of the environmental audit and management review will need to be prepared in a summary report to be made available to the public.

The EC draft Directive does not specify the role of the external verifier. It does, however, need to be designed in such a way that external verification is achievable. In the British context, this means that the BSI standard must be written in the form of a specification, to enable the standard to be used as a way of facilitating EC legislation.

## A MODEL PROTOCOL FOR ENVIRONMENTAL AUDITING: OVERVIEW

This section proposes a protocol for environmental auditing which combines the requirements of the proposed EC Eco-Audit Directive, the British Standard for Environmental Management Systems and best practice.

Figure 4 illustrates the basic stages in the model protocol. These stages are as follows:

(1) *Set the context*: commit top management to an environmental mission, the establishment of a corporate environmental programme and environmental unit, and environmental auditing.

(2) *Plan the audit*: prepare the audit team, determine the audit scope, identify background information, select methods for conducting the audit and define priority areas.

(3) *Undertake the audit*: through questionnaires, interviews, site inspections.

(4) *Evaluate findings*: describe impacts, establish links between them, assess their significance, explore alternatives, make recommendations.

(5) *Report*: prepare and make available a summary of findings and recommendations to decision-makers and stakeholders. This report focuses on the most pertinent factors and issues required for informed decision-making.

(6) *Implement action plan based on audit*: consider and implement changes to the organisation's operations and policies.

(7) *Verification and feedback*: review the accuracy and impartiality of the audit, and propose future improvements.

The term 'operation' is used throughout the model protocol as a generic term for the wide range of activities that could be audited: policies, programmes and plans,

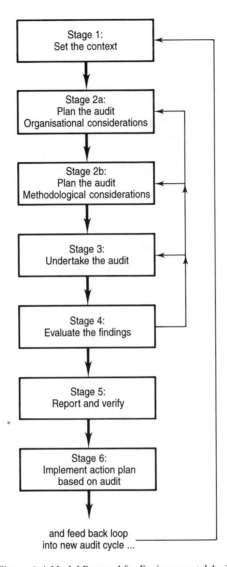

Figure 4. A Model Protocol for Environmental Audit.

site operations, plant, products, strategies etc.

This model cannot fit the vast diversity of cultural and strategic settings found across the hundreds of thousands of organisations undertaking these activities. It does, however, give a pattern which may be adapted to this variety. It generates a detailed system of observations and findings with which, by modification, managers can build up a detailed environmental audit procedure. Moreover, it provides a common reference point for internal and external environmental managers which can assist in negotiating the terms and conditions of the audit.

The term 'protocol' is deliberately borrowed from the laboratory sciences. It pertains in particular to rigorous tests or proofs which two parties in disagreement ('adversaries') can agree are reliable methods of arriving at mutually acceptable truth. In environmental audit such procedures are particularly important, in order that both managers and external auditors can have confidence in the quality of the information and findings.

A good protocol must start from the perspective that goodwill exists on both sides. As new compliance codes come into effect, all sides are motivated to ensure not only that temporary adequacy is achieved but also that predictable risks have been assessed which may compromise the financial, legal or liability position of the business at some future date. Directors and employed or consulting experts can also be found personally responsible in future court cases.

In summary, the following key assumptions in protocol must be kept in mind:

- there is no one perfect model;
- information is always imperfect;
- incremental improvement in decision-making is the overall goal; and
- patient review and reinterpretation of existing data can often reveal as much as new collection of data.

## Stage 1 Set the context

The investment of time and effort in laying the foundations for environmental audit can help to ensure that the audit can be conducted in a timely and efficient fashion, with good co-operation and an ultimately receptive and informed audience, inside and outside the organisation. There may be resistance to the imposition of the audit, which should be expected, as audit activities comprise both threats and opportunities for various people in the organisation. While audits can avoid costly and time-consuming surprises and problems downstream, they do impose new burdens on the planning and operational parts of the organisation. As well as extolling the virtues and necessities of environmental audit, the challenges, threats and difficulties should also be explicitly identified and addressed. Strategic networking, careful pre-planning and timely provision of required support can help to reduce anxieties and tensions, while promoting the teamwork vital to a good environmental audit.

- Gain top management commitment. Help establish environmental considerations on the normal 'agenda' of key managers and units responsible for corporate planning and development. Equip top management with appropriate knowledge, reference materials, environmental regulation, and policy documents and other briefing materials. Enhance their sensitivity to, and understanding of, environmental issues. Highlight linkages between environmental concerns and the core corporate objectives of the organisation.
- Establish a corporate environmental programme and an environmental unit. Make the organisation aware of the role and responsibilities of the environmental unit.
- Make environmental unit staff aware of the non-environmental aspects of the corporate context. Environmental auditors and their managers need to understand and appreciate the organisational and political realities faced by

strategic planners, and where the organisation's financial, social and legal responsibilities must be balanced with environmental considerations.

- Keep abreast of changes in environmental issues and regulation, and of comparable audits in other agencies and other strategy domains. Build networks with other units in the organisation, outside experts and other organisations to ensure that a ready capacity for planning and implementing audits is available on a stand-by basis.

## Stage 2a Plan the audit: organisational considerations

- Anticipate the need for environmental audits of:
  — newly acquired plant;
  — plant proposed for construction;
  — new investment programmes;
  — acquisition or divestment choices;
  — new corporate policies requiring major changes in the environment, e.g. expansion into national regulatory settings which have different environmental requirements from those of the home base.
- Review the scale and nature of the operation. The scope and level of effort of audit can vary considerably, depending on the anticipated scale and significance of environmental effects of the operation under consideration. In general, the more certain one can be about the environmental impacts of an operation, the more detailed and rigorous the audit can be. Conversely, if there is good reason to believe that the operation has no significant environmental effects, then a relatively cursory preliminary screening and audit may be all that is required. This would confirm initial assumptions and tentative conclusions.
- Establish the scope of the audit. Determine whether to audit the entire company; an individual site, department or process; or an issue of particular importance. Identify the kinds of technical issues involved, their scientific complexity and the level of existing knowledge concerning the operation's impacts on the environment. Determine how in-depth the audit should be, based on anticipated environmental effects and financial, time and technical constraints. Determine how long the audit will take, and how often to repeat it. In effect, even the decision of what level of effort should be applied to an audit constitutes a 'mini-audit' in itself.
- Determine stakeholders affected, their distribution, organisation and level of knowledge.
- Identify the auditing team, considering expertise and availability. Ideally, the team should comprise both environmental experts and people familiar with the workings of the operation being audited. Appoint a team leader. Allow the team to draw upon the expertise already existing in the company; this will not only improve the audit team's awareness of issues within the company, but will raise other employee's awareness of the audit and its associated issues.
- Identify the basic information, advice and experience that may be required for an audit. Identify contacts and sources that can meet these needs. If necessary,

identify outside experts to round out expertise: ideally any outside help should be used as part of the in-house audit team. Commission necessary background research at the earliest possible moment, to assemble pertinent knowledge and data.
- Set up arrangements for consultation with top management and with site staff. Inform site personnel of the audits purpose. Set up arrangements for obtaining permission if needed.
- Anticipate special needs *re* resources, staff, time etc.
- Prepare an audit plan and schedule. Build requirements for the audit into work programmes. Anticipate and secure the resources required.

**Stage 2b Plan the audit: methodological considerations**

- Gather relevant background information, including:
  — corporate environmental policy, charter, mission, strategy;
  — relevant planning documents, authorisations, monitoring records etc.;
  — relevant regulations and standards.
- Review the operation and its possible impact. Determine, to the extent possible, the form and nature of the operation, including such issues as product manufacture, distribution, timing, target markets and linkages with other operations. New operations, in particular, may present major new environmental impacts for the business. Environmental audit of major new operations should thus be addressed by more than one team, so that different and independent perspectives can be developed.
- Identify possible environmental impacts of the operation. Define priority areas: carry out preliminary screening and ranking of anticipated impacts.
- Select appropriate methods for conducting the audit, specifying any special requirements or considerations in their implementation. Take into account:
  — the objectives of the operation;
  — the scope and complexity of the operation;
  — the nature and significance of the operation's environmental impacts;
  — availability and reliability of data and knowledge;
  — level of scientific and stakeholder interest in the new programme; and
  — priorities, timing and available resources.
  The selection of an audit method is a strategic decision that typically must be made on the basis of educated guesswork, tempered by experience. Plan and prepare appropriate checklists, criteria and frameworks for audit that meet the unique needs of the organisation.
  Establish a data-gathering system.
- Establish control procedures for the audit: define testing and verification strategies.

**Stage 3 Undertake the audit**

Based on the agreed audit method, data on the operation's environmental impacts are then gathered. Ensure that information is collected about all key aspects of the operation. Be prepared to gather additional information about issues which come to light during this stage. Ensure that data gathered are factual and objective.

- Review background/baseline information. Ensure that all relevant documents exist, are up to date and accurate, and comply with pertinent regulations. Ensure that the company policy is adequately carried out; consider possible changes to the company's environmental policy.
- Undertake a questionnaire of staff to determine their level of environmental awareness, their operating procedures, perceived environmental impacts and any suggestions for change. These questionnaires should be accompanied by a letter explaining the aims of the study and specifying a time limit for returning the questionnaire.
- Interview staff, remembering to:
  - schedule the interview in advance so that staff will be prepared and have time;
  - interview in the workplace so that the interviewee is relaxed, relevant material is easily available and the auditor sees the facility; and
  - use good interviewing techniques (e.g. observe the interviewee's body language, ask open-ended questions).
- Inspect the operation. Where a large number of variables in the operation's outputs and emissions are being audited, a representative random range of variables should be audited using statistical sampling techniques. This will require, among other techniques, stratified sampling and random sampling. Using the principle of marginal selection, the auditor can choose to audit those activities which are deemed to be marginal to the main process, and which may well be ignored by local management as being unlikely to be monitored. This could be:
  - vehicle management, where engine tuning and emission controls may be seen as marginal to the operations of the local plant;
  - office control of waste paper, where this is not a main waste output of the local operation; or
  - nuisance at remote areas of the site, including boundaries.

  Where such marginal audits are pursued, they must be undertaken in the same spirit as the inspections of the main operations.
- Apply testing/verification strategies.

**Stage 4 Evaluate findings**

This evaluation should comprise an analysis of whether the operation complies with all relevant environmental regulations; a description of impacts, their significance and linkages; an assessment of alternative operations; and recommendations for change.

- Characterize and describe impacts. The list of impacts should constitute the widest possible range of characteristics, although in reality certain impacts will be either impossible to portray meaningfully or irrelevant for actual decision-making purposes.

- Establish a conceptual framework, in the form of a logic model, tracing all known or anticipated linkages from corporate strategy/policy to programme specifications to project/product/activity/service to environmental impact. In some cases the linkages may be virtually certain. In other cases they may be more speculative, relying upon emerging theories and speculative hypotheses regarding environmental impacts of new operations. Wherever possible, the rationale for the linkages should be made explicit, and should highlight the approximate degree of certainty which can be attributed to the assumed linkages. This enables decision-makers properly to consider the relative strength of arguments regarding environmental consequences, whether positive or negative. It also enables the audit to be revised as new data, knowledge or validated theories emerge. Summarise the evidence and rationale for the logic model and its cause/effect linkages.
- Appraise the significance of the impacts. The significance of each impact will hinge on the precise nature of the operation and on the strategic context in which it functions.
- Consider the need for a more systematic and rigorous analysis of anticipated environmental impacts focusing on:
  — high-priority impacts, including those that may be significant for key stakeholder groups, biotic systems, or marketing/reception of the operation, where greater precision and thoroughness is important;
  — 'suspect' impacts, where assumptions and projections may have been crude and unreliable, and which require further testing and confirmation before they can be brought fully into the logic model; and
  — newly identified impacts, whose consequences have not been detected or given appropriate importance.
- Explore alternatives to the operation; mitigatory, ameliorative and compensatory options that can help to minimise or offset anticipated negative impacts, or enhance the achievement of positive impacts. Ideally this should be achievable without significantly jeopardising core strategic or commercial objectives. Consider a range of optional configurations for the operation. Typically, these are developed with different performance and costings in mind; now they must also integrate environmental performance as a criterion when determining the preferred option.
- Assess the operation's future environmental performance, and that of the present operation which it is meant to displace. Appraise the implications of the improvements measures in terms of:
  — expected and potential environmental impacts;
  — technical feasibility;
  — financial implications;
  — the stakeholders affected and their relative values, concerns and priorities; and
  — strategic impacts on corporate aims.
  Discuss these findings and implications both within the auditing team and within the company.
- Make recommendations, stating an estimate of cost, resource needs and an optimum time for their introduction, as well as their expected effectiveness. Where appropriate, these should be discussed with the personnel directly concerned to

make them aware of proposed changes and to fine-tune recommendations, based on their experience.
● Ensure that the audit protocol documents are completed.


## Stage 5 Report

The key challenge of this stage is to translate and interpret findings in ways that are relevant to the decision-makers. The audit report should be structured and written to make clear distinctions between options, highlighting essential differences. Major issues and implications should receive the greatest attention, especially those for which there is meaningful choice or flexibility in approaches in strategy, design or operations. The report should identify issues requiring immediate decisions and attention, as well as those decisions which can be deferred, pending more information or experience at the subsequent implementation stage. The report should therefore indicate where decision-makers can set directions or conditions on subsequent implementation, while allowing progress to be made on the strategy itself. Finally, the report should identify issues requiring more specific audit at subsequent design and monitoring stages.

The environmental report and supporting documents should be written in clear language, avoiding unnecessary technical terms and jargon, keeping in mind that they must be read by a non-technical audience. Illustrations and case studies can help explain key points. The summary of findings should focus on the most essential factors, eliminating or playing down minor issues. Only data that help illustrate or explain a particular point should be included.

● Write up draft findings and recommendations in the form of a draft audit report. This report forms the core of the environmental audit's output. The format that is generally most useful consists of:
— executive summary (one to two pages);
— a statement of the objectives of the audit;
— exposition of the methods used to conduct and verity the audit;
— presentation of key information;
— analysis of information, using objectives and identified methods;
— main findings and conclusions; and
— recommendations.
Following the main body of the report will come:
— references used;
— technical appendices; and
— other supporting materials identified as relevant.
Prepare an executive summary for the board, which includes clear recommendations for action.
● Circulate the draft audit report and request comments, to ensure adequacy. Where possible and appropriate, provide a live briefing or presentation of the audit report for decision-makers and/or interested stakeholders. This may be taped for presentation to other audiences.

- Gain board approval of the report and recommendations.
- Prepare final findings. Where required, produce a public document summarizing the audit report. This should include as much information as possible within the strictures of commercial and political confidentiality. This document will form the basis on which external stakeholder groups, not directly involved in the decision, will trust the quality of the audit report and the decision-making setting. Therefore, it is not a minor output, but is in itself a major component of the process.
- Prepare and assimilate background materials supporting the environmental report. This will explain the rationale, sources, methodologies and related issues which support the audit. It will also assist in subsequent evaluation and audit initiatives.

### Stage 6 Implement action plan based on audit

Environmental audit does not end with the preparation of the report. Indeed, the report is a starting point, triggering a sharing of information and ideas. It should focus discussion and debate into a decision-making mode.

Intervention in the implementation process is, strictly speaking, not part of the audit process. However, it is a vital link that determines the relevance and effectiveness of the audit process. The process of intervention can also be used as an evaluative tool to develop better understanding about linkages between strategy and projects. Thereby intervention can improve the ability to forecast possible environmental outcomes. It can also build an understanding of factors and forces that may require the strategy to be modified.

- Address significant impacts first.
- Determine the need for intervention in strategic and project implementation. Assist in the translation of the audit recommendations into changes at different levels:
  — objectives and targets in an environmental management plan;
  — corporate environmental programme;
  — appropriate design and implementation guidelines.

### Stage 7 Verification and feedback

An investment of time and effort in evaluating substantive and procedural lessons learned can improve the knowledge base and methods for environmental audit. Monitoring and evaluation of the audit findings will:

- determine if outcomes matched predictions;
- assess the need for intervention to cope with unforeseen effects;
- determine if a reappraisal of design or strategy is warranted, in light of unforeseen or adverse outcomes; and

- ensure the collection of information that can assist future design and strategy information and their assessments.

By sharing the results with other parties, organisations can build valuable networks of allies whose knowledge, data and experience may help in future planning and audit initiatives.

- Appoint a verifier/monitor.
- Plan and carry out monitoring and follow-up processes, considering:
  — key issues and factors in implementation;
  — threshold indicators for intervention—unforeseen environmental impacts, restructuring of strategy or design, reappraisal of implementation;
  — priority areas for long-term environmental evaluation, leading to knowledge useful in future environmental audits.

  The monitoring should focus on the most critical elements of strategy or design, i.e. those with the greatest potential positive or negative impacts and especially those which were most subject to uncertainty during the audit. Monitoring should be structured to test specific conditions and circumstances within which the design was implemented, thereby allowing a comparison with the underlying assumptions upon which the strategy or design was based. This allows consideration of other factors such as:
  — cross-impacts of other operations or strategies;
  — scope for intervention, mitigation, amelioration or compensation;
  — reappraisal of the strategy/product in light of actual outcomes.
- Evaluate the audit. Compare anticipated outcomes and effects with actual results. Summarise and analyse mitigating factors and circumstances that may explain variances between anticipated and actual outcomes. Come to conclusions regarding:
  — the accuracy and appropriateness of the audit and factors that contributed to its success or shortcomings; and
  — implications for future strategic assessments, including new understandings regarding linkages between specific strategies and environmental impacts, and suggestions regarding improved procedures.
- Consider the future use of alternative audit methods.
- Plan the next audit, incorporating recommendations from this one.
- Evaluate and improve the criteria used to evaluate the audit.
- Share the above with appropriate stakeholders and decision-makers.

## SUMMARY

Auditing requires a balancing of facts and values, on a case-by-case basis, using appropriate input from both professional experts, and the affected workers and communities. Unlike scientific field research or financial audit, environmental auditing does not involve the application of hard and fast rules which dictate inclusion or exclusion in each and every case. Instead, it involves a creative, case-by-case development of specific audit designs, arising from discussions and agreements with decision-makers and stakeholders. Decision-makers and stakeholders must agree on findings separately for each case; these will be placed alongside other important concerns in the political or corporate arena, and a final decision will then be arrived at as a reflection of the balancing of many aspects.

That said, environmental issues in coming years will function both as compliance imperatives and ethically desirable end-states. Grave legal and financial consequences may result from corporate decisions which ignore the results of environmental auditing.

## REFERENCES

Gilbert, M. (1992) Inter-relationship with the new BSI Environmental Management Systems Standard. Conference Paper Westminster Management Consultants, London, January 1992.
Owen, R. and Mundy, D. (1991) Green and pleasant lands. *EuroDirector/The Director*, September.

# 14

# Accounting and Environmentalism: An Exploration of the Challenge of Gently Accounting for Accountability, Transparency and Sustainability

*Rob Gray*

Concern for the natural environment has not occupied a prominent role in accounting scholarship and practice. This paper attempts to redress this omission by investigating the implications for accounting of placing the environment at the centre of the analysis. The paper introduces the principles of this 'deep green' position and explores how accounting might articulate them. Whilst there may be no place for what we currently consider to be conventional financial accounting in any 'green utopia' the paper does attempt to operationalise, within a non-green world, certain of the principles of the green position. Emphasis is placed on an accounting's potential for contribution to accountability and transparency in participative democracy, the potential for non-financial accounts of the biosphere and, perhaps most contentiously, the use of current accounting techniques for the operationalisation of an accounting for sustainability.

Attempts to reintroduce protection and care for the environment into our thinking and into our ways of doing things lead slowly but inevitably to radical reconsideration of current attitudes, structures, beliefs and *modi operandi*. The extent to which we might choose to 'place the environment at the centre of all things' (as the 'deep greens' are increasingly accused of doing) will profoundly influence the impact of that reconsideration. However, even a pragmatic approach to survival (of the human species, of other species or of the planet) and to the sustainability of current human societies (as, for example, taken by the Brundtland Commission—United Nations, 1987) inexorably forces realisation that the roots of modern (especially Western) society are essentially incommensurable both with continued survival and with any sets of values other than those of (very) short-term (human and economic) self-interest.

Reprinted with permission from *Accounting, Organizations and Society*, Vol. 17, No. 5, 1992, pp. 399–425, Elsevier Science Ltd
© Elsevier Science Ltd, Oxford, England

The extent of this realisation seems well illustrated by the host of apparently incompatible commentators, from a wide range of seemingly contradictory backgrounds, offering fundamentally similar, but subversive, concepts as ways of responding to the environmental crisis. When a future king of England, the World Council of Churches, ecological humanists (e.g. Furkiss, 1974), the United Nations, holistic seekers of the Tao (e.g. Lovelock, 1982; Dauncey, 1988), conventional theologians (e.g. Daly and Cobb, 1990), and activists from the whole of the conventional political spectrum (e.g. Capra and Spetnak, 1984; Parkin, 1989) can broadly agree about a root issue and about the elements of its correction, then perhaps observers such as Robertson (e.g. 1978) are justified in suggesting that human society (especially in the developed world[1]) is in the process of experiencing a 'paradigm shift'.[2]

This paper is an attempt to explore one of the environmentally centred positions—that of the 'deep greens'—and some of the implications it might have for forms of accounting.[3] The paper is motivated by three strands. Firstly, I am trying to extend the project of developing a social accounting that takes an accountability, community and environment-centred approach (Gray et al., 1987, 1988, 1991; Gray, 1990a, c, d), whilst trying to begin the process of responding to the radical critique of this project (see below). Secondly, the splendid generosity and vision of Arrington's recent call for *solidarity* and his attempts to '...make those interested in public interest accounting feel good about their research...' (Arrington, 1990, p. 5) empowers and encourages the pursuit of new possibilities 'unfettered by the stifling and intellectually archaic methods of scholarship'. And whilst this is no excuse for poor scholarship it encourages the opening of different doors. Thirdly, the present intellectual climate now encourages openness about beliefs in green possibilities. The long-standing urgency of environmental issues (e.g. Gray, 1990d, chapter 2) has not overcome the considerable resistance there is to the concepts involved. This has tended to encourage the use of social accounting as the Trojan horse (although one which has not been warmly welcomed into the gates of the citadel). Environmentalism can now rise from its position as an 'also' issue in social—and indeed in conventional—accounting to a matter of central importance. This paper follows on from Gray (1990d) in trying to do this.

Before introducing the structure of the paper, I believe it is necessary to briefly acknowledge one very pertinent and important tension in the accounting literature—one which predominantly centres around the social accounting literature. This is the apparent, but probably unnecessary, tension between scholarly rigour and political action arising from scholarship. Despite the growing body of insightful analysis into the roles that accounting plays in organisational and social activity, and the increasing number of calls for the investigation of new accountings, the researchers who have offered their hostages to fortune by way of concrete proposals for actual new forms of accounting remain few in number. It is, it would seem, difficult to translate radical insight into suggestions for action, not least, I suspect, because speculation and proposal in accounting rarely maintain the rigorous level of critical and analytical sophistication associated with scholarly activity. Tinker et al. (1991) and Roslender (1990) note the importance of the distinction that must be drawn between 'intellectual' and 'political' radicalism. That is, intellectually radical insights may very well clarify, liberate and enable and thus encourage new discourse and perceptions (and thus creations) of new 'realities' but this is not the extent of the responsibility of the scholar. In the same way that 'positivists' may be accused of implicitly taking on the bias of the status quo, it seems to follow that the 'intellectual radical' takes on a dissatisfaction with the way things are. This suggests a desire for social change. But what social change? The 'political radical' recognises that his or her project is one of seeking social change and that insight and debate—of subverting discourse—are not the only means of seeking this. Such scholars will seek various means to try and move agendas, etc., and, it seems to me, will propose 'new ways of doing' that will also shift attitudes as well as shifting practice.

The social accounting literature contains some of the more obvious examples of these issues. Projects for social change through accounting change of one sort or another are generally coupled with theoretical flaccidity resulting from (1) an implicit, or at least underspecified value and belief base; (2) a lack of rigorous development of the proposals from some scholastic framework; and (3) a failure to fully explicate social structures and tensions and thus, as a result, a failure to articulate (or at least hypothesise) the mechanisms of social change. These criticisms are splendidly highlighted by Tinker *et al.* (1991) and by Puxty (1986), and are accurately targeted by the whole social accounting project.[4] This paper is an attempt to develop that project but tries to begin the process of taking these criticisms on board.

The paper is structured as follows. The next section examines the failures of 'conventional' economics (being the foundation of 'conventional' accounting) with particular regard to its inability to encompass adequately environmental issues. The section which follows then focuses on a particular failure with regard to 'externalities'. Next, a very brief critique of a 'conventional' Marxian analysis suggests that an approach based in this thought would also fail to give sufficient prominence to the protection of the environment. The 'deep green' position and the guiding principles of environmentalism are then outlined. Then the question of 'how to get there from here' is approached, first by exploring the sorts of actions that are open to the accounting scholar and then by specifying a number of limitations inherent in the ensuing discussion. The two sections which follow are attempts to move towards social action and explore, respectively, how accounting might contribute to accountability and transparency and how and why (if at all) we might account for sustainability. The final section contains conclusions.

The principal argument of the paper begins with an examination of conventional economics and it is to this that I now turn.


## LIMITATIONS OF TRADITIONAL ECONOMICS AND THE NEED FOR PARADIGM SHIFT

It would seem that a major part of the process of radically re-thinking the world must begin from the role that economics has played in constructing our world, the ubiquity of that role, the effects of that role and the profound limitations which economists, in general, have failed to notice and/or to sufficiently clarify. This is critically the case when we are considering environmental issues and when we are considering accounting. This is because our conceptions of 'environment', the steady but rapid destruction of the biosphere, the manner of that destruction and the way in which accounting is implicated in this (Gray, 1990d) must all, I suggest, be laid firmly at the door of 'modern conventional' economic thinking. We must, therefore, first identify the cage in which we place ourselves through economic thought, and then escape that cage if we are to adequately address either changes in accounting in general, and protection and enhancement of the environment in particular (Gray, 1990f; see also Maunders and Burritt, 1991).

The extent to which traditional economic thinking dominates our conceptualization, language and explanation of the world (both the world as is and the world as can be) has been widely remarked upon. It would seem that the extent of this colonisation must not be under-estimated. Any reasoning in the world of economics, politics, sociology and environmentalism that fails to explicitly explore the influence of traditional economic thinking seems, by default, to adopt the limitations and assumptions of traditional economics and all the baggage of the status quo, the world of business and the roles of organisations that currently pervade our world (Tinker et al., 1982, 1991). Perhaps this would not matter if traditional economic thought could be seen as principally benign to life and the planet, but there is an increasing amount of argument that suggests quite the opposite.

'Economic theory presents the guiding principles of "doing business" and the infrastructure of assumptions, values and beliefs that govern political and social behaviour' (Reilly and Kyj, 1990, p. 691; see also Owen, 1990). It presents a construction of the world that profoundly influences attitudes to and behaviour towards that world (Smith, 1980). Economic theory thus helps construct the world (see Hines', 1988, argument along the same lines for the role of accounting). It is founded in a faith about the world (McKee, 1986)—a faith that is maintained as implicit and unquestioned (McKee, 1986; Heibroner, 1984; Tinker, 1984a, c; Boulding, 1982; see also Hines, 1991a for exploration of the same phenomena in accounting). The faith is founded upon a severe simplification and reinterpretation of the founding ideals of, especially, Adam Smith and John Stuart Mill (Coker, 1990; Daly, 1980; Reilly and Kyj, 1990; Hardin, 1968; Held, 1987; Gray, 1989) and yet, as with any committed believer, the faith remains unexamined and is assumed to contain absolute truth (Schumacher, 1968).

There are a number of highly significant characteristics of traditional economics[5] which seem irrefutably to be neither *necessarily* of unqualified desirability nor logically supportable as immutable truths. These can be briefly rehearsed (but see also Gorz, 1989; Daly and Cobb, 1990). There is no necessary intrinsic desirability in rational economic man (Gambling, 1978; Reilly and Kyj, 1990). The exclusion of loyalty, compassion, altruism, sympathy, concern for others, etc., from any definition of human rationality could well exclude economics as having any pretensions to being a science of humanity (Reilly and Kyj, 1990; see also Armstrong, 1991). Similarly, ethical issues remain implicit (as a simplistic utilitarian version of consequentialist value-reasoning) and thus persuade to a view of value-freedom which is unsustainable (McKee, 1986; Raines and Jung, 1986; Heilbroner, 1984) and/or exclude other forms of moral reasoning from any analysis within an economics paradigm (Daly, 1980; Gray, 1990e; Turner and Pearce, 1990). Initial distribution of wealth, power and opportunity are ignored, 'efficiency' comes to mean only a very specialised, and perhaps irrelevant, type of activity (Schumacher, 1974) and, as Erlich and Erlich

(1978) argue from Boulding, perhaps we do efficiently that which should not be done at all (see also Machin and Lowe, 1983). Economic growth is seen as self-evidently desirable when there is no real argument to support it being any such thing (Daly, 1980), whilst technology is presumed to be neutral and to arrive *deus ex machina* when this is precisely what it is not (Dickson, 1974; Georgescu-Roegen, 1975). Furthermore, economic reasoning only achieves its considerable power by grossly simplifying and reducing the world (Smith, 1980; Daly, 1980), and whilst there may be much to applaud in such an approach to modelling complex systems, it is the case that reductionism necessarily violates structures (von Bertlanffy, 1956, 1971, 1972) and can have little to say about the complex world from which it was extrapolated (Tinker, 1984a, c; Silverman, 1970; Allen, 1975).[6]

One could continue but that is not the purpose of this paper. The foregoing comments provide a backdrop to assumptions about the ubiquity and intellectual integrity of economic reasoning. There is much to beware of in economic reasoning and, without an explicit awareness, we may so easily find ourselves—especially in accounting, business and management subjects—falling back into the categories and assumptions of reductionist, traditional economics (Tinker *et al.*, 1991; Tinker, 1984a, c). Thus the environmentalists' critiques of economic reasoning should not be seen as intellectually isolated—they build upon and extend a substantive critique of conventional thought that already pervades our discipline.

## ENVIRONMENT AS 'EXTERNALITY' OR AS 'INTERNALITY'

Although there is a considerable literature in which conventional economic thought addresses the issues arising from the physical environment (e.g. Fisher and Peterson, 1976; Fisher, 1981; Pearce *et al.*, 1989), it is in respect of environmental matters that traditional economic thought has received what is probably its most thorough attack. Boulding has long been a critic of economists' handling of environmental issues, highlighting their failure to distinguish between open and closed systems (Boulding, 1966) and thus failing to realise that there is much which an economist seeks to maximise (such as through-put and use of resources) that should, in the interests of life and the planet, not be *maximised* but *minimised*. Boulding later (Boulding, 1982) goes on to remind economists '...a law of economics that has been much neglected is: "goods and bads tend to be jointly produced".' Such compassionate and even fond criticisms are to be contrasted with broadsides by the like of Victor (1979). Victor effectively argues that economics and the physical environment are fundamentally incompatible (an argument echoed in, for example, Daly, 1980; Zaikov, 1986 and, in a different vein, Coppock, 1977). For example, whilst an economist will see environmental issues as arising from breakdowns in the market and seek therefore to repair or extend the market, Victor would argue that they represent breakdowns in economics itself (see also, for example, Schumacher, 1974; Smith, 1980; Georgescu-Roegen, 1975; Daly, 1985).

But to my mind, the most persuasive argument is that of Daly (1980, pp. 238 *et seq.*). In an argument which independently parallels that of Reilly and Kyj (1990) on the subject of ethical values, Daly questions how a matter as important as the physical environment can be treated as *external* to a subject which claims so much for human existence and behaviour. Surely the environment (and, for Reilly and Kyj, ethical values) must be most firmly embedded in—that is, *internal* to—any construct which purports to contribute to life and the planet:

> Such [dramatic environmental] phenomena have long been recognised (grudgingly) in economic theory under the heading of *externalities*—that is, interrelationships whose connecting links are external to the economists' abstract world of commodities but very much internal to the world in which we live, move and have our being. Perhaps 'non-market interdependence' is a more descriptive term.
>
> It would be easy to liken this concept to a *deus ex machina* lowered into the scene by our theoretical playwrights to save an awkward plot, but it is by no means easy to suggest a better treatment. A better treatment is called for, however, since externalities are spending more time center stage and less time in the wings than previously. Or, changing the metaphor, to continue theoretical development via continued ad hoc introduction of externalities is reminiscent of adding epicycles and in the long run will only lead to Ptolemaic complications in economic theory. Our economic cosmos is not one of uniform circular motion of commodities among men but one of elliptical orbits through interdependent ecological sectors (Daly, 1980, pp. 245–246).

The construction of a 'New Economics' thus becomes not only a daunting but an urgent project. There are, in fact, an increasing number of attempts to construct a new economic paradigm, building from the early inspiration of Shumacher (see, for example, Schumacher, 1968, 1973, 1974) and emboldened by The Other Economic Summit and The New Economics Foundation (arising out of Schumacher's thinking) they have many things in common—the most critical of which is a recognition of the need for there to be a root-reappraisal of assumptions before the exercise can be successful (e.g. Robertson, 1978, 1985; Goldsmith, 1988; Dauncey, 1988; Henderson, 1978, 1991; Daly and Cobb, 1990, Ekins, 1986).

## MARX AND THE ENVIRONMENT

As Heilbroner has continually and successfully argued (e.g. Heilbroner, 1983, 1984) the most cogent critique of the status quo, embedded as it is in liberal democracy and economics, must come from Marx.[7] However, the literature is far from clear about the extent to which Marxian analysis can be said to be compatible with or at variance with environmentalism.[8] The value and influence of the critique that Marxian analysis has supplied cannot be overvalued. However, the arguments such as that from (for example) Daly and Cobb (1990), that in the focus on employment, the derivation of value from labour, the attractions of centralisation, a belief in growth, a faith in techno-centrist solutions, the central position of conflict and an unconscious subscription to scientism, places Marx (from an environmentalist's view) closer to liberal economics than to environmentalism.

However, it is inevitable that such arguments will be rejected by some Marxist scholars. The principal grounds for this rejection centre on the recognition that Marx gave both to 'environmental' and to 'labour' as distinct from employment in his earlier writings. The development in Marx's thought led, however, to the recognition of the need to explicate the processes that generated the problems (whether 'social' or 'environmental', in so far as they can be distinguished) that one sought to address. Without an understanding of these processes, the recommendations of solutions would stand isolated and impotent.[9] It is certainly the case that the 'deep green' position (see below) offers little in the way of *detailed* analysis of the historical social processes that brought us to this point of environmental crisis and so stands accused of failing to recognise social tension, power and conflict (e.g. Sandbach, 1980). However, the significant contributions to the green debate from writers such as Ryle (1988), Gorz (1989), Frankel (1987) and Dobson (1990) show that, at a minimum, there are some important points of commonality. That is, there would seem to be little question that Marxian scholarship still provides a crucial input to the explication of the causes of environmental destruction and can continue to enlighten the environmental debate, *even though*, the position of the environmental issues is not considered by environmentalists to be sufficiently central in the analysis.

The extent of the shift in thinking that a deep green perspective is asking for is illustrated by recognition that this conclusion on the place of Marxian scholarship is much the same as the conclusion reached by Daly and Cobb (1990) and, for example Dauncey (1988) with respect to *liberal economics*—there is much that is *also* salvageable from liberalism for the development of environmentalism.[10]

The principal issue here, and the reason why I have not further developed the Marxist critique, is that whilst pluralism and liberal economy on the one hand, and socialism and Marxist reasoning on the other, have been seen as the major, and possibly only, substantive positions for analysing and reconstructing the western world (e.g. Heilbroner, 1983, 1984), the deep greens are attempting to define a *third* major position that draws from both the other two (see also Dobson, 1990). This is examined in the next section.


## DEEP GREEN AND THE PRINCIPLES OF ENVIRONMENTALISM


Harte *et al.* (1990) correctly note that environmental degradation is only one part of the environmentalism agenda—it just happens to be the most prominent and the one to which most parties are responding. However, whilst Harte *et al.* correctly identify that responses to this issue generally lie within the parameters of the current business and economics agenda (and therefore stands accused by the radical critique; Tinker *et al.*, 1991; Puxty, 1986), they fail to identify the essential separateness of the 'deep green' position from either the dominated agenda or the radical critique agenda.

A central factor in the thinking of deep greens[11] is the importance of systems theory and concepts (von Bertalanffy, 1971; Boulding, 1956; Beishon and Peters, 1972, 1981; Kemp and Wall, 1990; Gray, 1990d). General systems theory (von Bertalanffy, 1956, 1971) is primarily a way of thinking about the world. It has two principal characteristics. First, one recognises that all things are connected and thus total understanding of any one thing requires a complete understanding of all other things. Second, one recognises that such complete understanding is impossible and that issues must be addressed through the consideration of bounded subsystems—a complex process by which the universe of all possible events or things is reduced to more manageable systems, at a higher level of resolution. The selected subsystem is chosen by reference to the question of influenceability: given the issue of concern, what are the major sources of influence upon it and what are the major elements in the environment upon which the issue in turn has influence. This process inevitably involves leaving some issues of significance outside the systems boundary, and a major concern of systems thinking is attempting to identify the violence done to perception through the essential limiting of the elements considered in any subsystem (von Bertalanffy, 1956, 1971; Boulding, 1956; Emery, 1969; Beishon and Peters, 1972; Checkland, 1981; Carter *et al.*, 1984).

Systems thinking has had a major influence on ecology and environmentalism. The ecological view is perhaps best illustrated by the image of 'Spaceship Earth' (e.g. Ward, 1966; Boulding, 1966). The image of the Earth hanging in space illustrates the way in which our 'habitat' is finite, and whilst it is not a 'closed system' (subject as it is to, principally, the sun and the moon) it can be so considered for most purposes. That is, the Earth is a subsystem of the universe and whilst there is influence between the two, examination of most (for example) human issues from a planet-based level of resolution is unlikely to represent a serious limitation on any analysis. The subsystem Earth is a complex interreacting set of systems which support life. There are various subsystems of rain, cloud and water; of birth, growth, death and decay; of creatures and species interdependence; of species and habitat dependencies; and so on. Removal or interference with one of these elements will influence many, if not all others. For example, and rather simply, the extinction of one species allows the flourishing of a species upon which the extinct species grazed and the possible extinction of another species which depended upon the extinct species for its food. Such a break in the ecological chain can happen for many reasons—loss of habitat, use of insecticide, etc., but it takes little imagination to see that once started, the process is irreversible and will, potentially, accelerate. The process of extinction is now rapid. Mankind apparently does not have the wherewithal to stop it nor the knowledge to assess whether any ecological harmony will ever be possible again without man's constant interference to deal with excess manifestations (such as algal bloom, for example) or to artificially preserve habitats and species. (But see, for example, Lovelock, 1982, 1988.) This is summarised by Commoner in Table 1.

The ecological emphasis, however, is not only upon the biological systems and their interaction, survival, etc. Interacting with the ecosystems are the human, social, technical and economic systems. The interaction between all these systems is clearly

**Table 1.**  The four principles of ecology

- Every separate entity is connected to all the rest
- Everything has to go somewhere
- You cannot get something for nothing from it
- Nature knows best

*Source:* Commoner (1972).

complex but (the message of systems theory) you cannot look at one without considering the others.

General systems theorists have also held out claims that systems thinking would enable a uniting of the disciplines, but whilst systems thinking has provided powerful insights in the social sciences (e.g. Kast and Rosenweig, 1974; Lowe, 1972; Lowe and McInnes, 1971) its essentially scientistic, and hence functional, positivist basis has attracted considerable criticism (e.g. Hopper and Powell, 1985). It is important to recognise though, that the criticism of systems theory has applied, principally, to its applications in functional settings (e.g. organisational contingency theory), that is to 'hard' systems theory. On the other hand, the use of 'soft' systems theory, that is, as a way of seeing and thinking rather than as a problem solving tool, has remained largely untouched by the assault. Its protection (and thus, for some scholars, its ultimate weakness) has lain in 'soft' systems theory's level of generality and lack of specificity—its breadth rather than its depth. Whatever its purported weaknesses, systems thinking remains the basis for ecological perceptions and, as we shall see, the lack of analytical specificity is common to much of the deep green vision so that any failure of systems theory in this regard are by no means remarkable. It reduces, ultimately, to a matter of faith as to whether this lack of analytical specificity is to be considered as a strength or as a weakness. (For more detail of this in an accounting context, see Maunders and Burritt, 1991; Gray, 1990d, f).

This role of systems thinking in environmentalism will become increasingly obvious as the green ideas are discussed below, but there is one important manifestation of this that needs early introduction. Daly and Cobb (1990), echoing the famous dictum of Ackoff (1960) that 'we must stop behaving as though nature was organised in the same way as university departments are', are eloquent in their concern over disciplinarity—the reductionist tendency to divide up the world into defined subjects with each with its own varieties, methods, biasses and career tracks. This carries, of course, all the reductionist problems. Some way must be found to break out from this and re-privilege holistic attempts at thought, investigation and social change. The inevitable consequences of any such attempt, however, are (a) the failure to attract much support from the traditional cores of the individual subject divisions, and (b) the tendency to become rather generalist and thin, sacrificing reductionist depth for holistic breadth. One is conscious of this in what follows.

Despite the very widespread nature of the environmentalist movement in all its guises, and despite the very wide range of backgrounds underpinning aspects of the deep greens, it does appear that there are a substantial number of principles which can be said to underpin the deep green position and which command wide acceptance in green political movements, political parties and environmental groups generally throughout the world. These principles are central to the core manifestos of the green parties and are summarised in Table 2.[12,13]

The range of principles is both far reaching and radical but in (what amounts to) an attempt to re-design the world, the sheer enormity of the intellectual and empirical task leaves much undeveloped. Furthermore, this enormity must remain embedded in systems thinking and cannot resort to reductionism to simplify the problem. At the same time, many writers have resorted to almost spiritual (and, at times, even magical) assertion to overcome lacunae and the sheer complexity of the problem (e.g. Dauncey, 1988). Whether this appeal to other spirituality in place of scientistic logic is

**Table 2.** The principles of environmentalism

---

DEEP ECOLOGY: Holistic systems thinking; non-intrusive, soft, alternative technology; non-pollution; sustainable;—leads on to 'social ecology': recognition of individual and group systemic interactions; pursuit of 'wholeness'; non-hierarchical; humanity as part of environment;

SOCIAL RESPONSIBILITY: Including the economic domain; social justice; prevention of suffering through inequality in transition; social contract; social and civil rights of (especially) women and minorities;

GRASSROOTS DEMOCRACY: Participatory (as opposed to e.g. representative) democracy; autonomy; non-hierarchical; communication; openness; personal accountability; constraint of central power;

NON-VIOLENCE: Both personal violence and structural violence (oppression); non-exploitive economics; employee ownership and control; 'There is no way to peace, peace is the way', Gandhi;

DECENTRALIZATION: Need for more individual control over the complex interplay of social, ecological, economic, political forces; self-determinism (*not* individualism); resist centralisation which reduces democracy, increases power, bureaucracy, surveillance; reclaim power from centralised state; smaller countries/regions; 'Europe of the regions';

POSTPATRIARCHAL PERSPECTIVES: Feminist; non-aggressive politics; balance of 'masculine' and 'feminine' values *as well as* 'women's issues';—non-competitive, intimate, nurturing, instinctive, emotional;

SPIRITUALITY: beyond science; the oneness of life; Boulding's transcendental systems; human spirit as mode of consciousness connecting self to rest;

---

Adapted from Capra and Spretnak (1984, Chapter 2).

the (very proper) re-establishment of alternative modes of rationality, alternative means of establishing legitimacy in assertion and policy, or else simply a failure to use the traditions of Western reasoning (masculine modes of rationality?) is largely a matter of faith. The attempt by the deep greens to reintroduce the spiritual dimension is essential to the project but raises very difficult questions about how to legitimate discourse and assess competing truth claims when there is an elemental tension between this attempt and our usual means of arbitrating academic conflict through the use of analytic reasoning (see also Hines, 1991b).

This is the first, and perhaps most critical, vulnerability for the deep green position. Its appeal is only partly at an intellectual, analytic and empirical level and derives its principal power from emotional and spiritual appeal through the intervening variable of simultaneously de-emphasising consequentialist moral reasoning whilst championing a heightened emphasis on deontological ethics. This must have the effect of identifying *empathy* (or the existentialist concept of 'integrity') rather than rigorous analysis as the dominant determinant of outcome in discourse. Thus the 'objective' is de-emphasised and the 'subjective' emphasised. There is, clearly, a danger here that this may equally empower triviality and bigotry (for a related discussion see Hines, 1991b). Partly as a result of this, recognisably coherent, complete and traditionally rigorous expositions of the deep green world do not seem to be available in the literature. However, we do find that elements of the deep green vision emerge in a number of 'traditional' areas of scholarship. So, for example, the growing re-examination of economics (e.g. Daly and Cobb, 1990) and the exploration of soft-technology and the more radical re-appraisal of the forces of technological change (e.g. Dickson, 1974) accord well with, and are embodied in, the deep green perspective. Similarly, the exploration of participatory democracy in, especially, the work of MacPherson (e.g. MacPherson, 1973, 1977, 1978) and, more generally in the development of the 'neo-pluralist' conceptions of democracy (e.g. Held, 1987) have been essential foundations for the deep green conceptions of the organisation of social life. And there is a considerable harmony between environmentalism and the feminist literature. Feminism—especially its attempts to distinguish 'masculine' and 'feminine' from any necessary link with being male or female—has exposed the current modes of social, intellectual, business, financial and accounting ways of doing things as predominantly 'masculine' and unbalanced and unbalancing in the absence of 'feminine' traits from their practice (e.g. Maupin, 1990; Reed and Kratchman, 1990; Lehman, 1990; Bem, 1974, 1975, and also see, for example, Robertson, 1978, 1984; Hines, 1991b).[14] These concerns with the 'feminine' and with emancipatory forms of democracy have been significant elements in the growing attempts at the reestablishment of both the concept and the practice of 'community'. This would involve some more sharing conception of community ('Gemeinschaft' as Pallott, 1987, 1991, articulates it) that have strong implications for conceptions of property rights (MacPherson, 1973, 1978) and which may raise new consciousness of ambience such as 'solidarity' (Rorty, 1980, as articulated by Arrington, 1990; Hines, 1991a).[15] All of these projects are predicated upon a re-examination of ethical reasoning. The growing attempts to re-establish wider ethical bases for the assessment of the rightness of action, i.e. to re-expand the notions of utilitarianism as originally devised (Mill, 1857, 1859, 1863; but see also Daly, 1980; Donaldson, 1988; Held, 1987) and re-enable ethical conceptualisations within motivism and (especially) deontology are prerequisites for the emergence of the possibility of a deep green world. And finally, we find a profound re-examination of mankind's relationship with the planet, earth and biosphere is inherent in the re-examination of, and attempts to articulate, the notion of sustainability (e.g. Pearce et al., 1989; United Nations, 1987; Pezzey, 1989; Turner, 1989; Turner and Pearce, 1990; Gray, 1991).

Such a wide-ranging and ambitious agenda for the deep greens with its attempts to unify and integrate such diverse and difficult theorising offers great vision and possibility. For the deep greens, however, it is still a very long way to go in establishing its coherence, viability and truth claims and in dealing with the substantial criticisms that are levelled at it (e.g. Sandbach, 1980).

Maintaining the green vision at this level of generality, the paper now turns to attempting to assess any implications this might have for accounting and whether it is possible for accounting (in whatever guise) to either articulate or contribute to the process.

## ACCOUNTING IN ENVIRONMENTAL UTOPIA AND HOW TO GET THERE

The holistic radicalism of the deep green vision is such that anticipation of exactly how it might function owes more to day-dreaming than to reasoning.[16] Thus anticipation of 'truly green' accounting is unknowable.[17] At an extreme, however, some or all of the functions that accounting serves in some present-day societies (e.g. Burchell *et al.*, 1980) will be largely redundant. The formal and rather antagonistic accountability that accounting might be interpreted as currently serving would similarly be eschewed (Arrington, 1990, p. 2). Also, the conception of money in a green world and the role it serves might be very different (e.g. Dauncey, 1988).

Furthermore, it is not obvious that formal accounting would still be necessary as the informal accountability of deeper social relationships and attendant transparency took over.[18] So much so that 'accountants' as a separate tribe (Gambling, 1978, 1985) may be an entirely redundant breed in such a world.

What then for the role of accounting in the present world and its emancipatory possibilities to enable change towards 'utopia'—wherever, or whatever that might be? Without knowing the processes of social change, the pragmatism articulated by Gray *et al.* (1987) and Harte *et al.* (1990) appears to be the only solution. It seems that the Tinker *et al.* (1991) criticism that this simply embodies and enables the (at least Anglo-American) status quo may be addressed as follows. First, the vision towards which one might be pushing can be radical, as is the deep green vision articulated here. One then has two channels along which progress may be pursued—the intellectual and the immediately practical. The two need not be in tension but, as appears to be the case with many socialists, the two can be separately applied. That is, attempts to change intellectual and research agendas, to expose fallacies and limitations of the present hegemony, etc., become desirable activities but which do not preclude action on other fronts. On the immediately practical front, the deep greens, like all radical groups before them, face three possibilities:

(1)  the direct attempts to destroy the current system;
(2)  totally eschewing the present system and living and working in a separate system (the commune or colony model adopted by a number of greens throughout Europe and North America);
(3)  work with the present system and attempt to change it by attempting either to directly subvert education and agendas or to directly subvert current actions (current accounting practices).[19]

The subscription to non-violence by the greens and the emphasis on the integrity of process (as opposed to means-end calculations) ensures the exclusion of option (1). Option (2) is perhaps the most obvious one. The existence of this paper is evidence that this option has not been taken, as an examination of the current and possible roles of accounting (at least as traditionally conceived) becomes almost entirely redundant under such circumstances. There is also the tension felt throughout the green movement (e.g. Plant and Plant, 1991) over the relative merits of 'supping with the devil'. As has been identified above, the major criticism of the greens is that they have no systematic conception of how they are to bring about social change, and so the tendency is to try and seek change by any means possible. For many, including myself, working alongside the places where one imagines the power to lie—with governments and politicians, investors, company directors, civil servants and so on— seems likely to be more effective, if considerably more uncomfortable, than the more ideologically sound strategy of throwing elegantly crafted intellectual stones from the

**Table 3.** Environmental accounting and information systems

1. COMPLIANCE AND ETHICAL AUDITS are information systems designed to monitor whether the organisation meets legal requirements and its own code of conduct.

2. WASTE AND ENERGY AUDITS are a means of examining whether the organisation is making the best use of its inputs.

3. ENVIRONMENTAL BUDGETS can set green targets for activity centres and act as a part of the performance appraisal of the organisation.

4. ENVIRONMENTAL IMPACT ASSESSMENT, ENVIRONMENTAL HURDLE RATES, Best Practicable Environmental Option (BPEO), Best Available Technique Not Entailing Excessive Cost (BATNEEC), ENVIRONMENTAL RISK ASSESSMENT, etc., are techniques which bring environmental criteria into investment and project choice and post-audit.

5. ENVIRONMENTAL AND SOCIAL REPORTING would aid the discharge of the organisation's accountability and increase its environmental transparency. Reporting might consist of ENVIRONMENTAL POLICY, ENVIRONMENTAL CONTINGENCIES, ENVIRONMENTAL SPEND (possibly capitalised) and EMISSION STATEMENT, possibly in a COMPLIANCE-WITH-STANDARD REPORT, DISCLOSURE OF CRITICAL, NATURAL AND MAN-MADE ASSETS plus TRANSFERS BETWEEN THE CATEGORIES would probably also be essential if the organisation's environmental response was to be fully reported (see below).

6. ENVIRONMENTAL ASSET ACCOUNTING AND MAINTENANCE would attempt to capture the non-priced elements of *critical* and *natural capital*—both those that are entirely ignored by the pricing systems and those which are incorporated into the priced elements of man-made capital—e.g. the habitat/biodiversity cost of extracting a particular mineral. There is no necessary suggestion that this accounting need be in financial terms although there are both financial and non-financial implications. It should enable the organisation to assess the extent to which it is destroying natural capital to create man-made capital.

*Source:* adapted from Gray (1990d)

'outside' (e.g. Porritt, 1989). Hence the choice of option (3).

The articulation of option (3) for accounting derives from the recognition that as accounting helps to construct the world (in the big picture) and influences decisions and expresses accountability (in the more immediate picture) then accounting designed with environmentalism in mind can change these things. (How substantially or successfully is, obviously, unknowable.) Such was the intention in Gray (1990d), whose suggestions are summarised in Table 3. This project is continued here.

With this in mind, the paper now turns to look just at two specific elements of the deep green philosophy which can be articulated through a possible accounting. To do this, however, the limitations of the ensuing perception need to be considered briefly.

## AN INTERMEDIATE AND LIMITED CONCEPTION OF ORGANISATION

Having adopted, earlier in the paper, a position which applauds holism and denigrates reductionism, there is an imperative to ensure that what follows learns the lessons of systems thinking and takes care in specifying its limitations, systems boundaries and level of resolution.

Firstly, despite the analysis of Hines (1988) and Tinker (1985), a conception of 'organisation' is maintained. Thus 'company', 'university' and 'local authority' are retained as assumed social constructs having independent existence from those who give them life and the observer that creates them. (Thus individuals and groups can be said to be internal or external to the organisation at any one time for any particular act. Individuals and groups may operate in many roles, both internal and external, from time to time). In general, however, these conceptions will be treated as open systems with soft boundaries rather than as concrete, semi-closed systems with hard boundaries, as would normally be the case in the accounting literature.

Secondly, excluded from the analysis which follows are the critical questions of (1) how accounting defines and reinforces the power of exploitive relationships within the organisation, and (2) accounting as an expression of a 'masculine' rationality. Whilst it appears to be an increasingly widespread element of academic orthodoxy that accounting serves these functions, I am unaware of proposals for new accountings[20] that might deal with these issues, and the proposal 'there should be no (traditional or formal) accounting' is a fascinating, but different, paper. At an instinctive level only, I am unaware that what follows increases the pressure on these issues, and it may even soften them.

Thirdly, the organisation will be assumed to exist in fairly traditional space. That is, 'internal decision makers' will probably take decisions, probably in response to information. It is assumed that a change in information will change decision behaviour. I am not aware that any limiting objective function nor utility function is assumed. Furthermore, the organisation is placed in a pluralist (actually neo-pluralist; e.g. Held, 1987) world. That is, there exist individuals, groups, publics, States in the organisation's substantial environment who are influenced by and influence the organisation. Power asymmetry clearly exists, but (and here, I think, is the departure from both standard pluralism and Marxist conceptions) power can be exercised in some degree by all of these external participants. The neo-pluralist conception and, more particularly, the participative democratic process, see a future in which power is more widely shared with an emphasis on local democracy. Rather than democracy through representatives, participatory democracy requires much more active involvement by the demos (MacPherson, 1973, 1977). Held (1987) sees participatory democracy as a last, untried version of democracy and one which may unite much of the emancipatory power in both liberal and Marxist conceptions of society.[21] This paper, in line with the principles of environmentalism, is assuming the desirability of participatory democracy and seeking ways of moving towards it. For any power to be exercised in a participatory democracy there is an essential need for information, and this information will be an extension of that currently available. That is, the widest possible range of participants must be emancipated and enabled through the manifestation of existing but unfulfilled rights to information (e.g. Likierman, 1986; Likierman and Creasey, 1985).

Finally, the organisation is perceived as a flow-through system; drawing inputs from the social, industrial, legal, economic and environmental substantial environment, processing these, and producing outputs. Only some of these will be addressed here. The human, social and legal inputs will be considered only to the extent that they legitimate the organisation, determine rights and provide an assumed ethical framework and thus, as mentioned above, many of the important issues will be excluded. It is currently envisaged in this paper that different accounting systems are needed to 'capture' the inputs, the processing and the outputs of the organisation even for simply the physical environmental inputs (natural resources) and outputs (waste and pollution).[22]

## ACCOUNTING FOR ACCOUNTABILITY AND TRANSPARENCY

The accounting literature on accountability is of fairly recent vintage.[23] So much so, that before 1980 one would have been hard pressed to discover any significant analysis of a concept which seems, plausibly, so central to the practice of accounting. In principle, the notion of accountability was used in Gray (1983) and Gray *et al.* (1986, 1987, 1988, 1991) as an emancipatory concept helping to expose, enhance and develop social relationships through a re-examination and expansion of established rights to information. The difficulty that arises here is in determining some empirical base for those rights (Gray *et al.*, 1987). The trade-off is between (1) accepting some empirical basis for accountability, which must be flawed and reflect elements of a status quo that cannot necessarily be considered to be just or equitable, or else which fail on some other criteria or propriety (see Gray *et al.*, 1988, 1991, for more details), or (2) resorting to argument and assertion as to what one's own faith demands as rights. (See Likierman, 1986; Likierman and Creasey, 1985, for a nice introduction to this problem.) Gray *et al.* preferred to establish an elementary empirical basis and develop from that. The argument in essence was that anything which developed accountability practice from its current position *and* was justifiable within the status quo held out a practicable promise of evolution as a developing emancipation. That principle will be continued but extended here.

There are, however, some further substantive criticisms levelled at the accountability concept. The first is that most aggressively stated in Arrington (1990) but articulated in more detail by Roberts and Scapens (1985) and developed further in Roberts (1991). This is the observation that the process of 'being held to account' determines, reflects, reifies, strengthens and solidifies power relationships between the accountee and the accountor. The implication is that this is an odious activity— exploitive and suppressive. The second criticism arises from Tricker (1983) in which he argues that accountability only exists when the right to account is enforceable. Thus, in Tricker's view, the only true accountability relationships which currently exist are those which are empirically observable in flows of accounting information between accountor and accountee.

It seems that both of these observations have truth value but neither need be the case. Accountability is concerned with the right to receive information and the duty to supply it. The first is an essential element of any neo-pluralist or participatory democracy and the second, derived from the principle of personal accountability which is central to deep green thinking, is a tenet of personal development. So Tricker's arguments reduce to one of terminology which, whilst according with positive observation, does not necessarily exclude the possibility of many *unfulfilled* accountability relationships.

The criticism that accountability is necessarily exploitive largely presupposes an antagonistic and manipulative world. The deep green vision seeks to minimise and eventually replace such characteristics and thus sees accountability processes as social and liberating, a means of defining and re-defining community—Gemeinschaft as Pallot (1987, 1991) and Burkitt (1988) articulate it.[24] Such is also the world that was sought by John Stuart Mill and Adam Smith[25] and which has been profoundly and successfully developed by MacPherson.

> . . . MacPherson's theory of 'Developmental Democracy' . . . is non-extractive and developmental. It is non-extractive in that it does not depend upon the continued existence of class-based power-relationships. By developmental, MacPherson means that the theory implies the expansion of a person's power to use his ability to develop his supposedly essential human capabilities. These include a person's capacity for moral judgement and action, for aesthetic creation and contemplation, for friendship, love, and even religious experience. These rights, based on a person's potential ability must not be materially destructive. They are not the rights that everyone might like, especially not the Hobbesian right of any man to anything he desires. Developmental democratic theory, according to MacPherson, requires not the maximisation of individual utilities, but rather the ability of each to use and develop those capabilities, the use of which does not prevent others from using theirs (Clarke and Tilman, 1988, p. 187).

As, on the one hand, the deep green view demands the development of (and, indeed, the duty of) personal accountability (see Figure 2) and, on the other hand, the rights established by MacPherson suggests rights to information[26] it seems inescapable that the development of processes of accountability are essential to the deep green vision. The questions of 'for what?' , 'who?', 'to whom?' and 'how?' then present themselves for solution.

Gray et al. (1986, 1987, 1988, 1991) tried to solve these questions by reference to law and quasi-law. In particular, these papers argued that society at large had a right to information about the extent to which organisations had complied with the (minimum) standards of law and other regulation of a quasi-legal nature. The problem was, could this basis be extended further without resorting to opinion and assertion? Likierman (1986) and Likierman and Creasey (1985) argue that the existence of natural and moral rights is not disputed. (Although this is a contestable position, it is essential to the green vision.) What is disputed, and ultimately unresolvable, is what those rights actually are at any one time in any one place for any particular situation. The rights are social and ethical, but there are so many conceptions of what the social and the ethical implies that little resolution is forthcoming. Gray et al. attempt to allow the democratising forces of social change to take on the role of expanding democratic rights. That is, for example, the work on external social audits (Harte and Owen, 1987; Gray et al., 1991), on developments in ethical investment (Owen, 1990; Harte et al., 1990) and pressure group change such as the impact of Friends of the Earth and Greenpeace (Burritt and Maunders, 1990) all seek to expand those actions for which the organisation owes accountability. Gray (1990e) and Malachowski (1990) both suggest that barometers of public opinion can be *legitimately* interpreted as foundations for additional rights and accountability. Thus the empirical basis of accountability can be substantially extended from law and quasi-law to public domain matters of substance. This would not be uncontestable of course, but something closer to a particular specification of a community's moral and natural rights might begin to emerge.[27]

It is probably necessary to note that there are two, related, purposes behind the development of accountability systems. Firstly, as seen above, accountability is considered to be a means of developing closer social relationships and an element of bringing power back to the demos. Secondly, the development of accountability also increases the transparency of organisations. That is, it increases (or, in the green vision, should increase) the number of things which are made visible, increases the number of ways in which things are made visible and, in doing so encourages an increasing openness. The 'inside' of the organisation becomes more visible, that is, transparent.[28] The process of becoming more transparent is initially a painful process for the 'internal participants', but should encourage the diminution of the 'internal' versus 'external' tension as communities are all of owners, customers, management, employees, etc.

For the deep green vision, transparency and, thus, the right to information about actions which influence the society, other societies, future societies or the biosphere is not in question. This information must be in the public domain. Further, given the prominence of 'community' in the vision, the level at which information is reported—the level at which transparency must be sought—must be that of the community. Thus, we are now charged with the task of devising *local* accountability information systems; i.e. to what information about organisations do communities have rights? The argument in Gray *et al.* that the information content is governed by the categories recognised in law and quasi-law can probably now be expanded in the light of the above to include, particularly, social and environmental impact information. Remaining with the systems theoretic perspective, such information will be of three sorts:

*Input data:* on, for example, physical and human resources used; environmental impacts and disturbances caused (e.g. habitat destruction); ethical data on purchasing, investment and hiring activities.

*Processing data:* on, for example, efficiency (resource input to level of output or activity) data; accident data; control of employees.

*Output data:* on, for example, pollution emissions; waste produced and disposed or stored; influence and control exercised; stress caused, etc.

(Although this is clearly naïve in the current climate, it might act as a starting-of-discussion point.) This, with other compliance-with-standard data (including ethical code compliance data, e.g. Gray, 1990e; Malachowski, 1990) would form the basis of the accounting for accountability and transparency—informing the community about the use of its resources and the burdens (and benefits) it has been obliged to bear.

The next issue would appear to be the symbols used to encode the messages of accountability. It has long been argued (see also Gray *et al.*, 1986, 1987, 1988, 1991; and especially Gray, 1983) that the accountability need not be in terms of current financial units. Indeed it would be more in accord with a conception of participatory democracy if the events so described were described at the lowest level of resolution possible and thus the community could, collectively, exercise any 'valuation' process on the data as it saw fit.[29] In fact, the case for 'accounting' being a pre-dominantly financial activity is far from obvious; indeed a restriction to only financial accounts would critically limit the attempts at holism in the green vision.

Finally, there is the question of how the accountability will be communicated—

which channel(s) will be used for the transmission of the signal. Gray (1983) emphasises the point that the discharge of accountability can be achieved by simply making the information available in the public domain, the accommodating gymnastics of decision usefulness discussion are not essential to the process. However, the emphasis upon the duty to be personally accountable would tend, perhaps, to encourage the 'steward' towards seeking a more targeted accountability (see also Gray, 1990b).

Speculating about the possible shape of possible accounting systems loses its pertinence very quickly. The foregoing should be enough to begin the process of exploring whether such systems can be developed and/or applied and of seeking ways of moving accounting policy and practice towards the green ideals of personal accountability, participatory democracy and community transparency.

Whilst I would see the developments of these sorts of accountability systems as necessary conditions for the development of the green vision I cannot see that such systems represent sufficient conditions. As argued in Gray (1990d) there is an urgent need to develop environmental asset accounting and maintenance systems: to develop, in fact, sustainable accounting.

## ACCOUNTING FOR SUSTAINABILITY

Although the term 'sustainability' had been in wide currency amongst environmentalists for some time, the Brundtland Report to the United Nations of 1987 (United Nations, 1987) put the term firmly centre-stage of the economic, political and business agenda. Since then, whilst there has been considerable debate over what this terms means (e.g. Pearce *et al.*, 1989; Pezzey, 1989), the word has entered everyday speech (and is used to mean a very wide range of different things, most of them, in fact, not sustainable at all, e.g. Gray, 1991).

Sustainability, at its most general, relates to the planet and biosphere's ability to renew itself, to maintain its 'carrying capacity'. A sustainable action is thus one which does not disturb the essential ecology. However, all actions by all species *could be* considered as disturbing an ecology, which leaves us with the problem of deciding which actions disturb the ecology and which actions are *part of* the ecology. The issue is far from trivial and involves judgements about both the time necessary for an ecology to re-establish itself and the nature of the 'disturbance' versus 'transformation'. (For more details see Lovelock, 1982, 1988; Maunders and Burritt, 1991; and, on the 'entropy' and transformation issue, Georgescu-Roegen, 1971, 1975). However, sustainability is most usually considered in an anthropocentric context and such is the case in this paper. From an anthropocentric perspective, the level of activity which is sustainable then comes to mean that the current generation takes from the planet no more than the maximum which leaves the planet and future generations no worse off. Practice which sustains the planet must leave future generations with the same opportunities as we were bequeathed by our parents. Of course, it is accepted that, in an anthropocentric sense this is impossible (almost any action by man depletes the biosphere to some degree), unrealistic (is assumes that there will be no advances in technology, energy sources, etc.), underspecified (it does not clarify the question of whether substitution between elements is permitted) and imprecise (it assumes a static mode of action and does not allow for systemic change in social life). It seems inevitable that, faced with a concept of such importance and the obvious (to an environmentalist at least) observation that mankind's behaviour is anything but sustainable, some attempt will be made to try and operationalise it. This process of operationalisation has tended to be not only anthropocentric, but also calculative. There are clearly profound dangers in trying to employ calculation in a world where (1) the calculation can be identified as a root cause (e.g. Gray, 1990d) and (2) any calculation must run the risk of reinforcing analytic and scientistic solutions when, within a deep green context, one is attempting to do quite the opposite.[30] This is a critical problem but one which seems inevitable once one has taken the decision to work 'with the system' rather than around it. In general, the attempts at operationalising sustainability have not been directed towards finding precise answers but have rather been directed towards trying to better understand this idea and to assess, in broad terms, just how sustainable (Western) man is. This paper offers two further, pragmatic justifications—namely that the process will make visible that which is currently invisible in organisational settings (that is, the biosphere) and, secondly, the resultant data should be both disruptive and shocking.[31]

Moving to the more specific, Daly and Cobb argue (1990) that, at its simplest, sustainability is no more than an extension and re-interpretation of Hicksian income and traditional notions of capital maintenance. In effect, a level of sustainable activity is that level which maintains the planet's capital (see also Pearce *et al.*, 1989). Every action that uses limestone, oil, clay, peat, metals, etc.,—all finite raw materials— leaves mankind (and the current biosphere) potentially worse off. Every use of timber and timber products, clean air or water that is not replaced, every action involving energy based on fossil fuels, every product that produces waste which has to be physically disposed of, every personal or industrial action which removes habitat, and so one, leaves the planet with a depleted capital. In this scenario even the much-vaunted recycling is far from sustainable—each cycle loses raw material, and involves energy from finite (if potentially large) reserves. Ultimately, each action must lead to the use of the last of a resource or the last of a habitat and the extinction of yet another species.[32]

Environmental economists (see, for example, Turner, 1987, 1988, 1989; Turner and Pearce, 1990; Daly, 1980) propose that we start to deal with the problem by recognising that the planet will have to provide for the maintenance of three different types of capital before we can begin to count any residual as 'income'. These are:

*Critical natural capital:* that part of the biosphere that *must* be immutable. This includes such things as the ozone layer, a critical mass of trees (notably the rain forests, 'the lungs of the world'), the wetlands and critical habitats. The biologists seem to tell us that we *cannot* expend this capital without suffering the biggest loss of all (e.g. Goldsmith, 1988; Goldsmith *et al.*, 1972; Meadows *et al.*, 1972).

*Sustainable or substitutable (or 'other') natural capital:* that part of the biosphere which is renewable (e.g. water and air, timber, much land, the population of non-extinct creatures, agricultural products) or which can be substituted for its use-value; however, that might be defined (e.g. Pearce, 1977). Examples of substitutable capital might include mineral fuels or mineral building materials which can perhaps be substituted with some other means or material.[33]

*Man[34]-made capital:* Western capitalism has provided each subsequent generation, in the developed countries at least, with an ever-increasing amount of man-made capital—such things as machinery, technology and know-how, materials, housing, etc. This is what commercial activity appears to have set out to do and, for most people in the 'over-developed' Western 'democracies', does it *excessively* well (e.g. Henderson, 1981, 1991). However, there are non-priced aspects of the man-made capital stock which are also being treated non-sustainably; for example, infrastructure, built environment and, perhaps critically if ethnocentrically, ethical and aesthetic values, human freedom and self-actualisation, justice, community and so on. It is a moot question as to whether man-made capital; if measured by other than traditional National Income methods, has actually been increasing, even in the West (Daly and Cobb, 1990; Ekins, 1986; Dauncey, 1988).

There is some dispute about the level at which sustainability should be sought: planetary, national or community, for example. Such dispute is largely fruitless if it becomes an excuse for inaction. So one way forward might be to try and translate these concepts to the level of the individual organisation and seek ways in which to introduce them to our accounting. As organisations control much of the world's industrial capacity, are deeply implicated in environmental degradation and must, therefore, be part of any solution, it seem reasonable to explore organisational sustainability as a complement to, not a substitute for, sustainability at other levels.[35] It seems that any such accounting would have two major functions, both derived from the necessity of accountability and transparency discussed above. These functions would be (1) to keep organisational decision-makers informed of the extent to which their particular organisation was depleting the planet's capital. In effect, this would, to use economists' terms, be an attempt to 'internalise' what have previously been treated as 'externalities'; and (2) to keep society informed about the way its capital was being employed whether or not it was being maintained.

There are, it seems to me, two ways in which sustainability accounting could be approached based upon the foregoing. The first would be a non-financial accounting which attempted to identify and then track elements in the three categories of 'capital' which lay under the control of the organisation. The practical (and definitional) problems are clearly critical but, in principle at least, the very process of identifying critical, renewable or substitutable and man-made capitals would start the process of making biosphere interaction more visible. Thus, again in principle, it might be possible to identify the diminutions (and improvements) in both natural capitals (depletion of mineral resources, use of non-renewable and renewable energy, habitat destroyed or replaced, influence on air and water quality, etc.) which have been necessary to 'create' the increases in man-made capital as shown, for example, by changes in balance-sheet values.[36] There could be little precision in such accounts (and lack of precision might well be actually desirable), but they would point in the direction of sustainability.

An alternative account which has a much closer relationship with conventional accounting (and thereby suffers acutely from the earlier criticisms but has the advantage of being more immediately practicable, perhaps more acceptable, and thereby more subversive) is to attempt to calculate a sustainable cost. Whilst I have argued elsewhere about the critical problems that arise from considering environmental issues within a price-driven framework and thus the incipient dangers of a financial numbers-based solution to environmental issues (Gray, 1990d, f), it may well be that much progress can be achieved—and (with luck) little violence done—by employing some conventional-looking financial accounting concepts to address the environmental sustainability of organisational activity. That is, following Daly and Cobb's analysis of sustainability and their subsequent re-analysis of the concepts in Hicksian income, I wonder whether accounting might contribute to the development of sustainability by exploring the possibility of employing sustainable cost analysis as a shadow of current price-driven accounting information.[37] This might provide us with a starting point (and at a minimum it might stop some of the ridiculous claims for sustainable activity which are now being made).

This might work by trying to derive a parallel accounting system which provided calculations of what additional costs must be borne by the organisation if the organizational activity were not to leave the planet worse off, i.e. what it would cost at the end of the accounting period to return the planet and biosphere to the point it was at the beginning of the accounting period. On the face of it, there is much to recommend such an idea. Critical natural capital is irreplaceable; its 'sustainable cost' is infinite. Thus no 'economic' decision would ever choose to use it, and this is the answer that is required for a green, sustainable accounting. Other natural capital will obviously cause profound problems but as we are trying to move away from mechanistic calculative decision making, any information which broadly illustrates the sort of magnitude of costs which must be incurred to return the planet to the state in which it was before a transaction may well encourage a more sensitive approach to decision making.

To be effective, this shadow accounting system would, preferably, produce numbers which can be deducted from calculated accounting profit and be expended in the restoration of the biosphere. This will, thus, lead to a recognition that organisational income has been grossly overstated for some considerable time and that current generations have been benefiting at the cost of some future generation. *The probability is that no Western company has made a 'sustainable' profit for a very long time, if ever.*[38] (For more details see, for example, Daly, 1980; Daly and Cobb, 1990; Goldsmith *et al.*, 1972; Goldsmith, 1988; Ekins, 1986; Porritt, 1989; Robertson, 1978, 1984; Ward, 1979).

To illustrate the idea and to explore the notion just a little further, it might be worth a brief speculation on one or two aspects that might form part of this 'sustainable cost' of inputs method of dealing with sustainable activity.

There will be several categories of 'other natural capital' and they will differ from organisation to organisation.[39] These might be classified as:

*Primary resource inputs:* these would include minerals, timber, agriculture, fisheries, etc. The sustainable cost would only have to be calculated or estimated at the point of extraction, subsequent prices passing this on to secondary users. The need for sustainable fishing, agriculture and forestry is currently widely discussed. The cost of sustaining self-renewing species might be estimated as the cost of replenishment but discounted in some way to the point of maturity, i.e. to the point where the fish could be caught and eaten, the timber logged, etc.[40] The cost of (e.g.) over-logging or over-fishing (a state which is difficult to define) might therefore be so considerable as to prevent 'economically' worthwhile exploitation of the resource. For non-self-renewing resources, notably minerals, some decision about 'use-substitute' would have to be made so that (e.g.) energy mineral extraction was charged with some figure for (say) research into renewable energy resources—coal profits into solar panels or wind-power generation.[41] Similarly (whilst recognising that it is impossible to assess what future and essential use future generations might find for (e.g.) limestone or oil), the income from the activity would have to bear a charge for establishing an alternative source of renewable resource with the same use and use-substitute.

*'Input' of waste-sink capacity:* the use of air, sea, water, land, etc., for emissions and for waste disposal must be charged with correction of damage costs; that is, the costs necessary to return the sink to its original state. This may well tend to encourage organisations (as governments the world over are attempting) to reduce waste towards zero and, with developments such as the U.S.A. Superfund Act (e.g. Specht, 1991) these costs are being articulated through legislation. Where this is impossible or not directly possible (as, for example, in the contribution to the greenhouse effect), alternative ameliorating investment could be charged. This could, for example, be related to the re-establishment of forest to at least attempt to balance the carbon dioxide issue (if this is not naïve chemistry!).

*Stewardship assets:* such matters as land and habitats must be returned to their original condition or alternatives provided. There is an increasing amount of this in industry where these costs are now directly borne by the organisation, in re-landscaping or re-habitating after use of land (e.g. Elkington, 1987).

The practical and theoretical problems with this sort of approach are clearly monumental[42] but are offered here as suggestions, as stimuli and as a first approximation from which the essential but awesome task for accounting for sustainability might develop.


## CONCLUSIONS

Essentially, this paper, as it currently stands, has sought to make an explicit introduction of deep green thinking to the accounting literature and therefore begin a process of providing a more explicit and theoretical basis for the development of new accountings in the social and environmental public interest. As I started so I finish; the accounting literature is increasingly informed by scholarly critiques of accounting as it is but the radical developments have offered very few hostages to fortune in the form of detailed proposals of what accounting might look like. This has been the explicit project of Gray *et al.* (1986, 1987, 1988, 1991, forthcoming) and Gray (1990d). One explanation for the lack of the observation that it is profoundly difficult to begin to reconstruct the world through the imaginings founded upon (financial) accounting. I suspect this paper has illustrated this point rather clearly.


## ACKNOWLEDGEMENTS

I very gratefully acknowledge the helpful comments received on earlier drafts of the paper from Jan Bebbington, Jane Broadbent, Tony Clayton, David Collison, Sonja Gallhofer, Sue Gray, John Grinyer, Jim Haslam, Ruth Hines, Anthony Hopwood, Richard Laughlin, Linda

Lewis, Margaret Liston, Keith Maunders, Sheila Morrison, Rolland Munro, Ann Neale, Dave Owen, Mike Power, Tony Tinker, Diane Walters, David Weston and TOES, colleagues at the Universities of Edinburgh, Essex, Heriot-Watt and Manchester, participants at EIASM Workshop 1990, BAA Conference 1991, IPA Conference 1991 and the anonymous referees for IPA and *AOS*.

## NOTES

1. 'Developed world' is used here only because of the easy immediate referents which it connotes. I am conscious that it is a potentially pejorative term but the use of the preferred term 'over-developed world' will raise too many other issues that, for reasons of practicability, have been excluded from this paper. Ethnocentricity is a danger that every commentator must face and whilst I have tried to limit it, I must apologise in advance for the inevitable occasions upon which it creeps through.
2. For more detail on the case of paradigm shift see Goldsmith (1988), Daly and Cobb (1990), Dauncey (1988), Robertson (1978), Lovelock (1982).
3. The various shades of 'green' are eloquently explored in Plant and Plant (1991). The 'deep green' position employed in this paper must be distinquished from that of 'deep ecology', in that the former is anthropocentric whereas 'deep ecology' is ecology-centred. That is, this paper places the environment at the centre of *human* analysis but privileges human-kind, 'deep ecology' attempts to place human-kind on an equal footing with all species. For an especially good introduction to this and its implications in accounting see Maunders and Burritt (1991) and see also Dobson (1990).
4. And, in particular, at the project of Gray *et al.* (1986, 1987, 1988, 1990b, 1991).
5. 'Traditional' or 'conventional' economics refers here to capitalist economics as opposed to (say) Islamic economics. Reference to neo-classical economics, which might be an easier term to use, usually stands accused of being a straw-person (e.g. Gray, 1990f).
6. The whole issue of modelling and abstraction is clearly problematic in all discourse. The matter is side-stepped here but only for reasons of clarity.
7. Heilbroner, it seems, doubts whether other viable alternatives can be found. Daly (1980) attacks this notion and, effectively silences it (to my mind) in Daly and Cobb (1990). However, the ubiquity of these two, adversarial positions which might represent the whole of human possibility seems a fair reflection of most social science literature. The literature of environmentalism is a real attempt to move away from this two-sided debate and add a third, significantly different, dimension.
8. Such a concept is deeply apparent within the political movements themselves, see Capra and Spretnak (1984) and Parkin (1989).
9. I am especially grateful to Tony Tinker for taking the time to raise these issues with me.
10. The analysis later in this paper will draw equally from MacPherson, whose Marxist influences are obvious, Daly and Cobb, whose liberal and pluralist antecedents are explicit, as well as from Held, who has sought to tease out ways of drawing together both strands of analysis.
11. There are may terms for the deep greens—deep or radical or social ecologists, ecological humanists and all the shades of deep green (eco-greens, value conservatives, visionary/holistic greens, red greens). In the end the ideas intended by the term and the definition of that term will result in the usual tautology. However, 'deep green' (rather than more typically 'deep ecology') is used here because of its association with the Green political movement from which this paper draws its direction. Again, see Maunders and Burritt (1991) and Dobson (1990) for further development of this.
12. Although only apparently summarised from one source, a reading of such widespread sources as Parkin (1989), Kemp and Wall (1990), Schumacher (1968, 1973, 1974), Dauncey (1988), Robertson (1978), Goldsmith (1988), etc., will bring a very similar conclusion.
13. In what follows, an attempt will be made to illuminate and develop some of these themes.

However, the complexity and interrelatedness of the ideas counsels caution and leads at times to the treatment of matters under different headings and with different emphasis.

14. To open debate on this issue in the present climate is to beg many questions indeed. However, the terms as used here (and as used in much of the deep green literature) hypothesise wisdom and completeness of the human as deriving from a harmony of characteristics. The characteristics of apparent success in the current hegemony and which it seems are admired and sought after—characteristics such as intellect, traditional logic, aggression, cunning, 'calculated cleverness in the interests of self' (March, 1987, p. 158), energy and dynamism, accumulation and consumption of observable goods, insight, friendliness and warmth—can be considered 'masculine' traits, which have dominated to the exclusion of 'feminine' traits such as nurture, emotion, parenthood and family, spontaneity, physical well-being, calmness, stability, continuity, cheerfulness, happiness, childlikeness, innocence, etc. The acutal categorisation is obviously problematic and this categorisation does not fully accord with Bem. In part this is because the characteristics listed here need bear no relationship to sex or gender—whether socially constructed or not.

15. This then plays back into the economic system. That is, community may be incompatible with a dominant price-only exchange process which is generally alienating (see, for example, Dauncey, 1988, chapters 6 and 7), and thus non-financial economy, trust and personal contact through economic exchange would all re-establish community whilst removing much of traditional economic exchange as it currently exits.

16. This is not intended pejoratively. For example, the better science fiction literature has always had the aim—in which it has often succeeded—in exploring possible new futures unfettered by current contraints. Such speculation is what is needed here—see, for example, Moorcock (1984, pp. 191–201) and writing such as Samuel Butler's *Erehwon*. More specifically, a major theme in feminism is the empowering of the intuition and imagination (e.g. Hines, 1991b).

17. A similar point is made in the context of Marxist accounting by Laughlin and Puxty (1986).

18. A hint of this has emerged in the research following on from Gray (1990d). A series of interviews and working groups were established with some New Zealand companies. The smaller scale of operations, the small total population of the country and the different cultural attitudes to environmental issues seemed to place a very different emphasis on accountability. That is, as most communities could identify those organisations which were operating in ways counter to community values (over-cropping, polluting, flooding sensitive areas, noise, etc.) and could also identify employees up to and including senior management, there was not only no anonymity behind which the miscreant could hide, but the community values became the values of the employees and thus of the organisation. Transparency appeared to operate, thus making some aspects of formal accountability unnecessarily cumbersome.

19. The Marxist critique of the green movement is, once again, important here. Without a thesis about the essential structure of society, the forces that produced the status quo and the nature and process of change, the green attempts to seek change are, at best, empty and, at worst, may either produce a 'worse' situation or be captured by the institutional forces of reaction. There has been little green response to this charge, although Dobson (1990) represents a useful step in this direction (e.g. Tinker *et al.* 1991).

20. This is a generalised problem, I believe. That is, analyses of the functions of current accounting practice are not generally balanced by researchers offering hostages to fortune and proposing new accounting. It is not apparent to me that critique without proposal is entirely justifiable in the long term.

21. I acknowledge that provision of information to the demos will not ensure that the demos then behaves in a way I might approve. Subject to the constraints of power to act, it is fully accepted that the demos may continue along a path towards extinction. Despite the anthropocentric focus of the paper, I (and, I believe, most environmentalists) am content to let the human species wipe itself out. The point at issue is whether this was a democratically chosen path and (given the greater emphasis on deontological ethics in

the green vision) both the manner of the extinction and the state of the planet and other species at the time of extinction.

22. It is also recognised that this, and what follows, effectively concretises the organisation and, to a degree at least, accepts the organisation which accounting creates. Further, there is the hint of a suggestion that accounting captures reality (Hines, 1988). The 'organisation' remains the central unit of analysis for accounting and so is retained though, I would claim, in a softer form than is typical in accounting. Hines is not suggesting that accounting does not capture some aspects of some reality. I am making no claims to trying to do more than this. I am simply trying to throw up new realities which, in part, will reflect a different (and additional) set of aspects of some reality.

23. This is to be distinguished from the analyses of stewardship which did appear in the accounting literature but, in general, took the term as *ex cathedra* rather as a contestable notion whose precedents and implications required exploration. This should also be distinguished from the accountability literature outside accounting (e.g. public administration) in which accounting was implicated but not central (see, for example, Munkman, 1971; Greer *et al.*, 1978; and, for an exception, Gjesdal, 1981). The term 'accountability' has always had a high currency in the public sector accountability literature but this, again until recently, was very underdeveloped (e.g. Gray, 1983; Perrin, 1981).

24. This vision has been accused of naïvety and trying to side-step the critical issues (Sandbach, 1980). This may be so, but the importance of having and maintaining vision and emphasising process over ends does seem to counsel this sort of approach. Further, to talk of Gemeinschaft in isolation from Gesselschaft (formal contractual relationships) is perhaps overly simple. The green vision seeks to soften the Gesselschaft accountability in an attempt to develop something which looks more like Gemeinschaft.

25. Despite the terrible press they now receive and the perversion of their ideas which purportedly informs much that passes for Modernist (Arrington, 1990) thinking. I should also note in passing the similarity of tone between the following passage and that of Arrington's (1990) exposition of Rorty.

26. Information is essential to liberate, inform, enable and educate. From an alternative perspective, it would seem bizarre to grant rights to action but not rights to information concerning action.

27. Tricker's (1983) point concerning the enforcing of accountability upon organisations is clearly critical in this. The present discussion has a naïve faith about it that implies that all peoples will gladly open up when the 'truth' is demonstrated to them. This is clearly nonsense. It is anticipated that regulatory means would be necessary to take the process a long way down the road. The implications of this and the form that regulation must take in order to be compatible with the green vision are now explored in this paper.

28. The making of things visible must, inevitably make some things invisible. The more things made visible, and the more ways in which they are made visible should decrease invisibility. It is essentially experimental but this process should enable the creation of new, additional and more complex social realities.

29. This notion is largely informed by the (predominantly unsuccessful) exercises in valuing social activities in social accounting in the 1970s. See, for example, Gray *et al.* (1987), Estes (1976), Belkaoui (1984).

30. This parallels the reason examination of 'juridification', see, for example, Teubner (1987), Laughlin and Broadbent (1991), and see also Gorz (1989) and Power (1991).

31. Ultimately I can only offer a deontological position on this—any action which accords with the green vision, raises awareness of environmental issues and attempts to recapture 'sustainability' from the Western politicians and economists who see it as entirely consistent with more Western (old-style) economic growth, seems to me to be a right action.

32. The use of words such as 'loss' and 'depletion' are totally anthropocentric and conservative. Nothing is 'lost', it is merely transformed. In a 'total ecology' world, we would focus upon entropy and the transformation of elements in the biosphere. The antropocentric focus of the paper rejects the Lovelock Gaia hypothesis and sees actual

diminution of the biosphere's ability to sustain human and non-human life. At the opposite extreme, the more conventional environmental economists' position would be concerned with assessing transformation in an economic sense—from biosphere into goods, for example. The extreme version of this is rejected (e.g. Gray, 1990d, f) and the paper will reject absolutely the notion that there can be some equivalence between biosphere and goods that can be measured and assessed through prices. However, the persuasive thesis of Daly (1980) and Daly and Cobb (1990) counsels the careful use of some of the economists' tools and concepts. This will be obvious in what follows.

33. It must be noted that from a deep ecology perspective very nearly all natural capital is 'critical' in this sense. That is, first the introduction of an ethic which gives all lifeforms a reasonable right to life places all habitat—human and non-human—on a par. Second, in our world of increasing scientific ignorance (i.e. scientific and economic developments are advancing faster than mankind's ability to understand them and their interactions and implications) we cannot know which actions will be life threatening. Third, most, if not all, human interventions in the biosphere are major disruptions of the ecology (if only because of the scale of industrial activity and the levels of population) and, therefore, either directly or indirectly interferes with critical capital. For more details, see Maunders and Burritt (1991).

34. I apologise for the gender-specific term. No sexism is intended—even though the male may well be held principally responsible for the devastation we are witnessing. The continued use of this term is (a) to maintain consistency with other literature, and (b) because other terms—created capital, humankind-made capital, etc.—rather lack the directness and historical referents of the term 'man-made'.

35. It is possible, of course, that focus on sustainability at organisational levels might hinder essential developments at community and national levels, for example. It is far from obvious that this need be the case and recent research experience would suggest that the opposite is more likely—namely that assumptions that responsibility for sustainability lie at national levels *are* hindering experiments at the organisational level (e.g. Porritt, 1989).

36. New Zealand local authorities have been experimenting with these ideas through reporting physical qualities of types of land, natural leisure facilities and aspects of the built environment that fall into their dominion. The idea is still in early stages of development. An alternative approach, this time using principally financial data, is being explored in France. In this case the development of satellite environmental accounts is being constructed as part of the National Income accounting system, and then attempts are being made to link these through to the accounts of the individual enterprise (e.g. Christophe, 1989).

37. It is fully accepted that, in addition to all the other problems intrinsic to accounting and the use of calculative regimes to solve calculative problems, this suggestion is both potentially utterly conservative and, furthermore, relies upon prices, a pseudo-economic notion, and a concept 'income' which is a socially constructed accounting artifact anyway. I think it is apparent that the ideas which follow flow from the earlier discussions and are not entirely incompatible with them. Ultimately though, any justification must be largely pragmatic—something needs to be done, this is sufficiently like 'accounting' being a Trojan horse and, as we shall see, it produces the right sort of answers!

38. And this looks the sort of answer we might want. The desire to shock is probably achieved. It is also clear that this enables us to introduce consideration of the issues raised by 'lesser-developed' countries, but that is outside the scope of the present paper.

39. There are 'private' aspects of man-made capital that perhaps should also be dealt with here—notably built environment. This, however, raises severe problems of definition that will need to be dealt with and so are left for future analysis.

40. There are any number of obvious and perhaps not so obvious problems with this analysis but it might prove a starting point.

41. As is beginning to happen—at least in electricity generation industries.

42. And these problems to some extent echo earlier attempts and financially based social accounting (see, for example, Gray *et al.*, 1987; Estes, 1976).

# BIBLIOGRAPHY

Ackoff, R. L. (1960) Systems, Organizations and Interdisciplinary Research, *General Systems Theory Yearbook* pp. 1–8.

Allen, V. (1975) *Social Analysis: a Marxist Critique and Alternative* (Harlow: Longman).

Armstrong, P. (1991) Contradiction and Social Dynamics in the Capitalist Agency Relationship, *Accounting Organizations and Society* pp. 1–26.

Arrington, E. (1990) Intellectual Tyranny and the Public Interest: the Quest for the Grail and the Quality of Life, *Advances in Public Interest Accounting* pp. 1–16.

Beishon, J. and Peters, G. (1972, 1981) *Systems Behaviour* (London: Open University/Harper & Row).

Belkaoui, A. (1984) *Socio-Economic Accounting* (Connecticut: Quorum Books).

Bem, S. L. (1974) The Measurement of Psychological Androgyny. *Journal of Consulting and Clinical Psychology* pp. 155–162.

Bem, S. L. (1975) Sex Role Adaptability: One Consequence of Psychological Androgyny. *Journal of Personality and Social Psychology* pp. 634–643.

Bertalanffy, L. von. (1956) General Systems Theory, *General Systems Yearbook* pp. 1–10.

Bertalanffy, L. von. (1971) General Systems Theory, *Foundations, Development, Applications* (Hardmondsworth: Penguin).

Bertalanffy, L. von. (1972) General Systems Theory—a Critical Review, in Beishon, J. & Peters G. (eds), *Systems Behaviour* (London: Open University/Harper & Row).

Boulding, K. E. (1956) General Systems Theory—the Skeleton of Science, *Management Science* pp. 197–208.

Boulding, K. E. (1966) The Economics of the Coming Spaceship Earth, in Jarratt, H. (ed.) *Environmental Quality in a Growing Economy* (Baltimore: John Hopkins Press) pp. 3–14.

Boulding, K. E. (1982) Review of *Ecodevelopment: Economics, Ecology and Development—an Alternative to Growth-Imperative Models. Journal of Economic Literature* pp. 1076–1077.

Burchell, S., Clubb, C., Hopwood, A., Hughes, J. and Nahapiet, J. (1980) The Roles of Accounting in Organizations and Society, *Accounting, Organizations and Society* pp. 5–27.

Burkitt, W. P. (1988) Concept of Accountability, Paper presented to British Accounting Association, Bath.

Burritt, R. L. and Maunders, K. T. (1990) Accounting and Ecological Crisis, paper presented to the European Accounting Association Congress, Budapest.

Capra, F. and Spretnak, C. (1984) *Green Politics: the Global Promise* (London: Hutchinson).

Carter, R., Martin, J., Mayblin, B. and Munday, M. (1984) *Systems, Management and Change: a Graphic Guide* (London: Harper Row).

Checkland, P. B. (1981) *Systems Thinking. Systems Practice* (Chichester: Wiley).

Christophe, B. (1989) L'environnement naturel: Source de rapprochement entre la compatibilite nationale et al compatabilite d'enterprise? *Revue Francaise de Comptabilite* (Novembre) pp. 67–73.

Clarke, M. and Tilman, R. (1988) C. B. MacPherson's Contribution to Democratic Theory, *Journal of Economic Issues* (March) pp. 181–196.

Coker, E. W., (1990) Adam Smith's Concept of Social Systems. *Journal of Business Ethics* (February) pp. 139–142.

Commoner, B. (1972) The Social Use and Misuse of Technology, in Benthall, J. (ed.), *Ecology: the Shaping Enquiry*, pp. 335–362 (London: Longman).

Coppock, R. (1977) Life Amongst the Environmentalists: an Elaboration on Wildavsky's Economic and environmental/rationality and ritual, *Accounting, Organization and Society* pp. 125–129.

Daly, H. E. (ed.) (1980), *Economy, Ecology, Ethics, Essays toward a Steady State Economy* (San Francisco: Freeman).

Daly, H. E. (1985) Ultimate Confusion: the Economics of Julian Simon, *Futures* pp. 446–450.

Daly, H. E. and Cobb, J. B., Jr, (1990) *For the Common Good: Redirecting the Economy Towards the Community, the Environment and a Sustainable Future* (London: Greenprint).

Dauncey, G. (1988) *After the Crash: the Emergence of the Rainbow Economy* (Basingstoke: Greenprint).

Dickson, D. (1974) *Alternative Technology and the Politics of Technical Change* (Glasgow: Fontana).

Dobson, A. (1990) *Green Political Thought* (London: Unwin Hyman).

Donaldson, J. (1988) *Key Issues in Business Ethics* (London: Academic Press).

Ekins, P. (ed.). (1986) *The Living Economy: a New Economics in the Making* (London: Routledge).

Elkington, J. (and Burke, T.) (1987) *The Green Capitalists: Industry's Search for Environmental Excellence* London: Victor Gollancz).

Emery, F. E. (ed.) (1969) *Systems Thinking* (Harmondsworth, Penguin).

Erlich, P. R. and Erlich A. H. (1978) Humanity at the Crossroads, *Stamford Magazine.* Reprinted in Daly, H. E. (ed.). (1980) *Economy, Ecology, Ethics: Essays towards a Steady State Economy* (San Francisco: Freeman) pp. 38–43.

Estes, R. W. (1976) *Corporate Social Accounting* (New York: Wiley).

Fisher, A. C. (1981) *Resource and Environmental Economics* (Cambridge: Cambridge University Press).

Fisher, A. C. and Peterson, F. M. (1976) The Environment in Economics: a Survey, *Journal of Economic Literature* pp. 1–33.

Frankel, B. (1987) *The Post-Industrial Utopians* (Cambridge: Polity Press).

Furkiss, V. (1974) *The Future of Technological Civilization* (New York: Brazilier).

Gambling, T. (1978a) The Evolution of Accounting Man, *Accountants' Weekly* (10 November) pp. 30–31.

Gambling, T. (1978b) *Beyond the Conventions of Accounting* (London: Macmillan).

Gambling, T. (1985) The Accountants' Guide to the Galaxy, including the Profession at the end of the Universe, *Accounting, Organizations and Society* pp. 415–425.

Georgescu-Roegen, N. (1971) The Entropy Law and the Economic Problem. *Distinguished Lecture Series* No. 1 University of Alabama. Reprinted in Daly, H. E. (ed.) (1980) *Economy, Ecology, Ethics, Essays toward a Steady State Economy* (San Francisco: Freeman) pp. 49–60.

Georgescu-Roegen, N. (1975) Selections from 'Energy and Economic Myths', *Southern Economic Journal* (January). Reprinted in Daly, H. E. (ed.) (1980) *Economy, Ecology, Ethics: Essays toward a Steady State Economy* (San Francisco: Freeman) pp. 61–81.

Gjesdal, F. (1981) Accounting for Stewardship, *Journal of Accounting Research* pp. 208–231.

Goldsmith, E. (1988) *The Great U-Turn: De-industrializing Society* (Devon: Green Books).

Goldsmith, E. *et al.* (1972) *Blueprint for Survival* (Hardmondsworth: Penguin).

Gorz, A. (1989) *Critique of Economic Reason* (transl. Handyside, G. & Turner, C.) London: Verso).

Gray, R. H. (1983) Accountability, Financial Reporting and the Not-for-profit Sector, *British Accounting Review* (Spring) pp. 3–23.

Gray, R. H. (1989) Accounting and Democracy, *Accounting, Auditing and Accountability Journal* pp. 52–56.

Gray, R. H. (1990a) Greenprint for Accountants, *Certified Accountant* (March) p. 18.

Gray, R. H. (1990b) Corporate Social Reporting by UK Companies: a Cross-Sectional and Longitudinal Study—an Interim Report. Paper presented to British Accounting Association, University of Dundee.

Gray, R. H. (1990c) The Accountant's Task as a Friend to the Earth, *Accountancy* (June) pp. 65–69.

Gray, R. H. (1990d) *The Greening of Accountancy: the Profession after Pearce* (London: Chartered Association of Certified Accountants).

Gray, R. H. (1990e) Business Ethics and Organizational Change: Building a Trojan Horse or Rearranging Deckchairs on the Titanic? *Managerial Auditing Journal* pp. 12–21.

Gray, R. H. (1990f) Accounting and Economics: the Psychopathic Siblings—a Review Essay, *British Accounting Review* pp. 373–388.

Gray, R. H. (1991) Do you REALLY Want to Know what it Means? *CBI Environment Newsletter* (January) pp. 10–11.

Gray, R. H., Owen, D. L. and Maunders, K. T. (1986) Corporate Social Reporting: the Way Forward? *Accountancy* (December) pp. 6–8.

Gray, R. H., Owen , D. L. and Maunders, K. T. (1987) *Corporate Social Reporting: Accounting and Accountability* (Hemel Hempstead: Prentice-Hall)

Gray, R. H., Owen, D. L. and Maunders, K. T. (1988) *Corporate Social Reporting:* Emerging

Trends in Accountability and Social Contract, *Accounting, Auditing and Accountability Journal* pp. 6–20.

Gray, R. H., Owen, D. L. and Maunders, K. T. (1991) Accountability, Corporate Social Reporting and the External Social Audits, *Advances in Public Interest Accounting* pp. 1–21.

Greer, S., Hedlund, R. D. and Gibson J. L. (eds) (1978) *Accountability in Urban Society* (Sage: London).

Hardin, G. (1968) The Tragedy of the Commons, *Science* (December) pp. 1243–1248. Reprinted in Daly H. E. (ed.) (1980) *Economy, Ecology, Ethics: Essays toward a Steady State Economy* (San Francisco: Freeman) pp. 100–114.

Hardin, G. (1980) Second Thoughts on 'The Tragedy of the Commons', Ch. 7 in Daly H. E. (ed.), *Economy, Ecology, Ethics: Essays toward a Steady State Economy* (San Francisco: Freeman) pp. 115–120.

Harte, G. and Owen, D. L. (1987) Fighting De-industrialization: the Role of Local Government Social Audits, *Accounting, Organizations and Society* pp. 123–142.

Harte, G., Lewis, L. and Owen, D. L. (1990) Ethical investment and the Corporate Reporting Function. Paper presented at EAA Annual Congress, Budapest.

Heilbroner, R. L. (1983) *The Worldly Philosphers* (London: Pelican).

Heilbroner, R. L. (1984) Economics and Political Economy: Marx, Keynes and Schumpeter. *Journal of Economic Issues* (September) pp. 681–695.

Held, D. (1987) *Models of Democracy* (Oxford: Polity Press).

Henderson, H. (1978) *Creating Alternative Futures* (New York: Berkley).

Henderson, H. (1981) *The Politics of the Solar Age: Alternatives to Economics* (Doubleday: New York).

Henderson, H. (1991) New Markets, New Commons, New Ethics, *Accounting, Auditing and Accountability Journal* pp. 72–80.

Hines, R. D. (1988) Financial Accounting: In Communication Reality, we Construct Reality, *Accounting Organizations and Society* pp. 251–261.

Hines, R. D. (1991a) The FASB's Conceptual Framework, Financial Accounting and the Maintenance of the Social World, *Accounting, Organizations and Society* pp. 313–332.

Hines, R. D. (1991b) Accounting: Filling the Negative Space, *Proceedings of the Third Interdisciplinary Perspectives on Accounting Conference* Vol. 1 pp. 1.6.1–1.6.20.

Hopper, T. and Powell, A. (1985) Making Sense of Research into the Organisational and Social Aspects of Management Accounting: a Review of its Underlying Assumptions, *Journal of Management Studies* (September) pp. 429–465.

Kast, F. E. and Rosenweig, J. E. (1974) *Organisation and Management: a Systems Approach* (Kograkusha: McGraw-Hill).

Kemp, P. and Wall, D. (1990) *A Green Manifesto for the 1990s* (London: Penguin).

Laughlin, R. C. and Broadbent, J. (1991) Accounting and Jurisdiction: an Exploration with Specific Reference to the Public Sector in the United Kingdom, *Proceedings of the Third Interdisciplinary Accounting Conference*, Vol. 1, Manchester pp. 1.10.1–1.10.16.

Laughlin, R. C. and Puxty, A. G. (1986) The Socially Conditioning and Social Conditioned Nature of Accounting: Review and Analysis through Tinker's 'Paper Prophets', *British Accounting Review* (Spring 1986) pp. 77–90.

Lehman, C. (1990) The Importance of Being Earnest: Gender Conflicts in Accounting. *Advances in Public Interest Accounting* pp. 137–157.

Likierman, A. (1986) *Rights and Obligations in Public Information* (Cardiff: University College Cardiff Press).

Likierman, A. and Creasey, P. (1985) Objectives and Entitlements to Rights in Government Financial Information, *Financial Accountability and Management* (Summer) pp. 33–50.

Lovelock, J. (1982) *Gaia: a New Look at Life on Earth* (Oxford: Oxford University Press).

Lovelock, J. (1988) *The Ages of Gaia* (Oxford: Oxford University Press).

Lowe, A. E. (1972) The Finance Director's Role in the Formulation and Implementation of Strategy. *Journal of Business Finance* pp. 58–63.

Lowe, A. E. and McInnes, J. M. (1971) Control of Socio-Economic Organisations. *Journal of Management Studies* pp. 213–227.

McKee, A. (1986) The Passage from Theology to Economics, *International Journal of Social Economics* pp. 5–19.

MacPherson, C. B. (1973) *Democratic Theory: Essays in Retrieval* (Oxford: Oxford University Press).

MacPherson, C. B. (1977) *The Life and Times of Liberal Democracy* (Oxford: Oxford University Press).

MacPherson, C. B. (1978) *Property* (Toronto: University of Toronto Press).

Machin, W. and Lowe, A. E. (1983) *New Perspectives in Management Control* (London: Macmillan)

Malachowski, A. (1990) Business Ethics 1980–2000: An Interim Forecast, *Managerial Auditing Journal* pp. 22–27.

March, J. G. (1987) Ambiguity and Accounting: The Illusive Link between Information and Decision-making, *Accounting, Organizations and Society* pp. 153–168.

Maunders, K. T. and Burritt, R. (1991) Accounting and Ecological Crisis, *Accounting, Auditing and Accountability Journal* pp. 9–26.

Maupin, R. J. (1990) Sex Role Identity and Career Success of Certified Public Accountants, *Advances in Public Interest Accounting* pp. 97–105.

Meadows, D. H., Meadows, D. L., Randers, J. and Behrens, W. H. (1972) *The Limits of Growth* (London: Pan).

Mill, J. S. (1857) *Principles of Political Economy* Vol. II (London: John W. Parker).

Mill, J. S. (1859) *On Liberty* (London) Reprint (Hardmondsworth: Penguin, 1982)

Mill, J. S. (1863) *Utilitarianism* (London) Reprint (London: Fontana, 1962).

Moorcock, M. (1984) *The Opium General* (London: Harrap)

Munkman, C. A. (1971) *Accountability and Accounting* (London: Hutchinson).

Owen, D. L. (1990) Towards a Theory of Social Investment: a Review Essay, *Accounting, Organizations and Society* pp. 249–266.

Pallot, J. (1987) Infrastructure Assets as a Concept in Governmental Accounting. Paper given to AAANZ Canberra.

Pallot, J. (1991) The Legitimate Concern with Fairness: a Comment, *Accounting, Organizations and Society* pp. 201–208.

Parkin, S. (1989) *Green Parties: an International Guide* (London: Heretic Books).

Pearce, D. (1977) Accounting for the Future, *Futures* pp. 365–374. Reprinted in O'Riordan & Turner (*op cit*).

Pearce, D., Markandya, A. and Barbier, E. B. (1989) *Blueprint for a Green Economy* (London: Earthscan).

Perrin, J. R. (1981) Accounting Research in the Public Sector, in Bromwich, M & Hopwood, A. G. (eds.), *Essays in British Accounting Research* (London: Pitman).

Pezzey, J. (1989) *Definitions of Sustainability* (No. 9) (UK CEED).

Plant, C. and Plant, J. (1991) *Green Business: Hope or Hoax?* (Devon: Green Books).

Porritt, J. (1989) Accounting for the Planet's Survival. *Accountancy* (September) pp. 19–20.

Power, M. (1991) Auditing and Environmental Expertise: Between Protest and Professionalism. *Accounting, Auditing and Accountability Journal* pp. 30–42.

Puxty, A. G. (1986) Social Accounting as Immanent Legitimation: a Critique of Technist Ideology. *Advances in Public Interest Accounting* pp. 95–112.

Raines, J. P. and Jung, C. R. (1986) Knight on Religion and Ethics as Agents of Social Change, *American Journal of Economics and Sociology* (October) pp. 429–439.

Reed, S. A. and Kratchman, S. H. (1990) The Effects of Changing Role Requirements on Accountants. *Advances in Public Interest Accounting* pp. 107–136.

Reilly, B. J. and Kyj, M. J. (1990) Economics and Ethics, *Journal of Business Ethics* (September) pp. 691–698.

Roberts, J. (1991) The Possibilities of Accountability, *Accounting, Organizations and Society* pp. 355–377.

Roberts, J. and Scapens, R. (1985) Accounting Systems and Systems of Accountability, *Accounting, Organizations and Society* pp. 443–456.

Robertson, J. (1978) *The Sane Alternative* (London: James Robertson).

Robertson, J. (1984) Introduction to the British Edition, in Capra and Spretnak (*op cit*.) pp. xxiii–xxx.

Robertson, J. (1985) *Future Work: Jobs, Self-employment and Leisure after the Industrial Age* (Gower/Temple Smith).

Rorty, R. (1980) *Philosophy and the Mirror of Life* (Princetown: Princetown University Press).

Roslender, R. (1990) Sociology and Management Accounting Research, *British Accounting Review* pp. 351–372.

Ryle, M. (1988) *Ecology and Socialism* (London: Radius).

Sandbach, F. (1980) *Environmental Ideology and Policy* (Oxford: Blackwell).

Schumacher, E. F. (1968) Buddhist Economics, *Resurgence* (January–February). Reprinted in Daly, H. E. (ed.) (1980) *Economy, Ecology, Ethics: Essays towards a Steady State Economy* (San Francisco: Freeman) pp. 138–145.

Schumacher, E. F. (1973) *Small is Beautiful* (London: Abacus).

Schumacher, E. F. (1974) *The Age of Plenty: a Christian View* (Edinburgh: St. Andrews Press). Reprinted in Daly, H. E. (ed.) (1980) *Economy, Ecology, Ethics: Essays toward a Steady State Economy* (San Francisco: Freeman) pp. 126–137.

Silverman, D. (1970) *The Theory of Organizations: a Sociological Framework* (London: Heinemann).

Smith, G. A. (1980) The Teleological View of Wealth: a Historical Perspective, Ch. 14 in Daly, H. E. (ed.), *Economy, Ecology, Ethics: Essays toward a Steady State Economy* (San Francisco: Freeman) pp. 215–237.

Specht, L. (1991) What Auditors don't know about Environmental Laws can Hurt them! *Proceedings of the Third Interdisciplinary Perspectives on Accounting Conference*, Vol. 1, pp. 1.12.1–1.12.11.

Teubner, G. (ed.) (1987) *Juridification of Social Spheres* (Berlin: Walter de Gruyter).

Tinker, A. M., (1984a) Theories of the State and the State of Accounting: Economic Reductionism and Political Voluntarism in Accounting Regulation Theory, *Journal of Accounting and Public Policy* pp. 55–74.

Tinker, A. M. (ed.) (1984b) *Social Accounting for Corporations* (Manchester: Manchester University Press).

Tinker, A. M. (1984c) Accounting for Unequal Exchange: Wealth Accumulation versus Wealth Appropriation, in Tinker (ed.) (*op. cit.*).

Tinker, A. M. (1985) *Paper Prophets: a Social Critique of Accounting* (Eastbourne: Holt Saunders).

Tinker, A. M., Merino, B. D. and Neimark, M. D. (1982) The Normative Origins of Positive Theories: Ideology and Accounting Thought, *Accounting Organizations and Society* pp. 167–200.

Tinker, A. M., Neimark, M. and Lehman, C. (1991) Falling down the Hole in the Middle of the Road: Political Quietism in Corporate Social Reporting, *Accounting, Auditing and Accountability Journal* pp. 28–54.

Tricker, R. I. (1983) Corporate Responsibility, Institutional Governance and the Roles of Accounting Standards, in Bromwich, M. and Hopwood, A. G. (eds.), *Accounting Standards Setting—an International Perspective* (London: Pitman).

Turner, R. K. (1987) Sustainable Global Futures: Common Interest, Interdependence, Complexity and Global Possibilities, *Futures* pp. 574–582.

Turner, R. K. (ed.) (1988) *Sustainable Environmental Management: Principles and Practice* (London: Belhaven Press).

Turner, R. K. (1989) Interdisciplinarity and Holism in the Environmental Training of Economists and Planners, Symposium on Education for Economists and Planners, International Environment Institute, University of Malta (December).

Turner, R. K. and Pearce, D. W. (1990) Ethical Foundations of Sustainable Economic Development (London: International Institute for Environment and Development/London Environmental Economics Centre Paper 90–01, March).

United Nations World Commission on Environment and Development (1987) *Our Common Future* (The Brundtland Report) (Oxford: Oxford University Press).

Victor, P. A. (1978) Economics and the Challenge of Environmental Issues, in Leiss, W. (ed.), *Ecology versus Politics in Canada* (Toronto: University of Toronto Press). Reprinted in Daly, H. E. (ed.) (1980) *Economy, Ecology, Ethics: Essays toward a Steady State Economy* (San Francisco: Freeman) pp. 194–214.

Ward, B. (1966) *Spaceship Earth* (Hardmonsworth: Penguin).

Ward, B. (1979) *Progress for a Small Planet* (Hardmonsworth: Penguin).

Zaikov, G. (1986) Political and Economic Problems of Accounting for Ecological Factors in Social Production, *Problems of Economics*.

# 15

## Bankers Debate . . . Should Banks Lend to Companies with Environmental Problems?

*Jerry J. Kopitsky and Errol T. Betzenberger*

## THE CASE *AGAINST* MAKING LOANS WITH ENVIRONMENTAL RISKS

**Jerry J. Kopitsky**

Unfortunately, many manufacturing operations produce some type of waste disposal which is, or can be, classified as hazardous. Those operations are therefore subject to many federal environmental laws and regulations. As a result of these regulations, every financial institution, regardless of size and structure, must consider, as a part of their loan approval process, the ultimate risks and potential liabilities which the financial institution may become involved with.

It is not my intention in this article to discuss, in detail, the various local, state, and federal laws regulating hazardous waste. Instead, I merely want to address the inherent risks to the lender and, therefore, the possible conclusion that financial institutions may be more prudent, in many instances, not to lend to companies that are hazardous waste generators.

### Government Regulations

Environmental laws have existed as far back as 1924. Prior to the 1970s, however, the lender did not have to be overly concerned with government regulations controlling hazardous waste generation and disposal or the potential risks associated with financial businesses targeted by such regulations. Most of the laws governing control were minimal in nature and somewhat haphazardly enforced. However, since the establishment of the Environmental Protection Agency (EPA) in the 1970s and an ever growing public demand to control hazardous substances, national environmental acts have grown substantially.

Reprinted with permission from *The Journal of Commercial Bank Lending*, Vol. 69, No. 11, 1987, pp. 3–13
Copyright © 1987 Robert Morris Associates

*Three major Acts*

From 1970 to the present, there have been no less than 11 environmental laws that affect the private sector. Included in these are at least three major enactments which, when taken separately or combined, can seriously jeopardize a lender's position. They are the Resource Conservation and Recovery Act (RCRA), the Comprehensive Environmental Response, Compensation and Liability Act of 1980 (CERCLA)—also known as Superfund, and The Superfund Amendments and Reauthorization Act of 1986 (SARA).

*Summary descriptions of the Acts*

All the aforementioned acts were established to seek to control the disposal and transport of waste so as to protect human health and the environment.

RCRA gives federal authorities the ability to obtain temporary or permanent injunctions against a business halting facility operations or the right to issue compliance orders suspending or revoking the company's authority to operate.

CERCLA creates and imposes strict liability on the owners or operators of facilities for reimbursement of cleanup and related costs plus damages resulting from the release of a hazardous substance. The liability imposed by CERCLA is limited to $50 million in cost and damages in most instances.

Enacted in 1986, SARA assured that a great number of new sites would fall under CERCLA jurisdiction. Waste generators who previously avoided liability must now worry about becoming targets of CERCLA cleanup actions.

SARA also contains a new provision which allows landowners who acquired contaminated property without actual or constructive knowledge to avoid CERCLA liability by declaring to be an innocent landowner. The so-called 'innocent landowner' can establish a defense to liability where property was acquired after placement of hazardous wastes. However, the purchaser will not be allowed to stand on ignorance alone. Also, despite an innocent landowner's defense, those involved still remain Potentially Responsible Parties (PRPs).

**Impact of Environmental Acts**

One might wonder what all these regulations mean to lenders. If in the broad sense, a loan officer's major responsibilities are to structure a credit facility that meets the needs of the lender and borrower, collateralize such a credit facility, mitigate the risks to his financial institution, and provide alternate sources of repayment of debt other than cash flow (that is, liquidation of collateral), then the impact of environmental acts can be summarized in two words—*excessive risk.*

The impact of these regulations, not to mention unforeseen regulations, can have varying degrees of negative effects on the business viability of a borrower, the value of the borrower's collateral, and the potential loss of the lender's lien status. In addition, in certain instances, they can be a liability to the lender's financial institution causing it to be responsible for cleanup costs associated with the activities of its borrower. As a result, nonproductive costs due to strict environmental regulations can turn a productive loan into a nonperforming one.

## Impact on Business and Lender

Under RCRA, operating permits can be denied. In addition, the borrower may have to make substantial capital improvements to facilities in the form of machinery and equipment, provide worker protection equipment, make operational or production changes, be required to provide bonding for corrective action plans, and so forth. All these requirements could diminish or eradicate cash flow and net profits. Also, the lender's position could weaken as the lender finds himself in the position of possibly having to lend additional funds which could significantly exceed collateral values and future net income or foreclosing.

In the event of a foreclosure, the responsibilities and liabilities imposed by the acts may be imposed on those lenders who foreclosed or instituted actions against collateral. I am referring to those activities such as participating in day-to-day operations, frequent visits, and consulting that result in their ownership of the facility pledged as collateral.

### CERCLA liability

Under CERCLA, the lender's position can deteriorate further due to the broad category of responsible parties or PRPs that may be held liable for damages and costs plus interest.

The bank itself does not want to be put in the position of a PRP either through outright ownership of a contaminated site or by exercising management control to any degree. Active involvement in the daily business affairs of the credit or bank participation on the company's board of directors could lead to designation as a PRP and present or future liability. Regulations are so broadly written that future discovery of contaminations could result in retroactive assignments of guilt for those parties presently or previously involved in ownership or operation of the site.

Conceivably, if a lender as mortgagee initiated foreclosure proceedings and eventually acquired title ownership, the lender, as owner, might be held liable for damages and costs. CERCLA's liability is strict and joint and severable. Any person, including the secured lender, can be held liable for the full cost of the cleanup no matter how limited the lender's involvement.

Presently, the secured lender can avoid CERCLA liability if it does no more than hold a security interest in the contaminated property. However, if the borrower is bankrupt, it appears likely that the federal government would attempt to make recoveries from the lender regardless of its posture. Furthermore, the federal government could commence cleanup operations on the mortgaged property and deprive the owner of the property use.

Perhaps most important, all costs and damages for which a party is liable to the U.S. pursuant to the liability provisions of CERCLA shall constitute a lien in favor of the U.S. Although this lien, at present, is not a super priority lien, it is not too difficult to image what the value of the lender's collateral could be worth. However, regardless of federal liens in general, state law determines the federal lien priority. Presently, four states have super priority lien status over senior perfected debt. They are New Jersey, New Hampshire, Connecticut, and Massachusetts.

### Other risks

In addition to the potential risk for real estate loans, it is conceivable that other assets of a company (that is, receivables, inventory and machinery, and equipment) may become subject to federal and state liens. As more states enact more strenuous environmental laws, the potential exists that other assets of a business will not be available to lenders for recovery of loans.

Finally, if a facility is closed, a secured lender who gains ownership of a facility may be responsible for compliance with elaborate closure procedures, including post-closure care for an average of 30 years following closure.

## OTHER POTENTIAL LIABILITIES TO BUSINESSES AND LENDERS

In addition to the potential adverse impact to a borrower and lender under the environmental acts, a business can be further affected by citizen and worker suits as a result of contaminates causing unforeseen personal damage. The resultant lawsuits and new regulatory environmental acts that might be enacted could conceivably continue to erode a lending institution's ability to recover loans.

Recently, New York City enacted a law which will allow no improvements to existing real estate until asbestos has been removed from the facility. In short, no walls or other structures may be relocated without asbestos cleanup. It is presently estimated that asbestos removal costs in New York City could be as much as $1 million per floor.

## CONCLUSION

I have no doubt that lending institutions will continue to lend to companies that are hazardous waste generators. After all, a great deal of our economy depends on manufactured goods. However, as these credit decisions are being made, it should be recognized that the potential for any loan recoveries can be seriously affected by environmental risks.

Obviously, there are many steps that a financial institution can take to mitigate its exposure; however, in the final analysis, these loans should be recognized for what they are—potentially unsecured. Lenders could be placed in a position of standing by and watching a loan deteriorate beyond recovery as a result of environmental laws and possible financial consequences for their institutions.

# THE CASE *FOR* MAKING LOANS WITH ENVIRONMENTAL RISKS

## Errol T. Betzenberger

REIT, LBO, LDC, and DIDC are alphabet soup to some, but to the banking industry, these are initials that have caused confusion, consternation, and calamity. We are now beset with additional acronyms—EPA, DER, RCRA, CERCLA, and SARA. They will have a far more reaching effect and could potentially affect more banking institutions than all the rest of the alphabet put together.

It's the same old story of changing the rules of the game after play has begun. The Environmental Protection Agency, Department of Environmental Resources, Resource Conservation and Recovery Act, Comprehensive Environmental Response Compensation and Liability Act of 1980 (Superfund), and the Superfund Amendments and Reauthorization Act of 1986 sound more ominous than their cute abbreviations. But what do they have to do with banking? After all, we run a pollution-free and environmentally safe industry. But all financial institutions that provide commercial/industrial lending are affected regarding future lending practices as well as existing credits be they to a multinational chemical company or to a mom and pop gasoline station.

### Implications of Environmental Issues for Lenders

How important is environmental impact and how serious a problem do we as an industry face? This answer can be gauged by the number of seminars being offered and the fact that most banking publications have had at least one recent article about environmental contamination and lending. Read the articles and attend the seminars, or you will experience a rude awakening one day.

Should you or should you not make loans to businesses with actual or potential environmental problems to overcome? I feel strongly that lenders must continue to make these kinds of loans. But they should do so only when they have taken the appropriate steps to protect their bank and their loan applicants effectively.

#### State legislation

Every state has legislation concerning clean air, clean water, hazardous waste disposal, and worker notification. New Jersey has adopted an Environmental Cleanup Responsibility Act (ECRA), the most comprehensive in the nation, with many other states either passing or actively pursuing legislation. Some states have deed notification requirements that call for information to be included in the property deed concerning hazardous waste disposal or storage.

#### Significance for banking

What has all this to do with banking? Money, pure and simple, either through delinquencies, foreclosures, bankruptcies, or to deep pocket lawsuits aimed at the bank as an owner/operator of a contaminated site. Another possibility is a 'superlien' created by state or federal law that would take precedence over all prior liens, effectively placing the bank in a secondary lien position until mandated cleanup has been achieved and paid for.

## Looking at Existing Portfolio

Before discussing problems connected with future applications and loans, we must first look at our existing loan portfolio for potential environmental impact problems. If you are actively pursuing foreclosure action on a commercial/industrial loan, use the old cautionary approach: Stop, look, and listen.

*Stop* your action long enough to determine the primary and secondary business of your client and the impact on the environment. Does the client manufacture, store, transport, or otherwise handle hazardous substances?

If a yes answer is even a remote possibility, *look* at the site with wide open eyes for potential environmental problems.

Explain your fears to your legal counsel or hire an environmental engineer, and *listen* to their advice and input before continuing your action because if you step in and become an owner/operator you could be liable for the entire cleanup cost.

*Goals of an environmental assessment*

An environmental assessment should:

(1) Identify past practices.
(2) Evaluate regulatory compliance.
(3) Identify future problems.

It should include:

(1) Document screening.
(2) Site visitation and inspection.
(3) Site testing and evaluation.
(4) Recommendations to correct or forestall problems.

You may feel it is patently unfair for an innocent lending institution to bear the brunt of a costly cleanup program. However, the government feels that it is unfair to use public monies to correct environmental problems thereby enriching the lending institution. One reason for attempting to correct the problem on a private basis: It has been estimated the cost of cleanup will be 30% to 60% higher if undertaken by governmental agencies. It also will be much slower.

Once a problem is discovered, Pandora's box has been opened. Unfortunately from our standpoint, we are light years away from any definitive court decisions which will provide case law for guidance. The few cases now in litigation are sending conflicting signals regarding possible liability. By the time all the appeal processes have been exhausted, many of us will be retired.

*Need for an environmental risk rating*

If you are fortunate enough not to be involved in or close to a foreclosure action, it is still necessary to review your existing loan portfolio and assign an environmental risk rating to each loan. Two main purposes for flagging existing credits with a risk rating are to provide you with a forewarning of problems and to forearm you if any existing accounts request additional funding. Those accounts classified as a higher risk will require special handling to minimize the bank's exposure. If you are forewarned, you may be able to assist the client in correcting the problem before it becomes too great.

## Why Banks Must Continue to Lend Despite Environmental Liabilities

Obviously none of us today would finance the conversion of Love Canal into a housing site, but many of us are actively involved in financing the transformation of old industrial sites into housing tracts, condo units, or shopping malls. These purposes were approved without a second thought but second thought time has been forced on us.

The thrust of many seminars, books, and articles is that banking can no longer get involved in these projects because of the possibility of future problems. However, banking has too important a role to adopt such an attitude. By the same token we have too important a responsibility to our communities, employees, and stockholders to continue business as usual under our old policies and procedures.

The first automobile repossession was probably traumatic, but we didn't get out of the auto business. The depression taught us the folly of non-amortizing mortgages, but we stayed in the real estate business. Policies and procedures were adopted to minimize risk, and rate structures were adjusted to compensate for risk. Now we find ourselves on the eve of a new era of problem lending. Policies and procedures must be adopted to minimize risk and rate structures modified to compensate for risk.

*Two fallacies*

Two fallacies being touted today are environmental liability insurance protection and negative covenants. To begin with, liability coverage is becoming prohibitively expensive to acquire for most industries let alone those handling hazardous substances, and negative covenants won't be worth the paper they are written on.

For instance, the loan commitment may require liability insurance and contain negative clauses whereby your borrower faithfully promises to control environmental contamination. In real life, the borrower's liability carrier could refuse to renew (if coverage could be placed originally) or an accident could occur. These, of course, trigger your default provisions, and the bank can exercise its foreclosure options. No one has ever made money by foreclosing. And it will be very difficult to dispose of property without taking title—remember the owner/operator liability. Prudent banking requires the inclusion of these clauses, but a realistic approach is also necessary.

## How to Approve a Loan

How then do we go about approving a loan that may have future environmental problems attached to it. They key phrase is 'may have future environmental problems attached to it' because no one should pursue a loan that obviously will create problems. No longer will we be able to accept a commercial/industrial application, verify credit, calculate cash flow, evaluate an appraisal, and have a settlement all in the twinkling of an eye.

### The delay factor

Consider the delay factor. It's one of the first items to address. Anything additional to be considered in regard to loan applications and commitments always adds a degree of delay, and environmental issues are no exception. They could warrant no more than a momentary pause while reviewing an application to substantial delays encountered waiting for environmental inspections or responses from local and state agencies. Delay always increases expense.

### The ABCs of the application procedure

The following ABCs may help you develop a procedural guide and smooth out your application procedure. They probably cover the minimum questions to ask or facts to consider during the application procedure.

Applications require an in-depth discussion of the borrower's plans for the site and the possibility of future problems. Determine what the borrower knows of the previous usage of the site.

Before the applicant signs an agreement to purchase, require the seller or selling agent to provide in writing the previous history of the sites, its usage, and any contamination problems.

Caution the borrower to verify the information with pertinent state agencies, the EPA, or DER. Under the Freedom of Information Act, all incidents, investigations, permits, or pending actions must be disclosed. This requirement should be included as part of your commitment agreement.

Determine if any side collateral is available for additional protection against future impairment of the primary collateral. Perfect your lien.

Environmental audits will identify past practices, evaluate current regulatory compliance, and identify future problem areas. Require a current audit prepared by a qualified and reputable environmental engineering firm.

Face the fact that you may have to decline an otherwise qualified applicant because of unfavorable environmental information.

Gasoline stations are a prime potential source of contamination simply because of their function and because there are so many in place. Require your client to provide certification of tank age and to have a pressure test to ensure tank stability.

**H**old up any imminent foreclosure proceedings until after verification that no environmental cleanup problems exist.

**I**mplement immediately an environmental risk rating system for your existing commercial/industrial loan portfolio before problems occur.

**J**oin with representative banking groups and lobbyists to seek legislative amendments offering protection and secured lenders.

**K**eep in mind that the original aims of banking are to service our communities and customers and to earn a profit, but don't let either motive unduly influence your decision.

**L**ook for obvious site problems such as discarded drums, discolored vegetation, stained soil, and waste disposal areas, but don't substitute your judgment for that of a qualified expert.

**M**ake sure your borrower has the capacity to carry the debt load if a problem occurs.

**N**ever assume anything.

**O**bserve the first qualification of a good loan interviewer: ask questions.

**P**ut these regulations into perspective, and make informed, logical decisions based on facts.

**Q**ualified environmental engineers will not be inexpensive and may not work as rapidly as the buyer or seller expect but will be a necessary step in the application process.

**R**enovations to older existing office buildings or schools may encounter asbestos material. Asbestos abatement regulations require removal, enclosure, or encapsulation. This is an expensive process.

**S**tart the application process with an explanation of the need for various inspections and reports. Explain your concerns about past, present, or future contamination.

**T**ake notice of the extra time, effort, and potential loss factors connected with commercial/industrial loans and adjust the rate accordingly.

**U**nqualified waivers will not be obtainable from either state or federal agencies as to site purity. Neither will environmental engineers issue unqualified site reports. No one will be willing to certify compliance or completion of site cleanup because of their future liability.

**V**ery few of our institutions will escape without some loss experience. But we have existed with losses in the past, and by adjusting procedures, we will be able to minimize losses in the future.

**W**eigh alternatives as to existing loan problems. Remember your first loss is usually the best and cheapest loss. Don't take title to properties that may require extensive and expensive cleanup. Also remember that if the property value does outweigh cleanup costs, you probably won't be able to get a clean bill of health from any agency and will still be liable in the future.

**X**enophobic reaction, burying your head in the sand, or denying that problems could exist will only aggravate your potential environmental losses.

**Y**ou must realize that lending rules have changed, and if you don't adapt, losses will increase.

**Z**ero in on the possibilities of increased lending opportunities. If your competition declines loans out of hand, you may be able to acquire these loans if you plan and price accordingly.

## CONCLUSION

For all citizens, environmental contamination is a major source of concern but poses special problems for lenders. Now may be the time to add another factor to loan pricing; in addition to credit risk, rate risk, and market risk another risk category must now be added—environmental risk. Since some financial entity will continue to lend to companies that will perhaps face environmental risks, this may be the way to do so profitably.

## NOTE

This seminar, held in Philadelphia on December 16, 1986, was presented by JACA Corp., management & environmental consultants in Fort Washington, Pa.

# 16

# Not Paying for Our Past: Government, Business and the Debate on Contaminated Land in the UK

*Josephine Maltby*

It is difficult to overemphasize the extent to which battles over the availability of information played a fundamental role in environmental controversy (Hays, 1987: 537).

Since the 1990 Environmental Protection Act, there has been controversy in the UK about the extent to which businesses should be required to identify and clean up contaminated land. This paper examines the controversy in the context of wider debates about the function of corporate social reporting.

## INTRODUCTION

Various attempts have been made to explain the mechanisms prompting firms to make social and environmental disclosures. Tinker *et al.* (1991) identify five successive epochs in academic views of corporate social reporting (CSR). In the 1960s, companies' disclosures were seen as motivated by the interests of investors, prompted by critics of unsound stewardship such as Briloff. In the early 1970s, the 'caring society' era, CSR humanized capitalism by reporting the social costs of corporate activity. This was succeeded in the late 1970s by what Tinker *et al.* (1991) term the 'caring market' perspective; as opposed to narrow views of the market efficiency; research into CSR attempted to demonstrate that 'markets reacted positively to socially responsible behaviour' (Tinker *et al.*, 1991: 34). In the Reagan–Thatcher era of the 1980s, 'market re-regulation' reverted to the Friedmanite assumptions that shareholders' only interest was in profit maximization and that markets would identify and punish undesirable behaviour by managers. Monitoring of agents by self-interested principals meant that CSR was unnecessary. The last and current epoch identified and exemplified by Tinker *et al.* (1991) is one

Reproduced by permission of John Wiley & Sons, Ltd from Maltby, J., *Business Strategy and the Environment*, Vol. 4, No. 2, 1995, pp. 73–85
© 1995 John Wiley & Sons, Ltd and ERP Environment

of 'radical critique', which uses varying forms of social disclosure to document crises of capitalism and analyse the uses of CSR as an 'ideological weapon' (Tinker *et al.*, 1991: 39).

The third phase identified by Tinker *et al.* (1991), the 'caring market' approach, continues to command support as a means of analysing firms' CSR strategies. Preston and Post (1975) refer to the 'complex and interpenetrating relationships' which exist between large corporations and society. Each 'may take into account and seek to influence' the other's goals. Preston and Post (1975) regard this as an unproblematic relationship, devoid of the ideological implications of competing market contract or exploitation (i.e. Marxist) models of business in society. In their analysis, the organization uses a 'scanning' process to identify the social concerns that impinge on its activities. It then builds into its operations relevant control and accounting criteria and devises external reporting methods that disclose its social performance against targets. Legitimacy theory and stakeholder theory may both be seen as fitting into this framework. With different emphases, each explains CSR as a corporation's attempt to respond to society's demands.

Legitimacy theory 'suggests that organizations aim to produce congruence between the social values inherent (or implied) in their activities and societal norms...Corporate social disclosures may then be conceived as reacting to the environment where they are employed to legitimize corporate actions' (Guthrie and Parker, 1989). Patten (1992) used a case study—the effect on oil company environmental disclosures of 1989 *Exxon Valdez* oil spill—to test legitimacy theory. He found a significant increase in such disclosures in the annual reports of oil companies between 1988 and 1989 and concluded that 'at least for environmental disclosures, threats to firm's legitimacy do entice the firm to include more social responsibility information in its annual report' (Patten, 1992: 475).

Stakeholder theory refines legitimacy theory by narrowing its focus. The firm's stakeholders are 'any group or individual who can affect or is affected by the achievement of the firm's objectives' (Freeman, 1984)—investors and business contacts, employees, government and pressure groups. The objective of the firm is to 'balance the conflicting demands of various stakeholders' (Roberts, 1992), rather than to lubricate its relationship with society as a whole. Roberts looks at a sample of 'major corporations' and finds a significant relationship between CSR and three sets of variables—stakeholder power, strategic posture (i.e. the importance attached by the firm to CSR) and economic performance. What stakeholder and legitimacy theory have in common is the view of the firm as *reacting* to social demands and expectations.

Guthrie and Parker (1989) test the validity of legitimacy theory by tracking disclosures within a single company (Broken Hill Pty) over the period 1885–1985 and attempting to correlate them with contemporaneous events inside and outside the company. Stakeholder and legitimacy theory suggest that a pattern of disclosure in response to social concern should have emerged, but this seems not to be the case; the company has sometimes made reports where external events did not seem to warrant them, and is sometimes 'secretive and uninformative'. Guthrie and Parker (1989) concur with Tinker *et al.* (1991) that CSR disclosures are better explained by 'the political economy theory of accounting'. Corporate disclosure is 'a proactive process of information provided from management's perspective'. Disclosure is a contested terrain and information is provided or withheld as it serves or hinders the achievement of the firm's objectives. Firms do not merely respond to social demands for information; they seek to provide information that will further their interests and to suppress that which is harmful to them. This involves their active participation in creating the regime under which they will be required to make disclosures.

Hays (1987), writing about environmental politics in the USA, points to the significance of information as a weapon to be used by environmentalists and their opponents. 'Industry's most fundamental tactic (in opposing environmental movements)...was to control the acquisition, assessment, dissemination, and application of information. Every environmental issue was laced with technical information ... (M)uch of the strategy of the environmental movement and much of the drama and outcome of environmental controversy lay in the use of information and attempts to control it' (Hays, 1987: 319). Hays' account of the tactics used by businesses in what he calls the 'environmental opposition'—for instance, public-relations campaigns, the formation of 'tame' industry-sponsored environmental groups and educational programmes—is a reminder that corporate social disclosures are made through a variety of media, not only through financial statements.

The present paper examines the debate which began in the UK in the late 1980s about requiring the disclosure of ownership of contaminated land and about the ascription of legal liability for cleaning up contamination. This is only one of many debates surrounding the development of environmental reporting/accounting and it spills over from financial reporting proper (the reflection of environmental costs and liabilities in published financial statements) into other forms of disclosure—the publication of data in government registers, coverage in news media of legal liabilities, the disclosure to lenders and insurers of risks and contingencies. It is relevant to theories of CSR as evidence of the part played by corporations in setting the agenda for reporting. Both stakeholder and legitimacy theory assume implicitly that the pressures for disclosure that emanate from society and are mediated by government are reflected in corporate information. The story of the debate over contaminated land shows businesses as active players, creating legal and disclosure regimes that will promote their interests.


## DEFINING THE PROBLEM

### Identifying contaminated land

Contamination of land has been defined as 'the introduction or presence in the environment of alien substances or energy' (Beckett, 1993, quoting Royal Commission on Environmental Pollution, 1984). Heavy industry is not the only culprit; agriculture and transport are also implicated, and apparently innocuous activities may have undesirable consequences. 'Greenwich Council excavated a site of a former dental appliance manufacturer and found that (in addition to false teeth) the soil was heavily contaminated with mercury used to make dental amalgam' (POST, 1993: 11).

Contamination is 'a necessary, but not sufficient, condition for pollution' (POST, 1993); alien substances 'become pollutants only when their distribution, concentration or physical behaviour are such as to have undesirable or deleterious consequences' (POST, 1993). Much contamination has not been demonstrated to be harmful. 'Even when soils contain such extremely high concentrations of a contaminant that vegetables grown in them have at least 10 times the contaminant level of normal urban soils, it can be impossible to demonstrate any hazard at all to consumers of crops' (Cairney, 1993: 3).

On the other hand, contamination can involve pollution on a disastrous scale. Between 1942 and 1952, the Hooker Electrochemical Company dumped 210,000 tons of chemical waste, including caustic substances, alkalis and solvents, into Love Canal in Upper New York State. The dump was sealed with a layer of clay and subsequently used as the site of a school and housing estate. By the mid-1970s, the waste containers had begun to corrode and a series of heavy rains washed the chemicals into underground waterways and thence in gardens and cellars. In 1976, chemical contamination from Love Canal was detected in Lake Ontario. Levine (1982) documents the campaign undertaken by residents which culminated in the admission by the New York State commissioner of health that there was 'a great and imminent peril to the health of the general public residing at or near the site' (Levine, 1982: 7) and the evacuation in 1980 of 700 families. The story of Love Canal powerfully illustrates a number of problems of dealing with contaminated land.

### Contaminated land is not readily identifiable

In many instances, contamination does not affect the appearance of a site, or cosmetic measures can disguise its presence (Residents complained in 1952 of smells from the dump, but there were few protests after the site was capped in 1953, until government investigations were undertaken in 1976).

### Contamination can subsist long after the contaminating activity has ended

Love Canal was producing casualties more than 20 years after Hooker had ceased dumping. Many contaminants—not only radioactive contaminants—are long-lived. (POST quotes the case of villages in Somerset where lead and cadmium thrown up by Roman mine workings still make garden produce unsafe to eat.)

### Information and record-keeping are crucial to awareness and contamination

Land may change owners and uses after initial contamination has occurred—in this instance from waste dump to housing estate. The original owner may deliberately conceal (or be ignorant of) the condition of the site, or it may be thought irrelevant by the buyer. Subsequent buyers may have no idea of the site's history. 'By the mid-1970s, only a few old-timers remembered the whole history of the canal that had turned into a schoolyard and open fields' (Levine, 1982: 13).

*Ownership of contaminated land can impose high financial costs*

In addition to personal claims, Hooker faced a claim of $125 million from the US Environmental Protection Agency. Clean-up work on the site cost a further $1.3 billion.

## Quantifying the costs of contamination

The costs of cleaning up contamination are not only high; they are also subject to considerable uncertainty for a number of reasons. One factor is the difficulty in identifying sites which contain contaminants without carrying out thorough (and expensive) chemical analysis. A historical study of a site will identify potentially contaminating uses to which it has been put; to ascertain the actual level of contamination would require a site visit and analysis of soil and water samples. POST (1993: 27) estimates that this may cost £8,000–30,000 per hectare.

The interpretation of the data obtained will vary—a second reason for differing estimates of the extent of the problem. There is no world-wide consensus about the stage at which action needs to be taken if contamination is detected. One view is that if land contains substances which would not naturally occur, it should be restored to its pristine state, so that it is safe for any purpose, including sensitive uses such as growing food crops. This approach to the identification and treatment of land is described as the 'multifunctional' approach (POST, 1993: 24). Alternatively, the view taken of contamination may depend on the actual or intended use of the land; contamination which was acceptable on a factory site might require immediate clean-up if detected on a housing estate. This is the 'site-specific' or 'suitable for use' approach.

Finally, the costs of contamination will depend on the technology used for cleaning it up. Beckett and Cairney (1993) distinguish between two main approaches. The older and cheaper is the 'engineering-based' approach, which attacks contamination by isolating it physically. Most simply, contaminated soil may be dug out and tipped elsewhere; if left on site, it may be encapsulated or covered with impervious material.

Engineering approaches have the merits of being technically straightforward and quick to perform, but they typically contain or transfer pollution instead of eliminating it. 'Innovative techniques', in contrast, destroy contaminants—for instance, by using ore extraction, thermal stripping. In the USA, recent legislation has made the preferred option 'treatment (which) permanently and significantly reduces the volume, toxicity or mobility of the hazardous substances' (Stanford and Yang, 1989: 1.41).

## LEGAL REACTIONS TO CONTAMINATED LAND

### The US position

The US government's response to Love Canal was the enactment of the Comprehensive Environmental Response, Compensation and Liability Act (CERCLA, widely known as Superfund) in 1980, with funding of $1.6 billion. CERCLA identifies polluted sites and provides regulators with powers to seek clean-up through the courts by the responsible parties or to carry out clean-up and subsequently recover its costs. Its first five years of operation saw 'agreement of approximately $600 million in private party clean-ups, initiation of 580 removal actions at priority sites, completion of 470 remedial investigations/feasibility studies...filing of over 200 lawsuits by the government, and consideration by the EPA of 10 sites to be cleaned up'. (Meenan, 1993: 269–270). CERCLA was reauthorized by Congress in 1986 under SARA (Superfund Amendment and Reauthorization Act), which 'established a much more proscriptive program with a definite set of expectations' (Fortuna, 1989). Clean-up activity under CERCLA attracted criticism for being slow and uncertain; a five-fold increase ($8.5 billion) in its funding was intended to accelerate its operations. Deadlines were attached to certain activities and community involvement in identifying sites for clean-up was increased (for details, see Meenan, 1993).

The liability for contamination under the Superfund created anxieties among the business community in the USA for a number of reasons. The persons potentially liable for the costs of clean-up include 'current and past *owners* and *operators* of the contaminated site (in some cases including: parent companies; individual shareholders and directors; predecessor companies; and financial institutions exercising a degree of ownership and control' (McKenna & Co., 1989: 90). Liability is 'strict, joint and several, retroactive and essentially without regard to causation. ... Virtually no defences to liability are provided in statute.' (McKenna & Co., 1989). This means that not only are industrialists exposed to liability for actions with which they may claim to be only tenuously connected; providers of finance may also be implicated. A 'secured lender exemption' included in CERCLA does not extend to lenders who participate in the management of business. In *United States v Fleet Factors Corporation*, the definition of 'participation' was held to include the involvement of a secured creditor if 'it could affect hazardous waste disposal decisions if it so chose' (Kravitch, 1992).

The effects of US legislation have been the subject of controversy. Critics have pointed to the high costs, which result not only from clean-up efforts, but also from litigation, especially disputes between insurers. Litigation has also resulted in long delays in carrying out clean-up operations. In 1994, the Clinton administration began to modify the stringent legislative provisions by moving towards a 'suitable for use' approach, instead of the original multifunctional basis for clean-up, and by creating a fund, levied on insurers, which would meet a proportion of the clean-up costs. This was intended to give insurers a measure of certainty about their liabilities and help to clear the backlog of court cases as insurers and landowners argued about liability (*The Economist*, 7 May 1994).

Supporters of US legislation claim that, but virtue of the sanctions it imposes, the US regime has given businesses a powerful incentive to minimize land contamination and introduce safer practices. Fortuna (1989: 1.5) asserts that a unique feature of the US approach is 'shifting the relationship of costs and effectiveness by ensuring that we first establish the necessary level of effectiveness and then determine the least-cost method of achieving it, not the converse'. This has necessarily resulted in expense and delay, but as McKenna & Co. (1989: 76) comment '(i)t has also resulted in managements highly concerned to avoid such liabilities in the future' and hence created an incentive to minimize pollution. The ENDS Report (August 1994) comes to similar conclusions. 'Superfund has been an expensive and only partly successful experiment. But one of its chief merits has been to flush the debate on contaminated land...into the open'.

## The UK situation

No comprehensive survey of UK contaminated sites has been carried out, although partial studies have been carried out in Wales and Cheshire. On the basis of the information available, experts giving evidence to the Parliamentary Environment Select Committee in 1993 'estimated that there were between 50,000 and 100,000 potentially contaminated sites in the UK...more recent independent evidence suggests between 100,000 and 200,000 hectares' (POST, 1993: 11). POST (1993) concedes that 'only a small proportion of potentially contaminated sites, perhaps a few percent, pose an immediate threat to human health and the environment'. This still represents, however, a significant number of hazards. The documented cases that POST describes (1993: 6–7) are dramatic enough. They include: a landfill site releasing explosive gas; a petrol station leaking petrol over an area of 20,000 m²; and an underground fire on the site of a former steelworks which burned for five years and required expenditure of £1 million to contain.

No statutory guidance on land contamination was formulated in the UK before the 1990 Environmental Protection Act (EPA). Unlike Germany, Denmark, the Netherlands, Canada and the USA, the UK had no statutory definition of contamination. Voluntary guidelines were produced under the auspices of the Department of the Environment in the 1970s and 1980s, but were criticized for their limited scope—they covered only 20 contaminants—vagueness and inconsistency. Beckett and Cairney (1993: 69) describe the UK as having a 'free market' approach to the issue, compared with the countries mentioned earlier where 'more vigorous legislation and soil quality standards exist, where government funding for technology trials and reclamation is more abundant, and where the emphasis is on removing or reducing hazards to the wider environment'. The absence of government stimulus to achievement was, according to Beckett and Cairney, perhaps also reflected in a British preference for 'cost-effective' engineering-based solutions over innovative solutions.

## The UK legal regime: the EPA provisions

The EPA was a response to a general public perception that the UK Government was not doing enough to protect the environment. Its major contributions were contained in Parts I and II of the Act—the introduction of a system of integrated pollution control and extension of the potential criminal and civil liability of polluters. Part VIII of the Act, dealing with miscellaneous provisions, contained the first UK legislative provisions relating to contaminated land. EPA Section 143 placed a duty on local authorities to compile 'public registers of land which had been subject to contamination'. The wording is significant. The Government working party whose findings prompted the legislation concluded that it would be prohibitively slow and expensive to investigate the actual state of all UK sites. Instead, registration would be based on a site's history. If it had been subject to one of a list of 16 'contaminative uses' (see Table 1), it would qualify for registration. Because registration was based on past use, a site could not be deleted from the register if it were subsequently cleaned up. Local authorities would compile registers on the basis of desk research; owners of land would not be entitled to be informed about their inclusion, although they, like the rest of the public, would be allowed to inspect the registers.

Table 1.   Uses of land which may give rise to contamination (1991)

1.  Agriculture
    Burial of diseased livestock

2.  Extractive industry
    Extraction, handling and storage of carbonaceous materials

3.  Energy industry
    Producing gas from coal, lignite or oil

4.  Production of metals
    Production, refining or recovery of metals (manufacture or refining of lead or steel or an alloy of lead or steel)

5.  Production of non-metals and their products
    Manufacture of asbestos

6.  Glass-making and ceramics

7.  Production and use of chemicals
    Production, refining or recovery or storage of petroleum or petrochemicals. Manufacture, refining of other chemicals, excluding minerals

8.  Engineering and manufacturing processes
    Manufacture of metal goods; storage, manufacture or testing of explosives; manufacture and repair of electrical and electronic components

9.  Food processing
    Manufacture of pet foods or animal feedstuffs

10. Paper pulp and printing

11. Timber and timber products
    Chemical treatment and coating

12. Textile industry
    Preparing, treating and working leather; fulling, bleaching and dyeing

13. Rubber industry

14. Infrastructure
    Dismantling, repairing, maintaining railway rolling stock, marine vessels, road and air transport

15. Waste disposal
    Sewage treatment; storage, treatment and disposal of sludge, waste, scrap and radioactive material

16. Miscellaneous
    Dry cleaning; laboratories: demolition of buildings used for any of the scheduled activities

The consultation paper produced by the Department of the Environment (DoE) in May 1991 set out the perceived uses of registration. Registers would 'alert local authorities, landowners and potential purchasers or developers' to the chance of contamination; they would also be relevant to the needs of numerous other potentially interested parties, ranging from emergency services to 'insurers, financial institutions and others involved in land transactions and valuations'. It was recognized that registration might cause 'blight and alarm' by identifying land as contaminated, but '(i)t should be recognized that the potential for blight and alarm is always present. Much of the information to be included on registers is already public knowledge or could easily be discerned when sites are investigated... (I)n all but the very short term, it is better for everyone concerned to be aware of possible contamination' (DoE, 1991).

Registration of contaminated land may have seemed an obvious procedure to the DoE, acting on the recommendations of the House of Commons Environment Committee (1993) refers to 'an increasing consensus that... registers of contaminated sites are an essential first step' in tackling contamination. Registers or lists of sites have been in existence for some years in the USA, Germany and the Netherlands. However, reactions among certain sectors in the UK ranged from fear to indignation. Chakravorty (1992) referred to 'an element of panic amongst professionals involved one way or another in the property business'. The National Westminster Bank warned, in tones of dignified regret, that 'prudent financiers will stay away, as they always have done from areas of uncertainty, and neither the national economy or the environment will benefit' (Thompson, 1992). Property developers were concerned: 'Urban development corporations and some local authorities in the old industrial heartlands such as the West Midlands have told the DoE that the majority of land in their areas would be entered on the registers and would be open to the threat of blight' (ENDS Report, February, 1992).

In the consultation period before the proposed setting up of registers in April 1992, the UK Government was fiercely lobbied by interest groups. It was claimed that too many contaminative uses had been specified, that owners would suffer if they were not informed, but above all that 'the word *contaminative* could be misconstrued, thus creating concern (in some instances unnecessary concern) among all landowners and particularly the general public. This, possibly excessive, concern could result in over-reaction to the situation with, in some instances, catastrophic consequences for the owner of the property' (Thompson, 1992: 7). Land-owners, in other words, feared that the disclosure of additional information about the state of their property would depress its value as the market responded to the risks of high clean-up costs. The demise of the Mountleigh property group in 1992 was partly blamed on its failure to sell the Merry Hill shopping centre. The American buyers withdrew on finding the site, on an old railway sidings next to a decommissioned steelworks, to be potentially contaminated (*Financial Times*, 27 May 1992).

The UK Government reacted by delay and then by watering down its proposals. The April 1992 deadline was waived and a further consultation paper was issued in July 1992. The list of contaminative uses was cut to eight (listed in Table 2), which was expected to reduce the area of land registered to 10–15% of that previously envisaged. The format of the proposed registers was altered. They were to be in two

Table 2.   Specified contaminative uses (1992)

1. Manufacture of gas, coke or bituminous material from coke

2. Manufacture or refining of lead or steel or an alloy of lead or steel

3. Manufacture of asbestos or asbestos products

4. Manufacture, refining or recovery of petroleum or its derivatives, other than extraction from petroleum-bearing ground

5. Manufacture, refining or recovery of other chemicals, excluding minerals

6. Final deposit in or on land of household, commercial or industrial waste...other than waste consisting of ash, slag, clinker, rock, wood, gypsum, railway ballast, peat, bricks, tiles, concrete, glass, other minerals or dredging spoil; or where the waste is used as a fertilizer or in order to condition the land in some other beneficial manner.

7. Treatment at a fixed installation of household, commercial or industrial waste...by chemical or thermal means

8. Use as a scrap metal store

parts, Part A entries dealing with untreated land and Part B with land that had undergone treatment or investigation. David Trippier, the Minister of State for the Environment, 'confirmed that damage to property prices was at the root of the decision. He said "The Government were concerned about suggestions that land values would be unfairly blighted because of the perception of the registers"' (*The Guardian*, 12 March 1992). Environmentalists expressed surprise that the UK Government had addressed the 'unfairness' by removing several of the most polluting uses of land from the register—for instance, sewage works, petrol stations and tanneries (ENDS Report, August 1992).

In March 1993 the UK Government announced that, as a result of the second round of consultations, it had decided to withdraw its proposals for registers altogether. Three principal criticisms of the registers had prompted this. The use of *potentially* contaminating activities as a basis for registration was held to be misleading; some actually clean sites would be included and some actually contaminated ones omitted. The use of *past* contamination as a criterion would make it impossible to remove cleaned sites from the register. Thirdly, 'when sites are identified as actually contaminated, it remains unclear in some instances what action should be taken, what remediation measures should be carried out and by whom, which regulatory authorities should be involved, and where the liability for the cost of remediation or compensation should fall' (DoE, 24 March 1993).

None of the three objectives was insuperable. An extension of the list of contaminative activities might have addressed the first two, if taken in conjunction with a clear distinction between Part A and Part B registration. The third point, as will be discussed in the following, is valid, but there was no clear reason for the debate about liability to hold back registration; the issue of whether land may be contaminated and the issue of responsibility for its condition are separate and distinct. The UK Government announced itself deterred, however, and set up a further enquiry, this time 'a review of the legal powers of regulatory public bodies to control and tackle land pollution' (DoE, 1993).

# THE UK DEBATE OVER LIABILITY

Despite this vigorous temporizing by the UK Government, contaminated land continued to cause anxiety to the business community. The new cause for concern was the Green Paper on liability and compensation for environmental damage published by the European Commission in May 1993. This proposed a 'Community-wide system of civil liability for environmental damage' (Commission of the European Communities, 1993).

Civil liability may be fault-based or strict. Fault-based liability requires proof that the liable party caused damage by negligence or by committing a wrongful act. In the case of environmental damage, fault will tend to be determined by reference to environmental regulations and also to the current state of technical and scientific knowledge—for instance, about the riskiness of discharges. Strict liability, on the other hand, requires only that the injured party can prove a connection between the action taken and the damage caused. The Green Paper proposed that liability should be harmonized throughout the EC and should be strict, enforcing the so-called polluter pays principle. Where no liable party could be identified, or where the polluter was unable to pay, damages and remediation costs would be met out of a central fund, along the lines of that established by CERCLA. The Green Paper argued that harmonization was necessary to remove the competitive distortions that arose when some members' laws were more lenient than others. It recognized the drawbacks of strict liability—in particular its potentially high costs—but concluded that it would 'increase incentives for better risk management and provide legal certainty for ... enterprises subject to such a regime' (DoE, 1993: 25). A strict liability regime would need the limits of liability to be clearly defined, in terms of the economic sectors involved (e.g. certain hazardous industries) and perhaps also the maximum financial costs entailed. In addition to a joint compensation fund for cases where damages could not be recouped, the Green Paper proposed a compulsory insurance requirement for certain industries.

The Green Paper (and the EC's 1991 Draft Directive on civil liability for damage caused by waste) increased business anxiety and Government perplexity over contaminated land yet further. Five significant sets of proposals appeared in rapid succession, culminating in the production in late 1994 of a Government policy statement, *A Framework for Contaminated Land*. They deserve attention as an illustration of the shifting interplay between business and government, and as a case study of corporations attempting to control information disclosure in the furtherance of their interests.

## Advisory Committee on Business and the Environment: Report on the Financial Sector Working Group (February 1993)

The Advisory Committee on Business and the Environment (ACBE) was formed in 1991 by the DoE and Department of Trade and Industry to allow the UK Government to 'engage in closer dialogue with business on environmental policy'. It established a Financial Sector Working Group in January 1992 'to consider and advise on how financial institutions can encourage and assist their customers to improve their environmental performance; the implications for the sector itself of developments in environmental policy and regulation; and the debate on how best to apportion liability for environmental damage (ACBE, 1993a). The Group's composition reflected its title; of its 14 members, four were from a bank or building society, two from insurance companies, one was a lawyer and one an accountant.

The Group's report begins by noting the current low level of environmental disclosure and calling for companies to report on their environmental performance. It 'welcomes in principle' land registration, but expresses concern that '(e)ntries on the registers may distort land values by hindering—or even effectively preventing—some businesses or individuals from raising capital on the land' (ACBE, 1993a: 23). The term *contaminative use* could be misconstrued, and the Group accordingly recommends a title such as *Land Use Registers*. Landowners should be given notice if their land is to be included on the register, and an appeals system must be introduced.

On liability, the Group reviews the possibilities for change mooted by the EC and opposes most of them. Intriguingly, its discussion of liability hints that environmental issues are forcing a divergence between the interests of industry and finance. Lenders and insurers (reluctantly) operate in a strict liability regime; industry would oppose it. Banks are concerned that they 'could be faced with paying for their customers' liabilities', and they would like to see a statutory obligation for borrowers and vendors to disclose information about contamination to lenders and purchasers (ACBE, 1993a: 20).

The discussion of liability in relation to industry sounds a rather querulous note. Extensions of strict liability on sectoral basis 'would *unfairly* (my italics) categorize industries and subject them to differing concepts of liability based on potential rather than actual risks' (ACBE, 1993a: 20). (The distinction between a potential and an actual risk is subtle). An EC proposal that 'interest and amenity groups' might be empowered to bring civil suits for environmental damage 'would lead to costly, vexatious or vindictive claims' (ACBE, 1993a: 21). Retrospective liability would, the Group warns, 'have far more reaching adverse effects and in the long term lessen the availability of resources for improving environmental performance in the future' (ACBE, 1993a: 21).

In July 1993 the UK Government responded, reassuringly, to ACBE. It confirmed that its policy was to 'tackle actual contamination problems in a sensible way' (ACBE, 1993b: 67) and to 'consult fully' with industry in drafting environmental legislation.

### Response to the Communication from the Commission of the European Communities Green Paper on Remedying Environmental Damage (October 1993)

The UK Government's immediate expression of its 'sensible' approach rejected the need of harmonization of civil liability. Two themes emerge in its arguments. One echoes the anxiety expressed by ACBE that extending liability would be an additional burden on business. For instance, a requirement for compulsory insurance 'would seriously distort economic activity': 'insurers might simply refuse to insure companies operating in high risk areas, thereby circumscribing the activities such companies could undertake' (3.24). (The implication that uninsurably dangerous activities are fundamental to our economic well-being is sobering). The UK Government's other preoccupation is the avoidance of charges on 'the public purse'. This underlies its concern, which is shared by industry, to avoid high remediation standards. Looking presumably towards the Netherlands, the Green Paper response warns against 'excess remediation' and costs 'driving out of business the organization which would otherwise have met those costs' (3.10).

The UK Government and industry part company, however, on the issue of compensation funds. Polluter pays policy breaks down where the polluter has disappeared or is insolvent. The ACBE recommends firmly that, where the polluter cannot be made to pay, 'since all sectors of society have contributed to some degree of past pollution, either as financiers, insurers, traders, manufacturers or consumers, the financing of any... compensation fund should be on as wide a basis as possible' (ACBE: 41). In other words, clean-up should be publicly funded. The response to the Green Paper is far less open-handed. 'The public purse should not be treated as the easy answer in such circumstances, since that would weaken the responsibilities of operators and owners'. Instead, clean-up costs should be recovered from 'a hierarchy of liable persons... including owners, occupiers and, in some cases, the state' (3.21). The confiding relationship with business is being strained by EC demands. The ENDS Report (October 1993) commented that the UK Government was 'hedging its bets', and quoted a speech made by the then Junior Environment Minister warning bankers that the public purse was last resort', not 'a soft touch' (ENDS Report, October 1993: 21).

### *Firm Foundations:* CBI Proposals for Environmental Liability and Contaminated Land (October 1993)

The CBI's contribution to the debate is couched in the same embattled tones as the ACBE report. Its language constantly harks back to the 'sensible way'. Environmental policy should 'be... constructive', 'work with the grain of the competitive free market' (CBI, 1993: 4). Environmental improvement should be achieved through 'voluntary action' and 'at a pace which can be implemented and enforced' (CBI, 1993: 5). Like ACBE, the CBI warns, or threatens, that too much environmental protection will damage the environment; 'Stretch (civil liability) too far and the effects, as we are already seeing, begin to damage the economic development which ensures high environmental standards today' (CBI, 1993: 7). Industry should be protected from the consequences of contamination—'unforeseeable liabilities arising from our emerging understanding of the impact of human activity'; 'society will need to underwrite such liabilities' (CBI, 1993: 12). This is not merely a more ponderous version of 'can't pay, won't pay'; the CBI explains the moral justification for its stance: '(S)ociety has authorized business to carry out industrial activities on its behalf, and business should not be left to face the consequences alone' (CBI, 1993: 18).

*Firm Foundations* makes a number of recommendations for dealing with contaminated land, most of them involving the provision of incentives to business to clean up sites. Conspicuously lacking is any mention of the role of information in this. One rather baffling reference is made to the need for 'investors, environmental groups and the media' to 'contribute to realistic awareness of the problems to be tackled. The media attention given to the plight of home-buyers faced with unexpected contamination problems should help to avoid others being as severely affected' (CBI, 1993: 28). This sound like a more sophisticated restatement of *caveat emptor*; the public should be wary of pollution, but business is not under a duty to disclose it.

### *Paying for our Past:* a Consultation Paper from the Department of the Environment and the Welsh Office (March 1994)

Four years on from the EPA, *Paying for our Past* is still tentative about the central issues of disclosure and liability. It rehearses again the difficulties of strict liability, the need for cost-effectiveness and the desirability of market-based approaches 'integrating economic and environmental concerns'. It affirms the dangers of being too clean: 'disproportionate or unnecessarily early steps to treat land...may positively jeopardize wealth creation' (DoE, March 1994: 10). However, it sounds a new note in its discussion of the provision of information to markets.

The 1993 response to the Green Paper had touched on this sensitive area. Discussing possible limitations to the polluter pays policy, it suggested that it might be reasonable for a purchaser to assume liability for cleaning up a contaminated site, provided that the price paid had reflected the condition of the site (3.14). However, in the absence of registers, how can price-sensitive information be communicated to the market? Searches can be carried out privately, but are expensive, as was noted earlier. The high costs would be 'uneconomic' for domestic buyers or for small businesses. *Caveat emptor* would operate unfairly in situations where the purchaser could not be aware of contamination, or of its consequences, when entering into the contract. The purchaser of a house on a new development, for instance, would not be well placed to investigate the state of the land on which it was built. *Paying for our Past* enumerates these problems and the hazards for the 'innocent owner' who 'may find he has a liability without having had any opportunity to obtain an off-setting reduction in the price or a vendor's warranty' (DoE, March 1994: 35). This is admitted to be 'unfair...a disincentive to the marketing and use of potentially contaminated land' (DoE, March 1994). The imposition of a duty on the vendor to disclose contamination, together with an implied warranty by the vendor that land was not contaminated, would remove the purchaser's risk, but this 'would dissipate the current clear transfer of responsibility to each successive buyer which takes place at completion (DoE, March 1994).

### *Framework for Contaminated Land:* Outcome of the UK Government's Policy Review and Conclusions from the Consultation Paper Paying for our Past: Department of the Environment and Welsh Office (November 1994)

The *Framework for Contaminated Land* is the UK Government's policy statement, reflecting the responses it received to *Paying for our Past*, and accompanying a new

Environment Bill. It affirms the UK Government's commitment to the 'suitable for use' approach, which it glosses as requiring clean-up where 'contamination poses unacceptable actual or potential risks to health' and 'there are appropriate and cost-effective means available to do so' (DoE, November, 1994: 4). (Cost-effectiveness is not defined.) Further objectives include the promotion of an efficient market in land and the removal of 'unnecessary financial and regulatory burdens' (DoE, November 1994). The *Framework*, in addition to setting out a regulatory structure for identifying and taking action on contaminated land, again addresses the issues of liability and information. The UK Government has rejected the EC's Green Paper proposals for a defined strict liability regime. It will, as before, be left to the courts to decide upon common-law liability in cases of nuisance. There will be no rights for environmental organizations to claim for damage to the unowned environment; it will be the prerogative of regulatory bodies only to do so. Banks' worries are allayed. The UK Government does not intend to dip into 'deep pockets'—for instance, by pursuing secured lenders who have taken contaminated land as security. The financial memorandum accompanying the draft Environmental Bill states that it will not 'increase existing costs or place additional burdens on business'; this attitude is reflected in a rather evasive set of proposals on 'orphan sites', i.e. those where neither the polluter nor the owner/occupier can be made to pay. Orphan sites 'should be kept to a minimum, but not at the expense of pursuing "deep pockets" regardless of responsibility' (DoE, November 1994: 10). It is hard to see how the UK Government proposes to fund the clean-up of such sites; the costs must fall somewhere, but it is difficult for a Conservative government either to commit itself to increased public spending or to announce that businesses may face increased costs.

The *Framework* finally kills off the possibility of local authority registers of contaminated land. 'The Government does not ... see any need to undertake a survey of the whole country providing a snapshot of contaminated land, nor would it be cost-effective in relation to the pollution which it might relate' (DoE, November 1994: 12). The reasons for this assertion are not given; presumably, the UK Government's rationale is that the status of a site need only be known when it is to be sold or developed. However, this immediately raises the issues that were first aired by the DoE in 1991. Parties other than purchasers—local authorities, insurers, emergency services and others—have a valid interest in the status of land. Decisions about planning, or about the purchase or use of neighbouring sites, for instance, may be affected. The *Framework* is silent on these concerns. It does, however, address the difficulties faced by individuals and small businesses. They may lack the means and expertise to investigate the status of land they purchase, and they will be particularly hard-hit by finding themselves having to pay for clean-up if they buy a contaminated site. The *Framework* rejects the possibility of waiving *caveat emptor*. The onus will be on buyers to satisfy themselves of the state of land, assisted by (unspecified) improvements to the information held by regulatory authorities. The UK Government has abandoned its May 1991 position that 'it is better for everyone concerned to be aware of possible contamination'. Mandatory disclosure requirements have been defeated by a concerted campaign led by industrialists and developers.

What is also noteworthy is that the rejection of *compulsory* land registers has been accompanied by calls for *voluntary* disclosures by business. The ACBE's Fourth

Progress Report in October 1994 recommends that 'Every encouragement is given to businesses to report relevant environmental information' (ACBE, 1994a: 13): the UK Government's response (DoE, November, 1994) is 'We will continue to encourage consistent and cost-effective reporting'. The *Framework* refers approvingly to 'voluntary moves by the private sector', including improved standards of environmental reporting, under the aegis of ACBE.


## IMPLICATIONS FOR CORPORATE SOCIAL REPORTING


In November 1994, the ACBE organized a seminar which brought together industrialists and analysts to discuss environmental reporting. What emerges from the transcript of the seminar, sometimes with startling candour, is the business case for voluntary disclosure. John Gummer, the Secretary of State for the Environment, is quoted in a 'keynote speech': 'Pressure to deliver environmental improvement will come to business whether we like it or not. I want to see that the pressures are not those of constantly more and more regulation, greater and greater strictness, new ways of trying to catch business out. I want as much as possible to arise from business itself, setting its own standards and meeting those standards and being seen to meet them, so that in whole areas of environmental performance we shall be able to say we are delivering—we are delivering as a nation because business is delivering because business recognizes that the alternative is the kind of regulation against which this Government and most of the business community has set its face' (ACBE, 1994b: 37). Gummer's peroration looks to 'partnership between industry, commerce, the City and the Government' (ACBE, 1994b: 40) to develop environmental performance measures. However, Gummer's confidence in voluntary reporting is not shared by other participants. Contributors return constantly to the difficulties of developing a consistent framework for environmental reporting and to the adequacy or otherwise of accounting standards. The conclusions reached are diverse and often contradictory; an accountant calls for the 'financial community' to take a lead in defining the information needs, whereas a banker asks for industry to develop 'a coherent system of consistent environmental reporting and disclosure' (ACBE, 1994b: 12, 24). The executive director of a major plc states firmly that his company's environmental report is intended for internal management, not 'extraneous audiences' or ill-intentioned commentators' (ACBE, 1994b: 34), whereas others assert that reporting must respond to consumer interest in environmental issues.

The ACBE debate illustrates the impossibility of finding a basis for environmental reporting in the absence of a regulatory framework. No consensus can emerge without the identification of an audience for reports—shareholders, lenders, the public at large?—and of the nature of the information to be disclosed. The UK Government's rejection of a strict liability regime is implicated here—for instance, in the call by an ACBE speaker for 'legislative authorities... (to) determine the scale of the financial costs...we are attempting to evaluate' (ACBE, 1994b: 13). The accounting issues for the owner of a contaminated site, for instance, are summarized by Harris (1994) in the context of Royal Dutch/Shell: the criteria for the recognition of a liability/loss contingency; the basis for identifying different classes of environmental expenditure; the basis for determining what constitutes a reasonable estimate of cost; the treatment of expected recoveries from other parties; accounting implications of retrospective application of legislation; and gradual provisioning and creation of reserves/self-insurance. In the absence of both legislative and professional guidance, no authoritative basis exists for accounting for such situations.

Regulation in the USA has had a significant impact on business attitudes to environmental risks, and on their accounting and financial reporting practices. US accounting and reporting guidelines and regulation include: EITF Issue no 89–13 *Accounting for the cost of asbestos removal*; EITF Issue no 90–8 *Capitalization of costs to treat environmental contamination*; EITF Issue no 93–5 *Accounting for environmental liabilities*; SEC S-K item 1 requiring disclosure of the effects on earnings of compliance with environmental legislation; SEC S-K item 103 requiring disclosure of pending legal proceedings under environmental statutes; SEC S-K item 303 requiring discussion of the impact of environmental risks on a company's financial position; and SAS 54 *Illegal acts by clients* requiring the auditor to consider specifically any environmental derelictions on the client's part.

Articles in the US professional press deal with the implications of environmental regulation for the management accountant (Newell *et al.*, 1990), the financial accountant (Surma and Vondra, 1992; Zuber and Berry, 1992) and the auditor (Specht, 1992). This is not to exaggerate the quality or quantity of environmental disclosures in the USA—Surma and Vondra (1992: 51) note that only 11% of the major corporations they surveyed had accounting policies specifically on environmental accounting—but regulation has evidently impelled US accountants to address issues which, as Harris (1994) indicates, are ignored by UK practitioners.

One ACBE contributor, the managing director of BP, describes with grudging admiration the 'grilling' he received from the US SEC Commissioners about BP's environmental disclosures. (ACBE, 1994b: 26–27). Superfund registration gives US regulators a telling insight: 'When you are listed on several hundred sites and your annual report does not appear to include any provision for tackling those apparent obligations, very pointed questions by the financial regulators are easy, to try to understand how a board of directors is tackling those potential liabilities' (ACBE, 1994b: 27).

Gummer's appeal for business to set its own standards inadvertently echoes Guthrie and Parker's (1989) characterization of disclosure as 'information provided from management's perspective'. In the absence of government regulation, either to compel disclosure or create a liability regime that allows liabilities to be readily quanitified, the nature and scope of environmental reporting is to be determined by businesses alone. Pinfield and Berner (1994: 23) assert that 'incorporating the values and demands of external publics...is deemed essential in the new business climate of the 1990s'. Stakeholders and legitimacy theory both assume that society can formulate demands for information and performance which businesses must satisfy to survive, but this assumes that government will not intervene to deflect those demands. The UK debate has shown the systematic exclusion of the 'public' from access to information in the name of 'cost-effectiveness' and 'voluntary action'. What has emerged from the debate over contaminated land outlined above is not a regime of voluntary disclosure responsive to public demands, but a confusion of rhetorical assertions through which, in Guthrie and Parker's words, management can 'tell its own story or refrain from doing so, according to its own self-interest'.

## REFERENCES

Advisory Committee on Business and the Environment (ACBE) (1993a) *Report of the Financial Sector Working Group*, Department of Trade and Industry and Department of the Environment, London.
Advisory Committee on Business and the Environment (ACBE) (1993b) *Third Progress Report to and Response from the Secretary for the Environment and the President of the Board of Trade*, Department of Trade and Industry and Department of the Environment, London.
Advisory Committee on Business and the Environment (ACBE) (1994a) *Fourth Progress Report to and Response from the Secretary of State for the Environment and the President of the Board of Trade*, Department of Trade and Industry and Department of the Environment, London.
Advisory Committee on Business and the Environment (ACBE) (1994b) *Environmental Reporting: What the City Should Ask*, Department of Trade and Industry and Department of the Environment, London.
Beckett, M. J. (1993) Land contamination. In: *Contaminated Land Problems and Solutions* (Ed. T. Cairney), Blackie, London.
Beckett, M. J. and Cairney, T. (1993) Reclamation options. In: *Contaminated Land Problems and Solutions* (Ed. T. Cairney), Blackie, London.
Cairney, T. (1993) International responses. In: *Contaminated Land Problems and Solutions* (Ed. T. Cairney), Blackie, London.
Chakravorty, S. (1992) Commercial aspects of Section 143 of the Environmental Protection Act, *Journal of Planning and Environmental Law*, Jul, 624–627.
Commission of the European Communities (1993) *Communication from the Commission to the Council and Parliament and the Economic and Social Committee: Green Paper on Remedying Environmental Damage*, COM(93) 47 final, CEC, Brussels.
Confederation of British Industry (CBI) (1993) *Firm Foundations: CBI Proposals for Environmental Liability and Contaminated Land*, CBI, London.
Department of the Environment (DoE) (May 1991) *Public Registers of Land Which May Be Contaminated: A Consultation Paper*, DoE, London.
Department of the Environment (DoE) (24 March 1993) Michael Howard announces review of land pollution responsibilities, *New Release*, DoE, London.
Department of the Environment (DoE) (March 1994) *Paying for our Past: Arrangements for Controlling Contaminated Land and Meeting the Costs of Remedying the Damage to the Environment: a Consultation Paper*, DoE, London.
Department of the Environment (DoE) (November 1994) *Framework for Contaminated Land: Outcome of the Government's Policy Review and Conclusions from the Consultation Paper 'Paying for our Past'*, DoE, London.
*The Economist* (7 May 1994) Cleaning up, 103.
*ENDS Report 205* (February 1992) Delay Looms for Public Registers of Contaminated Land, 24–25.
*ENDS Report 211* (August 1992) Government's Climbdown on Contaminated Land Registers, 26–27.
*ENDS Report 225* (October 1993) Opening Shots in the Liability Debate, 19–22.
*ENDS Report 235* (August 1994) Groundwater Clean-up and the Art of the Possible, 21–23.
*Financial Times* (27 May 1992) Merry Hill interest the Richardsons.
Fortuna, R. C. (1989) Hazardous waste treatment come of age. In: *Standard Handbook of Hazardous Waste Treatment and Disposal* (Ed. H. M. Freeman), McGraw-Hill, New York.
Freeman, M. (1984) *Strategic Management: a Stakeholder Approach*, Pitman, Marshall.
Government of Great Britain and Northern Ireland (1993) *Response to the Communication from the Commission of the European Communities (COM(93) 47 final) Green Paper on Remedying Environmental Damage*.

*The Guardian* (12 March 1992) List of poisoned sites put on ice.

Guthrie, J. and Parker, L. (1989) Corporate social reporting: a rebuttal of legitimacy theory, *Accounting and Business Research*, **19**(76), 343–352.

Harris, G. J. (1994) Development of a corporate accounting policy—environmental clean-up obligations, *Unpublished Working Paper*.

Hays, S. P. (1987) *Beauty, Health and Permanence: Environmental Politics in the United States 1955–1985*, Cambridge University Press, Cambridge.

Kravitch, Circuit Judge (1992) Judgement in *United States v Fleet Factors Corp.* reported in *Journal of Environmental Law* **4**(1), 145–151.

Levine, A. G. (1982) *Love Canal: Science, Politics and People*, Lexington Books, Lexington.

McKenna & Co. (1989) A description of the laws of England, the USA and certain other countries concerning contaminated land, *Minutes of Evidence taken before the Environment Committee of the House of Commons, Monday 19 June 1989*, HMSO, London, 74–96.

Meenan, M. K. (1993) Introduction to the US waste management approach. In: *Contaminated Land Problems and Solutions* (Ed. T. Cairney), Blackie, London.

Newell, G. E., Kreuze, J. G. and Newell, S. J. (1990) Accounting for hazardous waste, *Management Accounting*, May, 58–61.

POST (1993) *Contaminated Land*, Parliamentary Office of Science and Technology.

Patten, D. M. (1992) Intra-industry environmental disclosures in response to the Alaskan oil spill: a note on legitimacy theory, *Accounting, Organizations and Society*, **17**(5), 471–475.

Pinfield, M. and Berner, M. (1992) Accountability and the corporate management of environmentalist publics, *Business Strategy and the Environment*, **1**(3), 23–33.

Preston, L. E. and Post, J. E. (1975) *Private Management and Public Policy*, Prentice-Hall, Englewood Cliffs.

Roberts, R. W. (1992) Determinants of corporate social responsibility disclosure: an application of stakeholder theory. *Accounting, Organizations and Society*, **17**(6), 595–612.

Stanford, R. and Yang, E. C. (1989) Summary of CERCLA legislation and regulations and the EPA Superfund programme. In: *Standard Handbook of Hazardous Waste Treatment and Disposal* (Ed. H. M. Freeman), McGraw-Hill, New York.

Surma, J. P. and Vondra, A. A. (1992) Accounting for environmental costs: a hazardous subject, *Journal of Accountancy*, March, 51–55.

Thompson, H. (1992) The legal and commercial implications of section 143 registers of contaminative uses, *Unpublished Press Release*, National Westminster Bank, London.

Tinker, T., Lehman, C. and Neimark, M. (1991) Falling down the hole in the middle of the road: political quietism in corporate social reporting, *Accounting, Auditing and Accountability Journal*, **4**(2), 28–54.

Zuber, G. R. and Berry, C. G. (1992) Assessing environmental risk, *Journal of Accounting*, March, 43–48.

# Part IV

Corporate Environmentalism in Practice

# CONTENTS

# Introduction to Part IV

*Pierre McDonagh and Andrea Prothero*

As well as considering the greening of organizations from a conceptual perspective, one must also discuss what it actually means for corporations in practice. The Readings in Part IV focus on the practicalities of greening management and are split into two areas. The first two readings provide some practical pointers for organizations to consider in their development and implementation of environmental policies, while the remaining readings focus on the development of environmental policies by companies and specific industries in recent years.

The ten steps to environmental excellence were published in *The Green Capitalists* at the height of renewed concern about the state of the natural environment in the late 1980s. Elkington and Burke (Reading 17) meant the steps to be considered as a framework and not an absolute means for companies aiming towards environmental excellence. The main issues of importance in actually putting environmental concerns into practice were addressed by the authors, and their ten steps to environmental excellence were then drawn up. The importance of developing and publishing environmental policies and preparing environmental audits can be linked with the importance of procedures and methods in developing an effective environmental management system, discussed in Readings 11–13. Another issue of importance is that of gaining the support and commitment of top management, which, while clichéd, is none the less vital (see also Burke and Hill, 1990; Shimel, 1991), as is maintaining good relationships with other stakeholders and institutions.

The Valdez Principles (now referred to as the CERES Principles), discussed by Barnard (1990) in Reading 18, were established by the Coalition for Environmentally Responsible Economies (CERES) in the USA in 1989 in response to the *Exxon Valdez* oil spill off Alaska. Some of the recommendations of Elkington and Burke are also reiterated here. The organization was aiming to persuade US companies to adopt ten principles of corporate environmental responsibility; these are discussed in the reading. The article also provides a discussion of some companies who fought the charter, including the Exxon company. It shows that while most of the principles were regarded as acceptable, two issues of controversy were the publishing of an annual 'environmental report card' and the appointment of an environmental manager at board level. However, as discussed in Reading 17, if environmental management systems are to be successfully integrated, the appointment of an environmental manager who has the support and commitment of the board (both personal and financial) and the development of some type of environmental report card are both vital elements within this process and should not be ignored. Any company that fails to take these issues on board will find themselves struggling in developing a fully integrated company-wide environmental management system. A discussion of an environmental scheme, 'Responsible Care', set up by the Chemical Manufacturers Association (CMA) in the US and adopted by over 170 companies, is raised. Finally, the author concludes by discussing problems of investing in environmental policies and how these may be addressed in the future.

These two readings provide a good practical starting point for looking at the issues organizations need to consider in order to develop a sound environmental management system. The remaining four articles of this section should be read while bearing in mind the issues raised in these two sets of environmental guidelines. It must be stressed, however, that other guidelines have also been developed, and these must be taken as a framework for consideration and not as the absolute way to introduce an environmental management system. While considering some of these practical issues, the importance of considering the overall 'soul' of the organization must not be forgotten, as discussed in Reading 10 (Fineman, 1996).

The article on the challenge to sustainable development (Reading 19) was written by three employees in environmental affairs at the Kodak company in the USA and considers the response the company has made towards achieving sustainability. The authors suggest companies who incorporate environmental concerns into all of their business activities can gain a number of benefits. Thus, the reader must be aware of both the opportunities and costs involved in 'going green'. Much of the popular press has only focused on the costs of going green: one only has to look at the success of 3Ms Pollution Prevention Pays programme to see that going green affords company opportunities as well as threats. The reading provides various examples of company activities that have been undertaken and illustrates Kodaks 'Environment Improvement Triangle'. This is linked to the way in which environmental management within the company has been established via the organization's structure. This provides a good starting point for illustrating what one company has done as far as integrating environmentalism into corporate activities is concerned. The practical issues discussed here should therefore be related to some of the theoretical issues raised in other readings in this volume. This is only one example of a specific organization's product stewardship and it is important to stress that readers may wish to pursue the development of environmental policies by other organizations (even their own!).

Reading 20 by Peattie and Ratnayaka (1992) is one of three that consider the recent historic response to the environmental challenge of particular industries that heavily influence our daily existence, namely chemicals, cosmetics and toiletries, and detergents and household products. The first two studies rely on questionnaires and the third is based on qualitative case studies. Recent empirical research on green issues has only just began to appear in the literature and the authors anticipate that more empirical studies will be conducted in the near future; there are also results of recent empirical research that are yet to be published.

Peattie and Ratnayaka (1992) consider the green challenge for the UK chemical industry and begin by reminding us that it provides both opportunities and threats, as discussed in Reading 19 by Poduska *et al.* (1992). Their article highlights the importance of companies not only considering their own environmental performance but also that of their suppliers (see also Prothero and McDonagh, Reading 21). Possible reasons for the attack on the environmental performance of the global chemical industry are raised, along with a discussion of the various responses from companies within the industry.

The telephone survey of 42 UK chemical manufacturers focused on three main issues: (1) awareness of green issues within the industry; (2) what environmental activities companies are engaging in; and (3) views on the environmental performance of the industry as a whole. After discussion of the green Ss of Success, the concluding section considers ways forward for the industry in the future; the main conclusion is that awareness of the issue in the industry has not yet been met by action. This is where the importance of holism (see the two articles by Shrivastava, Readings 2 and 9), organization-wide changes (see Fineman, Reading 10), integration of efforts (see McCloskey and Smith, Reading 11) and the developments of methods and procedures (see Roberts, Reading 12) become important.

Reading 21 by Prothero and McDonagh (1992) is an empirical piece based on a postal survey of cosmetics and toiletries organizations in 1990. The results of the survey are important for readers who wish to see how green issues have affected the strategies of cosmetic organizations in recent years. The article begins with a brief introduction to the social responsibility literature and its links with environmentalism before specifically considering the marketing department and environmental issues. The principal research issues from the study conducted centre around environmentally acceptable product issues (see also Dermody and Hanmer-Lloyd, Reading 22), production processes and suppliers, and other environmentally conscious activities by organizations—for example, packaging and cruelty-free issues. The main conclusions of this research suggested that the early adoption of piecemeal responses by companies to environmental issues was not enough in helping to solve the global environmental crisis. This conclusion again concurs with the main theme in this collection—that green is a holistic issue, which therefore means its impacts will permeate through all levels of the organization. Piecemeal responses, such as changing packaging, are not enough to appease the environmental movement nor stop the rapid deterioration of the natural environment.

Finally, in this part, Dermody and Hanmer-Lloyd (1995) (Reading 22) examine the development of environmentally responsible new products by the manufacturers of detergents and household products. The article provides a discussion of what environmental responsibility involves as far as new product development is concerned. Examples of some of the benefits of developing environmentally responsible new products are raised and the authors suggest that, while companies are aware of this, they are 'ill-equipped to deal with the complexities and difficulties that arise'. The aim of this reading is thus to provide guidelines for companies in developing environmentally responsible new products.

The recent spate of interest in environmental issues has meant that new research projects in the general area of greening management are developing all the time. It is thus vital that researchers in this area keep up to date with the results of new empirical research being published. Examples of specific environmental journals are provided at the end of the reader.

## REFERENCES

Burke, T. and Hill, J. (1990) *Ethics, Environment and the Company*, The Institute of Business Ethics, London.
Shimel, P. (1991) Corporate environmental policy in practice, *Long Range Planning*, **24**(3) 10–17.

# 17

# Ten Steps to Environmental Excellence

*John Elkington with Tom Burke*

Excellent companies are committed to people: their employees, their customers and those who are affected, in one way or another, by their operations. The difficulty they face in the environmental field, however, is in identifying everyone who is likely to be affected by their operations. Instead of concentrating on the area within the factory fence, or even on the communities living immediately around their manufacturing sites, such companies now recognize that their operations may have implications for people who they may never meet, either because they are geographically remote or, in some cases, because they are not yet born.

*The Green Capitalists* has concentrated on the manufacturing industry, rather than on agriculture or the investment community. This is not because farmers and investors do not have an impact on the environment: they most certainly do. Indeed, sustainable agriculture and other forms of sustainable development are only likely to emerge if investors can be persuaded that it is in their long-term interest to support them. An enormous amount of work still needs to be done if we are to have any hope of seeing the emergence of a new breed of 'green financiers' and 'green investors'.

Obviously, the companies described in earlier chapters cannot hope single-handedly to achieve the necessary shift in the world-view of those who work in the City of London or on Wall Street, the Paris Bourse or the Tokyo Stock Exchange. Post industrialists can have a profound influence by ensuring that their development proposals are environmentally acceptable and sustainable *before* they are submitted to potential investors. The investment community relies on entrepreneurs and industrial managements to tell it what is likely to be required for a business venture to proceed and succeed.

But how should a given company set about achieving environmental excellence? There is no guaranteed route, but all of the ten steps outlined below have been followed by almost every one of the environmentally excellent companies mentioned in previous chapters. We were indebted to Sir Peter Parker, chairman of Rockware and of the British Institute of Management, for the idea of using a checklist approach and for many of the individual steps. As he put it, 'there is an urgent need to simplify management ideas and action on this 360 degree challenge of the environment'.

These ten steps are not the complete answer as far as environmental excellence is concerned, but they do represent a framework within which excellence can be pursued with a real hope of success.

## 1.  DEVELOP AND PUBLISH AN ENVIRONMENTAL POLICY

The first step is to produce a company environmental policy. There is no standard format for such policies, with many of them being very short documents, but such a policy, adopted by the company's Board, effectively legitimizes all the subsequent steps.

'All industrial activity has an impact on the environment', ICI's environmental policy begins. 'It is the policy of ICI to manage its activities so as to ensure that they are acceptable to the community and to reduce adverse effects to a practicable minimum. This policy recognizes that the environment is able to absorb certain man-made effects, and is thus a resource to be used as well as one to be conserved'. The policy goes on to discuss the way in which ICI deals with the environmental aspects of its existing and new activities, its processes and its products. One interesting sentence notes that the Group will: 'Take positive steps to conserve resources, with particular regard for those which are scarce and non renewable.'

IBM's policy states that 'IBM will reduce to a minimum the ecological impact of all its activities. Management in IBM is expected to be continuously on guard against adversely affecting the environment and to seek ways to conserve natural resources.' The company also goes a long way towards ensuring environmental excellence by insisting that its various businesses match their environmental standards with the toughest prevailing anywhere in the world.

At BP, meanwhile, the Group's policy states that: 'It is a primary and continuing policy of the BP Group that in the conduct of its activities it will endeavour to protect the health and safety of its employees, customers and others who may be affected by these activities and endeavour to limit adverse effects on the physical environment in which its activities are carried out.' Each BP company then prepares its own policy, objectives and guidelines, appropriate to its own businesses.

## 2.  PREPARE AN ACTION PROGRAMME

A policy statement is a vital first step, but if it is to be implemented it needs to be spelled out in the form of a number of much more specific objectives for all company personnel, with guidelines on how these objectives should be met. At BP, for example, there are eight overall objectives:

(i)    to set standards which will at least meet the relevant statutory requirements for health and safety, product safety and environmental matters, as these may affect its own employees, customers, contractors and their employees and the public at large;

(ii)  to review and, where appropriate, develop these standards in the light of changes in technology, industry practices and trends in legislation, and to sponsor research and development to improve the rationale for the setting of standards;

(iii) to co-operate with the appropriate authorities and technical organizations on the formulation of standards and the means of compliance;

(iv) to ensure that the potential health and safety factors and environmental effects are assessed for all new products, projects, activities and acquisitions;

(v)  to ensure that all employees are properly informed of their responsibilities for health, safety and environmental matters and discharge them effectively and are encouraged to participate in the prevention of accidents;

(vi) to ensure that contractors working under the operational control of a BP Company are informed of its relevant standards, and that appropriate procedures exist for monitoring compliance without detracting from the legal responsibilities of the contractors;

(vii) to ensure that mechanisms are established and are used for consultation with employees on such matters; and

(viii) to ensure that these objectives are being fulfilled through the auditing of the Group's activities.

The purpose of an action programme is to determine where the immediate priorities for action lie and to ensure that the appropriate targets are clearly identified and the responsibilities for achieving them are given to people who have the power, initiative and resources to succeed in the task.

Where they do not already exist, environmental impact assessment procedures should be instituted to ensure that new projects, processes and products do not damage the environment in unsuspected ways.

## 3.  ORGANIZATION AND STAFFING

Most excellent companies which operate in environmentally sensitive businesses ensure that the responsibility for the environmental agenda is vested in top management. For example, the responsibility for determining BP's policies on health, safety and environmental matters lies with the Board, advised by the Group Health, Safety and Environment Committee.

Any company aiming for environmental excellence will need to identify a 'champion' for health, safety and environment, typically a Main Board Director. He or she will need the advice and support of a sufficient number of appropriately trained people, with access to all of the company's operations. But the responsibility for ensuring that individual plants or processes are environmentally acceptable must be pushed down to individual line managers. Their suitability for higher positions in the company should be explicitly assessed, as is now the practice in a growing number of companies, on the basis of their success in meeting health, safety and environmental targets, as well as other job- or task-related criteria.

## 4.   ALLOCATE ADEQUATE RESOURCES

If such environmental policies are to be translated into effective action, those responsible must be given adequate resources. As the 3M experience shows, such expenditures need not necessarily be a net drain on the company's resources. The key point, however, is that money spent in pursuit of environmental objectives should be subject to the same accounting procedures as the rest of a company's activities. Some of the benefits, particularly in the public relations and corporate image fields, may be hard to quantify, but the Board and shareholders must be assured that the environmental budget is being professionally managed.

## 5.   INVEST IN ENVIRONMENTAL SCIENCE AND TECHNOLOGY

Whether one thinks of acid rain or the impending choice between catalytic converters and 'lean-burn' engines for the cars of the future, sound environmental decision-making depends on the availability of sound scientific research. Industry must help ensure that the environmental debate is well-informed and that the necessary data bases exist to ensure that pressing questions about the potential environmental implications of particular decisions or activities can be assessed within a reasonable time-scale. A key development in this respect is the co-operation between the World Resources Institute (WRI) and the International Institute for Environment and Development (IIED) on the production of an annual series of *World Resources* reports on trends in the international environment.

New, environmentally acceptable technologies can be developed and deployed in an economically efficient manner if industry works closely with environmental interests and the regulatory agencies. The key objective must be to ensure that technology is designed from scratch to be cleaner, quieter or more energy-efficient, rather than having to be modified once in use. 3M's Pollution Prevention Pays Programme illustrates how product reformulation, process modification, equipment redesign and the recovery of wastes for re-use can help cut pollution and energy wastage dramatically. The example of Rolls-Royce shows how complex the process of technology development can be, with different environmental factors often needing to be traded off. But companies which fail to keep their technologies up to scratch environmentally risk going out of business.

## 6.   EDUCATE AND TRAIN

People are much more likely to respond to company objectives and action plans if they know exactly what is expected of them and how they should respond. Company policy should be spelled out fully and effectively, while progress with the environmental action programme should be regularly reviewed. 'I take the line that people in our companies are not just employees, not just trade unionists', noted Sir

Peter Parker: 'they are citizens at work, so the message of environmental quality must matter to them. At work, we are all environmentalists now'.

The important thing is to get people launched on the path towards environmental excellence, even if the early steps are fairly small. As the authors of *In Search of Excellence* noted in a different context, 'what's called "foot-in-the-door" research demonstrates the importance of incrementally acting our way into major commitment. For instance, in one experiment, in Palo Alto, California, most subjects who initially agreed to put a *tiny* sign in their front window supporting a cause (traffic safety) subsequently agreed to display a billboard in their front yard, which required letting outsiders dig sizeable holes in the lawn. On the other hand, those not asked to take the first small step turned down the larger one in ninety-five cases out of a hundred'.

The implications are clear, as Peters and Waterman pointed out, 'Only if you get people *acting*, even in small ways, the way you want them to, will they come to believe in what they're doing. Moreover, the process of enlistment is enhanced by explicit *management* of the after-the-act labelling process—in other words, publicly and ceaselessly lauding the small wins along the way. "Doing things" (lots of experiments, tries) leads to rapid and effective learning, adaptation, diffusion, and commitment; it is the hallmark of the well-run company.'

## 7.   MONITOR, AUDIT AND REPORT

Once the appropriate management systems are in place, their performance should be assessed regularly. This will involve a number of separate activities. The state of the environment will need to be monitored, to check that the company's controls are effective. But there will also be a need to check on the extent to which impacts which were predicted in the initial environmental impact assessment work have been borne out in practice, to ensure that the base of environmental science on which the company's procedures have been erected is sound.

As the Essochem Europe example showed, regular audits and surveys can help assess the extent of management involvement in, and support for, a company's environmental policy and action programme. The sort of questions Essochem Europe asks include the following:

(1)  In the planning of environmental conservation activities:
— Are all functions included?
— Who co-ordinates such activities? How is the plan stewarded?
— How are priority conflicts resolved?

(2)  With regard to legal requirements and developing legislation:
— Are laws available and understood?
— How is responsibility allocated?
— How is compliance audited internally?
— How is information obtained on developing legislation?
— How does the organization try to influence legislators?

(3)  In ensuring compliance:
— What monitoring programmes are conducted?

— Are records required by the authorities?
— What actions are taken following non-compliance episodes?
— Are legal and company standards well defined and understood?
— What changes in standards are anticipated?

(4) To maintain good relations with the public:
— Are there systems for recording, investigating and responding to complaints?
— Is there an effective emergency plan for accidental spills or emissions. When was it last tested? What was the result?
— What actions have been taken to inform the local community of your environmental conservation initiatives?

5.  In the area of training:
— What training has the environmental conservation co-ordinator received? Is it enough?
— Are there formal training programmes for operators, mechanical staff, technicians and contractors on the environmental policy and requirements?

(6) In the area of potential environmental hazards:
— Are the hazards associated with all chemicals and processes known and communicated to the appropriate people?
— How is the information updated? How often?
— Are protective measures widely known?
— Does the organization have discussions and exercises with local authorities in handling environmental emergencies?
— What waste disposal techniques are adopted? What are the relevant regulations? How are the dumps monitored?

(7) Where there are gaps or inadequacies in the available technology:
— How are they assessed?
— How are they followed up?

(8) What specific objectives exist in the area of developing 'clean technology'? What steps are under way to eliminate the use of undesirable chemicals and toxic materials?

(9) What work is under way on specific problems related to the need to eliminate or reduce the toxicity of plant and process effluents?


## 8.   MONITOR THE EVOLUTION OF THE GREEN AGENDA


The environmental agenda is constantly evolving. Any company which assumes the adequacy of information which it picked up two years ago, or even three months ago, may be in for an unpleasant surprise. As in any other area of business, the regular gathering and assessment of information is the intelligent approach. Excellent companies also keep up to date on international developments which may influence the environmental agenda in other countries in which they operate. Key publications here are the *ENDS Report*, published monthly by Environmental Data Services, based in London, and the *State of the World* reports, published annually by the Worldwatch Institute, based in Washington, D.C.

## 9.  CONTRIBUTE TO ENVIRONMENTAL PROGRAMMES

There are a tremendous range of projects and programmes under way in the environmental field which need help from industry, whether it is in the form of money, help in kind or seconded staff. The return on voluntary, charitable contributions to conservation organizations can be very high indeed, provided the corporate sponsor selects a well-run charity or other organization. Some companies, such as BP, are helping to train the staff of environmental charities and other non-governmental organizations in business management techniques. Internationally, too, industry should support programmes which make available environmental experts to countries which might not otherwise be able to afford them. Some of these experts should be drawn from industry itself.

## 10.  HELP BUILD BRIDGES BETWEEN THE VARIOUS INTERESTS

One of the most critical needs in today's business environment is to build bridges between business, government and environmental interests. 'There is a growing realization among business and environmental leaders that confrontation isn't helpful in achieving their ends', explained Monsanto chairman, Louis Fernandez. 'It is a time of transition and the climate is ripe for initiatives to be taken by industrialists and by responsible environmental leaders'.

Any company which has worked its way through the previous nine steps will have found such bridges beginning to form almost automatically. The key to environmental excellence is the recognition that such activities need not be a drain on the company's resources. Rather, they can help in training key personnel to operate effectively in today's world, in providing advance warning of impending pressures on core businesses and in identifying the business opportunities of tomorrow.

# 18

# Exxon Collides With the 'Valdez Principles'

*Jayne W. Barnard*

It has been a year and a half since the *Exxon Valdez* fouled Alaska's Prince William Sound with 11 million gallons of freshly pumped crude oil. For Exxon's management, the March 1989 spill was the beginning of a long night of public scrutiny of the company's environmental practices. Chairman Lawrence G. Rawl was summoned to appear before Congress. Angry demonstrators disrupted Exxon's annual shareholders' meeting. Environmentalists excoriated Exxon and investors watched helplessly as vast amounts of Exxon assets were redeployed to support the Alaska cleanup.

Now an influential group of environmental organizations, allied with some of the biggest shareholders in Exxon and other companies, has undertaken a major effort to redirect corporate environmental priorities.

The Coalition for Environmentally Responsible Economies (CERES), headquartered in Boston, includes such diverse groups as the Audubon Society, the Sierra Club, and the New York and California public employees' retirement funds. The Interfaith Center on Corporate Social Responsibility, headquartered in New York City and affiliated with the National Council of Churches, counsels churches and religious orders on the effective use of their proxy votes to advance social goals at corporate annual meetings. Together, CERES and the Interfaith Center are attempting to persuade thousands of American companies to adopt ten principles of corporate environmental responsibility: symbolically named 'The Valdez Principles.' These principles, announced by CERES in September 1989, are designed to minimize environmental damage and to maximize corporate accountability to employees, shareholders, and the public on matters of environmental concern.

The groups are using the mechanism of the 'shareholder proposal,' a method long used by social investors to promote various causes, such as discontinuing production of dangerous products or adopting anti-apartheid principles for companies doing business in South Africa. CERES and the Interfaith Center—and their stockholder members and clients—submitted shareholder proposals this year seeking inclusion of the Valdez Principles on the ballot at twenty-two companies. Some companies, including Exxon, fought the inclusion of the Valdez Principles on their corporate

Reprinted with permission from *Business and Society Review*, No. 74, 1990, pp. 32–35.
©1990 *Business and Society Review*

Box 1. The Valdez Principles

Leading environmental organizations—including the Sierra Club, National Audubon Society, and National Wildlife Federation—joined with the Social Investment Forum to form the Coalition for Environmentally Responsible Economics (CERES), whose first act was to draft the Valdez Principles for corporations to sign. The idea is to make the Valdez Principles a litmus test of corporate behavior. Companies are being pressured to abide by the following prescripts:

1.  Protection of the Biosphere
    We will minimize the release of any pollutant that may cause environmental damage to the air, water, or earth. We will safeguard habitats in rivers, lakes, wetlands, coastal zones, and oceans and will minimize contributing to the greenhouse effect, depletion of the ozone layer, acid rain, or smog.

2.  Sustainable Use of Natural Resources
    We will make sustainable use of renewable natural resources, such as water, soils and forests. We will conserve nonrenewable natural resources through efficient use and careful planning. We will protect wildlife habitat, open spaces, and wilderness, while preserving biodiversity.

3.  Reduction and Disposal of Waste
    We will minimize waste, especially hazardous waste, and wherever possible recycle materials. We will dispose of all wastes through safe and responsible methods.

4.  Wise Use of Energy
    We will make every effort to use environmentally safe and sustainable energy sources to meet our needs. We will invest in improved energy efficiency and conservation in our operations. We will maximize the energy efficiency of products we produce or sell.

5.  Risk Reduction
    We will minimize the environmental, health, and safety risks to our employees and the communities in which we operate by employing safe technologies and operating procedures and by being constantly prepared for emergencies.

6.  Marketing of Safe Products and Services
    We will sell products or services that minimize adverse environmental impacts and that are safe as consumers commonly use them. We will inform consumers of the environmental impacts of our products or services.

7.  Damage Compensation
    We will take responsibility for any harm we cause to the environment by making every effort to fully restore the environment and to compensate those persons who are adversely affected.

8.  Disclosure
    We will disclose to our employees and to the public incidents relating to our operations that cause environmental harm or pose health or safety hazards. We will disclose potential environmental, health, or safety hazards posed by our operations and we will not take any retaliatory personnel action against any employees who report on any condition that creates a danger to the environment or poses health or safety hazards.

9.  Environmental Directors and Managers
    At least one member of the board of directors will be a person qualified to represent environmental interests. We will commit management resources to implement these Principles, including the funding of an office of vice president for environmental affairs or an equivalent executive position, reporting directly to the CEO, to monitor and report on our implementation efforts.

10.  Assessment and Annual Audit
    We will conduct and make public an annual self-evaluation of our progress in implementing these Principles and in complying with all applicable laws and regulations throughout our worldwide operations. We will work toward the timely creation of independent environmental audit procedures which we will complete annually and make available to the public.

ballot, arguing that issues of environmental quality were matters of 'ordinary business operations' unsuited for shareholder input. When the Securities and Exchange Commission ordered that the proposal be printed, Exxon urged its shareholders to vote against it on the grounds that the Valdez Principles 'do not recognize the need to balance the importance of environmental protection with the importance of adequate energy resources and stable, healthy economies.'

## COMPROMISING PRINCIPLES

Other companies, including Waste Management, Amoco, Chevron, Mobil, and Texaco, took a more conciliatory position. They agreed to adopt a compromise version of the principles without requiring a shareholder vote. The Valdez Principles ultimately came to a vote at five companies. While none of the proposals passed in this first outing, they all received a surprising amount of support, given the difficulties and expense of soliciting votes for shareholder proposals. (Exxon, for example, has over 700,000 shareholders.)

CERES's long-term goal is to persuade 3,000 companies, principally through negotiation rather than by shareholder proposal, to adopt the Valdez package. Some major investors intend to support this effort—several state and city pension funds, controlling billions of dollars in assets, have passed resolutions to 'prefer' companies that have adopted the Valdez Principles.

The Valdez Principles are more than feel-good issues for shareholders. Exxon's clean-up costs following the Valdez oil spill have already passed the $2.3 billion mark—funds that otherwise would have been available for reinvestment or redistribution in dividends. California Comptroller Gray Davis, trustee of a fund holding over 8 million Exxon shares, stated in April that 'Exxon has yet to grasp fully the importance of improving its environmental record.'

Most of the Valdez Principles are uncontroversial—minimize pollution, recycle where possible, and use energy wisely, for example. Some, however, have generated heated resistance from management. One sticking point has been the requirement that companies circulate a comprehensive 'environmental report card' each year. There have also been strong objections to the twin demands that companies place on the board of directors a 'person qualified to represent environmental interests' and create an office of 'vice president for environmental affairs,' reporting directly to the CEO. Apparently, corporate managers find it more acceptable to embrace platitudes concerning their products and operations than to make concessions in the area of senior corporate governance. Shortly, after the Valdez oil spill, however, Exxon did put an environmentalist, oceanographer John H. Steele, on its board. In addition, in January 1990, Exxon appointed one of its top executives to the newly created position of vice president for environment and safety. Indeed, in its proxy statement, Exxon argued that these measures were 'consistent with several objectives' of the Valdez Principles. Other major oil companies, including Arco, Amoco, and Phillips, have also elevated responsibility for environmental policies to the vice presidential level.

California's Davis has been quoted as saying that the first companies to embrace the Valdez Principles in their entirely 'will increase market share and profit substantially.' While that seems unlikely, some consumer-oriented companies, including DuPont and Polaroid, are reportedly taking a hard look at adopting the principles. Presumably they see some marketing mileage to be gained from becoming corporate leaders in the environmental movement, as food processors did in embracing the low-fat/high-fiber/oat bran movements of the 1980s.

Among industrial companies, the chemical industry in particular has attempted to respond to pressures from environmentalists by creating its own set of principles, known as the 'Responsible Care' program. Nearly 200 chemical companies have signed on to Responsible Care. The program's sponsor, the Chemical Manufacturers' Association (CMA), recently saluted its members' efforts by placing full-page ads in newspapers across the country. The ads coincided with the observance of Earth Day.

## PRINCIPLE POSTURING?

Unfortunately, Responsible Care to date appears to reflect more public relations than progress. Though the program's 'Guiding Principles' (Box 2) were adopted in

Box 2. Not the Valdez Principles

---

The Chemical Manufacturers Association, an industry lobbying group, has developed ten 'guiding principles' concerning environmental matters. More than 170 member companies of the CMA have signed on to these principles as part of the group's Responsible Care program. Were these guidelines developed to preempt the imposition of a more potent set of principles on the industry?

- To recognize and respond to community concerns about chemicals and our operations.
- To develop and produce chemicals that can be manufactured, transported, used and disposed of safely.
- To make health, safety, and environmental considerations a priority in our planning for all existing and new products and processes.
- To report promptly to officials, employees, customers and the public, information on chemical-related health and environmental hazards and to recommend protective measures.
- To counsel customers on the safe use, transportation, and disposal of chemical products.
- To operate our plants and facilities in a manner that protects the environment and the health and safety of our employees and the public.
- To extend knowledge by conducting or supporting research on health, safety and environmental effects of our products, processes, and waste materials.
- To work with others to resolve problems created by past handing and disposal of hazardous substances.
- To participate with government and others in creating responsible laws, regulations, and standards to safeguard the community, workplace, and environment.
- To promote the principles and practices of Responsible Care by sharing experiences and offering assistance to others who produce, handle, use, transport, or dispose of chemicals.

1988, CMA is only now developing the 'Codes of Management Practice' with which to implement its larger goals. Moreover, the management codes, to be developed largely by 'chemical company experts,' are not intended to be enforced. That is, while all CMA members will be expected to work toward eventual compliance with the codes when they are written, CMA has not imposed timetables for compliance, nor does it intend to sanction members who fail to achieve compliance. Rather, the association will rely on company self-evaluations and will provide support to those companies making the least progress.

There is one advantage to joining Responsible Care. When representatives from CERES come knocking, urging chemical manufacturers to sign on to the Valdez Principles, the manufacturers can self-righteously decline. Companies can argue that they already have their own code of environmental conduct. Union Carbide did precisely this when first contacted by CERES during 1989. Pointing to the company's in-house Responsible Care program, Carbide spokeswoman Kay Phillips asserted that the Valdez Principles represented little more than a duplication of effort.

The real issue, however, is not which environmental reform program is the best. Rather, the issue is whether investors are willing to sacrifice some immediate profits in exchange for more responsible environmental practices. Thousands of investors supported this proposition when they voted for the Valdez Principles during proxy season this year. Many thousands more, however, did not. Can these investors be expected to change their views in the future? Will companies, without the support of investors, voluntarily embrace the Valdez Principles or similar stringent guidelines for environmental reform? These questions remain unanswered.

The Valdez Principles are backed by substantial moral and economic clout. In the end, however, it will be precisely the interests of the two types of sponsors— idealists and investors—which CERES has wisely assembled, that will have to be balanced if corporations are to make progress toward a cleaner environment. Exxon and others will find this delicate balancing act every bit as challenging as cleaning up Prince William Sound.

# 19

# The Challenge of Sustainable Development: Kodak's Response

*Richard Poduska, Richard Forbes and Maria Bober*

The last 20 years have seen a marked increase in environmental policy as a strategic tool in corporate policy. World class manufacturers in particular have woven environmental concerns into their corporate culture, their marketing strategies and their operations, to great effect. What they are finding is that waste reduction techniques, life cycle analysis and cradle-to-grave concern in the design process yield unexpected rewards. A case in point is Kodak, a study of which reveals the many benefits available to a company that wholly integrates environmental concerns into its corporate mandate.

The convening of the United Nations Conference on Environment and Development (UNCED) in Rio de Janeiro 20 years after the World Conference on the Human Environment took place in Stockholm marks a potential turning point in global affairs. Humanity is now being given its third chance in the 20th century to construct a new world order. And the health of the environment is of much greater concern today than it was in 1919 or 1946. The challenge is real and the response will set the course of future history. Only through unprecedented international cooperation can the peoples of the world attain the goal of Rio: Sustainable Development.

## KODAK'S STRATEGIC RESPONSE

Today, the issues surrounding sustainable development have made it essential that environmental considerations become an integral part of business planning. We at Kodak consider health, safety and environmental issues all to be part of our ethic of environmental responsibility. To reinforce and convey this important message to all parts of our diverse, worldwide corporate organization, we have articulated a corporate vision of environmental responsibility and a formal program to guide and assist managers in integrating environmental responsibility into their business operations. This is creating a new paradigm for our businesses.

Our program begins with a series of interlocking teams at the corporate and group levels. Each group works with and strengthens the other to form a cohesive whole. The Management Committee on Environmental Responsibility (MCER) is chaired by Mr. Kay R. Whitmore, our company's Chief Executive Officer; members include the group presidents and senior vice-presidents from staff organizations. This committee provides world-wide direction and review of health, safety and environmental policies and practices.

The Health, Safety and Environment Coordinating Committee (HSECC) provides advice and recommendations to the MCER, develops and administers programs under MCER's direction, and provides integrated support to MCER and to line organizations worldwide in health, safety and environmental issues. The HSECC includes members who represent the group and senior vice-presidents serving on the MCER. The chair of the HSECC also serves as the secretary to the MCER.

These corporate committees draw upon the resources and expertise of the company's Corporate Health, Safety and Environment (HSE) Organization. With a full-time staff of over 400, this corporate resource manages a growing agenda of responsibilities. In addition to providing corporate support, Corporate HSE offers advice to other company HSE teams that exist at the group and unit levels such as the Eastman Chemical Company Health, Safety and Environment Council, and the European Health, Safety and Environment Coordinating Committee.

All of these groups play vital roles in helping define, direct and encourage environmental sensitivity in the company's business planning and operations. To instill that sensitivity in line management, the company takes a three-part approach to continuous improvement, as depicted in the Environment Improvement Triangle in Fig. 1.

At all levels, on a worldwide basis, managers are encouraged to align their business practices with the company's Health, Safety and Environmental objectives in a process of continual improvement. These objectives are laid out as a series of corporate policies, guiding principles (which are consistent with principles established in the International Chamber of Commerce's Business Charter for

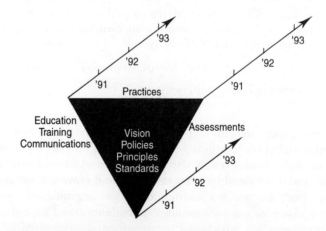

Figure 1. Environmental Improvement Triangle.

Sustainable Development and the Responsible Care initiative put forth by the association of chemical manufacturers worldwide) and performance standards. Education and training programs provide assistance, while a communications strategy helps increase employees' awareness of the company's intentions and achievements. Assessment programs, including the company's Corporate Health, Safety and Environment Assessment Program and our newly introduced HSE Self-Appraisal Program, are tools used to identify opportunities for further environmental improvement.

Our concern for the environment extends beyond our facilities and business through the donation of time and financial support to worthwhile environmental projects. Consistent with the company's goals, we focus our corporate environmental contributions primarily toward increasing environmental literacy. The most noteworthy is our contribution of $2,500,000 to World Wildlife Fund, one of the oldest and best known environmental groups, for the development of the program 'Windows on the Wild.' 'Windows' provides educational materials to zoos, aquariums and schools so that children can learn their place in and responsibility toward our planet.

## KODAK'S HISTORY OF ENVIRONMENTAL STEWARDSHIP

We believe that even one company can make a difference to the environment. Our corporate committees and ideals have translated into real environmental advancement within our products.

All of Kodak's products, from X-ray film to food packaging, meet human needs. And all are made from raw materials and use energy in their manufacture, distribution and use. The concepts of pollution prevention and the waste minimization hierarchy have become popular recently, yet they have been key to many of our programs and manufacturing operations for decades.

Source reduction has a long history at Kodak based on good business economics and technological innovation. The standard size of a professional photographic negative has been reduced from approximately 127 mm × 178 mm to today's 24 mm × 35 mm—producing the same or better image quality using only about 4% of the materials and allowing for smaller, more portable cameras. The introduction in 1982 of T-Grain technology for photographic film permitted us to produce a better quality product that contained less silver, thereby conserving a precious and nonrenewable resource. Since the late 1960s, Kodak innovations have resulted in a greater than 90% reduction of the amount of chemicals required to develop and print a roll of color film. These and other innovations have made it possible for photofinishers to reduce effluent discharges from 60% to 80% and to recover more than 99% of the available silver from their wastewater.

Kodak also responded to the need to reduce chlorofluorocarbon (CFC) emissions to prevent ongoing depletion of the stratospheric ozone layer. A corporate policy was established in 1990 that called for a 50% reduction in CFC emissions from our world-wide operations by 1993. An aggressive effort was launched and this target was met nearly two years in advance; a 48% reduction in emissions was achieved by 1991. In addition to reducing CFC emissions, we have a goal to eliminate use of CFCs in direct manufacturing by 1995 at the latest.

Recycling also has a long history at Kodak and is considered an integral part of our manufacturing and business activities. Silver recovery and reuse began in the early 1900s. The recovery and reuse of organic solvents used in manufacturing our photographic film products started in the 1920s. For example, over 97% of the solvents used to cast acetate-based film are recycled, saving the company millions of dollars each year. If Kodak were not recycling these solvents, costs for disposal and purchase of new materials would be seven times greater than the cost of recovery and reuse.

Waste acetate-based 'safety film' and nitrate-based films were recycled throughout the 1930s and 1940s. Cellulose triacetate motion picture film was introduced in the late 1940s, completing the phase-out of nitrate films. Waste safety film has been recycled ever since. The scrap from polyester-based film—a plastic introduced in the late 1950s—was saved, not landfilled, until a feasible recyling technology was developed. The initial recycling plant became operational in the early 1960s. This was replaced by a much larger methanolysis plant with improved technology in the mid-1970s. It was the first commercial facility of its type in the world. During its history, the methanolysis plant has recovered enough material to have filled landfill space equal to 100 football fields to a depth of over five yards. In addition to recycling Kodak photographic film base, including X-ray films from hospitals, the facility also handles polyester beverage bottles. And recently the U.S. Food and Drug Administration approved the reuse of the recycled materials to produce new food containers.

In total, we estimate that Kodak recycles over four billion pounds of materials annually, primarily in internal manufacturing operations.

Waste minimization efforts are also active at our phographic manufacturing plants outside the United States. For example, Kodak Australasia reduced emulsion coating melt waste by 33% through improved process control; Kodak Mexico (IFISA) reduced the amount of chromate used in some and completely eliminated its use in other water injection molding processes; and Kodak Limited, in Kirkby, England, reduced its wastewater pollutant discharges by 85% in 1992.

Our chemical manufacturing facilities are largely located in the United States and have been instrumental in initiating numerous internal and external waste reduction and minimization efforts. Texas Eastman Division cut its energy use per pound of product produced by 40% while increasing production by 50%. This cut resulted in a seven trillion BTU per year reduction in its overall energy requirements (equivalent to 3,300 barrels of crude oil a day) for which Texas Eastman was awarded the U.S. Environmental Protection Agency's prestigious Administrator's Award. Arkansas Eastman Division eliminated 100,000 pounds of methanol waste per year from its manufacturing operation by changing the process to use water as the solvent instead of methanol. Tennessee Eastman Division refined a by-product from its plasticizer production process and made a useable feedstock for Texas Eastman Division—eliminating 600,000 pounds of waste and the need for an equivalent amount of virgin materials annually. And Tennessee Eastman has also partnered with Waste Management of North America, Inc., to build a materials recovery facility that not only handles Tennessee Eastman's materials but has the capacity to handle recyclables from over 500,000 homes in the region. For this partnership, Eastman received the 'Keep America Beautiful' 1991 National Recycling Award.

Increasingly, more and more of our products and packaging are designed for recycling programs. The FUNSAVER Camera series is a fine example of a Kodak-initiated recycling effort. Over 6 million cameras have been returned to Kodak through an expanding worldwide recovery program. After exposing the roll of film contained in the camera, the consumer returns the entire camera to the photofinisher, who processes the film and returns the finished prints to the consumer. The photofinisher is then paid to return the camera and film spool to Kodak. After sorting, cleaning, and running quality checks on the components, Kodak then directly reuses or recycles 86% of the components into new FUNSAVER Cameras.

We have also recently initiated a nationwide program to ship the solid wastes associated with photofinishing (plastic film canisters, metal film magazines, plastic film cartridges and plastic spools) to three recycling centers in the United States. Our goal is to move beyond the 35 large photofinishing labs who participated in our pilot program—accounting for 30% of all U.S. photofinishing—to include all labs. We are involved in similar programs throughout the world.

Beyond the traditional sense of source reduction and recycling, there are other environmental benefits. Information storage and manipulation made possible by Kodak products has its own environmental story. Kodak copier-duplicators permit double-sided photocopying and their simple paper-path is conducive to copying on paper with recycled content. Microfilms and fiches permit the storage of vast quantities of data without the tonnage of paper previously required. And the recent introduction of Photo CD technology has the potential to bring information storage capabilities to new heights.

In the United States, Kodak is one of 13 founding principals of the National Office Paper Recycling Project (NOPRP), whose goal is to maximize the recycling of office waste paper and minimize its disposal. NOPRP gained national attention with the announcement of an industry challenge to triple the amount of office paper currently being recycled by 1995. Support for the challenge has been expressed by USEPA Administrator William Reilly: 'This is a tremendously important public–private partnership that has potential to reduce significantly the amount of waste our workforce in this country generates.' He went on to say, 'And, I want to sign EPA up.'

## NEW APPROACHES

The challenge of designing our products and processes to minimize their health, safety and environmental effects has resulted in new approaches. For example, the Imaging Group uses the Manufacturability Assurance Program (MAP), which provides a mechanism for newly considered products, and proposed changes to existing products, to be examined for health, safety and environmental impacts very early in their development. This allows our research and development scientists the information they need to modify products, as needed, throughout their development.

Regional standards and philosophies surrounding product packaging present another challenge for Kodak. Our response has been the formation of the Corporate Packaging Environmental Committee, a group of over 50 Kodak people from seven countries who represent all sectors of our company. Its mission is to facilitate the use of environmentally responsible packaging by our businesses worldwide. Examples of recent packing improvements include the redesign of the manufacturing process that produces 35 mm plastic film canisters to make them over 20% thinner without compromising performance, and the switch to 100% recycled fiber (30% post-consumer) for many of our consumer-film cartons.

Product stewardship offers yet another challenge that is being met by our many different businesses. For example, for their purposes, Eastman Chemical Company (ECC), our chemical group, had defined product stewardship as an effort that applies to both new and existing products. It begins with product research and continues through commercialization and disposal. Product stewardship involves the programs, actions and services related to health, safety and environment whereby we develop and provide information and assistance to customers to help assure the appropriate storage, handling, transportation, use, reuse and disposal of ECC products (and products containing ECC materials).

The life cycle of product stewardship has led us to 'close the loop' on several of our products. In 1987, Eastman Chemical Company formed a business group dedicated to advancing the recycling of one of its key products: polyethylene terephthalate (PET) plastic for beverage bottles. As a member of the National Association for Plastic Container Recovery (NAPCOR) in the United States, Eastman has worked to get PET plastics included in curbside recycling programs. In 1991, Eastman demonstrated to the U.S. Food and Drug Administration its ability to produce food-grade PET with reusable content. Although some PET beverage bottles are currently being recycled by Kodak to make photographic films, this demonstration paves the way for plastic beverage bottles to be recycled into new plastic beverage bottles—closing the loop.

Product stewardship has also resulted in the formation of the Customer Imaging Environmental Support Services, a Kodak organization dedicated to assisting our imaging customers with their health, safety and environmental concerns. This group shares Kodak's resources and years of environmental experience with photofinishers, printers, radiologists and other imaging professionals within the United States to minimize the environmental impact of the entire imaging industry. Kodak people in other organizations in other countries offer similar support to our customers around the world.

These are just a few of the environmental challenges faced by Kodak. We have the organizational structure in place to identify challenges as they arise and stand ready to meet them head on. Our intent is to do our part to help the world achieve sustainable development.

# 20

# Responding to the Green Movement

*Ken Peattie and Moira Ratnayaka*

The environment is an increasingly important issue for marketers in all areas of business. Consumer demand for more environmentally friendly products is growing, as is pressure for legislation requiring industry to 'clean up its environmental act.' This combined opportunity and threat has led marketers to acknowledge that the green challenge will force businesses to change dramatically. Companies are scrambling to generate or regain competitive advantage by proving their green credentials, and to back up their green rhetoric with improved environmental performance. But going green does not make a company secure from criticism; any 'green' company risks an embarrassing unmasking if its suppliers do their dirty work for them. So, environmental performance is a key issue for industrial marketers. This article explores the implications of the green challenge for industrial marketers by examining the chemical industry, a sector facing more than its fair share of green opportunities and threats.

## INTRODUCTION

A MORI poll published in July 1989 showed that over the previous 12 months environmental concerns had triggered the biggest change in consumer behavior since the oil price explosion of the early seventies [1].

Retailers and manufacturers of consumer goods were first in line when consumers began demanding greener products. This pressure quickly passed down the supply chain; green audits and pressure group action have prompted companies to assess their suppliers' environmental performance as well as their own. The battle is on to rise to the green challenge, and industrial marketers have suddenly found themselves on the front line. The situation is summed up by 3M's assertion that 'in stark terms the choice confronting manufacturing business is to develop a planned response which anticipates the environmental challenges of tomorrow, or face the prospect of potentially disruptive externally imposed solutions' [2].

Reprinted by permission of the publisher from Peattie, K. and Ratnayaka, M., *Industrial Marketing Management*, Vol. 21, No. 2, pp. 103–110 © 1992 Elsevier Science Inc.

## WHAT DOES ENVIRONMENTALISM MEAN FOR INDUSTRIAL MARKETERS?

During the late 1980s, marketers were pressured to improve the environmental performance of their product offerings, the processes that make them, and their companies. In responding to this pressure to go green, marketers are faced with a number of barriers to overcome and a variety of strategies from which to choose [3]; these are summarized in Figure 1.

| Green driving forces | Potential barriers to action | Potential green strategies |
|---|---|---|
| *Specific disasters:* e.g. Exxon Valdez; Bhopal; Chenobyl & Love Canal. | *Cost:* achieving global sustainability would cost $3–4 trillion over 20 years, according to the Worldwatch Institute. | *Head in the sand:* ignore problem; wait for 'return to normal'. |
| *Public opinion:* awareness; understanding; concern. | | *Defend:* dispute evidence; lobby; stress costs to customers. |
| *Green consumers:* demand for green products & willingness to pay a premium. | *Complex & interrelated issues:* in ecology 'everything connects with everything else' making the green agenda hard to tackle. | *Green lip-service:* sound concerned; green sponsorship & donations; but no changes to products, policies or practises. |
| *Internal pressures:* employee pressure (mainly from younger & women managers) | *Incomplete information:* on environmental problems, green customer behavior and companies' environmental impact. | |
| *Competitive pressure:* firms responding to competitors' green initiatives e.g. in car, supermarket & detergent industries. | *Lack of expertise:* Many firms lack the management skills to tackle green issues. | *Knee-jerk reaction:* comply with new regulations; respond to strong customer demands & pressure group lobbying. |
| *Legislation:* e.g. U.K.'s Environmental Protection Act, California's 'Big Green'. | | *Follow the herd:* keep up with competitors' products & promotions. |
| *Changing societal values:* away from consumerism to stewardship & conservation. | *Lack of commitment:* among poorly informed managers; or those who perceive a value clash between green and business. | |
| *Ethical investments:* worth $500 B in U.S. & £200 M in U.K. | | *Piecemeal initiatives:* sporadic changes to specific products, practises & promotion. |
| *Media interest:* ten-fold increase in green media coverage during late '80s. | *Timescales:* green problems may take decades to evolve and longer to solve. | |
| *Pressure groups:* increasing membership, wealth & sophistication. | *Disparities:* between regions, industries and companies in burden of environmental risks, costs and problems. | *Green selling:* stress green elements of existing product offerings. |
| *Rising costs of mishaps:* Exxon Valdez clean-up cost $2B; Love Canal cost $270M | | *Green marketing:* new product development; research customer needs; new marketing mix. |
| *Scientific evidence:* e.g. discovery of hole in ozone layer. | *Growth expectations:* among shareholders, and national & regional governments. | *Greening the company:* change company's structure, policies & practises. Use of green audits & support from top management. |
| *Opportunities:* global green technology market currently valued at over $300B. | *Organizational barriers:* including inertia and parochialism. | |

Figure 1. Responding to the Green Challenge—A Model.

It may be difficult for industrial marketers to respond correctly to the green challenge, since they are a step removed from green consumer pressure and may have to second guess their customers' response. The rapid and unpredictable evolution of the green agenda calls for new skills, information, and perspectives. According to Mitchell [4],

One of the big messages is 'suppliers watch out.' Nearly every sector is going to be scrutinizing their suppliers' activities from pesticides on food, animal testing on toiletries, polluting activities of vehicle components, to hardwood sources of builders. Brewers, consumer electronics, photographic, and clothing companies will all be trying to eliminate certain chemicals from their production processes; while food, toy, building, and industrial companies will be changing the components of their products (p. 34).

The green issue is potentially important for many industrial marketers, and is here to stay. *Marketing* suveyed 152 top marketers [4]:

- 80% believe that business will be forced to change dramatically in response to the growing ecological crisis;
- 20% see green ideas as a threat to a free market economy;
- 92% see the green movement as a permanent change in society and consumers, rather than a short-term fad.

Interestingly, this survey also asked which industry sectors face major opportunities or threats from the green movement. Chemicals were the most popular choice of industry for threats, but also the second most popular choice for opportunities (after the food industry). This makes the chemical industry particularly interesting to study. It may be hard to say whether green is a threat or an opportunity; but environmental performance will be a key issue for major producers and users of chemicals in the 1990s and beyond.


## THE CHEMICAL INDUSTRY AND THE ENVIRONMENT

### High profile and high pressure

'Our health, natural environment, and quality of life are threatened by chemical pollution of the food which nourishes us, the air we breathe, and our ocean waters. . . . These environmental problems arise from a common dependence on toxic chemicals in all aspects of the economy.' This introduction to California's Environmental Pollution Act demonstrates the high profile that chemicals have in the green debate [5]. The application of chemicals to the environment has increased dramatically in recent years. Since 1950, while industrial output rose sevenfold, use of chemical fertilizer increased ninefold and pesticide by a factor of 35 [6]. Many key environmental problems, such as ozone depletion and air, water, and land pollution, are linked to chemicals such as chlorofluorocarbons (CFCs), nitrates, and sulphur oxides. Often, these are simply by-products of other industries, but the result is that the term 'chemical' has become inextricably linked with pollution. The chemical industry is not the only major polluter, but 'the size of the business and the large amounts of waste products from chemicals factories make it an obvious sector to attack' [7]. Chemicals have been central to some of the worst environmental disasters, such as Love Canal and the pollution of the Rhine. The resulting green hostility has led to a 'siege mentality' within the chemicals industry [7].

Green pressure regarding chemicals is related both to products and the processes that make them. Waste is the key process issue. According to the *Economist,* 'it will be increasingly difficult and expensive to get rid of corporate waste. Big American chemical companies, faced with the threat of tough new laws to make them cut wastes, have been racing to show how well they can do the job voluntarily' [8]. Other process issues include energy use and plant safety. Key products under pressure are pesticides and herbicides. These have attracted media attention following discovery of traces of tecnazene and aldrin on foodstuffs [9] and evidence of accidental pesticide poisoning in developing countries [8, 10].

## Chemical industry reaction

The industry has tried to clean up its act in various ways:

(1) *Environmental protection investment.* European chemical companies spend 10% of their $23 billion annual capital expenditure on environmental protection. This figure is predicted to reach 20–25% in the next few years [11]. DuPont voluntarily spends an estimated $50 million a year beyond the legal requirements on environmental projects [11].

(2) *Clean-up programs.* Monsanto and DuPont have announced cuts in major pollutants by 70–90% over two years, and the Dutch chemical firm DSM was praised for a $270 million clean up [11]. Amoco Chemicals has cut its production of dangerous waste by 87% since 1983 (which saved $120 million).

(3) *New products and processes.* Money is being spent on new products and new processes. For example, DuPont has spent over $170 million searching for CFC replacements, anticipating a market worth $5.4 billion a year as a reward [12]. New processes include ICI's environmental award-winning clean ammonia synthesis technique and supporting services and systems such as ICI's expert system to advise farmers on correct use of agricultural chemicals [13].

(4) *Management changes.* Top management at such companies as DuPont and ICI have tied management reporting and rewards systems to the achievement of environmental targets. The French group Rhone Poulenc has developed an innovative green index covering every aspect of its environmental performance [14].

(5) *Policies and codes.* Environmental strategies, policies, and codes of practice are becoming commonplace. The Chemicals Industry Association has recently relaunched its 'Responsible Care' program in response to growing pressure from green campaigners [14]. The U.S. Chemical Manufacturers Association has listed 101 ways its members can contribute to environmental improvement [15].

Although these are all positive steps, the industry's reaction to green pressure has often been defensive. The British Aerosol Manufacturers Association, ISC Chemicals, and ICI complained about Friends of the Earth's CFC campaign, saying that 'conditions of the ozone layer over the Antarctic ... were unrelated to the use of CFCs in aerosols' [16].

## THE SURVEY—CHEMICAL COMPANIES' PERCEPTION OF ENVIRONMENTAL ISSUES

The aim of our research was to find out how aware people within the chemical industry are about green issues, what they are doing about them, and how they rate the performance of the industry in terms of improving environmental performance. The research consisted of a telephone survey of United Kingdom chemical manufacturers. Of the companies approached, 42 agreed to participate. The sample is not large compared to others conducted by major accounting firms and business institutes, and so the results must be treated cautiously. However, in its favor, this survey focused on one industry, and in terms of the responses it was an interesting exercise. We were surprised by individuals' genuine interest in the subject and willingness to talk. Environmental issues clearly occupy the minds of those in the chemical industry.

The person providing the response varied among companies. Most were marketers, while others came from purchasing, public relations, or technical management, and still others from senior management. Each respondent was asked several open and closed questions regarding their perceptions of environmental issues and their company's environmental performance.

## RESULTS AND IMPLICATIONS

*What specific environmental issues are companies aware of?* Table 1 summarizes awareness

Table 1.   Respondents' awareness of environmental issues

| Issue | % Respondents aware |
| --- | --- |
| Water quality | 84 |
| Rainforest clearance | 78.6 |
| Global warming | 76.2 |
| Pollution | 69 |
| Ozone layer depletion | 52.4 |
| Energy usage | 35.7 |
| Bleaching agents | 24 |
| Nuclear power | 23.8 |
| Soil erosion | 2.8 |
| Developing country debt | 2.4 |

of respondents, which was similar to that revealed in the management population as a whole by other suveys. There was unusual sensitivity to the issue of water quality, which focused more on inland waterways as distinct from the general public's recorded concern over sea pollution. One green issue significant by its absence is recycling. This suggests that chemical companies are more aware of the problems, threats, and responsibilities posed by the green agenda than the opportunities it presents. Opportunities for recycling within the chemical industry exists: ICI's Fluoropolymer Specialists Group recycles 1.36 million kg of plastics per year. The relatively low ranking of energy usage reflects a wider neglect of energy efficiency. Surveys have shown that only 37% of companies take energy-saving steps [17] and only 4% of marketers are aware of energy consumption as an important green issue [4].

*How important and urgent are environmental issues?* Just over 90% of respondents rated green issues as highly important; none rated their importance as low. In terms of urgency, 71.4% of respondents felt an immediate response was needed; 23.8% anticipating having to respond in the near future.

*To what degree are environmental issues integrated into companies' overall business strategies?* One third of all companies described integration of green issues as 'nonexistent'; only 28.6% felt they had achieved full integration. Green issues are often placed under one function or area such as marketing, production, public relations, health and safety, or social responsibility. Such compartmentalization encourages a narrow and weak definition of environmental performance. Developing a more substantial response to the green challenge involves consideration of the whole business and its suppliers, and requires the integration of green concerns into the overall business strategy.

*What specific measures are being taken to improve environmental performance?* Respondents mentioned the following areas:

52.4%—improving effluent and by-product measurement and control
42.8%—introducing lead-free distribution
35.7%—more environmentally friendly packaging
33.3%—improving energy efficiency
2.4%—using recycled paper.

In relation to energy efficiency, one respondent pointed out that many chemical reactions are exothermic, thus creating opportunities to harness and reuse the heat produced. This presents an opportunity to save money and energy and reduce heat pollution. Surprisingly, only a third of the sample are actively perusing energy efficiency improvements.

*How concerned is the chemical industry about the environment?* Nearly a third of respondents (30.9%) thought the industry was 'highly concerned,' while 14.3% detected little genuine concern. This left the majority describing concern as 'moderate.'

*How good is the performance of the chemical industry as a whole in responding to environmental issues?* Only 19% of respondents felt the industry is responding well, 54.8% felt the response is moderate and 26.2% felt that not enough is being done. The fact that 85.7% of our sample felt that the industry is at least moderately concerned is encouraging. However, the comments revealed that such concern is frequently prompted by existing regulations and codes of conduct rather than commitment to improving environmental performance.

Over 90% of respondents rated green issues as highly important, but only 19% felt that the industry was responding to this challenge well. Most viewed the industry as a whole as only moderate in its concern and performance. The difference in responses to questions 6 and 7 (below) shows considerable slippage between environmental concern and performance. This reflects a more general perception that industry is failing to convert environmental awareness into action [4, 18].

*How well does the government perform in responding to environmental issues?* Exactly half the respondents felt that the government's performance was 'poor' and only 21.4% felt it was doing enough. This perception provides 'a huge opportunity for major corporations to be seen as environmental saviors because individuals feel powerless, and they feel the government isn't doing enough' [19].

## HOW CONCERNED ARE CUSTOMERS ABOUT ENVIRONMENTAL PERFORMANCE?

Environmental performance is becoming increasingly important when companies choose their suppliers and over 80% of respondents thought it was of at least moderate importance to their customers. This supports a survey by 3M, which found it to be a major influence on the choice of suppliers among European companies. [1]. A company like IBM, for example, 'operates with what are probably the highest environmental standards of any major industrial company in the world ... the business uses over 3,000 chemicals including some extremely toxic and difficult substances' [20]. Selling to companies such as IBM will require an environmental performance that reaches the customers' benchmark.

## TURNING AWARENESS AND INTENTIONS INTO ACTIONS

For industrial marketers, the question is how to develop the right response to the green challenge. Going green can be costly, and the benefits are often long term and not guaranteed. A greener strategy won't work unless the customer finds it convincing, and the public is often skeptical of the green credentials of companies who have ignored or had previously damaging contact with the environment. Many companies are uncertain about how to proceed, and fear a consumer backlash if they get their greening wrong [21]: ICI launched a range of 'environmentally friendly' industrial cleaners, but met criticism because the production process was energy intensive and caused significant water pollution. Environmental groups are increasingly effective at exposing green bandwagon riders, and companies may find themselves in a difficult position trying to match yesterday's green noises with effective action.

### Raising understanding and awareness

The first green step taken by many companies is to develop greater understanding of the issues through an environmental audit, which provides an integrated, holistic snapshot of a firm's current environmental performance. This can help management to predict future pressure points, highlight opportunities, and form the basis of an environmental policy as part of corporate strategy. A slightly worrying finding from one survey was that only half the companies with an environmental policy had performed an environmental audit [17].

Generating awareness sounds simple enough in theory, but it can be difficult in practice. Environmental problems tend to be complex and intertwined. Their potential impact is mostly long term and either almost inconceivably profound or imperceptibly gradual. This makes such issues easier to talk about than deal with [22]. The perception of environmental problems and their causes also changes over time. CFCs were once widely promoted as exceptionally inert, harmless substances. Now, after having been tried and convicted of ozone depletion, CFCs are being replaced as targets of green activists by other 'ozone eaters' such as methyl chloroform.

## Key internal and external factors

An audit helps to identify the key internal and external influences on environmental strategy and performance. Since marketers are happy dealing with groups of 'P's,' it is perhaps useful to analyze these factors in terms of 'green P's.' The internal green P's that must be managed to improve green performance include the traditional marketing mix elements, provision of information on green issues, and ensuring that the company's people, policies, and processes become environmentally friendly. Externally, the green P's that must be monitored include the perceptions of paying customers and the public, politicians' legislative intentions, pressure group campaigns, the green performance of partners and providers, and the predictions and emerging problems identified by the scientific community. These factors interrelate to influence a company's environmental performance and can be used to aid diagnosis in much the same way that Peters and Waterman's seven 'S' framework can be used to analyze a business as a whole.

## Green performance

The way the interaction of the internal and external green P's produces environmental performance is illustrated in Figure 2. The model demonstrates that a switch from a traditional to a green marketing perspective involves a switch from managing the four P's for profit to managing the green P's for sustainable success.

## Practical steps

A green audit won't make a company green, in the same way a financial audit won't make it profitable. After an audit and sorting out the internal and external issues to watch, the company must take some practical steps forward. Elkington [23] suggests a

10-point plan to help companies raise their environmental sensitivity and develop more integrated green strategies.

(1) Develop and publish an environmental strategy.
(2) Prepare an action program.
(3) Lead from the top, reflecting green concerns throughout the firm.
(4) Allocate adequate resources.
(5) Invest in environmental science and technology.
(6) Educate and train.

| External green P's | Internal green P's |
|---|---|
| **PAYING CUSTOMERS**<br>needs & perceptions | **PRODUCTS**<br>raw materials; safety; quality; reusability; recyclability; lifespans; energy efficiency. |
| **PUBLIC OPINION**<br>of environment, industry & company. | **PRICE**<br>including component to cover environmental costs & risks. |
| **POLITICIANS**<br>legislative intentions. | **PROMOTION**<br>green advertising & PR; sales force understanding. |
| **PRESSURE GROUPS**<br>campaigns focus & tactics. | **PLACE**<br>energy efficiency of distribution. |
| **PREDICTIONS**<br>from scientific researchers & interest groups. | **PROVISION OF INFORMATION**<br>internally to decision makers; externally to customers and interest groups. |
| **PROBLEMS**<br>environmental disasters and damage. | **PROCESSES**<br>efficiency of material & energy usage; safety; pollution. |
| **PROVIDERS**<br>of materials, finance, energy & services. | **POLICIES**<br>on information, risk, purchasing, investment. |
| **PARTNERS**<br>in business & research. | **PEOPLE**<br>management attitudes & understanding; 'whistleblowing' risks. |

Green S's of success

SATISFACTION
of customers needs in relation to product & environment.

SAFETY
of products in manufacture, use and disposal; in relation to people (users & producers), & wildlife (habitants & species).

SUSTAINABILITY
of company's resource usage in the long term.

SOCIAL ACCEPTABILITY
of company's products, policies and image.

SHAREHOLDER APPROVAL
in terms of balancing financial and environmental performance.

Figure 2. A Model of Environmental Performance.

(7) Monitor, audit, and report.
(8) Monitor the evolution of the green agenda.
(9) Contribute to environmental programs.
(10) Help build bridges between the various interest groups.


## CONCLUSIONS

Chemical firms are at the forefront of green pressure, and so the trends within this industry may be relevant to the future of other markets.

(1) Managerial awareness of green issues is uneven, focusing on a few high-profile environmental symptoms while often overlooking the underlying causes.
(2) Awareness of the issues and their importance is not yet matched by actions, or by the integration of green issues into business strategy.
(3) More is expected from government in terms of supplying information, incentives, and fair but rigorous legislation to stimulate and guide the greening process.
(4) Most companies are so far adopting a relatively narrow range of piecemeal environmental improvements, mainly related to products, production, packaging, and distribution.
(5) Green pressure from customers in industrial markets is perceived as moderate but increasing. This suggests that much of the pressure to go green is internal or is being applied indirectly through pressure for legislation, from ethical investment trends, and from the rising costs of environmental mishaps.

For marketers concerned about the green challenge, awareness is the key factor. Internally, it is important to be aware of environmental performance as an issue encompassing all of a company's activities rather than specific products or processes. According to the director of environmental services for PA Consulting, greening involves a change in company culture, much like a switch to a total quality management focus [24]. Externally, companies need to understand the current and future levels of environmental performance required by customers, and by their customers; the current and emerging environmental issues and their relation to the company, its suppliers, and customers; and the environmental performance of competitors. Without such knowledge, companies' strategies will contain a large and potentially dangerous gap.

Wars, recessions, and other major world events may push environmental issues lower on the political and business agenda; a recent German election saw the previously successful Greens eclipsed by the issue of reunification. But the environment is unlikely to stay out of the limelight for long. Environmental disasters and companies that fail to live up to their green promises are newsworthy targets. Sadly, we are likely to see plenty of both in the next decade. According to the *Economist* [21], 'caring for the environment used to be a chore. It is now a market opportunity.' It is not an opportunity in all markets as yet, but green demand is setting up a supply chain reaction of pressure for better environmental performance that is affecting more and more companies. In future, being able to demonstrate a good environmental performance may be just as important as good products and balanced books when it comes to winning business, attracting investment, or even staying within the law. Companies who do not take the time to assess the green challenge and its potential impact run the risk of being surprised when the pressure to change arrives. Such gamblers may be labelled 'green,' not because they are environmentally friendly, but because they were naive.

# REFERENCES

1. Jackson, Sarah, Screaming Green Murder? *Director* **44**(11), 56–63 (May 1990).
2. Environmental Ethics: The Challenge for 3M, 3M Management Brief Publications, Bracknell, 1989.
3. Peattie, Ken, Painting Marketing Education Green. *Journal of Marketing Management* **6**(2), 105–125 (1990).
4. Mitchell, Alan, Milking The Greens, *Marketing*, 34–35 (September 14, 1989).
5. Baum, Rudy, Confusing Environmental Issues Face Californian Voters, *Chemical & Engineering News* **68**(39), 7–11 (September 24, 1990).
6. Mitchell, Alan, and Levy, Liz, Green About Greens, *Marketing*, 28–33 (September 14, 1989).
7. Marsh, Peter, A Very Visible Target, *Financial Times* **41**, 145, 4 (March 16, 1990).
8. Costing The Earth, *Economist* supplement, **312** (September 2, 1989).
9. Bangers 'n' Tecnazene? *Earth Matters* **3**, p. 13 (1989).
10. Myers, Norman, *The Gaia Atlas of Planet Management*, Pan Books, London, 1985, p. 122.
11. Blackburn, Virginia, Who Pays The Costs Of Going Green? *Investors Chronicle* **92**, 18–19 May 4 (1990).
12. Chambers, David, and Chester, Elaine, Clean Technology Challenge, *Business*, 111–113 (August 1990).
13. Hunt, John, Better Environment Awards: Six Winners Announced, *Financial Times* **41**, 145, 8 (March 16, 1990).
14. Kirkpatrick, David, Environmentalism: The New Crusade, *Fortune*, **121** (4) (February 12, 1990).
15. Cowe, Roger, How Green Grows The Chemical World, *The Guardian* **44**, 973, p. 15 (March 8, 1991).
16. Irvine, Sandy, Green Camouflage, *Campaign* **42–43** (February 16, 1990).
17. Peat Marwick McLintock, *Business and the Environment*, KPMG Peat Marwick McLintock, London (1990).
18. Touche Ross, *Head in the Clouds or Head in the Sand? U.K. Managers' Attitudes to Environmental Issues—A Survey*, Touche Ross, London (1989).
19. Bond, Cathy, Green Beanfeast, *Marketing* 45–47 (1989).
20. Good To Be Green, *Management Today*, 47–52 (February 1989).
21. The Perils of Greening Business, *Economist* **313** 109–110 (October 14, 1989).
22. Blowers, Andrew, The Environment—A Political Problem With No Solution? *Town & Country Planning*, **59**(5), 132–133 (May 1990).
23. Elkington, John, *The Green Capitalists*, Victor Gollanz, London, 1989.
24. Smith, David, Managing For A Better Environment, *Chemistry In Britain* **26**, 758–759 (1990).

# 21

# Producing Environmentally Acceptable Cosmetics? The Impact of Environmentalism on the United Kingdom Cosmetics and Toiletries Industry

*Andrea Prothero and Pierre McDonagh*

## INTRODUCTION

In recent years the activities of businesses and their impact upon the environment have become more apparent. Within society, organizations no longer face the problem of whether or not to behave in a socially responsible manner but rather which areas of responsibility should they be involved in; be it the amount of money they donate to their local charity or decisions as to where to dump their toxic waste. Problems have developed in the definitions of the concepts of both social responsibility and environmentalism, since each is perceived differently not only by academic writers but by the organizations themselves and individuals within those organizations (Arlow and Gannon, 1982).

The writings on social responsibility are vast and all suggest different activities for business, some advocating business proceed in a socially responsible manner and other criticizing such a role. The problem with those works that support social responsibility is, however, as Abratt and Sacks (1988) indicate, that few suggest what behaving in a socially responsible manner actually entails.

This paper is not aiming to consider the advantages and disadvantages of social responsibility but rather where the role of the marketing department fits and what activities it should be developing in the light of increased environmental awareness. It is however important for the reader to be aware of the social responsibilities of business where, if one considers social responsibility as a system, environmentalism and the response of business to environmental issues can be classified as a sub-set within that system.

If one accepts the trusteeship view of social responsibility (Smith, 1990), where business must be accountable for its activities, it becomes possible to develop this in

Reprinted with permission from *Journal of Marketing Management*, Vol. 8, 1992, pp. 147–166 the context of the marketing departments' function. As has been widely mentioned, business must consider the impact of its actions on society (Petit, 1967; Abratt and Sacks, 1988; Carroll, 1989). What does this then mean for the marketing department in terms of its response to environmentalism by assessing the effects of its activities upon the natural environment and ultimately society?

Many environmentalists, such as environmental lobby groups, green politicians and the environmentally conscious consumer are supporting the notion of sustainable development where such a practice 'meets needs of the present without compromising the ability of future generations to meet their own needs' (Source: Gro Brundtland, Report of World Commission on Environment and Development). It has been proposed that such sustainability will go some way towards eradicating global environmental problems.

The increased emphasis placed on the social responsibilities of business including greater concern for the environment has led to new business activities in many organizations, one of which includes the practice of societal marketing where in such instances:

Companies may be allowed to produce those goods that consumers need for day to day survival (and make a profit), but those goods and services that consumers want in the short term can only be provided on a long term basis so long as the production of such goods and services will have no adverse effects on the environment. (Prothero, 1990).

Adoption of such a strategy means businesses are beginning to change the context of their marketing function so that marketing now requires a wider definition to include the social as well as economic impacts of their activities (Nickels, 1974).

The global concerns of many groups have hence led to social responsibility being back on the corporate agenda (if it ever went away at all) where one element of such responsibilities is the practice of societal marketing by organizations who only produce goods at a sustainable level.

## ENVIRONMENTALISM AND THE MARKETING FUNCTION

Increased concern for the environment has then led to new debates surrounding the issue of societal marketing and the role of the marketing function in the 1990s. A look at some of the more important issues of environmentalism is thus required to enable the reader to consider such effects for the marketing function.

Since environmental issues are now a matter of concern on a global scale (Chuckman, 1990; Cope, 1990; Kirkpatrick, 1990; Krauer, 1990; Smith, 1990), industrialists can no longer be allowed to ignore the impact of their business activities on both society and the environment, whether or not they wish to be perceived as socially responsible institutions. In the next decade, most organizations will be faced with having to develop their business in a more environmentally sound manner, albeit the impact will be greater in some than in others.

The 'global crisis' has increased the number of green consumers (Smith, 1990) resulting in many companies developing greener products as a result of increased consumer demand. Kreitzman (1989) and Knappe (1990) proposed that companies that fail to produce environmentally friendly products will face difficult times and consumers will purchase products from those who address the issue more favourably.

The greening of consumers, along with a number of other factors (see Prothero, 1990), may lead to an increase in the number of companies practising societal marketing. Companies would still aim to make profits and satisfy customer needs, but the consequences of business activities on the environment would also be taken into consideration so as to eliminate any harmful effects for society and the environment (Abratt and Sacks, 1990).

As Krauer (1990) suggests, the environmental activities of a company must become part of the overall strategy of the organization and need to be integrated with all other major functions of the organization, where top management becomes involved with major environmental concerns (Glazer, 1990; Kenward, 1990) and as a result of such involvement organizations adopt the policy proposed by Wells (1990) of 'market-oriented environmental management'.

Such a strategy will impinge upon the marketing mix policies of the organization where these decisions will now have to include three considerations proposed by Shuptrine and Osmanski (1975) within the marketing mix; consumerism, clean-up and conservation. Definition of the marketing mix will be redefined so as to include societal considerations (Schwartz, 1971; El-Ansary, 1974) where the practice of societal marketing will enable the efforts of the marketing department to be more effective (Abratt and Sacks, 1988) in the new society in which business is operating.

## ENVIRONMENTAL IMPACTS UPON THE PRODUCT

The major mix element under scrutiny is the product itself and it has been suggested by numerous sources that organizations need to develop more environmentally acceptable products where such products will provide one of the most important marketing challenges of the 1990s (Foster, 1989). The problem arises however when one tries to find a definition for this term (Schlossberg, 1990). Peattie (1990) has gone some way in trying to clarify this problem by suggesting that the development of 'friendlier' products involves looking not only at the finished product but also, more importantly, the production processes involved. He proposes the adoption of a 4S strategy to enable production of more environmentally acceptable products.

(i)   *Satisfaction* of customer needs and wants;
(ii)  *Sustainability* of products consumption of energy and resources;
(iii) *Social acceptability* of both the company and its product offerings;
(iv)  *Safety* of the product.

The remainder of this paper concentrates on the effects of environmentalism on the United Kingdom's cosmetics and toiletries market and considers the steps taken by such companies in the following areas:

—products and their environmentally acceptable attributes;
—research of companies into the production of environmentally acceptable products;
—production processes of companies;
—environmentally conscious activities of companies.


## THE UNITED KINGDOM COSMETICS AND TOILETRIES INDUSTRY


Environmentalism has had a major impact upon some industries where such industries are involved in some of the major areas of concern such as

—depletion of natural resources;
—the use of substances which are harmful to/pollute the environment;
—waste generation through production processes; and
—cruelty to animals for cosmetic/scientific purposes
(McDonagh and Prothero, 1991).

The cosmetics and toiletries industry was seen as one industry for study as a result of the controversies surrounding animal based substances, the testing of ingredients and finished products on animals and the industry's use of harmful substances (such as CFCs).

The global market is estimated to be worth $60 million (Brady 1989), the UK industry £1.7 billion (National Westminster Bank 1990) and it has been proposed that the weekly household expenditure for cosmetics and toiletries is 2%. The combination of the controversies surrounding cosmetics and the size of the industry globally led to this research study.

Globally the cosmetics industry has been faced with many changes in recent years, one of the more notable being the increase in the number of mergers and acquisitions (Redmond, 1988). Acquisitions include that by L'Oreal of Helena Rubenstein, Unilever of both Rimmel and Faberge (Mintel, 1991), and Revlon of Max Factor and Almay (Key Note Report, 1989). Some large corporations are also moving towards mergers/acquisitions with pharmaceutical companies (Redmond, 1988) which has led to the development, in some instances, of the 'cosmeceutical market' (Levy, 1989).

The development of cosmeceuticals can be related with new products on a global scale. Two new market segments appear to be developing in the industry, the skin-care range of 'angi-ageing' creams (Larson, 1989) and the development of more environmentally acceptable products such as 'cruelty-free' and natural products (Mintel, 1991). New product development plays an important part in the industry itself, e.g. Revlon, one of the largest cosmetic companies, introduced 63 new products in 1988 (Anonymous, 1989a).

The move towards anti-ageing creams are attributed to a number of factors; namely the increase in the number of working women (Mintel, 1991) and hence increasing the number who can afford to purchase such products and demographic changes, i.e., the population is becoming older (Johnson, 1990): de Jouvenal (1989) estimates that by 2025 one in four Europeans will be aged 65 years or over.

The increase in more environmentally acceptable products may be attributed to the general rise in the number of green customers. A recent Mintel (1991) survey found that 39% of consumers look for green products. A survey of women (Dagnoli, 1990) in the US (women are the majority of purchasers for cosmetics, although the number of male purchasers is increasing, Mintel, 1991) found that 56% in 1989 refused to purchase a product for environmental reasons.

The strategies for companies adopting such new products are very different and involve many issues. This paper concentrates on the segment of the development of more environmentally acceptable products as a result of increased consumer demand for green products, whether they are newly developed products or modifications of existing ones, although the conclusions of this paper will also consider the anti-ageing segment.

## RESEARCH DESIGN

### Methodology

The sample consisted of 357 companies chosen from three main sources. The first 170 companies comprised cosmetic manufacturers and suppliers identified from the 1989/90 *Kompass* directory and the 1989/90 *Key British Enterprise Directory*. The remaining 187 companies were taken from the 1990/91 BUAV (British Union for the Abolition of Vivisection) approved product guide of cosmetics and toiletries. There are two classifications in the guide; those cosmetics companies who produce goods whose finished products and ingredients do not contain animal ingredients and have not been tested on animals during the past 5 years; the second somewhat smaller section includes companies whose finished products' and ingredients have not been tested on animals but where some of the products' ingredients include animal derived substances. Those companies who were in both the BUAV list and the business directories were included only in the BUAV sample for the purpose of analysis.

A self administered questionnaire was sent to the managing directors of all companies and was distributed during the summer of 1990. A reminder was also distributed approximately 2 weeks after the initial mailing had taken place.

From the selected sample of 170 companies identified from *Kompass* and *Key British Enterprise Directory*, 17 questionnaires were unusable either as a result of the firm no longer being at this address (questionnaires were returned by the post office stating 'gone away') or with the companies stating they were not in the cosmetics industry and should have therefore not been included in the initial mailing. The sample for these companies was then reduced to 153 companies. After both the questionnaire and the reminding letter had been sent out, the total response rate from these companies was 45 (29.40%). Of these responses there were only 23 (15%) completed usable questionnaires, six usable letter responses (3.9%), and 16 unusable letter/telephone responses (10.5%).

Various reasons were cited by these companies for non-completion of the questionnaire, the main one being that the company was 'too busy' to respond to questionnaires since they dealt with so many. The usable letters were helpful since although the respondent failed to complete the questionnaire, data were still provided on the company's policies on issues such as animal testing.

Of the 187 BUAV companies, three (1.6%) were no longer at the mailing address, (reducing the sample to 184 companies), three (1.6%) provided us with usable letter responses, two (1.1%) companies provided unusable letter response and 62 companies completed the questionnaire (33.70%). A summary of the total responses is shown in Table 1.

It should be noted that where the number of respondents is less than 62 or 23, respectively, in the research findings this indicates that some companies did not respond to the question being considered. In response to the call by Conant et al. (1991) for more accurate mail survey design information, Table 2 summarizes the mail survey design used.

Table 1. Response rate by respondent type

|  | Total responses (%) | BUAV (%) | Non-BUAV (%) |
|---|---|---|---|
| Unusable | 5.30 | 1.10 | 10.50 |
| Usable letter | 2.70 | 1.60 | 3.40 |
| Completed questionnaire | 25.20 $n = 85$ | 33.70 $n = 62$ | 15.00 $n = 23$ |
| TOTAL RESPONSE | 33.20 | 36.40 | 29.40 |
| Number [$n$] | 337 | 184 | 153 |

Table 2. Mail survey design information

| Overall response rate: | 33.20% | Usable response rate: | 27.90% |
|---|---|---|---|
| BUAV: [$n = 85$] | 36.40% | " | 35.30% |
| Non-BUAV: [$n = 23$] | 29.40 | " | 18.90% |

| Facilitation technique | Used | Not Used | Description |
|---|---|---|---|
| Preliminary notification | + | | |
| Foot-in-the-door | | + | |
| Personalization | + | | Addressed to Person resp. |
| Anonymity | + | | |
| Response deadline | | + | |
| Appeals | | + | |
| Sponsorship | | + | |
| Incentives | + | | Findings reported |
| Follow-ups | + | | Reminder |

| Type of postage—outgoing | 1st class |
|---|---|
| Type of postage—return | FREEPOST |
| Questionnaire length | 12 pages back to back |
| Questionnaire size, reproduction & colour | A4 B&W for Non-BUAV and A4 Green for BUAV |

## Research analysis

Initial comparison between the results from the two samples used percentages to consider any initial differences occurring. In order to reject the Null hypothesis,

(Ho—The proportion of environmental acceptability is the same in the two samples for the variables being considered)

the Chi-square ($\chi^2$) statistic was used to consider if there were any significant differences between variables that were not occurring simply by chance. Hence, if the Null hypothesis for each area of consideration cannot be rejected then one would expect the same proportion of environmental acceptability in both samples.

Chi-square values obtained were then compared with the $\chi^2$ distribution using the probability level of 0.001 and the appropriate degrees of freedom to establish if the value obtained was unusually large in order to reject the Null hypothesis. In a few instances the $\chi^2$ statistic was not used since the main criterion (only 20% or below of cells being considered can have an expected count of less than 5) could not be met. In these cases percentages only were examined. The $\chi^2$ values were also obtained using the frequency of occurrences and not the percentage in order to follow one of the major criteria laid down for the use of $\chi^2$ analysis.

Chi-square analysis was conducted for all responses (where possible by following the above criteria). For the purposes of this paper however, the results have only been included in areas where the Null hypothesis can be rejected, hence proving that differences between the two samples did not occur simply be chance. These results then show that there is a difference between the environmental acceptability of products in such instances for the two samples. Other $\chi^2$ figures were not included in order to allow a more general discussion of the findings.

## Respondents

A breakdown of companies by type of respondent is illustrated in Table 3.

The majority of respondents in both samples are either manufacturers, suppliers

Table 3. Type of respondents

|  | BUAV (%) | Non-BUAV (%) |
|---|---|---|
| Manufacturer | 30.5 | 50 |
| Supplier | 20.3 | 22.75 |
| Both | 37.3 | 22.75 |
| Retailer | 8.5 | 4.5 |
| Agent | 1.7 | — |
| Sub-contractor | 1.7 | — |
| Number | 59 | 22 |

Table 4. Average annual sales turnover of respondents

|  | BUAV (%) | Non-BUAV (%) |
|---|---|---|
| <£50,000 | 21.3 | — |
| £51–500,000 | 27.6 | 5 |
| £501,000–2 million | 34 | 10 |
| £2.1–5 million | 6.4 | 15 |
| £6–10 million | 6.4 | 25 |
| £11–25 million | — | 10 |
| £26–50 million | — | 15 |
| £51–100 million | 4.3 | 5 |
| £101+ million | — | 5 |
| Number | 47 | 20 |

or both of these. Respondents thus play a significant part in the shaping of the UK cosmetics and toiletries industry.

Average annual sales turnover for respondents has also been identified (Table 4).

There is then a sizeable difference between the two sets of respondents; the table indicates that non-BUAV companies are considerably larger in terms of sales turnover than the smaller BUAV sample. The impact of their actions will thus be far greater than that of the smaller organizations upon the industry.

The approximate annual sales turnover for 21 of the 23 respondents of the non-BUAV sample totals £515.2 million (1989 figures). In 1989 the anticipated sales turnover for the UK industry was estimated at £1,800 million. The respondents of the survey therefore hold a sizeable proportion (29%) of the industry in the UK. For this reason, the authors feel that despite a low response rate in the non-BUAV sample the results are still valid since the key players within the industry responded to the questionnaire.

## RESEARCH FINDINGS

In developing new products on an environmentally acceptable platform companies must not only consider the final product but also the manufacturing processes involved (Elkington with Burke, 1987). The major hypothesis considered by the authors therefore was that BUAV organizations would be responding to the issues outlined earlier in a more environmentally acceptable manner than other cosmetic companies.

### 1. Products and their environmentally acceptable attributes

Respondents were asked if they considered any of their products to be environmentally acceptable and if so what percentage of their product range is marketed on an environmentally acceptable platform. All respondents in both samples stated they had products considered by them to be environmentally acceptable; the percentages for the whole product range are listed below in Table 5.

Table 5. Percentage of products marketed on an
environmentally acceptable platform (Summer 1990)

|  | BUAV (%) | Non-BUAV (%) |
|---|---|---|
| Less than 50% | 9.7 | 56.5 |
| 51–75% | 12.9 | 21.75 |
| 76%+ | 77.4 | 21.75 |
| Number | 62 | 23 |

Ho—The proportions in the three categories for the percentage of products marketed on an environmentally acceptable platform are the same for BUAV companies as for non-BUAV companies.

$\chi^2 = 25.667$, df = 2, Probability 0.001, $\chi^2$ distribution value = 13.81.

Table 5 indicates that over three-quarters of BUAV products are marketed on an environmentally acceptable platform in comparison with less than a quarter of non-BUAV companies. The observed $\chi^2$ value in this instance is also much larger than the distribution value. Therefore the Null hypothesis of there being no relationship between variables can be rejected and it would appear that BUAV companies are more likely to market a larger percentage of products on an environmentally acceptable platform than their non-BUAV counterparts.

When asked how many products would be marketed on such a platform in 3 years time the 76%+ platform increased to 30.4% for non-BUAV companies; perhaps suggesting a trend where more products will be considered environmentally acceptable by non-BUAV companies in the future.

Whilst these indicates a possible trend for non-BUAV companies to market environmentally acceptable products this does not indicate how environmentally acceptable such products are but rather whether the company markets them on this platform. Respondents were thus asked which of the following attributes their environmentally acceptable products have (where more than one box could be ticked).

In all cases except one, over 75% of BUAV companies have the above attributes in their products. Figures are lower for non-BUAV companies and some attributes are

Table 6. Attributes of environmentally acceptable products

|  | BUAV (%) | Non-BUAV (%) |
|---|---|---|
| Not overpackaged | 74.2 | 52.2 |
| Recyclable packaging/container | 45.2 | 52.2 |
| CFC free | 75.8 | 82.6 |
| Not tested on animals | 98.4 | 78.3 |
| No animal based substances | 80.6 | 43.5 |

Table 7. When did company first introduce product
to attract environmentally conscious consumer

|  | BUAV (%) | Non-BUAV (%) |
|---|---|---|
| Pre 1987 | 54.2 | 21.7 |
| 1987–88 | 27.1 | 34.8 |
| 1989–90 | 18.7 | 26.1 |
| Never | — | 17.4 |
| Number | 59 | 23 |

in more companies' products than others. The high percentage of companies who do not test their finished products on animals will be considered in more detail in the 'cruelty-free' section of this paper.

Table 6 shows that BUAV companies' products have a greater number of environmentally acceptable attributes than those of non-BUAV companies although figures for these companies were higher than anticipated. These attributes are not the only ones that need to be considered as far as environmentally acceptable attributes are concerned, but at the time of this work, from their readings on the issue for the cosmetic industry, the authors considered them to be the most important.

In order to establish how long companies have been producing environmentally acceptable goods, respondents were asked when they first introduced a product to attract an environmentally conscious user (Table 7).

When we consider that nine BUAV organizations had not been established in 1988 it would appear that most BUAV companies have been tackling environmental issues since the mid 1980s, something which is not surprising when we consider this is the major strategy of these companies. A large proportion of the non-BUAV companies have only recently started to address the area of environmentalism for their product range. It is interesting to note here that 17.4% of the non-BUAV companies stated that they have never introduced a product for an environmentally conscious user although they did stress earlier that some of their products do have environmentally acceptable attributes.

It may be that some elements of a product are considered environmentally acceptable but not all of them since the company is not aiming to attract the 'real' green consumer but those who may be swayed by for example CFC-free goods but would not know or even be interested in the issue of animal testing.

Companies were asked to identify the major products that their company produced. This showed that a large number of BUAV companies concentrate on a small segment of the whole range of cosmetics and toiletries, for example soaps and skin care products, whereas non-BUAV companies tend to have a more diverse range of products in all of the major segments for the industry. This factor can be attributed to the sheer size difference between the respondents.

The survey asked if companies had phased out any of their products because they were not considered environmentally acceptable; responses in both instances were categorically no (88.3% BUAV and 87% non-BUAV) although reasons for such responses may be somewhat different. Most, if not all of the BUAV companies will have started their business on an environmental platform because of the very nature of their products. Hence most of these companies would not consider themselves to be producing environmentally unacceptable products.

What is interesting is the small number of other cosmetic companies who have phased out products, especially when one considers the intense pressure the industry has come under from environmental lobbyists in recent years.

Although very few non-BUAV companies have phased out products, 78.3% have modified some products during the past 3 years and 69.6% are expecting to make further modifications in the next 3 years. The modifications introduced or expected to be introduced are listed in Table 8 (bearing in mind that some respondents stated more than one modification would be taking place).

CFC removal was the area of most change, not a surprising factor when one considers the increased attention being paid to the issue recently. Changes during the next 3 years indicate that companies will be responding to the issue of 'cruelty free' products where some expect changes in both the removal of animal based substances and the introduction of vegetable substances. Packaging changes were also expected by both samples, again an area of important consequences in the cosmetics industry because of the bast importance placed on packaging by the industry especially the larger organizations, since it is often the package which persuades people to buy and not the product itself (National Westminster Bank, 1990). It is estimated that packaging costs may represent up to 35% of a product's total manufacturing costs in the cosmetics and toiletries sector (National Westminster Bank, 1990).

As far as environmentally acceptable products are concerned BUAV organizations appear to market more products on an environmentally acceptable platform, although not all products have environmentally acceptable attributes, which is highlighted, for example, by less than half of the packaging used by BUAV companies being recyclable.

This section of the findings concerning products and their environmental acceptability may indicate that the two samples equate environmental acceptability with different definitions; non-BUAV companies are more likely to equate the term with CFC-free goods (as a result of increased consumer pressure for these goods);

Table 8. Modifications of products

|  | Past 3 years | | Next 3 years | |
| --- | --- | --- | --- | --- |
|  | BUAV (*n*) | Non-BUAV (*n*) | BUAV (*n*) | Non-BUAV (*n*) |
| Packaging | 5 | 4 | 5 | 7 |
| Removal of CFC's | 1 | 15 | — | — |
| Removal of animal based substances | 3 | — | 3 | 2 |
| Change to vegetable substances | 6 | 4 | 2 | 6 |
| New formulae/ingredients | 1 | 2 | — | 1 |
| Monitoring of raw materials | — | 1 | 1 | 7 |
| Many changes | 4 | 1 | 6 | 2 |

*n* = Number

BUAV companies on the other hand would appear to equate the term with 'cruelty-free' products, with possibly some other attributes also included. What is apparent from Tables 5 and 6 is that organizations who are operating on a cruelty-free platform may not be environmentally acceptable when one considers other aspects of environmentalism, such as the use of recyclable packaging.

These issues then leave us with the question, 'Does being "cruelty-free" also mean an organization is producing environmentally acceptable products?' The answer to this seems to depend on the definition of environmental acceptability. What we may find happening in the future is products becoming more 'environmentally acceptable' in certain fields when customers demand such attributes from the products they are purchasing. In today's market it may be that as far as cosmetics and toiletries are concerned there may be three types of environmental purchasers; those who require the product they purchase to have as many environmental attributes as possible; those who only require 'cruelty-free' products; and those who require CFC-free products with consideration also made towards the environmental friendliness of the products' packaging. With increased emphasis being placed upon the environmental attributes of goods and services consumers in the future are expected to adopt a 'dark green' attitude when purchasing products. They will then be more likely to fall into the first of these categories, hence requiring both sets of respondents to improve the number of environmental attributes that their products contain.

## 2. Researching of environmentally acceptable products

Environmentalists have emphasized the importance of organizations researching the production of enviromentally acceptable products for future new product development. Respondents were asked if their company was currently researching the production of such products (Table 9). The data provide no significant evidence to suggest that one sample is more involved in the researching of environmentally acceptable products than the other.

What is interesting about this question however is that those BUAV respondents who replied no to this question stated they need not become involved in this research since the products they currently produce are already environmentally acceptable. In future years they may need to consider whether such products, their ingredients and the production processes involved will be considered

Table 9. Researching of environmentally acceptable products

|  | BUAV (%) | Non-BUAV (%) |
|---|---|---|
| Yes | 41 | 59.1 |
| No | 59 | 40.9 |
| Number | 61 | 22 |

environmentally acceptable (bearing in mind CFCs were the answer to many problems when they were first introduced (Kenward, 1990)). BUAV companies may therefore find themselves guilty of complacency if they consider themselves to be environmentally acceptable and see no urgent need to be monitoring future directions of environmentalism, assessing for example the future environmental performance of not only its final product but also the acceptability of the production processes involved. The BUAV sample may find that in future years they have no market for their product since they have not researched the possible future environmental requirements of their customers.

Of the non-BUAV companies who said they were involved in such research only two of these companies stated the research had a separate budget which may also highlight the importance (or lack of it) placed on the issue by non-BUAV respondents.

The questions asked only skim the surface of the subject and further investigation is required to discover what such research involves and what amount of resources is being ploughed into the researching of environmentally acceptable products. With the majority of BUAV organizations being very small in comparison with large non-BUAV companies the research processes of larger companies may have a greater impact upon the industry, simply because of the availability of resources. Globally the industry itself is estimated to be worth $60 million; the resources that may be available for research have the potential to be phenomenal. Many larger cosmetic companies are also part of a wider conglomerate of companies such as Unilever and Procter & Gamble, again highlighting the resources of such large multinational corporations.

## 3. Production processes and suppliers

A number of writers (Peattie, 1990; Elkington with Burke, 1987) have commented upon the need for production processes to be monitored and for the need to monitor or at least be aware of suppliers activities (Kenward, 1990).

This section considers the production processes of respondents and their relationship, if any with their suppliers. Respondents were firstly asked if they have total control over the production process for the products they market; 42% of BUAV and 36.4% of non-BUAV replied no to this question. Many of the cosmetic companies thus receive goods from suppliers. Whether these are for packaging purposes or ingredients for products is not known. What is important is that many companies do not have total control over their production processes and rely, at least to some extent, upon suppliers. All non-BUAV companies and 94.8% of BUAV ones receive packaging materials from suppliers even if some of them are suppliers of other products themselves. This research does not clarify how large a role suppliers play but it does indicate that suppliers are used.

Respondents were asked whether they monitor the supply of products they require: the answer was yes in all cases. Respondents were then asked how they would rate the importance of their company requesting the supply of environmentally acceptable items from their suppliers; a scale of 1–5 was used where 1 was not at all important and 5 very important. The mean score for BUAV and non-BUAV companies respectively was 4.6 and 4.2.

In order to delve further into this issue the authors tried to establish whether 'what companies say and what they do' are actually the same. The next section considers the environmentally conscious activities not just of respondents but also their suppliers.

## 4. Environmentally conscious activities

A number of areas were considered such as the ingredients of the product, the production processes involved and the packaging of the products; three areas which as outlined earlier should be of importance to environmentally conscious organizations.

### a. Production processes

Respondents were asked if they:

(i)  monitor waste generated as a result of their production processes, and
(ii) research the effects of their production processes on the environment (Table 10).

A large majority of respondents in both samples emphasized that they do monitor waste. It is interesting to note, however, that respondents in both samples were unsure as to the role of their suppliers in the monitoring of waste and in researching the effects of current production processes upon the environment. Some BUAV companies also did not respond to the question of researching the effects of production processes for their suppliers, perhaps suggesting they are again unsure about their suppliers activities.

Table 10. Production processes of respondents

|  | Monitoring of waste | | | | Researching effects of production processes | | | |
|  | Company | | Suppliers | | Company | | Suppliers | |
|  | BUAV (%) | Non-BUAV (%) | BUAV (%) | Non-BUAV (%) | BUAV (%) | Non-BUAV (%) | BUAV (%) | Non-BUAV (%) |
|---|---|---|---|---|---|---|---|---|
| Yes | 63.2 | 72.7 | 26.9 | 17.4 | 49.1 | 40.9 | 23.1 | 17.4 |
| No | 29.8 | 27.3 | 15.4 | 8.7 | 49.1 | 59.1 | 19.2 | 8.7 |
| Unsure | 7 | — | 57.7 | 73.9 | 1.8 | — | 57.7 | 73.9 |
| Number | 57 | 22 | 57 | 22 | 57 | 22 | 26 | 23 |

*b. Cruelty-free products*

Environmentally acceptable products in many industries are difficult to define since many groups argue over the properties of such products. For the cosmetics industry however this task is made easier in so far as cruelty-free products are concerned. It is suggested that cruelty-free goods have three characteristics; they should contain no animal based substances; they should not include ingredients tested on animals and their finished products should not be tested on animals (RSPCA, 1990). This area has caused great controversy within the industry since companies use different definitions of the term resulting in companies condemning each other's activities over dubious claims that have been made. Firstly, Hogan (1990) highlighted that most ingredients have been tested at some point in time, although testing on animals is currently decreasing (Anonymous, 1989). In 1988 there were 16,989 animal tests for cosmetic purposes (Source: Home Office Statistics) accounting for only 0.5% of the total number of annual animal tests (Hogan, 1990).

The controversy has led to some companies leaving the Cosmetics Toiletry and Perfumery Association (CTPA), the major association for companies in this industry, for example The Body Shop International plc and one of its suppliers, Creightons Naturally. Standard settings have also caused problems since the rules for animal testing are different; e.g., the 5 year rule of the BUAV organization means ingredients tested in 1985 can be included in their cruelty-free catalogue in 1991. Beauty without Cruelty have condemned companies such as The Body Shop for adopting the BUAV principle and state that companies should not use ingredients tested on animals after 1976 when the European Community (Law) Directive on cosmetics was introduced.

Considering all these factors and the confusion such disagreements have caused for consumers respondents were asked the following questions:

(i)  Does the company use non-animal based substances, and
(ii) Does the company not test its finished products on animals? (Table 11).

Table 11. Cruelty-free products?

|  | Non-animal based substances | | Finished products not tested on animals | |
|---|---|---|---|---|
|  | BUAV (%) | Non-BUAV (%) | BUAV (%) | Non-BUAV (%) |
| Yes | 90 | 31.8 | 96.7 | 82.6 |
| No | 10 | 68.2 | 3.3 | 17.4 |
| Number | 60 | 22 | 61 | 23 |

Ho—The proportions in the two categories for companies using non-animal based substances are the same for BUAV companies as for non-BUAV companies.
$\chi^2 = 28.603$, df = 1, Probability 0.001 $\chi^2$ distribution = 10.83.

As far as non-animal based substances are concerned there is a significant difference between the two sets of respondents i.e., the differences in $\chi^2$ values show that the Null hypothesis may be rejected. BUAV companies are more likely to produce products which do not contain animal based substances, a factor of vital importance to the environmentally conscious purchaser of cosmetics. Nearly all BUAV organizations also do not test their finished products on animals; however in this instance the figure for non-BUAV companies is also high. As mentioned earlier this may be attributed to the fact that most ingredients have been tested at some point thus not requiring the finished product to be tested unless new ingredients are used.

The $\chi^2$ statistic for 1985 (see footnote Table 12) could not be used since more than 20% of the cells had an expected count of less than five. Even so, if we consider the figure for 1980 (using only Yes and No answers) we can state that there is a difference between the $\chi^2$ statistic and the distribution figure allowing us to reject the Null hypothesis. BUAV companies are then more likely to use ingredients which have not been tested on animals since 1980; again an extremely important issue for the environmentally conscious cosmetics and toiletries consumer.

At this point it is important to state that some BUAV companies may be confusing customers by adopting the 5-year principle of the BUAV organization. Here companies operating under the BUAV logo may use in 1990 ingredients tested on animals before 1985. This issue has caused conflict amongst 'green' cosmetics companies themselves where some are happy to adopt the 5-year rule which is criticized by others as being misleading to consumers.

Respondents were asked all these questions for their suppliers as well. Very few answered these questions and those that did did not say anything unfavourable about their suppliers. This may mean that organizations may use cruelty-free products themselves but either they do not know about their suppliers activities or if they do are not saying anything about them because their suppliers activities may be less favourable than their own.

The results that were obtained show that there is considerable confusion within the industry and this needs to be tackled. In the case of new products it would appear that although many non-BUAV companies can claim they do not test the finished

Table 12. Does company use ingredients not tested on animals

|  | Since 1985 | | Since 1980 | |
|---|---|---|---|---|
|  | BUAV (%) | Non-BUAV (%) | BUAV (%) | Non-BUAV (%) |
| Yes | 94.9 | 47.8 | 85.5 | 17.4 |
| No | 3.4 | 43.5 | 14.5 | 60.9 |
| Unsure | 1.7 | 8.7 | — | 21.7 |
| Number | 59 | 23 | 55 | 23 |

Ho—The proportions in the two categories for companies using ingredients not tested on animals since 1980 are the same for BUAV companies as for non-BUAV companies.
$\chi^2$ for 1980 (without unsure).
$\chi^2$ 25.754, df = 1, Probability 0.001 $\chi^2$ distribution = 10.83.

product on animals a large proportion still use ingredients that have been tested on animals, especially if we go back further than 1985, 68.2% also profess to using animal based substances in their products.

With new developments in the market place increasing attention has been placed on the issue by major cosmetic companies; both Revlon and Avon for instance have recently stopped testing on animals. The CTPA also recommended the following changes:

(i)   to reduce the need for animal testing to an absolute minimum;
(ii)  to refine the tests to make them more acceptable;
(iii) to replace tests using live animals by alternative methods.

Companies such as The Body Shop state that these recommendations do not go far enough (Hogan, 1990) although they appear to be a step closer towards more environmentally acceptable products.


*c. Packaging*

As already highlighted, packaging plays an important role in the cosmetics and toiletries industry. It has been proposed that when considering such strategies packaging must not only be economical and ergonomical but ecological as well (see Miller, 1990). Following initial steps by environmentalists to encourage the use of recycled, recyclable and biodegradable packaging the terms have come in for some criticism as being no more than marketing ploys (Schlossberg, 1990). Miller (1990) has highlighted that there has been much 'misinformation about plastic and its disposal', she emphasizes the case of biodegradability where some plastic properties take years to degrade into plastic dust which is potentially more dangerous than the plastic itself. Another author argues (Anonymous, 1990) that surely something which takes 5 to 10 years to degrade is better than something which takes 300 to 400 years.

Despite such criticisms the aim towards more acceptable packaging is still being encouraged by environmentalists provided the strategies are conducted properly. Consumers are now also demanding more environmentally acceptable packaging (Kashmanian, 1990) which is another important reason for supplying it: a survey of US consumers in 1988 showed that 30% of respondents stated that recycling is an extremely important issue and another 50% said it was somewhat important (Lallande, 1988).

Respondents were asked whether they used recycled packaging and if the packaging is biodegradable (Table 13).

Table 13 (a, b) highlights the finding that both samples are aiming to increase their use of recycled and biodegradable packaging in the future. However BUAV companies tend to use more recycled and biodegradable packaging at present and this trend looks likely to continue. This factor may be attributed to the very nature of the BUAV companies' business which is to provide environmentally acceptable products in the first instance. However, with the non-BUAV sample representing a much larger part of the industry it seems that their influence will play a greater part than their non-BUAV counterparts on the future direction of the industry.

## IMPLICATIONS OF RESEARCH STUDY

From the research findings a number of points can be raised when one considers the actions taken by respondents towards environmental issues. Firstly, it can be noted that BUAV companies are more interested in the environmentally acceptable attributes of their products than their non-BUAV counterparts. However, there are discrepancies in some of the attributes of BUAV companies where the issue of cruelty-free products becomes complicated. In future years BUAV companies may be required by the environmentally conscious consumer to clarify such problems as consumers become better informed and require information on all of the attributes of a company's products. In such cases products may require more environmentally acceptable attributes, cruelty-free products packaged in an 'unfriendly-package' for example may not be deemed 'environmentally acceptable' to the newly emerging and better informed green consumer. Non-BUAV companies may find that one or two environmentally acceptable attributes are not enough to attract the market segment of the newly-informed environmentally conscious consumer.

Table 13. Environmentally acceptable packaging (a) BUAV companies

|  | Recycled | | | Biodegradable | |
|---|---|---|---|---|---|
|  | 1987 | 1990 | 1993 (expected) | 1990 | 1993 (expected) |
|  | (%) | (%) | (%) | (%) | (%) |
| 0–25% | 51.8 | 41.4 | 20.4 | 38.2 | 21.6 |
| 26–50% | 10.7 | 22.4 | 25.9 | 20 | 21.6 |
| 51–75% | 5.4 | 12.1 | 14.8 | 23.6 | 27.4 |
| 76%+ | 7.1 | 15.5 | 25.9 | 14.6 | 25.5 |
| Unsure | 8.9 | 8.6 | 13 | 3.6 | 3.9 |
| Co. did not exist | 16.1 | — | — | — | — |
| Number | 56 | 58 | 54 | 55 | 51 |

(b) Non-BUAV companies

|  | Recycled | Biodegradable | | | |
|---|---|---|---|---|---|
|  | 1987 | 1990 | 1993 (expected) | 1990 | 1993 (expected) |
|  | (%) | (%) | (%) | (%) | (%) |
| 0–25% | 85.7 | 59.1 | 38.1 | 50 | 40.9 |
| 26–50% | 4.8 | 22.7 | 23.8 | 22.7 | 22.7 |
| 51–75% | 9.5 | 18.2 | 33.3 | 13.7 | 18.2 |
| 76%+ | — | — | 4.8 | 9.1 | 13.7 |
| Unsure | — | — | — | 4.5 | 4.5 |
| Number | 21 | 22 | 21 | 22 | 22 |

Research by both samples into the production of environmentally acceptable products requires improvement. As outlined previously, environmentally acceptable goods now may become unacceptable as available information on environmental issues increases in the future.

When analysing the production processes and the environmentally conscious activities of companies again it appears that there is room for improvement in both samples. Marketing managers in these organizations should realize that an environmen-tal strategy is required for all of a company's activities, not only the finished product and its ingredients. Subsequently, they should help plan for the future by communi-cating the benefits of a rigorous environmental strategy which is regularly reviewed.

Very few respondents in either sample were clear as to their suppliers' strategies in environmental areas, despite both samples emphasizing the request of environmentally acceptable goods from suppliers being a very important issue. It may be that stricter specifications are required when accepting goods from suppliers, especially if companies are operating on an 'environmentally-friendly' platform.

If one considers the non-BUAV sample, whose sheer size and strength in the marketplace will have much more of an impact upon future developments than the smaller sized BUAV sample, a number of points may be raised.

It would appear that non-BUAV companies are only paying lip service to the issue of environmentally acceptable products (although the results obtained also suggest that BUAV companies are also paying lip service to certain environmental areas). 'Environment friendlier' goods for the non-BUAV sample are marketed to only one distinct segment amongst many others within the company's customer groups. The fact that these companies are currently developing new products aimed at the over 35 age group involving new animal testing of products and ingredients suggests that environmental issues are not a top priority.

The environmental segment is then isolated as a profit generating segment within non-BUAV companies, but environmental policies are not adopted across all of the organizations' activities. This situation is what environmentalists are seeking to reverse; where the practice of both sustainable development and the production of environmentally acceptable products requires the organizations' overall philosophy to consider environmental issues at all times and for *all* market segments.

Such a reversal would find itself manifested in increased resources allocation towards the environmentally acceptable resource budget. That this is not the case implies that such budgets are still discretionary and not compulsory.

From the environmentally conscious consumer's point of view it seems that overall production of cosmetics and toiletries by non-BUAV companies will remain environmentally unacceptable for some time yet if organizations continue to take a reactive action towards environmental issues. BUAV companies it seems may take more of a pro-active role when responding to environmental issues, their current environmental activities however require improvement if such companies wish to be perceived as environmentally acceptable to the green consumer of the future.

# CONCLUSIONS

From the practitioner's point of view the response of companies towards environmental issues in the future will be required to follow a number of routes which do not allow organizations to simply change a company's packaging, but rather to reorganize the whole structure of the firm. Any environmental scanning and analysis techniques will need to take on a new meaning for the marketing manager when s/he is considering new directions for the business.

Firms will not be expected to respond to certain environmental issues but rather to integrate environmentalism into the overall strategy of the organization. For the marketing practitioner this will require involvement in the environmental audit conducted by the company and adherence to new environmental strategies laid down by the company. This and only this action will ensure that the product or service offered will match and indeed anticipate the changing needs of the consumer.

Some possible areas of consideration for marketers include,

(a) assessing the promotional tools of the company to ensure no dubious green claims are made hence leading to claims of the marketing function adopting a window-dress strategy towards environmental issues;
(b) examining the pricing mechanism of products to ensure too high a price is not set simply because the product is green; but also ensuring any extra costs incurred by going green are included;
(c) New marketing research will be required to assess how environmentalism will proceed into the 1990s and beyond.

By far the most important tasks will be to develop an organization which is environment-led and the structure of which allows environmental issues and their impact upon society to be considered and acted upon not only by the marketing department but by the whole organization.

# REFERENCES

Abratt, Russell and Sacks, Diane (1988). 'The marketing challenge: towards being profitable and socially responsible', *Journal of Business Ethics*, **7**, No. 7, pp. 497–507.
Anonymous (1989a), '100 Leading Advertisers', *Advertising Age*, **60**, No. 42, pp. 108–114.
Anonymous (1989b) 'Alternatives to animals', *Economist*, **313**, December 2nd, pp. 97–98.
Anonymous (1990), 'Critics blast biodegradable plastic as 'marketing ploy', *Marketing News*, **24**, No. 6, p. 21.
Arlow, Peter and Gannon, Martin, J. (1982) 'Social responsiveness, corporate structure and economic performance', *Academy of Management Review*, **7**, No. 2, pp. 235–241.
Brady, C. (1989), 'Cosmetics consolidation characterises a moderately paced market', *Chemical Week*, **145**, pp. 20–21.
Carroll, Archie B. (1989) *Business and Society: Ethics and Stakeholder Management*, Cincinnati, Ohio, South Western Publishing Company, pp. 29–33.
Chuckman, J. W. (1990), 'The environment and the economy: aspects from an industry point of view', *Vital Speeches*, **56**, No. 21, pp. 657–661.
Conant, J. S., Smart, D. T. and Walker, B. J. (1991) 'Mail survey facilitation techniques: An assessment and proposal regarding reporting practices', *Journal of the Marketing Research Society*, **32**, No. 4, pp. 569–582.

Cope, David, in Kenward, Michael (1990), 'The green company can we manage it?' *Director*, December, pp. 92–96.

Dagnoli, Judann (1990), 'Green buys take root' *Advertising Age*, **61**, No. 36, p. 27.

de Jouvenel, Huges (1989), 'Europe's ageing population: trends and challenges to 2025', *Futures, Population Supplement*, pp. S5–S52.

El-Ansary, A. I. (1974), 'Societal marketing: a strategic view of the marketing mix in the 1970's', *Journal of the Academy of Marketing Science*, **2**, pp. 553–566.

Elkington, J. with Burke, T. (1987), *The Green Capitalists: Industry's Search for Environmental Excellence*, London, Victor Gollancz Ltd.

Foster, Anna (1989), 'Decent clean and true, *Management Today*, February, pp. 56–60.

Glazer, Walt (1990), 'Environmentalism will change course of research', *Marketing News*, March 19th, p. 19.

Hogan, Karen (1990), 'Testing time for cosmetics', *Marketing*, June 21st, pp. 22–23.

Johnson, Paul (1990), 'Our ageing population—the implications for business and government', *Long Range Planning*, **23**, No. 2, pp. 55–62.

Kashmanian, Richard M. (1990), 'Let's topple the recycling wall too', *Marketing News*, **24**, No. 6, p. 20.

Kenward, Michael (1990), 'The green company can we manage it?' *Director*, December, pp. 92–96.

Key Note Report, (1989), 'Cosmetics', *Key Note Publications*.

Kirkpatrick, David (1990), 'Environmentalism', *Fortune*, February 12th, pp. 44–51.

Knappe, Ernst G. (1990), 'Combining economic growth and environmental concern', *World of Banking*, **9**, No. 4, pp. 15–17.

Krauer, Alex (1990), 'Environmental leadership beyond supply and demand', *World of Banking*, **9**, No. 4, pp. 12–14.

Kreitzman, Leon (1989), 'Market research: green with guilt', *Marketing*, February 23rd, pp. 43–46.

Lallande, A. (1988), 'Environmental marketing: The next wave', *Marketing and Media Decisions*, **23**, December, pp. 174–176.

Larson, Melissa (1989), 'Packaging lures new cosmetic consumers', *Packaging*, **34**, No. 6, pp. 36–39.

Levy, Liz (1989), 'Cosmeceuticals: saving face', *Marketing*, August 3rd, pp. 22–23.

Market Intelligence, (1991), 'Make-up', *Mintel Publications*, January.

McDonagh, Pierre and Prothero, Andrea, (1991), 'The changing face of the United Kingdom cosmetics industry? strategic responses to environmentalism', *Proceedings of the 20th European Marketing Academy Conference*, **2**, pp. 385–403.

Miller, Cyndee (1990), 'Use of environment-friendly packaging may take a while', *Marketing News*, **24**, No. 6, p. 18.

National Westminster Bank, (1990), 'Cosmetics and toiletries industry brief', *Market Intelligence Department*, August.

Nickels, W. G. (1974), 'Conceptual conflicts in marketing', *Journal of Economics and Business*, **26**, pp. 140–143.

Peattie, Kenneth J. (1990), 'Painting marketing education green (or how to recycle old ideas)', *Journal of Marketing Management*, **6**, No. 2, pp. 105–125.

Petit, Thomas A. (1967) *The Moral Crisis in Management*, New York, McGraw-Hill.

Prothero, Andrea (1990), 'Green consumerism and the societal marketing concept: marketing strategies for the 1990's', *Journal of Marketing Management*, **6**, No. 2, pp. 87–103.

Redmond, Steve (1988), 'The fragrance industry: nothing to sniff at', *Marketing*, June 16th, pp. 24–25.

RSPCA, Pamphlet (1990) *Cruelty free cosmetics and toiletries—what you should know*, June 19th.

Schlossberg, Howard (1990), 'Greening of America awaits green light from leaders, consumers', *Marketing News*, **24**, No. 6, pp. 1, 16.

Schwartz, G. (1971), 'Marketing: the societal concept', *University of Washington Business Review*, **31**, pp. 33–38.

Shuptrine, F. K. and Osmanski, F. A. (1975), 'Marketing's changing role: expanding or contracting?' *Journal of Marketing*, **39**, pp. 58–66.

Smith, N. Craig (1990), *Morality and the Market: Consumer Pressure for Corporate Accountability*, London, Routledge, pp. 64–69.

Smith, Greg (1990), 'How green is my valley?' *Marketing and Research Today*, **18**, No. 2, pp. 76–82.

Wells, Richard P. (1990), 'Environmental performance will count in the 1990's', *Marketing News*, March 19th, p. 22.

# 22

# Greening New Product Development: The Pathway to Corporate Environmental Excellence?

*Janine Dermody and Stuart Hanmer-Lloyd*

WHY DOES business need to adopt an environmentally-responsible orientation throughout its policies, strategies and operations? Is there really a need to develop products with less harmful impacts on the natural environment? While the strategic importance of developing environmentally-responsible new products cannot be denied, to what extent is business recognising the opportunities and benefits arising from the environmental agenda?

This paper reports on qualitative research into the development of environmentally-responsible new products. It begins by considering the concept of corporate environmental responsibility and the strategic importance of environmentally-responsible new product development. On the basis of qualitative research findings, the evidence suggests that while manufacturers are attempting to integrate environmental responsibility into their new product development, it is a very complex and difficult task. Guidelines to assist the development of environmentally-responsible new products are identified as being critical, not only in new product development, but also in cultivating an environmentally-responsible orientation throughout the organisation.

## INTRODUCTION: CORPORATE ENVIRONMENTAL RESPONSIBILITY

CORPORATE responsibility involves the recognition that business objectives should reach beyond profit to include concern for the community and natural environment. Responsible companies set environmental standards above the requirements of legislation, incorporate environmental concerns into their mainstream operations, and have product stewardship policies, i.e. responsibility for products from cradle to grave. This product stewardship is based on the concept of 'clean design', i.e. aiming

Reprinted with permission from *Greener Management International*, Issue 11, July 1995, pp. 73–88
© 1995 *Greener Management International*

for minimal environmental impact through radical re-design of processes and product reformulations (see James, 'The Corporate Response'). This responsibility applies to all strategic and operational functions; greener marketing for example can be defined as:

. . . a holistic and responsible strategic management process that identifies, anticipates, satisfies and fulfils stakeholder needs, for a reasonable reward, that does not adversely affect human or natural environmental well-being (Charter, *Greener Marketing*).

This will involve matching the environmental performance of products and processes with stakeholder needs and environmental concerns (see Peattie, 'Painting Market Education').

Conceptually, therefore, it would appear that environmental responsibility within product development involves:

- Product stewardship, i.e. developing products with minimal environmental impact from cradle to grave
- Holistic development based on the principles of corporate responsibility
- Matching environmental performance with stakeholder needs
- Adopting a proactive approach to greener product development

However, while the concept of environmental responsibility is rooted in ethics and corporate responsibility, the development of environmentally-responsible new products would appear to be based more on business excellence and long-term vision rather than corporate altruism. Developing environmentally-responsible new products can improve the survival rate of both brands and companies by strengthening their competitive, strategic and financial positions.

## THE STRATEGIC IMPORTANCE OF DEVELOPING ENVIRONMENTALLY-RESPONSIBLE NEW PRODUCTS

A major challenge facing business in the 1990s is the need for new products that can improve the financial and competitive position of the company and at the same time reduce their negative impact on the natural environment (see Dermody and Hanmer-Lloyd, 'Developing Environmentally Responsible New Products'). Companies who respond positively to the challenge of improving environmental performance are likely to be at the forefront of industry. They will be developing new products in new markets as the EC envisage, satisfying the needs of their stakeholders and achieving advantage over their competitors. Environmental excellence is also increasingly being recognised as one route to total quality. Developing environmentally-responsible products can help achieve this environmental quality and excellence (see Coddington, *Environmental Marketing*; FitzGerald, 'Selecting Measures ...').

Developing environmentally-responsible new products may improve the survival rate of companies by strengthening their competitive, strategic and financial positions (see Dermody, *Guidelines* ...). Since the mid-1980s, companies have been

- Parent company
- Board of Directors
- Senior management
- Employees
- Customers
- The community
- Legislators
- Investors
- Suppliers
- Pressure groups
- Competitors
- The media
- Trade unions
- Professional bodies
- Pensioners
- Academia
- Dealers

Figure 1. Stakeholders Impacting on the Organization.

(*Source*: adapted from M. Charter, *Greener Marketing: A Responsible Approach to Business* (Sheffield, UK: Greenleaf Publishing, 1992), p. 67).

increasingly recognising the strategic opportunities that can arise from adopting an environmental orientation in their business practices and strategies. Companies who respond positively to the challenges of integrating environmental attributes into their product portfolios are likely to be at the forefront of their industry segments and as such will reap the rewards of first mover advantage.

Companies also need to respond to the increasing environmental pressures being exerted on them by their stakeholders. Charter (*op. cit.*) identified a number of potential stakeholders impacting on an organisation. As can be seen from Figure 1, the source of potential environmental pressures on an organisation is quite extensive.

However, Welford and Gouldson (*Environmental Management*), while recognising the range of stakeholder pressures impacting on an organisation, maintain that environmental legislators play a critical role in persuading organisations to adopt an environmentally-responsible orientation.

Regardless of individual impacts of specific factors, overall the ensuing environmental concerns and regulations have reshaped the business market. This has resulted in the revision and development of new management practices, strategies, and policies, and investment in science and technology in order to develop new products with minimal negative environmental impact.

The specific benefits of developing environmentally-responsible new products include:

- Corporate growth (sales and profit)
- Long-term corporate survival
- Competitive advantage from environmentally-responsible product and process opportunities
- Corporate expansion into new markets requiring environmentally-responsible products and processes

- Enhancing the reputation and position of the company as a product innovator who strives for continuous product improvement and total quality
- Reinforcing the 'responsible, caring' image of the company
- Encouraging investment in technology and science as a foundation to product advances
- Avoiding negative publicity about inactivity or an uncaring stance
- Avoiding fines and liability resulting from failure to comply with environmental legislation
- Reducing the environmental pressure from stakeholders by satisfying their environmental demands and needs and wants for environmental product features
- Environmental developments will encourage dialogue and involvement among interested parties. As a result, companies can become actively involved in the decision-making that will affect their new product development: for example, ecolabelling criteria.

So an environmentally-responsible new product would appear to be characterised by reduced environmental impact during the product's development, manufacture, use and disposal; satisfying the demands of a range of stakeholders; and providing strategic and financial benefits to the company. Developing environmentally-responsible new products would therefore appear to be based around business excellence and long-term vision rather than corporate altruism. Their development represents very good business practice (see Welford and Gouldson, *op. cit.*).

However, while business has been placed at the leading edge in providing realistic and effective solutions to minimise the environmental impact of its products, in reality how many companies are really capable of achieving this? The evidence to date suggests that, while companies are aware of the need to develop new products with minimal environmental impact, they are ill-equipped to deal with the complexities and difficulties that arise. Many companies do not possess the necessary experience, expertise, or lateral thinking required (see Dermody and Hanmer-Lloyd, 'Successfully Developing Environmentally Responsible Products'; 'Developing Environmentally Responsible New Products').

Given the strategic importance of developing environmentally-responsible new products, it is critical that guidelines are developed to assist organisations in developing these products. This was the primary purpose of the research study. The following sections of this paper will present a selection of the research findings and the guidelines developed.

## THE RESEARCH METHODOLOGY

The methodological approach adopted involved both secondary and primary research. The primary research was based on an inductive research paradigm using a qualitative research methodology. This approach was adopted because of its strengths in providing understanding and insight into the integration of environmentally-responsible attributes into the new product development process.

The qualitative exploratory and case study research methods were therefore adopted for their ability to provide in-depth examination of the research area. Qualitative research can dig deeper and can provide a richer understanding than a quantitative survey approach (see Moser and Kalton, *Survey Methods*). The case study approach is able to provide a wealth of detail, clues and ideas (see Yin, *Case Study Research*). These benefits of case study research are compounded by the qualitative research design used, because this will provide further insight and deeper understanding of the issues, practices, and problems of developing environmentally-responsible new products.

The first stage of the qualitative research involved exploratory depth interviews in ten UK organisations, including manufacturers and retailers, professional bodies, and design agencies. A judgement sampling approach was adopted. Respondents were either recommended, or identified from the secondary research. Respondents were selected for their new product development and/or environmental experience and expertise, and typically held senior positions within the organisations. Figure 2 provides further details of respondents and their responsibilities.

The second stage involved qualitative case study research with UK manufacturers of detergents and household cleaning products. The case study companies were required to be large, multinational organisations with leading brands within the marketplace. They were also required to be actively involved in developing environmentally-responsible new products. Five of the original sample of nine organisations participated in the research. Case study companies One and Two virtually dominated the UK detergents industry, and worldwide had between 70% and 90% of the market share (see *ENDS Report.* 226). None of the case study companies manufactured 'green' products; instead they were attempting to integrate environmentally-responsible attributes into their existing products. While it is recognised that discussions with manufacturers of 'green brands' would have been useful, the research was carried out at a time when brands such as Ark, Ecover and Greenforce were being withdrawn from sale and/or were undergoing revision of their distribution. Access to these organisations was therefore not possible during the data collection period.

Depth interviews were carried out with members of the new product development team, decision-making unit, or their advisors. Documentary evidence was also collected. Figure 3 provides further details of the organisations visited and products discussed.

## THE PRIMARY RESEARCH FINDINGS

The findings presented below include findings from both the exploratory and case study research.

### The principles underlying the development of environmentally-responsible new products

The case study companies are focusing on improving the performance of their existing brands to reduce environmental impact, rather than developing green (eco)

| Organisations | Respondents | Expertise/Responsibility |
|---|---|---|
| Government department (N = 1) | ● Civil Servant | **Environmental**<br><br>● Policy department<br>● Respondent responsible for eco-auditing policy |
| Trade/professional associations (N = 3) | ● Head of Environmental Management Unit<br>● Project Manager (Environmental Projects in Business)<br>● Special Adviser (Environment) | **Environmental**<br>● Associations involved in developing:<br>— Environmental policy<br>— Environmental guidelines for business<br>— EC directives<br>● Advising members/business on addressing environmental issues in business |
| Manufacturers (industrial and consumer products)<br><br>(Industrial: N = 2).<br>(Consumer: N = 2) | ● Health and Safety Director<br>● Business Executive<br>● Marketing Manager (x 2)<br>● New Product Development Manager | **Environmental and New Product Development**<br>● Two of the four manufacturers had integrated environmental responsibility into their operations and policy<br>● Of the remaining two, one manufacturer had recently revised its NPD approach, providing valuable info for the research.<br>● Health and Safety Director responsible for implementing environmental quality across company (industrial).<br>● Environmental knowledge/roles of Business Executive and Marketing Manager high (industrial).<br>● Environmental knowledge of respondents in Consumer Companies limited, focus on NPD. |
| Retailer (N = 1) | ● Marketing Manager<br>● Packaging Design and Development Controller | **Environmental and NPD**<br>● Environmental policy being translated into product development specifications |
| Design agency (N = 1) | ● Managing Director | ● Very active in NPD<br>● Recognised for its expertise in designing environmentally-responsible products<br>● Involved in policy development, e.g. eco-labelling |

Figure 2. Respondent Profiles (Exploratory Research).

cleaners or detergents. This involves evaluating product ingredients and the suppliers of these ingredients; substituting less harmful ingredients wherever possible; developing concentrated formulations to reduce chemical usage while retaining cleaning performance; using recycled and minimal packaging; developing biodegradable formulations and packaging; using butane propellants rather than

## Case Study One
Positioned within top fifty world companies
Positioned within top 150 rankings of UK top 1,000 companies
Headquarters USA
Health and household sales exceed £20 million
Pre-tax profits exceed £80 million
Number of employees exceeds 5,000
Product types discussed: detergent, household cleaning products and washing-up-liquid

Respondent:
*Marketing Director*, responsible for detergents in UK and internationally
*Environmental Communications Manager*, responsible for communicating and facilitating environmental
information throughout company and to a wider audience via conferences, etc. Advises on
environmental practices, EC legislation, etc. Also responsible for environmental PR

## Case Study Two
Positioned within top fifty world companies
Positioned within top twenty rankings of UK top 1,000 companies
Headquarters UK and The Netherlands
Turnover in detergents sector exceeds £60 million (1993)
Product types discussed: detergents, fabric conditioners and household cleaning products

Respondent:
*'Special Projects'*, responsible for marketing within division throughout Europe for past nine years. Now
a 'trouble-shooter' working on ad hoc specific problems. Currently attempting to rationalise
manufacturing of company's detergents and related products. Environmental issues are part of this

## Case Study Three
Positioned between 650 and 700 in the rankings of UK top 1,000 companies
Turnover exceeds £130 million
Number of employees exceeds 700 (UK)
Product types discussed: household cleaning and hygiene products

Respondent:
*Business Development Manager*, responsible for all company's household products. Essentially the
Marketing Manager for consumer and trade marketing in household products. Also responsible for
Catering Division

## Case Study Four
Positioned between 750 and 770 in the rankings of UK top 1,000 companies
Turnover exceeds £100 million
Pre-tax profit exceeds £12 million
Number of employees exceeds 3,800
Product types discussed: household cleaning and hygiene products, bleach

Respondents:
*Marketing Manager*, responsible for marketing and developing household cleaning and hygiene products.
Also responsible for facilitating environmental developments
*Technical team (R & D Division)*, responsible for technical development of cleaning and hygiene
products

Figure 3. Profile of the Case Study Companies and Respondents. *(Continued overleaf)*

**Case Study Five**
Positioned between 900 and 950 in the rankings of UK top 1,000 companies
Pre-tax profit exceeds £5 million
Number of employees exceeds 500 (UK division)
Product types discussed: household cleaning products, e.g. aerosol polishes and liquid cleaners, carpet cleaner and freshener

Respondent:
*Brand Manager (Consumer Division)*, responsible for marketing and NPD for carpet cleaner and freshener
*Marketing Manager (Air Care)*, responsible for marketing air care products, i.e. aerosols
*Team Leader (Regulatory Affairs)*, working within the R&D division, responsible for informing all members of the company of existing and changing environmental regulation and its impact on the company's products and practices. Works closely with NPD teams
*Environmental Officer*, working within the manufacturing and marketing divisions providing environmental information, education and training. Also responsible for advising and facilitating development of more environmentally-benign products. Works closely with NPD teams
*Life Cycle Analyst*, working within the R&D Division, responsible for developing LCA database and carrying out database searches

Figure 3. Profile of the Case Study Companies and Respondents.

CFCs, etc. The specific attributes of environmentally-responsible new products are detailed in Figure 4.

- Reducing environmental impact from cradle to grave
- Energy efficiency during production and use
- Biodegradable formulators and packaging
- Minimal use of solvents and other toxic ingredients
- Removal/reduction of known detrimental ingredients, e.g. CFCs, phosphates
- Minimal use of non-renewable resources, manufactured predominantly from renewable resources
- Minimal packaging
- Minimal waste outputs from product during manufacture, use and disposal
- Re-use, recycle, reduce: packaging and raw materials
- Developing concentrated formulations
- Integral part of health and safety requirements
- High performance
- Extended product lifespan: designed to last, be re-used, or recycled
- Not tested on animals
- Satisfying the needs and wants of the organisation's stakeholders
- Environmental information on product packaging

Figure 4. Environmentally-Responsible Product Attributes.

(*Source*: adapted from J. Dermody, Guidelines on Developing Environmentally Responsible New Products (PhD Thesis, Bristol Business School, University of the West of England, 1994)).

The primary research indicated that an environmentally-responsible new product is characterised by three fundamental goals:

- New product development should aim to reduce the environmental impact of the product from its initial conception through to final disposal, i.e. product stewardship from cradle to grave.
- The environmentally-responsible new product being developed must be able to satisfy the various needs of stakeholders without compromising the needs of future generations. For example, undiluted product performance would appear to be an essential consumer need.
- A proactive approach to environmentally-responsible new product development should be adopted where the organisation sets and meets environmental standards above those required by legislation. In doing so, companies will be aiming for environmental excellence and quality.

The concept of environmental responsibility therefore encompasses all stages of the products lifecycle and builds on brand reputation, strength and performance in order to achieve some differential advantage and to build on the needs and wants of the organisation's target market. So the key to the successful development of environmentally-responsible cleaners and detergents involves:

> Environmental Attributes + Product Performance
> = Product Quality
> = Consumer Satisfaction + Strategic and Financial Benefits = NPD Success
> (see Note 1)

Essentially, this equation represents the foundation of environmentally-responsible new product development (NPD). It indicates that environmental attributes and product performance must interrelate and complement each other. Reducing product performance, for example by substituting the solvents in household cleaning products with water- or plant-based substitutes is unlikely to satisfy consumer needs for high-performance, quality products. Consumers in turn will no longer purchase the product; for example, the demand for Ark and Ecover cleaners and detergents was limited to the very committed green consumer segments. This will threaten the strategic and financial position of the brand and company. Environmental responsibility therefore involves a variety of considerations revolving around.

- Reducing environmental impact throughout the product lifecycle
- Improving product performance through total quality goals based on continuous improvements
- Satisfying consumer expectations, values, needs and wants for a performance product with built-in environmental attributes
- Satisfying the demands of other stakeholder groups, for example conforming to or exceeding environmental legislation
- Strengthening the strategic position of the organisation

## STAKEHOLDER INFLUENCES ON THE DEVELOPMENT OF ENVIRONMENTALLY-RESPONSIBLE NEW PRODUCTS

While the development of new products is traditionally perceived in terms of satisfying consumer needs and wants, the primary research indicated that the development of environmentally-responsible new products also occurs in response to a range of other stakeholder influences. The primary influences are:

- **Parent company:** via corporate environmental policies and objectives
- **Environmental legislators:** EC and UK legislation, voluntary directives, etc.
- **Competitors:** via 'green' product ranges, improvements in performance of products, etc.
- **Consumers:** satisfying needs and wants by building in 'green' attributes into the performance and quality attributes of the product
- **Packaging suppliers:** informing manufacturers of changes in packaging technology with less environmental impact, etc.

The case study research indicated that the two principal reasons for adding environmentally-responsible product features are exceeding the requirements of environmental legislation and gaining competitive advantage. Essentially, this involves responding proactively to changing consumer needs and wants and environmental legislation ahead of competitors in order to achieve first mover advantage.

### Designing and developing environmentally-responsible new products

The primary research stressed the central role of cradle-to-grave considerations in the design of environmentally-responsible new products. Essentially, the whole environmental impact of the product needs to be considered, i.e. from the selection of raw materials, production, use and final disposal.

Figure 4 illustrated the range of environmental attributes spanning cradle-to-grave considerations. They include: energy efficiency during production and use; biodegradable formulations; durability; high performance during use; no animal testing; etc. The environmentally-responsible product designs of the case-study companies indicated that, while the mix of environmentally-responsible product attributes will vary by product and market type, there will also be attributes universal to a variety of products and markets. For example, the removal of phosphates is very pertinent to detergents, but the utilisation of recycled packaging materials has a much wider appeal. This is demonstrated in the examples presented below.

Case studies one and two have developed more concentrated detergent formulations (powders and liquids) and presented them in micro-packaging systems made from recycled paper (eco-bags), cardboard, or plastics. In addition, re-use of existing packaging is encouraged, for example eco-bags for refilling metal storage containers, and pouches or cartons containing liquids for refilling bottles, etc. These new product developments have resulted in a reduction in the use of resources, the toxicity of formulations, energy use in production, the quantity of detergent used by consumers, fuel usage during distribution because of weight savings, and the quantity and nature of waste sent to landfills. Case study one's ultra-powders have, for example, reduced the quantity of materials and packaging per wash by 30%. Cartons are made from a minimum of 80% recycled board. The plastic bottles for liquid detergents and fabric conditioner liquids are made from 25% recycled plastic from post-consumer waste. The refill packs for these liquids use 65% and 74% less packaging respectively than their equivalent bottles.

Case study five are making a variety of changes to their existing products to reduce environmental impact. These include the use of recycled plastic and chlorine-free (TCF) labels for their range of carpet fresheners. They also use PVC bottles for their brand of kitchen and bathroom cleaner in preference to polyethylene, thus replacing the use of a finite resource (oil) with a much more sustainable resource (salt water). The company removed CFCs from its aerosols in 1975 and volatile organic compounds (VOCs) were removed in 1992.

Overall, attempts by the case study companies to make their product and packaging designs more environmentally-responsible have involved:

- Product and packaging design based on reducing the environmental impact of the product throughout its life, i.e. from cradle-to-grave
- Extending the product's life by developing concentrated cleaning formulations and multiple-life packaging
- Minimising the nature and amount of finite raw materials used in packaging and product formulations
- Minimising land pollution by reducing waste through biodegradable packaging, or packaging designed for multiple lives via re-use or recycling
- Minimising air and water pollution by reducing and replacing formulation ingredients such as solvents, phosphates and CFCs with more environmentally-benign alternatives such as zeolites, butane, etc.
- Investing in innovations in biotechnology and packaging technology to improve the environmental status of the product and to achieve a competitive edge.

The development of environmentally-responsible new products was regarded as a very difficult and complicated task which went beyond the expertise and experience of the majority of personnel within the organisation. Exceptions are the R&D spectalists, the scientists and environmental experts, who, by the nature of their responsibilities within the organisation, possessed to a certain degree the environmental knowledge and expertise required. These complexities related to:

- Increased costs in sourcing less mainstream ingredients and materials
- Sourcing raw materials with reduced environmental impact
- The safety of alternative packaging and product formulations
- Assessing the environmental impact of new products
- Limited environmental expertise within the marketing and manufacturing functions and among senior management involved in new product development

## Increased costs in sourcing less mainstream ingredients and materials

Sourcing ingredients and packaging with reduced environmental impact typically resulted in the case study companies using less mainstream ingredients and materials. As a result, costs were significantly higher. For example, case study two bought a very expensive new ingredient to improve the biodegradability of their fabric conditioners. While the new product development project team were not averse to the increased costs, senior managers blocked the development for three years. Problems can therefore arise when senior managers will not authorise the increased expenditure because they cannot see the benefits to the company. In case study two, the NPD team eventually persuaded senior managers to authorise the additional expenditure on the grounds of competitive advantage rather than environmental benefits. This highlights the importance of emphasising the strategic advantages and opportunities that can be gained from developing environmentally-responsible new products. After all, as the marketing manager in case study four stressed, the predominant motivating principle in authorising the development of new products is profit potential.

## Sourcing raw materials with reduced environmental impact

The companies were experiencing problems sourcing recycled plastic for their bottles. Case study one stated that they would use a higher proportion of recycled plastic in their bottles if it was more readily available (see Note 2). Case study five highlighted a further problem of sourcing recycled post-consumer waste. The recycled waste they currently use is the right shade of green for their carpet freshener packs. However, the waste generated will not remain static over time. So as Radion becomes more popular, the colour will change. While case study five could recolour the waste, this will have environmental implications that will need to be addressed. It would therefore appear that the design and development of environmentally-responsible new products involves a regular assessment of raw materials and ingredients currently being used and the identification of replacements with the equivalent (see Note 3), or lower environmental impact.

## The safety of alternative packaging and product formulations

The case study companies stated that human health and safety would never be compromised in favour of reducing environmental impact, citing the need for both increased safety and lower environmental impact. However, they were experiencing a number of problems with recycled packaging and replacement ingredients. For example, packaging made from recycled materials may not be as strong as packaging using virgin materials. Paper labels, for example, could become part of the packaging wall causing product leakage. Using recycled materials can, therefore, have serious health and safety implications. Furthermore, companies were experiencing exploding aerosol canisters where CFCs had been replaced with butane. In addition, the environmental impact of these replacement ingredients is not always known and may not become apparent for a number of years.

## ASSESSING THE ENVIRONMENTAL IMPACT OF PRODUCTS

From the preceding discussion, it is apparent that the concept of reducing environmental impact throughout the life of the product, i.e. from cradle to grave, is central to the development of environmentally-responsible new products. However, the primary research indicated that it is very difficult to assess the environmental impact of a product in a scientific and systematic way. Three major barriers were cited. First, there is limited environmental experience and expertise within the organisation. Secondly, the factual information available is limited and contradictory. Thirdly, problems arise in trying to quantify environmental impact because of the limitations of environmental impact techniques, specifically lifecycle analysis (LCA). Respondents within the case study companies maintained that it is virtually impossible to quantify the environmental impact of the whole product at the current time. They can however use LCA, eco-toxicity tests and health and safety checks to evaluate the environmental impact of individual components of the product, for example formulation ingredients, packaging raw materials, etc.

Respondents maintained that, while the inventory phase of LCA is time-consuming and suffers from missing information, these problems virtually fade into significance compared with attempts to identify and improve environmental impact—stages two and three of LCA. The case study research indicated that it is virtually impossible to identify accurately the specific environmental impact of a product. There is insufficient available, scientifically-proven information on the environmental impact of products, their ingredients and packaging. For example, in case study four, the results of an enquiry the company were making into the energy used to manufacture a particular material indicated that nobody knew, not even the suppliers of the material. This lack of factual information makes the identification of environmental impact very difficult to achieve. These problems are exacerbated by the limited environmental expertise of some members of the new product development team, typically marketing and production.

Furthermore, even if environmental impact can be established, how can companies begin to compare the impact on different aspects of the environment, i.e. land, air and water pollution? Are they equally important, or do any have priority? This was a major concern expressed in the case study research. Improvement analysis therefore might require companies to trade off one environmental impact against another.

Problems also arise when companies misuse the LCA technique to their own advantage. The respondents were concerned that LCA was being manipulated to support the activities of particular industry segments, such as the phosphate manufacturers.

Overall, the primary research stressed that the assessment capability of LCA is still in its infancy. A direct result of this is that cradle-to-grave is very difficult and time-consuming to implement. This obviously has major implications for the speed of product development to market, which is considered a priority by the majority of companies.

A lot of these problems will be resolved in time as information becomes more widely available, the LCA technique becomes more familiar and the expertise and knowledge of users improve. The case study research indicated that simply by carrying out LCAs, knowledge and expertise will improve. This can then be fed back into the inventory, thus strengthening the application and benefits of using LCA in design decisions. It can therefore be regarded as a two-way process.

Furthermore, the case study research indicated that the questions that arise from LCAs are very beneficial to new product development decision-making. LCA enables appropriate questions to be asked, such as: 'Where did the plastic come from and how was it made?'; 'How did the suppliers get the ingredients to make it?'; 'How is it delivered?'; etc. LCA can also provide a foundation for alternative, more creative or radical product formulations and packaging. For example, LCA on aluminium tins carried out by case study two indicated that aluminium has a considerably lower environmental impact than the detergent packaging systems currently being used by companies in the marketplace (boxes made from recycled card, bottles made from recycled plastic, etc.). Yet consumer research indicated that consumers regarded aluminium as having a high environmental impact. The new product development project team in case study two were therefore concerned that their consumers would reject the detergents if they were packaged in aluminium tins. They actually overcame this barrier by presenting the tin as a refill storage container for their detergents packaged in 'eco-bags'. The data originating from the LCA had therefore enabled the project team to revise and re-think their packaging to further reduce environmental impact without alienating their customers.

## LIMITED ENVIRONMENTAL EXPERTISE WITHIN THE MARKETING AND MANUFACTURING FUNCTIONS AND AMONG SENIOR MANAGEMENT INVOLVED IN NEW PRODUCT DEVELOPMENT

The primary research indicated that all members of the new product development project teams are expected to consider the environmental impact of the product throughout the development process. It was stressed, however, that because of the more limited environmental knowledge of the marketing and manufacturing members of the team, R&D dominated the generation and development of environmentally-responsible new products and the assessment of their environmental impact. Environmental 'experts' also advised and supported the project team (see Note 4). A major concern of this R&D dominance is the need for new product development to achieve a balance between technical, environmental and marketing inputs, so that new products are developed that satisfy the needs and wants of consumers and other stakeholders; that have reduced environmental impact; and that are technologically and scientifically advanced.

A bias towards R&D can result in the sacrifice of the marketing inputs (meeting consumer needs and wants ahead of competitors), which in turn is likely to result in new product failure. It is therefore little wonder that respondents stressed the need for environmental education and training within all corporate functions from senior management through to employees on the shop floor. The need for top management involvement was emphasised because it is senior managers who authorise the new product development project. Their failure to understand the strategic and environmental importance of developing environmentally-responsible new products will result in projects being blocked, as happened in case study two with the new ingredient for the fabric conditioner. Respondents stressed that everyone within the company needs to understand what is going on and why. Therefore, the concept of environmental responsibility needs to be internally marketed throughout the organisation.

## CONCLUSIONS

It is apparent that while the development of environmentally-responsible new products is strategically important to the organisation, the difficulties involved are quite substantial once companies begin to move away from 'token gestures' towards environmental responsibility as an integral part of mainstream operations, strategies and policies. The selection of guidelines presented in Figure 5 have been developed to begin to assist business in successfully meeting the challenge of developing environmentally-responsible new products, the pathway towards corporate environmental excellence.

- Build environmental responsibility into the core of the organisation
- Base environmentally-responsible new product development on a long-term, proactive, strategic vision
- Cultivate the development of environmental expertise within new product development teams and decision-making units
- Cultivate the support of senior management in developing environmentally-responsible new products
- Integrate environmentally-responsible considerations throughout the new product development process
- Encourage innovative thinking and experimentation within new product development
- Aim for a balance in the origins of environmentally-responsible new product deas between the marketing and technical functions
- Be aware of the range of stakeholder demands that need to be satisified
- Base the development of environmentally-responsible new products on maximising product performance and quality, while minimising environmental mpact from cradle to grave
- Communicate the importance of developing environmentally-responsible new products throughout the organisation

Figure 5. Guidelines on Developing Environmentally-Responsible New Products.

(*Source*: adapted from J. Dermody, Guidelines on Developing Environmentally Responsible New Products (PhD Thesis, Bristol Business School, University of the West of England, 1994)).

# NOTES

1. Where NPD success represents the integration of environmentally-responsible product attributes, and quality and performance attributes to satisfy consumer needs, wants and expectations, thus resulting in competitive advantage and profit.
2. They currently use 25% recycled plastic in their liquid detergent bottles.
3. If an alternative needs to be found because the supply becomes exhausted or changes significantly.
4. These environmental 'experts' were individuals, or formed part of an environmental committee or department.

# REFERENCES

Charter, M. (ed.), *Greener Marketing: A Responsible Approach to Business* (Sheffield, UK: Greenleaf Publishing, 1992).
Charter, M., *Greener Marketing: A Responsible Approach to Business* (Alton, Hants, UK: KPH Marketing, 1990).
Coddington, Walter, *Environmental Marketing: Positive Strategies for Reaching the Green Consumer* (New York, NY: McGraw-Hill, 1993).
Dermody, Janine, and Stuart Hanmer-Lloyd, 'Developing Environmentally Responsible New Products: The Challenge for the 1990s', in M. Bruce and W. Biemans (eds.), *Meeting the Challenges of Product Development* (New York, NY: John Wiley, 1995).
Dermody, Janine,* and Stuart Hanmer-Lloyd, 'Successfully Developing Environmentally Responsible Products: The Response of UK Manufacturers of Detergents and Household Cleaning Products', in *Grøningen–UMIST Workshop: Meeting the Challenges of Product Development* (Manchester, UK: UMIST, May 1994).
* Published as Janine *Armstrong* and Stuart Hanmer-Lloyd.
Dermody, Janine, *Guidelines on Developing Environmentally Responsible New Products* (PhD Thesis, Bristol Business School, University of the West of England, UK).
ENDS, 'Sharp Growth Forecast for LCAs', in *ENDS Report*, No. 226 (25 November 1993).
FitzGerald, Chris, 'Selecting Measures for Corporate Environmental Quality: Examples from TQEM Companies', in *Total Quality Environmental Management*, Vol. 1 No. 4 (Summer 1992).
James, Peter, 'The Corporate Response', in M. Charter (ed.), *Greener Marketing: A Responsible Approach to Business* (Sheffield, UK: Greenleaf Publishing, 1992).
Moser, C. A., and G. Kalton, *Survey Methods in Social Investigation*, (London, UK: Heinemann, 1971).
Peattie, K. J., 'Painting Marketing Education (or How to Recycle Old Ideas)', in *Journal of Marketing Management*, Vol. 6, No. 2, pp. 105–25.
Welford, R., and A. Gouldson, *Environmental Management and Business Strategy* (London, UK: Pitman Publishing, 1993).
Yin, R. K., *Case Study Research* (Newbury Park, CA: Sage Publications, 1989).

# Part V

Green Marketing

# CONTENTS

# Introduction to Part V

*Pierre McDonagh and Andrea Prothero*

The final selection of articles in this volume considers the role of marketing in green management. By focusing on this one area the authors do not want the reader to consider that marketing is the most important function in developing an environmental management system. It is not! As we have already mentioned, developing an environmental orientation requires an integrated company effort (Shrivastava, 1994; Peattie, 1995). The fact that many companies who paid lip service to the ecological issue via the use of various green marketing strategies must, however, be considered. The main aim of this collection of readings is thus to show how successful green marketing should be conducted along holistic principles, as is the theme throughout the reader. Window-dress green strategies by company marketing departments will ultimately fail and embarrass if they are not backed up by an integrated approach throughout the whole organization.

The first reading (23) by Peattie and Charter (1994), was published in the latest edition of *The Marketing Book* (Baker, 1994), thus showing that the green agenda has now been integrated into mainstream marketing literature. There is a good introduction, discussing how environmental issues have changed since the 1970s, in which the green challenge for business is highlighted (see also Peattie and Ratnayaka, Reading 20). The authors attempt to explain why one cannot ignore the environment in business any longer (as in other readings in this volume). The importance of company-wide integration of efforts is raised, again making the point that it is not enough for one division of a company (in this case marketing) to be green—it must apply to the whole organization. Some practical examples of what green means for business—for instance, B&Q, Ecover and the life cycle analysis (LCA) for washing machines—are provided. The remainder of the reading considers green marketing in the two areas of marketing strategies and the main elements of the marketing mix. Finally, the reading provides some considerations for green marketing in the future, which links in with some of the issues raised in the next reading.

Reading 24, by Simintiras *et al.* (1994), centres on the marketing mix, considers existing environmental research in this area and discusses possibilities for future research progammes to develop around the emerging issues as contextualized by marketers. The authors provide a good introduction, suggesting sources of pressures upon companies to go green—for example, green consumers and green pressure groups. A discussion of what possibilities are involved as far as greening the marketing mix is concerned is also provided. Tables 1–3 are also good starting points for those wishing to gather further information on empirical research conducted in the areas of green products and pricing, consumer concern/behaviour and organization concern/behaviour towards environmental issues, and specific information on empirical research in the freight transport industry.

The third article (Reading 25) in this section is a practical piece by McDonagh and Prothero (1993), again showing the importance of organizations taking a structured holistic approach to green issues within their companies. It provides previously cited examples of environmentally responsible organizations in the UK. The reading begins with a brief introduction to the various stakeholders as far as green issues are concerned—namely, the media, the environmental movement, governments (nationally and internationally), industry and consumers. Environmental impacts upon the marketing function are discussed and the reading concludes with practical environmental checklists (Envir-Plots A and B) for organizations to consider. As with the proposals suggested by Elkington with Burke (1987) (Reading 17), the envir-plots are intended as guidelines and are not meant to be interpreted as the only way forward for companies wishing to assess their environmental performance.

The area of consumer buying behaviour is an important one: Reading 26 by Dembkowski and Hanmer-Lloyd (1994) provides us with a detailed account of a proposed framework (based on the value-attitude-system model of Vinson et al. 1977) in helping us understand environmentally conscious consumer behaviour. The authors highlight the complexities involved in the purchasing of environmentally sounder products and how individuals' attitudes to environmental problems are very different to their actual purchase behaviour.[1] Importantly, the framework proposed by the authors also enables us to see the complexities of the green issue from both the consumer and the business point of view.

The remaining readings focus specifically on marketing communications (the area most criticized for paying lip service to the environmental issue). The first of these, by McDonagh and Clark (1995) (Reading 27), examines the complex notion of organizations communicating with their ever better educated publics in a sensible and credible way. Drawing on practitioner insight, the authors suggest several management response strategies that are available and outline the process of 'sustainable communication'. Traditional theories of marketing communications have been modified to permit the focus to be on increasing environmental awareness in society as well as promoting sensible consumption patterns. As a result a new communication process, called sustainable communication, is proposed. McDonagh and Clark hope this brave alternative can assist those willing to invest in building credible relationships with their stakeholders (see also McCloskey and Smith, Reading 11).

Iyer and Banerjees (1993) reading (Reading 28) is an exploratory study of 173 print advertisements taken from a wide collection over a five year period. As with Reading 29, the advertisements under scrutiny are North American based: following a call for more European advertising research (O'Donohoe, 1996), a useful task for European researchers may be to consider the ideas raised in both readings in relation to European advertisements. The aim of the authors was to provide a framework in which advertisers would be able to categorize green advertisements, something which they stressed had not yet been conducted. Those studied were classed according to preservation in three broad areas—planet, animal life and personal health—and the article discusses the results of these three classifications in detail and concludes with a number of recommendations for advertisers to consider in the future use of green advertisements. The issues raised here should be read in conjunction with the final reading, discussed below.

Finally, Kilbourne (1995) (Reading 29) raises some of the major issues of importance surrounding green advertising in an excellent and insightful discussion. As noted in the introduction to the reader, one must not forget that the term 'green management' means different things to different people. The introduction to this reading should be read in conjunction with Readings 1 and 2 by Macnaghten and Urry and Shrivastava. It provides a useful description of the links between ecology and nature and the differences between anthropocentric and ecocentric views of the world. The author sees environmentalism as being anthropocentric and ecologicalism as ecocentric, in which your view of the world has fundamental implications for the way future research is conducted. The author considers ecologicalism from two positions, the *political* (a complete restructuring of society) and the *positional* (a need to consider the root cause of the crisis) and moves on to consider these in relation to green advertising. A number of advertisements are discussed in relation to their link with the dominant social paradigm and these are then related to the political and positional dimensions discussed at the beginning of the article. The advertisements discussed are US based and a useful task for European researchers may be to consider Kilbournes ideas in relation to European advertisements. The reading is a well rounded way of concluding this volume as it shows quite clearly that how one views green in the first instance (as discussed in Part 1 of the reader) will have fundamental implications on the development of environmental strategies of organizations right the way through to the communication of messages via advertising.

## NOTE

1. The issue of not placing too much emphasis on dubious market research reports into the green consumer is also raised in Reading 4 by Dunlap.

## REFERENCES

Baker, M. (ed.) (1994) *The Marketing Book*, 3rd edition, Butterworth-Heinemann, Oxford.
O'Donohoe, S. (1996) Advertising Research: Sins of Omission and Inaugurated Eschatology, in Brown, S., Bell, J. and Carson, D. (eds), *Marketing Apocalypse: Eschatology, Escapology and the Illusion of the End*, Routledge, London (in press).
Peattie, K. (1995) *Environmental Marketing Management: Meeting the Green Challenge*, Pitman, London.
Shrivastava, P. (1994) Industrial and environmental crises: rethinking corporate social responsibility, *Journal of Socio-Economics*, **24**(1).
Vinson, D.E., Scott, J.E. and Lamont, L.M. (1977) The role of personal values in marketing and consumer behaviour, *Journal of Marketing*, **41**, April, 44–50.

# 23

# Green Marketing

*Ken Peattie and Martin Charter*

Every one of us will have to face the challenges of the environment in some way during the decade of the 90s.—Sir Anthony Cleaver, Chairman of IBM (UK)

Corporations that think they can drag their heels on environmental problems should be advised; society won't tolerate it.—E. S. Woolard, Chairman of Du Pont

## INTRODUCTION

The black wall of depth which engulfed Prince William Sound, the Kuwait oilfields torched as a weapon of war, the eerie silence of the radio-active ghost towns around Chernobyl, the starving children of Ethiopia; many of the most powerful images of recent years stem from humankind's failure to live in harmony with the natural environment. As the cold war began to thaw, and the threat of nuclear war receded, concern about the environment, fuelled by increasing media coverage and scientific evidence, began to climb the social agenda. By 1991 the British Social Attitudes Survey revealed that 'damage to the environment' was the most serious problem now facing Europe in the eyes of over half the population.

Environmental concern has been reflected in a rising demand for less environmentally damaging products, to an extent which represents the most profound shift in consumer attitudes and behaviour since the oil crises of the early 1970s. Mintel's 1991 UK Green Consumer Survey and a 1992 McCann Erickson/Harris survey of European consumers both showed that over half of all consumers desired greener products, were willing to pay extra for them, and were willing to accept a limited trade-off between their functional quality and their environmental performance. In the UK the attitudes revealed by Mintel were translated into a change in consumer behaviour, even in mid-recession, which saw 46% of women and 31% of men actively seeking green alternatives while shopping. In the USA the situation is even more pronounced, a 1990 survey of 1000 consumers by J. Walter Thompson revealing that 82% were willing to pay a 5% premium for greener products, with 64% willing to boycott products from a 'dirty' company.

Environmental concern and green consumer demand has led to the emergence of 'green marketing', which attempt to balance the pursuit of sales and profit with a concern for the environment and society. As a marketing concept, green marketing is still in its infancy, but by the beginning of the 1990s it had become an important influence on marketing practice. One measure of its impact comes from America, where 10% of all products launched during 1990 claimed to be in some way green (Davis, 1991). Within Europe, a survey of multinationals by Vandermerwe and Oliff (1990) found that in response to the green challenge:

- 92% had changed their product offerings.
- 85% had changed their production systems.
- 78% had changed the focus of their marketing communications.

This chapter marks green marketing's debut in *The Marketing Book*, and will attempt to explain what it is, why it is important, what makes it different to traditional marketing approaches, how to put it into practice, and why it has a vital role to play in the future development of marketing.

## GREEN MARKETING IN CONTEXT

The study and practice of business activity has long been dominated by economic and technical systems perspectives which concentrate on products, production and profits. The role of businesses in society and as social systems themselves has been recognized with the emergence of disciplines like organizational behaviour, human resource management and societal marketing. The fact that businesses are also physical systems which exist within a finite and vulnerable physical environment has largely been ignored as a management and a marketing issue. Green marketing extends societal marketing to embrace society's increasing concern about the natural environment (Prothero, 1990). We can define it as:

The holistic management process responsible for identifying, anticipating and satisfying the needs of customers and society, in a profitable and sustainable way.

The difference between the green marketing concept and societal marketing lie in:

- An emphasis on the physical sustainability of the marketing process, as well as its social acceptability.
- A more holistic and interdependent view of the relationship between the economy, society and the environment.
- An open-ended rather than a long-term perspective.
- A treatment of the environment as something with intrinsic value over and above its usefulness to society.
- A focus on global concerns, rather than those of particular societies.

The concept of combining environmental concern (which traditionally involves encouraging conservation) with the discipline of marketing (which aims to stimulate and facilitate consumption) can appear somewhat paradoxical. Sustainability is the keystone of the green marketing philosophy, which resolves this apparent paradox. A sustainable approach to consumption and production involves enjoying a standard of living today, which is not at the expense of the standard of living that can be enjoyed by future generations. It is a deceptively simple concept comprising two parts:

1 Using natural resources at a rate at which environmental systems or human activity can replenish them (or in the case of non-renewable resources, at a rate at which renewable alternative can be substituted in).
2 Producing pollution and waste at a rate which can be absorbed by environmental systems without impairing their viability.

Green marketing's central concepts of sustainability and holism are both apparently simple but can be extremely difficult to translate into action. This is largely because they go against the accepted management wisdom, which depends upon reductionalism and specialism, and which is founded on economic theories that mistakenly treat environmental resources as limitless, free (beyond the cost of extraction) or, for marketless commodities like stratospheric ozone, worthless.

## GREEN DRIVING FORCES

The engine driving green consumer demand and green marketing can broadly be termed the 'Green Movement'. It has evolved from the environmentalism which was most prominent during the early 1970s and which created the 'ecological marketing' concept (Hennison and Kinnear, 1976). This ancestry often causes green marketing to be treated with a sense of *déjà vu* by marketing academics and practioners. However, there are some important differences between the 1970s and the 1990s which are summarized in Table 1.

Developing an appropriate response to Green for any business involves:

- Gauging the strength of the pressures to become greener, from a range of sources including customers, legislation and competitors.
- Understanding the counteracting real and perceived technical, economic and organizational barriers to change.
- Selecting a response from the range of options open to a company, which vary from doing nothing to greening the entire company.

Table 2 summarizes this process, and although space constraints prevent detailed discussion of the model's components, the underlying principles are described in Charter (1992a,b) and Peattie and Ratnayaka (1992).

The extent to which green concern is a relevant issue for marketers is shown by a 1989 *Marketing* survey of top marketers of whom 80% expected businesses to 'change dramatically in response to the growing ecological crisis', with only 6% expecting Green to be 'a fad which will all die down in a year or two' (Mitchell, 1989).

Table 1. The evolution of environmental concern

| Factor | 1970s environmentalism | 1990s Green |
| --- | --- | --- |
| Emphasis | On 'environmental' problems | On the underlying problems with our social, economic, technical or legal systems |
| Geographic focus | On local problems (e.g. pollution) | On global issues (e.g. global warming) |
| Identity | Closely linked to other anti-establishment causes | A separate movement embraced by many elements of 'the establishment' |
| Source of support | An intellectual elite, and those at the fringes of society | A broad base |
| Basis of campaigns | Used forecasts of exponential growth to predict future environmental problems (e.g. Limits to Growth) | Uses evidence of current environmental degradation (e.g. the hole in the ozone layer) |
| Attitude to business | Business is the problem. Generally adversarial | Businesses seen as part of the solution. More partnerships formed |
| Attitude to growth | Desire for zero growth | Desire for sustainable growth |
| View of environment/ business interaction | Focused on negative effects of business activity on the environment | Focuses on the dynamic interrelationship between business society and the environment |

## A NEW PERSPECTIVE ON BUSINESS: ECO-PERFORMANCE

Good environmental performance is not an optional extra . . . No business has a secure future unless it is environmentally acceptable (Sir Bob Reid, while Chairman of Shell UK).

Green marketing introduces into marketing strategy the concept of 'eco-performance', which represents the impact that products and businesses have on the human and natural environment within which they exist. Eco-performance is not a straightforward concept. A question like 'What constitutes a green product?' has no simple answer. Is it one that has achieved sustainability? One that is better than its competitors? One that is less harmful than the product it replaces?

The eco-performance of businesses and products, like the demand of consumers, comprises many different shades of green. Trying to identify a company as either green or 'dirty' is rather misleading, in the same way as trying to classify a company as marketing orientated or not. Such 'black or white' distinctions are inappropriate for

Table 2. The green challenge for businesses

| Green driving forces | Potential barriers to action | Potential green strategies |
|---|---|---|
| *Specific disasters*: e.g. *Exxon Valdez*; Bhopal; Chernobyl and Love Canal | *Cost*: achieving global sustainability would cost $3–4 trillion over 20 years, according to the Worldwatch Institute | *Head in the sand*: ignore problem; wait for a 'return to normal' |
| *Public opinion*: awareness; understanding; concern | | *Defend*: dispute evidence; lobby; stress costs to customers |
| *Green consumers*; demand for green products and willingness to pay a premium | *Complex and interrelated issues*: in ecology 'everything connects with everything else', making the green agenda hard to tackle | *Green lip-service*: sound concerned; green sponsorship and donations; but no changes to products, policies or practices |
| *Internal pressures*: employee pressure (mainly from younger and women managers) | | |
| *Competitive pressure*: firms responding to competitors' green initiatives (e.g. in car, supermarket and detergent industries) | *Incomplete information*: on environmental problems, green customer behaviour and companies' environmental impact | *Knee-jerk reaction*: comply with new regulations; respond to strong customer demands and pressure group lobbying |
| *Legislation*: e.g. UK's 1990 Environmental Protection Act and over 450 EC Green Laws. | *Lack of expertise*: many firms lack the management skills to tackle green issues | *Follow the herd*: keep up with competitors' products and promotions |
| *Changing societal values*: away from consumerism to stewardship and conservation | *Lack of commitment*: among poorly informed managers; or those who perceive a value clash between green and business | *Piecemeal initiatives*: sporadic changes to specific products, practices and promotion |
| *Ethical investments*: worth $500 billion in USA and £320 million in UK | | |
| *Media interest*: tenfold increase in green media coverage during late 1980s | *Timescales*: green problems may take decades to evolve and longer to solve | *Green selling*: stress green elements of existing product offerings |
| *Pressure groups*: increasing membership, wealth and sophistication | *Disparities*: between regions, industries and companies in burden of environmental risks, costs and problems | *Green marketing*: new product development; research customer needs; new marketing mix |
| *Rising costs of mishaps*: *Exxon Valdez* clean-up cost $3 billion; Love Canal cost $270 million | *Growth expectations*: among shareholders, and national and regional governments | *Greening the company*: change company's structure, policies and practices. Use of green audits and support from top management |
| *Scientific evidence*: e.g. discovery of hole in ozone layer | *Organizational barriers*: including inertia and parochialism | |
| *Opportunities*: global green technology market currently valued at over $300 billion | | |

Adapted from Peattie and Ratnayaka (1992).

a performance continuum, and the relatively of eco-performance is reflected in Charter's (1992a) concept of 'greener' rather than 'green' marketing.

The pursuit of sustainability is the underlying principle of green marketing, and a company can justifiably claim green credentials if it is demonstrably and consistently moving towards sustainability. Achieving sustainability is not a prerequisite for a valid claim to be green, just as 100% customer satisfaction is not a prerequisite to claim a marketing orientation. In many markets, economic and technical considerations preclude sustainability as a short-term objective for green companies, even though sustainability is their ultimate goal.

Measuring and managing the eco-performance of products is made difficult by the variety of factors which can contribute to a good or bad customer perception of eco-performance. Some companies have run into problems by claiming their products as 'green' by focusing simply on the product itself, while ignoring the environmental performance of the means of production or the company as a whole. For example, the £8 million advertising campaign launching Ariel Ultra as a green detergent was somewhat negated by front-page news coverage highlighting that it had been tested

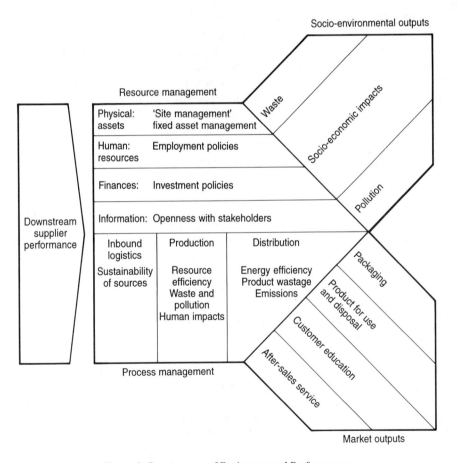

Figure 1. Components of Environmental Performance.

on animals. Companies whose green strategy is product-orientated or one-dimensional, instead of holistic, are prone to exposure by green interest groups, to charges of hypocrisy and green hype, and to a loss of consumer confidence in their green message. Developing a more holistic green strategy requires an appreciation of the product itself, what goes into it, and what goes into, and out of, the environment as a result of its production and use. This process is analogous to Porter's Value Chain approach, as shown in Figure 1.

## WHY THE ENVIRONMENT AND ENVIRONMENTAL PERFORMANCE COUNT

At the simplest level, the environment affects businesses because it represents the physical space within which they and their customers exist, and it provides the resources which they depend upon. A dramatic rise in sea level caused by global warming or the exhaustion of key non-renewable resources will disrupt the economic system, and it is clearly in businesses' interest to avoid such developments. Although global issues such as climate change and ozone depletion dominate public perceptions, the green agenda contains a vast array of issues, each of which creates marketing opportunities and threats for different businesses. So while concern over the thinning ozone layer has posed a major threat to CFC producers, the ensuing warnings about the increased risk of skin cancer has provided a somewhat grim opportunity for the manufacturers of skin-care products. Some issues are industry-specific, while others have a much wider impact. If EC proposals for an 'energy tax' to help combat global warming come to fruition, the entire business community will begin to directly feel the consequences of environmental degradation.

For the marketing strategist it is vital to understand both the potential impact of the green agenda on the business and its customers and the competitiveness of its eco-performance. The cost of poor eco-performance was vividly demonstrated by Exxon's combined bill for clean-up costs, fines and legal costs estimated at $3 billion in the aftermath of the *Exxon Valdez* disaster, which also left 41% of Americans describing themselves as 'angry enough to boycott Exxon products' (Kirkpatrick, 1990). Good environmental performance has become an important issue in many markets because it provides:

- *New market opportunities,* through access to growing green markets. Estimates for the expenditure on environmental technologies and services between 1991 and 2000 are £140 billion for the UK, £860 billion for the EC and £1060 billion for the USA (source: The Centre for Exploitation of Science and Technology, 1991).
- *Market access*: Countries like Germany with relatively tough environmental legislation have developed strong clean-technology sectors, whose companies have been able to penetrate emerging export markets. German companies hold an estimated 37% of the European market for pollution control and clean-up technology and 70% of the US air pollution control market.
- *Differentiation opportunities.* AEG increased their sales by 30% within an otherwise static white-goods market following an advertising campaign stressing the relative energy and water efficiency of their products.

- *Cost savings.* 3M's famous Pollution Prevention Pays campaign has saved the company almost a billion dollars since its inception in 1975.
- *Protection from legislation.* Industries with a poor eco-performance can face increasingly tough and costly legislation. German legislation means that German chemicals companies face 20% more compliance costs than their EC competitors. Companies that rely on mere compliance also risk being left behind by the upward 'ratcheting' of legislation, leading companies like IBM to develop production facilities worldwide which surpass every nation's environmental standards.
- *Improved access to capital.* In the USA the introduction of retrospective clean-up costs for environmental damage has increased the financial risks of companies in 'dirty' industries to the extent that bank lending and insurance coverage are increasingly dependent on an ability to demonstrate good environmental performance.

## GOING GREEN—THE PHILOSOPHICAL CHALLENGE

Adopting green marketing as a response to the needs of customers and other stakeholders requires the development of new products, processes and philosophies which should reflect the organization's overall commitment to environmental improvement. In its underlying quest to satisfy consumers, and in terms of the steps in the marketing process, green marketing resembles conventional marketing. The difference between the two lies in a philosophy which tries to balance a techno-economic market perspective with a broader socio-environmental approach. This requires a re-evaluation of some of the most fundamental marketing concepts including:

- *Consumers.* Fayol once quipped about sending out for workers, but human beings turning up instead. Similarly, green marketers need to reconsider their approach to consumers. The word 'consumer' epitomizes a view of customers, not as people but as a means of consumption. Marketing theory tends to deal with one customer want or need at a time. However, people have various wants, some of which may conflict, such as a desire to own an ivory necklace and for their grandchildren to see living elephants. Just as a product is more accurately analysed as a 'bundle of benefits', a customer should be considered as possessing a 'bundle of wants and needs'. In the face of conflicting desires to consume and conserve, customers may increasingly seek satisfaction through non-purchase decisions (such as repairs). By contributing to reduced environmental degradation, green consumer behaviour addresses an inherent human need for a viable environment, which may sometimes be at the expense of more explicit material wants. Recent years have witnessed an increasing range of conservation-orientated behaviour among consumers, from the recycling of cans and bottles to the boom in returning consumer durables to the supply chain through small ads or car boot sales.
- *Customer satisfaction.* In the past, customer satisfaction has been judged in terms of the performance of the product at the moment (or during the period) of consumption. Green consumers may reject a product because they become aware of the environmental harm that the product causes in production or disposal. They may

also avoid a product because of activities of a producer, its suppliers or investors. The UK's Green Party recently advised its members to avoid Ecover detergent products, despite their environmental excellence, following alleged violence by staff from the parent company Group 4 against green protesters at Twyford Down.

- *The product concept.* If green consumer satisfaction depends upon the production process and on all the activities of the producer, we are approaching the situation where the company itself is becoming the product consumed. Drucker's (1974) famous concept that 'Marketing is the whole business seen from its final result, that is from the customers' point of view' seems set to become an enforced reality for many businesses, because the green movement means that customers (or those who influence them) are now actively looking at all aspects of their company.
- *Strategy.* The strategy concepts which underpin marketing and general management theory mostly originate from military warfare. Concepts of aggression, eradicating 'the enemy' and disregarding the environmental consequences have been accepted in business, just as they are in battle. However, the business/warfare analogy is flawed. For example, for an industrial marketer, another company may be their key competitor in one market, sole supplier in another and partner in a third. Such interrelationships make the all-out aggression of warfare inappropriate for business. As marketing theory becomes greener we may witness a more ecological approach to strategy, where other companies are regarded as 'natural competitors' rather than as enemies to be destroyed. A significant trend within many green markets is an unprecedented level of collaboration between rivals in the development of new technologies to solve common environmentally related problems.
- *Criteria for success.* Traditional marketing theory implies that if the four Ps are right, then success will follow in the form of a fifth P, 'Profits'. Green marketing success involves ensuring that the marketing mix and the company meet four 'S' criteria (Peattie, 1990):

(1) *Satisfaction* of customer needs.
(2) *Safety* of products and production for consumers, workers, society and the environment.
(3) *Social acceptability* of the products, their production and the other activities of the company.
(4) *Sustainability* of the products, their production and the other activities of the company.

- *Demarketing.* One unavoidable conclusion of green marketing logic is that where a product is being consumed and produced in an unsustainable way it may have to be demarketed (either voluntarily or forcibly) to reduce consumption. This may sound unlikely, but within tourism, destinations such as Cyprus have developed a successful policy of attracting fewer but wealthier tourists in an effort to conserve the quality of the destination itself (Clements, 1989). Taxation increases on fossil fuels have also been justified by governments as a 'conservation measure'.
- *An opportunity focus.* In the past the environment has been viewed in terms of legal responsibilities and cost burdens by businesses. However, green marketing should be a positive approach. It provides a firm with a chance to reassess what business it is in and to rethink its strategic positioning. A proactive approach can even turn

perceived threats into opportunities. For example, Evode, the producer of adhesives, have developed a water-based adhesive for shoes, which they were able to test market through Marks & Spencer. This opportunity was created by the need to respond to toughening legislation covering VOCs (Volatile Organic Compounds) in manufacturing processes.

## CREATING A HOLISTIC GREEN PHILOSOPHY

Achieving environmental excellence requires the development of an explicit green business philosophy, as demonstrated by The Body Shop:

> Our products reflect our philosophy. They are formulated with care and respect. Respect for other cultures, the past, the natural world, and our customers. It's a partnership of profits with principles (Anita Roddick, from The Body Shop promotional literature, 1990).

A company's environmental commitment can be communicated through an environmental policy, strategy or statement. By 1991 over half of all European companies surveyed by Touche Ross had developed an environmental policy. A survey of the UK's top 150 companies revealed that over two thirds had amended their mission statements to reflect increased environmental concern (Peattie and Ringler, 1993).

## AN ENVIRONMENTAL POLICY IN ACTION: B&Q

B&Q have produced a detailed environmental policy statement which defines the responsibilities of different functions including marketing, finance, personnel, logistics and systems. It also demonstrates the leadership role that marketing should play in the greening process:

> The marketing director is the main board director responsible for environmental issues and is therefore ultimately responsible for researching the issues, writing the policy and auditing progress. As marketing director he also has responsibility to ensure that the environmental policies and targets of marketing are implemented.
>
> In market development B&Q shall monitor through market research, customers' concerns and perceptions on environmental issues and customers' understanding and appreciation of B&Q's response to them. Market development will also incorporate environmental considerations into the strategic planning in the company and refer to strategic environmental issues in the five year plan.
>
> Marketing services is responsible for most of the purchasing decisions handled by marketing. They shall ensure that 'Point of Sale' material, carrier bags and all their other purchases consider environmental specifications. These include use of recycled post consumer waste, recyclability, and waste minimisation. Marketing services will ensure that no misleading environmental statements or claims are made on any POS material or other communications such as press enquiries. Marketing recognises that some of the products it sells have distinct environmental attributes, for energy efficiency equipment and home composting. We also recognise a need to inform our customers more about our environmental policies and the environmental performance of all products (*source*: 'How green is my hammer', *B&Q's Environmental Review*, 1993).

## GOING GREEN—THE PRACTICAL CHALLENGE

The main practical differences between green marketing and conventional marketing concern three areas:

(1) *Holism.* Green marketing requires marketers to have an appreciation of, and influence over, all aspects of a business, its products and its production system. How energy efficient is our production system. How energy efficient is our production process? Where are raw materials sourced from? Where is spare capital being invested? Such questions were once not the concern of marketers, but they have become relevant because the answers could now influence consumer behaviour.
(2) *Information.* Green marketing requires a variety of information which may be new to marketers concerning the environmental impact of products, supplies, production processes and competitors.
(3) *Timescales.* A 'cradle-to-grave' view of products may mean that their performance must be considered over a period of years instead of moments. Going green is also not a quick fix. It took Dow Chemicals in Switzerland five years to ge their waste-minimization programme fully operational.


## TOWARDS HOLISM—BROADENING THE SCOPE OF MARKETING IN PRACTICE

Conventional marketing focuses mainly on the 'magic triangle': the interrelationship between the company, its customers and its competitors. External factors from the wider business environment are only considered in relation to the direct effect that they have on these 'three Cs'. Internally, the company is considered only in terms of its ability to support the marketing strategy and mix.

The green marketing process (Peattie, 1992), as illustrated by Figure 2, calls for a much broader agenda for marketers both internally and externally. Since marketers seem to be comfortable dealing with groups of Ps, the model presents an agenda of 'green Ps'. Each P factor provides an area where the prospective green marketer needs to address a variety of questions. The external green Ps that must be monitored and evaluated include:

- *Paying customers.* How green are they? How well informed about green issues are they? Which issues concern them? Do they want greener products, and if so, what sort? What environmentally related information do they require?
- *Providers.* How green are the companies who supply the business with everything, including raw materials, energy, office supplies and services such as waste disposal?
- *Politicians.* What legislation is being proposed? Is political lobbying necessary?
- *Pressure groups.* What issues are they currently highlighting? Who and what are they campaigning about? What new areas of concern are emerging?
- *Problems.* Has the company or any of its competitors been linked with environmental and social problems?
- *Predictions.* What environmental problems might affect the company in future? What current research might prove relevant?

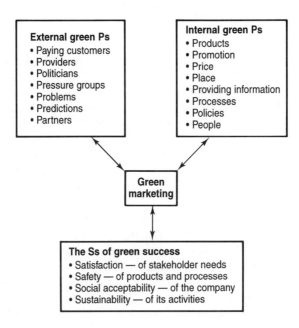

Figure 2. The Green Marketing Process.

- *Partners.* Is the company linked to any other organization whose activities might affect perceived environmental performance?

The internal green Ps represent an expanded marketing mix which needs to be audited, managed and, hopefully, improved to support a green strategy:

- *Products.* How safe are they in use and disposal? How durable are they? What are the environmental impacts of packaging and raw materials sourcing?
- *Promotion.* Do we/should we use green promotional messages? Can they be substantiated? Will they be credible?
- *Price.* Do prices need to be changed to reflect the differences in cost or demand for green products? How price sensitive are customers? What is an acceptable price for a green product?
- *Place.* Are channels with suitably green credentials available? Can we improve distribution efficiency? Can wastage be reduced?
- *Providing information.* What information does the rest of the business require about green consumer behaviour, competitors' environmental performance and the evolution of the green agenda?
- *Processes.* Could the production technology be cleaner, or the processes involved made more efficient?
- *Policies.* Do they help to motivate, monitor, evaluate and control eco-performance improvements?
- *People.* Do they understand environmental issues, the company's performance, and their role in the greening process? Are the necessary green management skills available?

## STAKEHOLDER INVOLVEMENT

A 'stakeholder approach' is vital for the development of appropriate green philosophies, strategies and policies. Internally and externally organizations face an increasing depth of interest in their eco-performance and an ever-increasing range of interested parties. Table 3 demonstrates the perceived importance of a selection of key stakeholders in terms of the proportion of surveyed companies that cited their influence.

A green firm needs to take a holistic view of its various stakeholders and their relationships with the firm and each other, with each being viewed as a customer. Creating an appropriate and balanced response to stakeholders requires:

- *Internal commitment.* Internally it is essential that stakeholders are won over before a green message is taken outside the firm. As emphasized by Edgar Woolard, Chairman of Du Pont, 'No company can be truly innovative until everyone in the company had adopted an environmental attitude'.
- *Clear priorities.* The nature and importance of different stakeholders' concerns will vary among companies and industries. Those in sensitive sectors, such as the manufacture and distribution of chemicals, will face considerable external pressures from legislation and pressure groups. A bank, by contrast, might be driven more by internal pressure from employees.
- *Research and monitoring.* To ensure that stakeholders' awareness and attitudes are clearly understood.
- *Openness.* Stakeholders increasingly demand information about eco-performance which companies have traditionally been reluctant to provide. A 1991 sample of 670 UK companies' annual reports analysed by *Company Reporting* revealed only 3% highlighting environmental information, most of which was meaningless. Satisfying the green customer (and the terms of the EC Directive 90/313, Freedom of Access to Information on the Environment) requires a new openness which will force marketers away from a 'black box' view of the production process. This is particularly the case in industrial markets, where companies such as IBM insist upon environmental auditing reporting by all suppliers.

Table 3. Perceived importance of stakeholder influence on environmental policy development (%)

| | |
|---|---|
| Customers | 75 |
| Employees | 70 |
| Suppliers | 55 |
| Government | 48 |
| Media | 46 |
| Pressure groups | 30 |
| Trade unions | 18 |

*Source*: Charter (1990).

## INFORMATIONAL ISSUES

Successful greening is very much a data-driven exercise. The early phase of green marketing witnessed a somewhat *ad hoc* approach to information and decision making. A 1990 Peat Marwick McLintock survey of major chemical producers and users showed that although 39% had an environmental policy and 26% had amended their marketing strategy, only 19% had conducted any form of environmental audit. Meeting the needs for environmentally related information, both as an input into the development of marketing and corporate strategy and as an output for stakeholders, involves:

- *Environmental scoping reviews and audits* for existing facilities.
- *Environmental Impact Assessments (EIAs)* conducted as part of the development process for new products or facilities.
- *Environmental information systems (EIS)* to support management decision making.
- *Risk analysis* to determine the likelihood and potential impact of environmental incidents and the costs of prevention and contingency measures.
- *An action-orientation* to ensure that the gathering of information is translated into positive action. Conducting environmental audits will not make a company green, just as conducting financial audits will not make it profitable.

It is essential for a company to focus on the environmental outcomes of decision making, as well as the 'hard' eco-performance of products and process. This involves answering such questions as:

- What are the environmental impacts of our marketing decisions?
- What information is needed to improve the quality of those decisions?
- Where do we get that information?
- What information do we have in-house?
- What do we need to acquire from outside?

## A NEW TIMEFRAME

Green marketing focuses on the performance of products before purchase and after use, which requires a new time perspective for marketers. For consumer durables, the question of actual durability assumes a new importance. Evidence suggests that many products currently exist only as semi-durables. A survey examining the lifecycles of domestic appliances found that a high percentage of appliances discarded on rubbish dumps had little wrong with them and required only simple and cheap repairs (source: *New Scientist,* 24 December 1988). Creating more durable products can form an important part of a green strategy. Agfa Gevaert switched from a policy of selling photocopiers to leasing them on a full-service basis. This led to a product redesign brief based around durability, and the upgrading of the copy drums from a lifespan of under 3 million to over 100 million copies.

Improving the post-use eco-performance of products requires the integration of opportunities for some or all of the 'five Rs' into the product concept:

(1) *Repair.* A modular design approach and good after-sales service provision can make repairing products cost effective and extend their useful life.
(2) *Reconditioning.* In the automotive market a wide range of reconditioned parts, from tyres to engines, can be purchased.
(3) *Re-use.* The average dairy milk bottle is used twelve times.
(4) *Recycling.* Products ranging from beer cans to BMWs are now designed to be recyclable.
(5) *Re-manufacture.* To create new from old, such as the re-manufacture of used laser printer cartridges performed by Onyx Associates.

The need to examine the impact of products from cradle to grave is leading towards the concept of re-marketing or even closed-loop (waste-free) marketing. Various tools are being developed to aid the green marketer to assess the full environmental impact of products, the best known being Lifecycle Analysis and Eco-balance Analysis. The greatest difficulty for the marketer is to know how far forward or back, and down how many of the branches of the supply chain, such an analysis should go. An example of a cradle-to-grave lifecycle is provided in Figure 3.

## DEVELOPING A GREEN MARKETING STRATEGY

The majority of companies worldwide appear to be taking a reactive and tactical approach to green issues, unless they are in 'front-line' sectors such as oil, chemicals, power and cars. However, a 1992 survey of *Fortune 500* companies conducted by Abt Associates revealed a shift away from a technical, compliance-orientated approach towards a more proactive green strategy orientation (Hochman *et al.*, 1992). Companies were increasingly pursuing competitive advantage and product differentiation by increasing investment in green marketing and green design, and improving overall corporate environmental performance.

For those companies that are serious about green marketing, the success factors can be summarized as the seven Cs, creating a strategy that is:

(1) *Customer-orientated*; in addressing environmental issues that concern customers and creating product offerings that balance improved eco-performance with customer needs for functionality, value and convenience.
(2) *Commercially viable*; in ensuring that any technical and economic barriers can be overcome to produce a product offering that will both meet customer needs and make a profit.
(3) *Credible*; to customers, senior managers and other stakeholders.
(4) *Consistent*; with corporate objectives, strategies and capabilities.
(5) *Clear*; it should not be shrouded in environmental or technical jargon. The use of mysterious claims for green detergents such as 'contains no NTAs' has been heavily criticized by the Consumers' Association.
(6) *Coordinated*; with the operational strategies and plans of the other business functions.
(7) *Communicated*; effectively internally and externally. Internal marketing does just

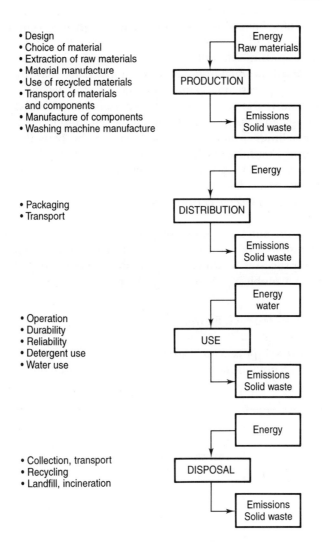

- Design
- Choice of material
- Extraction of raw materials
- Material manufacture
- Use of recycled materials
- Transport of materials and components
- Manufacture of components
- Washing machine manufacture

Energy
Raw materials

PRODUCTION

Emissions
Solid waste

Energy

- Packaging
- Transport

DISTRIBUTION

Emissions
Solid waste

Energy
water

- Operation
- Durability
- Reliability
- Detergent use
- Water use

USE

Emissions
Solid waste

Energy

- Collection, transport
- Recycling
- Landfill, incineration

DISPOSAL

Emissions
Solid waste

Figure 3. A Washing Machine's Life Cycle (*Source*: DTI/DoE, 1992).

not mean launching environmental policies to staff; it also means keeping the momentum going as the environment becomes just another key business issue.

## KEY ISSUES IN MANAGING THE GREEN MARKETING MIX

### Green products

What makes a product green? Inevitably, there are a range or eco-issues that surround different products and services, and these will produce different impacts from cradle to grave. For example, ingredients, packaging and animal testing are the central issues for lipsticks, while efficiency of powder, water and energy use account for 90% of the environmental impact of washing machines (*source*: PA Consulting). To solve intractable eco-conundrums it will be essential to refocus on customer-orientated needs as opposed to product-orientated solutions. This may mean refocusing a business towards a 'purer' marketing orientation, for example away from car manufacturing towards the provision of transportation and mobility. Electrolux in Belgium have instigated a programme of installing centralized 'textile care centres' of leased washing machines in apartment buildings, on the basis that people have no innate desire to own a washing machine but instead simply require clean clothes.

Analysing the eco-performance of a product needs to be multi-dimensional, since it is influenced by many factors, and it also should be done with reference to competitors' offerings. A Green Performance Matrix, like the one shown in Figure 4, can aid this process.

Green product attributes fall into two general categories. First, there are those relating to the tangible product (or service encounter) itself. Second, there are those that relate to the processes by which the product is developed and the attributes of the producer itself. Combining these creates the total green product concept.

## Creating a total green product: Ecover

The challenge in developing a total green product is to improve eco-performance while producing acceptably comparable levels of functionality and service, at a

| Product attribute | Comparative green performance | | | | |
|---|---|---|---|---|---|
| | Best possible | Among the best | Above average | Better than some | Poor |
| Raw materials | | | | | |
| Energy efficiency | | | | | |
| Waste | | | | | |
| Pollution | | | | | |
| Packaging | | | | | |
| Lifespan | | | | | |
| Re-usability | | | | | |
| Recyclability | | | | | |
| Effect on customer behaviour | | | | | |
| Green associations and linkages | | | | | |
| Socio-economic impact | | | | | |

Figure 4. The green performance matrix

competitive price. This is not an easy task, but one which has been accomplished by some pioneering green companies such as Ecover within the highly competitive green detergent market. Their approach involves adopting cleaner technologies that design out waste in the manufacturing processes, rather than using 'end-of-pipe' solutions which inevitably represent an added cost.

In October 1992 in Belgium, Ecover launched the world's first ecological factory. Their approach was to ensure that all processes, products and philosophies are sufficiently green to meet increasingly close stakeholder scrutiny. Innovations range from the use of factory bricks derived from coal slag to monetary incentives given to employees for the use of company bicycles. Ecover are also championing the concept of a zero-impact business park which produces no, or minimal, environmental pollution and has energy efficiency and recycling 'built-in'.

## Green packaging

Packaging has been an obious starting point for many companies' green marketing efforts, since packaging can often be safely reduced without expensive changes to core products or production processes and without a risk of disaffecting customer. So where shampoos like 'Head and Shoulders' once came in a stout plastic bottle housed within a cardboard box, they are now sold in only a bottle.

Reducing and recycling packaging is also a key feature of government policy within Europe. The UK government has a target to recycle 25% of household waste by the year 2000, while the controversial German Waste Packaging Ordinance forces producers and retailers to accept all waste packaging returned by consumers and includes mandatory deposits on many containers to encourage returns.

In addition to the removal of unnecessary layers and provision for recycling, there are a range of ways in which the design of packaging can be made greener which can be identified using the following checklist (Chick, 1992):

*Checklist for choosing or designing a greener pack*

- Does the production of the packaging material have an adverse effect on the environment? e.g.
  —Does the material come from a scarce or seriously declining source?
  —Is production of the material energy-intensive?
- Design or choose packaging where the materials can be easily re-used or recycled. Does the combination of materials create difficulty for recycling?
- Avoid *coloured* polyethylene terephthalate (PET).
- Ensure the chemicals used in a pack do not cause environmental damage (e.g. CFCs), or choose a chemical-free alternative pack (e.g. pump-action sprays).
- Do environmental protection laws in any proposed market either constrain the use of chosen materials or increase their production or disposal costs?
- Can concentrated products that fit into smaller packages by developed?
- Avoid excess packaging: only use what is necessary.
- Use reclaimed (secondary) materials wherever possible, which encourages the development of the recycling industry.

- Support resource-efficient reclamation schemes; consider whether material identification would help. It is vital that any collection system coincides with the development of markets and that companies start to 'sell' the re-usability or recyclability of their product.
- Give proper consideration to pollution that may be caused during manufacture or as post-consumer waste, e.g. pigments formulated with cadmium, lead or chromium.
- Ensure the pack, the information and the overall appearance encourages the efficient use, re-use and disposal of the contents and the pack.
- Consumer education material and advertising should be considered as an accompanying option to the pack.
- Establish a system for checking and collating information about the environmental implications of different materials, processes, etc.
- Ensure appropriate training has been given to designers, marketers, advertisers, packaging engineers, etc.

## Green promotion

There are a range of issues in managing the green communications mix:

- *Advertising*: do our products lend themselves to convincing and distinctive green images?
- *Direct mail*: how can we avoid being labelled 'junk mailers'?
- *Sales promotion*: can consumers be offered incentives to change their purchasing and product-use decisions in favour of green products and the environment? (For example, Lever's offer of the Persil EcoBox to encourage the use of Persil refills.)
- *Personal selling*: have the salesforce been made aware of the environmental implications of the company and its products and processes?
- *Public relations*: has an environmental audit been undertaken? Are results accessible?
- *Sponsorship*: is there an environmental project that fits our communications objectives?

Green issues provide good opportunities for both informative and emotive marketing communications. Fort Sterling's green brand Nouvelle captured 3% of the £500 million toilet-tissue market in its first year with a modestly funded advertising campaign which used such hard-hitting copy as 'It feels a little uncomfortable using toilet tissue that wipes out forests'. The key is to understand the concerns of stakeholder audiences and then to communicate effectively and efficiently.

## Green pricing

Going green may affect the cost structures of a business with a knock-on effect on prices, particularly if pricing is on a 'cost-plus' basis. Developing new sustainable raw material sources, complying with legislation, writing off old, 'dirty' technology, capital expenditure on clean technology and the overheads associated with greening the organizations can impose a heavy cost burden. However, this can be counterbalanced by the savings made by reducing raw materials and energy inputs, by reducing packaging by finding markets for by-products and by switching to lead-free distribution.

Consumer demand for green products can also allow for the addition of a green price premium, as applies to free-range egges and dolphin-friendly (rod-and-line-caught) tuna. However, marketers should exercise caution in taking advantage of such opportunities, as any suggestions of profiteering may undermine the development of a credible green image.

If costs are looked at holistically and managed on a portfolio basis, then wider eco-efficiency process benefits when added to premium demand benefits can counterbalance the costs of greening to make a positive contribution to profitability.

## GREEN LOGISTICS

An example of logistics forming a key component of a greening strategy comes from B&Q, whose logistics functions has been rewarded with several major awards for environmental excellence. Their 1993 *Environmental Review* included:

- The development of 'Centralized Distribution' at B&Q bringing environmental benefits such as reduced vehicle movements and a reduction in transit packaging.
- The establishment of a policy and targets aimed at reducing vehicle emission impacts.
- The reduction of transit packaging in conjunction with suppliers, aiming for a 30% reduction in the total corrugated board used by UK suppliers within the first year.
- A cost and benefit analysis undertaken into the practicalities of store-based collection and recycling systems for packaging materials.
- Insistence that logistics subcontractors operate an environmental policy consistent with B&Q's and commission their own comprehensive environmental audit.
- The promotion of environmental awareness within both B&Q's Logistics Department and its subcontractors.

## GOING GREEN—THE ORGANIZATIONAL CHALLENGE

Although the marketing philosophy embraces the entire business, the sphere of influence of marketing and marketers in practice is often more limited. Carson's (1968) observation that, for many companies, marketing is 'the integration, just below senior management levels, of those activities related primarily towards customers' unfortunately still holds true today. A range of organizational forces tend to restrict the influence of marketing, or split it into operational marketing tasks handled by marketers, and strategic marketing decisions handled by top management (Peattie and Notley, 1989).

As green issues have increasingly come to influence customers and competitiveness, green marketing and the management of eco-performance need to escape their functional boundaries to become pan-organizational management concerns, in much the same way that quality slipped its functional bonds to become Total Quality Management. Within the USA there is now a trend towards the merging of quality with green marketing management to create the philosophy of Total Quality Environmental Management (TQEM) (Hochman *et al.*, 1993).

To be effective, the implementation of greening needs to be:

- *Led from the top.* Although marketers may be the first to instigate the greening process as a result of marketing intelligence which reveals a greening of the market, the process requires top-level organizational commitment. Unless the chief executive or a senior executive takes responsibility for environmental issues then the resulting policies and initiatives will not be taken seriously.
- *Integrated.* To be successful, green marketing needs to become an integrative management philosophy which instills 'green management' throughout the company. As yet, relatively few organizations have progressed very far down the path of integration.
- *Marketing-led.* All the management functions have an important part to play in the greening process. Marketers have a natural leadership role to play reflecting their status as the consumers' advocate and because marketing already provides a focus for the type of crossfunctional coordination that greening requires.
- *Backed by actions.* There needs to be leadership in words and action from the company and its leaders to ensure that eco-issues permeate throughout the organization.

## THE FUTURE OF GREEN MARKETING

A key question for marketers is 'How will the green challenge evolve?' Environmental concern has always moved up and down society's agenda according to the perceived state of the environment and the importance of other issues in society. However, a 'ratchet effect' operates, ensuring that short-term fluctuations in green interest translate into a long-term deepening of concern.

For anyone who thinks that the environment will somehow go out of fashion as an issue for marketers, there are two important points to be aware of. The first is Ehrlich and Ehrlich's (1990) IPAT model which expresses the overall impact of economic activity on the physical environment as:

$$\text{Impact} = \text{Population} \times \text{Affluence} \times \text{Technology}$$

According to UN forecasts, the world's population could reach 8 billion as early as 2015, a 60% increase from 1985 levels. This would mean that just to restrict the rate of environmental damage to current levels, there would have to be a drastic adjustment in either the standard of living that we enjoy or the environmental impact of the technologies used to satisfy our demand for goods and services. If humankind were to continue current rates of population growth, consumption and methods of production, then by 2030 critical natural resources would last less than a decade more, and humankind would generate 400 billion tons of solid waste each year, enough to bury Los Angeles 100 metres deep (Frosch and Gallopoulos, 1989).

The second factor is the arrival of a new generation of more environmentally literate consumers, employees and investors. This results from the integration of the environment into education, and the 'Blue Peter Effect' of practical environmentalism becoming integrated into popular children's entertainment. The Henley Centre's 'Young Eyes: Children's Vision of the Future Environment' studying 10–14-year-olds revealed high levels of environmental concern, a belief that environmental problems are urgent and likely to affect society directly in their lifetime, and a tendency towards realistic and pragmatic values rather than woolly idealism. Among undergraduates there have also been measurable increases in environmental concern and an increasing tendency to consider eco-performance when considering potential employers (Charter, 1992c).

Green consumerism and green marketing is likely to evolve in three phases:

(1) *Substitution.* Characterized by green consumers differentiating between products on the basis of perceived eco-performance, much confusion over concepts and terminology, and with a great deal of sales and public relations activity dressed up as green marketing. The result has been increasing consumer cynicism about green claims, as demonstrated by Gerstman & Meyers' *Third Annual Environment Survey* finding that 91% of US consumers rated marketers as 'the least concerned about the environment'. There has also been a great deal of 'spotlighting', the singling out of particular industries, companies and products for praise or condemnation, sometimes with little relation to the actualities of eco-performance. Environmental improvements are often limited to end-of-pipe changes to production systems, the substitution of damaging ingredients such as CFCs and the elimination of excess packaging.
(2) *Systemization.* The establishment of BS 7750 for Environmental Management Systems and the EC Ecolabel Scheme should move the entire 'game' onto a new plane of recognized (if flawed) performance criteria and evaluation. Businesses will move towards the re-design of products and production systems, and the implementation of environmental reporting and management systems. Better information for consumers will allow more informed and consistent green purchasing. Provision of environmental information and provision for the recycling of products will become standard practice, and governed by increasingly stringent legislation.
(3) *Societal change.* The deepening environmental crisis will eventually lead to a more radical shift in consumer behaviour challenging the very basis of demand and consumption. This will be part of a wider social, political and economic upheaval to develop a more sustainable society. Consumers will increasingly become conservers and will seek opportunities to recycle or recondition products, and to achieve satisfaction through non-purchasing-based activities.

When any given market will reach the first or the second phase of green consumption is anyone's guess. However, the longer the delay before reaching phase 3, the greater will be the upheaval involved. Marketers are faced with a very simple

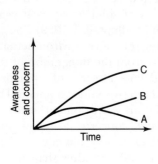

| Greener marketing Scenarios | Without | With |
|---|---|---|
| A | No change | No change |
| B | Gradually forced to adopt greener strategy — may lose market share | Possible market gains available — strong future likely |
| C | Loss of market share likely and long-term survival unlikely | Secure market share — secure future likely |

Figure 5. Potential Scenarios for Environmental Awareness and Concern. (*Source*: Charter, 1990).

choice, to pursue improved environmental performance or not. The consequences of that choice will depend upon the evolution of the green agenda in relation to their industry, as demonstrated by Figure 5.

Some environmentalists have criticized green marketing on the basis that 'Changing our shopping habits will not save the world'. This is true, but if it creates improvement in the eco-performance of businesses it will buy much-needed time in which to understand how to make the more important changes to our economic, technical and political systems, in order to manage our environment in a sustainable way.

Currently, green marketing is viewed as one of many options for generating competitive advantage. This rather ignores one important factor—the customer. People want greener products from greener companies. If a company is not improving its eco-performance as fast as constraints of cost, technology and consumer understanding allow, it is questionable as to whether they are practising marketing at all.

Green marketing's early progress has concentrated on the greening of the tangible marketing mix, along with the production system that underpins it. What many companies have yet to recognize is that greening represents a massive internal marketing challenge. Marketers have a duty to voice the consumer's demands for improved environmental performance within all aspects of the business, and to take a lead in making it happen. A tall order for marketers? Perhaps, but this is what the marketing philosophy is all about—getting the entire business behind the effort to satisfy the customer. It is a familiar rallying cry for marketers, but this time the stakes are a little higher, and winning the battle just might help to save the world!

## REFERENCES

Carson, D., 'Marketing organisation in British manufacturing firms', *Journal of Marketing*, **32**, 268–325 (1968).

Charter, M., *The Greener Employee*, KPH Marketing, Alton (1990).

Charter, M., 'Emerging concepts in a greener world', in Charter, M. (ed.), *Greener Marketing*, Greenleaf, Sheffield (1992a).

Charter, M., 'Greener marketing strategy', in Charter, M. (ed.), *Greener Marketing*, Greenleaf, Sheffield (1992b).

Charter, M., 'Greener people', in Charter, M. (ed.), *Greener Marketing*, Greenleaf, Sheffield (1992c).

Chick, A., 'Greener packaging', in Charter, M. (ed.), *Greener Marketing*, Greenleaf, Sheffield (1992).

Clements, M. A., 'Selecting tourist traffic by demarketing', *Tourism Management*, June, 89–95 (1989).

Davis, J. J., 'A blueprint for green marketing', *Journal of Business Strategy*, **12**(4), 14–17 (1991).

Drucker, P. F., *Top Management*, Heinemann, London (1973).

Ehrlich, P. R. and Ehrlich, A. H., *The Population Explosion*, Simon & Schuster, New York (1990).

Frosch, R. A. and Gallopoulos, N. E., 'Strategies for manufacturing', *Scientific American*, September, 144–152 (1989).

Hennison K. and Kinnear, T. *Ecological Marketing*, Prentice Hall, Englewood Cliffs, NJ (1976).

Hochman, D., Wells, R. P., O'Connell, P. A. and Hochman, M. N., 'Total quality management: a tool to move from compliance to strategy', *Greener Management International*, **1**, 59–70 (1993).

Kirkpatrick, D. 'Environmentalists', *Fortune*, 12 February (1990).

Mitchell, A. 'Milking the greens', *Marketing*, 14 September, 34–35 (1989).

Peattie, K. J., 'Painting marketing education green: or how to recycle old ideas', *Journal of Marketing Management*, **6**(2), 105–127 (1990).

Peattie, K. J., *Green Marketing*, Pitman, London, 1992.

Peattie, K. J. and Notley, D. S., 'The marketing and strategic planning interface', *Journal of Marketing Management*, **4**(3), 330–347 (1989).

Peattie, K. J. and Ratnayaka, M., 'Greener industrial marketing', *Industrial Marketing Management*, **21**(2), 103–110 (1992).

Peattie, K. J. and Ringler, A., 'Management and the Environment in the United Kingdom and Germany: a comparison', Cardiff Business School Working Paper in Marketing and Strategy (1993).

Prothero, A., 'Green consumerism and the societal marketing concept—marketing strategies for the 1990s', *Journal of Marketing Management*, **6**(2), 87–104 (1990).

Vandermerwe, S. and Oliff, M., 'Customers drive corporations green', *Long Range Planning*, **23**(6), 10–16 (1990).

## FURTHER READING

Carson, P. and Mouldson, J., *Green Is Gold*, HarperCollins, Canada (1991). Uses the experiences of Canada's Loblaw and a range of other companies to paint an illuminating picture of the contemporary green scene on the other side of the Atlantic. Good coverage of the process of developing greener products and the opportunities it can create.

Charter, M., *Greener Marketing*, Greenleaf, Sheffield (1992). An edited collection which provides detailed coverage of the strategic implications of the greening of marketing, and follows through the practicalities in terms of the extended marketing mix. The themes of the text are reinforced through a collection of 20 detailed case studies covering a wide range of organizations.

Charter, M., 'Scott Limited: measuring environmental performance', *Greener Management International*, **1** (1993). A case study which demonstrates how to tackle the problem of downstream environmental performance by integrating green issues into supply chain management.

Coddington, W., *Environmental Marketing*, McGraw-Hill, New York (1993). Takes a very practical approach to developing competitive advantage from improved environmental performance, mostly from the perspective of American consumer goods companies. Provides useful coverage of the problems of developing a greener organization as a foundation for the greening process.

Develter, D., *Ecover Manual*, 2nd edn, Ecover Publications, Oostemalle, Belgium (1992). A comprehensive manual covering Ecover's experience in developing the world's first ecological factory. Demonstrates the wealth of detail that must be dealt with to ensure that the means of production, as well as the product itself, is environmentally sound.

Mitchell, A. and Levy, L., 'Green about green', *Marketing*, 14 September, 28–35 (1989). A brief but thought-provoking analysis of the implications of environmental concern for marketers and marketing strategy, which is followed by the results of a survey of marketing professionals' opinions on the subject of greening.

Peattie, K., *Green Marketing*, Pitman, London (1992). A book in the succinct M&E handbook style which provides an ideal introduction for students or practitioners to the principles and practice of green marketing. Each chapter uses a highly structured format, a variety of brief examples and test questions to aid understanding and learning. The coverage of issues goes beyond the implications of greening for marketing strategy and the management of the mix to consider organizational, international and legal issues.

Peattie, K., 'Painting marketing education green: or how to recycle old ideas', *Journal of Marketing Management*, **6**, Autumn, 105–127 (1990). Examines the range of forces acting on a company which promote or prevent the greening of marketing strategy, and discusses the ways that both marketing principles and practice can be amended in response. 'A good starting point for the green marketer. Many helpful examples and a useful literature review' said Anbar.

Wehrmeyer, W., *Environmental References in Business*, Greenleaf, Sheffield (1993). An invaluable steeping-stone to 'everything you ever wanted to know about business and the environment but were afraid to ask', with over 2700 classic and 'cutting-edge' articles indexed and referenced.

# 24

# 'Greening' the Marketing Mix: A Review of the Literature and an Agenda for Future Research

*A. C. Simintiras, B. B. Schlegelmilch and A. Diamantopoulos*

## INTRODUCTION

During the last decade, the 'environment' has become an important issue and the world has experienced a dramatic increase in campaigns focusing on the effects of environmental deterioration (Sand, 1990). These campaigns appeal for action towards environmental protection and conservation and have already had an influential effect upon consumers' attitudes and behaviour (Jowell, Witherspoon and Brook, 1988; Bidlake, 1990). Furthermore, predictions that the environment will become the most important issue of this decade (Cope, 1990; Kirkpatrick, 1990) suggest that it will have an even greater impact on the way of thinking and behaving of the individual and society as a whole in the future.

With the advent of the 'green movement' and increased government regulation, many companies have attempted to introduce environmental policies and to present themselves in an 'environmentally friendly' light. However, while firms have been criticised for rushing into green marketing without much planning (Davies, 1991), marketing researchers are also said to have been left somewhat behind by the spread of the green thinking in marketing practice (Peattie, 1990). Thus, while there is a substantial body of literature on green marketing issues, it is largely disjointed and normative in nature. There appears, therefore, to be a need for integrating the existing literature on green marketing, in order to lay the foundations for a coherent research agenda.

This article aims to provide a state-of-the-art review of the green marketing literature by using the marketing mix elements as an integrative framework. More specifically, its purpose is threefold; firstly, to discuss the available green marketing literature pertaining to the various elements of the marketing mix; secondly, to highlight research gaps under each element; and thirdly, to draw up an agenda for future research.

The paper is divided into three parts. In the first part, the sources of green

Reprinted by permission of John Wiley & Sons, Ltd from Baker, M. J. (ed.), *Perspectives on Marketing Management*, Vol. 4, 1994, pp. 1–25 pressures are identified and the concept of 'green marketing' is defined. In the second part, the green literature is reviewed around each component of the marketing mix. Finally, in the third part, a discussion of the identified research gaps is provided and suggestions for a possible future research agenda are made.

## THE PRESSURE FOR GREENNESS

The idea that the environment should be protected is now gaining wide recognition by companies and has led to efforts to improve environmental performance. Examples from different industry sectors include the Swedish car manufacturer Saab, which is wooing environmentalists with the launch of its new 'lean burn' engine which is claimed to be extremely efficient in burning off a high percentage of noxious gases (Dwek, 1992); General Motors which has already announced its intention to mass produce an electrical car; General Mills, which requires the use of recycled paper in all of its cereal box boards; and Kodak which plans to recycle disposable cameras (Coddington, 1990). Furthermore, large US retailers such as Wal-Mart and K-Mart have instituted programmes to promote environmentally responsible packaging (Kashmanian, Ferrand, Hurst and Kuusinen, 1990), while a number of UK retail chains (e.g. Sainsbury's) actively promote 'green own label' products. Company responses along the above lines have come about as a result of a number of internal and external pressures (Figure 1). In this context, the magnitude and impact of these pressures depend upon the industry in which a company operates. For example, firms in 'environmentally sensitive' industries, such as nuclear energy, waste disposal or chemicals are more likely to be targeted by green

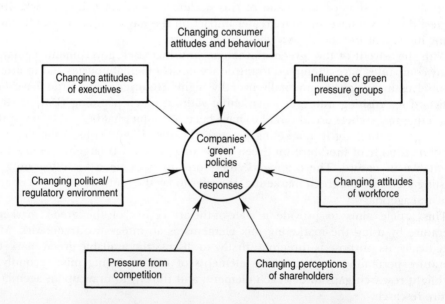

Figure 1. Sources of Pressure for the 'Greening' of Companies.

organisations' campaigns and controlled by government legislation than in less environmentally sensitive sectors. Nevertheless, as will become clear below, no company can any longer afford to ignore the 'environmental message'.

## The greening of consumers

Smith (1990) has pointed out that there is now a group of consumers who are genuinely concerned about the food they eat, their everyday habits and the impact these will have on the environment. Evidence for this claim can be found in numerous surveys. For example, a study by Brand New Products showed that 73% of UK consumers were concerned about the environment and that 40% considered, on a regular basis, environmental matters in some of the products they bought (Lloyds Bank, 1989). Furthermore, in July 1989 a Mori poll indicated that the proportion of UK consumers choosing products on the basis of their 'environmental performance' had increased from 19% to 42% in less than one year while, a month earlier, a Mintel survey concluded that 27% of British adults were prepared to pay up to 25% more for 'environmentally friendly' products (Prothero, 1990).

However, although the environment is becoming a persistent public issue worldwide (Fierman, 1991; McIntosh, 1991) and the increased base of green consumers has been well documented in the literature (Anderson and Cunningham, 1972; Brooker, 1976; Corrado and Ross, 1990), the translation of these widespread concerns into action varies from country to country. For example, although 70% of Canadian consumers would be willing to participate in household recycling programmes, only 33% would pay more for environmentally safe products (Welds, 1991).

Environmental concern and activism differ among green consumers and result in different shades of 'greennees' within the population. For example, one of a number of classification schemes in the UK suggested the following spectrum: (i) 'green activists', who are members or supporters of environmental organisations (5–15%); (ii) 'green thinkers', who actively seek out 'green' products and may engage in time-consuming support activities such as having multiple bins at home (25–30%); (iii) the 'green consumer base', who feel that they have taken special action to express their environmental concern through, for example, the purchase of non-CFC aerosols (45–60%), and finally; (iv) the 'generally concerned', which includes everyone who voices concern for the environment (80–90%) whether it is followed by action or not (Murphy, 1989). Similar typologies of 'green consumers', based on demographic and psychographic profiles, have been proposed by, amongst others, Ogilvy and Mather (Peattie, 1992).

## Political and regulatory pressures

'With 10 million voters Europe-wide, and 15% of UK voters going green in the European elections, environmental concern has become a major item on the political agenda' (Peattie, 1990, p. 111). The increasing environmental concern of individuals has led politicians to address the issue and express publicly their own views. For example, Margaret Thatcher, the ex-Prime Minister, has stated that 'no generation has a freehold on this Earth. All we have is a life tenancy—with a full repairing lease. And this government intends to meet the terms of that lease in full' (Thatcher, 1990, p. 10). Meanwhile, international political pressures for a cleaner environment continue to build up, and recently the World Environment and Development Convention in Brazil (the Rio summit) has established guidelines and action plans which are required in order to preserve the world's environment (Hunt, 1991a).

At a regional level, in an attempt to achieve a better integration of environmental policies in particular industrial sectors (i.e. energy, transport, agriculture, etc.), the European Community is exerting efforts to ensure implementation of current legislation (Delbeke, 1991; Prothero and McDonagh, 1993). In addition to the EC's environmental policies, several member states have already introduced their own pieces of legislation for environmental protection. For example, individual countries ban certain environmentally damaging products such as paraquat, a weedkiller forbidden in Germany but allowed in Britain and France (*The Economist*, 8.9.1990). Furthermore, Great Britain is to become the first country to introduce an official national standard for evaluating the environmental performance of its business and industry by the British Standards Institution (Hunt, 1991b).

## Competition

In recent years, many company boards have spent time thinking out green strategies and setting up management systems to make sure that environmental performance goals are met (*The Economist*, 8.9.1990). According to Peattie (1990), however, for many firms, an environmental response is simply a way of catching up with competitors who have already gone green. For example, Ever Ready's and Panasonic's response of launching mercury-free batteries following Varta's innovative introduction (Peattie, 1990), demonstrates the effect of competitive pressures on the greening of firms.

## Green pressure groups

Pressure groups such as Greenpeace, Friends of the Earth and the World Wide Fund for Nature, to name but a few, have been playing a significant role in putting pressure on companies to improve on their environmental performance (Peattie, 1990).

The nature and size of green organisations vary considerably. The green movement in the UK alone comprises over 1000 organisations with a combined membership of more than 3 million (Peattie, 1990). By far the largest subset are the pressure groups which, in turn, either campaign for a wide range of green causes (for example Friends of the Earth and Greenpeace), confine themselves to particular interests (for example the World Wide Fund for Nature and the Council for the

Protection of Rural England), or strictly focus on one specific issue (for example the Royal Society for the Protection of Birds and the Campaign for Lead-Free Air). All of these groups claim to be non-party political with the objective of influencing politicians and voters of all persuasions (Porritt, 1987).

In the mid and late 1980s, green organisations experienced a growth in support of 20–30% per year, with Greenpeace recruiting between 3,000 and 4,000 members a week (Nelson, 1989). The 13 largest environmental bodies in the UK have nearly 5 million supporters and a combined income of over £160m per year (Nelson, 1989). Greenpeace UK alone grew from just 30,000 members in 1985 to 385,000 in 1990 and reached 414,000 in 1992. The growth in membership of Greenpeace UK, however, dropped from 30–40% during 1985–86 to 5.5% in 1992 (telephone enquiry to Greenpeace, August 1992).

## The greening of shareholders

The spread of environmentalism in recent years has also had an impact on investment practices. According to Elkington, Burke and Hailes (1988), environmental investment funds have been growing rapidly as an increasing number of individual investors seek to fulfill a desire to invest in a way which reflects their personal convictions. Environmental investments are, however, regarded as a subdivision of ethical investments since as Tennant (1991, p. 33) points out, 'environmental equity cannot exist without the first principles of human equity'.

The proliferation of ethical investment funds in the UK is indicated by the fact that in the first half of 1990, there were 23 ethical funds in existence with a combined value of £227 million (*The Ethical Investor*, Summer 1990), whereas now, in 1992, there are 32 funds and more than £440 million is invested in them (The Ethical Investment Research Service, 1992). However, while the UK market is relatively young, the USA market is well established. In 1988, Elkington, Burke and Hailes reported that the Calvert Social Investment Fund, a leader company in this field, reaped $350 million in ethical investments, whilst in the first half of 1990 the value of ethical funds reached $400 billion (Dunham, 1990).

## The greening of executives

Pressure for improving environmental performance also comes from within the firm itself. For example, Touche Ross Management consultants found that an increasing number of UK companies appointed board members responsible for environmental management, although they appeared to move less quickly than some of their European counterparts (*Market Research Society Newsletter*, 1990). Although such appointments are not unambiguous manifestations of internal pressures, it could be argued that allocation of responsibilities for stimulating green thought and action is in itself a source of future green pressure within the firm.

Assessing the attitudes of directors toward the environment, Nash (1990) has pointed out that directors were more aware than ever before of green issues. Despite the high levels of awareness, however, a substantial number were taking little or no action towards environmental protection as part of their company's operations. Nonetheless, his survey also revealed that 53% and 39% of non-manufacturing and manufacturing industry directors respectively felt under increasing pressure from their families to improve the environmental performance of their company. Such pressure can be expected eventually to filter through company policy, creating a further impetus toward environmentally responsible management.

### The greening of employees

Employees who hold strong views about the environment are another source of internal pressure. A survey carried out by KPH Marketing, in which 101 marketing personnel and administration managers were interviewed, indicated that 76% of the sample considered that a socially responsible image was important, whereas more than half believed that a 'green office policy' was important. Moreover, the survey showed that 23% of the sample would actually consider taking a pay cut in order to work for a more environmentally friendly company (Reeves, 1990). Similarly, a poll drawn from the marketing directors and managers of the UK's top 300 advertisers found that 43% of respondents would be willing to accept a smaller company car for environmental reasons (*Marketing*, 21.6.1990).

### THE CONCEPT OF GREEN MARKETING

Prothero (1990) has argued that societal marketing is the fourth phase in the evolutionary development of marketing as it allows management to consider the concept of responsible consumption. According to Kotler (1979, p. 85) 'the societal marketing concept calls for a consumer orientation backed by integrated marketing activity aimed at generating consumer satisfaction and long-run consumer well-being as the key to achieving long-run profitable volume.' He argues that the objective of societal marketing 'is not to maximise consumption, consumer satisfaction, or consumer choice. The objective is to maximise the quality of life.'

From a similar perspective, Henion (1979, p. 34) used the term 'ecological marketing' to describe the role and importance of green marketing in serving the long-term interests of companies. More specifically, he considered green marketing as a subset of social marketing and asserted that 'ecological marketing can be considered a marketing strategy for the environmental crisis. It is based principally on engaging the profit motive of producers of environmentally beneficial products. These producers then are seen as marketing such products to target markets, which initially would consist of a subset of the population called the ecologically concerned consumer.'

More recently, Pride and Ferrell (1991, p. 88) have provided a definition of green marketing which centres around the marketing mix elements, namely: 'the specific development, pricing, promotion and distribution of products that do not harm the environment'. Furthermore, Peattie (1992, p. 11) has postulated that green marketing is 'the management process responsible for identifying, anticipating and satisfying the requirements of consumers and society, in a profitable and sustainable way'.

At this point it might be argued that any concept or definition of green marketing is contradictory in itself. To a lesser or greater extent, any production or marketing process which uses up scarce resources and creates waste as a by-product is damaging the environment; seen under this light, for most companies, claims regarding 'environmentally friendly' products must be false in the strict interpretation of the term (Roberts, 1991). The question, however, is not 'how to eliminate' but rather 'how to minimise' the adverse impact of products on the environment and it is in this context that green marketing assumes its role.

Reflecting on the concept and fundamental objectives of green marketing, it can be postulated that green marketing is a managerial philosophy which starts with a careful examination of variables that are related to environmental concerns of society and consumers and extends into a never-ending effort to improve on the environmental performance of a company. The number of companies which decide to go green and the degree of their greenness will depend, of course, upon an evaluation of the threats and opportunities associated with environmental action versus environmental inaction (Peattie, 1990). For example, research findings suggested that during 1990 in the USA, sales of green products accounted for $1.8 billion, whereas the potential unfulfilled demand of up to 18 million green households was in the region of $7 billion more (Peattie, 1992). Such findings reveal marketing opportunities for companies which decide to respond to the changing needs of consumers. On the contrary, predictions that environmental pollution will be the most serious problem facing the motor industry in the 1990s (Peattie, 1992) denote possible threats which may arise as a result of environmental inaction by car manufacturers.

## THE GREEN MARKETING MIX

Companies adopting a green marketing philosophy must consider environment-related issues before products are produced and made available to customers. Unlike traditional marketing which emphasises the product during its usage, green marketing emphasises how the product is produced and its disposal at the end of its life cycle (Peattie, 1990). Given the broader range of responsibilities of green marketing, its overall impact on the marketing mix becomes of primary importance. The following analysis focuses on the marketing mix and examines the 'green literature' for each of its components.

### Product

Although the 'product' itself has been acknowledged as the most important challenge of green marketing (Foster, 1989), there are difficulties in finding a widely accepted operational definition of 'environmentally friendly products' (Schlossberg, 1990). Mainly, the difficulties lie in the areas of determining particular specifications and attributes that green products should possess and in evaluating their degree of contribution towards environmental protection and sustainability (Shuptrine and Osmanski, 1975; Kinnear, 1982). In an attempt to address this problem, Peattie (1990, p. 124) suggested that the product should be judged against four critical Ss: 'Satisfaction—of consumers' needs and wants. Sustainability—of the product in terms of the consumption of energy and resources. Social acceptability—of the product and company in terms of not destroying species, habitats, peoples or other countries. Safety—of the product in terms of not endangering the health of individuals or damaging the environment, through use or disposal.'

'Green products' compose minority offerings in the marketplace (*Marketing*, 12.4.1990), despite the fact that they come from a wide range of industrial and service sectors (agriculture, chemicals, transport, food, etc.). Some sectors, however, are perceived to be more 'environmentally responsible' than others. For example, in a survey of 50 marketing managers and 102 marketing directors examining the perceptions of environmental responsiveness of different industries, it was found that, petrol companies and aerosol manufacturers aside, no major industry was perceived to have responded particularly well (Mitchell, 1989).

With regard to product and product-related aspects, companies' responses towards the environment can be classified into two broad categories: (i) production processes; and (ii) finished products or services. Environmental responses concerning manufacturing processes can be identified in the areas of waste-management, materials used and production processes. Although these non-marketing operations are of vital importance for the environmental performance of companies, their analysis is beyond the scope of this study. As to companies' responses concerning finished products the notion of different product levels (e.g. core, tangible and augmented product) lends itself as a useful analytical framework.

The core product of the 'green' offering is related to the anticipated benefits and/or satisfaction which is derived from buying, consuming and disposing of products which either do not damage the environment or which are less harmful than others. In this respect, some companies have managed successfully to capitalise on the environmental concern of consumers, whereas others got their product responses wrong. On the successful side are the legendary stories of shoppers who bought large quantities of biodegradable washing powder (e.g. Ecover), organically grown food, and low-mercury batteries (e.g. Varta). Among the green casualties, on the other hand, are Bradford and Bingley, the building society, which launched a Green Personal Equity Plan in July 1989 and had to withdraw it two months later due to lack of interest (Prestridge, 1989).

Packaging as part of the overall offering has also attracted the attention of environmentally friendly companies. Packaging decisions, according to Miller (1991), should include economical, ergonomical as well as ecological considerations. With regard to the latter, the main issues are: (i) reduction of materials used; (ii) making packaging reusable; and (iii) recycling (Lauson, 1989).

With regard to refillable and concentrated packages progress has been made by several companies and this is now big news for reducing and reusing packaging material (Lauson, 1989). For example, Vizir, a Proctor & Gamble product in the fabric softener market, uses a refillable pack, a 5-litre bag in a box which improves the ratio of product to package (Lauson, 1989). Recycling has also been seen by many companies as an alternative in minimising the impact their packaging has on the environment. For example, the cosmetics giant Estèe Lauder, which has recently launched a 'green' skin care and cosmetics line under the name 'Origins', offers its customers the chance to return empty bottles, tubes and caps to the Origins counter for recycling (Miller, 1991). In addition, Pepsi and Coke will soon introduce bottles made partly from recycled plastic in a new bid to give plastic packaging its first green tint (Britt, 1990). The backing card for the Varta batteries blister pack has already changed to recycled board. Similarly, ICI is pressing ahead with its Biopol compostable 'nature's plastic'. This uses a micro-organism which converts glucose to a plastic and it is recyclable. Wella has collaborated with ICI and is now using Biopol to package its hair care products (Cobb, 1991).

The remaining characteristics of the tangible product (i.e. brand name, quality, styling, etc.) have also attracted the attention of environmentally responsible firms. For example, Procter & Gamble have managed successfully to offer real environmental benefits (e.g. to reduce the quantity of materials used, encourage reuse and incorporate post-consumer waste in the packaging materials) without compromising the quality, brand name and consumer convenience of products such as Ariel Ultra detergent (Mackenzie, 1992).

In contrast to the widespread discussion in the trade and normative literature concerning 'green' product issues, empirical studies on the topic appear to be rather limited (Table 1).

The findings of the studies listed in Table 1 provide linkages between consumer behaviour and green products or green product attributes. However, it appears that additional research examining, amongst others, issues such as product redesign, new product development, evaluation of green products' social and environmental impact (El-Ansary, 1974; Varble, 1972), and the relationship between consumer behaviour and green product attributes in other product categories is needed.

In the area of services, apart from three studies conducted by Schlegelmilch and Diamantopoulos (1990), Schlegelmilch, Diamantopoulos and Bohlen (1992), and Bohlen, Diamantopoulos and Schlegelmilch (1992), no other study was found in the literature. Therefore, further research examining consumers' behaviour toward a wide range of green services is also needed.

**Price**

The role of pricing in the context of green marketing is primarily to cover the additional environmental costs that might be incurred, to offer good value for money, and to achieve profit objectives.

Cost is one of the most important factors which affect pricing decisions. However, the extra cost which a company is likely to incur in the short run as a result of the introduction of green policies may, in the long term, lead to cost reductions. For

Table 1. Empirical research relevant to green product attributes and environmental concern/behaviour of consumers or organisations

| Author(s) | Year | Product/service | Sample | Research objectives |
|---|---|---|---|---|
| Prothero and McDonagh | 1992 | Cosmetics and toiletries | 85 companies | Environmental consciousness of companies in producing environmentally acceptable products |
| DuPreez, Diamantopoulos and Schlegelmilch | 1992 | Cars | 306 consumers | Cross-country comparison of consumers' preferences towards 'green' product attributes |
| Schlegelmilch, Diamantopoulos and DuPreez | 1992 | Cars | 410 'ordinary' consumers and students | Cross-country comparison of consumers' preferences towards 'green' product attributes |
| Bohlen, Diamantopoulos and Schlegelmilch | 1993 | Freight transport | 34 consumers | Consumer perceptions of environmental nuisances arising from the freight transport |
| Schelegelmilch, Diamantopoulos and Bohlen | 1992 | Freight transport | 65 key decision makers and opinion formers | Analysis of the perceived environmental impact of road and rail freight transport |
| Grunert and Kristensen | 1992 | Food | 1476 consumers | Consumers' environmental concern and attitudes and their buying behaviour of organically grown food |
| Diamantopoulos, Schlegelmilch and DuPreez | 1992 | Cars | 262 consumers | Cross-country comparisons of the role of 'green' product attributes on consumer preferences |
| Kristensen and Grunert | 1991 | Food | 312 consumers | The effect of ecological consciousness on the demand for organic foods |
| Fritzsche and Duehr | 1982 | Deodorants | 449 students | Product attribute utility between environmentally concerned and unconcerned consumers |
| Kerin and Peterson | 1974 | Detergents and soft drinks | 250 housewives | The relationship between environmental consciousness and preferences for selected product attributes |
| Kinnear and Taylor | 1973 | Detergents | 500 consumers | Effects of ecological concern on brand perceptions |
| Mazis, Settle and Leslie | 1973 | Detergents | 130 consumers | Consumer response to the elimination of phosphate laundry detergents |
| Henion | 1972 | Detergents | 4 supermarkets | Purchasing behaviour of consumers when exposed to information about phosphate content of detergent brands |
| Kassarjian | 1971 | Gasoline | 242 consumers | Consumers' attitudes and responses towards air pollution and 'green' petrol |

example, 3M's policy of adding up small contributions of many small energy savings, waste elimination, or pollution prevention initiatives, saves rather than costs them money (Peattie, 1990).

When the introduction of green policies implies extra costs for the industry, this may be reflected either in lower profit margins and/or in higher priced products for customers. On the one hand, findings that individual consumers are willing to pay higher prices for goods which will not damage the environment demonstrate that they are prepared to go some way to meet the extra costs involved (Research 2000, 1990). On the other hand, many top-level managers believe that society at large is ready to absorb the extra costs. For example, Mr Carl Hahn, chairman of the management board of Volkswagen, has pointed out that: 'we have reached an economic position in which it is entirely reasonable to anticipate that our societies can afford the added costs which are unavoidable in connection with the protection of the environment' (Griffiths, 1991).

Empirical research with a main focus on pricing decisions of green products has been very limited; only a few studies were found which examined the relationship between green product attributes, price variance and consumer purchase behaviour (Table 2).

Herberger and Buchanan (1971) found that consumers were reluctant to pay a premium for more ecologically compatible products. Kerin and Peterson (1974) reported that two consumer groups, based on their environmental consciousness (high vs low), placed price ahead of ecology. The above findings are contradictory to those of Henion Gregory and Clee (1980) who found that environmentally concerned consumers were willing to subordinate price to ecology, whereas unconcerned consumers placed price and function ahead of ecology. Additional research is needed to clarify the relationships between the environmental consciousness of consumers and their responses to different price levels. In addition, empirical evidence is needed to ascertain whether 'ecological price elasticity' differs between different product categories and services.

Table 2. Empirical studies examining the relationship between green product attributes, price and consumer buying behaviour

| Author(s) | Year | Product/ service | Sample | Research objectives |
|---|---|---|---|---|
| Henion, Gregory and Clee | 1980 | Detergents | 110 consumers | Buying behaviour of environmentally concerned and unconcerned consumers towards different price levels of ecological and non-ecological detergents |
| Kerin and Peterson | 1974 | Detergents and soft drinks | 250 housewives | The relationship between environmental consciousness of consumers and different price configurations |
| Herberger and Buchanan | 1971 | Detergents and soft drinks | 202 housewives | The effect of price variance on products which are associated with environmental compatibility |

## Communications mix

Addressing the importance of good communication for environmentally friendly organisations, Thomas (1992, p. 24) has stated that 'good communications will ... eventually allow consumers to associate particular companies with environmental responsibility'.

Thus far, however, not all of the environmental claims made by organisations have been accurate (see below). Therefore, companies considering making environmental claims about their products must also address broader questions of company behaviour such as consumption of energy and resources, environmental investments, and so on, in order to ensure consistency and integrity (Mackenzie, 1992). The following section provides a review of the green literature relating to the four elements of the communications mix.

*Advertising*

Advertising has often been used successfully to promote the environmental performance of green products and/or production processes of companies. A well-publicised example is Peaudouce's TV and press advertising campaign aimed at promoting their 'environmentally friendly' nappies. The advertising message was so potent that the company has been acknowledged by other businesses as one of the leaders in the league of companies who have responded well towards the environment (Buck, 1989).

None the less, firms advertise their environmental 'achievements' to an audience which has grown increasingly sceptical about their claims. This is evidenced in survey results (based on 1,200 face-to-face interviews throughout the UK) which indicated that 56% of all consumers are suspicious about 'environmentally friendly' claims (Burnside, 1990). This reflects the fact that a number of misleading claims have been made by firms jumping on the green bandwagon (*Marketing*, 21.2.1991). For example, criticised misleading claims include BP's Supergreen petrol which was shown to contain several toxic chemicals despite its 'pollution-free' tag (Peattie, 1990), and Procter & Gamble's green nappies on the grounds that disposables still destroy trees (*Management Consultancy*, September 1989). In addition, ICI, Eagle Star and Shell have been criticised for proclaiming their greenness while dumping waste in waterways, destroying Brazilian forests, and producing the pesticides Aldrin and Dieldrin (Corrigan, 1989). Similarly, Greenpeace urged consumers to boycott Tesco Supermarkets on the grounds that the stores sell Icelandic fish products while Iceland is killing whales and defies the international moratorium (Corrigan, 1989). In an attempt to publicise inaccurate or misleading environmental claims, Friends of the Earth have established a 'Green Con of the Year' award. The 1991 'winner' was Fisons plc for misleading and unjustifiable claims in the horticultural trade press which downplayed the damage caused by its peat-cutting operations. ICI was also highlighted for the involvement of its subsidiary ICI (India) in the marketing of an ozone-destroying chemical in certain developing countries, despite its claims that it is firmly committed to the protection of the environment (Friends of the Earth, 1991).

To reduce the number of misleading claims, Germany has developed a labelling system where an expert jury under the auspices of the Federal Environment Ministry awards to consumer products an offficial environmental quality label that may be used for commerical advertising and packaging (Sand, 1990). Furthemore, in the UK the ITV companies and the Advertising Standards Authority (ASA) have expressed their concern and plan to establish guidelines for TV advertisers (Kavanagh, 1990)

Apart from the literature which focuses on the environmental claims of advertising campaigns and legislative controls for refining the quality of consumer information, no empirical studies were found in the broad area of 'green product' advertising. Therefore research examining issues such as consumer's perceptions of 'green' advertising, 'green' advertising effectiveness, types and impact of 'green' advertising appeals for different products/product categories is needed.

## Sales promotion

Unlike advertising, sales promotion of green products has attracted less attention from the media. None the less, several sales promotion programmes have already been or will be introduced in recent years. A sales promotion scheme has been introduced by the Vauxhall car manufacturers who have offered the owners of Vauxhall models built since August 1985 the opportunity to have their cars converted to run on both lead-free and leaded petrol, free of charge (Hall and Sturges, 1988). Other examples include Nouvelle, who plan to deliver to households throughout the UK a million trial size mini-packs of its paper products and 1.5 million money-off leaflets (Hoggan, 1991). Also the UK's biggest packaging exhibition, Reed Exhibitions' *Pakex '92*, plans to use the Pavilion Hall at the National Exhibition Centre, Birmingham, for promoting green issues and to run an international conference on the subject (Gofton, 1991).

According to Croydon (1992), the key difficulty of green sales promotions is one of credibility. That is, the degree of compatibility and reconciliation between the long-term environment-related commitments of companies and short-term sales promotions for sales gains strategies. No empirical study was found to address issues of sales promotions of green products. There appears, therefore, to be a need for research if the effectiveness of 'green' sales promotion programmes for different environmentally friendly products is to be analysed.

## Publicity

During the last decade there has been a dramatic increase of media coverage on green issues. For example, a sample of newspapers and magazines in June 1985 indicated that the word 'green' was used 3,617 times; the same survey conducted in June 1989 revealed that the usage rate had increased to 30,777 (Mitchell and Levy, 1989). Such findings show that publicity for environmental issues has grown substantially.

The environmental performances of several companies have received much attention from the media. Perhaps one of the most successful stories is that of 3M. 3M have attracted media coverage for developing environmentally sound business strategies in anticipation of present and future challenges (Peattie, 1990). They pioneered a companywide effort to reduce solid and hazardous waste, which now has become a standard model for corporations (Coddington, 1990). Another example is Wal-Mart's decision to stock environmentally safe products and packaging, which was publicised widely in the form of magazine articles, newspaper acknowledgements and TV coverage (Pride and Ferre, 1991).

The consequences of adverse coverage, however, must not be overlooked. A good example is the Heinz case. Heinz attempted to boost its green image through major donations to the World Wide Fund for Nature and by sponsoring Green Consumer Week. When environmentalists pointed out the contribution a Heinz subsidiary was making to needless slaughter of whales and dolphins in tuna production, the company was forced to withdraw from Green Consumer Week to minimise bad publicity (Peattie, 1990).

Apart from the study conducted by Mitchell and Levy (1989) and despite significant increases in media coverage, no other empirical study was found in the literature to examine 'green' publicity. Therefore, empirical research is needed to examine, amongst other things, 'consumers' perceptions and attitudes towards 'green' publicity, the effectiveness of 'green' publicity for different products/services, and the impact of positive/negative 'green' publicity on consumer behaviour.

*Personal selling*

According to Stanton, Etzel and Walker (1991), salespeople go far beyond simply making transactions; amongst other tasks, they are involved in explaining product benefits to customers. However, although there is evidence to support that 'green marketing' has broadened its scope in many respects, the role and contribution of personal selling in promoting green products attributes has not been empirically investigated. Therefore, the contribution of salespeople in providing customers with information concerning environmental performance of their products and/or environmental commitments of their companies needs to be examined and assessed.

**Distribution**

Among the various elements of physical distribution, transportation has been seen by companies as a key area with considerable potential for environmental contributions. For example, the Norfolk-based Start-rite shoe manufacturer has expanded its EDI (electronic data interchange) system to achieve more efficient delivery in terms of less fumes and fewer transport hazards (Knight, 1992).

Companies which are involved in the transportation business have also taken several steps in an attempt to minimise the environmentally damaging effects of their operations. Evidence can be found in a survey of 250 companies which indicates that the vast majority want to introduce more environmentally friendly logistics activities (Szymankiewicz, 1993). For example, in the car rental business, both Avis and Hertz claim to be ahead in the race to have the cleanest fleet. Also, both claim to have been the first to convert their entire fleet to run on unleaded petrol (*Marketing*, 30.8.1990). The TNT transportation group has dedicated personnel seeking to reduce usage of fossil fuels by improving efficiency in the maintenance and operation of motor vehicles and by reducing the number of motor vehicles they use (TNT Ltd, Annual Report, 1990). The UK's largest road transport company, BRS, has also revamped its environmental image. With the assistance of the corporate identity consultants Lloyd Northover, the company is eager to use its new fleet of 'environmentally friendly vehicles' to combat public perceptions of road haulage as a dirty business (*Marketing*, 6.9.1990).

In addition to various initiatives taken by companies, the government's White Paper on the environment which was introduced in 1989 investigates several transport-related problems and puts forward propositions such as: 'to extend the MOT test to cover vehicle emissions and so improve the tuning of the engines', 'to work in the EC to improve the fuel consumption of vehicles', etc. (Roberts, 1991). Criticism of these plans has been extended by Porrit (1990), Rogers (1991) and the Friends of the Earth (1990), on the grounds that the government ignores the potential of rail for easing the congestion on roads.

In the academic literature, the environmental problems which are associated with transport have been discussed by Seymour and Giradet (1988), and Elkington and Hailes (1989). Environmental problems specifically related to rail and/or road freight transport (i.e. emission levels, congestion, noise, etc.) have been empirically researched in the studies listed in Table 3.

Apart from the above studies, no other empirical study was found in the literature. This clearly indicates a research gap in the broad area of 'green physical distribution and channel management'. Therefore many marketing issues which are related to green distribution and channel management (e.g. examining the objectives, structure and functions of green marketing channels; identifying potential sources of conflict and areas for closer cooperation in green channel relations; determining criteria for measuring performance of green distribution channels, etc.), need to be addressed and empirically researched.

Table 3. Empirical studies examining perceptions of the environmental impact of the freight transport industry

| Author(s) | Year | Product/ service | Sample | Research objectives |
|---|---|---|---|---|
| Baughan, Hedges and Field | 1983 | Road transport | 2198 members of the general public | Perceived environmental disturbance caused by lorries |
| Huddart and Baughan | 1987 | Road transport | 200 members of the general public | Public attitudes to drawbar goods vehicles |
| Schlegelmilch, Diamantopoulos and Bohlen | 1992 | Freight transport | 65 key decision makers and opinion leaders | Analysis of the perceived environmental impact of road and rail freight transport |
| Bohlen, Diamantopoulos and Schlegelmilch | 1993 | Freight transport | 34 consumers | Consumer perceptions of environmental nuisances arising from the freight transport |

## CONCLUSIONS: A GREEN RESEARCH AGENDA

Despite the fact that the overall level of concern of both researchers and marketing managers towards the environment appears to have risen steadily, empirical research conducted in green marketing is still rather limited. Although previous contributions have provided a number of important insights, these did not provide a framework for the development of an effective green marketing mix. Based on the preceding analysis of the literature, several recommendations for additional research are now provided and discussed around each of the four marketing mix elements.

### Product

Research efforts in this area have mainly focused on the relationship between green product attributes and the buying behaviour of consumers (see Table 1). However, besides these contributions, which need to be extended to other product categories and services, there are more issues in the area of green product or product mix decisions that need to be empirically examined. The following list of research questions provides a guideline for the needed research; however, it is by no means all-inclusive.

- What are the similarities and differences of consumer responses towards green product attributes for different product/service categories?
- What are the possibilities for benefit segmentation along green criteria?
- What is the rate of adoption of new green products/services and what factors facilitate/hinder the diffusion process?
- What is the rate of success/failure of green products/services and what are the determinants of new product success?
- What are the added costs and benefits associated with the development and marketing of green products?

### Price

The literature review has revealed that the number of empirical studies in the area of 'green' pricing decisions and consumer behaviour to green product price variations is very limited. Additional research is required to identify the relationship between price variations of competing green and non-green products and consumer responses for several environmentally friendly products; such research also needs to be extended to services. Further research questions include:

- What are the pricing objectives, strategies and methods of companies practising green marketing?
- What is the role of pricing on the positioning of green products?
- What is the impact of competition in influencing the price adaptation strategies of green products?

● To what extent do social interests and moral concerns of management affect pricing decisions of green products?

## Communications mix

### Advertising

Despite the intense media coverage of vicarious 'green' advertising campaigns, government regulations, and pressures from organised green groups, no empirical study has been found in the literature to address issues related to advertising of green products. Therefore, there are several research opportunities, and potential topics can range from some widespread current issues (i.e. regulation for advertising green products) to more management-oriented questions. The following list provides some research questions on green advertising:

● How do consumers react to green advertising claims?
● What are the advertising objectives and strategies of companies practising green marketing?
● What are the criteria for evaluating the effectiveness of green advertising?
● What do organisations need to know about advertising their green products (i.e. what, when and how green claims should be made)?

### Sales promotion

No empirical studies were found to focus on sales promotion of green products. Given that the primary objective of a sales promotion programme is to stimulate demand in the short term and the core principle of environmentalism is to preserve the environment in the long run (i.e. less waste and reduced consumption), it appears that both empirical research and conceptual development in the area of sales promotion are required. For example, questions such as the following need to be addressed.

● What are consumers' attitudes towards green sales promotion?
● What sales promotion vehicles (i.e. coupons, free samples etc.) are relevant for promoting green products?
● How can the overall effectiveness of green sales promotion be maximised?
● To what extent do sales promotion techniques need to be modified in order to reflect the changes in green consumers' attitudes and buying habits?
● What are the similarities/differences between consumer-related and trade-related green sales promotion methods?

### Publicity

As in green advertising and green sales promotion, no study was found in the literature to address green publicity. Lack of empirical research offers many opportunities at a time when publicity of green issues has increased dramatically in the recent past and is still growing (Plachta, 1991). Some important questions for research include:

- What is the effect of green publicity on consumer perceptions and purchasing behaviour?
- What are the characteristics of green publicity themes (i.e. marketing developments, company policies, product endorsements, etc.), and what is their relative effectiveness?
- How can adverse publicity best be avoided?

*Personal selling*

Again, no empirical study was found in the literature to address the role of salespeople in the green companies. Given the fact that an increasing number of companies are turning green and that the effectiveness of a salesforce is an important determinant of an organisation's success, research focusing on the role and contribution of green salespeople could provide significant insights. Since salespeople occupy a boundary role position, they can contribute a lot in developing and maintaining a green marketing mix which could satisfy both customers and the firm. Consequently, issues such as the following need to be addressed:

- Should the objectives of a green salesforce be different from those of a conventional salesforce?
- What is the contribution of salespeople in the greening of companies?
- What are the determinants of a green ethical conduct of salespeople?
- What type of salespeople should green sales representatives be?

**Distribution**

Empirical research on ecological problems in physical distribution is limited, despite the growing concern about transport-related issues. Thus, research is needed to address issues of physical distribution activities and channel management. Possible research questions include the following:

- What are the distribution and channel management objectives and strategies of companies practising green marketing?
- What are the associated costs and expected benefits of a green distribution system?
- How will implementation of green logistics affect channel members (e.g. what are the possible sources of conflicts and how might such conflicts be resolved)?
- What criteria should be used to evaluate the performance of green distribution systems?

The above discussion has identified several gaps which were found in the literature dealing with the green marketing mix, and has offered some suggestions for future research. The purpose of this study was neither to suggest specific guidelines for the development of an effective green marketing mix nor to identify possible sources of support and resistance to the needed changes. What needs to be emphasised is that undesirable consequences resulting from the implementation of an incomplete green marketing mix can be prevented if additional information on how to go about it becomes available. To this end, a comprehensive literature review has been provided and several areas for further research have been suggested.

Marketing managers who wish to focus on the needs of green consumers must develop a marketing mix that accurately matches their expectations. The likelihood of developing a successful green marketing mix increases with additional information and knowledge. Researchers, therefore, have a key role to play by generating empirically based guidelines for designing, implementing and evaluating the various components of the green marketing mix.

# REFERENCES

Anderson, W. T., Jr and Cunningham, H. W. (1972) The socially conscious consumer. *Journal of Marketing*, **36** (July), 23–31.

Baughan, J. C., Hedges, B. and Field, J. (1983). A national survey of lorry nuisance. Transport and Road Research Laboratory, Digest SR 774, Department of the Environment/Department of Transport.

Bidlake, S. (1990) Still looking after Number One. *Marketing*, 29 November, 24–25.

Bohlen, G. M. Diamantopoulos, A. and Schlegelmilch, B. B. (1993) Consumer perceptions of the environmental impact of an industrial service. *Marketing Intelligence and Planning*, **11**, No. 1, 37–48.

Britt, B. (1990) Colas crack a green plastic bottle. *Marketing*, 13 December.

Brooker, G. (1976) The self-actualising socially conscious consumer. *Journal of Consumer Research*, **3** (September), 107–112.

Buck, C. (1989) Nappy wars. *Survey* (Winter), 14–17.

Burnside, A. (1990) Keen on green. *Marketing*, 17 May.

Cobb R. (1991) A problem that won't go away. *Marketing*, 31 January, 29–30.

Coddington, W. (1990) It's no fad: Environmentalism is now a fact of corporate life. *Marketing News*, 15 October, 7.

Cope, D. (1990) The green company: Can we manage it? in M. Kenward, *Director* (December), 92–96.

Corrado, M. and Ross, M. (1990) Green issues in Britain and the value of green research data. *ESOMAR Annual Congress*, Vol. 43, pp. 347–369.

Corrigan, K. (1989) They've got to be green. *Marketing News*, 15 October, 74.

Croydon, D. (1992) Are green offers dead and buried? *Marketing*, 26 March, 11.

Davies, J. (1991) A blueprint for green marketing. *Journal of Business Strategy* (July-August), 14–18.

Delbeke, J. (1991) The prospects for the use of economic instruments in EC environmental policy. *The Royal Bank of Scotland Review* (December), No. 172, 16–29.

Diamantopoulos, A., Schlegelmilch, B. B. and DuPreez, J. P. (1992) The relative importance of country-origin and ecological product attributes in two European countries: A partially individualised conjoint analysis. *Working Paper EBMS/1991/33*, European Business Management School, University of Wales, Swansea.

Dunham, R. (1990) Ethical funds, no bar to profits. *Accountancy* (June), 111.

DuPreez, J. P., Diamantopoulos, A., and Schlegelmilch, B. B (1992) The role of 'made in' and 'green' product features in automobile purchases: A cross-country comparison between Korea, Spain and France. *Annual Meeting of the Academy of International Business*, Brussels, 20–22 November.

Dwek, R. (1992) Saab revs up green turbo engine. *Marketing*, 26 March, 3.

El-Ansary, I. A. (1974) Societal marketing: A strategic view of the marketing mix in the 70s. *Journal of the Academy of Marketing Science*, **2**, No. 4, 553–566.

Elkington, J., Burke, T. and Hailes, J. (1988) *Green Pages: The Business of Saving the World.* London: Routledge.

Elkington, J. and Hailes, J. (1989) *Universal Green Office Guide.* London: Gollancz.

Fierman, J. (1991) The big muddle in green marketing. *Fortune*, 3 June, 91–101.

Foster, A. (1989) Decent, clean and true. *Management Today* (February), 56–60.

Friends of the Earth (1990) *How Green is Britain?—The Government's Environmental Record.* London: Hutchinson Radius.

Friends of the Earth (1991) Green Con of the Year Awards 1991. Press Release, 19 December.

Fritzsche, D. J. and Duehr, R. (1982) The effects of ecological concern on product attribute utility. *American Marketing Association Proceedings*, pp. 364–369.

Gofton, K. (1991) Pakex '92 Exhibition goes green. *Marketing*, 12 December, 11.

Griffiths, J. (1991) A prime target. *Financial Times Survey*, 13 March, p. VII.

Grunert, S. C. and Kristensen, K. (1992) The green consumer: Some Danish evidence. In *Marketing For Europe—Marketing For The Future*, Proceedings of the 1992 Annual European Marketing Academy Conference, 26–29 May, Denmark, pp. 525–539.

Hall, N. and Sturges, J. (1988) Going clean for green. *Marketing Week*, 10 June, 37.

Henion, E. K. (1972) The effect of ecologically relevant information on detergent sales. *Journal of Marketing Research*, **IX** (February), 10–14.

Henion, E. K. (1979) Ecological marketing: Will the normative become descriptive? In G. Fisk, J. Arndt and K. Gronharg (eds), *Future Direction for Marketing*. Boston: Marketing Science Institute, pp. 280–291.

Henion, E. K., Gregory, R. and Clee, A. M. (1980) Trade-offs in attribute levels made by ecologically concerned and unconcerned consumers when buying detergents. *Advances in Consumer Research*, **8**, 624–629.

Herberger, A. R. and Buchanan, I. D. (1971) The impact of concern for ecological factors on consumer attitudes and buying behaviour. *American Marketing Association Proceedings*, pp. 644–646.

Hoggan, K. (1991) Green Nouvelle attacks Andrex with money-off. *Marketing*, 19 September.

Huddart, L. and Baughan, J. C. (1987) Public attitudes to drawbar goods vehicles. *Transport and Road Research Laboratory*, Digest of Research Report 108, Department of Transport.

Hunt, J. (1991a) Industry and the environment: Rising levels of concern. *Financial Times Survey*, 13 March, p. 1.

Hunt, J. (1991b) Yardstick for environmental performance. *Financial Times*, 10 June.

Jowell, R., Witherspoon, S. and Brook, L. (eds) (1988) *British Social Attitude: The 5th Report*, London: Gower.

Kashmanian, R. M., Ferrand, T., Hurst, K. and Kuusinen, T. L. (1990) Let's topple the recycling 'Wall', too. *Mrketing News*, **24**, No. 6, 20.

Kassarjian, H. H. (1971) Incorporating ecology into marketing strategy: The case of air pollution. *Journal of Marketing*, **35** (July), 61–65.

Kavanagh, M. (1990) TV fights fake green ads. *Marketing*, 15 March, 1.

Kerin, A. R. and Peterson, R. A. (1974) Selected insights of ecologically responsible behaviour. *American Institute for Decision Sciences Proceedings*, **6**, 33.

Kinnear, C. T., and Taylor, R. J. (1973) The effect of ecological concern on brand perceptions. *Journal of Marketing Research*, **X** (May), 191–197.

Kinnear, C. T. (1982) A new milk jug. In D. A. Aaker and G. S. Day (eds), *Consumerism: Search for the Consumer Interest*. New York: Free Press.

Kirkpatrick, D. (1990) Environmentalism. *Fortune*, 12 February, 44–51.

Knight, P. (1992) Numbers plucked out of the sky. *Financial Times*, 11 March, p. 15.

Kotler, P. (1979) Axioms for societal marketing. In G. Fisk, J. Arndt and K. Gronharg (eds), *Future Directions for Marketing*. Boston: Marketing Science Institute, pp. 33–41.

Kristensen, K. and Grunert, S. C. (1991) The effect of ecological consciousness on the demand for organic foods. In *Marketing Thought Around the World*. Proceedings of the 1991 Annual European Marketing Academy Conference, 21–23 May, Ireland, pp. 299–318.

Lauson, C. (1989) Packaging and the environment. *Survey* (Winter), 18–20.

Lloyds Bank (1989) Being economical with the environment. *Lloyds Bank Economic Bulletin*, No. 129, September.

Mackenzie, D. (1992) Greener than thou. *Marketing Business* (April), 10–13.

*Management Consultancy* (1989) Keep your head in the green revolution. September, pp. 56–57.

*Marketing* (1990) Nielsen: Green product. 12 April.

*Marketing* (1990) Marketing forum. 21 June.

*Marketing* (1990) Green battle accelerates with Avis move. 30 August.

*Marketing* (1991) Consumers grow skeptical of advertisers' green campaigns. 21 February.

Market Research Society (1990) Attitudes to environmental issues. *MRS Newsletter*, October.

Mazis, B. M., Settle, B. R. and Leslie, C. D. (1973) Elimination of phosphate detergents and psychological reactance. *Journal of Marketing Research*, **X** (November), 390–395.

McIntosh, A. (1991) The impact of environmental issues on marketing and politics in the 1990s. *Journal of Market Research Society*, **33**, No. 3, 205–217.

Miller, C. (1991) Cosmetics industry's marketing approach says colour me green. *Marketing News*, **25**, No. 12, 10 June, 2.

Mitchell, A. (1989) Milking the greens. *Marketing*, 14 September, 34–35.

Mitchell, A. and Levy, L. (1989) Green about green. *Marketing*, 14 September, 28–35.

Moore, K. (1993) An emergent model of consumer response to green marketing. In J. Chias and J. Sureda (eds), *Proceedings of the 22nd European Marketing Academy Conference*, vol. II, pp. 955–974.

Murphy, O. (1989) Green is the colour. *Survey* (Winter), 9–11.

Nash, T. (1990) Green about the environment? *Director* (February), 40–43.

Nelson, E. (1989) Shades of Green. *Survey* (Winter), 9–11.

Peattie, J. K. (1990) Painting marketing education (or how to recycle old ideas). *Journal of Marketing Management*, **6**, No. 2, 105–125.

Peattie, K. (1992) *Green Marketing*, The M+E Handbook Series. London: Longman.

Plachta, J. (1991) Relations improve in a poor climate. *Marketing*, 24 January, 23–24.

Porritt, J. (1987) *Friends of the Earth Handbook*, London: McDonald.

Porritt, J. (1990) On the road to ruin. *Country Life*, 18 October, 126–129.

Prestridge, J. (1989) Green and ethics sprout forth. *Money Management* (November), 63–71.

Pride, M. W. and Ferrell, C. O. (1991) *Marketing: Concepts and Strategies*. Boston: Houghton Mifflin.

Prothero, A. (1990) Green consumerism and the societal marketing concept: Marketing strategies for the 1990s. *Journal of Marketing Management*, **6**, No. 2 (Autumn), 87–103.

Prothero, A. and McDonagh, P. (1992) Producing environmentally acceptable cosmetics? The impact of environmentalism on the United Kingdom cosmetics and toiletries industry. *Journal of Marketing Management*, **8**, No. 2, 147–166.

Prothero, A. and McDonagh, P. (1993) The European Community and environmentalism—the impact of EC environmental policies upon the marketing function. In M. J. Baker (ed.), *Perspectives on Marketing Management*, vol. III. Chichester: Wiley, pp. 91–117.

Reeves, I. (1990) Going green. *Business Marketing Review* (November), **1**, No. 7, 30–31.

Research 2000 (1990) Consumers and the environment: The impact of environmental change on attitudes and purchasing behaviour. *Environmental Attitudes Research Survey*, No. 1, September.

Roberts, H. L. (1991) Environmentalism in the UK: A review. Unpublished MPhil Thesis, European Business Management School, University of Wales, Swansea.

Roberts, J., James, N. and Rawcliffe, P. (1991) Railroading the environment? *Town and Country Planning* (May), **60**, No. 5, 159–160.

Rogers, D. (1991) More roads? The Government's road programme reconsidered. *Planner*, **77**, No. 9 (March), 7–9.

Sand, H. P. (1990) Innovations in international environmental governance. *Environment*, **32**, No. 9, 16–20, 40–45.

Schlegelmilch, B. B. and Diamantopoulos, A. (1990) The perceived environmental impact of rail and road freight transport: A qualitative analysis. European Business Management School, University of Wales, Swansea.

Schlegelmilch, B. B., Diamantopoulos, A., and DuPreez, J. P. (1992) Consumer preferences as barriers to standardising marketing programmes in the single European market: The role of country of origin and ecological product attributes. In V. L. Crittenden (ed.), *Developments in Marketing Science*, vol. XV. Proceedings of the Annual Conference of the Academy of Marketing Science, 21–26 April.

Schlegelmilch, B. B., Diamantopoulos, A. and Bohlen, G. M. (1992) Environmental issues in the freight transport industry: A qualitative analysis of stakeholders' perceptions. *Proceedings of the 1992 MEG Annual Conference*, July, pp. 619–632.

Schlossberg, H. (1990) Greening of America awaits green light from leaders, consumers. *Marketing News*, 19 March, 1, 16.

Seymour, J. and Girardet, H. (1988) *Blueprint for a Green Planet*. London: Dorling Kindersley.

Shuptrine, K. F. and Osmanski, F. A. (1975) Marketing's changing role: Expanding or contracting? *Journal of Marketing*, **39**, 58–66.

Smith, G. (1990) How green is my valley? *Marketing and Research Today*, **18**, No. 2 (June), 76–82.

Stanton, J. W., Etzel, J. M. and Walker, J. B. (1991) *Fundamentals of Marketing*. New York: McGraw-Hill.

Szymankiewicz, J. (1993) Going green—the logistics dilemma. *Focus on Logistics and Distribution Management*, **12**, No. 5 (June) 36–41.

Tennant, T. (1991) The ethical issue. *Planned Savings*, February, 31–33.

Thatcher, M. (1990) *Our Threatened Environment: The Conservative Response*. London: Conservative Political Centre.

The Economist. (1990) Cleaning up. *A Survey of Industry and the Environment*, 8 September.

The Ethical Investment Research Service (1992) What is ethical investment? *EIRIS Information Sheet*, p. 3.

*The Ethical Investor* (1990) Ethical investors go for green variety (Summer), p. 1.

Thomas, M. L. (1992) The business community and the environment: An important partnership. *Business Horizons*, **35**, No. 2 (March–April), 21–24.

TNT (1990) *TNT Limited Annual Report 1990*.

Varble, L. D. (1972) Social and environmental considerations in new product development. *Journal of Marketing*, **36** (October), 11–15.

Welds, K. (1991) Unwrapping the environment. *Canadian Grocer* (June), 18–23.

# 25

# Environmental Marketing: Some Practical Guidelines for Managers

*Pierre McDonagh and Andrea Prothero*

How should a firm respond to the rising tide of environmentalism? Is it primarily a marketing problem or opportunity, or a company wide one? Should firms appoint an environmental manager? There are many issues at play and the responses of the various players—government, EC, industry, and consumer—must be examined. A basic requirement is a communications regime of integrity and clear-sightedness both within companies and between companies and their relevant publics.

The best 'environmental' strategem for companies to pursue is a structured holistic approach rather than a fragmented piecemeal one. Indeed a piecemeal approach is often likely to backfire on the firm. A number of environmentally responsible firms in the UK are profiled. Finally, in order to assess a firm's environmental 'blood pressure', a straightforward diagnostic tool is proposed that allows the marketing manager to assess whether or not her company has a structure in place upon which it can develop a proper environmental orientation.

## RESPONSES TO ENVIRONMENTALISM

*Marketing* magazine has recently pointed out that, of the newspapers and magazines monitored by its database, the term 'environment-friendly' was used only once in June 1985; by June 1989 this figure however had increased to the use of the term thirty times a day.[1] The combined mixture of increased concern about environmental problems on a global scale and increased pressure from environmental groups has meant increased attention being paid to 'green' issues in the media. This attention is also reflected in the domain of marketing.

The environmental movement has seen a dramatic change in recent years; environmentalists are no longer seen as 'embittered, scruffy, anti-business street fighters',[2] but as a respected group trying to influence the concern being paid to the environment by various interest groups. This environmental concern has

Reprinted from *Irish Marketing Review*, Vol. 6, pp. 120–126 with permission triggered responses from national governments, the European Community, industry and the consumer.

The UK government has responded to the environmental challenge by being one of the first governments in the world to introduce a comprehensive environmental statement, with the publication of its White Paper *This Common Inheritance* in September 1990, backed up by a first year report in September 1991. Along with the publication of the planned strategies of the government in the environmental area there has also been increased environmental legislation, for instance, the 1990 Environmental Protection Act. It should also be noted at this point that much of the UK legislation introduced has been as a result of EC Directives. Although the government has introduced new environmental policies, it has been criticised by environmentalists for only paying lip service to the issues; while it has also been criticised by the European Commission for not introducing Directives quickly enough.

For member states within the EC, environmental legislation is becoming increasingly dictated by Community wide initiatives. EC environmental legislation has moved beyond the traditional concerns of monitoring pollution and waste to areas like agriculture and transport, and to the marketing of specific products.[3] Among the Environmental Directives which have been proposed or are currently under discussion, and which will affect industry, are eco-auditing, eco-labelling, and the launch of a new European environmental agency. The eco-auditing initiative proposes a framework for encouraging and monitoring environmentally sound management among businesses. It will be a voluntary system which will allow a firm to apply for EC-approved 'green' status. This process for winning approval is outlined in Figure 1.

Industry has also been responding as a result of increased pressure 'to be seen to be green'. Indeed companies have been promoting more environmentally acceptable goods and services, publishing environmental policy documents, conducting environmental audits and environmental impact assessments, whilst also providing increasing support to local community projects. Firms have become more efficient in the use of raw materials, energy and so on, and have modified products to take into account environmental considerations, for example the removal of CFCs and animal ingredients from cosmetic and toiletry products. In general, however, industry has been criticised by environmentalists for only paying 'lip service' to environmental issues. Many companies have lost out by promoting themselves as green only to be awarded *The Green Con of the Year* by Friends of the Earth for what they call dubious green claims. It would seem that industry has much further to go before it will satisfy the environmentalists.

Consumers in recent years, have responded to the environmental challenge by voting with their pockets and purchasing more environmentally acceptable goods and services. Research has shown a potential of twelve to fifteen million green consumers in the UK.[4] A Mintel survey had shown forty per cent of respondents to be dark green consumers; i.e. consumers who always or nearly always buy or use 'environment-friendly' products; with a further twenty per cent of respondents being pale greens; i.e. consumers who sometimes buy or use 'environment-friendly' products.[5] Consumers then are playing a significant role in the rise of importance of environmental issues. As Knappe stresses: 'The value system of the consumer creates

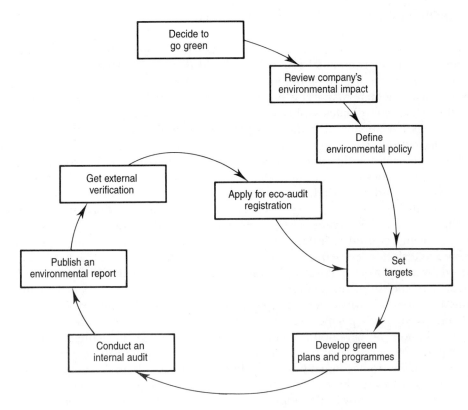

Figure 1. The EC Eco-Auditing Registration Process. (*Source*: Peattie, K. (1992), *Green Marketing*, Pitman, London, p. 305).

the social attitudes that, in turn, result in political consequences that restrict the behaviour of business throughout the world.[6] However, consumers are still said to be not purchasing enough of the alternative products available on the market; this is in part a result of the premium price being charged for many green products, and also of fears by consumers that green products may be somewhat inferior to the alternatives. Consumers have also been hindered by many dubious claims by organisations and whether or not they can trust such claims.[7] Consumers have difficulty, for example, in distinguishing between terms such as 'environment-friendly' and 'environment-friendlier'. As Penzer points out consumers are beginning to attack green sponsors for making unsubstantiated green claims.[8]

In general, then, it would appear that the major criticism of environmentalists is that environmentalism is not at the top of the agenda of government, the EC, industry (including agriculture), or, for that matter, the consumer. If this is the case they fear that global environmental problems cannot be cured if environmental issues are continually treated as window dress strategies by the various interest groups involved. What seems to be important is that green cannot be seen as 'just a colour put on a product as an afterthought. It has to be a company philosophy that the whole staff can get behind.'

## ENVIRONMENTAL IMPACTS UPON MARKETING

What then are the consequences for marketing departments which are trying to respond to the environmental challenge? Should they, and indeed how do they, go about green marketing? Environmental/green marketing may in fact be seen by many as a misnomer. Marketing has been perceived as Machiavellian[9] and as the function which coordinates sophisticated advertising campaigns aimed at disguising what effects a company actually has upon the natural environment, as much as informing customers about current environmental practices. Marketing may be its own worst enemy for this public perception. A 1990 survey conducted by Kaagan Environmental Monitor indicated that only 8% of Americans surveyed viewed business and industry leaders as very believable sources of information on environmental issues.[10] Some logical explanation for such scenarious may be found in what measures a company takes to communicate with its various publics. If the message being received or indeed broadcast is clouded, confused or muddled, there will be unsatisfactory consequences. It is in the firm's best interest to be believed and trusted by the various publics with which it interacts on a daily basis—as with a personal relationship, the existence of trust among the firm's publics is a major foundation for the environmentally acceptable and successful company.

Thus, from the perspective of the marketing manager, the quality of communication is paramount. There is first the need to gather marketing intelligence from the market, and second the requirement to coordinate the communication from company to the targeted market. Internal, communications and coordination are also crucial. The environmently conscious marketing manager will be involved not only in developing new products, but also in overseeing changes in attitude and culture in an organisation. People skills and the ability to communicate clearly are key.[11,12]

Because of the complexity, sensitivity and personnel expertise—not to mention the investment of time—involved in managing environmental issues successfully for the firm, companies are increasingly appointing environmental managers within their organisations. In Germany and the Netherlands, this is becoming widespread. It is not yet so alas in the UK and Ireland. There are many advantages in having such a 'dedicated' manager. In particular, it facilitates a holistic and coordinated approach to managing a firm's environmental policy. A piecemeal approach is simply often not successful, and can sometimes backfire.

Many organisations responding to the environmental challenge have been responding in a fragmented way to only a few issues within the broad spectrum of environmental concerns. It is for this reason that many companies are beginning to move away from considering environmental issues for fear of being attacked on some grounds, other than those addressed, by environmentalists. Procter and Gamble, for example, introduced a new 'environmentally friendly' detergent Ariel Ultra only to be criticised by environmentalists because the product had been tested on animals. Indeed many environmental organisations are 'waiting in the wings' to attack the activities of business. Sheridan has emphasised that 91.2% of US executives sampled recognised the importance of 'buying green' and saw a strong connection between good environmental stewardship and creating the right corporate image in the market-place.[13] However, marketing managers who take on the role of emphasising the 'greenness' of a company's products will come under heavy criticism from environmentalists if other activities within the organisations are seen as environmentally unacceptable. One way of countering this and overcoming the 'dilemma of commitment' to environmentalism is to appoint an environmental manager charged with achieving a company-wide environmental orientation.

## ENVIRONMENTAL INFORMATION RESPONSE

The importance of communicating environmental information throughout the organisation has already been stressed. Figure 2 illustrates an environmental information response model which may be of use to marketing departments when considering the environmental challenge. Stages one and two in the model are phases which are already happening within the business environment today. In other words, awareness of the environmental challenge has been raised and communication within organisations, regarding environmental issues, are beginning to take effect.

Stages three of the model however—cooperation between all various interest groups on the natural environment, from the suppliers through to the end-consumer—seems mainly to be a matter of discussion rather than action. In the relevant literature, the recognition of cooperation between functions within the organisation and external 'influencers' is being raised from respective functional standpoints. During stage three management effectively acknowledges the need to do something in respect to its interaction with the human and natural environments. Stage four is obviously the most productive from an environmental viewpoint, in so far as strategies decided upon as a result of stage three are implemented. Examples of companies who have reached this stage include, for example, the cosmetics and toiletries firm Beauty Without Cruelty.

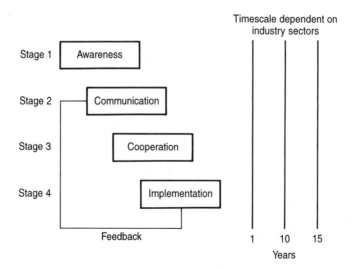

Figure 2. Environmental Information Response Model.

It is possible for a company to go from stage one to stage four and make incorrect environmental decisions; thus management requires a *ceteris paribus* approach to assist it in stages one to four. As well as making incorrect environmental decisions some companies choose to implement partial policies relating to environmental management (see company examples further on). It is indicated that, in the UK, grocery multiple retailers avoid addressing environmental problems in their entirety.[14] There are three main reasons for this. Firstly, after an initial surge of selling green labelled products companies are wary of the complexity of the environmental issues that emerge. Secondly, firms begin to feel inhibited by the 'green image' they may possess, as this may lose them valuable non-green customers. Thirdly, these companies lack organisational commitment and control in the environmental area.

The response of the grocery retailing sector is somewhat at odds with the response found in the US hotel industry. As Rowe notes when the Miami Marriott Dadeland converted 19 of its 303 rooms to 'green' rooms the response was overwhelming.[15] Demand for rooms with equipment designed to purify the air and drinking water was phenomenal, leading Marriott to increase the number of such rooms to 28. This confirms the sectoral pattern in Figure 2. There is no doubt that stage four of the model is the most difficult to handle but also the most vital. Research for the Brunel management programme short courses on environmental management supports this. Whilst there was agreement amongst managers of the importance of the environment within company strategies, very few companies had actually undertaken any plans to implement environmental decisions and were unclear as to what steps they should take when addressing the environmental challenge.

## ENVIRONMENTALLY RESPONSIBLE COMPANIES

Many companies are, however, responding to the environmental challenge. In the first instance, this may arise from a desire to cut costs through, say, an energy conservation programme. But it initiates the process. Many firms are hiring environmental consultants to help them develop sound environmental practices and are beginning to see the difference.[16] Examples of companies which have responded to the environmental challenge in some way include the following.

- Peter Lane Transport has tried to adopt good environmental management with subsequent increased profitability and a better profile in the community. It has began using more environmentally acceptable trucks, is involved with local schools, and has initiated employee training schemes on several environmental issues.
- Borley Park Hotel has a statement of the hotel's environmental concerns placed in all hotel rooms and has managed to attract a series of European environmental conferences resulting from some of its green practices.
- British Airways and Norsk Hydro won environmental reporting awards in 1991, sponsored by the Chartered Association of Certified Accountants, for making available to shareholders and the general public, environmental information on

core business activities. This was conducted by each company and validated by external consultants.

- Procter and Gamble have implemented a number of product changes; refill packages have reduced packaging and recycled plastics are used in the manufacturing of bottles for different products.
- National Westminster Bank is expecting savings of almost a million pounds from the introduction of a new energy-efficient cheque processing site, as well as a 12% saving from making visiting cards out of recycled paper.

A leading group of companies including IBM, Costain, ICI, Tesco, and British Telecom have formed a group called 'Business and the Environment' to cooperate in helping to solve environmental problems. Other organisations have also been joining forces to help combat environmental problems. The Confederation of British Industry has been coordinating an effort between environmentalists, academics and business people in the development of independent evaluation techniques to measure the environmental impact of goods and services. A number of organisations, BASF, Enichem, Proctor and Gamble, Shell, and Unilever, are all supporting the development of a society which will promote the use of life-cycle development, where companies assess the environmental impact of products from 'conception to the grave'. In the US, although many firms have been criticised for talking about environmental issues but not actually acting on them, several companies operating environmental policies have been rewarded by cutting down on waste, selling recycled products and conserving energy. All these activities have led to increased profits.[17]

## A STRUCTURED APPROACH TO ENVIRONMENTALISM

These examples show a number of strategies that companies have adopted in response to the global environmental challenge. They indicate a clear integration, communication and implementation of a new environmental orientation. However, such organisations are in the minority. The greater proportion of companies have not addressed environmental issues, have addressed them wrongly, or have tackled them in a piecemeal fragmented way which is ultimately unsatisfactory. What is required is a more structured approach to environmentalism on the part of both companies and regulatory authorities.

Due to the complexity of addressing the environmental issues it is unrealistic for individual organisations to undertake all of the work themselves unless they have vast reserves, or are willing to invest monies heavily in this area. It would appear that in order to simplify the stages of responses taken by organisations, clearer incentives need to be developed in moving from one stage to another. For instance, governments could offer tax savings for companies operating in an improved environmental manner. Firms undertaking eco-audits and using eco-labels could be given financial support for doing so.

The authors have developed a straightforward diagnostic tool to allow the marketing manager to asses whether or not the company has a structure in place upon which it can develop an environmental orientation (see Figures 3 and 4).

Clearly, the best approach to developing an objective environmental orientation is to pursue an eco-audit within your company (as outlined, say, in Prothero and McDonagh[18]) and display the eco-label as a way of communicating your strategy to various publics. This however requires a dedicated and enlightened management and staff team to implement such exemplary strategies. Thus, the objective here in using the simple diagnostics is to tackle the initial hurdles in deciding the scope of the task to be undertaken. After completing the diagnostics, if the company scores poorly in the 'sitting ducks' or 'talkers not achievers' categories, then it is the time to

For each of the following questions score +5 points for a YES answer and −5 points for a NO answer. Then do an 'environment' plot on the diagnostic to see how your company is performing.

Q.1. Has your company been visited by an environmental consultant in the past 12 months? YES/NO

Q.2. Does your organisation have an environmental director/manager? YES/NO

Q.3. If NO to last question, does some board member take charge of researching environmental issues? YES/NO

Q.4. Are findings researching the firm's environmental impact reported back to the board of directors? YES/NO

Q.5. Is any environmental reporting incorporated into the firm's business planning? YES/NO

Q.6. Does your company have an integrated PR programme dealing with environmental issues? YES/NO

Q.7. Do you inform any of the following publics of your stance on environmental issues?

| Pressure groups | YES/NO | Media | YES/NO | The trade | YES/NO |
|---|---|---|---|---|---|
| Customers | YES/NO | Suppliers | YES/NO | The community | YES/NO |
| Investors | YES/NO | Competition | YES/NO | Legislators | YES/NO |

Now sum up your scores for questions 1 to 5 and plot your firm's environmental position on the vertical axis of Envir-Plot A. Then sum up your scores for questions 6 & 7 and plot your firm's external communications scores on the horizontal axis of Envir-Plot A.

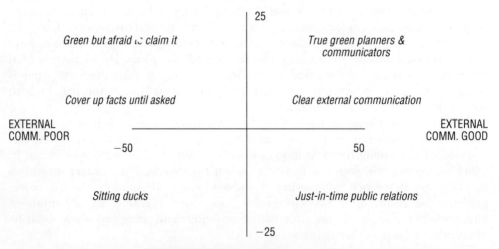

Figure 3. Envir-Plot A

call in an environmental expert and sit down to address the environmental challenge. It is hoped that the diagnostics may well trigger off the management to respond to the need for a job description for someone to act as an environmental expert for the company. The tool is not meant to be a rigorous health check, more a way of assessing the firm's environmental blood pressure.

For each of the following questions score +5 points for a YES answer and −5 points for a NO answer. Then do an environment plot on the diagnostic to see how your company is performing.

Q.1. Does your company have a written environmental policy document (EPD)?   YES/NO

Q.2. If NO to last question, is there acknowledgement of environ. issues in the firm's mission statement? YES/NO

Q.3. Are all functions involved in writing the EPD?   YES/NO

Q.4. Does each functional area have environmental targets to be met?   YES/NO

Q.5. Are these reviewed?   YES/NO          If YES, are reviews weekly? YES/NO;   monthly? YES/NO;
                                           6 monthly?  YES/NO;   annually?  YES/NO

Q.6. Is the EPD communicated throughout the company? YES/NO

Q.7. Is the EPD communicated by any of the following?

    Inter-departmental meetings  YES/NO       Memos       YES/NO       Noticeboards  YES/NO
    Departmental meetings        YES/NO       Newsletters YES/NO       Personnel     YES/NO

Q.8. Does the company run environmental training courses for its employees? YES/NO Are the courses for

    Senior management?  YES/NO       Junior management  YES/NO       Support staff?  YES/NO
    Middle management?  YES/NO       Operational staff?    YES/NO       Trades unions?  YES/NO

Now sum up your scores for questions 1 to 5 and plot your firm's level of environmental concern on the vertical axis of Envir-Plot B. Then sum up your scores for questions 6, 7 & 8 and plot your firm's scores for internal communications relating to environmental issues on the horizontal axis of Envir-Plot B.

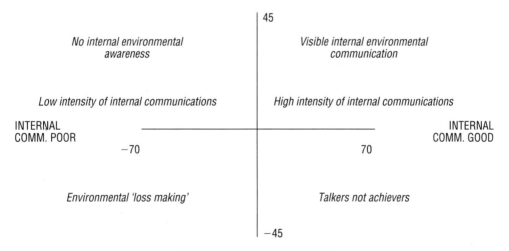

WRITTEN ENVIRONMENTAL POLICY

Figure 4. Envir-Plot B

## REFERENCES

1. Prothero, Andrea (1990) 'Green consumerism and the societal marketing concept—marketing strategies for the 1990s', *Journal of Marketing Management*, vol. 6 no. 2, pp. 87–102.
2. Kirkpatrick, David (1990) 'Environmentalism'. *Fortune*, February 12th, pp. 44–51.
3. Peattie, Ken (1992) *Green Marketing*, Pitman, London, pp. 302–305.
4. Butler, Dan (1990) 'A deeper shade of green', *Management Today*, June, pp. 74–79.
5. Hailes, Julia (1991) 'Shopping for a Euro-label to help consumers', *Independent* September 10th, p. 4.
6. Knappe, Ernst G. (1990) 'Combining economic growth and environmental concern, *World of Banking*, vol. 9 no. 4, pp. 15–17.
7. Bond, Cathy (1989) 'Green beanfeast', *Marketing*, September 28th, pp. 45–47.
8. Penzer, Erik (1990) 'Turning "green"', *Incentive Marketing*, vol. 164 no. 7, pp. 26, 28, 128.
9. Hunt, Shelby D. and Chonko, Lawrence B. (1984) 'Marketing and Machiavellianism', *Journal of Marketing*, vol. 48, Summer, pp. 30–42.
10. Davis, Joel J. (1991) 'A blueprint for green marketing', *Journal of Business Strategy*, vol. 12 no 4, pp. 14–17.
11. Friedman, Frank B (1992) 'The changing role of the environmental manager', *Business Horizons*, vol. 35 no. 2, pp. 25–28.
12. Shimel, Pamela (1991) 'Corporate environmental policy in practice', *Long Range Planning*, vol. 24 no. 3, pp. 10–17.
13. Sheridan, John H. (1992) 'Environmental issues sap executive time', *Industry Week*, vol. 24 no. 6, pp. 44–48.
14. Simms, Christine (1992) 'Green issues and strategic management in the grocery retail sector', *International Journal of Retail and Distribution Management*, vol 20 no. 1, pp. 32–42.
15. Rowe, Megan (1992) 'Greening for dollars', *Lodging Hospitality*, vol. 48 no. 4, pp. 36–38.
16. McIntosh, Malcolm (1991) 'Switch the lights off: save the planet', *Director*, vol. 45 no 3, pp. 89–94.
17. Smith, S. L. (1991) 'The greening of American business', *Occupational Hazards*, vol. 53 no. 9, pp. 112–118.
18. Prothero, Andrea and McDonagh, Pierre (forthcoming 1993) 'The European Community and Environmentalism', in Baker, Michael, J., (ed.), *Perspectives on Marketing Management*, vol. III, John Wiley & Sons, Chicester.

# 26

# The Environmental Value-Attitude-System Model: a Framework to Guide the Understanding of Environmentally-Conscious Consumer Behaviour

*Sabine Dembkowski and Stuart Hanmer-Lloyd*

Business writers such as Charter in 1992 predict that addressing the environmental consciousness of consumers will be one of the most important issues industry will face in the 1990s, and was seen by Ottmann in 1992 as the marketing trend of the decade. In 1993 Coddington judged much of green consumer potential to be latent as the environmental concern expressed in surveys was not clearly visible in current consumer behaviour. How best to respond to this new challenge and exploit the potential market is still causing confusion amongst marketers. However, it is a practical business concern as consumers may become more explicit in their demand and use their purchase power as an economic vote to effect social and environmental change. It is argued that marketing conclusions can only be drawn from a thorough understanding of the phenomenon. In this paper, the value-attitude-system model of Vinson *et al.* in 1977 is applied and extended to provide an insight into the complex phenomena affecting environmentally-conscious purchase behaviour by integrating the underlying influences from the individual belief system.

## INTRODUCTION

The environment is, without doubt, one area which is being subjected to greater public scrutiny, and therefore the influence of environmental issues on marketing is an area of increasing significance to industry and commerce.

Numerous opinion surveys show a clear growth of environmental consciousness among the public. In the UK, Market & Opinion Research International (MORI) has, since its founding in 1969, 'tracked the view of the British public towards environmental matters' (Worcester, 1993, p. 2). In 1992, research showed that 69%

Reprinted with permission from *Journal of Marketing Management*, Vol. 10, 1994, pp. 593–603.

of the British population think pollution and other environmental damage are affecting their day-to-day life. The same study also found 'a bewildered British public, with nearly four in 10 (39%) agreeing with the statement " I don't fully understand environmental issues" ' (Worcester, 1993, p. 2). A survey conducted on behalf of the EC found that 82% of citizens in the UK rated the environment as an immediate and urgent problem, and only 10% of the British population thought it more a problem for the future. Comparing those figures with the two previous surveys from 1986 and 1988 one can find that the urgency of the problem for the public has increased (INRA, 1992). Citizens in the UK are amongst those within the EC most likely to have heard of different environmental problems and to be most sensitive towards them (INRA, 1991).

These continually-expressed concerns have a potential long-term implication for business as consumers increasingly force companies to adopt an environmentally-sensitive approach. However, the translation of concerns into action is only slowly diffusing through the marketplace. This provides an opportunity for the development of new marketing strategies. To exploit the potential of this social trend, it is important for marketers to have an in-depth understanding of the development of environmental consciousness within the individual's belief system.

## UNDERSTANDING ENVIRONMENTAL CONSCIOUSNESS

Before describing the value-attitude-system model, it is important to clarify what is meant by environmental consciousness. The term environmental consciousness does not have a standardized definition in the body of international literature (Fietkau, 1984 and 1991; Hofrichter, 1992; Monhemius, 1992; Schuster, 1992; Schahn and Giesinger, 1993) as the term arose out of political and everyday language (Hofrichter, 1992). Nevertheless it is one of the central constructs in the literature used to explain environmentally-conscious consumer behaviour (Schuster, 1992). Environmental consciousness is an element of the individual belief system. Environmental consciousness is a part of the social consciousness and is in itself, a complex system of values and attitudes (Monhemius, 1992; Wimmer, 1992; Schahn and Giesinger, 1993).

To aid the explanation of the relationship between attitude and behaviour, psychologists have constructed several models of the composition of attitudes: the factors underlying them and the interrelationships of those factors. To portray the factors underlying environmental consciousness, the three component model can be applied. This suggests that environmental consciousness is a multidimensional construct with a cognitive, affective and conative component (Schuster, 1992; Tiebler, 1992; Wimmer, 1992; Schahn and Giesinger, 1993). The cognitive component encompasses the ideas, thoughts or knowledge that a person has about the attitude object and involves the information processing activities of the mind. In the scope of this paper, the cognitive component refers to the possession of subjective knowledge by the consumer about the environmental consequences of his actions. In the literature there appears to be a conflict about the degree of influence of knowledge on behaviour. One body of literature suggests that there is only a weak relationship between environmental knowledge, behavioural intentions and behaviour (e.g. Maloney *et al.*, 1975; Borden and Schettino, 1979; Balderjahn, 1985). However, the other body implies that the cognitive component plays a significant part in influencing environmentally-conscious behaviour (e.g. Billig *et al.*, 1986). The emotions or feelings that an individual has towards the object are described as the affective component, sometimes also referred to as the feeling component (Kinnear and Taylor, 1987). With respect to environmental issues, the affective component includes the anxieties, expectations and emotive responses of an individual (Billig *et al.*, 1986). The component also encompasses the emotional judgement of the individual about the consequences of his actions to the biophysical environment (Bruhn, 1978). This implies that environmentally conscious behaviour is not necessarily the consequence of a rational insight into the appropriate action (Urban, 1986). The final part of the trichotomy, the conative component, makes reference to the behavioural tendencies of the individual with regard to the object (Borden and Schettino, 1979; Silberer, 1983). Environmentally-oriented behaviour requires an individual to have concrete behavioural tendencies towards making a personal contribution to environmental solutions (Bruhn, 1978). This trichotomous concept can also be applied to the construct of values (Kluckhohn, 1951; Rokeach, 1973).

## APPLICATION OF THE VALUE-ATTITUDE-SYSTEM MODEL TO ENVIRONMENTAL CONSCIOUSNESS

The results of the surveys outlined in the introduction show only a change of values on a global level but these are not always reflected in the consumers purchase behaviour. It would seem that, at the moment, consumers do not translate their conviction into actual purchase behaviour. The environmental value-attitude-system outlined in the following paragraphs attempts to explain how this affects the actual consumer behaviour and why further investigations into other levels described in the model are essential.

The increased awareness may be causing people to re-evaluate values within their belief systems. To provide a framework for understanding how this 'new' value may be influencing consumer behaviour, the relationships between values, attitudes and behaviour are examined using the environmental value-attitude-system. It is not the author's intention to develop a new model, rather to extend an existing comprehensive descriptive model to aid the understanding of the impact of environmental considerations on purchase behaviour. To describe the model, important studies and findings from international literature from a range of social science disciplines are integrated to demonstrate the relationship between the different elements of the individual belief system.

To aid the understanding of ecological consumer behaviour, Professor Dr Frank Wimmer (1988 and 1992) argues that the phenomenon should be viewed as part of an extensive value-attitude-system of humans which exists on various hierarchical levels. The system Wimmer (1992) applied to understand environmentally-conscious purchase and consumption behaviour, is based on the value-attitude-system from Vinson *et al.* (1977). This is regarded as 'perhaps the most noteworthy' study in understanding values in relation to behaviour in the field of marketing (Munson and

McQuarrie, 1988, p. 381). In Germany, 3 years after Vinson *et al.* (1977), Dahlhoff (1980) enhanced the original value-attitude-system model by adding the behavioural component. The purchase and behavioural component is shown as a dependent variable in Figure 1.

## Description of the environmental value-attitude-system model

The three levels of the model are arranged in the form of a hierarchical value network where all the levels are interrelated and represent different degrees of abstraction. In the system, the levels are referred to as global or generalized personal values, domain specific values and evaluation of product attributes. Figure 1 shows the systematization of values and suggests the influence of the social and cultural environment on the composition and development of the individual value-attitude-system. A classic starting point of approaches in social sciences is to define values using the work of Kluckhohn. He defined a value as '... a conception, explicit or implicit, distinctive of an individual or characteristic of a group, of the desirable which influences the selection from available modes, means, and ends of action' (Kluckhohn, 1951, p. 395). In his original work, Kluckhohn points to a cultural basis for particular values as each society may have a different concept of that which is desirable. Individuals may also each have their own private interpretation of a value. Later research supports this understanding of values by suggesting that human values are not solely based on an individual's own needs rather they capture the effects of societal and other external demands on the person (Rokeach, 1973). Therefore the concept of values integrates elements both on a sociocultural and a personal level (Kluckhohn, 1951; Scholl-Schaff, 1975; Graumann and Willig, 1983; Schuermann, 1988a). As sociocultural factors are beyond the immediate domain of the individual, values must also encompass some broad situational and external factors.

Values on an individual level can be understood as 'internalized values' (Scholl-Schaaf, 1975), which are gained in a complex socialization and cultural process (Schuermann, 1988b). It is also suggested by Vinson *et al.* (1977) that internalizing values is a sociocultural process and that variations in the value orientation will lead to modifications in preferences for products and brands. The value-attitude-system shows a clear theoretical linkage between the general global values and product related attitudes. In an empirical study with marketing students, especially on the domain specific value level, significant differences in the belief system of liberal and traditional oriented students could be demonstrated (Vinson *et al.*, 1977). This finding can be interpreted as giving empirical evidence for the validity of the value-attitude-system (Dahlhoff, 1980). The linkage between the basic levels of the system as well as the variables influencing an environmentally-conscious purchase and consumption behaviour will be described in this paper.

### Global values

The Vinson *et al.* (1977) approach aims to link the rather abstract global values and attitudes directly related to the product. In their system they start out from the global, and in numbers limited, values as a central order concept forming the top

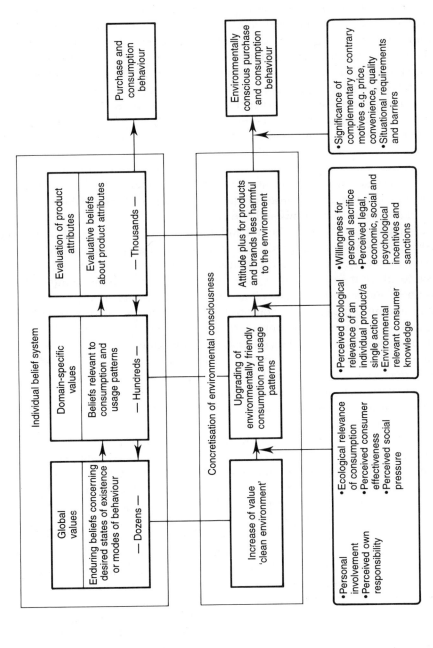

Figure 1. Environmental Value-Attitude-System.

level of the hierarchy. These global values are interpreted within the value-attitude-system as 'enduring beliefs concerning desired states of existence or modes of behaviour' (Vinson et al., 1977, p. 46).

The authors recognize the interest of various disciplines e.g. sociology and anthropology in the conceptualization of values. The system adopts the psychological definition of values and, in particular, the view of Rokeach whose research has been a major influence on value research in the area of marketing and consumer behaviour. Rokeach (1968, p. 161) defined '... a value as a centrally held, enduring belief which guides actions and judgements across specific situations and beyond immediate goals to more ultimate end states of existence.' Rokeach's definition clearly points to the immediate function of values and value systems which are guiding human action in daily life and providing criteria and standards by which judgements are made. Values can therefore be seen as global beliefs about desirable end states which influence attitudinal and behavioural processes. This understanding of values is fully reflected in the value-attitude-system. Vinson et al. (1977, p. 45) view the function of global values in their concept as to 'consist of closely held personal values which are of high salience in important evaluations and choices.'

Global values are on a more general and abstract level than generally held beliefs, relatively small in number and form the central core of an individual's belief system (Vinson et al., 1977). In an empirical study Vinson et al. (1977, pp. 47–48) found evidence for their theoretical thoughts in the sense, that 'several of the global and consumption values seem logically related to the differentially evaluated automobile attributes and the appeal of various products or services.' In a research project undertaken in Germany, Schuermann (1988a and 1988b) found significant correlation between the importance of global values, domain-specific values and the evaluation of product attributes for automobiles. He concluded that in extensive purchase decisions e.g. the purchase of an automobile, the influence of the importance of values is, in many cases, confirmed.

The observation that, in many opinion polls, people rate the environment as a matter for serious public concern shows that the value 'clean environment' is held on a general, global level (Wimmer, 1992). The growing importance of the value 'clean environment' belongs to the category of 'terminal values' in the terminology of Rokeach (1973). Although opinion polls seem to suggest that the value 'clean environment' is held as a public aim, it is not clear to what extent it is transferred into action (Schuster, 1992). However, research into consumer behaviour indicates that terminal values guide choice criteria within a product class i.e. weight given to specific product attributes (Pitts and Woodside, 1983; Louden and Della Bitta, 1993). This could mean that the ecological product features will grow in importance in comparison to traditional features. However, one has to differentiate between the global values themselves and the strength and importance of the global values for the person. If, in a concrete situation, various conflicting values exist which can not be achieved at the same time, then the person decides according to the importance placed on the values (Herker, 1993). An individual may also decide to emphasize different values for himself and for society in general. Although this would seem to be inconsistent it merely serves to demonstrate that an individual is capable of viewing different values as appropriate for himself and for society (Cotgrove and Duff, 1981).

Howard (1977) explained the purchase intention in a partial model of consumer behaviour. In the model he showed that the purchase intention stemmed from values and attitudes. In a differential analysis of the consumer's purchase-making decision process, he differentiated three levels: 'extensive problem-solving', 'limited problem-solving' and 'routinized response behaviour'. He found that values exert more influence over extensive purchase decisions (e.g. car purchase) than those which are seen to be more mundane. It can be deduced from Howard's models that a time lag exists between value and behavioural changes. New judgements, for example about environmental compatibility, occur only after the consumer has developed an awareness of the inconsistency between values and product choice criteria. This can be explained by reference to learning theory which suggests that behavioural changes are brought about through habituation. In terms of the development of environmentally-conscious purchase decisions, this could imply that consumers are still passing through the 'learning stage'.

As Figure 1 shows, global values like 'clean environment' are relatively far away from the actual purchase behaviour. It is assumed that as there is a growth of concretization towards less centrally held values the behavioural relevance of those values increases. Global values give a broad orientation to behaviour but whether or not they actually cause a change of behaviour depends on a range of variables which can act as barriers to change.

*Domain-specific values*

The domain-specific values are an intermediate value construct bridging the gap 'between the traditional concept of closely held, but very general, global values and the less closely held descriptive and evaluative beliefs about product attributes' (Vinson *et al.*, 1977, p. 45). These domain-specific values are, in relation to global values, more numerous and less abstract and are related to specific domains of human life e.g. consumption (Wimmer 1992). Vinson *et al.* (1977) clearly point out that the levels do not exist as sharply separated and unconnected as the visual appearance of the system might suggest. Rather 'they coexist in an interconnected hierarchical structure with the more durable and closely held global values exerting influence on each other as well as affecting the more peripherally located domain-specific values. These domain-specific values, in turn, are interconnected along the central-peripheral dimension and further influence the individual's evaluative beliefs associated with the attributes of products or brands' (Vinson *et al.*, 1977, p. 46). Also here Vinson *et al.* (1977) contend, in line with the value system understanding of Rokeach, that values exist in a hierarchical interconnected structure. Munson and McQuarrie (1988, p. 381) explain that the 'values within each hierarchy are rank ordered according to their importance as guiding principles in the individual's life.' These explanations of the value system structure imply that whilst all values are relevant for the individual and interconnected, some are more important than others and in different situations different values can gain the upper hand. Cotgrove and Duff (1981) indicate that different values achieve prominence for an individual within each domain of life. In addition, the significance of the value will vary according to the domain. It is also suggested that the more central and hence salient elements are more resistant to change but when they do change, they have a wide-ranging effect on the whole system. In other words, the central elements are pivotal in influencing an individual's belief system.

In the social psychological literature the distinction between values and attitudes is not always clear and can sometimes seem rather arbitrary. Indeed, some authors, for example Oerter (1978), seem to use the term synonymously. Within the value-attitude-system the use of the term 'value' is also not clearly separated from that of 'attitude'. When describing the third category of values Vinson *et al.* (1977) refer to less centrally held values which could be viewed as attitudes as they are linked to product attributes. Although the two terms may be seen to be used interchangeably some authors do point to clear distinctions. Boote (1981, p. 30) regards values as 'more durable than attitudes because they are acquired over a longer period of time and they are likely to be thoroughly "internalised" by the time the individual reaches adulthood.' The most important distinction that can be made between the two terms is that attitudes are linked to a specific object whereas values are related to more abstract concepts (Silberer, 1983).

The intermediate value construct reflects the belief that behaviour can only be understood and efficiently predicted in the context of a specific social environment (Schuermann, 1988a and 1988b; Herker, 1993; Schahn and Giesinger, 1993). If consumers show environmental consciousness in relation to the purchase, usage and disposal of goods then this becomes more concrete on this level and one can speak of environmental consciousness in the sense of consumption-related basic attitudes (Wimmer, 1992). If held on the domain-specific level the value 'clean environment' could upgrade environmentally-friendly consumption and usage patterns (Schuster, 1992). However, this does not mean that an environment conscious purchase takes place. If the domain-specific value of an environmental friendly consumption style is to be actually transferred to the evaluation of specific product features it depends again on various influencing variables.

## Evaluation of product attributes

The third category of values is of much interest to industry and of specific relevance to marketing. This is because the values are far less abstract and are comprised of descriptive and evaluative beliefs about products (Vinson *et al.*, 1977). This third level is important in the final product judgement and purchase behaviour. Application of the value-attitude-system to environmentally-conscious purchase behaviour e.g. the purchase of a car, illustrates that the significance of environmental product features (e.g. waterbased paint, reusable materials) and other product features (e.g. acceleration, speed, design) are dependent on the importance of environmental values (e.g. desire to live in harmony with nature) and other, contrary values related to the product (e.g. independence, fun, pleasure, comfort). Depending on the importance placed on environmental values in relation to other competing values, environmental product features are judged as more or less significant in relation to other product features. However, beliefs on this level are less centrally held and as a consequence easier to change in relation to product judgement and purchase behaviour (Dahloff, 1980; Schuermann, 1988). Values on this level are related to a point of reference, that can be a specific object, a subject, a concept or a specific situation (Schuster, 1992) and therefore closer to the actual behaviour. 'Among the many kinds of beliefs in this category are evaluative beliefs about the desirable attributes of product classes as well as specific brands' (Vinson *et al.*, 1977, p. 46). Attitudes may predispose individuals to respond in a preferential manner as they are based on a number of beliefs all centring on a particular object or situation (Clawson and Vinson, 1978). In an extensive literature review of the relationship between attitudes and behaviour, Schuermann (1988a) concluded that attitudes more directly congruent with a specific behaviour could be used as more accurate predictors of that behaviour. This finding stresses the importance to industry of understanding this third level of values. If consumers reject products or have a negative attitude towards them because they do not hold specific ecological features then environmental consciousness is evident on this more concrete level of product-related attitudes (Wimmer, 1992). However, even if environmental consciousness is evident on this level it does not mean that the consumer is making an ecologically-conscious purchase. This is because complementary or contrary motivations as well as situational requirements can act as barriers towards an environmentally-conscious purchase decision (Adelwarth and Wimmer, 1986).

The relationship between the levels can be shown to be that global values have an effect as an imperative or standard for the subordinate levels (Schuster, 1992). This implies an influence of centrally held values towards less centrally held values. However, there is limited feedback from the less centrally held values to the more general levels (Dahloff, 1980; Silberer, 1983; Schuster, 1992). According to the understanding of Rokeach (1973) behaviour is instrumental to the achievement of a specific-value state. Consequently if somebody strives to live in harmony with nature (global value), he would prefer ecologically sound products (domain-specific value) and gives a high priority to ecological product attributes. However, in reality numerous partly non-compatibile values exist next to each other when judging a concrete product. In these situations the person decides according to the importance given to specific values.

Hence, one can conclude that the importance placed on environment-related product features and an environmentally-conscious purchase and consumption behaviour depends on competing values and the significance placed on environmental-related values.

## CONCLUSION

The environmental value-attitude-system model has been shown to have evolved from a sound theoretical base. Its application serves three groups each of which has a specific need to gain further insights into a very complex social phenomenon.

For those involved in academic marketing research, the model provides a framework for future research in the field of environmentally conscious purchase behaviour. There is much scope for investigation of the interrelationships between variables, for understanding the complex phenomenon in relation to specific products and for investigating cultural influences on environmentally conscious purchase behaviour.

The model may also be of value to those working within institutions promoting environmentally-conscious behaviour.

Finally, the model demonstrates the rather limited value to marketers of using the results of opinion polls as a guide to consumers' actual purchase behaviour. Such surveys only examine environmental consciousness on a global level which is rather abstract and far removed from actual purchase behaviour. An examination of the model reveals why there is such a gap between expressed environmental values and actual behaviour. If it is seen to be desirable to include environmental considerations in future marketing strategies then marketers will need to gain an in-depth understanding of the variables which may act as barriers to environmentally-conscious consumer behaviour.

## ACKNOWLEDGEMENTS

The authors would like to thank Professor Dr Wimmer and his assistant Heiko Wahl from the Otto-Friedrich Universitaet in Bamberg (West Germany) for their kind support and hospitality during a research trip in the Summer of 1993.

## REFERENCES

Adlwarth, W. and Wimmer, F. (1986) 'Umweltbewusstsein und Kaufverhalten—Ergebnisse einer Verbraucherpanel—Studie' ('Environmental Consciousness and Purchase Behaviour—Results of a Consumer Panel Study'), *Jahrbuch der Absatz—und Verbraucherforschung*, No. 2, Nuerenberg, Gesellschaft fuer Konsumforschung, pp. 166–192.

Balderjahn, I. (1985) 'Strukturen sozialen Konsumbewusstseins—Reanalyse und Versuch einer Bestimmung' ('Structures of Social Consumer Awareness—Re-analysis and an Attempt of a Determination'), *Marketing ZFP*, **4**, July, pp. 253–262.

Billig, A., Briefs, D. and Pahl, A. D. (1986) 'Das oekologische Problembewusst-sein umweltrelevanter Zielgruppen—Wertewandel und Verhaltensaenderung' ('The Ecological Problem Awareness of Environmentally Relevant Target Groups—Value Change and Behavioural Changes'), Berlin, Forschungsbericht 101 07033 Umweltbundesamt.

Boote, A. S. (1981) 'Market Segmentation by Personal Values and Salient Product Attributes . . . Demographics tell only Part of the Story', *Journal of Advertising Research*, **21**, February, pp. 29–35.

Borden, R. T. and Schettino, A. P. (1979) 'Determinants of Environmentally Responsible Behaviour', *Journal of Environmental Education*, **10**, No. 4, pp. 35–39.

Bruhn, M. (1979), 'Das soziale Bewusstsein von Konsumenten. Erklaerungsansaetze und Ergebnisse einer empirischen Untersuchung in Deutschland' ('The Social Awareness of Consumers. Explanation Attempts and Results of an Empirical Study in Germany'), Doctoral thesis, University of Muenster.

Charter, M. (1992) 'Emerging Concepts in a Greener World'. In: *Greener Marketing—a Responsible Approach to Business*, (Ed) Charter, M. Sheffield, Greenleaf Publishing, pp. 55–94.

Clawson, C. J. and Vinson, D. E. (1978) 'Human Values: a Historical and Interdisciplinary Analysis', *Advances in Consumer Research*, **5**, pp. 78–96.

Coddington, W. (1993) *Environmental Marketing—Positive Strategies for Reaching the Green Consumer*, New York, McGraw-Hill.

Cotgrove, S. and Duff, A. (1981) 'Environmentalism, Values and Social Change', *British Journal of Sociology*, **32**, March, pp. 92–105.

Dahlhoff, H. D. (1980) 'Individuelle Wertorientierung—Analyse und Aussagewert personenspezifischer Werthierachien im Marketing' ('Individual Value Orientations—Analysis and Statement Value of Person Specific Value Hierarchies in Marketing'), Working Paper No. 23, Institute of Marketing at the University of Muenster.

Fietkau, H. J. (1984) *Bedingungen oekologischen Handelus—Gesellschaftliche Aufgaben der Umweltpsychologie (Requirements of Ecological Behaviour—Societal Tasks of Environmental Psychology)*, Weinheim, Verlag Psychologie.

Fietkau, H. J. (1991) 'Umweltbewusstsein' ('Environmental Consciousness'). In: *Umwelt und Oekonomie (Ecology and Economy)*, (eds) Seidel, E. and Strebel, H. (Wiesbaden), Betriebswirtschaftlicher Verlag, pp. 144–150.

Graumann, C. F. and Willig, R. (1983) 'Wet, Wertung, Werthaltung' ('Value, Evaluation, Value Position'). In: *Enzyklopaedie der Psychologie*, Serie IV, Motivation and Emotion, Bd, 1, (Ed) Thomae, H. Goettingen, Hogrefe, pp. 312–396.

Herker, A. (1993) 'Eine Erklaerung des umweltbewussten Konsumentenverhaltens' ('An Explanation of Environmentally Conscious Consumer Behaviour'), Europaeische Hochschulschriften, Reihe V Volks- und Betriebswirtschaft, Frankfurt, Peter Lang Verlag.

Hofrichter, J. (1992) 'Umweltbewusstein/Umweltverhalten' ('Environmental Awareness/Environmental Behaviour'). In: *Umwelt Handwoerterbuch* ('Environmental Handbook'), (Ed) Dreyhaupt, F. J. Berlin, Walhalla.

Howard, J. A. (1977) *Consumer Behavior: Application of Theory*, New York, McGraw-Hill.

INRA (1991) 'European Opinion and the Energy Question in 1991', Report produced for the Commission of the European Communities Directorate General XVII Energy, Bruxelles.

INRA (1992) 'Europeans and the Environment in 1992', Report produced for The European Commission Directorate-General 'Environment, Nuclear Safety and Civil Protection' Unit XI/C/4: 'Communication and Training', Bruxelles.

Kinnear, T. C. and Taylor, J. R. (1987) *Marketing Research—an Applied Approach*, 3rd Edition, New York, McGraw-Hill.

Kluckhohn, C. (1951) 'Values and Value-orientations in the Theory of Action'. In: *Toward a General Theory of Action*, (Eds) Parsons, T. and Shils, E. A. Cambridge, MA, Harvard University Press, pp. 388–433.

Louden, D. L. and Della Bitta, A. J. (1993) *Consumer Behaviour—Concepts and Applications*, 4th Edition, New York, McGraw-Hill.

Maloney, M. P., Ward, M. P. and Braucht, G. N. (1975) 'A Revised Scale for the Measurement of Ecological Attitudes and Knowledge', *American Psychologist*, **30**, July, pp. 787–790.

Monhemius, K. Ch. (1992) 'Umweltbewusstes Kaufverhalten von Konsumenten' ('Environmentally Conscious Purchase Behaviour of Consumers'), Frankfurt, Peter Lang Verlag.

Munson, J. M. and McQuarrie, E. F. (1988) 'Shortening the Rokeach Survey for use in Consumer Research', *Advances in Consumer Research*, **15**, pp. 381–386.

Oerter, R. (1978) '*Struktur und Wandlung von Werthaltungen (Structure and Change of Values)*, Muenchen, Auer.

Ottman, J. A. (1992) *Green Marketing—Challenges and Opportunities for the New Marketing Age*, Lincolnwood, NTC Business Books.

Pitts, R. E. and Woodside, A. G. (1983) *Personal Values and Consumer Psychology*, Lexington MA, Lexington.

Rokeach, M. J. (1968) *Beliefs, Attitudes, and Values*, San Francisco, Jossey Bass.

Rokeach, M. J. (1973) *The Nature of Human Values*, New York, Free Press.

Schahn, J. and Giesinger, T. (1993) 'Einfuehrung' ('Introduction'). In: *Psychologie fuer den Ummweltschutz (Psychology for Conservation)*, (Eds) Schahn, J. and Giesinger, T. Weinheim, Beltz Psychologie Verlags Union.

Scholl-Schaaf, M. (1975) *Werthaltungen und Wertesystem. Ein Plaedoyer fuer die Verwendung des Wertekonzepts in der Sozialpsychologie (Values and Value Systems. A Proposal for the Use of Value Concepts in Social Psychology)*, Bonn, Bouvier.

Schuster, R. (1992) *Umweltorientiertes Konsumentenverhalten in Europa (Environmentally Oriented Consumer Behaviour in Europe)*, Hamburg, Verlag Dr Kovac.

Schuermann, P. (1988a) 'Werte und Konsumverhalten' ('Values and Consumer Behaviour'), Doctoral Thesis, University of Munich.

Schuermann, P. (1988b) 'Werte und Konsumverhalten' ('Values and Consumer Behaviour'), *Werbeforschung & Praxis*, **5**, pp. 157–161.

Silberer, G. (1983) 'Einstellungen und Werthaltungen' ('Attitudes and Values'). In:

'Enzyklopaedie der Psychologie—Band 4; Marktpsychologie als Sozialwissenschaft' ('Encyclopedia of Psychology—Volume 4: Market Psychology as Social Science'), (Ed) Irle, M. Goettingen, Hogrefe, pp. 533–625.

Tiebler, P. (1992) 'Umwelttrends im Konsumentenverhalten' ('Environmental Trends in Consumer Behaviour'). In: *Handbuch des Umweltmanagements (Handbook of Environmental Management)*, (Ed) Steger, U. Muenchen, Vahlen Verlag, pp. 183–206.

Urban, D. (1986) 'Was ist Umweltbewustsein?—Exploration eines mehrdimensionalen Einstellungskonstruktes' ('What is Environmental Awareness? Explanation of a Multidimensional Attitude Construct[2]), *Zeitschrift fuer Soziologie*, Oktober, pp. 363–377.

Vinson, D. E., Scott, J. E. and Lamont, L. M. (1977) 'The Role of Personal Values in Marketing and Consumer Behaviour', *Journal of Marketing*, **41**, April, pp. 44–50.

Wimmer, F. (1988) 'Umweltbewusstsein und konsumrelevante Einstellungen und Verhaltensweisen' (Environmental Awareness and Consumption Relevant Attitudes and Behaviour'. In: *Oekologisches Marketing (Environmental Marketing)*, (Eds) Brandt, A., Hansen, U., Schoenheit, I. and Werner, K. Frankfurt, Gabler Verlag, pp. 44–85.

Wimmer, F. (1992) 'Umweltbewusstes Verbraucherverhalten' ('Environmentally Aware Consumer Behaviour'). In: *Vahlens grosses Marketinglexikon (Vahlens Big Marketing Lexicon)*, (Ed) Diller, H. Muenchen, Vahlen Verlag, pp. 1167–1169.

Worcester, R. (1993) 'Public and Elite Attitudes to Environmental Issues', Paper from MORI, London.

# 27

## Corporate Communications about Sustainability: Turning Clever Companies into Enlightened Companies[1]

*Pierre McDonagh and Alison Clark*

THIS ARTICLE examines the complex issue of how to deal with environmental issues when an organisation is communicating with its publics. By means of practitioner insight coupled with academic theory, the authors offer several possible management response strategies for an organisation confronting the environmental challenge with its communications policy. The major argument put forward it that companies can move from merely being 'clever' in the face of the green challenge to a more enlightened approach. This move has been conceptualised in a previous publication by the author as a radical new process called 'sustainable communication'. After briefly explaining the main facets of this process, the article considers how to manage the green communications gap credibly. The conclusions highlight that the organisational consequences of addressing the environmental challenge in such a new manner are not as simple as is often suggested.

### INTRODUCTION

The old adage about market research being like a lamppost used by a drunkard ('more for support than illumination') is especially true for the new and complex area of environmental understanding. To some analysts, current data suggest that environmental concern has dropped down the rankings of public opinion, so management—having survived thus far—need not bother about it. This paper suggests that there are underlying structural reasons in present value systems which will ensure that environmental concerns will repeatedly, if not consistently, be expressed by consumers.

For this reason, the interpretation of 'dying environmentalism' may be comfortable, but it is possibly terminally naive and dangerous. This conclusion is

Reprinted with permission from *Greener Management International*, Issue 11, July 1995, pp. 49–62.

supported by evidence concerning the impact of environmental issues on business and management (see Coddington, *Environmental Marketing*; McDonagh and Prothero, 'Why Bother ...', Peattie, *Green Marketing*; Welford and Gouldson, *Environmental Management*). Shrivastava, ('Castrated Environment') strongly counters the 'fad' argument by detailing the implications that the environmental challenge has for organisation studies:

> Organisations can no longer be treated primarily as rational, neutral, technical systems of production, as is done in traditional OS [organisational studies]. They must also be seen as systems of destruction. They systematically destroy environmental value. This destruction cannot be dismissed . . . as an 'externality' of production. Organisations must become accountable for these externalities, which are a central and systematic feature of organized economic activity (p. 721).

It is a truism to say that people have a 'worry quotient'. If this quotient is used up on immediate pressures—such as unemployment and recession—more distant concerns fade on a relative scale. This does not mean they go away completely.

Concerns will fade, on the other hand, if the public perceives that there are proper company planning systems in place to understand and manage the issue, and their disquiet can be allayed. Research may not reveal blatant concern over, say, the use of child slave labour, but any company translating that as public acquiescence would soon draw international media attention.

There continues to be debate about whether, in any democracy, government action should ameliorate public concern. Less debatable is the notion that voluntary industrial action is ethically essential. There also is the need for industry to acknowledge its role in developing the public concern for environmental issues (see Thomas, 'The Business Community').

Cycles in public opinion about the environment may be more predictable than at first evident. It is difficult to find out what the real concerns are until they become activated by specific situations and events or disasters. However, it is possible to gain insight into what marketing planners may be facing in coming years by looking at 'personal values' and examining the 'green case' (see Yearley, *The Green Case*).

There is evidence that environmental consciousness (see Krause, 'Environmental Consciousness'; Selman, 'Canada's Environmental Citizens') and concern for the planet is getting a firm foothold in the value sets of the public. In the near future a well-'environmentally-educated' management will be faced with an extremely well-'environmentally-educated' consumer. Recent research, for instance (reported in *The Independent* newspaper, 14th February 1995) shows that 91% of Europeans aged between 16 and 34 identify environmental issues as a matter of personal concern to them. This trend presents company directors with an environmental challenge which has been categorised as an instance of the JIMM theory, with JIMM standing for a 'jolly interesting moment for management' (Clark, 'The Environmental Challenge').

The two key premises for this environmental challenge are: first, that education increases awareness of a topic, and secondly, that this awareness helps form personal values. Environmental education is becoming commonplace in Britain (see Smith, 'Business and the Environment'). The growing influence of The Greening of Higher Education Council is attempting a radical change in the way business and post-secondary education deal with environmental issues in the curriculum. This can be depicted in Figure 1, which illustrates the desired impact of an increased environmental focus in the educaiton system.

The environmental challenge for managers does not depend on precision of numbers, but on the general nature of the curve in the diagram (Figure 1). As far as the authors are aware, all UK children—for at least the last 10–15 years—have received formal environmental education at school. That takes the reader back to around the mid-1970s, when, for instance, the 'Keep Britain Tidy' campaign had successful schools projects focusing on how to avoid litter and waste.

That history of the two decades explains the first part of the curve. The small peak around the age of 35 occurs because of the phenomenon where children may 're-educate' their parents by asking them for help with homework or questioning why certain things in their lifestyles happen in a particular way.

The graph (Figure 2) has superimposed on it a suggested peak period of purchasing activity: the period when people are considered likely to increase levels of consumption. In this respect there are more purchasing decisions made during this

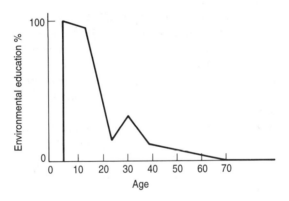

Figure 1. Environmental Awareness.

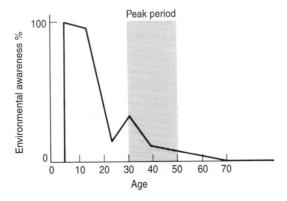

Figure 2. Purchasing Activity.

time, so consumers have more opportunities to influence the market and express environmental values. In theory, although the reality is more complex (see Bocock, *Consumption*), this conflux arises partly because of increased affluence after their days in education, and because they may have young families and are setting up home.

Based on this hypothesis concerning purchasing activities, for the 'baby boom' generation (born c. 1945–1965), the first signs of environmental awareness should have been observable in the marketplace a few years ago. This view of the mounting environmental challenge seems consistent with actual experience of the heightened attention of green issues in the late 1980s and early 1990s with the rise of green consumerism (see Prothero, 'Green Consumerism').

## THE 'LESS IS MORE' PRINCIPLE

Environmentally-aware consumers are more likely to use less if they follow the principle that less consumption is more acceptable for society (see Charter, *Greener Marketing*; Peattie, *op cit*; Prothero, *op cit*).

The full force of the environmental challenge relates to the extent the environmentally-aware consumer might adopt this 'less is more' philosophy. This can be illustrated by the 'banana example', which relates to the cumulative effect of small changes in consumption by large numbers of people who purchase goods and services on a regular basis. The overall impact will have a much greater effect on the marketplace than that experienced by the purchasing behaviour of more radical 'dark green' consumers who may be smaller in number.

The 'banana example' reflects how environmental education bridges the generation gap. A mother learned her housekeeping skills in wartime and austerity. If she buys three bananas from a shopkeeper, the family eats three bananas. One child is a product of the affluent '70s. She or he buys three bananas, goes off the idea of eating bananas and throws one away. But her or his nieces—in the vanguard of the next environmentally-aware generation—buy only two bananas, based on the reasoning that this avoids waste or over-consumption.

The implications for business as a whole if such consumption practices were taken up by a large proportion of the population with environmental values are considerable. Growth in such practices would be a challenge to the high-consumption economy of recent years. Given the logic for this proposed decrease, management is faced with the complexities of justifying consumption to an audience that is becoming more environmentally conscious.

The progressive movement of purchasers with strong environmental values into the period of high purchasing activity itself is a significant challenge for management and marketers. This is specifically the case for management because the period of maximum personal business influence comes from people who have lower levels of environmental values rather than the crusading green consumer.

In this respect, business may not yet understand or estimate what is going on, or how significant and permanent the market shift will be as a result of increased levels of environmental consciousness. Clearly research on this area will be crucial in informing management.

# MANAGEMENT RESPONSES TO THE ENVIRONMENTAL CHALLENGE

From a marketing communications perspective, we identify four possible positions for companies confronting the environmental challenge.

## Issue attack

Companies who have had to manage a particular environmental issue—for example, the use of CFCs in aerosols—will typically respond with technical solutions—for example, by replacing CFCs with butane. Unfortunately, butane is a volatile organic compound (VOC) and just coming under an issue attack of its own. The issue-attack response is a short-term solution to a very complex situation and may lead to more consumer confusion than clarification (see Prothero *et al.*, 'Green Marketing Communications'). It may disguise the changing public value set underlying the issue. Cosmetics companies retailing anti-perspirants and deodorants such as 'Mum', 'ZR', 'Body Mist' and 'Natrel Plus' have adopted this approach.

## Simple or naïve

Some companies look hopefully at the top line of opinion research and say that environment was a flash-in-the-pan issue which has now expired. 'Simple' is the kindest word for their approach, but 'naïve' may be a better description. There are examples of companies, such as Kyocera, the Japanese printer company, that switched from an initial focus on environmental claims to one of low price in their advertising campaigns (see Cane, 'Putting Price before Conscience'). These companies may later discover that environmental performance is important to many of their buyers and may wish to reclaim this ground.

## Clever

The prevalence of environmental values in the general public is starting to increase and will further increase sharply in about five years' time, it is predicted (see World Commission on Employment and Development and Brundtland, *Our Common Future*; Rehak, *Greener Marketing and Advertising*). Those companies that we might describe as 'clever' will start planning how to do business with a consumer and regulatory marketplace where environmental values are predominant.

There are several recent examples of clever initiatives, such as the introduction by Varta Batteries of the mercury-free battery as an alternative that delivered identical performance but avoided potential problems in disposal (see Peattie, *op. cit.*). The glass industry's initiative of bottle banks addressed a real consumer concern. Consumers felt guilty using non-returnable bottles that seemed identical to returnables. By providing bottle banks, the industry provided an outlet for that guilt without the expense of collection and cleaning. Thereby they created an approach to cost-effective consumer recycling and an advance in waste management.

The benefits of being a clever company were illustrated when Shell was fined over the Mersey oil spill in the early 1990s. It was estimated that it would take the River Mersey a decade to recover from the environmental consequences of the spill. The court, however, mitigated the fine to £1 million, based on awareness of the company's strong environmental policies and contributions. While £1 million remains by far the largest green fine in the UK, it was small in relation to the magnitude of the incident.

## Enlightened

Those companies that know that environmental values will be prevalent and that hope to be seen as leading-edge companies are taking the environmental challenge seriously. They understand the issues from their audiences' viewpoints and engage in sustainable communication.

Among many North American companies active in this area, Frankel ('Environmental Excellence') identifies four US companies that have embarked on such a process. They are:

- Fetzer Vineyards, whose products are eliminating herbicide and pesticide usage from the entire grape-growing industry
- Church & Dwight, the $500-million New Jersey-based bakng soda company, which supplies industrial and consumer products
- AT&T, with its strong environmental management programme
- Dow Chemicals, with its ground-breaking innovations in environmental management in the area of public outreach and dialogue.

Even enlightened companies face problems, however. In spite of its twenty-year effort in the environmental and product-liability areas, in May 1995 Dow was forced through the threat of medical-product liability litigation to file for protection from bankruptcy.

## CONFRONTING THE ENVIRONMENTAL CHALLENGE: SCENARIOS FOR CLEVER COMPANIES AND ENLIGHTENED COMPANIES

Let us first consider the situation facing clever companies. The process of clever management has already been well defined, by the Confederation of British Industry (CBI) in its Environmental Business Forum Agenda for Voluntary Action. The agenda for how enlightened companies will react to the environmental challenge is far from agreed. The CBI and other industrial organisations offer guidelines for those companies.

Essentially, the CBI agenda requires a company to undertake four steps.

- Commit at board level to accept responsibility for the company's environmental impact.
- Measure the impacts of operations to ensure the best possible understanding of them.
- Set up systems to manage the environmental impact and reduce it.
- Report to the public on the steps taken and their results.

## ENVIRONMENTAL COMMUNICATIONS

The question of public reporting is defined for professional communications managers (see Clark, *op. cit.*): communication is the transmission of information of interest to receiving audiences. Four of these words have crucial implications.

### 1. Audience

The first thing to notice is how many target audiences there are. This is not a definitive list.

 (1) Own staff
 (2) Customers
 (3) Consumers
 (4) Neighbours
 (5) Suppliers
 (6) Journalists
 (7) Local politicians
 (8) Parliamentarians
 (9) Civil service
(10) Regulators
(11) Special interest groups

### 2. Interest

The special significance of 'interest' is that each of the eleven audiences will have their own special set of interests and they will set the agenda to be discussed. To put it crudely, there is no point in reporting about your policy to use recycled office paper when the external audiences really want to know why the river goes purple on Thursdays.

### 3. Information

Information is necessary for communications. There is a real need for supportive facts rather than assertions or appeals to emotion. Many people are disinclined to trust in industry, and explanation supported by hard facts is really the only choice. It is worth pointing out that the amount of environmental information that becomes available to external audiences is going to expand greatly, as a result of both legislation and government policy. The forthcoming British Environmental Protection Agency will require companies to communicate with many publics about their environmental performance.

Interestingly, working parties have in the past been involved ahead of the legislation to sort out the technical details of getting the data available for easy, on-line access to outsiders. For instance, the UK Government has announced the setting-up of the Chemical Release Inventory; which will increase ease of access to all data collected under Integrated Pollution Control.

There will shortly be no choice between revealing environmental impact figures or not (see Beecham and SustainAbility; *Coming Clean*). The choice is whether they go naked and unexplained, or clothed in context.

## 4. Transmission

There are more ways to transmit information than are commonly recognised. The process can be informal or formal, and range from action to words. In extreme cases, the transmission can be accidental rather than deliberate. Put another way, the continuum reaches from brochure to explosion.

All of these are forms of public reporting which can be used by clever companies and ought to be actively managed by enlightened companies. There is a systematic way that can be used to help you work out *how* to say *what* you want to *whom* you want. Controlling *when* to communicate is preferable in all circumstances from a business point of view. The radical new way forward, suggested in this article, has been conceptualised as the process of sustainable communication.

## SUSTAINABLE COMMUNICATION: A RADICAL NEW WAY FORWARD

In order to make this concept explicit, McDonagh ('Towards an Understanding ...') illustrates a utopian framework of the process of sustainable communication (see below) and explains how this process might work without a results-driven emphasis:

> Sustainable communication is an interactive social process of unravelling and eradicating alienation that may occur between an organisation and its publics or stakeholders. Based on the notion of totality or holism, it embraces conflict and critique through information disclosure, access to, and participation in organisational policies and processes, and structures allowing open-ended dialogue. Thus by use of 'green, eco- or environmental marketing communications,' the organisation builds trust in the minds of those in society and permits the approach of a utopian situation, of high levels of environmental consciousness and consensus as to how humankind should exist ('Towards an Understanding . . .', p. 4).

McDonagh's (*op cit.*; 'Sustainable Communication' recent research) involves global environmental communications experts and specifically documents the work of Medianatura, the leading London-based communications agency dealing with environmental issues and social justice campaigns. The existence of Medianatura and the communications of its client groups corroborates the potential influence of this new process for communication. Medianatura's client organisations include:

- Equal Exchange, Oxfam Trading, Traidcraft and Twin Trading with their fairly-traded Cafédirect
- The World Society for the Protection of Animals with its 'Libearty' campaign
- Anti-Slavery International
- The Earth Centre

While this communications dialogue process is similar to what Harrison ('Achieving Sustainable Communications') has mentioned as a results-driven exercise, it highlights the role of green marketing communications without seeking to measure results over time. While outcomes are ultimately important, they are felt to be inappropriate for benchmarking in the early stages. Competitors, a twelfth category of audience, can be included in the process of environmental marketing communications. These developments can be seen as the operationalisation of 'relationship marketing' (see Gummesson, 'Making Relationship Marketing Operational').

This framework would seem to be broadly matched with what Welford and Gouldson (*Environmental Management and Business Strategy*) suggest is a direct outcome of green marketing practices: consumers demand that companies give information about their environmental claims on a right-to-know basis. They state that 'this means that firms must be both open and honest in their communication with the public'.

This approach compares with the definition of green marketing by Peattie (*op. cit.*): 'the management process responsible for identifying, anticipating and satisfying the requirements of customers and society, in a profitable and sustainable way' (p. 11). It also parallels the trend that Clutterbuck *et al.* (*Actions Speak Louder*) have noted as socially-responsible activities yielding 'mutual benefit' with both companies and voluntary organisations seeking genuine partnerships. It is consistent with Bernstein's request (In the Company of Green) to make communication participative wherever possible.

The utopian framework depicted illustrates the organisation interacting with its various publics or stakeholders. This interaction is highlighted by the overlapping circles at the centre of the illustration (Figure 3). It is at this focal point that sustainable communication is occurring. This is drawn from the central principle that for effective communications both sender and receivers of messages need to share overlapping fields of experience. This is a precondition for messages that can produce meaningful responses (see Munter, *Business Communication*).

In this respect it is important that the gap between what the organisation's publics expect from green marketing communication and what they are getting is negligible (see Kim, 'The Meaning of Green'). The main principles for sustainable communication are:

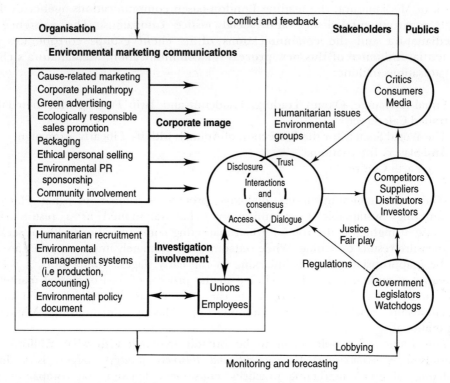

Figure 3. Understanding Sustainable Communication (*Source*: P. McDonagh 1994: A Utopian Framework).

*Trust*

With the continuing loss of trust and confidence in businesses and business leaders leading to legitimation crises, sustainable communication aims to rebuild that trust and establish it in society generally.

*Access*

Openness and disclosure of information have become necessary criteria on which to create and build trust, according to people assessing socio-environmental performance, such as investors.

There are legislative measures afoot that should improve the level of access to a firm (see the European Union Freedom of Access Directive 90/313). Publics are also likely to ask a company to substantiate its claims.

*Disclosure*

It can be argued that more and more organisations are being assessed by their publics, who judge them by what they are freely prepared to reveal about their activities. This is evidenced by trends in corporate environmental reporting. The benefits of 'coming clean' are receiving much discussion (see Beecham and SustainAbility, *op. cit.*). This may have a direct consequence on how they are perceived in such things as the Corporate Standing Monitor (see Sturges, 'Who Will Top the Corporate League?'). It is felt that companies who have disclosed the truth about what they do are more likely to be trusted than those organisations where the truth has been found out. People might feel that in the latter case there is much more still hidden by the firm.

### Dialogue

Another principle of the sustainable communication process is that of dialogue between an organisation and its publics. The benefits of displaying to your publics, for example that you are an equal opportunities employer working in a democratic and non-exploitative way, can be highlighted through dialogue. The credibility of the organisation's stated values is increased when individuals can air their views directly to representatives of the organisation and gain their immediate reactions. In this respect, companies undertaking sustainable communication programmes will draw their audiences into the decision-making process, ultimately leading to a situation of management by external consensus.

### Promotion

It is still acknowledged that most marketing communications in Western society aim to increase levels of consumption. Whatever the company discloses about its organisation, its agenda will always be promotion of its product to the end-consumer or its other publics. This promotion, however, may be different in nature because it consists of environmental or green marketing communications (see McDonagh, *op. cit.*).

## MANAGING THE GREEN COMMUNICATIONS GAP

It is self-evident that the truth will, to an interested audience, be somewhere on a scale between good and bad news (Figure 4). If people find out about the truth, they tend to assume that it has been concealed from them and they therefore believe that hidden aspects remain which they would class as bad news. In other words, when you get found out, people perceive the truth to be closer to 'bad news' than it really is.

On the other hand, if you communicate the truth, you can explain it in context in a positive way. Coupled with this, your audiences are likely to be flattered by being sought out. Together these two factors lead to perceptions being positive and messages producing meaningful responses (see Munter, *op. cit.*).

The simple analogy; suggested by Peter Morgan of Cardiff Business School, of management using a one-way mirror to communicate with its publics explains the situation well. Consider that the intensity of information that leaks out about a

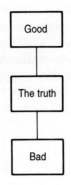

Figure 4. The Communications Gap.

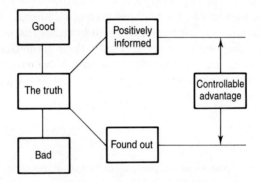

Figure 5. Controllable Advantage.

company is equal to the brightness behind the one-way mirror where the company is located. In this way, at present, the person outside the company sees a reflection in the mirror. Put simply, because the brightness is low, one does not see inside the company. However, if the light inside the company's observation room is switched on accidentally, then people can see what the company is doing as an unintended consequence. The task of the enlightened company is to put the light on deliberately and let people see that this is being done. The gap between the perception that arises from those two communications strategies is indicated as the controlled 'communications advantage' (Figure 5), which is similar to what others have termed competitive advantage (see Porter, *Competitive Strategy*) or have described as being market-driven (Day, *Market-Driven Strategy*). This communications advantage is available to everyone who manages their communications in a systematic professional way.

## CONCLUSIONS

Sustainable communication has clear implications for marketing and strategic management in contemporary business organisations. From a marketing viewpoint, the process of sustainable communication that is presented here allows the organisation legitimately to discuss and operationalise any major programme involving the transition to environmental management or green marketing. Sustainable communication will involve marketers in much more detailed market research to assess public attitudes. Likewise, one would expect the process to yield a better chance of new products matching consumer needs. This process permits the development of communications that are credible, clear and avoid clichéd imaged or meaningless statements. From a strategic management perspective, the process brings a new dimension to competitive positioning and how an organisation might compare itself with the main companies that share similar business interests. Finally, from a human-resource management point of view, in the short run, the process of sustainable communication has significant implications for how management structures itself in relation to dealing with its externalities (see Shrivastava, *op. cit.*). There will be a need to emphasise staff training in communication skills, both internally and externally. In the longer term, sustainable communication may well represent the isomorphic change (see Dimaggio and Powell, 'The Iron Cage Revisited') that brings organisations towards some homogenisation in dealing with the complexities of environmental communications.

## NOTE

1. This paper is based on an earlier presentation by Clark at a Confederation of British Industries conference, London, 1992.

## REFERENCES

Beecham, K., and SustainAbility Ltd (eds.), *Coming Clean: Corporate Environmental Reporting* (London, UK: Deloitte Touche Tohmatsu International/International Institute for Sustainable Development, 1993).
Bernstein, D., *In the Company of Green: Corporate Communications for the New Environment* (London, UK: ISBA, 1992).
Bocock, R., *Consumption* (London, UK: Routledge, 1993).
Cane, A., 'Putting Price before Conscience: A look at a Japanese Printer Campaign in which Environmental Concerns have Lost Out to Cost', in *Financial Times, Management Section*, 1 September 1994.
Charter, M. (ed.), *Greener Marketing: A Responsible Approach to Business* (Sheffield, UK: Greenleaf Publishing, 1992).
Clark, A., 'The Environmental Challenge or the Jolly Interesting Moment for Management (JIMM) Theory' (Presentation to the Confederation of British Industry, February 1992).
Clutterbuck, D., D. Dearlove and D. Snow, *Actions Speak Louder: A Management Guide to Corporate Social Responsibility* (London, UK: Kogan Page, 1992)
Coddington, W., *Environmental Marketing: Positive Strategies for Reaching the Green Consumer* (New York, NY: McGraw-Hill, 1993).
Day, G., *Market Driven Strategy: Processes for Creating Value* (New York, NY: The Free Press, 1990).
Dimaggio, P. J., and W. W. Powell, 'The Iron Cage Revisited: Institutional Isomorphism and Collective Rationality in Organisational Fields', in *American Sociological Review*, Vol. 48 (April 1990), pp. 147–60.

Frankel, C., 'Environmental Excellence: Four Top Guns', in *Tomorrow*, Vol. 4 No. 4 (October–December 1994), pp. 10–15.

Gummesson, E., 'Making Relationship Marketing Operational', in *International Journal of Service Industry Management*, Vol. 5 No. 5 (1994), pp. 5–20.

Harrison, B. E., 'Achieving Sustainable Communications', in Peter B. Erdmann (ed.), 'Corporate Environmentalism (Focus Issue)', in *Columbia Journal of World Business*, Vol. 27 Nos. 3 and 4 (Fall–Winter 1992).

Kim, P., 'The Meaning of Green: How Environmental Advertising Works', in JWT *Greenwatch USA* No. 3 (Spring–Summer 1991).

Krause, D., 'Environmental Consciousness: An Empirical Study', in *Environment and Behaviour*, Vol. 25 No. 1 (January 1993), pp. 126–42.

McDonagh, P., 'Towards an Understanding of What Constitutes Green Advertising as a Form of Sustainable Communication' (Paper presented at The First Marketing Education Group Doctoral Colloquium, University of Ulster, 1994), pp. 1–10.

McDonagh, P., 'Sustainable Communication: Pipe Dream for Green Advertisers or the New Way for Business to Communicate?', in M. Bergadáa (ed.), *Marketing Today and for the 21st Century, Proceedings of the 24th European Marketing Academy Conference*, Vo. I (1995) pp. 731–51.

McDonagh, P., and A. Prothero, 'Why Bother with Environmental Marketing? Some Practical Guidelines for Managers', in Irish Marketing Review, Vol. 6 (1993), pp. 120–26.

Munter, M., *Business Communication: Strategy and Skill* (Englewood Cliffs, NJ: Prentice Hall, 1987).

Peattie, K., *Green Marketing* (London, UK: Pitman, 1992).

Porter, M. E., *Competitive Strategy* (New York, NY: The Free Press, 1980).

Prothero, A., 'Green Consumerism and the Societal Marketing Concept: Marketing Strategies for 1990s', in *Journal of Marketing Management*, Vol. 6 No. 2 (1990), pp. 87–103.

Prothero, A., P. McDonagh and K. Peattie, 'Green Marketing Communications: Dressing Windows or Opening Doors?, in J. Bell, *et al.* (eds), *Marketing: Unity in Diversity* (Proceedings of the 25th Marketing Education Group Annual Conference, University of Ulster, 1994), Vol. II, pp. 766–76.

Rehak, R., *Greener Marketing and Advertising: Charting a Responsible Course* (Houston, TX: Rodale Press, 1993).

Selman, P., 'Canada's Environmental Citizens', in *British Journal of Canadian Studies*, Vol. 9 No. 1 (1994), pp. 44–52.

Shrivastava, P., 'Castrated Environment: Greening Organisational Studies', in *Organisation Studies*, 15 May 1994, pp. 705–26.

Smith, D., 'Business and the Environment: Towards a Paradigm Shift?', in D. Smith (ed.), *Business and the Environment* (London, UK: Paul Chapman, 1993).

Sturges, J., 'Who Will Top the Corporate League?', in *Marketing Week*, February 1992, p. 1.

Thomas, L. M., 'The Business Community and the Environment: An Important Partnership', in *Business Horizons*, Vol. 35 No. 2 (1992), pp. 21–24.

Welford, R., and A. Gouldson, *Environmental Management and Business Strategy* (London, UK: Pitman, 1993).

World Commission on Employment and Development and G. H. Brundtland (eds.), *Our Common Future* (New York, NY: Oxford University Press, 1987).

Yearley, S., *The Green Case: A Sociology of Environmental Issues, Arguments and Politics*, (London, UK: Routledge, 1992).

# 28

# Anatomy of Green Advertising

*Easwar Iyer and Bobby Banerjee*

## ABSTRACT

Much work has been published, both in scholarly journals and the popular press, about the greening of the American consumer. Most of the past work, if not all, deal with consumer profiles; none deal with 'green' advertising. This work is the first attempt to analyze 'green' print advertisements. In this study we first provide a framework for analyzing green ads and then use that very framework to analyze a sample of print ads.

## INTRODUCTION

Green is in, no question about it. The term 'green', as we intend it, implies an underlying concern for preservation of the environment and a noninvasive lifestyle. Generally targets for concerns are the preservation of the planet earth, personal health, and animal life. Moreover, the goal of preservation is generally accompanied with a belief that noninvasive methods have to be employed in achieving those goals. Thus, activities causing the least damage to the planet earth, its environment, human and animal life are preferred.

Concern along these target dimensions have been rising steadily over the past few decades (Bremner, 1989) and is having a major impact on consumer purchasing behaviors (Roper, 1990). According to the Roper Organization study (1990) 11% of all Americans are True-Blue Greens and yet another 11% are Greenback Greens (see Figure 1). These segments are identified by their environmental attitudes and behaviors and represent the two greenest segments in the 5-way classification scheme used in the Roper study. Together, they represent a little under one-quarter of all consumers—a very significant market segment especially when one compares it to the market shares of very successful national brands. For example, many heavily advertised and promoted cigarettes turn in a handsome profit with market shares varying

Reprinted with permission from *Advances in Consumer Research*, Vol. 20, 1993, pp. 494–501.

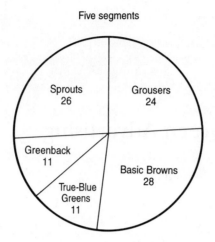

Figure 1. Green Consumers. (*Source:* The Roper Organization (1990)).

between 1% and 3%. Many lesser known brands of household products such as soap and toothpaste survive on market shares as low as 5% or less (Simmons Market Research Bureau, 1990). The point is that the green segment is big enough to accommodate quite a few brands. Further, the two greenest segments, i.e., True-Blue Greens and Greenback Greens comprise of the most lucrative and desirable consumers—affluent and college educated. While the national median income is $27,100, the median income of these two segments is $31,850 (Schwartz and Miller, 1991). Likewise, only 19% of all Americans have a college degree; over 27% of these two segments have graduated from college (American Demographics, February 1991).

Many factors have contributed to the growth of the green movement, but none could be more important than the emerging perception that the world is a more polluted place than it was 20 years ago (New York Times/CBS News Poll, April 1990). According to this poll, not only did 75% of the respondents feel that the air was more polluted and 80% feel that the water was more polluted, but that 41% feel that both air and water would be more polluted 20 years hence unless something is done right now. Such pessimistic perceptions have sent a message to political and business leaders who are scrambling to create platforms and programs that placate the environmentally conscious segment. For example, corporations have responded to this shift in the consumer attitudes and the resultant emergence of a new market by launching new products with a green appeal at an ever growing rate. In 1984, 54 new green products were launched; in 1988 178 new green products were introduced (Hinds, 1989). This represents a 230% growth in that 4-year span.

## WHO IS GREEN?

Consumer researchers have done an excellent job in identifying the green consumer. One of the most detailed studies was carried out by the Roger Organization in which many behaviors deemed environmentally friendly, i.e., using biodegradable/recycled products, and recycling bottles, cans and newspapers, were reported. The list also included behaviors indicative of environmental concern such as reading packaging labels, contributing to environmental groups and lobbying politicians. Cluster analysis was used to identify five distinct segments: True-Blue Greens (11%), Greenback Greens (11%), Sprouts (26%), Grousers (24%), and Basic Browns (28%). This study also confirmed that green consumers tend to be better educated, earn higher incomes, and hold professional/white collar jobs (see Table 1 for details), making them a very desirable target market.

Yet, others prefer to classify green consumers in terms of their motivation (Ottman, 1991). Based on a careful analysis of the different type of activist groups and causes, Ottman (1991) postulates three distinct consumer motives: preservation of the planet, preservation of personal health, and preservation of animal life. The first group, 'planet passionates', are likely to belong to 'Keep America Beautiful' and engage in recycling bottles, cans, and newspapers; whereas the second group, 'health fanatics', are likely to belong to 'Americans for Safe Food' and buy organic product only. Lastly, the third group, 'animal lovers', are most likely members of the 'Humane Society' and buy 'cruelty-free' cosmetics and boycott fur coats. (See Table 2 for details.) Such a classification scheme is very useful in terms of understanding the primary motives that drive a green consumer. It is also helpful in creating new product positions.

## GREEN ADVERTISING

Although much is known about the green consumer, very little is known about green advertising. There are three very compelling reasons why it is timely and important to study and analyze green advertising. First, the new media has picked up on the green theme and is reporting very extensively on the subject. For instance, the *Tyndall Report* found that there was an increase of 76% from 1988 to 1989 in the number of minutes devoted by network television to environmental issues. Second, and a closely allied factor, most consumers get information on environmental issues from the mass media (TV, newspapers, magazines, and radio) far more so than either environmental newsletters or government publications (Scott Paper Company study, March 1990). Third, despite the high dependence on mass media for information, consumers do not find that information believable or reliable. In fact, from a survey done by Abt Associates (March 1990) it was reported that the most credible source of information was an environmentally active organization and the least credible was an advertisement place by a major company.

Given the growing attention placed on environmental issues and the heavy reliance of the consuming public on mass media, the dire lack of credibility in green advertising is a shocking state. We believe this to be a strong signal calling for an analysis of green ads. Thus, our paper is about the anatomy of green advertising. At first we present a framework to categorize green ads. Next, we use this framework to analyze our sample of print ads. The results, we believe, will help us understand some of the trends in green advertising.

Table 1. Segmentations by environmental attitudes and behaviors

|  | Total adults | True-Blue Greens | Green-back Greens | Sprouts | Grousers | Basic Browns |
|---|---|---|---|---|---|---|
| Total | 100% | 100% | 100% | 100% | 100% | 100% |
| Share of adult population | 100% | 11% | 11% | 26% | 24% | 20% |
| **Sex** | | | | | | |
| Male | 47% | 34% | 42% | 48% | 46% | 55% |
| Female | 53% | 66% | 58% | 52% | 54% | 45% |
| **Education** | | | | | | |
| Less than High school | 21% | 11% | 11% | 15% | 26% | 30% |
| High school graduate | 38 | 39 | 35 | 33 | 43 | 39 |
| Some college | 22 | 22 | 28 | 25 | 19 | 20 |
| College grad. or more | 19 | 28 | 26 | 28 | 12 | 11 |
| **Occupation** | | | | | | |
| Executive/Professional | 16% | 25% | 17% | 22% | 13% | 11% |
| White collar | 18 | 18 | 28 | 19 | 18 | 15 |
| Blue collar | 28 | 19 | 24 | 22 | 31 | 36 |
| **Marital status** | | | | | | |
| Married | 62% | 69% | 62% | 71% | 55% | 59% |
| Single | 37 | 30 | 38 | 29 | 44 | 41 |
| **Political/social ideology** | | | | | | |
| Conservative | 39% | 43% | 37% | 41% | 40% | 36% |
| Middle of the road | 37 | 26 | 33 | 35 | 39 | 41 |
| Liberal | 20 | 28 | 29 | 21 | 18 | 16 |
| **Region** | | | | | | |
| Northeast | 22% | 31% | 24% | 25% | 23% | 17% |
| Midwest | 26 | 27 | 26 | 29 | 26 | 22 |
| South | 33 | 18 | 28 | 28 | 30 | 48 |
| West | 19 | 24 | 23 | 18 | 21 | 13 |
| **Race** | | | | | | |
| White | 85% | 82% | 92% | 91% | 80% | 82% |
| Black | 10% | 11 | 3 | 6 | 13 | 13 |
| Other | 4% | 3 | 4 | 4 | 6 | 3 |
| With children under age 13 | 34% | 34% | 43% | 33% | 33% | 32% |
| Median age (in years) | 41 | 44 | 34 | 42 | 39 | 42 |
| Median income (in thousands) | $27.1 | $32.1 | $31.6 | $32.0 | $24.9 | $21.2 |

*Source:* The Roper Organization, New York, NY.

## METHODOLOGY

Being the first attempt at classifying green advertising, there was no categorizing scheme to fall back upon, although there were quite a few studies categorizing advertisements in general. For example, Shimp, Urbany and Camlin (1988) have categorized print ads for mass-marketing products in the U.S.A., while Tse, Belk, and

Table 2. Segmentaton by consumer motives

| Planet passionates | Health fanatics | Animal lovers |
| --- | --- | --- |
| Likely to belong to: | Likely to belong to: | Likely to belong to: |
| Sierra Club<br>Natural Resources Defense<br>   Council<br>American Rivers<br>Rainforest Alliance<br>Friends of the Earth<br>Keep America Beautiful | Americans for Safe Food<br>Mothers and Others<br>   Against Pesticides<br>National Coalition Against<br>   the Misuse of Pesticides | Greenpeace<br>World Wildlife Fund<br>National Audobon Society<br>Earthwatch<br>Humane Society<br>The Nature Conservancy<br>People for the Ethical<br>   Treatment of Animals |
| Likely environmental<br>behavior: | Likely environmental<br>behavior: | Likely environmental<br>behavior: |
| Conserve energy, water<br>Recycle bottles, cans<br>Buy recycled paper<br>Avoid excessive packaging<br>Buy cloth diapers<br>Read *Garbage* magazine | Buy organic foods and<br>   bottled water<br>Use sunscreens<br>Buy unbleached coffee<br>   filters<br>Read *Organic Gardening*<br>Read *Prevention* | Boycott tuna, ivory<br>Buy 'cruelty-free' cosmetics<br>Avoid fur<br>Boycott Exxon<br>Read *Animal Agenda* |

*Source:* J. Ottman Consulting

Zhou (1989) have used content analysis to compare three 'similar' societies. Yet others (Pollay, 1985) have employed content analysis to develop and describe a history of print advertising in the USA. Thus, even though there is a tradition of employing content analysis in the literature, there were no ready-made categories for our purposes. Therefore, we had to adapt available categories and create some new ones as we went along.

Among a host of critical issues on methodology, two stood out. First, we had to identify ads that would be included in our study and second, we had to develop a set of relevant categories to classify the ads. These two steps are loosely the equivalent of data gathering and scale development.

## CHOICE OF ADS

We decided to focus on print ads for a variety of reasons. The print medium has a broader base than television. This is manifest in two separate ways. First, print medium accounts for more volume of advertising than any other medium, and second, it has a larger array of advertisers, including small businesses and local businesses, participating. The first factor, i.e., volume of advertising, is important in that we could generate a large sample of ads for our analysis. The second factor, i.e., array of advertisers, is important in that it represents a larger spectrum of participants thereby ensuring that our sample ads was adequately representative of the advertising community.

Over and above those were practical considerations. We were given access to a personal library that was the store house of thousands of ads, articles and reports that addressed the issues of environment, health, and animal life preservation. We selected the ads for our study from this vast pool, using three cardinal principles. First of all, it had to be an ad; we rejected all articles and reports from this collection. Second, we included an ad in our study only if it addressed any one of the three issues, i.e., preservation of the planet, personal health or animal life. Third, and finally, multiple occurrences of the same ad were eliminated by including each ad only once. It is important to note here that we did include multiple ads for the same product/brand/company as long as they were not identical. The result was a collection of 173 ads that were used in the study. Although this procedure was dictated by a matter of convenience, it is not entirely flawed. The original collection was a large assortment of ads, articles and reports compiled over five years or more. Thus, we believe that the specific ads selected for our study represents a fair cross-section of green ads in general.

## MAIN TAXONOMY AND SUB-CATEGORIES

The main taxonomy used in this study was derived from past literature as well as our interest in the subject matter. There were four broad items in the main taxonomy: AD TARGET, AD OBJECTIVE, ECONOMIC CHAIN, and AD APPEAL.

The first item, AD TARGET, was used to identify the target of the ad. Based upon past literature (Ottman, 1991) we identified three targets. These three sub-categories are:

PLANET PRESERVATION
ANIMAL LIFE PRESERVATION
PERSONAL HEALTH PRESERVATION

The second item in the taxonomy was AD OBJECTIVE. This was used to identify whether the ad promoted a CORPORATE IMAGE or the PRODUCT/SERVICE itself; these constituted the two sub-categories were identified. Inputs, the first minor category, was defined when the ad highlighted the raw material or production processes used. The second minor category, packaging, was defined when the product's packaging was emphasized in some manner. Finally the overall product/service itself was defined as a minor category when the product/service was promoted in general. Following is a summary of the sub-categories and minor categories.

CORPORATE IMAGE
PRODUCT/SERVICE CHARACTERISTIC
Inputs
Packaging
Overall Product/Service

The third item in the main taxonomy was ECONOMIC CHAIN. This was used to identify the different activities involved in the closed loop of an economic system. Our identifying this item in the taxonomy is in response to the call to expand the focus of marketing from that of a purely selling institution (Kotler and Levey, 1969). Nicosia and Mayer (1976, p. 69) used the terms buying, using, and disposing in their theory on the sociology of consumption. We have adapted that trilogy for our purpose and the sub-categories we use are PRODUCTION, CONSUMPTION, and DISPOSITION. Essentially we have changed the emphasis from buying to production, while retaining the other two categories. This is because motivating a consumer to buy is the implicit goal of all advertising, and hence that sub-category may not be very useful. However, ads that emphasize production would be worthy of being identified as a separate sub-category. We wish to point out that there is a logical sequence to these sub-categories in that production typically precedes consumption and both of them precede disposition.[1] Thus, the three sub-categories are:

PRODUCTION
Raw Materials
Process
CONSUMPTION
DISPOSITION

Only in the case of PRODUCTION, we identified two minor categories, i.e., Raw Materials and Process. Ads that emphasized the inputs to a production process would be classified under the first minor category, whereas those that emphasized the actual process itself would be classified in the second minor category.

The fourth and final item in the main taxonomy was AD APPEAL. This was used to categorize the type of appeal employed in the ad. Based on the literature (Russell and Lane, 1991; Ottoman, 1991) and our own analysis of the ads, we identified five sub-categories, with each sub-category encompassing a few minor categories. Those that could not be easily classified were coded under a catch-all category. The sub-categories and the minor categories are as follows:

ZEITGEIST
Mere Statement
Bandwagon
EMOTIONAL
Fear
Guilt
You Make a Difference
FINANCIAL
Money-Off
Cause Subsidy
EUPHORIA
Health
Natural

MANAGEMENT
Control
Social Responsibility
OTHERS
Comparison
Exemplar
Celebrity Endorsement


ZEITGEIST is defined as the general climate prevailing at a time. Thus, any ad that merely tried to ride on the current wave of the green movement was classified in this category. An ad was placed in the first minor category if there was nothing more than a bland statement, e.g., Brand X is environmentally friendly. It was placed in the second minor category if there was an obvious attempt to hitch the company to the green movement, e.g. In response to the growing demand for an environmentally friendly product, we are proud to offer Brand X. All ads that heavily relied on an emotional appeal to stimulate a consumer were classified in the second sub-category, i.e., EMOTIONAL. Those using the emotions of fear or guilt were placed in the respective minor categories. Ads that made the consumer the focal point were placed in yet another minor category. The next sub-category, FINANCIAL, was used to identify all of those ads that emphasized the financial aspects either directly through money-off coupons (first minor category) or through subsidizing certain causes (second minor category). The theme in the next sub-category, EUPHORIA, was intended to capture all the ads emphasizing a sense of well-being. Typically a sense of euphoria was invoked either by emphasizing the health aspects or the use of natural ingredients; these determined placement of an ad in the appropriate minor category. The last sub-category, MANAGEMENT, was used to identify ads implying that the corporate entity was, in some sense, proactively involved in the green movement. If the message ascribed a fair degree of management control through a conscious programmatic effort, then the ad was placed in the first minor category, i.e., control. However, an ad was placed in the second minor category, i.e., social responsibility, if the message generally emphasized that characteristic of the corporate sponsor.


## CODING


The two researchers themselves acted as the two coders in this study. This does not pose any particular problem of a bias since there were no *à priori* hypotheses to be tested. Rather, this study is in the tradition of grounded theory (Glaser and Strauss, 1967) wherein the data are analyzed, not with any preconceived hypothesis to support, but with the intent of seeing a pattern emerge. Both the coders simultaneously coded the ads, and any discrepancies were discussed till there was agreement. This one-step procedure was possible because the coding scheme was quite simple. Moreover, being a preliminary attempt at analyzing green ads, we felt that our coding method was satisfactory and adequate.

# RESULTS

Given the nature of the data and the exploratory ground-up orientaiton of this study, (Glaser and Strauss, 1967) analysis of frequencies and cross-tabulation were thought to be the most appropriate techniques. The overall analysis of frequencies is presented in Table 3 and the cross-tabulation in Table 4.

From the analysis of AD TARGET, it is evident that planet preservation is the most extensively used target. This is consistent with the general perception that the green movement grew from environmental concerns. Witness, for instance, the description of the most visible green event, i.e., Earth Day, in the popular press (Begley, Hager, and Wright, *Newsweek*, March 26, 1990). The entire report speaks of the movement wherein corporations can be seen as 'friends of the Earth' and corporation have set up 'Save The Planet Departments' (*ibid.* p. 60). The green movement, in order to sustain momentum and growth, will have to expand its target to include other concerns as well.

Advertisers appear to emphasize corporate image slightly more often than product/service itself, but the difference is relatively small. We are not exactly sure about the implication of this finding; we can merely offer a speculative view. Stern and Resnik (1991) replicated an earlier study by Resnik and Stern (1977) and found that other than institutional advertising, information content in advertising had generally increased. In the case of institutional advertising, the reduction in the number of information cues was dramatic (Stern and Resnik, 1991, p. 41, Table 1). Since we found more than one-half of the green ads emphasizing corporate image, we can speculate that green advertising may suffer from low information content, thereby leading to its low credibility (Ottman, 1991) and it being perceived as deceptive exploitation (*Newsweek*, March 26, 1990, p. 60).

Based upon our analysis of ECOCHAIN, one striking conclusion was that the three-way categorization was not applicable to over one-half of the ads. For those ads that could be categorized using this scheme, most emphasis was placed on the production phase of the chain.

Within this category, advertising copy typically emphasized the use of ecologically friendly raw materials most often. It is clear that advertisers view the production emphasis as a key one in wooing the green consumer. Disposition was emphasized less frequently than production, although it was moderately frequent in and of itself. With the increasing awareness on subjects like landfill wastes and ever growing laws that regulate disposal behavior (e.g., bottle redemption) it is hardly surprising that disposition is emphasized in over one-third of the green ads.

The concept of locus of control can be gainfully used to shed additional light on the distribution of the ecochain categories. Emphasis on production, whether it be raw materials or process, clearly places the locus of control with the corporate sponsor. That message suggests that the corporate entity is behaving responsibly and being sensitive to the green issues. On the other hand, an ad emphasizing disposition, suggests that the locus of control is shared by the corporate entity and the consumer, although the onus of responsibility lies with the consumer. The implication is that the consumer must behave in a responsible manner and contribute her/his mite by regulating her/his disposal behavior. This approach has the advantage of bringing a consumer into the green movement thereby benefiting the corporate sponsor as well.

Table 3. Analysis of frequencies.

|  |  | No. of ads | % | % Not incl. N/A |
|---|---|---|---|---|
| I. | *Ad target* | | | |
|  | Planet Preservation | 135 | 78.0% | |
|  | Animal Life Preservation | 26 | 15.0 | |
|  | Personal Health Preservation | 12 | 7.0 | |
|  | *Total* | 173 | 100.0% | |
|  | | | | |
| II. | *Ad objective* | | | |
|  | Corporate Image | 96 | 55.5% | |
|  | Product/Service Characteristic | 77 | 45.5 | |
|  |   Inputs    28 (36.4%) | | | |
|  |   Packaging    26 (33.8%) | | | |
|  |   Overall    17 (22.0%) | | | |
|  |   Others    6 (7.0%) | | | |
|  | *Total* | 173 | 100.0% | |
|  | | | | |
| III. | *Ecochain* | | | |
|  | Production | 49 | 28.3% | 59.0% |
|  |   Raw Materials    37 (75.5%) | | | |
|  |   Process    12 (24.5%) | | | |
|  | Consumption | 6 | 3.5 | 7.3 |
|  | Disposition | 28 | 16.2 | 33.7 |
|  | Not Applicable | 90 | 52.0 | — |
|  | *Total* | 173 | 100.0% | 100.0% |
|  | | | | |
| IV. | *Ad appeal* | | | |
|  | Zeitgeist | 55 | 31.8% | |
|  |   Mere Statement    29 (52.7%) | | | |
|  |   Bandwagon    26 (47.3%) | | | |
|  | Emotional | 36 | 20.8 | |
|  |   Fear    9 (25.0%) | | | |
|  |   Guilt    10 (27.7%) | | | |
|  |   You    17 (47.3%) | | | |
|  | Financial | 14 | 8.1 | |
|  |   Money-off    7 (50.0%) | | | |
|  |   Cause Subsidy    7 (50.0%) | | | |
|  | Euphoria | 15 | 8.7 | |
|  |   Health    6 (40.0%) | | | |
|  |   Natural    9 (60.0%) | | | |
|  | Management | 38 | 22.0 | |
|  |   Control    19 (50.0%) | | | |
|  |   Social Resp.    19 (50.0%) | | | |
|  | Others | 15 | 8.7 | |
|  |   Comparison    4 (26.6%) | | | |
|  |   Exemplar    10 (66.7%) | | | |
|  |   Celebrity    1 (6.7%) | | | |
|  | *Total* | 173 | 100.0% | |

Table 4. Crosstabulation of frequencies

I. AD APPEAL × AD OBJECTIVE

| Ad objective | Zeitgeist | Emotional | Financial | Eu |
|---|---|---|---|---|
| Corporate | 29 | 20 | 10 | 1 |
| Prod./Serv. | 26 | 16 | 4 | 14 |
| Total | 55 | 36 | 14 | 15 |

II. AD APPEAL × ECOCHAIN

| Ecochain | Zeitgeist | Emotional | Financial | Euphoria | Managem |
|---|---|---|---|---|---|
| Production | 10 | 7 | 0 | 13 | 14 |
| Consumption | 1 | 4 | 0 | 1 | 0 |
| Disposition | 14 | 4 | 3 | 0 | 5 |
| Total | 25 | 15 | 3 | 14 | 19 |

a This crosstabulation was not applicable to 90 of the 173 ads, and hence the smaller grand total.

We felt that AD APPEAL was the most important variable. Hence, we decided crosstabulate the frequency distributions of AD OBJECTIVE and ECOCHAIN respectively, with AD APPEAL. These results are presented in Table 4; both the results were significant ($p < 0.001$). Rather than describe all aspects of these results, in this portion of the discusson, we will selectively highlight aspects worthy of discussion.

The financial appeal, for example, was skewed more toward corporate image advertising. A further breakdown of the financial appeal into its two subcomponents, i.e., cause subsidy and money-off, was very striking. All those that were categorized as 'cause-subsidy' (7) were used to promote a corporate image exclusively, whereas 'money-off' ads (4) were exclusively used in the case of product/service promotions. Clearly corporate image is better promoted by associating the corporate name with visible and/or major causes (Ross, Patterson, and Sutts; 1992). The other distribution of interest was that of Euphoria; it was mostly used for promoting product/services rather than a corporate image. The one exception was a case when an attempt to build a corporate image was made by emphasizing the use of only natural ingredients.

The crosstabulation of AD APPEAL and ECOCHAIN resulted in many sparse cells since a large number of ads could not be classified under this scheme. In light of this, emphasis on statistical significance must be softened. Nonetheless, there were interesting patterns worthy of discussion. For instance, consumption was rarely used in many of the appeals. However, production and disposition were more extensively used. The use of financial appeals (3) was exclusively related to disposition; even more interesting was that all these appeals were of the 'money-off' type. Euphoria was

...vertisers found it easy to
...ilities.

...less we cautiously
...rs of the green
...d with planet
...f the green
...he target of
...mendation
...nd more
...sustain

...oduct
...account for
...by low credibility
...probes (Lawrence and
...ld be for the advertising
...lexicon for many over used words
...able', 'safe', and 'natural'. In fact,
...nitiated work in this regard. The advertising
...assuaging consumers' feeling and ward off potential
...ctive and cooperative stance.
...hat consumption was rarely emphasized in green ads; the
...mphasis was on production. This is almost like a throwback to the pre-
...era from which we have emerged. Our third and final recommendation
...ld be that green advertisers adopt the fundamental marketing maxim, i.e.,
emphasize the consumer and consumption, not the producer and production.

## NOTE

1. Actually 'buying' (or purchasing) will be in between these two activities, but has been omitted for reasons already specified.

## REFERENCES

Abt Associates, Inc. (1990) *Environmental Consumerism in the US.*
Begley, Sharon, Mary Hager, and Lynda Wright (1990) 'The Selling of Earth Day', *Newsweek*, 26 March, pp. 60–61.
Bremner, Brian (1989) 'The New Sales Pitch: The Environment', *Business Week*, 24 July, p. 50.
*The Economist* (1990) 'Marketing Greenery. Friendly to Whom?' 7 April, p. 83.
Glaser, B. J. and A. L. Strauss (1967) *The Discovery of Grounded Theory*, Chicago: Aldine.

Hinds, Michael de Courcy (1989) 'In Sorting Trash, Householders Get Little Help From Industry', *New York Times*, (July 29).

Kotler, Philip and Sidney J. Levy (1969) 'Broadening the Concept of Marketing', *Journal of Marketing*, **33**, (January), 10–15.

Lawrence, Jennifer and Laurie Freeman (1990) 'Marketers Study State Guidelines', *Advertising Age*, Vol. 61 (47), (November 12), 74.

New York Times/CBS News Poll (1990) (April).

Nicosia, Francesco M. and Robert N. Mayer (1976) 'Toward a Sociology of Consumption', *Journal of Consumer Research*, 3, (September), 65–75.

Ottman, J. (1991) *Environmental Consumerism: What Every Marketer Needs to Know*, J. Ottman Consulting, Inc.: New York:

Pollay, Richard W. (1985) 'The Subsiding Sizzle: A Descriptive History of Print Advertising, 1900–1980,' *Journal of Marketing*, **49**, 24–37.

Resnick, Alan J. and Bruce L. Stern (1977) 'An Analysis of Information Content in Television Advertising', *Journal of Marketing*, **41** (1), 50–53.

The Roper Organization (1990) *The Environment: Public Attitudes and Individual Behavior*, commissioned by S. C. Johnson and Son.

Ross, John K., Larry T. Patterson, and Mary Ann Stutts (1992) 'Consumer Perceptions of Organizations that use Cause-Related Marketing', *Journal of the Academy of the Marketing Science*, (Winter), Vol. 20 (1), 93–97.

Russell, Thomas J. and Ronald Lane (1991) *Kleppner's Advertising Procedure*, Englewood Cliffs, NJ: Prentice Hall.

Schwartz, Joe and Thomas Miller (1991) 'The Earth's Best Friends', *American Demographics*, (February), 26–35.

*Scott Paper Company Study* (1990), (March) cited in Ottman (1991).

Shimp, Terence A., Joel E. Urbany, and Sarah E. Camlin (1988) 'The Use of Framing and Characterization for Magazine Advertising of Mass-Marketed Products', *Journal of Advertising*, Vol. 17 (1), 23–30.

*Simmons Market Research Bureau, Inc.* (1990).

Stern, Bruce L. and Alan J. Resnick (1991) 'Information Content in Television Advertising: A Republication and Extension', *Journal of Advertising Research*, (June/July), 36–46.

*The Tyndall Report*, cited in Ottman (1991).

Tse, David K., Russel W. Belk, and Nan Zhou (1989) 'Becoming a Consumer Society: A Longitudinal and Cross Cultural Analysis of Print Ads from Hong Kong, The Peoples Republic of China and Taiwan', *Journal of Consumer Research*, **15**, (4) (March), 457–472.

# 29

# Green Advertising: Salvation or Oxymoron?

*William E. Kilbourne*

The purchase of this paper is to clarify the nature of green advertising, thus demonstrating that the concept is far more complex than the extant marketing literature suggests. Green is characterized here as a two dimensional concept with political (reformism to radicalism) and human positional (anthropocentric to ecocentric) dimensions. It is argued here that there are at least five different types of green, including environmentalism, conservationism, human welfare ecology, preservationism, and ecologism. To understand the greenness of an advertisement, it is useful to position it within this framework; and each type suggests a different human position with respect to nature and a different political orientation. The proposed framework is useful for defining terms such as 'green,' 'environmental,' and 'ecological' which are often used interchangeably in the marketing and advertising literature.

## INTRODUCTION

Much has been written within the marketing/ecology domain in the last twenty years. Beginning with Fisk's (1974) seminal book, *Marketing and the Ecological Crisis*, interest in the area developed and evolved into a series of ecological marketing workshops beginning in 1975 and repeated in 1979. Special issues of such journals as the *Journal of Business Research* in 1994 and the *Journal of Public Policy and Marketing* in 1991 have focused on ecology, the environment, and on green marketing.

There appears to be, however, an anomalous development within this particular field of study. Unlike other areas of investigation where a theoretical framework is developed to direct further research, a similar pattern has not developed in the green marketing literature. Research tends to be fragmentary and highly specific with common goals focusing on the identification of ecologically conscious consumers as a target market or the development of scales to assess the level of environmental concern among consumers. Of the twenty-two papers within the Ecological

Reprinted with permission from *Journal of Advertising*, Vol. 24, No. 2, 1995, pp. 7–19

Marketing Workshop and the environmental issue of the *Journal of Public Policy and Marketing*, none addressed the issue of a theoretical framework for environmental studies in marketing. Marketers do not appear to be compelled to define clearly what is encapsulated under the general rubric of 'ecological concern.' A notable exception to this is Iyer and Banerjee (1993), who explore the possibility of developing a framework for categorizing green advertisements.

As is evident from the first two paragraphs, the terms ecology, environment, and green appear synonymous. This is characteristic of the literature cited. The purpose of this paper is to bring into the advertising literature a clearer delineation of what an ecological perspective entails and how it is qualitatively different from an environmental perspective. It will be demonstrated that, within the ecology literature, environmentalism and ecologism are not only different, but that they are virtually political antitheses. Once this distinction is made clear, the relationship between ecology and advertising can be examined in a fruitful way drawing from a rich literature in ecology, ethics, political science, economics, and philosophy of science. An attempt is made to offer a synthesis which will define the ecological domain in such a way that its true richness and diversity can be understood. From this starting point, a research agenda can be developed.

## MARKETING AND ECOLOGY

Before embarking on the primary task of the paper, a slight diversion into the context of the problem is in order. This is considered necessary since advertising can be viewed as a subsystem of marketing practice. While it is not the intent of the paper to focus on the whole area of marketing, it is essential to recognize that advertising cannot be effectively separated from its marketing context. This would be anti-ecological in itself. What is advertised and how it is advertised are driven by and interact with products, prices, and distribution practices. Thus, there can be no truly green advertising if there is not something green about the product (e.g., use of resources, packaging, energy efficient transport system). The greening of marketing will not take place until consumers and producers recognize the imminent ecological crisis. When these groups change their behavior and priorities, then new social institutions informed by ecological consciousness can evolve. Such marketing institutions would produce more ecologically benign products, develop modes of promotion that do not encourage ecologically destructive consumption, as well as develop modes of distribution that minimize ecological impact on both the environment and resource use. Thus, the problems lie within the domain of marketing practice, and advertising is only one interdependent piece of that domain.

While marketing technology has contributed significantly to the ecological crisis, mitigation of that same crisis is immanent in the marketing process as well (Fisk, 1974). Partially because of the reductionist solutions imposed on the problems, the ameliorative power of marketing had not appeared when Fisk (1974) first offered his ecological analysis of the marketing process. From outward appearances, it has not materialized in the ensuing twenty years except, as Fisk suggested, under duress from government or consumers.

It has been argued that advertising has the power to effect social change; but if advertisers continue to misuse their power in promoting false ecological claims, then its power to mitigate the imminent crisis will be diminished (Fisk, 1974). This is evidenced by the fact that consumers have suggested the least credible source for environmental information is an ad by a major company (Iyer and Banerjee, 1993). This should not be surprising since Kangun, Carlson and Grove (1991) found that 58% of environmental ads sampled contained at least one misleading or deceptive claim. It would appear that Fisk's warnings were not headed.

## WHAT DOES GREEN MEAN?

To develop a clear distinction between environmentalism and ecologism, a framework within which the nature of 'Green' can be established is developed. It will be shown that the concept is not uni-dimensional as implied by the contemporary business literature. There are two dimensions which will be developed for purposes of this paper, the political and the positional (position of humans in nature) (see Figure 1). Depending on one's particular intellectual bent or purpose, others might be established as well.

The political dimension reflects the relative positions one might take regarding how change is to be effected and how much change is acceptable. The question is whether political reform is sufficient. If it is, then all necessary change can be brought about by enacting new legislation on such problems as pollution control, recycling, and toxic waste disposal. This tradition, reformism, accepts as axiomatic that the dominant social paradigm, and through it, the *status quo*, should be maintained. The opposite extreme on the scale is referred to as radicalism, which calls into question the paradigm itself, maintaining that politicial reform is

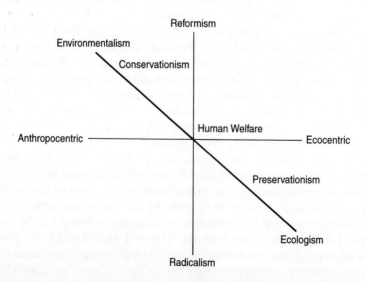

Figure 1. Levels of Ecological Concern.

insufficient to engender the magnitude or type of change necessary to preserve the environment in the long run. Thus, in the political dimension, reformism and radicalism, are at opposite ends of the continuum (Dolbeare and Dolbeare, 1976). Lying between these extremes is reform liberalism which offers a modest challenge to the stock assumptions of the dominant social paradigm, but its proponents consider that social ills can be alleviated with political reform. The difficulty in reform liberalism, according to Dolbeare and Dolbeare (1976), is that it seeks reform using the established procedures that resulted in the conditions denounced. Real, substantive change refers to changes in the dominant ideology (social paradigm) regarding 'poverty, unemployment, war, racism, deterioration of the physical and natural environment' (Dolbeare and Dolbeare, 1976, p. 73).

The second dimension is the positional which means the position that humans consider themselves to occupy in the ecology *vis à vis* the rest of the biotic community. The prevailing view within the dominant social paradigm is anthropocentrism (Dobson, 1990; Porritt, 1984; Capra, 1982). This perspective is closely aligned with others such as technocentrism (O'Riordan, 1976) and human centeredness (Fox, 1986). Each tends to see in nature instrumental value for purely human purposes. The contrary view is referred to here as ecocentrism which reflects the idea that the ecology is characterized by inherent value rather than human instrumental value. This is not to suggest that eccocentrism had no anthropocentric properties since any concept that is the product of human rationality is, by definition, anthropocentric to some degree (O'Riordan, 1976; Dobson, 1990).

Before proceeding further, one terminology problem should be resolved. As suggested earlier, one of the difficulties in evaluating the green properties of any aspect of marketing is the somewhat indiscriminate use of the term. This problem is recognized even in the ecological literature. Eckersley (1992), for example, states:

> Of course, the label *Green* is an extraordinarily elastic one that has been applied to, or appropriated by, all manner of environmental and political positions over the past decade (p. 8).

The difference between types of green can best be described as anthropocentric green and ecocentric green, or what Dobson (1990) refers to as green with a 'little g' and Green with a 'capital G,' respectively. In the present paper, the two positions will be referred to as environmentalism and ecologism. Within the framework developed here, environmentalism is in the upper left quadrant and ecologism is in the lower right quadrant as shown in Figure 1. When the term 'Green' is used, Dobson's convention will be followed. With these concepts in hand, the discussion will now turn to their political and positional dimensions.

## POLITICAL DIMENSION

As Eckersley (1992) states, '. . . from the point of view of the participants in the Green movement and in Green political parties, the work *Green* represents a distinctive body of ideas and a new political force' (p. 8). This suggests that environmentalism represents an ideology of political reform motivated by a world view that deviates dramatically from that within which ecologism was developed. It evolved out of deficiencies of social and political theory development which were primarily concerned with distributional justice and democratic participation. Rodman (1980) describes environmentalism as having been:

> . . . domesticated by mainstream political science, reduced to the study of pollution control policy and environmental interest groups, and eventually absorbed within the framework of 'the policy process' and the 'politics of getting' (p. 65).

A casual examination of the contemporary business literature reveals the validity of the criticism. Within the dominant socio-political agenda, we find unlimited economic growth (Schmookler, 1993; Kassiola, 1990) and technological rationality (Habermas, 1971; Marcuse, 1964) as the sustaining ideologies of the dominant social paradigm which is the intellectual framework within which environmentalism has evolved. There is, within environmentalism, virtually no allusion to the *root causes* of the current ecological crisis. England and Bluestone (1972) suggest this results from economic reductionism defining a socio-political problem as a technical one.

While the paucity of socio-political critique within the marketing/advertising domain is evident, it is not at all clear why this should be the case. Part of the explanation for this paucity of critique, it is argued here, lies in the ideology of industrialization and resistance within the dominant social paradigm which eschews the anti-industrial implications of radical social critique (Porritt, 1984; Marcuse, 1964, 1969). Reformism is the preferred mode of critique within the dominant social paradigm since it does not challenge the liberal, technological foundations upon which it rests. The solution set derived from this mode of analysis always lies within technological rationality motivated by unlimited economic growth and consumption (Kassiola, 1990). England and Bluestone (1972) refer to this state as follows:

> As a consequence, though middle-class acceptance of the urgency of the environmental issue is widespread, there is also a tendency to perceive the problem of protecting the environment in technical, rather than political, terms (p. 203).

And in a confirmation and critique of this a-political posture, Winner (1986) adds:

> A crucial failure in modern political thought and political practice has been the inability or unwillingness even to begin . . . the critical evaluation and control of society's technical constitution (p. 57).

This sentiment regarding the 'techno-fix,' a term referring to the prevailing view that every problem can and will be solved by advancing science/technology (Ehrenfeld, 1978) is prevalent today. Further, within the *status quo*, it is considered the reform of choice (Dobson, 1990; Trainer, 1985). To do otherwise would call into question the basic tenets of liberal democracy and capitalism (particularly the unequal distribution of wealth and power) and the industrial ideology that evolved through them and continuously reinforces them. The prevailing ideology is inimical to such investigations, however, and analytical methods different from those commonly used for inquiry are necessary. Among those methodological extensions with emancipation potential are critical theory (Murray and Ozanne, 1991; Rogers,

1987) and Marxist/feminist critique (Rothschild, 1983; Hirschmun, 1993). With these approaches, the ideological basis of the ecological problem can be examined effectively mobilizing 'the critical evaluation and control of society's technical constitution' and helping to establish Fisk's (1973) call for rational consumption.

Environmentalism, as a social concept, circumscribes the domain of social critique within the prevailing view of post-industrial society as the technological, affluent, service society in opposition to the radical version of post-industrial society as low technology, agrarian, and decentralized (Dobson, 1990). The environmentalism concept limits the scope of political analysis to quantitative change within the dominant social paradigm suggesting changes in methods of operation within the framework of the *status quo* (Porritt, 1984). Within this mode of thought, for example, it is believed that what technology and economic growth cannot solve, legislation can (Milbrath, 1984). Environmentalism does not present a challenge to the dominant paradigm, and Porritt and Winner (1988) state further:

> . . . the most radical [Green aim] seeks nothing less than a non-violent revolution to overthrow our whole polluting, plundering and materialistic industrial society and, in its place, to create a new economic and social order which will allow human beings to live in harmony with the planet (p. 9).

Ecologism, on the other hand, challenges the foundations of the paradigm itself demanding a new paradigm in place of the old (Dobson, 1990). As such, ecologism represents a new paradigm (Kuhn 1970) that will replace the one that evolved from Enlightenment thought and is still dominant today. The new paradigm demands a restructuring of the whole of social existence entailing nonviolent, radical (as opposed to reformist) transformation of the social, political, and economic structure of post industrial society (Dobson, 1990). Rather than navigating within the dominant social paradigm, it seeks *qualitative* change in the systems of thought that have structured the consciousness of Western industrial society for the past three centuries (Pirages, 1977; Cotgrove, 1982). As such, it represents a *change in consciousness* rather than a change in behavior. While little attention has been paid within the advertising literature to the connection between the prevailing mode of thought embedded in the dominant social paradigm and current environmental conditions, the link should become evident upon closer examination of the positional dimension.

## POSITIONAL DIMENSION

To examine this dimension, a brief historical analysis of the development of the dominant, social paradigm will be developed. This will be followed by an assessment of its impact on green thought as it exists today.

The development of the contemporary world view in Western industrial societies has manifested itself through an evolutionary process beginning in early industrialization and the Enlightenment and continuing through to the present time. As the Enlightenment project unfolded, its effects systematically and progressively eroded religious, social, political, and economic beliefs and, through them, the prevailing view of nature (Dobson, 1990; Kassiola, 1990; Rifkin, 1980; Capra, 1982; Merchant, 1982). The development of Enlightenment science and English liberalism sounded the death knell of feudalism and religious hegemony (Dumont, 1977) and ushered in a new world view that has prevailed to the present time (Merchant, 1992). Among the basic axioms that evolved in the process were possessive individualism (MacPherson, 1962), unlimited accumulation of material wealth (Locke, 1963), and free markets (Smith, 1937). Each axiom must be reexamined in the context of contemporary society (Eckersley, 1992) before any progress can be made in developing a sustainable society based on sound ecological principles. About these historical developments, Leeson (1979) states:

> It was the unleashing of the passion for material abundance, legitimized by Hobbesian natural right, amplified by Locke, combined with the rejection of the classical commitment to reason and proper limits that caused the ecological crisis (p. 317).

The historical process through which the prevailing world view was transformed from organic to mechanical is described in detail by Merchant (1982, 1992), Leiss (1972), and Dobson (1990). Kassiola (1990) provides a political perspective on the changes. In addition, each describes how the prevailing attitude toward nature was transformed from one of reverence and harmony to one of exploitation and domination. It is a direct consequence of this shift in world view that nature has been stripped of intrinsic value as described by Regan (1981) and, consequently, ravaged in the name of human progress. Goldsmith (1988) refers to the consequences of this process as the creation of a surrogate world of 'material goods and technological devices.' This transformation from organicism to mechanism and its attendant consequences, both social and physical, motivated the development of anthropocentrism and is now the force against which ecocentrists align themselves. From the perspective of ecologism, it can be concluded that environmental reform as currently practiced within the framework of Western industrial ideology may achieve too little, too late. This is not to say that environmentalism, as traditionally conceived, is wrong, but that it is deficient. As Porritt (1984) suggests,

> Concern for the environment provides as good a starting point as any for green politics. But unless it then encompasses fundamental social and economic issues, it will contribute little towards eliminating the root causes of that crisis (p. 228).

These 'root causes' can be visualized as multiple links in an ideological chain going back to the Enlightenment (Kassiola, 1990; Dobson, 1990; Rifkin, 1980; Leiss, 1972; Capra, 1982; Merchant, 1992). While it is not the intent of this paper to provide a complete analysis of the evolution of the root causes, it is only through such a comprehensive analysis that a clear sense of the socio-political nature of the problem can be obtained. Only in doing this can it be seen that the techno-fix and legislative action (a social form of techno-fix referred to in the more general sense of technique [Winner, 1977; Ellul, 1964]) will be impotent in the solution of ecological problems if not accompanied by fundamental cultural change. This suggests a true shift away from the dominant social paradigm and toward an ecologically based world view— ecologism. To do otherwise is to address the symptoms of a culturally based ecological crisis while leaving the root causes intact. The end result of this truncated evaluational process is that the symptoms will reemerge in a different time, place, or form (Ophuls, 1977).

The foregoing suggests neither that the achievements of the Enlightenment were culturally inconsequential nor that we should somehow return to pre-Enlightenment modes of thought. While the long tradition of humanist ideals has led to unprecedented success in human endeavor, it has also led to accelerated ecological degradation. More recently, this has led to increasing environmental philosophical inquiry into the nature of human existence and, specifically, intrinsic value theories of nature. But the philosophical inquiry has been directed almost exclusively toward the human condition. As a consequence, the perspective that 'intrinsic value is generally taken to reside exclusively, or at least preeminently, in humans,' has motivated and directed the inquiry, shrouding it with a veil of arrogance (Ehrenfeld, 1978).

The consequences of this path require that the domain of inquiry be expanded to the non-human world as well, or the reduction of nature to pure instrumental value is inevitable. Within the dominant social paradigm, the supremacy of humans over non-human entities is the primary assumption and stems from the Enlightenment tradition. It remains a stock assumption within the industrial ideology despite mounting evidence that conditions of the past no longer exist. Even though Copernicus removed the Earth from the center of the Universe and Darwin removed humans from the center of the Earth, we still envision ourselves as the center of the universe yielding the belief that 'We are superior to nature, contemptuous of it, willing to use it for our slightest whim' (White, 1967, p. 1204). This has become part of our 'inherited intellectual capital,' and we must dis-abuse ourselves of the impediment if we are to develop more productive inquiry (Gouldner, 1973). In particular, the anthropocentric and cornucopian assumptions of the Enlightenment must be challenged from the perspective of the contemporary world. To begin the critique, an examination of the main streams of ecological thought will be developed. O'Riordan (1976), Rodman (1983), and Eckersley (1992) provide the framework from which the following was developed. This will be followed by an assessment of the different perspectives falling within the framework developed here.

## RECENT DEVELOPMENT IN GREEN THOUGHT

The three major streams of ecopolitical thought that have developed over the last three decades are contained in the themes of participation, survival, and emancipation (Eckersley, 1992). The rise of Green parties can be seen as the emancipatory phase and gives a new dimension to political debate that does not reside within the older left/right politics of the past (Porritt, 1984). While emancipatory Green is still somewhat amorphous, it embodies new ideas and 'a new political force' (Porritt, 1984, p. 8). Further, within the 'Green,' ambit there is debate over the spectrum of potential positions within the dimension.

Within the participation view, old assumptions of unlimited economic growth (Kassiola, 1990), technological rationality (Marcuse, 1964; Habermas, 1970), and free market mechanisms were not addressed, and the basic cause of environmental degradation was considered poor planning or bad management. Nature as resource is left intact and anthropocentrism is the social value in this perspective.

The survivalist perspective of ecopolitical thought arrived through the limits to growth debates of the 1970s, primarily *The Limits to Growth* (Meadows *et al.*, 1972) and *Blueprint for Survival* (Goldsmith *et al.*, 1972). In addition, critiques by Heilbroner (1974), Ophuls (1977), and Hardin (1968) reasoned that dramatic, Draconian political measures would need to be taken if the human race is to survive in the long run. While each preferred less politically repressive solutions, these were not considered likely to be effective, so the only real choice was between 'Leviathan and oblivion' (Ophuls 1973). While most reject the authoritarian response to ecological crisis, survivalists have heightened the intensity of the debate and challenged the limits of extant social values and political institutions in dealing with the crisis.

The emancipation position expands upon the survivalist tradition to include not just survival, but survival under conditions of freedom which are perceived to have been eroded under the hegemony of instrumental or technological rationality. Leiss (1978), for example, suggests that the limits to growth should be viewed, not as a problem, but as an opportunity for 'qualitative improvement in the course of creating the conserver society' (p. 112). Rodman (1980) further suggests that the role of government should not be to repress economic growth but to stop forcing it through economic policy. This would allow the limits of consumption to be exposed as deficient in the satisfaction of true human needs. Roszak (1979) adds that the needs of the person and the needs of the planet have become unified, thus offering the opportunity for cultural renewal. Within the emancipatory tradition, the ecological crisis is also a crisis of culture. Its challenge is to 'overcome the destructive logic of capital accumulation, the acquisitive values of consumer society, and, more generally, all systems of domination (including class domination, patriarchy, imperialism, racism, totalitarianism, and the domination of nature)' (Eckersley, 1992, p. 21).

As can be seen, emancipatory theorists offer a challenge to both liberalism and Enlightenment science/technology which are perceived as the means through which the domination of inner and outer nature has evolved. Existing power relations within the dominant social paradigm serve to disempower the individual in the name of freedom and growth. The idea that human self-realization can be achieved through the domination and transformation of nature is part of the intellectual baggage of the Enlightenment that must be discarded for the development of a sustainable society. The argument in emancipatory theory is for a post-liberal, trans-industrial society (Kassiola, 1990).

A fundamental disagreement among the emancipatory proponents, however, relates to the perspective to be taken regarding anthropocentrism. The first is the position that the objective is '*human* emancipation and fulfillment in an ecologically sustainable society' (Eckersley, 1992, p. 26). The second acknowledges the same objective but with a recognition of the moral standing of the nonhuman world and its right to continue evolving. The primary point of departure between the two views is the position of humans in the biosphere with ecocentric theorists postulating that the current ecological crisis stems from an over inflated sense of human value, or, as Ehrenfeld (1978) calls it, 'the arrogance of humanism.'

While the anthropocentric view falls short on positional and political criteria, it surpasses the participation and survivalist traditions by allowing the critique of industrialism and unlimited economic growth. Consequently, it still falls within the emancipatory position. The key element distinguishing the ecocentric positions from the more conservative ones is their insistence that the free market liberalism of the dominant social paradigm be subordinated to the conditions of ecological (Porritt, 1984) and social justice (Bookchin, 1980, 1990).

As suggested, within the emancipatory tradition, the spectrum ranges from environmentalism to ecologism with multiple positions between. The following will delineate several of these intermediate positions beginning toward environmentalism and moving toward ecologism. None of the types should be considered mutually exclusive as they sometimes maintain similar ideas in limited areas. Nor are they exhaustive, as others could be divined in the literature.

## Resource conservationism

Next to environmentalism discussed earlier, the most anthropocentric and reformist position is that of resource conservationism which was formed out of the scientific and utilitarian perspectives. Consequently, its focus is on the efficient management of natural resources so that they will be available for future human centered development and use. One of its premises is the Lockean perspective that resources unused are resources wasted. This approach to environmental management is firmly embedded within the dominant social paradigm since its basis lies in science and liberalism; and, consequently, it is well within the limits of acceptable critique. Nature considered as a resource naturally ties this form to contemporary modes of production and consumption and reduces the concept of value in nature to instrumental value only. The essential values of this mode of thought are rationality, efficiency, control, and progress. These are the essential elements of the 'ideology of technocentrism' based on 'faith in the technology of intervention and manipulation' (O'Riordan, 1976, p. 17). The ecological crisis is thereby reduced to a management problem in the efficient allocation of resources while ignoring ecological diversity and stability (Hayes, 1959) and soft variables such as aesthetic and spiritual needs and the intrinsic value of nonhuman life-forms. Eckersley (1992) concludes.

> While the recognition of the use value of the nonhuman world must form a necessary part of any comprehensive environmental ethic, resource conservation is too limited a perspective to form the exclusive criterion of even a purely anthropocentric environmental ethic (p. 36).

To move to a more ecologically based position, the soft variables should be included, at least implicitly. Human welfare ecology provides this remedy (Eckersley 1992).

## Human welfare ecology

This position argues for an enhancement of conditions to include those factors beyond the narrow economistic vision of resource conservation's efficiency in resource allocation. It argues against the degradation of the physical and social environment by reintroducing the soft variables. Consequently, it is much more critical of technological rationality and economic growth as policy. It compels the revaluation of human needs to include the aesthetic and spiritual aspects of life with the recognition that nature degraded cannot provide them. While this position is still anthropocentric, it is argued that that biotic community can benefit indirectly if the human welfare position is adequately defined.

Fox (1990) suggests that this is only a short run perspective because it maintains the view that what is of value in the environment is also what is of value to humans. In the inevitable case of conflict between the human and the nonhuman, the nonhuman will ultimately lose. Rodman (1983) argues similarly in his evaluation of moral extensionism, an even stronger position than human welfare ecology, that ' "subhumans" may be accorded rights, but we should not be surprised if their interests are normally overridden by the weightier interests of humans,...' (p. 87). It should not be surprising if human interests supplant nonhuman rights when the entities involved have not been provided a definitive moral standing. And as Fox (1990) states, 'one is contributing to losing the ecological war by enforcing the cultural perception that what is valuable in the nonhuman world is what is useful to humans' (p. 186). To reconcile this potential ecological dilemma, an additional character must be added to the human welfare position. This results in the preservationist position.

## Preservationism

To move to the preservationist perspective, the aesthetic and spiritual dimensions must be introduced into the evaluation of nature. This is the spirit of preservationism extolled by Muir. The fundamental difference between preservation and conservation is the purpose for which it is effected. In conservationism, nature is preserved *for* future human development and in preservationism it is preserved *from* development. The position might be expanded to include two forms. If the motivation for preservation is to provide human spiritual resuscitation, weak preservation is implied. If the motivation is inherent value regardless of human use, then strong preservationism is implied. The political ramifications of this position have been pointed out by Eckersley (1992), who concludes that it reflects both a reaction against monoculturalism and materialism, two characteristics of the dominant social paradigm, and a political statement for a particular set of social values regarding these positional and political dimensions.

While preservationism is a reaction for or against certain political or social positions, it still lacks a true ecocentric basis since it remains firmly anthropocentric in the sense that we, as humans, pick and choose which aspects of our environmental conditions are worth preserving. At the end of the continuum, ecologism provides the conditions for an all encompassing view of nature and, as such, represents the full blown political philosophy (Dobson, 1990) described earlier in the Political Dimension section.

## CAN ADVERTISING BE GREEN?

We are now in a position to return to the question posed in the title of the paper—Green Advertising: Salvation or Oxymoron? For the remainder of the paper it will be assumed that advertisers are sincere in their efforts to be ecologically responsible. From the foregoing discussion, it should be clear that the question posed is not as simple as it appears from a casual reading of the marketing/advertising literature that systematically fails to define the ambit of green. While most would consider any advertisement promoting 'environmentally benign' products, recycling behavior, or energy conservation to be green, the foundation of the conclusion depends on the particular type of Green one is. Hence, however, we must consider both the political and positional dimensions. The difficulty in labeling a particular ad as green (environmentalism), Green (ecologism), or neither is that the explicit message and the meta-message (reading between the lines) can, and often do, conflict. A second difficulty is that most ads do not necessarily fall clearly into one or another category, but maintain elements of several. This is most likely a product of the lack of consistent terminology which has been addressed in this paper. To demonstrate this point, several ads from the 'Dow Lets You Do Great Things' campaign by Dow Chemical Company will be examined for their green content.

If a particular company advocates a 'techno-fix,' promotes recycling, or promotes its products as biodegradable or recyclable, most would consider this to be a Green ad in the customary sense of the word. From the perspective of the framework developed here, it would be green only in the weakest sense. From the production standpoint, the ad deals with a marginally useful, albeit necessary, ecological device. It requires no political or social reform, and even the responsibility for the behavior is shifted from the producer, who should be responsible, to the consumer. From the consumption standpoint, the message is to consume with a minimum of ecological impact. This is not an accurate depiction of the production/consumption process which is hidden beneath the meta-message: consuming is good, more is better, and the ecological cost is minimal. Each aspect of this meta-message is anathema to the ecologist who considers all dimensions of the process. Such an ad, which is only weakly green, would fall at the environmentalism end of the diagonal in Figure 1. An example of this type of ad used the following text: 'It sounds like my kind of research. Finding new ways to grow more food.' The ad advocates human centered consumption behavior and only minimally reformist production behavior employing the essence of the 'techno-fix,' more chemicals to increase food production. A second ad in the series states, 'She'll also learn about protecting our environment. Through a recycling program of the National Park Service and its recycling partner, ...' It is clear this ad only promotes recycling behavior and is characteristic of the environmentalism position.

The environmentalism position can be transcended somewhat by adding a conservation perspective. If the reasoning in the ad is based on preserving resources so that we can maintain consumption standards (and profitability) for a longer time period, then the ad represents conservationism and adds to the greenness of the previous example. Recognition that future generations have some rights to the environment shifts this ad down on reformism and to the right on anthropocentrism, but it is still tied to 'nature as resource' and management efficiency and, therefore, still within the dominant social paradigm. Thus, the ad may be green with a little 'g' since it is still advocating increased production and consumption and nature as instrumental. The exemplar from the chemical company series actually bridges several categories defined here. The ad states, 'We are committed to joining hands with federal agencies, communities, states, and other industries across the country to recycle and conserve our resources, ...' The conservation principle is clearly in evidence in this statement, but it is combined with recycling. This implies concern for future generations thus moving to the right on the positional axis. It also suggests working within the political framework to effect some marginal changes in perceptions. The ad also contains an additional statement that moves it further down the continuum to human welfare ecology, exemplifying the problem of categorizing such ads.

Moving to human welfare ecology is problematic since it requires that motivation for change be known. The ad discussed in the conservation classification also contains a human welfare ecology dimension with the statement, '... improve our environment, and ensure the beauty of these lands for generations to come.' While the consequences may be similar to conservationism in the short run, an additional non-economic evaluation of the resource is appended. The change is on the order of reform liberalism which questions the stock assumption about purely economic, instrumental value and focuses on the inherent value of the resource in yielding human welfare. This aspect also renders human welfare actions anthropocentric since it is 'human' welfare that is preserved. The consequence of human welfare ecology must be tempered with Fox's (1990) admonition that in a confrontation, nature will lose and we will revert to anthropocentrism. To 'preserve' the resource in question, it must be revalued in non-economic terms based on intrinsic values. This change moves the position lower and to the right in Figure 1.

Once we have descended the diagonal past the origin in Figure 1, we move into the area of Green. From here, changes will represent challenges to the dominant social paradigm; and the balance shifts from anthropocentrism to ecocentrism on the positional scale and to radicalism on the political. And, an unprecedented definition of nonhuman legal and moral rights enters the analysis. Advertisements in this domain will generally come from non-profit social/ecological organizations such as the Sierra Club or Greenpeace but can come from other sources as well. The problem in assessing ads in this cateogy is one of intentionality. To be truly preservationist, an intrinsic value motivation must be present. The stock assumptions regarding free markets, material accumulation, and profits within the dominant social paradigm will begin to come under attack. Arguments will tend to be deontological rather than utilitarian, focusing on what is inherently 'right' rather than the 'greatest human good' (Eckersley, 1992). This violates both liberalism and Enlightenment science and technology, thus representing a radical transformation. We cannot legislate aesthetics and spiritualism required in preservationism. The ad ostensibly representing this position makes the statement, 'When I was growing up, Mom and Dad taught me that we've only got one planet, and we'd better take care of it. Now I'm about to join a company that's committed itself to helping people preserve our wildlife ... and to protect the earth.' The motivation is not that we, as humans, will be better off it we do not destroy the environment, but that doing it is simply not what our parents taught us. This is a more deontological position, and the human instrumental dimension in the previous ad is missing. Caution in classifying this ad as preservationist must be exercised since, as stated earlier, motivation plays a large part in this area.

From here we move to the ecologism position at the lower right end of the diagonal representing a full blown political philosophy as described earlier. Since this position requires a virtual overthrow of the dominant social paradigm, few, if any, advertisements will be found supporting the position. Major advertisers would view this as virtual economic suicide, and its advocates would see it as so extreme as to be ineffective in promoting their position. These ads would promote such things as appropriate technology, voluntary simplicity in consumption, soft energy paths, and trans-industrial existence. The theses of these ads are that we cannot consume ourselves out of an over-consumption problem, we cannot techno-fix our way out of problems caused by technology, and nothing ecologically viable can be sustained without global redistribution of wealth.

With these scenarios in mind, we can now determine whether ads can be Green. Based on the foregoing analysis, the answer depends on where you stand. If individuals' eco-philosophies place them in the upper left quadrant, an anthropocentric reformist, then green advertising will be seen as an ecologically useful addition to the advertisers' arsenal, providing benefits to the individual consumer and the ecology. If individuals' philosophies position them in the lower right quadrant, then what others consider to be a Green ad would be considered an oxymoron. Advocating green consumption is advocating more consumption, more technology, and more economic growth all considered anathema to the ecological position. To ecologists, the only Green advertising would be promoting their socio-political agenda; and the only Green product is the one that is not produced.

## IMPLICATIONS

The implications of the proposed definition/categorization scheme fall in two domains, one for marketers and the other for Greens interested in promoting ecological values within the marketplace. With respect to marketers who would be Green, it is imperative that a clear understanding of what Green really entails be developed. As was suggested twenty years ago by Fisk (1974) and more recently by Kangun, Carlson, and Grove (1991) and Iyer and Banerjee (1993), the credibility of Green advertising is relatively low. This indicates that a significant problem exists for marketers who truly desire to be environmentally proactive. Because there is so much confusion about what that means, both within the marketing world and the consumer world, a clearly identified concept must be developed and followed. Building consumer confidence once it is lost is a difficult and expensive task at best, but under conditions of confusion and deception it is virtually impossible.

Marketers must start rebuilding trust by adhering to more rigid ethical and environmental standards within their entire domain, not just advertising. As suggested earlier, consumers cannot be deceived indefinitely by ads touting traditional products as Green. Marketers must develop Green marketing programs encompassing the production, consumption, and disposition dimensions using Iyer and Banerjee's (1993) framework. Until it is understood that there can be no Green advertising in a brown marketing mix, no progress will be made, even at the environmentalist, or lowest level of green.

Fisk (1973) was one of the first to recognize the role of responsible consumption in the environmental framework; and, if Iyer and Banerjee's (1993) results suggesting that consumption is the least often emphasized factor in green ads are any indication, Fisk may have been one of the last as well. Even ecologists have been slow to recognize the necessity of transforming the consumption process (Durning, 1992). While Fisk (1974) thoroughly assessed the role of more ecologically benign consumption, he fell short by failing to emphasize the necessity for limiting levels of consumption. This is the most difficult challenge marketers will face, and it is one of the most critical in moving from an environmentalism position to the Greener positions in the framework proposed here. From the ecologism position, it would be argued that the only truly Green product is the one that is produced from renewable resources at rates lower than the resource's replacement rate for non-frivolous human needs. While such a position is not on the immediate marketing horizon, a commitment to work in that direction is necessary. Engendering this commitment in both producers and consumers is partly the task of Greens themselves.

From the perspective of Greens who proffer their position, the task is commensurately difficult. They must recognize that the positions they are most frequently advocating are in the lower right corner of Figure 1. As such, they represent an extreme position in the minds of producers and consumers steeped in the dominant social paradigm. From an understanding of marketing and advertising theory, they might better position themselves relative to their targets. While their desires are admirable and essential, any movement in the direction from green to Green must be incremental.

Any advertising strategy focusing, for example, on extreme fear appeals is generally unsuccessful in effecting enduring attitude change (Janis and Feshbach, 1953; Ray and Wilke, 1970). By moving their appeals in the direction of the upper left, environmental quadrant where the majority of consumers and producers reside, Greens are more likely to achieve small but effective attitude changes. Because the changes necessary are both positional (where humans fit in nature) and political (political reform or radical transformation), these are the dimensions that should be addressed specifically in Green advertising campaigns. Focusing on things far away and uncontrollable in advertising can lead to feelings of helplessness and hopelessness in consumers. It is ironic indeed that the Green aphorism, 'Think Globally Act Locally,' is not followed by Greens in their own approach to advertising. This is, after all, what targeting is all about.

Thus, we see that marketers, consumers, and Greens can gain a great deal by adopting a consistent framework within which to assess and guide their behavior. Such a formal framework has been lacking in both Green and marketing literature. With it comes the recognition that the changes necessary will be both difficult and slow in coming because they represent, not only a change in behavior, but, in the long run, a paradigm shift. It is a cultural revolution on a global scale that the twenty-first century will require of us. It is the *ecological imperative* of the next century and not a whimsical choice of a novel idea. The social power to exacerbate or ameliorate the ecological crisis is immanent in the marketing and advertising processes. Those in marketing who persist in pretending there is a choice should recall Fisk's (1974) admonition, '... ecological sanctions don't read public-relations releases.'

## SUMMARY AND CONCLUSION

Before it can be determined whether green advertising exists and is useful in developing ecological awareness, it must be established what green is. The purpose of this paper was to develop a framework within which the greenness of advertising could be established. An examination of the advertising and ecology literatures revealed a discrepancy between the views of advertisers and those of ecologists. An advertising perspective considers green to be a uni-dimensional concept encapsulating environmental, ecological, Green, and environmentally oriented behaviors such as recycling. The ecological literature suggests that this approach is too simplistic since ecology is a multi-dimensional concept containing at least two dimensions: political and positional. Using this framework, five different types of green were established each with a different human and political agenda. The types, from least to most political and human positional were environmentalism, conservationism, human welfare ecology, preservationism, and ecologism. These range from green with a little 'g' to Green with a big 'G.' For an advertisement to be classified as green in any sense, it must be placed within the framework. It was also shown that this can be problematic since intentionallity plays a part in the decision.

It appears that green advertising does exist and would be considered, even by the ecologist, necessary and useful in promoting environmentally-oriented consumption behavior. However, only a small first step has been taken which in no way represents a solution to the ecological crisis. The solution requires addressing the 'root causes' of the crisis, and such factors as pollution and ozone depletion are symptoms, not causes. While these symptoms can be fatal if left unattended, they will reemerge in the future if the root causes are not considered. The only form of green which addresses the root causes is ecologism requiring political and positional radicalism. The position extols profound change in the dominant social paradigm, and this is change that the power elite within the industrial system will not embrace. This is where environmentalism and ecologism part company, and a compromise seems unlikely because their positions represent virtual political and positional antitheses. For the time being, it seems, we must content ourselves with green advertising and consider it a necessary, if not critical, first step.

Unfortunately, even that first step is yet to develop in any meaningful way. Marketers, consumers, and Greens have failed to consider the complex nature of the crisis confronting them. Consequently, little progress has been made by marketers in developing Green marketing programs, by consumers in developing Green values, or by Greens in effectively presenting their position to prospective targets. At least part of this problem can be attributed to divergent perceptions of the nature of the problem. In failing to recognize the positional and political dimensions as interrelated parts of an integrate whole, each group has failed to achieve its potential. The framework offered here represents a first step in reconciling the pieces of the ecological puzzle and providing a common ground for ecological discourse within the discipline of marketing.

# REFERENCES

Bookchin, Murray (1980) *Toward an Ecological Society*, Montreal: Black Rose Books.
— (1990) *Remaking Society: Pathways to a Green Future*, Boston: South End Press.
Capra, Fritjof (1982) *The Turning Point*, London: Fontana Flamingo series.
Cotgrove, Stephen (1982) *Catastrophe or Cornucopia: The Environment, Politics and the Future*, New York: John Wiley & Sons.
Daly, Herman E. (1972) *Toward a Steady-State Economy*, San Francisco: W. H. Freeman and Company.
Dobson, Andrew (1990) *Green Political Thought*, London: Harper Collins Academic.
— (1991) *The Green Reader*, San Francisco: Mercury House, Inc.
Dolbeare, Kenneth M. and Patricia Dolbeare (1976) *American Ideologies*, Boston: Houghton Mifflin Company.
Dumont, Louis (1977) *From Mandeville to Marx: The Genesis and Triumph of Economic Ideology*, Chicago: University of Chicago Press.
Durning, Alan (1992) *How Much Is Enough?* New York: W. W. Norton & Company.
Eckersley, Robyn (1992) *Environmentalism and Political Theory*, Albany, NY: SUNY Press.
Ehrenfeld, David (1978) *The Arrogance of Humanism*, New York: Oxford University Press.
Ellul, Jaques (1964) *The Technological Society*, J. Wilkenson, trans., New York: Vintage Books.
England, Richard and Barry Bluestone (1972) 'Ecology and Social Conflict,' in Herman Daly, ed., *Toward a Steady-State Economy*, San Fransisco: W. H. Freeman and Company.
Fisk, George (1973) 'Criteria for a Theory of Responsible Consumption,' *Journal of Marketing*, **37** (April), 24–31.
— (1974) *Marketing and the Ecological Crisis*, New York: Harper & Row, Publishers.
Fox, Warwick (1990) *Toward a Transpersonal Ecology: Developing New Foundations for Environmentalism*, Boston: Shambhala.
Goldsmith, Edward, Robert Allen, Michael Allaby, John Davoll, and Sam Lawrence (1972) *Blueprint for Survival*, Boston: Houghton Mifflin.
Goldsmith, Edward (1988), 'De-industrializing Society,' in *The Great U-Turn: De-industrializing Society*, Bideford: Green Books.
Gouldner, Alvin (1973) *The Coming Crisis of Western Sociology*, London: Heinemann.
Habermas, Jurgen (1971) *Toward a Rational Society: Student Protest, Science and Society*, J. Shapiro, trans., London: Heinemann Educational Books.
Hardin, Garrett (1968) 'The Tragedy of the Commons,' *Science*, **162** (December), 1243–48.
— and John Baden (1977) *Managing the Commons*, San Fransisco: W. H. Freeman and Company.
Hayes, Samuel P. (1959) *Conservation and the Gospel of Efficiency*, Cambridge, MA: Harvard University Press.
Heilbroner, Robert L. (1974) *An inquiry into the Human Prospect*, New York: Norton.
Hirschman, Albert (1977) *The Passions and the Interests: Political Arguments for Capitalism Before Its Triumph*, Princeton: Princeton University Press.
Hirschman, Elizabeth C. (1993) 'Ideology in Consumer Research, 1980 and 1990: A Marxist and Feminist Critique,' *Journal of Consumer Research*, **19** (March), 537–555.
Iyer, Easwar and Bobby Banerjee (1993) 'Anatomy of Green Advertising,' L. McAlister and P. Andrews, eds., *Advances in Consumer Research*, Provo, UT: Association for Consumer Research, 491–501.
Janis, Irving and Seymour Feshbach (1953) 'Effects of Fear-Arousing Communications,' *Journal of Abnormal and Social Psychology*, **48** (January), 78–92.
Kangun, Norman, Les Carlson, and Stephen Grove (1991) 'Environmental Advertising Claims: A Preliminary Investigation.' *Journal of Public Policy and Marketing*, **12** (Fall), 47–58.
Kassiola, Joel (1990) *The Death of Industrial Civilization*, Albany, NY: State University of New York Press.
Kuhn, Thomas (1970) *The Structure of Scientific Revolutions*, Chicago: Chicago University Press.
Leeson, Susan (1979) 'Philosophic Implications of the Ecological Crisis: The Authoritarian Challenge to Liberalism,' *Polity*, **11** (March), 303–18.
Leiss, William (1972) *The Domination of Nature*, New York: George Braziller.

— (1978) *The Limits to Satisfaction: On Needs and Commodities*, London: Marion Boyars.

Locke, John (1963) *Two Treatises on Government*, P. Laslett [ed.], Cambridge: Cambridge University Press.

MacPherson, Crawford B. (1962) *The Political Theory of Possessive Individualism*, Oxford: The Clarendon Press.

Marcuse, Herbert, (1964) *One Dimensional Man*, Boston: Beacon Press.

— (1969) *An Essay On Liberation*, Boston: Beacon Press.

— (1972) *Counter-revolution and Revolt*, Boston: Beacon Press.

Meadows, Donella H., Dennis L. Meadows, Jorgen Randers, William W. Behrens III (1972) *The Limits to Growth: A Report for the Club of Rome's Project on the Predicament of Mankind*, New York: Universe.

Merchant, Carolyn (1982) *The Death of Nature: Women, Ecology and the Scientific Revolution*, London: Wildwood House.

— (1992) *Radical Ecology: The Search for a Livable World*, New York: Routledge.

Milbrath, Lester (1984) *Environmentalists: Vanguard for a New Society*, Albany, NY: SUNY Press.

Murray, Jeff B. and Julie L. Ozanne (1991) 'The Critical Imagination: Emancipatory Interests in Consumer Research,' *Journal of Consumer Research*, **18** (September), 129–144.

Ophuls, William (1973) 'Leviathan or Oblivion?' in Herman Daly, ed., *Toward a Steady-State Economy*, San Francisco: Freeman.

— (1977) *Ecology and the Politics of Scarcity: A Prologue to a Political Theory of the Steady State*, San Francisco: Freeman.

— and Stephan Boyan, Jr. (1992) *Ecology and the Politics of Scarcity Revisited: The Unraveling of the American Dream*, New York: W. H. Freeman and Company.

O'Riordan, Timothy (1976), *Environmentalism*, London: Pion Limited.

Pirages, Dennis (1977) 'Introduction: A Social Design for Sustainable Growth,' in D. C. Pirages, ed., *The Sustainable Society: Implications for Growth*, New York: Praeger Publications.

Porritt, Jonathon (1984) *Seeing Green: The Politics of Ecology Explained*, Oxford: Basil Blackwell.

— and David Winner (1988) *The Coming of the Greens*, London: Fontana.

Ray, Michael and William Wilke (1970) 'Fear: The Potential of an Appeal Neglected by Marketing,' *Journal of Marketing*, **34** (January), 54–62.

Regan, Tom (1981) 'The Nature and Possibility of an Environmental Ethic,' *Environmental Ethics*, **3** (Spring), 19–34.

Rifkin, Jeremy (1980) *Entropy*, New York: Bantam Books.

Rodman, John (1980) 'Paradigm Change in Political Science: An Ecological Perspective,' *American Behavioral Scientist*, **24** (September), 65.

— (1983) 'Four Forms of Ecological Consciousness Reconsidered,' in Donald Scherer and Thomas Attig, eds., *Ethics and the Environment*, Englewood Cliffs, NJ: Prentice-Hall, Inc.

Rogers, Everett M. (1987) 'The Critical School and Consumer Research,' in M. Wallendorf and P. Anderson, eds., *Advances in Consumer Research*, Vol. 14, Provo, UT: Association for Consumer Research.

Roszak, Theodore (1979) *Person/Planet: The Creative Disintegration of Industrial Society*, London: Paladin.

Rothschild, Joan (1983) *Machina ex Dea: Feminist Perspectives on Technology*, New York: Pergamon Press.

Scherer, Donald and Thomas Attig (1983) *Ethics and the Environment*, Englewood Cliffs, NJ: Prentice-Hall.

Schmookler, Andrew B. (1993). *The Illusion of Choice: How the Market Economy Shapes Our Destiny*, Albany, NY: SUNY Press.

Schumacher, E. Fritz (1973) *Small is Beautiful: Economics as if People Mattered*, New York: Harper & Row.

Smith, Adam (1937) *An Inquiry into the Nature and Causes of the Wealth of Nations*, New York: Random House.

Trainer, Ted (1985) *Abandon Affluence!* London: Zed Books.

Winner, Langdon (1977) *Autonomous Technology*, Cambridge, MA: The MIT Press.

— (1986) *The Whale and the Reactor: A Search for Limits in an Age of High Technology*, Chicago: University of Chicago Press.

White, Lynn (1966) *Medieval Technology and Social Change,* New York: Oxford University Press.
— (1967) 'The Historical Roots of our Ecological Crisis,' *Science,* **155,** 1203–1207.

# Further Sources of Information

*Pierre McDonagh and Andrea Prothero*

We list below some other sources of environmental information, ranging from general environmental texts and books on green management to texts specifically in the marketing field, the internet, journals and magazines. This is a personal choice of further information which the authors have found to be beneficial in their research and teaching of green management issues and is not meant to be seen as an exhaustive list of further reading in the green management area. Please let us know if you feel any particularly helpful source has been left out.

Contact:

Pierre McDonagh and Andrea Prothero
Department of Marketing
Faculty of Management
University of Stirling
FK9 4LA
Pierre—Tel: [44] 1786 467395, Email: p.b.mcdonagh@stirling.ac.uk
Andrea—Tel: [44] 1786 467402, Email: a.i.prothero@stirling.ac.uk

## BOOKS (GENERAL AND GREEN MANAGEMENT)

Buchholz, R.A. (1993) *Principles of Environmental Management: The Greening of Management.* Prentice Hall, Englewood Cliffs, New Jersey.
This text was written in North America and is divided into three broad areas covering basic environmental concepts, a discussion of some of the major global environmental problems (for example ozone depletion and deforestation) and concluding with examples of environmental strategies for business and society. The third section of the text is the weakest with only one chapter focusing on business and society; however, the first two sections provide excellent starting points for learning about basic environmental concepts and global environmental problems.

Dobson, A. (ed.) (1991) *The Green Reader.* André Deutsch, London.
This is a wonderful book and one of the first edited volumes of the writings of

experts on the environment discussing what they feel are the issues affecting green consciousness. It has a wide range of contributors, ranging from the late Petra Kelly to Schumacher, and contains excerpts from classic pieces by Rachel Carson and Murray Bookchin.

Fischer, F. and Black, M. (eds) (1995) *Greening Environmental Policy: The Politics of a Sustainable Future.* Paul Chapman Publishing, London.
This is an edited book (Reading 11 is taken from it) with chapters on a range of issues in the environmental field, including sustainability, environmental policy making (examples include environmental policy in Chile and the North American Free Trade Agreement), and environmental values.

Hansen, A. (ed.) (1993) *The Mass Media and Environmental Issues.* Leicester University Press, Leicester.
This edited collection provides the reader with an overview of current thinking and research from Europe and North America on the role of the mass media in the rise of the environment as a social issue.

Hopfenbeck, W. (1993) *The Green Management Revolution: Lessons in Environmental Excellence.* Prentice Hall, Hemel Hempstead.
This text was initially written for a German market in 1990. It was rewritten with a European market in mind in 1992, and the text includes company examples from Europe and North America. The first section of the book considers general green management issues such as proactive environmental management, environmental policies and information systems. Specific organizational functions are also considered—examples include marketing, personnel and logistics management.

Kemp P., Wolf, F.O., Juquin, P., Antures, C., Steigers, I. and Telkamper, W. (1992) *Europe's Green Alternative: A Manifesto for a New World.* Green Print (Translated by Julia Sallabank), The Merlin Press, London.
This is a visionary and revolutionary text which argues that the core values and insights of socialism are still essential tools with which to combat the life-threatening forces at work in the world today. The authors propose '*cultural dialogue to be at the heart of a struggle to build new relationships with the Third World that break with the old imperialist and capitalist ties of dependence and development*'.

Roberts, P. (1995) *Environmentally Sustainable Business: A Local and Regional Perspective.* Paul Chapman Publishing, London.
A good starting point for those wishing to focus on environmental issues in business (reading 12 is taken from this text). The first four chapters look at wider environmental issues—major trends and issues, problems and opportunities, economics and socio-political issues. Remaining chapters focus specifically on business and consider areas such as environmental strategies and operational practices and the response of business to environmental strategies.

Smith, D. (Ed.) (1993) *Business and the Environment: Implications of the New Environmentalism.* Paul Chapman Publishing, London.

This edited book covers an array of environmental issues—business, politics, accounting, legislative issues, corporate social responsibility—as well as including examples of particular industry responses to the environment, e.g. the chemical industry.

Wehrmeyer, W. (1994) *Environmental References in Business.* Interleaf Publications, Sheffield.
This bibliography contains references for over 2,700 articles from a variety of journals and is a must for anyone interested in the green management area. Sections include: general references and sources of data, society, state and the environment, industry and the environment and social perceptions of the environment. There is also a useful author index at the end of the book.

Welford, R. and Gouldson, A. (1993) *Environmental Management and Business Strategy.* Pitman, London.
A useful text which includes a good introduction to the environmental challenges facing business before analysing specific environmental areas. Topics covered include environmental impact assessment, environmental auditing, waste minimization issues, life-cycle analysis and green marketing issues. The text also includes chapters on environmental management for small businesses and environmental management issues in relation to regional development.

## BOOKS (MARKETING)

Bernstein, D. (1992) *In the Company of Green, Corporate Communications for the New Environment.* Incorporated Society of British Advertisers, London
Described by Kenneth Miles, Director General of the ISBA, as all a company needs to understand about corporate communication on environmental subjects, this text provides a humorous and informal look at the task of green communications.

Charter, M. (Ed.) (1992) *Greener Marketing: A Responsible Approach to Business.* Interleaf Productions, Sheffield.
This edited book contains a number of useful chapters relating directly to green issues in marketing. The book is divided into three sections: the strategic implications of greener marketing, the practical implications of greener marketing and case histories.

Grunert, S. C. (1995) *Environmental economics, sustainable development, 'green' marketing, eco-management, and the like.* CeSaM Working Paper No. 5.
This is a highly selective, partly annotated bibliography of research conducted in Europe, and North America since the 1970s. It contains some 800 references on various aspects under the general heading 'ecology and economy'. Books, readers, articles, working papers, and conference papers are listed.

Peattie, K. (1995) *Environmental Marketing Management.* Pitman, London.
An excellent starting point for those who wish to update their knowledge on what going green means for marketing management. The text includes a good introduction to the issues surrounding environmental marketing before looking specifically at both strategic and operational marketing issues. Good up to date examples and mini case studies are included throughout the text.

Rehak, R. (ed.) (1993) *Greener Marketing & Advertising: Charting a Responsible Course.* Rodale Press, Emmaus PA.
This is an edited book by the Senior Vice President of Ogilvy & Mather/Houston with the non-profit Environmental Marketing and Advertising Council and the Center for Resource Management. The book gives good practical insight, with hundreds of examples, into how many leading-edge companies have promoted environmental awareness while maintaining or increasing their profitability.

## OTHER BOOKS

Ball, S. and Ball, S. (1991) *Environmental Law.* Blackstone Press, London.
Bunyard, P. and Morgan-Grenvill, F. (1987) *The Green Alternative.* Methuen, London.
Cairncross, F. (1991) *Costing the Earth.* Business Books, London.
Chisholm, A. (1972) *Philosophers of the Earth. Conversations with Ecologists.* London
Clark, J. (Ed.) (1990) *Renewing the Earth: The Promise of Social Ecology.* Green Print, London.
Coddington, W. (1993) *Environmental Marketing: Positive Strategies for Reaching the Green Consumer.* McGraw Hill, New York.
Confederation of British Industry (1990) *Environment Means Business.* CBI, London.
Davis, J. (1991) *Greening Business—Managing for Sustainable Development.* Basil Blackwell, Oxford.
ECO Directory of Environmental Databases in the UK (1995) ECO Environmental Information Trust, Bristol.
Ekins, P. (1986) *The Living Economy: A New Economics in the Making.* Routledge and Kegan Paul, London.
Elkington, J. with Burke, T. (1987) *The Green Capitalists: Industry's Search for Environmental Excellence.* Victor Gollancz, London.
Elkington, J. Knight, P. and Hailes, J. (1991) *The Green Business Guide.* Victor Gollancz, London.
Good, B. (1991) *CEST—Industry and the Environment.* Centre for Exploitation of Science and Technology, London.
Hannan, M. and Freeman, J. (1989) *Organizational Ecology.* Harvard University Press, Boston.
Irvine, S. (1989) *Beyond Green Consumerism.* Friends of the Earth, London.
Johnson, C. (1991) *Green Dictionary.* Optima, London.
Kemball-Cook, D., Baker M. and Mattingly C. (1991) *The Green Budget.* Green Print, London.
Newman, O. and Foster, A. (1993) *European Environmental Statistics Handbook.* Gate Research International, London.

Newman, O. and Foster, A. (1993) *European Environmental Information Sourcebook.* Gate Research International, London.

Nieuwenhuis, P. and Wells, P. (eds) (1994) *Motor Vehicles in the Environment.* John Wiley & Sons, Chichester.

Pearce, D., Markandya, A. and Barbier, E. B. (1989) *Blueprint for A Green Economy.* Earthscan Publications, London.

Peattie K. (1992) *Green Marketing.* Pitman, London.

Porritt, J. (1984) *Seeing Green: The Politics of Ecology Explained.* Basil Blackwell, Oxford.

Porritt, J. and Winner, D. (1988) *The Coming of the Greens.* Fontana, London.

Porteous, A. (1992) *Dictionary of Environmental Science and Technology.* John Wiley & Sons, Chichester.

Stead, W. E. and Stead, J. G. (1992) *Management for A Small Planet: Strategic Decision Making and the Environment.* Sage, London.

Steiner, D. and Nauser, M. (1993) (Eds) *Human Ecology: Fragments of Anti-fragmentary Views of the World.* Routledge. London.

Winters, G. and Ewers, H. (1988) *Business and the Environment: A Handbook of Industrial Ecology.* McGraw-Hill, Hamburg.

World Commission on Environment and Development (WCED) (1987) *Our Common Future.* WCED, Oxford.

## THE INTERNET AND ORGANIZATIONS

Listed below is a collection of information about various environmental issues included on the World-Wide Web, as well as some e-mail addresses for a number of environmental organizations. This information is not meant to be a comprehensive guide but rather should be seen as providing some examples of readily available information on the natural environment generally and green management issues specifically.

**EMAS (The European Eco Management and Audit Scheme)** **http://www.quality.co.uk/emas.htm** Includes information on EMAS and a comparison between EMAS, ISO 14001 and BS 7750.

**The Earth Centre http://www.shef.ac.uk/vec** Kilners Bridge, Doncaster Road, Denaby Main, Nr Doncaster, South Yorkshire, DN12 4DY. Tel: [+44] 1709 770566.

**The Enviroweb http://envirolink.org** The enviroweb (envirolink) has been described as 'a clearing house of all environmental information available on the internet'. It is an excellent starting point to discovering further information via the environmental library and the very useful search facility available.

**Environmental organizations on line http://www.envirolink.org/orgs/** *'Comprehensive listing of all environmental organizations on the internet'.*

**European Environment Agency   http://www.eea.dk//.**

**Friends of the Earth   http://www.foe.co.uk/** 26–28 Underwood Street, London, N1 7JQ. Tel: [+44] 171 1490 1555.

**Green MarketAlert** Published monthly by The Bridge Group, 345 Wood Creek Road, Bethlehem, CT 06751, USA. Tel [+1] 203 266 7209.

**Greenpeace   http://www.greenpeace.org/** Greenpeace House, Cannonbury Villas, London, N1 1MB. Tel: [+44] 171 354 5100.

**International Institute for Environmental Development (IIED).** 3 Endsleigh Street, London, Tel: [+44] 171 388 2117.

**Institute for European Environmental Policy (IEEP)** 158 Buckingham Palace Road, London, SW1W 9TR. Tel: [+44] 171 824 8787.

**International Institute for Sustainable Development** http://iisd1.iisd.ca/ Electronic clearing house for information on past and upcoming international meetings related to environment and development.' Topics include 'What is Sustainable Development', 'Global News on Sustainable Development' and 'Sustainable Development, Policy and Practice'.

**LCA (Life cycle analysis)** http://www.cfd.rmit.edu.au/research/LCA.html Includes definitions and list of other LCA sites on the net.

**MediaNatura** http://www.oneworld.org/misc/saynon/medianatura_top.html Contact: 21 Tower Street, London WC2H 9NS. Tel: [+44] 171 240 4936. MediaNatura is a professional media and communications consultancy which works at greatly reduced rates with people and organizations working in the social justice and environmental fields. As part of its ongoing work Medianatura is the official co-ordinator for the British Environment and Media Awards (BEMAS) each year.

**SGS Yarsley International Certification Services Ltd** http://www.sgs.co.uk/bs7750.htm Information on British Standard for Environmental Management Systems, BS 7750.

**SustainAbility Ltd** 91–97 Freston Road, London. Tel: [+44] 171 243 1277. Environmental consultants founded by John Elkington and Julia Hailes, authors of the *Green Consumer Guide.*

**World Society for the Protection of Animals (WSPA)** http://www.way.net/wspa/ 2 Langley Lane, London SW8 1TJ. Tel: [+44] 171 793 0540.

**World Wide Fund for Nature (WWF UK)** Panda House, Weyside Park, Godalming, Surrey GU7 1XR. Tel: [+44] 1483 426444.

Below is an extract from two other internet sites, EcoNet! And E Magazine, to let you see a small sample of what is available.

**Econet** http://www.igc.apc.org/econet/

*Welcome to EcoNet!*

EcoNet serves organizations and individuals working for environmental preservation and sustainability. EcoNet builds coalitions and partnerships with individuals, activist organizations and non-profit organizations to develop their use of the electronic communications medium. For further details, send a blank e-mail message to econet-info@igc.apc.org, or find out about EcoNet and its sister networks in the Institute for Global Communications and the Association for Progressive Communications.

We offer the resources on our World-Wide Web page as a public service to the environmental community on the Internet. We invite your contributions and feedback to econet@igc.apc.org.

*EcoNet News Of Note.* Editor's pick of articles and postings found among the thousands of conferences (aka newsgroups) available to EcoNet subscribers. Updated twice weekly.

*EcoNet New and Featured Items.* EcoNet coordinators think these links are of particular current importance. We update this frequently, based on your suggestions.

*EcoNet Issue Resource Center.* Environmental resources on the Internet and through EcoNet sorted by category.

*Organizations.* List of environmental organizations with resources on EcoNet's World-Wide Web and Gopher services, and elsewhere on the Internet.

*EcoNet's Environment Gopher.* The EcoNet Gopher is a means for EcoNet members to disseminate news and information about their projects and campaigns and a starting point to browse environmental issues on the Internet.

**E Magazine    http://www.igc.apc.org/emagazine/**

This is the electronic edition of E Magazine, the premier bimonthly environmental magazine published in Norwalk, Connecticut. E Magazine was formed for the purpose of acting as a clearing house of information, news and commentary on environmental issues for the benefit of the general public and in sufficient depth to involve dedicated environmentalists. It is our intent to inform and inspire individuals who have concerns about the environment and want to know what they can do to help bring about improvements. In doing so, we hope to advance ecological perspectives, increase attention paid to the issues and enlist greater popular support for environmental protection efforts.

Contact E Magazine directly at <ean@econet.apc.org>.

**USENET, Newsgroups**

Two examples of environmental newsgroups found using the *Infoseek Guide* in *Netscape* are:

(1)  Sci.environment newsgroup: 'discusses major environmental issues'
     http://guide-p..infoseek.com/DB?&dbid=1&grp=sci.environment&st=O&s&st=
     0&sv=N1&lk=noframes&col=NN
     (no gaps throughout)
(2)  Talk.environment 'discusses environmental policy and issues such as pollution, global population, natural resources and recycling.'
     http://guide-p.infoseek.com/DB?&dbid=1&grp=talk.environment&st=O&s&st=
     0&sv=N1&lk=noframes&col=NN

## JOURNALS

Environmental journals on a range of issues, not just management include the following.

*Business Strategy and the Environment,* John Wiley & Sons
*EC Environmental Policy Monitor,* Environmental Policy Consultants
*Ecological Economics,* Elsevier
*The Ecologist,* Ecosystems
*Eco-Management and Auditing,* John Wiley & Sons
*Environment and Behaviour,* Sage Publications
*Environment and Development Economics,* Cambridge University Press (new in 1996)
*Environmental Conservation,* Cambridge University Press
*Environmental and Ecological Statistics,* Chapman & Hall
*Environmental Policy and Practice,* Environmental Policy and Practice (EPP) Publications
*Environmental Politics,* Frank Cass
*Environmental and Resource Economics,* Kluwer Academic
*European Environment,* John Wiley & Sons
*Global Environmental Change,* Butterworth-Heinneman
*Greener Management International,* Interleaf Publications
*International Journal of Environmental Studies,* Gordon and Breach Science Publications
*Journal of Business Ethics,* Kluwer Academic
*Journal of Environmental Economics and Management,* Academic Press
*Journal of Environmental Management,* Academic Press
*Journal of Macromarketing,* Business Research Division, University of Colorado
*Journal of Waste Management and Resource Recovery,* EPP Publications
*Society and Natural Resources,* Taylor & Francis
*Sustainable Development,* John Wiley & Sons
*UK Ceed Bulletin,* UK Centre for Economic and Environmental Development

## MAGAZINES

**Earth Matters**  Friends of the Earth, 26–28 Underwood Street, London, N1 7JQ. Tel: [+44] 171 490 1555. Up to date on a wide variety of environmental issues and information on how to become actively involved in a mixture of green campaigns.

**Ethical Consumer**  ECRA Publishing Ltd, 16 Nicholas Street, Manchester M1 4EJ. Tel: [+44] 1612 371630. Examines specific companies and industries and rates them according to a number of criteria split into three broad areas: environmental, ethical and social issues.

**New Internationalist**  New Internationalist Publications Ltd, 55 Rectory Road, Oxford, OX4 1BW. Tel. [+44] 1865 728181. E-mail newint@gn.apc.org. Monthly magazine that focuses on one global theme per issue. Environmental issues are discussed in various contexts, although not necessarily in every issue. Examines the injustices that exist between developed and developing nations.

**Red Pepper**    3 Gunthorpe Street, London, E1 7RP. Tel: [+44] 171 247 1702. Email redpepper@online.rednet.co.uk. Monthly magazine founded by the Socialist Movement. Regular features on green issues and updates on forthcoming events.

**Tomorrow**    Tomorrow Publishing AB, Kungsgatan 27, S-111 56 Stockholm, Sweden. Tel [+46] 8 24 3480. Email 100126.3133@compuserve.com. Practical up to date information on what is happening in the environmental field.

**Which?**    2 Marylebone Road, London NW1 4DF. [+44] 171 830 6464. Monthly magazine published by the Consumers Association. Occasionally examines environmental issues as they relate to consumers—for example, energy issues were covered in February 1994.

## NEWSPAPERS

Most major broadsheets now have a specialist environment editor and weekly columns on environmental issues. Check out Fridays edition of the *Guardian* for an up date on general environmental issues. See also the *Independent on Sunday*, *Scotland on Sunday*, and the *Daily Telegraph* for balanced reporting on environmental issues.

## AUDIOVISUAL

### Radio

Radio 3 runs a weekly environment education programme and the *Today* programme on Radio 4 regularly covers environmental issues. Radio 4 ran, for example, programmes in 1994 on *Winning Rights* and in 1995 on *Environmental Secrecy*. Also worth listening to is 1995's *Special Assignment: Green BackLash* from BBC Radio Policy and Social Programmes [ed. G. Williams] and 1995's BBC Education *In the News* [ed. J.A. O'Hagan].
See also **http://oneworld.org/tvandradio/radio_current.html**

### Television

There are various programmes on television that cover green issues in management, such as Channel 4 News, ITN and BBC Scotland's Reporting Scotland. There are also specialist videos that you can buy; here are just a few:

(1994) *Lifeschool: G is for Green*, A Workhouse Production for BBC Education.

(1995) Car Wars, *World in Action*, Granada TV.
(1995) Africa's Big Game: *Gardeners in Eden*, Scorer Associates for BBC2.
(February 1996) The BBC's *Money Programme* special feature on organic farming.
(1995) *Future File: Earth Centre Project*, Contact: European Business News, 10 Fleet Place, London, EC4M 7RB. Tel: [+44] 171 653 9309.
See also **http://www.oneworld.org/media/television.html**

# Index

Page numbers in italics refer to tables and illustrations.